£11·88

DA?E DUE FO?

15 DE

N
K
Y

STUDIES IN EIGHTEENTH-CENTURY
FRENCH LITERATURE

Robert Miklaus

STUDIES IN EIGHTEENTH-CENTURY FRENCH LITERATURE

presented to ROBERT NIKLAUS

Edited by

J. H. FOX, M. H. WADDICOR and D. A. WATTS

UNIVERSITY OF EXETER

1975

ISBN 0 85989 050 3

Set in Monotype Bembo 270, 11 on 12 point
Printed in Great Britain by James Townsend and Sons Limited

Contents

CONTENTS

vi

CONTENTS

The Contributors

W. H. BARBER
  Professor of French, University of London (Birkbeck College)

D. G. BERRY
  Lecturer, Department of French Studies, University of Leeds

Th. BESTERMAN
  Director of the Voltaire Foundation

M. T. CARTWRIGHT
  Associate Professor, McGill University

JANE MARSH DIECKMANN
  Cornell University Press

ENID L. DUTHIE
  formerly Lecturer in French, University of Exeter

O. FELLOWS
  Avalon Foundation Professor in the Humanities, Columbia University

J. H. FOX
  Professor of French, University of Exeter

B. J. GUY
  Professor of French, University of California, Berkeley

D. R. HAGGIS
  Reader in Modern French Literature, University of Exeter

SUSAN HAYWARD
  Assistant Professor, Simmons College, Boston

R. A. LEIGH
  Professor of French, University of Cambridge, and Fellow of Trinity College, Cambridge

JENNIFER LONGHURST
  Lecturer in French, Leeds Polytechnic

J. LOUGH
  Professor of French, University of Durham

R. MORTIER
Professeur à la Faculté de Philosophie et Lettres, Université Libre de Bruxelles

LYNETTE R. MUIR
Lecturer, Department of French Studies, University of Leeds

VIVIENNE MYLNE
Reader in French, University of Kent at Canterbury

NORMA PERRY
Lecturer in French, University of Exeter

J. PROUST
Professeur à la Faculté des Lettres et Sciences Humaines, Université de Montpellier III

R. SHACKLETON
Bodley's Librarian, and Fellow of Brasenose College, Oxford

CHRISTINE M. SINGH
Laboratoire d'Automatique et d'Analyse des Systèmes, Toulouse

J. S. SPINK
Emeritus Professor of French Language and Literature in the University of London

L. W. TANCOCK
Fellow of University College, London, formerly Reader in French at University College

R. S. TATE
Associate Professor of French, University of South Carolina

P. M. W. THODY
Professor of French Literature, University of Leeds

P. VERNIÈRE
Professeur à la Sorbonne

M. H. WADDICOR
Lecturer in French, University of Exeter

D. A. WATTS
Reader in Classical French Literature, University of Exeter

P. J. YARROW
Professor of French, University of Newcastle upon Tyne

Preface

This volume was proposed to the Publications Committee of the University of Exeter in 1971, as a tribute to Professor Robert Niklaus on the occasion of his retirement in 1975 as Head of the Department of French and Italian. Initially the editors had the choice of inviting contributions on all aspects of French literature, or of limiting them to the eighteenth century. It was the second alternative that was chosen, as likely to ensure greater unity of subject-matter, and because this century is Professor Niklaus's own favourite (though by no means only) field of specialisation. Invitations to contribute were then sent to as many as possible of Professor Niklaus's colleagues, pupils and friends, who responded with great enthusiasm.

The articles presented here, although bearing on the eighteenth century, are varied in content and method, but there is an emphasis on Diderot and on the theatre, two of Professor Niklaus's main interests. Uniting those two themes, Dr Michael Cartwright studies an important but rather neglected aspect of Diderot's æsthetics, the idea of the performer, while Dr David Berry provides an analysis of the *philosophe*'s visual imagery. Mrs Jane M. Dieckmann throws light on Diderot's attitude to music, and Professor Philip Thody gives a new interpretation of the figure of Le Neveu. Mrs Christine Singh looks at Diderot's debt to Lucretius, and, in quite a different vein, Miss Susan Hayward looks forward to the twentieth century in her comparison of *Jacques le Fataliste* and Beckett's *Molloy*.

Voltaire also receives an important share of the contributions. Professor William Barber reassesses his interests in the 1730s and 1740s; Dr Norma Perry examines how far his view of the relative status of the merchant in France and in England corresponds to historical reality, while Dr Robert Tate studies his attitude to the *parlements* and Dr Theodore Besterman pursues the bibliographical investigations in which, along with so many other aspects of Voltaire, he has specialised. There are two articles on Montesquieu: his political attitudes are evoked by Dr Robert Shackleton in his critical assessment of a letter attributed to the *Président,* and Dr Mark Waddicor looks at his attitude to the theatre. Rousseau's attitude to his friends and to society emerges from Dr Ralph Leigh's investigation of an aspect of his stay in England.

Philosophy and architecture are linked by Professor Otis Fellows in an article on Berkeley, while Professor Basil Guy, Professor Roland Mortier and Professor Philip Yarrow examine the careers and importance of three minor but representative figures: Ligne, Dupaty and Dutens. Also in the historical field, Dr Derek Watts draws attention to the interest to be found in the memoirs of four exiled Huguenots. Professor J. S. Spink gives us a number of important *inédits* throwing light on the Prades affair.

Four articles deal with the novel. Mrs Jennifer Longhurst studies the Spanish influences on *Gil Blas;* Dr Leonard Tancock submits the sequel of Marivaux's *Le Paysan parvenu* to close literary scrutiny, and Professor Paul Vernière gives us a new perspective on *Les Liaisons Dangereuses;* in a more general survey, Dr Vivienne Mylne analyses the use of dialogue in eighteenth-century fiction.

Several parallels are drawn between the eighteenth and other centuries. Dr Donald Haggis evaluates the extent to which Balzac was influenced by Beaumarchais. Two articles look back at previous ages: Dr Lynette Muir examines the fortune of the Arthurian legends in the eighteenth century while Professor John Fox calls attention to a scholar who interested himself in the Middle Ages and Renaissance: Bernard de La Monnoye. Both these articles provide material for a reassessment of eighteenth-century attitudes to the past. Dr Enid Duthie, on the other hand, looks forward to the romantic movement in her commentary on a passage from Barthélemy, and Professor Jacques Proust to Revolutionary Russia in his comparison of plays by Maréchal and Maiakovsky. In view of this diversity of treatment, it is appropriate that Professor John Lough should have given us a thorough analysis of what constitutes a *philosophe.*

The book as a whole is evidence of the continuing vitality of the Enlightenment and we therefore hope that it makes a fitting complement to Professor Niklaus's own lively and important contribution to eighteenth-century studies.

★   ★   ★

The editors' task has been considerably eased by the contributors' warm and prompt response to the invitations; by the patience and skill of the Departmental Secretaries, Miss Stephanie Clarke and Miss Jakki Langdon; above all, by the wisdom and experience of Professor J. H. Brumfitt and Mr R. A. Erskine, whose advice has helped the editors so greatly in the course of this complicated venture. Finally the editors would like to thank the Publications Committee of the University of Exeter, who so readily agreed to sponsor this volume.

Robert Niklaus

The retirement of Professor Robert Niklaus from his position as Head of the Department of French and Italian at Exeter University brings to an end an active and distinguished career of over forty years in university teaching. Born in London in 1910 of Swiss parents, Robert Niklaus was educated at the Lycée Français de Londres. He took his Licence-ès-Lettres at the University of Lille in 1930, followed by a B.A. in French with First Class Honours at the University of London in 1931. Three years later the same university awarded him a PhD for his thesis on Jean Moréas. In 1932 he was appointed to an assistant-ship at University College, London, which he left in 1938 in order to take up a post as assistant lecturer, and subsequently lecturer, in the University of Manchester, where he remained until 1952. In that year he succeeded Professor Graeme Ritchie as Head of the Department of French at the University College of the South-West. Henceforth he was to play a prominent role in the history of that institution up to and well beyond its achieving university status in 1956. Under Professor Niklaus's guidance, the Department of French at Exeter has increased over three-fold in size since the university college days, and emphasis has shifted away from formal 'History of Literature' towards a compre-hensive study of texts from the Middle Ages to the present day. He has also been instru-mental in developing the study of Spanish and Italian in this University, and has fostered the establishment of a new Language Centre.

The administrative duties of a Head of Department during the expansionist years of the fifties and sixties were particularly heavy, and Robert Niklaus fulfilled them with character-istic energy and competence. He was Dean of the Faculty of Arts from 1959 to 1962 and Deputy Vice-Chancellor from 1965 to 1967, serving at the same time as a member of many of the committees on which a modern university depends for its smooth running. His devotion to the constantly developing University of Exeter did not prevent him from becoming Visiting Professor at University of California, Berkeley, during the academic year 1963–4, and at Case Western Reserve University, Cleveland, in the Autumn Semester of 1971. That he never allowed administrative and lecturing duties to detract from his academic research is shown by the long list of publications which follows this memoir. While his own studies have been concerned principally with eighteenth-century French literature, and with Diderot in particular, as General Editor of the series of *Textes français classiques et modernes*, published by the University of London Press, he has rendered out-standing service to the study of French literature as a whole; over thirty titles have appeared in this series, ranging from the seventeenth century to the contemporary period. The remarkable scope of his activities becomes evident when we add that he has been a member of the Society for French Studies since its inception, that he was its President from 1968 to 1970, and its Vice-President from 1967 to 1968 and again from 1970 to 1971. He was also a founder member and first President of the British Society for Eighteenth-Century

Studies, Treasurer of the International Society for Eighteenth-Century Studies from 1969 to 1975, President of the International Association of University Professors and Lecturers from 1960 to 1964 and its Vice-President from 1954 to 1956, and from 1958 to 1960, President of the Association of University Teachers from 1954 to 1955 and its Vice-President from 1953 to 1954 and from 1955 to 1956. He also served on the Executive Committee of the Modern Humanities Research Association from 1956 to 1970 and on the Postgraduate State Studentships Committee from 1956 to 1961.

His former students, numbers of whom are established in university posts in this country and abroad, will remember with gratitude his skilful fostering of their particular qualities so that each gave of his best, and the warm interest he took in their subsequent careers, while students and colleagues alike have long benefited from the advice he so generously gave, unfailingly shrewd, witty, tinged frequently with a gentle, teasing and always perceptive irony. His guiding force throughout has been a deeply felt interest in his fellow men, whom he has served loyally and well in his chosen profession.

In his private life he suffered a terrible tragedy with the death after a long illness of his first wife in 1970. Robert and Thelma Niklaus formed an excellent team, as readers of their joint edition of Marivaux's *Arlequin poli par l'amour* know, and as all will remember who had the privilege of being entertained by them in their many lively and stimulating soirées. Happily this tradition is being very ably maintained by his second wife Kathy, who, together with his three children by his first marriage, and seven grandchildren, ensures him a contented family life.

Robert Niklaus is not one to remain satisfied with memories of a highly successful career. His academic interests are being pursued now as energetically as ever, and we hope that many happy and fruitful years lie ahead of him still.

JOHN FOX
MARK WADDICOR
DEREK WATTS

List of Publications by Robert Niklaus

1936   *Jean Moréas, poète lyrique*, Les Presses Universitaires de France, 251 pp.
French Prose Composition: Extracts from Modern and Contemporary English Writers for Translation into French, G. Duckworth (In collaboration with Dr J. S. Wood). Reprinted in 1940, 1946, 1951, 1955, 1961, etc.

1937   'The Nineteenth Century (Post-Romantic) and After', in *The Year's Work in Modern Language Studies*, Cambridge University Press, 7, 80–108.

1938   'The Nineteenth Century (Post-Romantic) and After', in *YWML*, 8, 101–126.

1939   'The Nineteenth Century (Post-Romantic) and After', in *YWML*, 9, 64–112.

1940   'The Nineteenth Century (Post-Romantic) and After', in *YWML*, 10, 65–76.
French Unseens: Extracts from Contemporary French Writers for Translation into English, G. Duckworth (In collaboration with Dr J. S. Wood). Reprinted in 1947, 1950, 1953, 1960, 1963, etc.

1941   'The Social Structure of France', *Geography*, No. 132, t. 26, June.
Les Pensées philosophiques de Diderot, Manchester University Press and The John Rylands Library. (Reprinted from the *Bulletin of the John Rylands Library*, Manchester, 26, no. 1, October–November).

1942   J.-J. Rousseau, *Les Rêveries du promeneur solitaire*, Manchester University Press, pp. xxii–125 (*French Classics*). Second edition 1946, third edition 1952, fourth edition 1961. Many reprints.

1950   Denis Diderot, *Pensées philosophiques*, E. Droz et G. Giard. Critical edition with introduction, notes and bibliography (*Textes Littéraires Français*). Second edition 1957, third edition 1965. Many reprints.
'The Nineteenth Century (Post-Romantic) and After', in *YWML*, 11, 114–132.

1951   Denis Diderot, *Lettre sur les aveugles*, E. Droz et F. Giard. Critical edition with introduction, notes and bibliography (*Textes Littéraires Français*). Revised edition 1963. Many reprints.
'The Nineteenth Century (Post-Romantic) and After', in *YWML*, 12, pp. 63–73.

1952   *Diderot and Drama*, an inaugural lecture published by the University College of the South West of England.
'Baron de Gaufridi's Refutation of Diderot's *Pensées philosophiques*', *Romanic Review*, April.
'The Nineteenth Century (Post-Romantic) and After', in *YWML*, 13, pp. 74–89.

1953   *Encyclopædia Britannica*. Articles on: Mme du Deffand, Diderot, Mme Geoffrin, La Mettrie, Mlle de Lespinasse, Mme Riccoboni, Restif de la Bretonne, Jean Moréas, Mme de Graffigny.

1958 *Modern Method French Course*, iv, Nelson (In collaboration with C. E. Loveman). Many reprints.

1959 *Modern Method French Course*, v, Nelson (In collaboration with C. E. Loveman). Many reprints.

'Pre-University Studies. A consideration of desirable modifications in VIth form curriculum and in Post-Ordinary Level school examinations and the effects of these on the selection of students of French', *Modern Languages*, September.

Marivaux, *Arlequin poli par l'amour*, University of London Press, edited in collaboration with Thelma Niklaus (*Textes Français Classiques et Modernes*).

1960 J.-J. Rousseau, *Confessions*, 2 volumes, Dent. Introduction to the English translation in the *Everyman* series. Revised edition.

1961 'Diderot et le conte philosophique', *Cahiers de l'Association Internationale des Études Françaises*, No. 13.

'Le *méchant* selon Diderot', in *Saggi e ricerche di letteratura francese*, Vol. II.

Assistant Editor, *The Status of University Teachers*. (Report from sixteen countries prepared with the assistance of UNESCO under the general editorship of Professor R. H. Shryock). International Association of University Professors and Lecturers, 1961, 223 pp.

'L'Organisation des études et des examens universitaires en Grande-Bretagne', *Communication*, 27, Brussels.

1962 'The University of Exeter, its Governing Structure, Finances and General Programme', *Canadian Association of University Teachers Bulletin*, 10, No. 4, April.

Presidential address, XIth University Conference of the International Association of University Professors and Lecturers, *Communication*, 30, December.

'The Provision for the Training of Future University Teachers, with special reference to the recruitment of scientists to the staff of universities and institutions of scientific research', Fifth International Seminar, *University Today*, published by the League of Yugoslav Universities and the Federation of Students of Yugoslavia in co-operation with the National Commission of UNESCO, Belgrade.

'Le Recrutement et la formation des cadres pour l'enseignement supérieur et la recherche scientifique', *Communication*, 31, December.

1963 'Diderot et Rousseau: Pour et contre le théâtre', in *Diderot Studies*, 4, Droz.

'La Portée des théoriques dramatiques de Diderot et de ses réalisations théâtrales', *Romanic Review*, February.

'Diderot et la peinture: Le critique d'art et le philosophe', *Europe*, January–February.

'The Mind of Diderot: an inquiry into the nature of Diderot's understanding and thought', *Filosofia*, 56, November.

'La Propagande philosophique au théâtre au siècle des lumières', in *Studies on Voltaire and the Eighteenth Century*, 26 (Geneva).

Presidential address, XIIth University Conference of the International Association of University Professors and Lecturers, *Communication*, 35, December.

'The Status of University Teachers', *The British Universities Annual*, 1963.

1964   'Présence de Diderot', in *Diderot Studies, 6.*

'La Comédie italienne et Marivaux', in *Studi in Onore di Carlo Pellegrini,* Società Editrice Internazionale, Biblioteca di *Studi Francesi,* 2.

1966   'Teaching Methods and Modern Aids to University Teachers, a General Survey', in *Communication,* 48, pp. 21–34, 105–108, July.

'Diderot's Moral Tales', in *Diderot Studies,* 7, pp. 309–318.

Chambers's Encyclopædia. Articles on: Diderot, Maurice de Guérin, Eugénie de Guérin, G. d'Houville, Gustave Kahn, Jean Moréas, Anna de Noailles, Péguy, Edmond Rostand, Francis Vielé-Griffin.

1967   'The Age of Enlightenment', *The Age of Enlightenment, Studies presented to Theodore Besterman,* St Andrews University Publications, No. 57, Oliver & Boyd, pp. 395–412.

The Encyclopedia of Philosophy, The Macmillan Co. Articles on: Boulainvilliers and Clandestine Philosophical Literature in France.

'La Genèse du *Barbier de Séville*', in *Studies on Voltaire and the Eighteenth Century,* 57, pp. 1081–95.

1968   *Beaumarchais: Le Barbier de Séville, Studies in French Literature,* No. 13, General Editor: W. G. Moore (Edward Arnold).

'Drama', in *A Critical Bibliography of French Literature,* Supplement to Vol. IV, *The Eighteenth Century,* edited by R. A. Brooks, Syracuse University Press. Chapter 3, pp. 29–40.

Diderot, in *French Literature and its Background,* edited by John Cruickshank, Oxford University Press. Vol. 3, Chapter 7, pp. 100–16.

'L'Esprit créateur de Diderot', in *Cahiers de l'Association Internationale des Études Françaises,* No. 19.

1969   '*Tableaux mouvants* as a technical innovation in Diderot's experimental novel *Jacques le Fataliste*', in *Eighteenth-Century French Studies, Literature and the Arts,* edited by E. T. Dubois, Elizabeth Ratcliff, P. J. Yarrow, Oriel Press, pp. 71–82.

'Observations sur le style expressif de Diderot', an introduction to *Diderot critique d'art et le problème de l'expression,* by Michael T. Cartwright, in *Diderot Studies,* 13.

'Diderot and the *Leçons de clavecin et principes d'harmonie par Bemetzrieder* (1771)', pp. 180–94, in *Modern Miscellany presented to Eugène Vinaver,* edited by T. E. Lawrenson, F. E. Sutcliffe and G. F. A. Gadoffre, Manchester University Press and Barnes and Noble, New York.

Pensées philosophiques, Vol. I, pp. 267–311; and *Lettre sur les aveugles,* Vol. II, pp. 163–233 in *Denis Diderot, Œuvres Complètes,* Le Club Français du Livre.

Encyclopædia Britannica. Articles on: J.-J. Barthélémy, Mme du Deffand, Diderot, Lamettrie, Mlle de Lespinasse, Jean Moréas, Restif de la Bretonne. (Revised edition 1972).

xvii

1970   'L'Édition des œuvres de Diderot fondées sur les seuls imprimés', *Revue de l'Université de Bruxelles*, Octobre 1969–Janvier 1970. Paper read at the *Colloque International relatif aux problèmes d'édition de textes français du dix-huitième siècle*.

      A Literary History of France: The Eighteenth Century, Ernest Benn Ltd. London, and Barnes & Noble Inc. New York, xx—435 pp. In the six-volume *Literary History of France*, General Editor: P. Charvet.

      'Beaumarchais: *Le Mariage de Figaro*', *Romanic Review*, Vol. 61, no. 2, pp. 146–9, April.

      M. J. Sedaine: La Gageure imprévue, édition critique, xxiv – 78 pp., 1 pl., University of Exeter (*Textes littéraires*, General Editor: Keith Cameron).

      'The Enlightenment: An Interpretation', *Journal of the History of Philosophy*, Vol. 8, No. 4, pp. 482–7, October.

1972   'Rousseau', *Contemporary Review*, pp. 87–91, February.

      'Crébillon fils et Richardson', in *Studies on Voltaire and the Eighteenth Century*, 89.

1973   'Beaumarchais et le drame', in *Missions et démarches de la critique*, *Mélanges offerts au Professeur J. A. Vier*, Librairie C. Klincksieck, Publications de l'Université de Haute-Bretagne, pp. 491–9.

1974   'The Pursuit of Peace in the Enlightenment', in: *Essays on Diderot and the Enlightenment, in honour of Otis Fellows*, edited by John Pappas, Geneva.

      'Ériphyle and Sémiramis', in forthcoming *Festschrift* in honour of Ira O. Wade, Princeton University Press.

      Reviews and review articles in: *Modern Language Review, French Studies, Diderot Studies, Romanic Review, Modern Languages, The Manchester Guardian, The Manchester Evening News, The Universities Review, The Tutor's Bulletin, The Adelphi, Revue d'histoire littéraire de la France, Études Anglaises*, etc.

      Encyclopædia Britannica, 15th edition. Article on Diderot.

I

Voltaire at Cirey: Art and Thought

W. H. BARBER

Much has been written during recent decades concerning the years Voltaire spent with madame Du Châtelet, and Professor Wade in particular has conclusively shown how important a stage in Voltaire's intellectual development this period in his life represents.[1] This modern emphasis on Cirey as a power-house of enlightenment, rather than an amorous retreat, has taken us several long steps further towards a full understanding of Voltaire. It inevitably derives, however, from a selective examination of Voltaire's activities in the years from 1734 onwards, concentrating upon his newly developing concern with philosophical and scientific matters, and with biblical scholarship, and leaving somewhat in the background his continuing activities in such fields as drama, poetry, and historiography, where his interest and reputation were already well established. It may therefore seem worth while to attempt to take a broader view of this phase in Voltaire's career, and to try in particular to explore what relationships may exist between his intellectual preoccupations and his work in the genres of imaginative literature during these years.

The Protean nature of Voltaire's genius is a familiar notion, but even so the variety and fertility of his output at this period is a striking phenomenon. In the seven years 1734–40 alone, he was engaged upon the composition or revision of one serious and one burlesque epic, five tragedies, four comedies, two operas, two major poems of moral and philosophical reflexion, two *contes philosophiques*;[2] two works on metaphysics, a handbook on Newtonian science, a prize essay based on original research into a contemporary scientific problem;[3] a major contribution to French historical literature, a literary biography, an essay on contemporary economic theories, and the editing of Frederick of Prussia's attack on the politics of Machiavelli.[4] In addition, of course, these years saw the continuation of Voltaire's usual steady output of occasional verse, polemical journalism, and minor pieces on a wide variety of topics, and we know that he was also then engaged in the wide reading in the fields of secular and religious history, including biblical studies, which bore fruit in such major works of the following decades as the *Essai sur les mœurs* and the *Dictionnaire philosophique*. A similar analysis of the seven years 1741–47 would show a comparable fertility and variety, but with a clear shift of emphasis away from philosophical and scientific interests towards greater preoccupation with historical studies, and the emergence of the *conte philosophique* as a major vehicle for Voltaire's creative powers.

Such a multiplicity of intellectual and artistic pursuits can scarcely have been indulged in, even by a man of Voltaire's vitality, without some sense of strain. And indeed there is evidence, from the early part of the period, that he was himself aware of a certain tension created by this diversity. In June 1734, in the first weeks of his exile from Paris in consequence of the condemnation of the *Lettres philosophiques,* he wrote to his friend Formont, who had apparently caught some rumour that he was at work on a new epic (in fact, *La Pucelle*), to explain that his new poem, 'plutôt dans le goût de l'Arioste, que dans celui du Tasse', was a private work, intended only for his intimate friends: 'J'ai voulu voir ce que produirait mon imagination, lorsque je lui donnerais un essor libre, et que la crainte du petit esprit de critique qui règne en France ne me retiendrait pas.' He is also, however, at work on a philosophical essay (the *Traité de métaphysique*), inspired by a re-reading of Locke; and he clearly sees these two activities as contrasting but complementary:

Il serait bien doux, mon cher Formont, de marcher dans ces terres inconnues avec un aussi bon guide que vous, et se délasser de ses recherches avec des poèmes dans le goût de l'Arioste; car, malheur à la raison si elle ne badine quelquefois avec l'imagination. (Best.D764)

The critical powers of the mind are in some way sustained and refreshed by the unfettered creativity of poetic fantasy. Nevertheless, sharp as the contrast may be in tone and theme between *La Pucelle* and the *Traité de métaphysique,* there is a certain amount of common ground between the two works: burlesque epic and philosophical essay are both critical in spirit, directed towards calling into question accepted notions, whether they are the heroic sanctity of Joan of Arc or the spirituality and immortality of the soul. If philosophy and poetry are to be seen here as work and play, then they are certainly activities taking place under one roof.

   Ten months later, when for a brief visit he is again caught up in the whirlpool of Parisian social and intellectual life, he writes to Cideville in terms which show a greater awareness of the difficulties involved in the simultaneous pursuit of the intellectual and the artistic. It is not merely that, predictably, the dissipations of the social round inhibit the poet's inspiration: current fashions too are hostile:

Les vers ne sont plus guère à la mode à Paris. Tout le monde commence à faire le géomètre et le phisicien. On se mêle de raisonner. Le sentiment, l'imagination et les grâces sont bannies. [. . .] Les belles lettres périssent à vue d'œil. Ce n'est pas que je sois fâché que la philosofie soit cultivée, mais je ne voudrois pas qu'elle devint un tiran qui exclût tout le reste. Elle n'est en France qu'une mode qui succède à d'autres et qui passera à son tour, mais aucun art, aucune science ne doit être de mode. Il faut qu'ils se tiennent tous par la main, il faut qu'on les cultive en tout temps. Je ne veux point payer de tribut à la mode, je veux passer d'une expérience de phisique à un opera ou à une comédie, et que mon goust ne soit jamais émoussé par l'étude. (Best.D863, 16 April 1735)

Voltaire is clearly aware that the diversity of his own interests constitutes a challenge, that science and belles lettres, in particular, may not move easily in harness together; but it is a challenge which he is anxious to meet, and his output over the following years shows how effective a stimulus it proved to be.[5]

If Voltaire thus took pleasure, whatever the dictates of fashion, in appearing before his public and his friends as in turn poet, dramatist, historian, philosopher and scientist, he surely did so because each of these roles expressed some aspect of his complex personality; and one might expect to find in the varied writings of the Cirey period at least some hints of a unifying force which derived from the deeper levels of his nature, some traces of fundamental assumptions and attitudes, transposed as it were into different keys as they move from one context to another.

One is tempted to see such an integrating theme in a profound sense of contentment which can be perceived in him at this stage in his career. At the level of human relationships and personal circumstances, this contentment is very plain in the early years at Cirey. Life of course contained many surface irritations and misfortunes, as it always did for Voltaire: his health was often poor, there were continuing feuds with such literary enemies as J.-B. Rousseau and Desfontaines, he frequently attracted the attention of spongers and sometimes of would-be blackmailers, his dealings with printers seldom went smoothly, the attitude of the French authorities towards him varied between thinly veiled mistrust and active hostility. But his liaison with madame Du Châtelet was a stable one for many years, based on deeply felt affection and admiration on both sides, and the studious tranquillity of Cirey was highly congenial, even if he sometimes missed his Paris friends. There are several direct assertions of his feelings of happiness to be found in Voltaire's letters to close friends at this time. In June 1735, for instance, he writes to Cideville giving an account of his various literary and intellectual activities—*Alzire, La Pucelle,* a little metaphysics and science, above all at this date *Le Siècle de Louis XIV,* which he calls his 'principal employ [. . .]: c'est là, la sultane favorite, les autres sont des passades'—and he concludes: 'Voylà mon cher amy un comte exact de ma conduitte et de mes desseins. Je suis tranquile, heureux et occupé, mais vous manquez à mon bonheur' (Best.D885). And two months later he writes in very similar terms to Thieriot: 'Je vis heureux dans une retraitte charmante, fâché seulement d'être heureux loin de vous. [. . .] Je goûte dans la paix la plus pure, et dans le loisir le plus occupé, les douceurs de l'amitié et de l'étude avec une femme unique dans son espèce qui lit Ovide et Euclide, et qui a l'imagination de l'un et la justesse de l'autre' (Best.D899).

The linking here of happiness with activity is characteristic, and very significant. It seems likely that a further element in the euphoria of these years was a sense of creative exuberance: of having set free within himself, in the favourable circumstances of Cirey, powers of intellect and imagination which had lain dormant earlier, or at least had been in some degree cramped by the distractions of Parisian social life and the restraints imposed by any attempt to avoid shocking conventional opinion. The great fertility of this period, and the intellectual and artistic development which took place in Voltaire, may be seen as the products of an emotional fulfilment and security never before experienced, coupled with a new sense of liberation and inner tranquillity.

Another aspect of this mood is a strengthened sense of benevolence towards mankind in general. Voltaire was never lacking in generosity towards the needy, and especially towards young artists of potential talent, but the number of such individuals whom he unobtrusively helped and encouraged seems if anything greater than usual during these years—one thinks

of Baculard d'Arnaud, 'Gentil' Bernard, Desforges-Maillard, La Marre, Lefèvre, Linant—
and it took the hostile activities of such an ungrateful protégé as Desfontaines to inhibit the
impulse completely. It is not merely, however, a matter of kindness to individuals; Voltaire
seems at this period to have become fully aware for the first time of the strength of his
desire to work for the betterment of the human race. The 'Discours préliminaire' published
with the first edition of *Alzire* in 1736, an unusually self-revelatory document for Voltaire
(as indeed, it would have been for any dramatist of the time), contains a declaration of faith
which is none the less genuine for being placed under the protection of Christian orthodoxy:

La religion d'un barbare consiste à offrir à ses dieux le sang de ses ennemis. Un chrétien mal instruit
n'est souvent guère plus juste. [. . .] Celle du chrétien véritable est de regarder tous les hommes comme
ses frères, de leur faire du bien et de leur pardonner le mal. Tel est Gusman au moment de sa mort; tel
Alvarez dans le cours de sa vie; tel j'ai peint Henri IV, même au milieu de ses faiblesses.
    On trouvera dans presque tous mes écrits cette humanité qui doit être le premier caractère d'un
être pensant; on y verra (si j'ose m'exprimer) le désir du bonheur des hommes, l'horreur de l'injustice
et de l'oppression; et c'est cela seul qui a jusqu'ici tiré mes ouvrages de l'obscurité où leurs défauts
devaient les ensevelir. (M.III, 379)

Voltaire's contentment at this time seems, moreover, to extend beyond any merely
personal sense of well-being and benevolence to others, to embrace optimistic attitudes of a
more broadly intellectual kind. The foundations of his interest in Newtonian cosmology
are undoubtedly complex, and include a distaste for over-confident speculation issuing in
metaphysical dogmatism in the manner of the Cartesians, admiration for the intellectual
rigour and the intellectual modesty of Newton's empirical method, and a predisposition to
think favourably of things English which were unfamiliar, and unwelcome, to Frenchmen
of orthodox outlook; but a major factor must certainly have been the appeal of a cosmology,
exclusively grounded in clear induction from observed fact, which not only imposed a
rational pattern on the universe, but infused it with a dynamic power of divine origin in the
force of gravitation. Nothing could have been more congenial to Voltaire in the Cirey
years than a world-view which both proclaimed the triumph of reason and order and
attached a great significance to spontaneous activity.[6] In this context, the *Éléments de la
philosophie de Newton* can be viewed as at once an act of homage, a personal declaration of
confidence in the ultimate nature of reality, and a missionary effort in the cause of enlightenment and reassurance, as well as a contribution to the spread of scientific knowledge.
    As Voltaire was so fond of insisting, however, at this period his chief preoccupation was
not so much metaphysical as moral: less with the universe than with man.[7] And here too
his mood of contentment seems to colour his views, sometimes strengthening earlier
attitudes. His long-standing rejection of the Christian view of man as a fallen and divided
being, strongly expressed in the attack on Pascal in the *Lettres philosophiques,* found its
positive counterpart in the belief, shared with Pope, that man was as he was intended to be,
passions and all, and occupied his rational position in the divinely ordained scheme of the
universe. His praise of the pleasures and refinements of civilization in *Le Mondain* rests upon
this, and the discussion of the function of the passions and the nature of virtue in the *Traité
de métaphysique* and the *Discours en vers sur l'homme* makes the case in some detail, not

without some internal contradictions, but in a general tone of modest cheerfulness concerning the possibility for mankind of achieving the degree of happiness appropriate to the limitations of his nature—and that nature is such that happiness is not really separable from activity. In the sixth *Discours* Voltaire writes:

> Peut-être qu'autrefois
> De longs ruisseaux de lait serpentaient dans nos bois,
> La lune était plus grande, et la nuit moins obscure;
> L'hiver se couronnait de fleurs et de verdure;
> L'homme, ce roi du monde, et roi très fainéant,
> Se contemplait à l'aise, admirait son néant,
> Et, formé pour agir, se plaisait à rien faire.
> Mais pour nous, fléchissons sous un sort tout contraire.
> Contentons-nous des biens qui nous sont destinés,
> Passagers comme nous, et comme nous bornés.
> Sans rechercher en vain ce que peut notre maître,
> Ce que fut notre monde, et ce qu'il devrait être,
> Observons ce qu'il est, et recueillons le fruit
> Des trésors qu'il renferme et des biens qu'il produit.
>
> (ll. 149–62)

Man is capable of the good life, possessing moral freedom, reason, and natural benevolence: all he needs is encouragement:

> Sûr de ta liberté, rapporte à son auteur
> Ce don que sa bonté te fit pour ton bonheur.
> Commande à ta raison d'éviter ces querelles,
> Des tyrans de l'esprit disputes immortelles;
> Ferme en tes sentiments et simple dans ton cœur,
> Aime la vérité, mais pardonne à l'erreur;
> Fuis les emportements d'un zèle atrabilaire;
> Ce mortel qui s'égare est un homme, est ton frère:
> Sois sage pour toi seul, compatissant pour lui;
> Fais ton bonheur enfin par le bonheur d'autrui.
>
> (Second *Discours*, ll. 127–36)

It is not difficult to find echoes of this optimistic view of human nature and human destiny in Voltaire's drama at this period. If one leaves aside *Mérope*, where Voltaire is treating a subject from antiquity, and *L'Envieux* and *Mahomet*, where his intentions are essentially satirical, the plays on which he was working in the years 1734–40 are dominated to a striking degree by the themes of compassion, forgiveness, and reconciliation; nobility of feeling and behaviour proves to be within the capacity of almost all, and simple wickedness is a rarity.

This can be seen even within the traditionally simplistic and grandiose conventions of the opera. In the libretto of *Samson*, the sordid villainy of the biblical Delilah, who betrays her lover's life for a bribe, is transformed. Voltaire's Dalila is the daughter of the king of the Philistines: she falls in love with the Hebrew hero, and sees her marriage to him as a means to peace between the two nations. But she is tricked by the Philistine high priest into obtaining

Samson's secret as a condition of her father's consent to the wedding, without realising the sinister significance of the request;[8] and when she discovers that she is responsible for Samson's downfall, she kills herself, and grief for her becomes an additional motive for her lover's act of suicidal vengeance. By an odd mixture of biblical and classical mythology, the whole tale is elevated, for operatic purposes, to a symbolic struggle between Mars and Venus, with the catastrophe representing the dangerous aspect of the power of love.

In tragedy, there is scope for a much fuller exposition of humanitarian optimism, especially where the subject of the play is entirely of the author's own devising. *Adélaïde du Guesclin* presents a plot centring upon the relationship of Adélaïde to three suitors, two of whom, Vendôme and Nemours (whom she loves) are leaders of opposite factions in a civil war. The dramatic action leans heavily upon misunderstandings and concealments for its effects; very necessarily, since, apart from a phase during which Vendôme is overcome by jealousy, authentically tragic conflict between the characters is inhibited by the nobility, sensitivity, generosity and self-sacrifice which they all exhibit in their dealings with each other. Nemours is saved from the effects of his brother's fit of jealous rage by Coucy's discreet failure to carry out Vendôme's orders for his execution; Vendôme, in remorse, is reconciled with Nemours, blesses the union of the true lovers, and abandons his rebellion against the French King; and Coucy, never a hopeful suitor, is consoled for the loss of Adélaïde by the success of his own efforts to avert general disaster. Reason, order, benevolence and happiness prevail.

Alzire enshrines a similar idealism in a dramatic situation involving much deeper and more genuine conflicts, political and religious. The opening discussion between the retiring Spanish governor of Peru, Alvarez, and his son and successor, Gusman, begins with debate as to whether oppressive severity or humane conciliation is the better policy for consolidating colonial rule; but Alvarez raises the problem from the political to the religious and ethical level by pointing out that it is paradoxical for the Spaniards to impose a cruel tyranny on the Inca people when their moral justification for conquering the country is their duty to spread the true religion; for Christianity is essentially a religion of mercy:

> Ah! Dieu nous envoyait, quand de nous il fit choix,
> Pour annoncer son nom, pour faire aimer ses lois:
> Et nous, de ces climats destructeurs implacables,
> Nous, et d'or et de sang toujours insatiables,
> Déserteurs de ces lois qu'il fallait enseigner,
> Nous égorgeons ce peuple au lieu de le gagner.
> Pour nous tout est en sang, pour nous tout est en poudre,
> Et nous n'avons du ciel imité que la foudre.
>
> (I, i, 75–82)

And the paradox is heightened by the revelation, as the play proceeds, that, Alvarez excepted, *anima naturaliter christiana* is to be found among the Peruvians rather than their Spanish rulers. The emphasis upon clemency as the political expression of the central truth of Christianity—'Et le vrai Dieu, mon fils, est un Dieu qui pardonne' (I, i, 134)—is paralleled at the personal level by the dénouement provided to resolve the triangular relationship between Alzire, the Inca princess; her betrothed Zamore, the leader of resistance to the invaders; and Gusman, whom she marries (for the sake of reconciling the two nations) in the mistaken belief that Zamore is dead. Zamore, deeply wronged both as a lover and as a national leader by the arrogant and cruel Gusman, succeeds in assassinating him; but Gusman, as he dies, remembers his father's exhortations and, all passion spent, brings himself to forgive his attacker and Alzire, and gives his blessing, Mithridate-like, to their future marriage.

Of *Zulime* one cannot speak with complete assurance in relation to the Cirey years: the play was begun in December 1738 (Best.D1685) and first performed in 1740, but not published until 1761, and then without Voltaire's consent; the first authoritative edition is that of 1763, following the stage revival of late December 1761. The 1761 and 1763 editions differ considerably in the construction of the dénouement,[9] and Voltaire clearly never felt very satisfied with the work. Whatever the details of the original conception, however, the central features of the plot can scarcely have been changed. The situation is essentially that of *Bajazet,* with the concealment from Zulime that Ramire, whom she loves, is already married to Atide, but the emotional climate could scarcely differ more. Zulime's father, Bénassar, is no Amurat but a noble-minded and pathetic elderly monarch cast in the mould of Lusignan, hurt by his daughter's disobedience, but ultimately ready to forgive both her and Ramire. Zulime is torn between her passion for Ramire and remorse at the suffering she causes Bénassar; first suspicions of the true nature of Ramire's relationship to Atide inevitably provoked jealousy, but the fifth act develops a situation in which she and Atide vie with each other in forgiving self-abnegation, and her remorseful suicide[10] restores the moral order, acknowledging both the sanctity of Ramire's marriage to Atide and the claims of filial duty. As in earlier tragedies, the ravages of egoistic passion are atoned for, if here not entirely overcome, by sensibility, forgiveness and self-sacrifice.

Comedy provides similar opportunities for stressing the human potential for good, in a setting closer to everyday private life. In *L'Enfant prodigue,* Voltaire offers a combination of traditional *comédie de mœurs* and the newly fashionable sentimental style of Nivelle de la Chaussée, applied to the dramatic presentation of a Christian parable in modern dress. The litigious Baronne de Croupillac, Euphémon's younger son the vain and pompous magistrate Fierenfat, and to a lesser extent Lise's wealthy bourgeois father Rondon, are comic figures descended from Molière and Regnard. They acquire a new aspect, however, with their hard-hearted predatory obsession with money and property, as members of a society whose values have become corrupt and dehumanized, in contrast with the representatives of the newer type of comedy in the play. Euphémon *père* is a noble, benevolent and somewhat pathetic father-figure, in many ways the equivalent of such characters as Lusignan, Alvarez and Bénassar in the tragedies; his elder son, the returning prodigal, is all too sorrowfully conscious of the suffering his earlier misdemeanours have caused, and has lost all taste for the pleasures wealth can bring; while Lise, in the manner of comedy heroines but with rather more independence of mind, firmly rejects a marriage of loveless opulence with Fierenfat and immediately recognizes the fundamental integrity of the long-lost Euphémon *fils,* her former betrothed. Remorse, virtue, sensibility predominate, authentic human values are reasserted, and if moral enlightenment does not universally prevail, at least the incorrigible Fierenfat and madame de Croupillac are paired off together, out of harm's way, by the dénouement, and the play can end with a declaration of faith that potentially all is right with the world and human nature:

> rendons grâces aux cieux,
> Dont les bontés ont tout fait pour le mieux.
> Non, il ne faut (et mon cœur le confesse)
> Désespérer jamais de la jeunesse.

If the hopeful view of human nature, and the value attached to compassion, forgiveness and love in the plays reflect something of Voltaire's personal feelings at this time, this outlook is also coloured in some degree by certain of his intellectual preoccupations. *Alzire*, in particular, reflects a familiar Voltairian critical attitude concerning religion, in emphasising the contrast between the behaviour of the Catholic rulers of Peru and the central moral precepts of the Gospels. This line of attack, deriving ultimately perhaps from Bayle, was that pursued in the *Lettres philosophiques*, with their depiction of the Quakers as people who, whatever their eccentricities, succeed in living the authentically Christian life in spite (or rather, it is implied, because) of their rejection of all ecclesiastical organization. The specifically anticlerical emphasis is absent in *Alzire*, though present marginally in *Samson*, and more strongly in the earlier libretto *Tanis et Zélide*, but *Alzire* is Voltaire's only play which directly presents political oppression as unchristian and indirectly attacks catholicism for condoning it when it assumes the cloak of missionary zeal. Perhaps it was the geographical and historical remoteness of the subject, as much as the general indifference of the age concerning what would now be termed colonial problems, which allowed *Alzire* to achieve popular success without any apparent shadow of official censure, but the subversive implications of the play were not entirely lost on Voltaire's friends.[11]

The optimistic moral attitudes that we have found in the plays can similarly be related, not only to Voltaire's mood at this period, but to his intellectual concern with ethics and even, in some degree, with the problem of free will. In the *Traité de métaphysique* Voltaire insists, following Shaftesbury, that all men are endowed with a natural feeling of benevolence towards their fellows: a benevolence which is one of the roots of human society, along with the natural bonds of sexual and family love. It is liable, however, to come into conflict at times with the equally natural instinct for self-assertion and self-preservation which is *amour-propre,* and social wisdom consists in maintaining a proper balance between the two:

L'homme n'est pas comme les autres animaux qui n'ont que l'instinct de l'amour-propre et celui de l'accouplement; non seulement il a cet amour-propre nécessaire pour sa conservation, mais il a aussi pour son espèce une bienveillance naturelle qui ne se remarque point dans les bêtes. [...] Il est vrai que ce sentiment de pitié et de bienveillance est souvent étouffé par la fureur de l'amour-propre: aussi la nature sage ne devrait pas nous donner plus d'amour pour les autres que pour nous-mêmes; c'est déjà beaucoup que nous ayons cette bienveillance qui nous dispose à l'union avec les hommes.

(Chapter 8. M.XXII, 222)

It is not merely *amour-propre,* however, which can inhibit the activity of *bienveillance.*

Other selfish passions, love, jealousy, envy, can do the same, overlaying the fundamental qualities of the personality to the extent that the individual ceases to be in command of himself, is no longer truly free:

Nous avons souvent des passions violentes qui nous entraînent malgré nous. Un homme voudrait ne pas aimer une maîtresse infidèle, et ses désirs plus forts que la raison le ramènent vers elle; on s'emporte à des actions violentes dans des mouvements de colère qu'on ne peut maîtriser; on souhaite de mener une vie tranquille, et l'ambition nous rejette dans le tumulte des affaires. [. . .]

Lorsque vous aviez cette passion furieuse, votre volonté n'était plus obéie par vos sens: alors vous n'étiez pas plus libre que lorsqu'une paralysie vous empêche de mouvoir ce bras que vous voulez remuer. Si un homme était toute sa vie dominé par des passions violentes, ou par des images qui occupassent sans cesse son cerveau, il lui manquerait cette partie de l'humanité qui consiste à pouvoir penser quelquefois ce qu'on veut; et c'est le cas où sont plusieurs fous qu'on renferme, et même bien d'autres qu'on n'enferme pas.

Il est bien certain qu'il y a des hommes plus libres les uns que les autres, par la même raison que nous ne sommes pas tous également éclairés, également robustes, etc. La liberté est la santé de l'âme; peu de gens ont cette santé entière et inaltérable.

(Chapter 7. M.XXII, 218)

Such a theory of human behaviour seems to shed a good deal of light on the actions of the characters in the plays we have discussed. Love and pride provoke Vendôme, in *Adélaïde,* to acts of jealous anger which temporarily deny his natural feelings for his brother; in *Alzire,* a harsh arrogance prevents Gusman from seeing Alzire and Zamore as fully human beings, until the approach of death brings home to him the vanity of his pride and the true nature of his actions; Zulime's passion for Ramire blinds her to any awareness of his relationship to Atide, and turns her, to her great distress, into a disobedient daughter; Samson is betrayed by his love for Dalila, but she too is a victim of deception through her longing to marry him; and in *L'Enfant prodigue,* Euphémon *fils,* with the passionate follies of youth behind him, emerges as a generous and sensitive, as well as remorseful, human being, even though the comic figures, madame de Croupillac and Fierenfat, remain locked in the grip of their obsessive passions. For Samson and Zulime the situation is indeed irretrievable, but for both of them suicide is a positive act, an assertion of liberty recovered, whether as Old Testament vengeance in the destruction of the Philistines or as conscious self-sacrifice in atonement for disobedience and in tribute to the sanctity of marriage. In other cases, a happy outcome is possible, not, as one might at first glance imagine, through the intervention of an implausibly miraculous 'conversion' of such men as Vendôme and Gusman, but because the events of the play are such as finally to release them from the dominance of passion, allowing them to recover freedom and their true selves. They speak of themselves, at the crucial moment, in very similar terms. For Vendôme, it is the cannon-shot supposedly announcing Nemours's execution which breaks the spell, and brings home to him the true nature of his acts: he exclaims:

Il est mort, et je vis! Et la terre entr'ouverte,
Et la foudre en éclats n'ont point vengé sa perte.
Ennemi de l'État, factieux, inhumain,
Frère dénaturé, ravisseur, assassin,

> Voilà quel est Vendôme! Ah! vérité funeste!
> Je vois ce que je suis, et ce que je déteste!
> Le voile est déchiré, je m'étais mal connu.
>
> *(Adélaïde du Guesclin, v.3)*

For the dying Gusman, it is the sight of his father and the recollection of what Alvarez stands for:

> Le ciel, qui veut ma mort, et qui l'a suspendue,
> Mon père, en ce moment m'amène à votre vue.
> Mon âme fugitive, et prête à me quitter,
> S'arrête devant vous ... mais pour vous imiter.
> Je meurs; le voile tombe; un nouveau jour m'éclaire;
> Je ne me suis connu qu'au bout de ma carrière;
> J'ai fait, jusqu'au moment qui me plonge au cercueil,
> Gémir l'humanité du poids de mon orgueil.
> Le ciel venge la terre: il est juste; et ma vie
> Ne peut payer le sang dont ma main s'est rougie.
> Le bonheur m'aveugla, la mort m'a détrompé.
> Je pardonne à la main par qui Dieu m'a frappé.
>
> *(Alzire, v.7)*

It is in the cooler atmosphere of comedy, however, that the process of release from passion can be most clearly defined. In *L'Enfant prodigue,* Lise sounds out the father's reactions by describing in hypothetical terms the change that has taken place in the prodigal son:

> Monsieur, si son expérience
> Eût reconnu la triste jouissance
> De ces faux biens, objets de ses transports,
> Nés de l'erreur, et suivis des remords;
> Honteux enfin de sa folle conduite,
> Si sa raison, par le malheur instruite,
> De ses vertus rallumant le flambeau,
> Le ramenait avec un cœur nouveau;
> Ou que plutôt, honnête homme et fidèle,
> Il eût repris sa forme naturelle;
> Pourriez-vous bien lui fermer aujourd'hui
> L'accès d'un cœur qui fut ouvert pour lui?
>
> *(L'Enfant prodigue, v.5)*

Once reality has penetrated to the individual's sensibility—usually, as with Vendôme, through the agency of an emotional shock—the veil falls, lucidity reasserts itself, and the personality can once again assume, in full freedom, 'sa forme naturelle'. These plays end in enlightenment and reconciliation, affirming the existence in all men of a fundamental generosity of spirit which can lead them, if released, to harmony and freedom. There is nothing here as negative as, for instance, the despairing suicide of Orosmane at the end of *Zaïre,* and authentically evil characters seem to occur at this period only in *Mérope,* where the classic story requires a ruthless tyrant, Polyphonte, and *Mahomet,* where the prophet himself is the focus of hostility in what is essentially a propaganda play.[12]

Voltaire's compassionate and ultimately hopeful view of human nature, as it manifests itself in the plays of this period, thus seems to reflect both his own contentment and the optimistic moral attitudes formulated intellectually in the *Traité de métaphysique*. The wider problem of human destiny is one that does not appear to trouble him deeply at this stage: the cosmic optimism implied in Newtonian deism, and memorably expressed by Pope in the *Essay on Man,* seems to satisfy him (though with certain hesitations), and in the *Traité de métaphysique* he attempts to dismiss the problem of evil by exonerating God from any specific moral responsibility for the behaviour of his creatures: the framework of the cosmos is rational and orderly, and within that framework man must conduct his affairs as best he can (M.XXII,228). 'Les horreurs du destin' which overshadow *Œdipe* are now no longer present. It is interesting, indeed, that in the only dramatic work of these years which raises such issues, the opera libretto *Pandore,* 'le Destin' appears, personified, as a beneficent, rational power who outwits the machinations of the selfish and tyrannical Jupiter and preserves the world from destruction by him. Here, evil is launched into the world by the selfish malice of the Olympian gods, but man in compensation is given the pleasure of love, and the capacity for hope. Voltaire's first *conte philosophique,* the brief *Songe de Platon,*[13] leads to similar conclusions: the cosmos, if not perfect in detail, is as perfect overall as its inevitable limitations allow, and must be accepted as it is.

Voltaire's idealism and personal contentment during these years thus seem to underlie both the moral atmosphere of his major imaginative works and the more precise conceptions of his writings on ethics; and some of the latter are themselves exemplified by patterns of behaviour in the plays. And all this seems reinforced by the cosmic structure of order and rationality confirmed for him by Newtonian science. Art and thought are not, in fact, as much in a state of tension as was suggested by some of the comments, by Voltaire and others, we examined earlier. Or rather, such tension as there is exists, not at any profound level of his personality, but rather at the level of expressivity. His fundamental outlook is quite strongly coherent (more so, one suspects, than in his early years of literary and social ambition, or during the disillusionments and upheavals of the 1750s), his multifarious activities reflect a single vision. But the literary forms whereby they are expressed, being for the most part rooted in tradition, inevitably offered some resistance to the material to be conveyed. Burlesque epic was a perfectly conventional genre to adopt for the purpose of making fun of a saintly national heroine, and the development of tragedy during the earlier years of the century made it a ready enough receptacle for the effusive melodrama of *Adélaïde du Guesclin* and the political and moral conflicts of *Alzire;* but to attempt to use the public theatre to attack religious fanaticism in *Mahomet* was a bold venture in more ways than one.

'Faire des vers' was an irrepressible impulse in Voltaire, and the adaptation of the moral *épître* to somewhat unorthodox philosophical views in the *Discours en vers sur l'homme* has perhaps a certain originality.[14] Most important of all, however, is the fact that it was during these years, when Voltaire's full intellectual and moral personality was emerging, that he made his two major innovations in the field of literary form. His growing concern with humanity at large, reflected in the 'Discours préliminaire' of *Alzire,* took him again to the study of history, but now with an angle of vision much wider than the traditional pre-occupation with the exploits of heroic warriors which still largely dominated his *Charles XII*. *Le Siècle de Louis XIV*, begun at Cirey, was intended from the first to be a new kind of history, concerned with all the achievements of French civilization, proclaiming, in fact, a new scale of social values; and as such, in effect, a new art form. And with *Le Songe de Platon*, and *Le Voyage du Baron de Gangan*, the first version of *Micromégas*, he began to adapt prose fiction in a quite new way, to become a stimulus to critical thought for the reader and a vehicle for the expression of his own beliefs, questions and satirical hostilities, over a wide range of moral and philosophical issues. To have invented both social and cultural history and the *conte philosophique* can be seen as the most fruitful achievement to which Voltaire was led by the tensions of the Cirey years; by finding, in this way, new literary vehicles for the expression of his concern with humanity and with enlightenment, he also, as time has shown, assured himself of immortality, for these genres have lived where much else in Voltaire's *œuvre* has disappeared from the sight of all but scholars.

NOTES

1 In *The Intellectual Development of Voltaire* (Princeton, 1969), I. O. Wade summarizes the conclusions arrived at in his earlier writings.

2 *La Henriade* (revised edition 1736), *La Pucelle* (begun in 1734, ten cantos written by August 1735); *Adélaïde du Guesclin* (revised after first performance, 1734), *Alzire* (1734–6), *Mérope* (1737–8), *Zulime* (1738–40), *Mahomet* (1739–41); *Le Comte de Boursoufle* (1735), *L'Enfant prodigue* (1736), *L'Envieux* (1738), *La Prude* (1739–40); *Samson* (under revision, 1734–6), *Pandore* (1740); *Le Mondain* (1736), *Discours en vers sur l'homme* (1737–8); *Le Songe de Platon* (1737); *Voyage du baron de Gangan* (1738).

3 *Traité de métaphysique* (1734–7), *La Métaphysique de Newton* (1739–40); *Éléments de la philosophie de Newton* (1736–40); *Essai sur la nature du feu* (1738).

4 *Le Siècle de Louis XIV* (1735–40); *La Vie de Molière* (1734–9); *Observations sur Mm. Jean Lass, Melon et Dutot* (1738); *L'Anti-Machiavel* (1739–40).

5 Madame de Graffigny suggests that, in 1738 at least, Voltaire was the object of conflicting pressures on this issue within the household at Cirey. She writes in December: 'J'ai enfin achevé Newton, je suis bien aise de savoir que Voltaire sait aussi bien rêver qu'un autre; mais je le persécute pour ne plus rêver. Nous disputons souvent pour cela, il ne demande pas mieux, car il me dit encore hier: "Ma foi! laissez là Newton, ce sont des rêveries, vivent les vers!" Il aime à en faire avec passion, et la belle dame le persécute toujours pour n'en plus faire. La grosse dame et moi, nous la contrarions tant que nous pouvons: c'est affreux d'empêcher Voltaire de faire des vers!' (Best.D1725). If madame Du Châtelet really did discourage Voltaire in this way, the reason may well have been in part that she felt that works on physics were less likely to involve Voltaire in trouble than *La Pucelle* and *Le Mondain*.

6 It is not clear whether Voltaire was tempted to see gravitational attraction as an analogue of divine and human love: some other French Newtonians certainly did so.

7 The *Traité de métaphysique,* in spite of its title, purports to be primarily an analysis of man; and I shall hope to show in a forthcoming edition of this text that there are grounds for thinking that the 'anthropological', social and ethical elements in it grew in relative importance in Voltaire's successive drafts over the years 1734–7.

8 The religious fanatic and the ambitious tyrant, Voltaire's lifelong favourites as dramatic villains, either separately or rolled into one character, would seem to make their début, oddly enough, here and in Voltaire's slightly earlier opera, *Tanis et Zélide.*

9 In the 1761 text, it is Atide, not Zulime, who kills herself: M.IV,90.

10 That this was a feature of the first version of the play seems attested by Voltaire's letter to Mlle Quinault of 19 April 1740, Best.D2200.

11 See Cideville's letter to Voltaire, *c.* 5 February 1736, Best.D1002.

12 Even Mahomet, however, conforms in some degree to the pattern of behaviour we have been describing. In the final scene of Act v, under the shock of the suicide of Palmire, whose conquest was to be for him one of the fruits of his crimes in causing the deaths of her father and brother Zopire and Séide, he for the first time feels remorse and guilt; but he is too much in love with power to admit the truth about himself in public and accept the consequences; like Shakespeare's Claudius, he 'cannot repent'; true freedom is not accessible to him:

> Il est donc des remords! ô fureur! ô justice!
> Mes forfaits dans mon cœur ont donc mis mon supplice!
> [. . .]
> Je me sens condamné, quand l'univers m'adore,
> Je brave en vain les traits dont je me sens frapper.
> J'ai trompé les mortels, et ne puis me tromper.
> [. . .]

(to Omar)   Et toi, de tant de honte étouffe la mémoire;
> Cache au moins ma faiblesse, et sauve encore ma gloire:
> Je dois régir en dieu l'univers prévenu;
> Mon empire est détruit si l'homme est reconnu.

13 The arguments for assigning the composition of this work to the late 1730s seem on the whole plausible: see J. Van den Heuvel, *Voltaire dans ses contes* (Paris, 1967), pp. 61–7.

14 The *Épître à Uranie* is of course an earlier, and more virulent, example; but it was never meant for publication.

2

Diderot's Optics: An Aspect of his Philosophical and Literary Expression

DAVID BERRY

Among the many important contributions which Professor Robert Niklaus has made to research in the field of eighteenth-century studies, one of the most valuable for both scholar and student is his critical edition of Diderot's *Lettre sur les aveugles*.[1] The excellence of this edition is acknowledged by the editor of the recent complete works of Diderot who publishes the text of the *Lettre sur les aveugles*, as established by Professor Niklaus, in the second volume of the new *Œuvres Complètes*.[2] The *Lettre sur les aveugles* focuses our attention on a problem which was to preoccupy Diderot in many areas of his writing, the problem of physical vision and its relationship to both philosophical vision and imaginative vision. In the *Lettre sur les aveugles* the discussion of the physical serves as a pretext for speculations on the metaphysical, with the psychological problems of sightlessness becoming a springboard towards philosophical insight and illumination. Thus, as Professor Niklaus remarks: 'L'aveugle de Diderot [. . .] est un symbole commode pour approfondir certains aspects de la doctrine sensualiste et propager certaines théories matérialistes rien moins que nouvelles. Diderot n'a vraiment pas voulu qu'on lise sa *Lettre* pour résoudre les problèmes de la cécité'.[3] The theme of blindness in Diderot's work has been examined by G. Norman Laidlaw,[4] who shows how, æsthetically, blindness becomes a useful symbol for the limitation of man's mental and spiritual powers, a blindness which can be induced through submissiveness to authority or through faith in something other than human reason and so vividly illustrated, for example, in *La Promenade du sceptique* by the various allusions to the *bandeau* with which the Church blindfolds its victims or by an image in which creatures spiritually benighted are dazzled by the light of truth: 'Présenter la vérité à de certaines gens, c'est [. . .] introduire un rayon de lumière dans un nid de hiboux; il ne sert qu'à blesser leurs yeux et à exciter leurs cris [. . .]; leur aveuglement est systématique' (*O.C.,* I, 317–18). However, for Diderot, this theme of blindness is simply an aspect, albeit important and provocative, of his ever-present concern with the visual, the ocular and the optical.

Diderot's fascination with the visual is strikingly evident. On the one hand it is revealed by his various discussions of the expressive power of mime, notably in his *Entretiens sur le Fils Naturel*: 'Le pantomime joue; et le philosophe transporté s'écrie: "Je ne te vois pas

C

seulement. Je t'entends. Tu me parles des mains"' (*O.C.*, III, 139); in the section devoted to 'De la pantomime' in the *Discours sur la poésie dramatique*; and in his review in 1779 of a pamphlet by Cochin, *Pantomime dramatique*: 'de mettre en pantomime tout ce qui se comprend par les yeux, sans avoir besoin de l'interprétation vocale' (*O.C.*, XII, 753), where he also emphasizes the importance of imaginative grouping on the stage, a notion which is linked to his earlier stress, in both the *Discours* and the *Entretiens,* on the need for exploiting the expressive possibilities of *tableaux vivants* and *tableaux mouvants* in the theatre.[5] From his remarks in the *Lettre sur les sourds et muets,* we know also that Diderot stopped up his ears in the theatre in order to surrender himself fully to the emotions communicated by the gestures of the actors. On the other hand Diderot's whole involvement with art-criticism, his powerful response to the visual arts, and his growing sense of awareness that through his examination of painting he was able to discover the rich resources of his own creative imagination provide a further indication of his absorption with the world of the visual.[6]

Thus, as Diderot makes abundantly clear, the importance of the eye, for the philosopher, dramatist and painter, is paramount. Of all the senses, vision is the one which he discusses most fully and whose manifold aspects spread into all areas of his writing. In the *Éléments de physiologie* the section on the eye occupies twice as much space as that devoted to all the other four senses; its anatomy and physiology are minutely described, together with various related anomalies, with the whole section developing into a curious optical miscellany (*O.C.*, XIII, 771–5).

The eye has enormous interest for Diderot both as one of the most striking examples of natural physiological complexity, appealing to his scientific curiosity: 'cet œil, cette machine admirable' (*O.C.*, XI, 55); and also as a fascinating object in its own right, appealing to his imagination, as we see from a passage which, through the alliteration and assonance, goes beyond scientific statement to become a quasi-poetic description:

[. . .] il n'y a point de peintre assez habile pour approcher de la beauté et de l'exactitude des miniatures qui se peignent dans le fond de nos yeux, [. . .] tout le temps nécessaire aux humeurs de l'œil pour se disposer convenablement; à la cornée, pour prendre la convexité requise à la vision; à la prunelle, pour être susceptible de la dilatation et du rétrécissement qui lui sont propres; aux filets de la rétine, pour n'être ni trop ni trop peu sensibles à l'action de la lumière. (*O.C.*, II, 210–11)

Among the myriad of references to the eye we discover that, even though it is a highly complex organ, it is perhaps the most superficial of the senses: 'je trouvais que de tous les sens l'œil était le plus superficiel' (*O.C.*, II, 525), easily duped by optical illusions: 'Le peuple se sert mieux de ses yeux que de son entendement' (*O.C.*, XIII, 503), the most lascivious and flirtatious, the sense which, of all others, is essentially that of the *femme galante,* 'celle dont l'âme est tantôt dans le bijou, et tantôt dans les yeux' (*O.C.*, I, 594). In a moment of fantasy, Diderot imagines the senses transformed into geometers, with the eye rapidly resorting to its obsession with colours: 'Bientôt l'œil bigarrera son discours et ses calculs de couleurs' (*O.C.*, II, 573). At the same time Diderot frequently stresses that the faculty of sight must be sharpened before philosophic insight can be obtained: 'il faut [. . .] que l'œil apprenne à voir' (*O.C.*, II, 207), specifically defining the philosopher as 'un homme clairvoyant qui a longtemps réfléchi sur la meilleure manière d'user de ses yeux, selon les différentes circonstances' (*O.C.*, XI, 564),[7] and showing how, as soon as the philosopher has trained himself, like Dorval, to look at the world with a perceptive and penetrating gaze, he will begin to experience a sense of discovery and joyous surprise: 'Il s'était abandonné au spectacle de la nature. [. . .] Ses yeux attentifs se portaient sur tous les objets. Je suivais sur son visage les impressions diverses qu'il en éprouvait; et je commençais à partager son transport' (*O.C.*, III, 136).

If at times Diderot, the scientist, underlines the delicate and vulnerable nature of the eye: 'L'œil est un organe délicat qui ne veut pas être fatigué' (*O.C.*, III, 729), then at others its fragility and complexity provoke a response from Diderot, the poet. In *Mystification ou Histoire des portraits,* during a discussion of the Epicurean notion that vision is the result of the transference of simulacra from the object to the eyes, the retina inspires an image which later, in *Le Rêve de d'Alembert,* is to recur with even more vivid relevance: 'Qu'est-ce qu'une rétine? [. . .] C'est une toile d'araignée tissue des fils nerveux les plus déliés, les plus fins, les plus sensibles du corps, qui tapisse le fond de l'œil' (*O.C.*, VII, 457). In the *Rêve* the spider's web image is extended to the whole nervous system, with the spider representing the brain; whilst the conjunction of the retina with the web is comparable in tone to the delicate juxtaposition, in this same context, of eyes and flowers: 'Vos yeux, ces beaux yeux, ne ressemblaient non plus à des yeux, que l'extrémité d'une griffe d'anémone ne ressemble à une anémone' (*O.C.*, VIII, 104). The eye not only attracts images but creates images, most of which are fairly commonplace, involving the idea of spiritual vision or intellectual perception: 'L'entendement a ses yeux' (*O.C.*, I, 59) or 'Et l'œil de mon entendement continua d'être ouvert' (*O.C.*, II, 701); or expressing the notion that nature keeps a close watch on human behaviour and is always prompt to punish those who go against natural laws: 'la nature a ses vues; et [. . .] vous verrez sa vengeance sur tous ceux qui les ont trompées; les hommes punis du célibat par le vice, les femmes par le mépris et par l'ennui' (*O.C.*, III, 294). The essential figurative use of the eye is concerned with the inner eye, the eye of the imagination, and is well illustrated in the chapter on imagination in the *Éléments de physiologie* where Diderot begins with the traditional notion of the inner eye and then proceeds to elaborate it through a series of optical associations:

L'imagination [. . .] est l'œil intérieur, et la mesure des imaginations est relative à la mesure de la vue. Les aveugles ont de l'imagination, parce que le vice n'est que dans la rétine.

[. . .] Celui qui a les yeux microscopiques, aura aussi l'imagination microscopique. Avec des idées très précises de chaque partie, il pourrait bien n'en avoir que de très précaires du tout. (*O.C.*, XIII, 790).

Not unexpectedly, in the context of visual and æsthetic discussion, the *Salons* provide several allusions to the eye of the imagination: 'L'imagination passe rapidement d'image en image; son œil embrasse tout à la fois' (*O.C.*, VII, 103), together with the profusion of references to the eye in the multiplicity of activities it performs when confronted by a painting: 'L'œil est partout arrêté, récréé, satisfait' (*O.C.*, V, 436), 'l'œil est arrêté, il se repose. Satisfait partout, il se repose partout; il s'avance, il s'enfonce, il est ramené sur sa trace' (*O.C.*, VI, 270), and 'Ce qui achève d'augmenter la confusion, la discordance, la fatigue de l'œil' (*O.C.*, VII, 212). This personification of the eye, frequently demonstrated in the *Salons,* is obviously, in the language of art-criticism, simply a kind of expressive shorthand for communicating the critic's mental and emotional response to a painting. Nonetheless it does help to indicate the emphasis which Diderot places on the eye as a creature functioning, it seems, in its own right, a sort of living animal, as is vividly shown in the *Éléments de physiologie*:

L'œil nous mène; nous sommes l'aveugle. L'œil est le chien qui nous conduit; et si l'œil n'était pas réellement un animal se prêtant à la diversité des sensations, comment nous conduirait-il?[. . .] C'est que l'œil est un animal dans un animal exerçant très bien ses fonctions tout seul. (*O.C.,* XIII, 809)

Also in the *Salons* Diderot often comments on the skill of certain artists in investing the eyes of their figures with the feelings appropriate to the event depicted, an aspect which he underlines in his chapter on artistic expressivity in the *Essai sur la peinture*: 'L'œil s'allume, s'éteint, languit, s'égare, se fixe; et une grande imagination de peintre est un recueil immense de toutes ces expressions' (*O.C.* VI, 278–9). As a creative artist himself, Diderot exploits the expressive language of the eyes in his own fiction, notably in *La Religieuse,* where, apart from the various pictorially inspired *tableaux vivants* à la Greuze which help to give visual relief to the heroine's emotional torments, we also find a whole network of disturbing ocular effects: 'elle lut apparemment dans mes yeux [. . .] que le sentiment profond que je portais en moi était au-dessus de ses forces' (*O.C., IV*, 537), 'on me suivait de l'œil; je ne faisais pas un pas qui ne fût éclairé' (ibid., 549), and 'ses yeux, dont l'un, c'est le droit, est plus haut et plus grand que l'autre, sont pleins de feu et distraits' (ibid., 613).

A further aspect of Diderot's preoccupation with the visual is revealed through his references to optical science. The principal discoveries in the field of experimental optics in the eighteenth century were made known with the publication in 1704 of Newton's *Opticks,* describing his analysis of white light into the several colours of the spectrum and virtually initiating research into colour vision. Optics and its two main branches, catoptrics, concerned with reflected light, and dioptrics, concerned with refracted light, feature in the list of scientific subjects presented in the *Prospectus de l'Encyclopédie* (*O.C.,* II, 308). However, Diderot himself is not particularly interested, on the scientific level, in the problems of optics: 'L'optique, la dioptrique, la catoptrique, ne sont que trois problèmes généraux à résoudre. Combien l'algèbre abrège de discours et de temps' (*O.C.,*XI, 781).[8] He is more concerned with the general development of visual aids in scientific research and with the technical refinement of optical instruments, which, apart from Newton's discoveries and the creation of photometry by Pierre Bouguer, a branch of optics dealing with the intensity of light and put forward in his *Essai d'optique sur la graduation de la lumière* of 1729,[9] represents the eighteenth century's major contribution to optical science.

This general contemporary interest in optics is reflected in a number of places in Diderot's work. During the Age of the Enlightenment, telescopes, microscopes, prisms and lenses become the illustrious symbols of scientific progress. In *La Promenade du sceptique,* after the 'Discours préliminaire', the opening paragraph of the work proper includes two optical references: the first to the superior quality of the contemporary telescope and its importance to posterity: 'des avantages que la géographie, la navigation, l'astronomie retireront, dans deux ou trois mille ans, des prodiges de mon quart de cercle et l'excellence de mes lunettes' (O.C., I, 325); the second to the value, to the philosopher, of cultivating his powers of observation to a degree of almost microscopic intensity in order to apprehend the true nature of the world around him: 'Tout ce qui nous environne est un sujet d'observation. Les objets qui nous sont les plus familiers, peuvent être pour nous des merveilles; tout dépend du coup d'œil. S'il est distrait, il nous trompe; s'il est perçant et réfléchi, il nous approche de la vérité' (ibid., 326). In this same work telescopes, not surprisingly, are a part of the scenery along the 'allée des marronniers', the pathway which leads symbolically to the domain of philosophical reflection and speculation: 'Dans l'allée des marronniers, on a des sphères, des globes, des télescopes, des livres' (ibid., 330). In the chapter given over to the celebrated allegorical dream of Les Bijoux indiscrets, a chapter which Diderot himself describes as 'le meilleur peut-être, et le moins lu de cette histoire', the gigantic figure symbolizing experimental truth, in its apocalyptic advance across the centuries, is seen to wield, in imitation of Galileo and Newton, both the telescope and the prism: 'Dans le progrès de ses accroissements successifs, il m'apparut sous cent formes diverses, je le vis diriger vers le ciel un long télescope, [. . .] et, le prisme à la main, décomposer la lumière' (O.C., I, 604-5). Later in this same novel we are told of an astronomer who, obsessed with the desire not to miss the passing of a certain comet, dies with his eye still glued to the end of his telescope: 'il est mort [. . .] la main gauche sur l'œil du même côté, la droite posée sur le tuyau du télescope, et l'œil droit appliqué au verre oculaire' (ibid., 673).

It is logical, therefore, as we see in the Suite de l'apologie de l'abbé de Prades, that any possible weakening of the tolerant attitudes of the Enlightenment, particularly towards scientific research, and any subsequent return to the dark ages of religious persecution would best be represented for Diderot by the destruction of those very instruments which have done so much to transform and enrich our knowledge of the material world: 'Si, à la première découverte qui se fera, [. . .] nous devons renouveler dans la personne de l'inventeur l'injure faite autrefois à la philosophie dans la personne de Galilée, allons, brisons les microscopes, foulons aux pieds les télescopes, et soyons les apôtres de la barbarie' (O.C., II, 636). The idea of the telescope as a weapon which has played heretical havoc with religious doctrines is again evoked in the Réfutation d'Hemsterhuis. To Hemsterhuis's statement that the greatest revolution in ideas took place when the world was shown to be merely a planet like so many others, Diderot retorts: 'Vous avez raison: le quart de cercle et le télescope furent deux machines bien impies' (O.C., XI, 87). The Lettre sur les aveugles, on the other hand, shows us optical instruments not so much as weapons in an ideological war but rather as obstacles in a conceptual struggle. How can objects which are essentially optical fit into a world in which the optical has no place? If, to the blind man of Puiseaux, the mirror is conceived in tactile terms as a complex piece of machinery, then the microscope and telescope become even more amazing and elaborate: 'Il nous fit cent questions bizarres sur ces phénomènes. Il nous demanda, par exemple, s'il n'y avait que ceux qu'on appelle naturalistes qui vissent avec le microscope, et si les astronomes étaient les seuls qui vissent avec le télescope' (O.C., II, 167).

The prism in its turn has a place among Diderot's collection of optical devices. As we
have noticed in *Les Bijoux indiscrets,* the prism seems to become in Diderot's mind a kind of
metonymy for Isaac Newton. Its importance is highlighted in *Pensée* 23 of the *Pensées sur
l'interprétation de la nature*:

Nous avons distingué deux sortes de philosophie, l'expérimentale et la rationnelle. L'une a les yeux
bandés, marche toujours en tâtonnant, saisit tout ce qui lui tombe sous les mains et rencontre à la fin
des choses précieuses. L'autre recueille ces matières précieuses, et tâche de s'en former un flambeau:
mais ce flambeau prétendu lui a jusqu'à présent moins servi que le tâtonnement à sa rivale; et cela
devait être. L'expérience multiplie ses mouvements à l'infini; elle est sans cesse en action; elle met à
chercher des phénomènes, tout le temps que la raison emploie à chercher des analogies. La philosophie
expérimentale ne sait ni ce qui lui viendra ni ce qui ne lui viendra pas de son travail; mais elle travaille
sans relâche. Au contraire la philosophie rationnelle pèse les possibilités, prononce et s'arrête tout
court. Elle dit hardiment: *On ne peut décomposer la lumière*; la philosophie expérimentale l'écoute, et
se tait devant elle pendant des siècles entiers; puis tout à coup elle montre le prisme, et dit: *La lumière
se décompose.* (O.C., II, 728)

In this *Pensée* Diderot discusses the general nature of two systems of thought, Newtonism
and Cartesianism, and shows how the inductive approach of the former is infinitely preferable to the deductive approach of the latter. This is not to say that Diderot revolted against
rationalism as such but simply against the belief, held by many of his contemporaries, that
the reason was so infallible that the observation of natural phenomena was superfluous.
His analysis proceeds through a series of expressive antitheses, with the two abstract systems
being thrown into relief by means of personification. At the same time an element of
deliberate paradox gives additional piquancy to the stylistic presentation. In a seemingly
contradictory manner it is the figure of experimental philosophy who, blindfolded, gropes
his way towards the treasures of truth whilst the figure of rational philosophy remains
static, with the torch with which he attempts to illuminate the world finally going out
through lack of energy and fuel. Thus blindfolded empiricism is shown to achieve vision
whilst perceptive rationalism is ultimately kept in the dark. In the final lines the prism makes
its appearance and triumphantly justifies the experimental approach. Thus, in a *Pensée* in
which the abstract notion is rendered concrete through predominantly visual and optical
figurations, the initial idea is itself decomposed, so to speak, into a number of literary
refractions, finally invoking, through some strange collusion of matter and manner, the
instrument of refraction itself.

Apart from their function as important pieces of scientific apparatus, optical instruments
in the eighteenth century were also considered as fascinating objects of beauty. In the
Salon of 1765 a painting by Chardin, *Les Attributs des sciences,* wins warm praise from Diderot
for both the subject and the treatment, depicting, as it does, among other things, the
principal accessories of optical science:

On voit, sur une table couverte d'un tapis rougeâtre, en allant, je crois, de la droite à la gauche, des
livres posés sur la tranche, un microscope, une clochette, un globe à demi caché d'un rideau de taffetas
vert, un thermomètre, un miroir concave sur son pied, une lorgnette avec son étui, des cartes roulées,
un bout de télescope.

C'est la nature même, pour la vérité des formes et de la couleur; les objets se séparent les uns des autres, avancent, reculent, comme s'ils étaient réels, rien de plus harmonieux; et nulle confusion, malgré leur nombre et le petit espace. (*O.C.*, vi, 89)

This quality of a harmonious and sensuous reality which Diderot responded to so intensely in Chardin's work is in the same æsthetic vein as the poetic realism which caused him such rapturous delight in the painting of Vernet. In the *Salon* of 1763 Diderot is particularly enchanted by Vernet's *Le Port de la Rochelle*, with its ravishing sense of perspective and its truthfulness to nature, above all in respect of the sky, which seems to be suffused with light— 'Qui est-ce qui entend la perspective aérienne mieux que cet homme-là?', he exclaims—; and in order to communicate to the reader his admiration for the way in which the artist has captured reality in his painting, has created a beautiful microcosm of nature, he calls upon the aid of a telescope:

Regardez *le Port de La Rochelle* avec une lunette qui embrasse le champ du tableau et qui exclue la bordure, et oubliant tout à coup que vous examinez un morceau de peinture, vous vous écrierez, comme si vous étiez placé au haut d'une montagne, spectateur de la nature même: 'Oh! le beau point de vue!' (*O.C.*, v, 440)

Later in this *Salon* the same injunction is made to the reader with regard to Greuze's portrait of his wife, another masterpiece of naturalism: '[. . .] regardez-le avec une lunette, et vous verrez la nature même; je vous défie de me nier que cette figure ne vous regarde et ne vive' (*O.C.*, v, 452). Thus for Diderot the telescope becomes a means to æsthetic as well as scientific truth, with optics put at the service of art. Elsewhere in the *Salons* the only way he can imagine one particularly dull and disorderly painting, *La Construction de la nouvelle halle* by Machy, as serving any useful purpose is to consign it to the realm of optics by considering it as an image projected by a magic lantern: 'c'est un vrai tableau de lanterne magique. Comme il montre des grues, des échafauds, du fracas, et qu'il papillote bien d'ombres noires, très noires, et de lumières blanches, très blanches, projeté sur un grand drap, il réjouira beaucoup les enfants' (*O.C.*, vi, 113).

Further references to optics occur in a number of figurative contexts.[10] Microscopes and telescopes are, as images, transformed into instruments of wider philosophical vision, transcending the limits of the purely optical. The role played by such objects in Diderot's metaphorical expression reveals his more personal response to eighteenth-century optics, suggesting an interest which went beyond a merely superficial knowledge of microscopy and a taste for the fashionable pursuit of star-gazing, and showing the degree to which scientific activities appealed to his creative imagination. The stress which Diderot, at the opening of *La Promenade du sceptique*, places on observation as an essential part of philosophical enquiry has already been noted. The eye of the philosopher must be constantly on the alert, scrupulously seizing the minutiæ of material reality with his probing glance, subjecting it to his own self-developed microscopic vision, and bringing into clear focus previously disregarded truths about the world around him.

In the same way microscopic vision represents an important element in Diderot's æsthetic theories, particularly those concerned with literary realism, in which the illusion of truthfulness is often created by the expressive detail, as we see from remarks on the nature of literary genius in the *Éloge de Richardson*:[11] 'l'art du grand poète et du grand peintre est de vous montrer une circonstance fugitive qui vous avait échappé. [. . .] Sachez que c'est à cette multitude de petites choses que tient l'illusion' (*O.C.*, v, 133). In a work characterized by its use of physiological imagery, the *Lettre d'un citoyen zélé*, Diderot argues on behalf of a closer relationship between medicine and surgery; and, in keeping with the scientific images in which his discussion is couched, he refers to his own view-point as a microscope which attempts to see the problem in close-up: 'Du moins c'est ainsi que je me peins la plupart des médecins et des chirurgiens d'aujourd'hui, et que vous les verrez comme moi, si vous avez la bonté de les considérer un moment avec mon microscope' (*O.C.*, II, 151). Elsewhere, in a section of the *Réfutation d'Helvétius* devoted to a discussion of the interaction of the senses and the manner in which one highly developed sense might affect the others, Diderot evokes both the microscope and the telescope in order to intimate the power, influence and sensitivity of refined faculties: 'Une sensation fortuite n'est qu'un fait de plus; mais une sensation produite par un organe exquis et prodigieux est une multitude prodigieuse de faits; c'est la réunion du télescope et du microscope'; and then, as if to show up the absurdity of Helvétius's views on the limitations of the senses, he caps his statement with the ironic question: 'Le microscope n'a-t-il enrichi la physique d'un fait?' (*O.C.*, XI, 514–15).

Likewise telescopes help Diderot to bring certain airy philosophical abstractions down to earth and closer to the mind of the reader. In his translation of Shaftesbury's *Essay on Merit and Virtue*, the ability to look at life optimistically and broadly is represented as a telescope through which injustice and misfortune are placed in a more tolerable perspective: 'A travers ce télescope, on aperçoit les accidents particuliers, les injustices et les méchancetés, dans un jour qui dispose à les tolérer et à conserver dans le cours de la vie toute l'égalité possible. Ce tour d'affection et ce télescope moral sont donc vraiment excellents; et la créature qui les possède est bonne et vertueuse par excellence' (*O.C.*, I, 127). It is significant that, even in what is a fairly free translation of Shaftesbury's essay, this image of the telescope is not present in the original work and has been inserted by Diderot to give more concrete relief to Shaftesbury's notions. However, telescopes vary in their powers of magnification, a fact which Diderot uses in the *Pensées philosophiques* to underline that human beings consider the world in a variety of different ways, each through his own private telescope, the lenses of which place things in a different focus to those of others. Thus the broad moral outlook provided by the wide-angled telescope of the *Essai sur le mérite et la vertu* has, in the *Pensées*, been narrowed down by the lenses of personal prejudice:

Chaque esprit a son télescope. C'est un colosse à mes yeux que cette objection qui disparaît aux vôtres: vous trouvez légère une raison qui m'écrase. [. . .] Sont-ce mes lunettes qui pèchent ou les vôtres? (*O.C.*, I, 285)

The idea, encountered in the *Réfutation d'Helvétius,* that the senses are like optical instruments is also found in the *Lettre sur les aveugles,* where those that see are shown to have one more telescope than the blind: 'ils ont un télescope de plus' (*O.C.*, II, 188), not that the blind man of Puiseaux considers his deficiency as a particular disadvantage since he believes that the sense of touch is a more powerful telescope than the sense of sight, a belief which he illustrates with the amusing remark: 'Si la curiosité ne me dominait pas, [. . .] j'aimerais bien autant avoir de longs bras: il me semble que mes mains m'instruiraient mieux de ce qui se passe dans la lune que vos yeux ou vos télescopes' (ibid., 170). In a related image Diderot reveals his own fervent belief in the creative vision of the imagination by endowing it with supra-telescopic power: 'je ne connais pas la limite de ce que l'imagination peut embrasser. Le monde est trop petit pour elle; elle voit au-delà des yeux et des télescopes' (O.C., x, 130). Thus, as Diderot explains in the Salon of 1767, the eye of the artist and the poet works in the opposite way to that of the scientist and philosopher, the one subjecting the world to a process of magnification, the other to a process of reduction; artistic creation and scientific research are therefore, as he aphoristically points out, the two ends of a telescope:

Les poètes, prophètes et presbytes, sont sujets à voir les mouches comme des éléphants; les philosophes myopes à réduire les éléphants à des mouches. La poésie et la philosophie sont deux bouts de la lunette. (O.C., vii, 272)

Telescopes and microscopes in Diderot's imagination become appropriate symbols of personal vision, philosophical perception and creative revelation. Associated with the telescope there are a number of astronomical images. These mainly involve references to planets and their satellites, as, for example, when Diderot sees Grimm as the satellite of Catherine the Great: 'satellite d'une planète qu'il fallait accompagner partout' (O.C., xi, 1186).[12] These telescopic discoveries are counterbalanced in Diderot's work by the revelations of the microscope. We find a profusion of references to the minute, the minuscule and the microscopic. The discovery of a world previously invisible to the naked eye has had a profound effect on philosophical speculation. Through the improved quality of lenses in the eighteenth century, the natural world is suddenly shown to be more complex and intricate, more highly structured and organized than had previously been imagined. Insect life in particular seems to cause Diderot great fascination. A section of La Promenade du sceptique, for example, takes us into a kind of entomologist's paradise where bees, silkworms, flies and caterpillars are evoked to sustain an argument on behalf of divine order in the universe, an order which seems to be further substantiated by their anatomical complexity, which has been disclosed by the microscope:

[. . .] depuis qu'à l'aide du microscope on a découvert dans le ver à soie un cerveau, un cœur, des intestins, des poumons; qu'on connaît le mécanisme et l'usage de ces parties; qu'on a étudié les mouvements et les filtrations des liqueurs qui y circulent, et qu'on a examiné le travail de ces insectes, en parle-t-on au hasard à votre avis? Mais laissant là l'industrie des abeilles, je pense que la structure seule de leur trompe et de leur aiguillon présente à tout esprit sensé des merveilles qu'il ne tiendra jamais pour des productions de je ne sais quel mouvement fortuit de la matière. (O.C., i, 375)

However, it is in Le Rêve de d'Alembert that Diderot's use of microscopic vision achieves its apotheosis. This work draws much of its power from the fact that we are allowed to enter a world which has been revealed by the microscope, a world to which we gain access, like Alice stepping through the looking-glass, through the lens of a microscope. The scientific reality of this microscopic world is subsequently transformed and transfigured by d'Alembert's oneiric imagination into an enthralling, portentous and at times prophetic philosophical vision. In *Le Rêve* the spider at the centre of its web reappears as an even more brilliant image for the brain at the centre of the nervous system: 'Les fils sont partout. Il n'y a pas un point à la surface de votre corps auquel ils n'aboutissent; et l'araignée est nichée dans une partie de votre tête, que je vous ai nommée, les méninges, à laquelle on ne saurait presque toucher, sans frapper de torpeur toute la machine' (*O.C.*, VIII, 100). Similarly the image of the cluster of bees is shown to represent the contiguity of the senses, with the world itself envisaged as a gigantic bee-hive: 'Le monde ou la masse générale de la matière est la grande ruche. [. . .] Les avez-vous vues s'en aller former à l'extrémité de la branche d'un arbre, une longue grappe de petits animaux ailés, tous accrochés les uns aux autres par les pattes . . . Cette grappe est un être, un individu, un animal quelconque' (ibid., 82). At one point d'Alembert himself in his dreaming state reveals that his visions are directly inspired by the microscope:

Il avait imité avec sa main droite le tube d'un microscope, et avec sa gauche, je crois, l'orifice d'un vase; il regardait dans le vase par ce tube; et il disait: [. . .] J'en crois mes yeux. Je les vois. Combien il y en a! [. . .] Le vase où il apercevait tant de générations momentanées, il le comparait à l'univers. Il voyait dans une goutte d'eau l'histoire du monde. Cette idée lui paraissait grande. Il la trouvait tout à fait conforme à la bonne philosophie qui étudie les grands corps dans les petits (*O.C.*, VIII, 88–89)

a fact which shortly afterwards is consolidated and enhanced by Bordeu in a significant choice of metaphor: 'mais comme on voit tout à travers la lunette de son système' (ibid., 121). The above lines provide one of the several references in *Le Rêve* to minute phenomena conceived as microcosms of the universe. Indeed d'Alembert is reported to have uttered the key word: 'sa goutte d'eau qu'il appelait [. . .] un microcosme' (ibid., 90).[13] In addition there is a host of allusions to atoms, molecules, spermatozoa: 'les molécules qui devaient former les premiers rudiments de mon géomètre [. . .] se filtrèrent avec la lymphe, circulèrent avec le sang' (ibid., 60), animalcules or creatures only visible under a microscope: 'Suite indéfinie d'animalcules dans l'atome qui fermente' (ibid., 89), together with a nightmarish notion about tiny human polyps which could be easily disposed of and replaced: 'des polypes humains [. . .]. L'homme se résolvant en une infinité d'hommes atomiques qu'on renferme entre des feuilles de papier comme des œufs d'insectes qui filent leurs coques [. . .]. Si l'homme se résout quelque part en une infinité d'hommes animalcules; on y doit avoir moins de répugnance à mourir; on y répare si facilement la perte d'un homme qu'elle y doit causer peu de regret' (ibid., 87). Thus, in *Le Rêve de d'Alembert,* the miracles and marvels of the microscope are given an even greater intensity of magnification by the magic of dream. Science in a way becomes science fiction. Although the crucial mental activity of the dreaming d'Alembert is crystallized in the optical, or microscopic, images; nonetheless, sleep, memory and imagination act as basic areas of refraction and illusion, with Diderot consequently achieving philosophic truth through a technique of *trompe-l'œil*.

On a more general level, it is possible to suggest that the science of optics has been assimilated by Diderot in his literary techniques, revealing itself in what might be termed the art of reflection and the art of refraction. To a certain extent the art of reflection in Diderot's work has become a critical cliché, simply showing his primary need for some kind of literary mirror in which his own thoughts are reflected with varying degrees of clarity and brilliance, like the sensuous mirror he himself at one point describes: 'ce miroir sentant, pensant, jugeant, terni, obscurci, brisé, à la décision duquel toutes nos sensations sont soumises' (*O.C.*, XI, 558). Among the most well-known of these literary mirrors are Shaftesbury's *Essay on merit and virtue,* Bougainville's *Voyage autour du monde,* Hemsterhuis's *Lettre sur l'homme et ses rapports,* and Helvétius's *De l'homme,* some perfectly reflecting Diderot's own thoughts, others, like Batteux's *Les Beaux-arts réduits à un même principe* and La Mettrie's *L'Homme Machine,* distorting them and thus provoking the radical re-adjustment of focus performed respectively in the *Lettre sur les sourds et muets* and *Pensées sur l'interprétation de la nature.* Indeed, it is perhaps in the *Essay on Merit and Virtue* that Diderot first saw the literary expression of this process of reflection and learned initially of the importance of a self-regarding attitude in the achievement of philosophical truth: 'toute créature qui pense est nécessitée par sa nature à souffrir la vue d'elle-même et à avoir à chaque instant sous ses yeux les images errantes de ses actions, de sa conduite et de son caractère' (*O.C.,* I, 191), a notion which he himself, in the *Lettre sur les sourds et muets,* has stated more critically and which implies his own full realization of the process of literary *dédoublement,* itself an integral aspect of the art of reflection: 'Il m'a semblé qu'il faudrait être tout à la fois au-dedans et hors de soi, et faire en même temps le rôle d'observateur et celui de la machine observée (*O.C.,* II, 575). The art of reflection is developed in a more consciously creative manner through this device of *dédoublement* whereby Diderot employs a variety of characters to embody certain of his own attitudes and opinions. Thus, in some cases, these characters become simple projected images of Diderot himself, as, for example, with both Ariste and Cléobule in *La Promenade du sceptique* or with Dorval in the *Entretiens sur le Fils naturel*; in others, they represent more genuinely independent beings in whom, during the process of creation, a powerfully imagined personality has triumphed over the authorial persona, as, most obviously, with the Neveu de Rameau. In fact most of Diderot's dialogues can be considered as a game of mirrors in which, as Peter France has shown, dramatic *dédoublement* allows him to distance himself safely from the exaggerated exposition of his own ideas.[14]

Linked to the art of reflection is the art of refraction, which we have already briefly touched upon in relation to *Pensée* 23 of the *Pensées sur l'interprétation de la nature.* The art of refraction is closely connected to Diderot's predilection for free forms and may be seen as an aspect of his overall discursive and digressive style, with its characteristic tendency to discuss several subjects simultaneously. It is most apparent in certain works whose structure might be defined as 'prismatic', that is to say, a form in which the initial idea is split up into several separate yet interrelated thoughts, at once short, sharp, intense, allowing

Diderot the maximum of intellectual variation and expressive brilliance within a clear-cut and narrowly defined framework. Such a form is to be found mainly in Diderot's various involvements with the *pensée*. For example, in Diderot's first original work, the *Pensées philosophiques,* we are struck initially by the looseness of composition but on closer examination discover that these dispersed and scattered thoughts are in fact refractions of the same philosophical ray, that each individual *pensée* has a balanced, often axiomatic, quality that revokes what at first appears to be total disorderliness, and that the various clusters of *pensées* are linked together by an underlying plan.[15] In this medium, ideas frequently flash before us in the form of images. If we look at *Pensée* 39 of the *Pensées philosophiques*: 'Le vrai martyr attend la mort; l'enthousiaste y court' (*O.C.,* I, 291); here Diderot sets up in a maxim an antithesis between the true believer and the religious fanatic. The ironic twist of the line depends on the verb 'courir' in the final position. This is then refracted at a slightly different angle in the subsequent *pensée*:

Celui qui, se trouvant à La Mecque, irait insulter aux cendres de Mahomet, renverser ses autels et troubler toute une mosquée, se ferait empaler à coup sûr, et ne serait peut-être pas canonisé. Ce zèle n'est plus à la mode. Polyeucte ne serait de nos jours qu'un insensé. (*O.C.,* I, 291)

Pensée 40 is more concrete and pictorial, has a touch of scriptural exoticism that adds to the humour and a gruesome verb 'empaler' that brings out the madness of the martyrs. A short sentence tersely states that martyrdom is no longer fashionable, with the final allusion impishly reducing the classical Christian hero to the level of a madman. In this way the *Pensées philosophiques* is able to introduce a variety of philosophical shadings into what is largely a deistic spectrum, becoming, in Roger Lewinter's words, 'un dialogue à quatre voix—entre un déiste, un sceptique, un chrétien et un athée—réglé par un chef d'orchestre, l'écrivain, qui, par un subtil jeu de réfractions, met un argument en lumière au détriment d'un autre' (*O.C.,* I, 269). Similarly the *Pensées sur l'interprétation de la nature,* where the proliferation of *pensées* accords structurally with the very aims expressed at one point in the work: 'Nos travaux doivent avoir pour but [. . .] de multiplier sur le terrain les centres de lumières' (*O.C.,* II, 725); and the *Pensées détachées sur la peinture,* where all those notions concerning æsthetic theory, which Diderot has developed haphazardly in his *Salons,* are now brought together and intensified through a series of maxims, images and unexpected associations, both provide illustrations of the art of refraction.

In Diderot's work, therefore, optics establishes itself as a subject which embraces physics, physiology, psychology and æsthetics; its laws and terminology are shown to be particularly appropriate for describing human perception and artistic processes; and it helps to underpin Diderot's concern with perceptual, rather than conceptual, knowledge. What Roger Shattuck says of Proust in his brilliant study, *Proust's Binoculars,* is equally applicable to Diderot, for whom 'truth is a miracle of vision'.[16] This affinity with Proust is further justified when we remember that, on numerous occasions, Proust draws on optical imagery to give greater clarity to the expression of his artistic intentions. The work of literature itself he says, is an optical instrument: 'L'ouvrage de l'écrivain n'est qu'une espèce d'instrument optique qu'il offre au lecteur afin de lui permettre de discerner ce que, sans ce livre, il n'eût peut-être pas vu en soi-même';[17] Marcel, in the closing pages of *A la recherche du temps perdu,* compares himself as a writer to the optician with his magnifying glass: 'mon livre n'étant qu'une sorte de ces verres grossissants comme ceux que tendait à un acheteur l'opticien de Combray';[18] whilst his own creative aims are described as telescopic rather than microscopic: 'Bientôt je pus montrer quelques esquisses. Personne n'y comprit rien. Même ceux qui furent favorables à ma perception des vérités [. . .] me félicitèrent de les avoir découvertes au "microscope", quand je m'étais au contraire servi d'un télescope pour apercevoir des choses, très petites en effet, mais parce qu'elles étaient situées à une grande distance, et qui étaient chacune un monde'.[19] In a similar fashion Diderot, in each of his works, attempts to provide the reader with a lens of revelation and discovery, 'si vous avez la bonté de les considérer un moment avec mon microscope' (O.C., II, 151), 'on voit tout à travers la lunette de [mon] système' (O.C., VIII, 121). At the same time he recognizes, along with Proust, whose famous statement on style stresses that it is primarily a personal and idiosyncratic mode of vision: 'le style, pour l'écrivain aussi bien que la couleur pour le peintre, est une question non de technique mais de vision'[20], that the most vital optical instrument for the artist is his own consciousness and imagination to which he should always remain faithful: 'Chaque artiste ayant ses yeux, et par conséquent sa manière de voir, devrait avoir son coloris' (O.C., IV, 407), and that artistic creation is, therefore, simply an 'optical' illusion of truthfulness, the projection of a unique inner vision:

Éclairez vos objets selon votre soleil, qui n'est pas celui de la nature; soyez le disciple de l'arc-en-ciel, mais n'en soyez pas l'esclave. (O.C., XII, 346).

NOTES

1 Geneva, 1st edition 1951; 2nd edition 1963.
2 D. Diderot, *Œuvres Complètes,* édition chronologique, introductions de Roger Lewinter (Paris, 1969–73), in 15 volumes. This edition will subsequently be referred to as O.C.
3 op. cit., 2nd edition, pp. xl–xli.
4 See *Elysian Encounter*: *Diderot and Gide* (Syracuse University Press, 1963), pp. 97–120.
5 See Robert Niklaus's article, '*Tableaux mouvants* as a technical innovation in Diderot's experimental novel, *Jacques le Fataliste*', in *Eighteenth Century French Studies*: *Literature and the Arts,* presented to Norman Suckling (Newcastle upon Tyne, 1969), where we find that 'The importance in [Diderot's] eyes of *tableaux* and *pantomime,* and his view of the theatre, as of life itself, as a spectacle, led him to use in his novels what was an essentially dramatic technique [. . .]. The novel in fact provided him with greater scope for mingling narrative, dialogue and tableaux' (p. 74).
6 See in particular Michael T. Cartwright, *Diderot critique d'art et le problème de l'expression, Diderot Studies* , 13, 1969.
7 Contrast 'Le myope sera moins bon observateur des astres, moins bon peintre, [. . .] moins bon juge d'un tableau que celui qui a la vue excellente' (O.C., XI, 510).
8 See Jean Mayer, *Diderot: homme de science* (Rennes, 1959), pp. 148–50.
9 See G. Hanotaux, 'L'Optique au dix-huitième siècle', in *Histoire de la Nation Française* (Paris, 1924), XIV, 220–6.

10 Eric Steele, in *Diderot's Imagery* [1941] (New York, 1966), discusses some of these references without giving a complete list or fully assessing their implications, pp. 108–11.

11 Compare similar comments in *Les Deux amis de Bourbonne*: 'Mais que l'artiste me fasse apercevoir au front de cette tête une cicatrice légère, une verrue à l'une de ses tempes' (*O.C.* VIII, 711).

12 Compare: '(M. Gaschon) n'aura pas encore résigné sa charge de satellite du plaisir, la plus excentrique de toutes les planètes, qui le promène avec elle sur toutes sortes d'horizons' (*O.C.*, XI, 1042).

13 Compare: 'Quelle comparaison d'un petit nombre d'éléments mis en fermentation dans le creux de ma main, et de ce réservoir immense d'éléments divers, épars dans les entrailles de la terre, à sa surface, au sein des mers, dans le vague des airs' (*O.C.*, VIII, 91).

14 Peter France, *Rhetoric and truth in France: Descartes to Diderot* (Oxford, 1972), pp. 214–15.

15 See Robert Niklaus's critical edition of the *Pensées philosophiques* (Geneva, 1965), p. xi. Also René Étiemble, 'Diderotesques—Signification et structure des *Pensées philosophiques*', *Le Disque vert*, May 1953, pp. 46–7.

16 Roger Shattuck, *Proust's Binoculars* (London, 1964), p. 6.

17 *A la recherche du temps perdu* (Paris, Bibliothèque de la Pléiade, 1954), in 3 volumes, III, 911.

18 ibid., 1033.

19 ibid., 1041.

20 ibid., 895.

3

Three Additions to Voltaire Bibliography

THEODORE BESTERMAN

. . . And so *ad infinitum*! Hardly had the fourth (and, so far as I am concerned, final) edition been published of my *Some eighteenth-century Voltaire editions unknown to Bengesco*,[1] which extends to 361 items, than I acquired a little booklet containing five pieces. Two of them are

1. *Ordonnance de Momus, portant défenses de rire de la conduite du chapitre d'Orléans*, has yet not been precisely identified.

2. *Eloge funébre de monsieur le président de Montesquieu*, 1755, attributed by Barbier to Pierre Lefèvre de Beauvray.

This is not a bad beginning, but the extraordinary thing is that the remaining three pieces form no mean contribution to Voltaire bibliography, two of them being unrecorded editions, and the third no less than an unrecorded title.

I

[174a] (Th. D.N.B.)

POËMES / SUR / LA RELIGION / NATURELLE, / ET SUR LA DESTRUCTION / DE LISBONNE. / [*double rule*] / *Par M. DE V****. / [*double rule*] / [*typographic ornament*] / [*ornamental triple rule*] / M. DCC. LVI. /

pp. 44; sig. A–B⁸, C⁶; cm. 16.5.

this edition clearly has some affinity with Bengesco 616, and more with Besterman 174 and Библиотека Вольтера no. 3716.

29

II
[186a] (Th. D.N.B.)

ÉPÎTRE / DU / *DIABLE*, / A / M. DE V★★★. / *A Genève.* / [*etching*] / M. DCC. LX.

pp. 21. [iii blank]; sig. A–B⁶; cm. 16.5.

this may well be the first edition, and certainly preceded Bengesco 685 (1) and Besterman 187.

III
[362] (Th. D.N.B.)

[*begins:*] [*double rule*] / CHANSONS / GRIVOISES, / *SUB LA PRISE DU PORT* / MAHON, / *PAR M. V★★★.* / [*ornamental rule*] /

pp. [4]; no signature; cm. 16.5.

in the third line SUB is of course a misprint for SUR. In case anyone can provide any information about this unknown leaflet, let me record the fact that it contains the words of two songs, one beginning 'T'nez, Messieurs les Anglois,' the other 'Enfin on a pris l'Port Mazon'. Neither is by Voltaire.

NOTE

[1]*Studies on Voltaire and the eighteenth century*, vol. cxi: (Voltaire Foundation, 1973).

4

Diderot and the Idea of Performance and the Performer

MICHAEL CARTWRIGHT

Cependant, comme il fallait faire quelque chose, je lui prenais les mains que je lui plaçais autrement; je me dépitais, je criais, *sol, sol, sol,* mademoiselle, c'est un *sol.* LA MÈRE: 'Mademoiselle, est-ce que vous n'avez point d'oreilles? Moi qui ne suis pas au clavecin et qui ne vois pas sur votre livre, je sens qu'il faut un *sol.* Vous donnez une peine infinie à monsieur . . .'

This passage from *Le Neveu de Rameau* occurs about a third of the way through the dialogue and forms part of what has been described as the *leçon de musique.* The famous procuration episode has just passed and there follows a period where MOI, reduced to a state of outraged silence, realizes for the first time the full moral implications of his encounter with LUI. The conversation slowly picks up momentum once more, but in a lower key and a more personal one. The subject will be that of education, or rather of factitious education, since the music lesson given by the Neveu is, like all his outward activities, a process of adaptation to the empty values of a corrupt and corrupting society.

Although the scene is not one that draws our attention in quite the same way as the frenzied moments of pantomime where LUI acts out his would-be powers of genius, it has the charm of delicate irony and of very careful aural and visual observation. It is a small *tableau* in the style so often repeated by Diderot when his powers of fictional invention are at their highest intensity. Furthermore, the music lesson is clearly part of Diderot's own family experience, and we can have little doubt that the figure of his daughter Angélique was in his mind as he wrote. We are tempted to believe that this domestic scene is a species of antidote, a reflex action on the part of the 'philosophe', an effort to forget or at least to place at a certain distance the possible danger to the virtue of his own child in a social structure where the wiles practised by LUI were all too apparent and all too easily set in motion.

It must be admitted that there is a danger in finding, in the pages of *Le Neveu de Rameau,* the confirmation of almost any hypothesis that one cares to formulate, but at the very least one must admit that the image and the context of the music lesson are striking. If we care to look closer, and few can deny that *Le Neveu* is of a density that invites the most careful scrutiny,[1] we may visualize the figure of the supposed music-master leaning over the shoulder of his pupil to place her hands in a different position so that the 'correct'

31

note shall be struck on the keyboard. The interjection of '*sol, sol, sol,* mademoiselle, c'est un *sol,*' is intended to make the reader himself hear the note G, but that illusion is then cast in doubt by the pretensions of the pupil's mother who is clearly tone-deaf but anxious to establish her own importance through a coquettish show of maternal severity. The hands of the pupil move hesitantly and the desired sound, if it is struck at all from the harpsichord, is lost in the meaningless chatter and the gestures that bring the lesson to the speedy close that the Neveu intends.

The scene is a fleeting one, certainly, but it symbolizes a dilemma to which Diderot returns constantly, both as a theorist of æsthetics and as an artist in his own right. From the vignette may be deduced questions of the following order: How is the creative process of art to be controlled? What forces of temperament, of physiology even, condition its generation and its evolution? To what moral dictates must it be subjected if it is to be for the ultimate benefit of the collective human condition without compromising the freedom of individual expression? And springing from this problem are those considerations which are readily identified with specific issues treated by Diderot: the nature of genius and of the poet-artist; the inter-relation and the control of expressive forces in literature, in music and in the plastic arts.

In confronting the problem, or paradox as it has come to be considered through identification with *Le Paradoxe sur le comédien* where it is discussed with great intensity, critics and commentators have tended to concur in finding a positive value in the very disparate nature of Diderot's pronouncements. The notion of an æsthetic based on that variety of sensory and intellectual perceptions that go to make up the system of 'rapports' suggested in the article 'Beau' of the *Encyclopédie* is certainly close in spirit to the free-ranging nature of all of Diderot's methods of enquiry. Add to it the concept of movement, the dimension of time and recollection, and one has a 'dynamic' system of æsthetics that fits practically every formulated principle and almost every chance contingency that arises in Diderot's writings on the nature of Beauty. Thus, in a general way, although not perhaps entirely for the reasons he advances, one may agree with Professor Belaval that the case for *L'Esthétique sans Paradoxe de Diderot*[2] has been established. If we return for a moment to our point of departure in *Le Neveu de Rameau,* we may admit the multiple arguments of both MOI and LUI as forces subject to the value of the *total* dialogue which comes alive and has meaning only when it is viewed as a whole. In this way the work provides its own explanation and its own justification.

There remains, however, a nagging doubt that penetrates even the most carefully arranged theses and the most ingenious interpretation of texts. *Le Neveu de Rameau,* reflecting the human condition, is much more an exploration of frailties and flaws than an affirmation of perfections. There rings in our ears the strident '*sol, sol, sol,* mademoiselle,' the search for a moment of absolute, undeniable truth which transcends even the posturing of the instructor and which the pupil, in spite of her ineptitude, must bring forth from her instrument. And there remain in our mind's eye the moments of pantomime through which LUI tries to rip aside the veils of commonplace reality and show us the ultimate verity that is the core of Art.

The struggle is, of course, a practical one, and for that very reason it is of the greatest importance. Viewed in its most immediate terms, it is Diderot's effort to communicate his own experience of artistic endeavour. The anguish of both MOI and LUI is his own, first and foremost on the moral level, but so too is the hesitation of the pupil as her hands stray over the keyboard in search of the note which, in spite of interruptions, false prompt-ings, distractions, pretensions and her own shortcomings, must be found and struck in its correctly-timed sequence. It cannot be forgotten that the last words of the dialogue are 'rira bien qui rira le dernier', and even as they are pronounced the sounds of the opera bell summon us to more posturing, more pantomime, a continuation of the dialectical and æsthetic struggle.

Yet, in spite of this, Diderot's own creative effort and the rigours it undoubtedly entailed, indicates that he was intimately aware of a species of calm, a sentiment (and the analogy is perhaps audacious) close to the Wordsworthian 'emotion recollected in tranquillity'. Faced with the order and the organization necessary to the completion of the *Encyclopédie,* with the sense of narrative cohesion inherent in *La Religieuse,* we are forced to recognize a kind of endeavour that transcends the tumult of argument and the vagaries of human actions. Ultimately, it is difficult indeed to abandon the entire Diderot æsthetic canon to a solely dynamic principle. He himself would never commit himself to the eccentricity of a simple formula or a Line of Beauty such as that propounded by Hogarth, but there does seem to be evidence that may lead us to a clearer understanding of that unity and harmony of the æsthetic experience that he knew very well and that he tries, not always with perfect clarity, to communicate to his reader.

We have chosen to place the weight of our hypothesis on the words 'performance' and 'performer'. These embrace the realms of the theatre and of music without giving particular semantic emphasis to the one artistic form rather than to the other. They may be given added force by translation: 'exécution' and 'exécutant' will form a useful part of our enquiry, although there, of course, music and painting take semantic precedence over the drama. Our goal will be to indicate an æsthetic constant that runs through Diderot's theories and his own imaginative work, a set of conditions under which the artist, without lessening the acuity of his observation and the range of his imagination, may bring to fruition his particular vision. Similarly, these conditions will ensure the transmission of that vision to the widest possible audience.

Before proceeding further, let us review briefly the principal difficulties that Diderot encounters in his exploration of the acknowledged fields of artistic expression. Appropriately enough, the debate opens in earnest with the *Lettre sur les sourds et muets* where the primary theme is a discussion of language. The Poet, whose achievement ranks highest in artistic importance, must use the imprecise tools of words, grammar and syntax which cannot always match the sublimest thought and which are severely limited by geographical and ethnic boundaries. The Painter has, at first sight, a distinct advantage, since figurative representation has for so long been part of the human tradition that it is immediately recognized and its content is swiftly understood. However, the very material nature of the plastic arts makes them vulnerable through the vicissitudes of technique—the laborious translation of swift inspiration into carefully applied pigment, chiselled stone or a delicately wielded stylus on the engraver's plate.

As for the Actor, he is himself the instrument of his creation within the confines of the play he is interpreting. To reach perfection in his art, he must produce the illusion of 'otherness' to the point where his own identity must disappear. This process of alienation, to which we shall return, was a source of no small disturbance at profound levels of Diderot's consciousness. The actor as artist is a phenomenon that, morally and psychically, he is unwilling to accept, and his response, most notably in the *Paradoxe sur le comédien,* is to produce an elaborate system of rules that will seek to govern every aspect of dramatic expression.

There remains the field of music. As Diderot knew it and as it relates to his æsthetic principles, the subject is improperly understood. The main stumbling-block is that literary criticism and musicological expertise rarely go hand in hand. Moreover, it requires musicological skill of a particular kind to render absolutely clear the complex and often idiosyncratic theories that the eighteenth century brought forth. The definitive thesis on Diderot and music remains to be written.

Happily, in the present context it is sufficient to reiterate the fact that Diderot did indeed have a thorough and a far-reaching knowledge of musical theory and to examine the degree to which he understood the nature of musical practice. For it is here, in the little-explored field of music, that we find our first evidence that he was aware of an æsthetic mode that combines liberty of expression and stringent discipline—a mode where *performance,* both on the part of the individual artist and on the part of the artist acting *in concert,* can bring forth moments of overwhelming emotion beyond the power of words and of plastic representation.

*   *   *   *

'La musique est ma folie, ma vie, mon existence, mon être.'

Using as a point of departure this quotation from the *Leçons de clavecin et principes d'harmonie par Bemetzrieder,* Robert Niklaus has argued most persuasively that Bemetzrieder's methods of musical instruction were fully understood by Diderot who adopted and transmuted them, making them more accessible to the reader through the familiar technique of a lively dialogue involving Le Maître (Bemetzrieder), L'Élève (Diderot's daughter, Angélique) and Le Philosophe (Diderot himself).[3] Furthermore, a definite link between this work and *Le Neveu de Rameau*[4] establishes the *Leçons* as a text where Diderot's imaginative powers were certainly as strong as his desire to explain and communicate musical theories. In fact, this is apparent from the very beginning where the tone is easy and the identity of the protagonists is firmly and realistically portrayed. Even at those points where abstruse details of pædagogical exposition become necessary, the engaging nature of Diderot's fully-developed narrative technique draws our full attention. In the first *leçon,* for example, we find an echo of the article 'Beau' from the *Encylopédie*:

[Le chant] est une succession de sons agréables, parce qu'ils réveillent en nous quelques sentiments de l'âme ou quelques phénomènes de la nature. Toute musique qui ne peint ni ne parle est mauvaise, et vous en ferez sans génie. (O.C., IX, 139)[5]

This sort of generality is a recurring feature of the dialogue, breaking up the long sections relating exclusively to harmony and giving the conversation a wider æsthetic application. However, in the very first pages it is established by *Le Maître* that excellence in musical performance is not a matter of impenetrable mystery:

Le disciple

M'avez-vous entendu? Ai-je de la disposition?

Le maître

Vous êtes mon disciple, et vous en doutez? Sachez, monsieur, que pour vous conduire à ce qu'il y a de plus sublime dans la science de l'harmonie et des accords, je n'exige qu'autant d'intelligence qu'il en faut pour concevoir que deux et trois font cinq, qu'entre les trois barres d'une grille il n'y a que deux intervalles, et que vous deviendrez un virtuose, si vous avez deux mains, cinq doigts à chacune, deux yeux, deux oreilles et un pied, encore le pied est-il de trop. (O.C., IX, 136)

It would seem that Diderot is almost on the point of re-examining many of the themes of the *Lettre sur les aveugles,* the *Lettre sur les sourds et muets,* and even of the *Rêve de d'Alembert,* but this train of thought quickly gives way to lengthy technical discussions interrupted only by demonstrations that *Le Disciple* is making excellent progress under the guidance of his instructor.

After this initiation, and not until the fourth *leçon* does l'Élève make her appearance. This is charmingly arranged so that the young woman shall receive *Le Maître* in her father's temporary absence and from this moment on the dialogue becomes a carefully staged domestic tableau. The theoretical preoccupations remain dominant, of course, but through them we are very much aware that these are *practical* lessons involving the well-being and edification of the beloved Angélique, and leading toward a perfection of her musical talents that may well bring her to the point of inspired composition and hence to the rank of artistic genius.

However, at no point is it suggested that some divine spark will render arduous practice and thorough understanding superfluous. On the contrary, the emphasis of both instructor and parent (the latter, it must be noted, having now acquired a good measure of musical enlightenment) is upon rigorous discipline, intelligently applied and understood, but above all upon simplicity. The following exchanges are very revealing:

Le philosophe

Vous l'avez entendue, qu'en dites-vous? Parlez-moi net, j'aime la vérité, et je l'écoute avec autant de plaisir que je la dis. Je mets beaucoup d'importance à la droiture de l'esprit, à la bonté du cœur, aux connaissances utiles; médiocrement aux talents agréables. [. . .] Soyez persuadé que ma fille ne me sera pas moins chère, quand vous m'aurez appris qu'elle ne sait rien, et qu'elle ne saura jamais rien en musique.

Le maître

La pièce que mademoiselle vient d'exécuter est belle et difficile; elle a les mains très bien placées; il ne tiendra qu'à elle d'exceller. Sa physionomie vive annonce de la pénétration. Je ne sais si elle composera jamais; mais si elle compose, ce sera de la musique forte; car je vois que son goût la préfère à la musique fine et délicate.

L'élève

C'est peut-être que je trouve celle-ci d'une exécution plus difficile.

Le maître

Son intelligence, son énonciation aisée promettent beaucoup d'agrément à un maître; et il ne dépendra pas de moi qu'elle n'acquière incessamment ce qui lui manque.

Le philosophe

[. . .] Croyez-vous qu'en s'appliquant, ma fille puisse se mettre au-dessus de toute difficulté?

Le maitre

Au-dessus de toute difficulté? Il n'y a peut-être personne qui en soit venu là [. . .].

(O.C., IX, 262–64)

Time and again, forming a complement to the exposition of the theory of harmony, the question of excellence of performance is raised and its implications debated. If we wish to apply to the process a term culled from modern educational practice, it can be said that the *Leçons* are a demonstration of a 'direct method'. This is clearly explained at the very end of the work when, before taking leave of *Le Maître,* father and pupil discuss the merits of the particular form that their instruction has taken. *Le Maître* summarizes his achievement in a way that indicates how his knowledge has been assimilated by his pupils, and he does not hesitate to widen the scope of his method beyond the strict sphere of music:

Le maître

[. . .] La musique est une langue; ne faut-il pas savoir parler, avant que d'apprendre à lire et à écrire? Le clavier, c'est l'alphabet; les touches, ce sont les lettres. Avec ces lettres, on forme des syllabes; avec ces syllabes, des mots; avec ces mots, des phrases; avec ces phrases, un discours. Je ne quitte mes élèves que quand ils en sont là et comme vous savez, je ne les garde pas longtemps. Il vient un moment où je leur dis: Parlez; et ils parlent. [. . .].

L'élève

Tout ce que vous dites est vrai, et vrai à la lettre. Qui le sait mieux que moi? Avec tout cela, il se passera du temps, et l'on aura entendu grand nombre de vos élèves, avant qu'on cesse de regarder comme le plus étrange paradoxe qu'on ait jamais avancé, la possibilité d'apprendre l'harmonie sans connaître une note de musique. (O.C., IX, 539–40)

Music is, then, a language of a particular sort whose perfection can be achieved through the comprehension of a 'grammar' (whose laws are absolute) and through the acquisition of a technique that involves the performer in a highly personal and rigorously disciplined exercise of skills, progressively acquired. At one point *l'Élève,* now far advanced in her studies, cannot suppress a cry of joyous impatience:

Quel rigorisme! Voilà un jansénisme musical que vous n'aviez pas en m'enseignant le catéchisme. (*O.C.*, IX, 522)

It is not difficult to see how musical performance would please Diderot's sense of æsthetic excellence. The discipline involved, combined with a definitive theory, guarantees a firm sense of morality—even if (to anticipate an objection) that morality becomes a morality *à rebours,* as is the case of the musical mime sequences of *Le Neveu de Rameau.*

Confusion only arises with Diderot's persistent failure to deal adequately with the difference between vocal and instrumental music.[6] The former, unfortunately, colours his every pronouncement on the subject. It must be remembered that the 'Querelle des Bouffons' reached its peak in 1752 and that even in *Les Bijoux indiscrets,* published in 1748, the whole of Chapter 13, 'De L'Opéra de Banza', is devoted to a discussion of the works of Utmiutsol and Uremifasolasiututut who are respectively Lulli and Jean-Philippe Rameau. For the greater part of his life, Diderot thought of music in terms of the opera whose composite form leads to a distinct lack of clarity when it comes to musical and æsthetic analysis. At one point in *Le Neveu* there is an effort made to distinguish the true nature of those twin elements that appear so often in eighteenth-century musical criticism, 'chant' and 'déclamation':

Il faut considérer la déclamation comme une ligne, et le chant comme une autre ligne qui serpenterait sur la première. Plus cette déclamation, type du chant, sera forte et vraie; plus le chant qui s'y conforme la coupera en un plus grand nombre de points; plus le chant sera vrai; et plus il sera beau. (*O.C.*, x, 379)

The nebulousness of these pronouncements needs hardly to be underscored, but in the *Leçons de clavecin,* 'chant', despite its obvious vocal emphasis, has come to mean music in general, as the following passage testifies:

Le philosophe
Quoiqu'il y ait des nations où les gens du peuple, où les habitants de la campagne chantent en partie, sans la moindre étude pratique de l'art; chantent comme ils parlent; aussi ignorants en musique, qu'ils le sont en grammaire; on niera qu'on puisse faire ici par institution ce qui se fait ailleurs par habitude. (*O.C.*, IX, 540)

The distinction between opera and instrumental music is important, since much of what we have established regarding performance leans decidedly away from the broadest vein of Diderot's musical experience and gives emphasis to the performer expressing himself through the medium of an instrument. On the whole, music critics and theorists of the eighteenth century had great difficulty in seeing all music in terms other than those dictated by an extension of Horace's 'ut pictura poësis erit.' Music had a purpose similar to that achieved in painting—to portray in as realistic a way as possible human emotions and accompanying states of nature.

It is depressing to find that much of Diderot's musical partisanship is based upon this simplistic idea, and we are forced to admit that the 'Coin de la Reine' were attracted more to melody, easily-identified rhythms and theatrical effects than to music in the absolute sense that we understand it to-day. In the rambling article 'Exécution' that Cahusac contributed to the *Encyclopédie,* one passage is sufficient to illustrate this tendency:

Qu'on ne m'oppose point les sourdines dont on se sert quelquefois dans les orchestres d'Italie. Ce n'est point pour faire les *doux* qu'on y a recours. C'est pour produire un changement de son, qui fait tableau dans certaines circonstances, comme lorsqu'on veut peindre l'horreur d'un cachot sombre, d'une caverne obscure, etc.

If more concrete evidence is needed, one has only to listen to the airs of Rousseau's *Le Devin du Village* which are charming but facile. Happily, Cahusac does make a distinction between 'exécution' in its vocal and its instrumental sense, but his general conclusions are historical rather than analytical. Lulli is chastised for his rigour in perfecting the art of recitative at the expense of

ce chant brillant, léger, de tableau, de grande force, les chœurs de divers desseins, et à plusieurs parties enchaînées les unes aux autres, qui produisent de si agréables effets, ces duo, ces trio savants et harmonieux, ces ariettes qui ont presque tout le saillant des grands *aria* d'Italie.

Against the overwhelming conformity of this contemporary modishness, Diderot's ideas, although hesitant, are progressive. He realises that inherent in the notion of performance lies the possibility of transcending the vagaries of immediate human emotion to touch artistic truth of a higher order. We have seen his preoccupation in the *Leçons* with theories of harmony, and there the harpsichord is an ever-present instrument, necessary to illustrate and to put into immediate practice every phase of Angélique's instruction. The plates describing musical instruments in the *Encyclopédie* were also her father's concern, and it is impossible to forget that fascinating invention, the 'clavecin oculaire' of Père Castel that appears as a leitmotiv in Diderot's comparative æsthetics.[7] The instrument is thus of crucial importance in the act of musical performance, and the greater the degree to which that instrument can be made reliable, obedient to the dictates of human invention and imagination, the greater the chances of artistic excellence.

At this point a dilemma of no mean proportions arises. To argue for instrumental performance with force tends to diminish the rôle of human emotion to a point that is clearly at odds with Diderot's humanitarianism. As fascinating as he found the 'clavecin oculaire', he cannot be seen as sharing an æstheticism of a proto-Huysmans variety; even less can he be imagined approving any manifestation originating in mechanical or purely random phenomena and labelled as art. Art in its widest sense is obviously the supreme human endeavour, but human frailty betrays art just as surely as it creates it. Diderot is far from the syntheses of Wagner, Nietzsche, and Schopenhauer, although the latter does indeed express in a simple fashion a notion toward which Diderot was surely evolving:

Music does not, therefore, express this or that particular and definite joy, this or that sorrow, or pain, or horror, or delight, or merriment, or peace of mind; but joy, sorrow, pain, horror, delight, merriment, peace of mind *themselves,* to a certain extent in the abstract, their essential nature, without accessories, and therefore without their motives.[8]

For Diderot, human frailty in art was an all-too-present danger and he sought to come to terms with it in a variety of ways. The roots of the problem go deep and can be traced ultimately to the early influence of Shaftesbury and the *Essai sur le mérite et la vertu* where the moral implications of human emotions and passions are discussed at length. At the risk of over-simplification, we can say that Diderot became ever more wary of the absolute freedom that the artist must be given if he is to pursue his vocation. *Le Neveu de Rameau* states the problem in a remarkably frank and penetrating way. The fact that the date of composition of the dialogue can only be determined approximately and that Diderot undoubtedly returned to it over a number of years, indicates how present the dilemma was in his mind.

At least in *Le Neveu,* a carefully-balanced discussion is maintained and the equivocal nature of the artist is explored from all sides. Elsewhere in Diderot's writings, the particular nature of an art-form leads to a different reaction and different conclusions. Much has been made of the *Paradoxe sur le comédien* and the debate will no doubt continue,[9] but there can be little question that Diderot held the theatre of his time in low esteem and that he mistrusted the actor. When the latter is untutored and spontaneous he is unpredictable:

Le comédien de nature est souvent détestable, quelquefois excellent. En quelque genre que ce soit, méfiez-vous d'une médiocrité soutenue. Avec quelque rigueur qu'un débutant soit traité, il est facile de pressentir ses succès à venir. Les huées n'étouffent que les ineptes. (*O.C.,* x, 424)

In a multitude of different ways, often with the actor partially forgotten or assimilated into the theatre viewed as a whole, the obsessive theme of instability returns:

Qu'est-ce donc que le vrai de la scène? C'est la conformité des actions, des discours, de la figure, de la voix, du mouvement, du geste, avec un modèle idéal imaginé par le poète et souvent exagéré par le comédien. (*O.C.,* x, 435)

Qu'est-ce donc qu'un grand comédien? Un grand persifleur tragique ou comique, à qui le poète a dicté son discours. (*O.C.,* x, 445)

At times, the argument takes on a universality that is at the same time a source of philosophical consolation:

Dans la grande comédie, la comédie du monde, celle à laquelle j'en reviens toujours, toutes les âmes chaudes occupent le théâtre; tous les hommes de génie sont au parterre. Les premiers s'appellent des fous, les seconds qui s'occupent à copier leurs folies, s'appellent des sages. (*O.C.,* x, 430)

However, only the actor who uses his talents as a species of instrument or who reaches perfection in his art through a purely fortuitous accident of inspiration of which he is not fully conscious, finally gains Diderot's acceptance. One revealing passage shows the aftereffects of a theatrical performance where the actor has used his body to the limits of its capacities and who afterwards lapses into a mindless state, his energy having been transferred to the spectator:

Le socque ou le cothurne déposé, sa voix est éteinte; il éprouve une extrême fatigue; il va changer de linge et se coucher; mais il ne lui reste ni trouble, ni douleur, ni mélancolie ni affaissement d'âme. C'est vous qui remportez toutes ces impressions. (*O.C.*, x, 431)

In another, the performance of la Clairon is described as having a dream-like quality whose value, however, difficult to define, cannot be denied:

Il n'en est pas de la Dumesnil ainsi que de la Clairon. Elle monte sur les planches sans savoir ce qu'elle dira; la moitié du temps elle ne sait ce qu'elle dit; mais il vient un moment sublime. Et pourquoi l'acteur différerait-il du poète, du peintre, de l'orateur, du musicien? Ce n'est pas dans la fureur du premier jet que les traits caractéristiques se présentent; c'est dans des moments tranquilles et froids, dans des moments tout à fait inattendus. (*O.C.*, x, 428–29)

It is interesting to note that the actor is given, fleetingly, a place beside the poet, the painter, the orator and the musician, but his importance is presented in a rhetorical question. Overwhelmingly, the actor is seen as a form of monster who must be constrained, directed, made to fit the stringent rules that Diderot advocates in his reform of the theatre. In fact, the actor must become the instrument of a *total* performance involving a carefully-governed text, minutely-controlled gesture and diction, realistic costume, décor and lighting.[10]

Clearly, the essence of dramatic presentation, *le jeu,* cannot be constrained in this way. It will always escape in large measure the dictates of the playwright and the wishes of the most solicitous and comprehending director. For the actor, launched before his public in the situation that creates dramatic illusion, is the complete master of that illusion. Unlike the poet or the painter, he cannot modify his work in a reflexive way, as he produces it, and then present it as a finished, material entity that will bear leisurely, dispassionate and reasoned scrutiny. Rather, he dominates an irrevocable moment in time, striving to charge it with the greatest possible emotional intensity.

Diderot could not but be fascinated by this process, and his sensibility prompted him to the sincerest applause when the 'moment sublime' manifested itself upon the stage. He even identifies himself with it, at a distance. Although the famous autobiographical references to his early intentions of making a career for himself as an actor must be seen as the kind of daydream in which we all indulge, they cannot be dismissed entirely.[11]

What is at issue here is a plain conflict of nature between the man of letters who projects his vision of the world into the written word and in so doing reinforces his identity, and the actor who transmits a text and loses sight of his identity in the mirror-images of himself that his rôles impose. Ultimately, there is no reason why Diderot should not have come to better terms with this difficulty of æsthetic and moral conscience. It is possible, of course, to point to the influence of Rousseau whose views on the morality of the theatre were extreme. There is also documentary evidence to support the idea that Diderot's particular way of looking at the actor's craft and the whole of his programme for reform of the theatre were prompted by the cavalier treatment he received at the hands of the theatrical profession when he was attempting to stage his own plays. However, nothing can be proved definitively in this regard, and the question is best left at the level of temperament and personal experience.

We have allowed ourselves to dwell at some length on performance and the actor because Diderot's reaction to this form of art throws into much stronger relief his attachment for musical performance. Now it can be seen more clearly why instrumental music should have achieved a greater significance in his preferences had not current operatic squabbles led him to take up dogmatic positions in so many of his writings. Hopefully, the *Leçons de clavecin* will be given added weight, over and above their significance as a work of theory, for the instrumentalist executing a work is much more akin to the writer labouring over his manuscript than is the singer or the actor before his public. Writer and instrumentalist perform in accord with 'rules' which are discernible, subject to analysis. Although they may appear absolute and inflexible they serve, as Angélique finds in the *Leçons,* and as Diderot certainly discovered in the discipline of his literary efforts, to guide inspiration and to heighten imaginative powers. Through their intelligent application the human bases of art are not stifled but directed and nourished, made above all virtuous in the widest sense of the term, and reasonable.

If we look for a brief moment at the plastic arts where the word 'performance' can hardly be applied, but where 'exécution' has a definite place, it is clear that Diderot's critical preferences lean very heavily toward those artists who are masters of a highly individual style that nonetheless conveys a swift and unequivocal pictorial message. Chardin, Greuze and Vernet were known to him personally and they doubtless explained their painterly techniques carefully and with precision. Painting therefore, despite the limitations imposed by its very material nature, offers a form of artistic expression where the 'performer' is present in every aspect of the work produced but is absent in person, leaving his efforts to be contemplated and their echoes and resonances to proliferate in the memory and the imagination of the beholder.

★   ★   ★   ★

Where do these hypotheses lead us? It would be demonstrably false to claim that notions of performance and the performer as we have attempted to describe them constitute an overwhelming portion of Diderot's æsthetic doctrine. Our purpose has been to show that within that doctrine a little-known but not inconsiderable mode of feeling does exist. Certainly, the unbridled enthusiasm, the multiplication of ideas, the advocacy of emotion and passion are elements of Diderot's thought that struck his contemporaries, as they strike ourselves, with the greatest force. But in the eye of the creative whirlpool, as it were, is a place of order and of calm where the artist may look inward upon himself and where he may abstract from the turmoil of his endeavour a feeling of deep commitment that is at one and the same time intense and strangely impersonal. At that moment he is at one with the instrument of his art and is its unique and highly individual performer. Diderot undoubtedly knew this sentiment, but perhaps because of its intimate place in his own creativity, he merely hints at its presence, placing it in that capacious but important drawer of his unpublished works and leaving to his reader the task of seeking out its traces and attempting its definition.

NOTES

1 The Introduction to the critical edition by Jean Fabre (Geneva, 1963), remains the best starting-point for exploration of the complexities of *Le Neveu de Rameau,* but much more exhaustive treatment of important themes is provided in *Entretiens sur'Le Neveu de Rameau'*, prepared under the direction of Michèle Duchet and Michel Launay (Paris, 1967). See especially the contribution of Françoise Levaillant, 'Problèmes d'Esthétique dans *Le Neveu de Rameau*' pp. 207-218.

2 Yvon Belaval, *L'Esthétique sans Paradoxe de Diderot* (Paris, 1950).

3 Robert Niklaus, 'Diderot and the *Leçons de Clavecin et Principes d'Harmonie par Bemetzrieder* (1771)' in *Modern Miscellany* (Manchester University Press, 1969).

4 ibid, p. 183.

5 References to Diderot's works are taken from the new chronological edition of the *Œuvres complètes* edited by Roger Lewinter (Paris, 1969–73). They are given the sigla 'O.C.,' in the text.

6 See A. R. Oliver, *The Encyclopedists as Critics of Music* (New York, 1947). Several parts of this thesis have been superseded by articles emphasizing a particular theory or theorist, but its historical perspective remains most useful and Chapter 5, 'Instrumental Music', is of special importance to the ideas developed here with regard to Diderot.

7 Mention of this instrument is made in *Les Bijoux indiscrets,* Chapter 19, in *Le Rêve de d'Alembert* and in the article 'Clavecin oculaire', *Encyclopédie*, Vol. III.

8 Arthur Schopenhauer, *The World as Will and Idea,* Book III, Second Aspect, Section 52.

9 'Il n'est pas d'œuvre de Diderot plus lue, plus glosée, plus contestée, et plus sûre de survivre, que le *Paradoxe sur le comédien.* Tant qu'il y aura des théâtres et des acteurs—*genus irritabile*—le paradoxe fera scandale.' Paul Vernière, Introduction to the *Paradoxe* in Diderot, *Œuvres esthétiques* (Classiques Garnier).

10 At one point the comparison between actor and instrument is made concrete: 'Un grand comédien n'est ni un piano-forte, ni une harpe, ni un clavecin, ni un violon, ni un violoncelle; il n'a point d'accord qui lui soit propre, mais il prend l'accord et le ton qui conviennent à sa partie, et il sait se prêter à toutes.' (*O.C..* x, 460)

11 The basis for the legend rests principally on the famous passage from the *Paradoxe*: 'Moi-même, jeune, je balançai entre la Sorbonne et la Comédie. J'allais, en hiver, par la saison la plus rigoureuse, réciter à haute voix des rôles de Molière et de Corneille dans les allées solitaires du Luxembourg' (*O.C..* x, 462). However, it is significant to note that the reminiscence arises in a discussion of the generally dubious social background and education of the actor.

5

'A Zerbina penserete':
A Note on Diderot's Epigraph

JANE MARSH DIECKMANN

A number of Diderot's early works have a motto inscribed above the text. In each case the motto points to a principal theme of the work in question and elucidates it. For his early philosophical works, for example, the *Pensées philosophiques,* the various 'allées' of the *Promenade du sceptique,* the *Lettre sur les aveugles,* the *Lettre sur les sourds et muets,* Diderot frequently used Latin quotations as mottoes. Usually the passages chosen are brief and are taken from classical poets such as Virgil or Horace. The use of the motto virtually disappears in the later period of Diderot's writings; two notable exceptions are the *Supplément au Voyage de Bougainville,* where a long citation from Horace figures in several manuscript copies, and the *Neveu de Rameau,* where the quotation from Horace's satire characterizes a distinct trait of the nephew's personality and points to one of the meanings of the genre.

Diderot composed the *Paradoxe sur le comédien* in 1773, as an expansion of a review, the *Observations sur une brochure intitulée: Garrick ou les acteurs anglais.* This redaction of the *Paradoxe* also had a motto: *A Zerbina penserete. La Serva Padrona.* The epigraph was not carried into the final version of the work. In view of Diderot's use of other mottoes, the question may be raised concerning the meaning of the reference and its relevance to the themes of the *Paradoxe sur le comédien.*

The genesis of the *Paradoxe* goes back to the autumn of 1769, when Diderot received from Grimm a series of papers to review for the *Correspondance littéraire*; among them was a brochure on Garrick and the art of acting. In the space of about one week, Diderot composed the *Observations.*[1] The review appeared almost one year later in the October 15th and November 1st issues of the *Correspondance littéraire.*[2] Diderot developed extensively the *Observations* several years later, in 1773, and named his work on the art of the actor *Paradoxe.* We have a manuscript copy of this version, showing two stages of the text and written in the hand of Jacques-André Naigeon, Diderot's disciple and friend. This copy is the only one which contains the motto.[3]

A Zerbina penserete (Diderot uses here as in *Le Neveu de Rameau* an italianized form of the French Zerbine) is an aria of *La Serva Padrona,* an intermezzo in two acts by Giovanni-Battista Pergolesi (1710–36), which attained great popularity in France in the middle of the eighteenth century. The *Serva Padrona* was first played in 1733 in Naples at the theater of

43

San Bartolomeo. In 1746 the members of the *comédie italienne* at the Hôtel de Bourgogne produced the intermezzo for the first time in Paris. Not very much notice was taken of it.[4] On 1 August 1752, however, the *Serva Padrona* was produced again in Paris by a troupe of travelling Italian players called 'les bouffons'[5] as the opening work of their season. The critics were very favorable to the work of Pergolesi, and many extended their praise to Italian music in general. It was the performance of the 'bouffons' in Paris and the great success of their repertory that touched off the 'querelle des bouffons,' a violent exchange of pamphlets which divided the music lovers of Paris into two opposing camps.[6] The controversy was over the merits of Italian music (with its flexible rules, predominant lyricism and emphasis on melody) as opposed to French music (which was characterized by strict regulations, emphasis on harmonic progression and a certain static quality). The great popularity of *La Serva Padrona* (as well as of other Italian operas) and the beauty of its music led many to believe that French opera was in need of reform and that, in addition, the French language perhaps was not suitable for lyric expression in opera. Large audiences flocked to the performances of the 'bouffons' and the quarrel raged on for several years. The crowning success of Pergolesi's intermezzo came in 1754 when the work was produced at the *Théâtre Italien* in a French translation entitled *La Servante Maîtresse*. The operetta had about 150 successive performances and was also produced in Versailles that same year.[7] In one way this great success settled the argument about the appropriateness of the French language in opera; the translation was excellent and in no way detracted from the music. Also those who felt that their national honor was questioned could openly support this production because the words were in French. There is no question that the influence of Pergolesi's music on the French style was great. As the Abbé Raynal states in his *Nouvelles littéraires* (he was reviewing this French production in August of 1754): 'On ne peut disconvenir qu'il ne se soit fait une révolution dans le goût pour la musique depuis le séjour des bouffons, et qu'on ne peut attribuer qu'à eux'.[8]

Most of Diderot's circle of friends greatly admired Pergolesi. Grimm, who had to a certain extent initiated the quarrel with his *Lettre sur Omphale* (1752), found additional ammunition in the success of the Italian operas. Rousseau, who had led the attack on the use of the French language in opera, acknowledged the influence of Pergolesi on his own operetta, *Le Devin du Village,* and supervised the printing of a revised version of *La Serva Padrona* in 1752.[9] The musician Grétry declared his debt to the Italian composer and Jean-Philippe Rameau, whose music was a leading example of the French style, admitted that 'si j'avais trente ans de moins, j'irais en Italie. Pergolèse deviendrait mon modèle'.[10]

The aria 'A Serpina penserete' comes in the second act of the intermezzo. Serpina, a young and tyrannical servant, lords over her much older master, Uberto. When he declares that he will marry to escape from her domination, she answers that he must marry *her*. He refuses, although he is truly fond of Serpina. She retires to prepare her attack and returns to declare that, as he is firm in his purpose, she must depart. She sings a slow, sad and pleading aria, which states that he should think of her when she has gone, that perhaps she had acted wrongly against him and that she is truly sorry. This expression of sad regret is followed by a rapid allegro aside where Serpina notes with a certain pleasure that Uberto's

heart and resolution are rapidly softening. Indeed they are, for after the aria and the introduction of a pseudo-fiancé for Serpina, who (without uttering a word) threatens and dupes
Uberto completely, the latter agrees to marry his servant. The aria thus marks the turning
point in the intermezzo and in the relationship between the protagonists, and stands out in
sharp contrast to the rest of the work, where the music is quick and light, reflecting the
amusing quarrels and verbal skirmishes that have been going on for years between master
and servant. The slow, lyrical, pleading tone and words show Serpina's ability to move her
master, but, in the context, also suggest conflicting emotions—she does indeed want to
trap him but she also cares for him.

We are now ready to ask the question, in which way does the aria show a relationship to
Diderot's *Paradoxe sur le comédien*? We note in the first place that Serpina's aria stands out
in marked contrast to the rest of the work, because it shows her capacity to play a double
role and because the scene reflects a variety of emotions. This complex situation finds its
expression in the words she sings (she reveals sadness, regret, almost longing, directly to
Uberto and then in an aside her awareness that he is beginning to yield). The music illustrates this by a change of tempo from Largo to Allegro. The instrumental accompaniment
reflects Uberto's emotions by a sobbing tremolo in the violins and Serpina's pleading by a
sentimental, almost tragic tonality in the harmony.

The theme of the actor's emotional self-control and of his ability to express feeling and
evoke it in the audience without being moved or carried away himself is central in the
Paradoxe. Serpina's aria illustrates this well. She 'plays' true feelings: she deeply moves
Uberto and at the same time observes the effect; she seemingly pleads with her heart and in
reality observes with her eyes.

There also exists a parallel between 'A Serpina penserete' and a scene in Diderot's *Paradoxe
sur le comédien*. When he expanded the *Observations,* he dealt at length with the moral and
personal qualities of the great actor. By argument and examples he demonstrates to his
reader the actor's ability to express emotions which have no relation to his own personal
state of feelings. To illustrate this ability, Diderot included the 'a-parté' section, where he
describes the way in which an actor and actress who are husband and wife performed a
scene from Molière's *Le Dépit amoureux*. Alternating with the lines of Molière, which
convey the deep and anguished torment of a lover's estrangement and separation, are the
asides of the performers, who are engaged in a violent personal quarrel. An actor and
actress express deep feelings so successfully that the audience enthusiastically applauds their
performance, while at the same time their asides (which only they hear) reveal emotions
which are in complete contrast to what is happening on the stage: a striking illustration of
the thesis that the great actor is the one who is capable of this 'dédoublement'. In Serpina's
aria with its aside to the audience Diderot was happy to find another illustration of this
theory: Uberto must feel that Serpina repents her past behavior, that she is sad and filled
with regrets; he never must become aware of her scheme to win him over to marrying her.
The audience, however, must understand fully the simultaneity of reality and play. Pergolesi
achieves this by the use of the aside, and the contrast, both musically and verbally, between
what is expressed to Uberto and what Serpina reveals as her true motive.

The *Serva Padrona* had its great success in the 1750s and the question arises why Diderot, after a lapse of almost twenty years, should think of the aria as an appropriate epigraph for the *Paradoxe sur le comédien*. Though there is in his correspondence during that period no reference to the musical controversy surrounding Pergolesi's intermezzo, nor to the quarrel of the 'bouffons', nor to the reception of the *Serva Padrona* in Paris, we have evidence that he remembered Pergolesi's work and the issues which it raised. Recent scholarship has shown that during the period between 1769 and 1773 Diderot revised the *Neveu de Rameau*, a work where the controversy of French versus Italian music is reviewed. Indeed the nephew, in one of his monologues, refers to a group of famous arias from French and Italian opera, citing together the three major airs of *La Serva Padrona*, among them 'A Serpina penserete'.[11]

In 1771 Grimm sent a 'carton' of music to Diderot's daughter, Angélique, who was an accomplished pianist and who liked to study scores. In the box were several works of Pergolesi (Diderot mentions the music of the *Stabat* in a letter to Grimm of March 1771). In a subsequent letter to Grimm, he writes: 'Je vous renvoye, mon ami, *la Serva padrona* que vous aviez permis à mad^lle Diderot de séparer du carton'.[12] Pergolesi's intermezzo was thus in Angélique's hands during the early months of 1771, and she may well have played and sung parts of it.

Finally, Diderot when in Russia recommended to Catherine II that the young girls of the Smolna convent school perform the *Servante Maîtresse*. In a letter of late 1773, he speaks highly of the children's remarkably good performance.[13]

The epigraph *A Zerbina penserete* was omitted from Diderot's final revision of the *Paradoxe sur le comédien*. The motto would have served well, as did those of his early works, to point out a central theme of his most famous work on the actor.

NOTES

1 Diderot refers to the composition of the *Observations* in two letters to Grimm, dated November 14 and 19; see *Correspondance*, edited by Georges Roth and Jean Varloot, 16 volumes (Paris, 1955–1970), (CORR), IX, 213 and 219.

2 See *Correspondance littéraire, philosophique et critique*, par Grimm, Diderot, Raynal, Meister, edited by Maurice Tourneux, 16 volumes (Paris, 1877–1882), (C. L.) IX, 133–41 and 149–57.

3 In a letter to Mme d'Epinay of August 1773, Diderot writes that 'un certain pamphlet sur l'art de l'acteur est presque devenu un ouvrage' (CORR, X, 46). The Naigeon copy was discovered in 1902 by Ernest Dupuy, who subsequently published an edition of the *Paradoxe* based on this text (Paris, 1902). The full title, *Paradoxe sur le comédien*, appears only in the later copies which are in the Leningrad and Vandeul collections.

4 François Riccoboni (son of the famous Luigi Riccoboni), who is mentioned by Diderot at the end of the *Observations* and in the *Paradoxe*, played the role of Uberto. The *Mercure* (Octobre 1746, p. 161) mentions that 'la Serva Padrona est une espèce d'opéra comique italien mêlé de prose; la musique en a été trouvée excellente; elle est d'un artiste ultramontain mort fort jeune'. According to Antoine d'Origny 'cette pièce attira pendant longtems de brillantes & nombreuses assemblées' (*Annales du Théâtre Italien*, Paris, 1788, I, 217).

5 They played comic opera, *opera buffa*.

6 For information on the 'querelle des bouffons', consult Auguste Poulet-Malassis, *La Querelle des Bouffons* (Paris, 1876), and Louisette Reichenburg, 'Contribution à l'histoire de la "Querelle des Bouffons"' (Dissertation, University of Pennsylvania, Philadelphia, 1937). A contemporary discussion of the quarrel is given by D'Alembert in 'De la liberté de la musique'; in paragraph 23, he writes in detail about the art of the recitative with examples from *La Serva Padrona*. See *Œuvres de d'Alembert* (Paris, 1821), I, 515.

7 See Alfred Loewenberg, *Annals of Opera 1597–1940*, (Geneva, 2nd edition, 1955).

8 C. L., II, 176. For the judgment of Grimm, see pp. 408–9. Compare also *Anecdotes Dramatiques*, 3 volumes (Paris, Duchesne, 1776), II, 167.

9 See Jean-Jacques Rousseau, *Œuvres complètes,* edited by Bernard Gagnebin and Marcel Raymond (Paris, Pléiade, 1959), I, 383 and n. 5, p. 1446. Rousseau also used examples from Pergolesi in his *Dictionnaire de musique*; cf. the articles 'Dessin' and 'Duo'.

10 Quoted in Paul-Marie Masson, *L'Opéra de Rameau* (Paris, 1930), p. 88. For André-Modeste Grétry's comment, see *Mémoires ou essais sur la musique,* edited by Paul Magnette (Liège, 1914), p. 127.

11 See *Le Neveu de Rameau,* edited by Jean Fabre (Geneva, 1950), pp. 79–80 (where the nephew refers to Pergolesi and the musical quarrel) and p. 83.

12 CORR, X, 244.

13 CORR, XIII, 125.

E

6

L'Orage

(from Barthélemy's *Voyage du jeune Anacharsis en Grèce*, 1788)

E. L. DUTHIE

Cependant l'horizon se chargeait au loin de vapeurs ardentes et sombres; le soleil commençait à pâlir; la surface des eaux, unie et sans mouvement, se couvrait de couleurs lugubres, dont les teintes variaient sans cesse. Déjà le ciel, tendu et fermé de toutes parts, n'offrait à nos yeux qu'une voûte ténébreuse que la flamme pénétrait, et qui s'appesantissait sur la terre. Toute la nature était dans le silence, dans l'attente, dans un état d'inquiétude qui se communiquait jusqu'au fond de nos âmes. Nous cherchâmes un asile dans le vestibule du temple, et bientôt nous vîmes la foudre briser à coups redoutables cette barrière de ténèbres et de feu suspendue sur nos têtes; des nuages épais rouler par masses dans les airs, et tomber en torrents sur la terre; les vents déchaînés fondre sur la mer, et la bouleverser dans ses abîmes. Tout grondait, le tonnerre, les vents, les flots, les antres, les montagnes; et de tous ces bruits réunis il se formait un bruit épouvantable qui semblait annoncer la dissolution de l'univers. L'aquilon ayant redoublé ses efforts, l'orage alla porter ses fureurs dans les climats brûlants de l'Afrique. Nous le suivîmes des yeux, nous l'entendîmes mugir dans le lointain: le soleil brilla d'une clarté plus pure; et cette mer, dont les vagues écumantes s'étaient élevées jusqu'aux cieux traînait à peine ses flots jusque sur le rivage. (Chapter 59)

If it is the sign of a successful description to be self-explanatory, then this description of a storm possesses the necessary qualification. But its concision suggests that its function is not exclusively descriptive, and in fact in its context it has several uses. It occurs in an episode of the *Voyage du jeune Anacharsis,* one of the most popular of the works in which eighteenth-century scholars in France expressed that renewal of interest in Greco-Roman art and civilization to which the discoveries of Herculaneum and Pompeii had given a powerful impetus. This vast compilation, begun by the abbé Barthélemy on his return from his stay in Italy with his patron the Duc de Choiseul, did not appear till 1788 and owed its immediate success partly to the political climate in which it was published. Unintentionally Barthélemy pleased the Republicans by a work 'où sont rappelés avec tant de séduction les beaux jours de la Grèce et ces mœurs républicaines qui produisaient tant de grands hommes et de grandes choses.' It was on these grounds that, after temporary imprisonment in 1793, he was set at liberty and subsequently offered the post of librarian of the Bibliothèque Nationale. But it was essentially his deep interest in classical antiquity in its plastic forms that had inspired the 'gardien du cabinet de médailles' to undertake this vast work, whose originality and lasting appeal lay primarily in the fact that the social and esthetic values of

Greek civilization were evoked through visual media rather than allowed to remain in the realm of abstractions.

The passage under consideration comes towards the end of a chapter in which Anacharsis and his friend Apollodore, who has an estate near Eleusis, have visited the plains of Attica and the silver mines of Sunium. Accompanied by Plato, they arrive at Cape Sunium, from which they have a magnificent view of the sea and islands. Plato seems specially attentive to the sea. The onset of the storm gives a dramatic turn to the narrative. At the same time it provides the immediate occasion for Plato to expose his views on the origin of the world, which form the culminating stage of the episode.

But if this passage is an integral part of the whole chapter, it exists none the less in its own right as an arresting and significant piece of descriptive writing. Within the compass of seven sentences, it encloses the whole course of the tempest, from the ominous calm that heralds its onset to the different calm that succeeds when it finally moves away towards the African coast.

The description is given from the point of view of an eye-witness. From the promontory the spectators see the insidious approach of the storm, the darkening sky, the changing colour of the ocean. But they cannot brave the full fury of the elements, and it is from the entrance hall of a 'superbe temple consacré à Minerve' that they witness the fiercest paroxysms of the tempest and finally watch it subside.

The effect of the description is to give the impression of an authentic storm. The language is classic in its generality, but that very generality suggests a cosmic disturbance: the principal actors in this drama are the sun, the sea, the winds, thunder and lightning. The presence of elemental forces is conveyed without any proliferation of detail, in terms appropriate to the classic conventions of the 'style noble'. The livid colouring of the sea is accentuated by the absence of any attempt to define its 'couleurs lugubres, dont les teintes variaient sans cesse'. The claustrophobic effect of the lowering sky is realized to the full when it becomes first 'une voûte ténébreuse' and then 'cette barrière de ténèbres et de feu suspendue sur nos têtes'.

It is in keeping with the classic generality of the description that it should depend for its effect predominantly on the harmony of words and phrases and the conscious orchestration of the whole movement. The first three sentences constitute a prelude, whose music is characterized by the modulation of the long vowels, the alliteration of liquids and voiceless consonants and above all by the increasing pace of the whole, which quickens, from the near-lethargy of the initial binary movement to the ternary rhythm of the transitional phrase: 'Toute la nature était dans le silence, dans l'attente, dans un état d'inquiétude qui se communiquait jusqu'au fond de nos âmes'. The measured syllables and the long vowels of the clause that immediately follows provide a pause which momentarily arrests the action and reaffirms the security found by the spectators in the shelter of the temple. But it is at once followed by a rapid and complex ternary movement, in which each clause fans out in a manner suggestive of the growing fury of the natural forces which are successively evoked: fire, air and water. The fifth and climactic sentence echoes in sound and movement the full force of the storm, as the rapid pace of the initial enumeration, with its dark and sonorous vowels, builds up to a mingling of stridency and harmony whose vibrations seem to correspond to the threat of cosmic catastrophe: 'un bruit épouvantable qui semblait annoncer la dissolution de l'univers'. In the succeeding phrase there is a sudden change of tempo, introduced by the use of the past definite, which had previously been used to mark the onset of the storm and now heralds its departure. The return of order to the natural scene is mirrored in the firmer and slower rhythm. In the concluding lines the pace slows down till it is no quicker than it had been at the beginning, but the tonality of the vowel sounds is very different and there is no hint of discord to disturb the final harmony, as the thunder dies away in the distance: 'Le soleil brilla d'une clarté plus pure; et cette mer, dont les vagues écumantes s'étaient élevées jusqu'aux cieux, traînait à peine ses flots jusque sur le rivage.'

This is a striking evocation of a storm, remarkable for its finished artistry. But it does not only suggest the elemental power of nature, shown in the ferocity of the unleashed forces of the tempest; it communicates the repercussions of the scene on the spectators, 'un état d'inquiétude qui se communiquait jusqu'au fond de nos âmes'. This deep disquiet is not caused by any fear for their personal safety, nor are they in a state of mind which predisposes them to an emotional reaction. It is the sense of cosmic disturbance which first holds them for a time 'immobiles et muets' and then prompts them to interrogate the mysteries of the universe: 'Pourquoi ces écarts et ces révolutions dans la nature? [. . .] Est-ce une cause intelligente qui excite et apaise les tempêtes? [. . .]' These questions lead them to cosmical speculation: 'De là nous remontions à l'existence des dieux, au débrouillement du chaos, à l'origine de l'univers'. They turn to Plato to rectify their confused ideas and he expounds his cosmical theories. They occupy far more space in the chapter than the actual description of the storm, but the descriptive passage forms the natural transition to the Platonic cosmogony, for it contains implicitly the depth of questioning out of which philosophies grow.

The theme of the storm, always a favourite one with artists, was to acquire increasing importance with the development of Romanticism. The year before the publication of the *Voyage du jeune Anacharsis,* Bernardin de Saint-Pierre had anticipated the seascapes of Chateaubriand with his dramatic description of the wreck of the Saint-Géran. But Barthélemy's picture does not look forward to the great Romantic frescoes. The personal fate of his heroes is not involved, like that of Paul and Virginie, with a ship foundering in the tempest. Nor does the tumultuous sea of his description serve as a backcloth to the hero's personal emotions, as it does for René, who spends his last night in Europe watching the waves beating on a deserted shore and wonders if storms are always to accompany him. Barthélemy's true theme is less the storm itself than the perpetual state of flux in nature, of which it is an outstanding example. Not a shipwreck but a philosophy is the outcome of the tempest which Anacharsis and his companion watch from the shelter of the temple of Minerva, and which Plato interprets for them.

The final impression left by the passage is not of storm but of calm. There has been the suggestion of cosmic catastrophe in the fury of the elements, and the subsequent reflections of the spectators show their awareness of this and their recognition that such threats are bound to be recurrent. Yet they also recognize with wonder that '[. . .] sur le point de se briser mille fois, la chaîne des êtres se conserve toujours'. The re-emergence of the sunlight, the subsiding of the waves are the proof of this, and so quite as impressive as the violence that preceded. The fury of the elements was a magnificent spectacle, but a disquieting one, disquieting particularly because it threatened not only human survival but human values. It is with evident relief that Anacharsis and his companion watch the storm-clouds being driven towards 'les climats brûlants de l'Afrique'. After the traumatic experience of something akin to primitive chaos, they are all the more ready to listen to Plato's account of the creative activity which produced order in the universe. Sunlight and calm seas are not only natural phenomena, they are the assurance of the continuance of an order which may and indeed will be menaced again, but which will survive.

Like Heredia later in his sonnets, Barthélemy has fixed a philosophic vision in a plastic form, whose masterly concision and grace of finish recall the perfection of an antique medallion. Intercalated between a far more lengthy account of Attic agriculture and silver mines and an exposition of Platonic cosmogony, it is not well placed to receive the attention it merits, in spite of its relevance as a transitional passage. But considered, as it deserves to be, as poetic prose of a high order, this is not the least charming of the visions that have been seen from 'Sunium's marbled steep'.

7

George Berkeley, His Door and the *Philosophes*

OTIS FELLOWS

Mais je pense, entre nous, que vous n'existez pas. Voltaire, *Les Systèmes.*

George Berkeley has, down through the years, remained one of the five or six great British philosophers. This is so despite the fact that during his lifetime as well as today there has been an unending diversity of opinion regarding the man himself, and little agreement on the interpretation of his metaphysics and his science. The future Bishop of Cloyne may well have protested that, basically, he was 'with the mob', and he may have written his friend, the American philosopher Samuel Johnson, that two or three readings of anything he had written would make its meaning eminently clear. The truth is that Berkeley's deceptively simple but remarkably subtle thought processes have been subject to various interpretations, evaluations, and superimposed shades of meaning. Today, just as 250 years ago, Berkeley appears easy to grasp as a philosopher, dialectician and man of God: in reality he is extremely difficult.

It is beyond the competence of the present writer to delineate the fine-spun metaphysics of Berkeley or to bring a semblance of order to the explication of a philosophy on which respected authorities are not themselves in accord. The purpose of this inquiry, therefore, is simply to: (1) review how available or accessible Berkeley's ideas were to the French *philosophes*; (2) note, whenever possible, any influence he may have had on their thinking—an influence that hitherto may have been given insufficient stress or, in some instances, no stress at all; and (3) assess the impact of the Bishop of Cloyne on Diderot's equally daring, and, quite likely, equally fertile mind.

Finally, it is hoped that there may be established here and there new rapprochements between the great British metaphysician and some of the most enlightened figures of the French eighteenth century. Berkeley's 'door' will, at least in a symbolical sense, be used—for the first time—and to open portals on to the task that confronts us.

When, in 1729, Dean Berkeley came to colonial America with his recent bride, he already had behind him three works that would be essential to his metaphysics and to his contribution to eighteenth-century knowledge: the *Essay towards a New Theory of Vision* (1709), *A Treatise concerning the Principles of Human Knowledge* (1710), and *Three Dialogues between Hylas and Philonous* (1713), as well as *De Motu* (1721).

The *Essay* was written when Berkeley was not yet twenty-three. It was, as Ernst Cassirer has said, a prelude to all of Berkeley's philosophy with its main tenets implicitly or explicitly stated in this earliest of his works. The great significance it acquired during the eighteenth century was due to its presentation of a particularly challenging study of epistemology and psychology grouped around one common center which was so much in evidence at the time. This focal point consisted of a question: could perception in one field offer sufficient perception in a totally different field?[1]

For over a century, scholars have regarded Berkeley as being fundamentally the defender of subjective idealism whose main contribution as a philosopher was his immaterialism. In consequence, the *Principles* and the first of the *Three Dialogues* have been the most widely read of all Berkeley's writings, to the detriment of the *Essay towards a New Theory of Vision*. But of late the *New Theory* has again been receiving warm critical attention, and only recently A. D. Ritchie in his posthumous study, *George Berkeley: A Reappraisal,* has called the *Essay* the most important of the philosopher's works.[2]

To pick up the thread of our story, we must go to Newport off the tip of Rhode Island. In the eighteenth century, Boston, New York, and Newport were the most thriving seaport towns of what was to become, half a century later, the north-east corner of the United States of America. Today, Newport and its environs remain filled with reminders of almost three years of Berkeley's presence on the island. Among the more striking mementoes of his sojourn is his house, 'Whitehall', still some three miles outside the teeming port town, and in an excellent state of repair.

Despite occasional assertions to the contrary, architecturally and historically speaking, the mysteries of 'Whitehall' are pretty well cleared up. Berkeley's statement that he had 'built' a house in a nearby valley was not quite exact.[3] It is now known that he had bought a seventeenth-century farmhouse and had let his mind play over it both inside and out with the result that a number of oddities of plan and construction have persistently intrigued historians of American colonial architecture.

Berkeley was not the first philosopher who fancied himself something of an architect, and the most pronounced of his architectural changes is the entire frontal façade of 'Whitehall'.[4] Two leading authorities on colonial houses in New England, commenting on 'Whitehall,' find that 'the building presents certain unsolved problems'. Chief among these, and the one of greatest concern to us here, is outlined as follows: 'The peculiarity of the wide divided front doorway, half of which is false and extends beyond the parlor wall at the left, is still unexplained'.[5]

I submit that the puzzlement of architectural historians derives from the fact that this rare pedimented door with its false left leaf is far less an architectural phenomenon than it is a philosophical demonstration. It may have been a quiet little jest on Berkeley's part, and one he kept to himself, for, so far as is ascertainable, neither he nor any of his compeers ever made any reference to it in writing.

In his *New Theory of Vision,* Berkeley in turn—for, since Descartes, it had been an intellectually fashionable thing to do—examined the cognitive value of the senses but, of course, on his own terms. These terms were to be embroidered upon in his subsequent writings. And his exquisite dialogue, *Alciphron or the Minute Philosopher* (1732), which was written behind Berkeley's own frontal façade in a room with a low ceiling and a fireplace with old-fashioned painted tiles, is a particularly delightful 'translation' of the *Essay*.

Without reviewing the complex ramifications of *A New Theory*, we might, for present purposes, merely keep in mind that it stresses certain essential points: that there is a general misuse of vision, that the eyes see a visible object whereas the hands manipulate a tangible object, and what we see is distinct and different from what we feel. In short, the visible and the tangible are two separate fields of experience; it is a serious mistake to suppose that only the visible is real, and that the other senses, notably those of hearing and touch, count for naught.[6]

Paragraph by paragraph, almost without fail throughout the *Essay towards a New Theory of Vision*, 'Whitehall's' pedimented front door could, in one way or another, illustrate Berkeley's philosophy or his insights in the field of psychology. We shall limit ourselves, however, to a few instances, some of which will have a particular interest for the *philosophes*.

In paragraph 130, Berkeley gently calls John Locke to task for his assertion in the *Essay on Human Understanding* (Book III, chapter 9, section 9) that sight is 'the most comprehensive of all our senses'. Distance and shape, Berkeley notes, can be ascertained through the sense of touch, and distance alone through hearing. But if we examine the matter closely, we are told, there is no object perceived by sight save by light and colors.

We ourselves could use a common example to illustrate the validity of Berkeley's statement that Locke is mistaken in believing sight to be the most comprehensive of the senses. A rose in a vase on a table in a pitch black room would appear non-existent to the eye. But it could immediately be recognized as a rose through either the sense of touch or of smell. And so a blind man, or indeed anyone at all, coming down the gravel walk to Berkeley's house in the dark of night could, through the sense of touch, perceive there was only a single door. But the visitor approaching 'Whitehall's' façade—as visitors still do in numbers—gains the distinct, even positive, visual impression that he is facing a handsome pedimented double door. It is plain that by the mere act of vision a person cannot tell whether both leaves make up the door, or only the right leaf. To one depending upon the sense of sight, the left side under the pediment would itself be a door; but to one relying solely upon touch the truth would emerge, and the so-called left leaf would be part of the unmoving and unmovable front wall. Clearly, seeing is not necessarily believing. To paraphrase Berkeley slightly in paragraph 137 of the *New Theory*, 'Visible figure and extension have been demonstrated to be of a nature entirely different and heterogeneous from tangible form and extension.' There is no need to belabor further the illustration of 'Whitehall's' unusual door, even though it could be pushed to the extreme consequences of the youthful author's brilliant essay on vision whose opening sentences are: 'My design is to show the manner wherein we perceive by sight the distance, magnitude, and situation of objects. Also to consider the difference there is betwixt the ideas of sight and touch, and whether there may be any idea common to both senses' (¶ 1).

It is generally known that the *philosophes* were aware of Berkeley and that they were only too prone to greet his ideas with mixed sentiments. Almost to a man, they strove to be intellectually honest by their own lights, earnest in their endeavors, and dedicated seekers of the truth in all its manifestations whether factual or metaphysical. With each passing year, they saw scientific hypotheses and verities piling up on all fronts, and the fact often gave them hope that through this accumulation of knowledge the human condition could, perhaps, after all, be bettered. They were afforded hope and inspiration in particular by two great British philosophers, Newton and Locke. Moreover, the *philosophes,* with few exceptions, were themselves in varying degrees common-sense materialists in much of their speculation. Berkeley was a British philosopher too, but he tried to set both Locke and Newton straight in their thinking; and hadn't Bolingbroke said that Berkeley was 'one of those geniuses who showed their madness by boasting a revelation superadded to reason?'[7]

The *philosophes* had respect and even grudging admiration for Berkeley's metaphysics, much as they did for Pascal and Malebranche, and at times they seemed almost to fear his ideas. Furthermore, they would, now and then, in an explosion of irritation scoff at his philosophy. Still, they found it difficult to dismiss him as a thinker of little consequence, and even more difficult to refute his immaterialism. It has been recently noted that the *philosophes* reading Pascal through the mists of the Port-Royal version of the *Pensées,* could not grasp the extent of his pyrrhonism, the boldness of his speculations or those aspects of his thinking that brought them closer than they realized to their own modes of thought.[8] Malebranche too was an impressive figure in the evolution of French metaphysics or French philosophico-religious meditation. And the *philosophes* treated him with the distant respect they felt he so well deserved, a respect so completely characterized by d'Alembert's remark: 'Chez le commun des philosophes chrétiens c'est la raison qui défend la foi; ici, par une disposition d'esprit singulière, c'est la foi de Malebranche qui a mis à couvert sa raison et qui lui a épargné l'absurdité la plus insoutenable'.[9] This seemed to particularize one whole aspect of Berkeley as well, whose metaphysics the *philosophes* were too often given to confusing with that of Malebranche.[10] The Irish Bishop's metaphysical account of the material universe was entirely foreign to their own views. To add to the difficulty, Berkeley, like so many British metaphysicians of the day, had an extensive vocabulary where specific words were frequently lacking in precision or terms had startlingly new meanings. Then too, Berkeley was a distinguished churchman in whose thinking, as might be expected, theology and metaphysics were, more often than not, along with psychological insights, inextricably intertwined with abstract intelligence and scintillating dialectic. Such an approach could be but a source of futility and despair for the *philosophes* whose systems commonly represented a mixed bag of deism, Spinozism, pantheism and atheism; this was true especially if they had only a vague familiarity with Berkeley's writings.

And how much acquaintance did the *philosophes* have with Berkeley and his works? The Bishop of Cloyne was far more in the thoughts of those in the French Enlightenment than some critics in the history of ideas have been led to suppose. As a matter of fact his writings were easily available both in the original and in translation,[11] partial summaries of his *New Theory* were at times amazingly competent,[12] and commentaries on his philosophy, even if usually tinged with a trace of disapproval, were not a rarity. A recent scholar, following the lead of others, assumes, however, that such an important *philosophe* and *encyclopédiste* as Diderot, for instance, did not know Berkeley's work at first hand but came into contact with him through Voltaire's *Éléments de la philosophie de Newton*.[13]

Molyneux and Cheselden are the two names that figure most prominently in the spectacular rise of Berkeley as a philosopher of the first magnitude. The story of William Molyneux has been repeated too often to be presented in detail here. Suffice it to say that he was a friend of Locke's, who in the *Treatise of Dioptrics* (1690) launched a celebrated question and gave a tentative 'no' by way of answer. The question asked was whether a man blind from birth, if his sight were suddenly restored, would be able without hesitation, to distinguish and identify familiar objects without recourse to touch, and relying solely on his eyes. Locke first answered 'yes', and then, in agreement with young Berkeley, answered 'no'. But Berkeley as a philosopher and an independent thinker drew scant attention in England or on the Continent until certain conclusions of his 1709 *Essay* seemed to find thorough justification after Dr Cheselden successfully operated on a boy of fourteen for congenital cataract. Cheselden's account as it appeared in the *Philosophical Transactions* of the Royal Society of London[14] was undeniably dramatic, scientifically challenging and full of human interest. The lad, with sight restored, could not at first, without the aid of touch, differentiate between a sphere and a cube. When a pet entered the room, he could not tell whether it was his beloved cat or his faithful dog until he stroked the familiar animal; he assured the cat that he would do his best to remember it upon seeing it a second time. Upon being shown pictures, and running his fingers over the flat surfaces, he was filled with perplexity and cried out asking what he should believe, that which his eyes told him—here was a face, for example, with all its features—or what his touch had to say, that this was nothing but a piece of paper or canvas with colors and shadings.

Among the *philosophes,* Voltaire was the first to bring up the name of Berkeley, and, for various reasons, to mention it with the greatest frequency. Berkeley was already in London when the Frenchman, fresh from the Bastille, arrived in 1726, and Voltaire could see for himself, with the publication of Cheselden's experiment, that the author of the *New Theory of Vision* was, like the clergyman's good friend Jonathan Swift, something more than a Dean of the Anglican Church. Furthermore, Berkeley, ten years Voltaire's senior, was, in his ideas on vision, reflecting one of the great interests of the day. Clearly, here was a mind to be reckoned with.

Voltaire took pains to point out more than once that he knew Berkeley personally, had found him to be a man of charm and distinction and had even entered into philosophical discussion with him. Moreover, he had read carefully and, upon several occasions had acknowledged that he owed a considerable debt to the British philosopher for the latter's views on the sense of sight. This debt has been emphatically expressed in chapter 6 of his *Éléments de Newton* in which he gives thought to the manner in which we know distances, magnitudes, figures and situations. More specifically, in the *Éclaircissements nécessaires sur les Éléments de la philosophie de Newton,* in the development, 'Sur un cas très singulier de catoptrique', he says that his own arguments are drawn from a little treatise by the Bishop on the *Théorie de la Vision,* and adds that he himself has been reproached for leaning on Berkeley, who had accused English mathematicians of being incredulous in matters of religion, and too credulous in those dealing with calculus. Voltaire, who did not agree with Berkeley's views on fluxions, nevertheless asks the reader whether a person who may be in error on one point of his thinking should be deemed mistaken in all others. His conclusion here is: 'Faudra-t-il haïr le vrai, parce qu'un homme qu'on n'aime point nous le présente? J'ose dire que, dans sa *Théorie de la vision,* la profondeur, et la subtilité ne se trouvent point aux dépends de la vérité.'

In his correspondence Voltaire turns time and again to the fact that the Abbé Desfontaines had read Berkeley superficially and, unable to follow the dialectic involved, had drawn the conclusion that the author of *Alciphron* was nothing but a young libertine. No doubt this running defence of the Bishop of Cloyne was in reality a continued attack on the despised Desfontaines, since as late as 2 May 1776, Voltaire calls Berkeley 'un des plus profonds écrivains qui aient défendu le christianisme' (Best. 18958).

But despite whatever other estimable qualities a man might have, his passion for theology and metaphysics sooner or later made him an object of Voltaire's derision, and Berkeley was no exception. Northrop Frye has written '[. . .] philosophical pedantry becomes, as every target of satire eventually does, a form of romanticism or the imposing of over-simplified ideals on experience'.[15] Voltaire, the most devastating wit and the keenest satirist in the *parti des philosophes,* sought out the good Bishop in what was to the *philosophes* themselves his most vulnerable spot, his immaterialism. Well concealed in the *New Theory,* it emerged full-blown in some of Berkeley's other works, especially the popular and widely read *Three Dialogues between Hylas and Philonous,* the 1750 translation of which Voltaire had in his library.[16] Voltaire's attack came openly and with a touch of the ribald in the article 'Corps' in his *Dictionnaire philosophique.* Charging Berkeley with trying to prove that bodies do not exist, and that only ideas are real, Voltaire could not resist adding, 'De sorte que, selon ce docteur, dix mille hommes tués par dix mille coups de canon ne sont dans le fond que dix mille appréhensions de notre entendement; et quand un homme fait un enfant à sa femme, ce n'est qu'une idée qui se loge dans une autre idée dont il naîtra une troisième idée.' The refutation is not too far different from that of the celebrated Dr Johnson who, according to Boswell, answers Berkeley by kicking a stone. In the world of Johnsonian physics—and in Voltaire's—for every action there is an equal and opposite reaction.[17]

This is not the place to review the many references to Berkeley that appear in Voltaire's writings and are readily at hand.[18] It might be more profitable here to touch upon the possible influence of Berkeley—hitherto unremarked by scholars—on certain aspects of Voltaire's views.

From the time of his English sojourn Voltaire had been enthusiastic about Swift and, as Ira Wade has noted, there is overwhelming evidence that *Gulliver's Travels* in many ways inspired the short philosophical tale, *Micromégas.*[19] In fact few would disagree with Professor Wade that 'one can scarcely escape the conclusion that the English satirist must have been uppermost in the Frenchman's mind when *Micromégas* was composed' (p. 86).

What concerns us here is that two scholars appear persuaded that George Berkeley had at least a partial influence on *Gulliver's Travels*. One asserts that the *Theory of Vision* was, quite possibly, an origin of 'the relativity of human life and its values which was given such emphasis in the contrast between Lilliput and Brobdingnag'.[20] As proof, the following passage is quoted:

Phil. A mite therefore must be supposed to see his own foot, and things equal or even less than it, as bodies of some considerable dimension; though at the same time they appear to you scarce discernible [. . .] and to creatures less than the mite they will seem yet larger. [. . .] Insomuch that what you can hardly discern, will to another extremely minute animal appear as some huge mountain.[21]

Insect imagery is fairly common but widely scattered in the first two books of *Gulliver's Travels*. A Lilliputian lark is smaller than a 'common fly'. In Brobdingnag Gulliver feasts upon 'snails and other insects'. A mischievous giant-dwarf releases 'flies' under Gulliver's nose, so that the enormous insects will terrify him. Here, wasps are 'insects as large as partridges', and, for the King of the Brobdingnagians, Gulliver is but a 'diminutive insect'.

It is, of course, entirely possible that Swift appropriated this insect imagery from the *Dialogues*. But it seems equally likely that Voltaire, who had conveniently at hand the Berkeley passages in French, and an excellent command of English as well, drew directly from the British philosopher for certain words and terms in *Micromégas* that are far closer to Berkeley than to the texts in *Gulliver's Travels*.

Preceding the passage already quoted from the first of the *Three Dialogues*, Philonous enters upon a disquisition concerning 'those inconceivably small animals perceived by glasses', who 'see particles less than their own bodies'. Moreover, in his discussions on insects, 'mite' is a recurring word, just as it is for Micromégas and his companion, whereas it is absent from Gulliver's vocabulary. Furthermore, there is the title of Voltaire's *conte* itself. As Professor Wade has suggested, it was doubtless carefully chosen with 'micros' signifying the small and 'mégas' the large or great.[22] Shortly following the second of Philonous's two discussions of mites and 'lesser creatures' (Voltaire uses 'atomes'), the interlocutor repeats the terms '*great* and *small*' (the italics are Berkeley's) ending with '*great* or *small*'.[23] Mindful of the above, after rereading *Micromégas*, chapters 5–7, it is difficult not to feel that some of the dry discourse of Berkeley's Philonous on humans and insects has been fleshed out and dramatized in Voltaire's philosophical and moral tale of giants among men and men among giants.

Everything taken into consideration, the fact remains that Voltaire was, from the time of his stay in England to the end of his life, well acquainted with Berkeley and his works. He had praised and utilized the British philosopher frankly and openly when occasion warranted, and, as was often his wont when he was convinced of the absurd, had ridiculed him as well. There was something honest and above-board in the procedure.

On the periphery of the philosophic movement were three men of mark who owed a debt to Berkeley; without him something would have been lacking in what they wrote. All three, though fervidly interested in advanced modes of thought, enjoyed virtual independence and, through personal choice, remained more or less apart from their fellow *philosophes*. They were Maupertuis, La Mettrie and Buffon.

Of these, Georges-Louis Leclerc, comte de Buffon—the very essence of intellectual and social self-confidence—was, as was his custom in such matters, considerably less forthright than Voltaire in dealing with the philosophical churchman. In *Du Sens de la vue*[24] Buffon's references to Cheselden, whom he calls the 'fameux chirurgien de Londres', lend an air of authority to his essay on sight. But neither in this essay nor in *Des Sens en général* (II, 126–37) where his indebtedness to the *New Theory of Vision* is clearly apparent, is there any mention of Berkeley. This privilege had already been reserved for the *Préface* of his translation of Newton's treatise on calculus, which begins: 'On était tranquille depuis plusieurs années, lorsque dans le sein même de l'Angleterre, il s'est élevé un Docteur ennemi de la science qui a déclaré la guerre aux mathématiciens'. He concludes: 'Tout le monde conviendra pour lui, en lisant ses ouvrages, que sa fausse métaphysique l'a conduit à une mauvaise morale, et qu'à force de bien penser de lui-même, il est venu à fort mal penser des autres hommes' (XII, 151–2).

The considerable number of assertions in the *Histoire naturelle de l'homme,* for example, 'L'existence de notre corps et des autres objets extérieurs est douteuse pour quiconque raisonne sans préjugé' (II, 2), are sometimes direct echoes of Berkeley's writings. Then again, they are ricochets of Berkeley's ideas bouncing off the *Traité de l'âme* of La Mettrie. Buffon was of that breed of men who through wilful silence often ignore the real sources of their ideas the better to emphasize their own originality of mind. It may even be that Berkeley and La Mettrie were among that select number of contemporaries who were decidedly more important to the Sage of Montbard than he has led us to suppose.

Pierre-Louis de Maupertuis was not an intellectual jack-of-all-trades but a true scientist among the *philosophes*; many of his far-reaching theories were scientifically sound. Shortly before his death, in an *Épître à Monsieur Duvelaër,* he wrote: 'Les sciences auxquelles je me suis le plus long-temps appliqué, nous présentent le superflu & nous refusent le nécessaire: elles nous découvrent quelques vérités peu intéressantes, & laissent dans les ténèbres celles qui nous intéressent le plus.'[25] Maupertuis was here referring to the limits that the nature of things imposes on our knowledge. He strove to push back these limits to more distant boundaries through his own insights and those of some of the most original thinkers of the age.

One of these was Berkeley. As Franco Venturi has shown,[26] Maupertuis felt obliged to lean heavily on Berkeley in opening up new views on a great and challenging question of the eighteenth century as well as of today: how the problem of language is connected with that of knowledge. The Frenchman's debt to the Irish prelate is particularly marked in the *Réflexions philosophiques sur l'origine des langues et la signification des mots* (op. cit., I, 259–85). Maupertuis explains the origin of words as entities with perception as the point of departure. But the same signs are used to express both a perception ('je vois un arbre'), and what causes the sensation in the first place ('il y a un arbre'). This, he reasons, is a misuse of language, for there has been established a duality between the exterior world, and subjective, unextended perception. He is following Berkeley closely here and concludes that the misuse or neglect of the meaning of words is at the heart of our errors. Thus he manages to deny the existence of the external world. Maupertuis was of course entirely unaware of Berkeley's door in the New World, but through the use of 'un arbre', he arrived at an over-all conclusion of the

New Theory of Vision which could be applied to the Newport portal. He tells us in the *Réflexions philosophiques*: 'Si l'on n'avoit jamais rien touché de ce qu'on a vu, & qu'on le touchât dans une nuit obscure, ou les yeux fermés, on ne reconnoîtrait pas l'objet pour être le même; les deux perceptions *je vois un arbre, je touche un arbre* [. . .] seroient absolument différentes' (I, 282). On the other hand, Maupertuis had no need of the door at 'Whitehall', for Berkeley had himself called up the tree image both in the *Principles of Human Knowledge* (¶ 23) and in the first of his *Three Dialogues*.

Unlike La Mettrie, Buffon and Maupertuis, d'Alembert was very much a member of the philosophic party as well as an *Encyclopédiste* generally held in high regard. Had he been a superficial thinker as well as a lighthearted, lightheaded sceptic, rather than a persistent seeker into the nature of ideas and one of the great mathematicians of the Enlightenment, he would doubtless have brushed aside Berkeley without further ado.

Mathematicians and defenders of mathematics were inclined—and with reason—to look upon the Bishop of Cloyne as one of their most inflexible enemies.[27] He who abhorred abstractions was nevertheless an immaterialist, a spiritualist, and, according to d'Alembert, one of those moderns who has pushed pyrrhonism to its ultimate consequences. Despite this seeming inconsistency, he was a mainstay of the Church of England in the face of those he referred to as the 'philomathematical infidels' of the day. As we have seen, this was more than enough to incur the hostility of a Buffon.

It is not within the scope of the present inquiry to account for d'Alembert's repeated references to Berkeley in such *Encyclopédie* articles as 'Corps' and 'Égoïstes'. This has been sufficiently indicated by Lois Gaudin.[28] Professor Gaudin places emphasis on the British philosopher—as he emerges from the pages of the *Encyclopédie*—as a veritable thorn in the side, not only for d'Alembert, but also for his fellow collaborators. This was unquestionably so but, I think, Ronald Grimsley gives a truer picture, at least of d'Alembert, both through the latter's *Encyclopédie* articles and the *Éléments de philosophie,* by stressing the fact that Berkeley had raised 'a number of teasing problems concerning the vexed question of the existence of the external world'. He had, according to Professor Grimsley, clearly made d'Alembert feel the force of his arguments and may even 'have had some influence in reinforcing the phenomenalist strain in his thought'.[29] It is doubtful, however, whether twentieth-century advocates of phenomenalism would accept Berkeley as their precursor. But the Grimsley remarks could serve as an excellent beginning for anyone wishing to study *à fond* the involved course of d'Alembert's thinking in relation to the man he once accused of daring to contradict 'ou d'ébranler les vérités fondamentales' (article 'Corps').

Condillac is often held to be the only bona fide philosopher of the French Enlightenment, an acknowledged age of *philosophes*. This appears to have been the view of Diderot who, in a famous passage of the *Lettre sur les Aveugles* (1749), considers the author of the *Essai sur l'origine des connaissances humaines* (1746) and the *Traité des systèmes* (1749) eminently qualified to take a clear stand on the absurd but seemingly irrefutable philosophy of idealism so frankly and clearly expounded by Dr Berkeley in his *Three Dialogues*.[30]

Diderot was well acquainted with Condillac as a friend and fellow *philosophe* and saw that the latter had combated with ingenuity the Bishop of Cloyne's *New Theory of Vision* in judging that the eye is naturally capable of figures, magnitudes, situations, and distances.[31] The first of three points I should like to make, then, is that Diderot with his high regard for Condillac as a philosopher encouraged him, after reading the *Essai* and the first *Traité*, to look into Berkeleian notions of man and the universe.

Much has been made of the fact that Condillac did not know English and so depended on Voltaire's résumé in the *Éléments de Newton* for his ideas on Berkeley's *Theory of Vision*. But whether Condillac was totally beholden to Voltaire or also took into account the complete translation—available since 1734—the fact remains that, in what he was later to regard as his prejudiced view, he criticized in his *Essai* of 1746 four well-known figures of the European Enlightenment: Molyneux, Locke, Voltaire, and Berkeley. Yet despite the title of the chapter in which he did so—'De quelques jugemens qu'on a attribués à l'âme sans fondement ou solution d'un problème métaphysique'—he gave little or no evidence of being aware of Berkeley's philosophy of idealism. This brings us to the second point. Berkeley had prudently exposed almost nothing of his immaterialism in the *New Theory of Vision,* knowing full well that his views on vision would have far less chance of being accepted if they were immediately associated with his startling metaphysics. He was convinced that in his essay on vision he was dealing with the facts and only the facts of the senses of sight and touch. It was the *Principles of Human Knowledge* and the *Three Dialogues* that were to offer the Bishop's developed philosophy with its doctrine that the tangible world is comprised of objects that cannot be independent of the mind. This was the metaphysical system, with its 'esse est percipi', and not Berkeley's discussions of vision and touch, that so disturbed Diderot in the *Lettre sur les aveugles.* The *Principles* would not be translated during the life-time of either Condillac or Diderot, and the *Three Dialogues* only in mid-century.

And so we come to the third point. In 1750 with the translation, *Trois dialogues entre Hylas et Philonous contre les sceptiques et les athées,* conveniently at hand, Condillac could seriously consider Diderot's invitation to shatter idealism, that 'système extravagant [...] qui, à la honte de l'esprit humain et de la philosophie, est le plus difficile à combattre' (A.T., I, 304). This was a splendid reason for composing *Le Traité des sensations* (1754), which, according to Georges Le Roy, constitutes an attempt to draw from a sensory impression, as it is felt within, knowledge of the exterior world; and the author, by linking the faculties one to the other, posits the passage from idealism to realism. Professor Le Roy concludes:

Or, par une suprême ironie, les arguments, qui permettent d'établir la continuité du développement psychologique et de rejeter cependant les conclusions de l'idéalisme, sont empruntés à Berkeley lui-même. Dans l'*Essai d'une nouvelle théorie de la vision,* publié en 1709, Berkeley s'était efforcé de définir le rôle du toucher et celui de la vue dans la perception de la distance, de la grandeur et de la situation des objets. En ce qui concerne la perception de la distance, il avait opposé les données visuelles aux données tactiles: les sensations visuelles, avait-il dit, ne font que rappeler les sensations tactiles, auxquelles elles ont été fréquemment associées, et, par conséquent, ce que nous croyons voir n'est que ce que nous nous souvenons d'avoir touché. Nul n'avait pu méconnaître, après ces remarques, la valeur du toucher, ni l'importance de son apport. (*Œuv. phil.,* I, xx-xxi)

For the present there seems nothing to add to this except to say that Buffon thought Condillac owed a debt to his invention of a 'premier homme' who comes into possession of his senses one after the other. Condillac in the *Traité des sensations,* as we know, endowed a statue with one sense at a time. But we can also recall Diderot's 'muet de convention' in the *Lettre sur les sourds et muets* and conclude that, by the middle of the century, the idea had become more or less commonplace. However, it is conceivable that it would have been far less widespread as a device during the Enlightenment had not Berkeley's *New Theory of Vision* already been known throughout Europe for some two decades.

If the scope of this study permitted, Diderot and Berkeley could easily serve as its *pièce de résistance.* Franco Venturi has, in fact, opened the way for just such a presentation. In his aforementioned *Jeunesse de Diderot* he has splendidly summarized the role played by the *New Theory of Vision* in relation to both the *Lettre sur les aveugles* and that on *Les sourds et muets.*[32] Rather than follow in Professor Venturi's footsteps, it would be preferable, I believe, to touch upon possible aspects of the relationship that have had little or no place in his critique.

For instance, valid evidence seems to be lacking that any of the *philosophes* except Diderot had, during the first half of the century, any substantial awareness of Berkeley as a leading exponent of the philosophy of idealism. Berkeleianism, that is to say, the doctrine that corporeal reality exists only as the object of an apprehending mind—in brief, that there is no matter independent of mind—had been stated definitively only in the *Principles* and the *Three Dialogues.* The *Principles* was not translated while the *philosophes* were still alive.

Before 1750 Voltaire—along with Diderot—was the only figure of note among the *philosophes* to show a pronounced awareness of Berkeley. As we have already seen, with his lucid intelligence and his sense of taste, Voltaire had perceived *Alciphron* for what it was, a beautifully wrought series of dialogues where objections to the Christian religion are presented fully and forcefully, but clash head on with equally devastating logic and persuasive arguments for religion in general and the Church of England in particular.

But even Voltaire had concentrated on the British philosopher as author of the *Essay* on vision. It was well after the 1750 translation of the *Three Dialogues between Hylas and Philonous* that Voltaire—trailing the Condillacs and the d'Alemberts by several years—devoted some three pages to the immaterialist Bishop who, he said, claimed with a hundred sophisms to have proved that bodies do not exist. In doing so, Voltaire quoted directly from the *Trois dialogues* itself, in the article 'Corps' of the *Dictionnaire philosophique* (1764), fifteen years after Diderot had elaborated on philosophic idealism as an extravagant system (A.T., I, 304).

Diderot alone of the *philosophes*—according to evidence at hand—had read the *Principles* and the *Three Dialogues* in the original, and the *New Theory* and *Alciphron* either in English or in translation. But what of *Alciphron*?

It has long been considered that Diderot's *Promenade du sceptique* was his last work composed under the direct influence of Shaftesbury. But direct or even indirect influence of Berkeley has gone comparatively unnoticed. Though points of comparison could be multiplied, we shall limit ourselves to a mere handful.[33] In the first place, in the *Discours préliminaire* of *La Promenade,* Cléobule-Diderot suggests that his own series of dialogues could be conceived 'sur le ton de [. . .] Barclay' (A.T., I, 185). Equally challenging is the role that the name 'Alciphron' plays in both works. The word 'sceptique' figures in Diderot's title, and Berkeley's title, *Alciphron,* stands for 'strong head', 'free-thinker', 'skeptic' in ancient Greek; and though in Diderot's *Promenade* Alciphron is mentioned by name only once, his part is clearly established at the outset when we read in the *Discours préliminaire:* '[. . .] le jeune sceptique Alcyphron survint [et] se proposa pour arbitre de notre différend' (A.T., I, 186).

The 'différend' is, as Diderot states, on 'la religion, la philosophie et le monde'. These are the same topics—the world of revealed religion, of the mundane and of philosophy— around which the discussions revolve in the seven dialogues of Berkeley's *Alciphron.*

Despite the fact that, in the two works, the divergent viewpoints on theology are at once obvious, one could, with a little patience, spell out the arresting similarities in the initial rural settings, in the satirical portraits, in illustrations of points made and even, upon occasion, in the very phraseology used. Stylistically, Diderot tried to follow Berkeley more closely than the less inspiring Shaftesbury. But Diderot, still something of a neophyte in both style and argumentation, has offered in *La Promenade* a cliché-ridden, somewhat slipshod piece of writing. Berkeley's *Alciphron,* however, has remained an outstanding example of acutely tuned observation, sparkling dialectic and esthetic and moral equipoise.

Had Berkeley been able to read what Diderot was to say about him as the idealist, Zénoclès, in the 'Allée des marronniers' (A.T., I, 231–2), and by name in both the *Lettre sur les aveugles* and the *Entretien entre d'Alembert et Diderot,* he would have protested that he was not a solipsist. The reason given would have been that in postulating the mind of God he was saying that God's mind contained the reality that Berkeley himself observed. Other beings were ideas in the mind of God and in his own mind. It could also be said that Berkeley would never have thought of himself as a 'clavecin sensible' nor would he have had such moments of delirium as suggested by the author of the *Rêve de d'Alembert.*

Diderot was a materialist and Berkeley an idealist. There was no difference in what each admitted as facts, the kinds of objects experienced. The difference came rather in the theory each would introduce to account for the fact or the set of facts under consideration.

In reading Berkeley, the *philosophes*—especially Diderot—did see that he was bent on denying universals. For him, all words were meaningful in terms of specific references. With Berkeley, then, we are dealing with a specific book, a specific tree, or a specific door.

The Bishop of Cloyne was bound to be intriguing to the *philosophes,* led on as they were by Diderot, for these works, in spite of their perplexing and even displeasing metaphysics, revealed a mind as acute as it was analytical. But these same *philosophes* could not be expected to go along with them when he postulated spiritual reality. Nevertheless—and the paradox is striking—Berkeley could have gone along with Diderot and his fellow *philosophes* who posited material reality. Addressing his friend, the American Samuel Johnson, Berkeley wrote: 'I had no inclination to trouble the world with large volumes. What I have done was rather with a view of giving hints to thinking men, who have leisure and curiosity to go to the bottom of things and pursue them in their own minds' (op. cit., II, 273).

But Berkeley was subtle, elusive and extremely difficult. Yet he proved to be of much use to the *philosophes* by seeking answers, even to questions no one had asked.

One might say in conclusion that Berkeley's philosophy—like his pedimented door—

remains as elusively tantalizing as ever. Both door and philosophy, despite their subtle ambiguities, or perhaps because of them, continue to pique the imagination of those who still number themselves among the quick.

NOTES

1 Ernst Cassirer, *The Philosophy of the Enlightenment* (Princeton, 1951), pp. 108–17.

2 A. D. Ritchie, *George Berkeley: A Reappraisal* (Manchester, 1967). On page 2 we read: 'NTV is not just the first, it is the main, central, constructive, and most strictly scientific work; also, in Berkeley's own view, the most strictly theological.'

3 In a letter of 9 March 1730, the good Dean wrote Thomas Prior: 'I live here upon land I have purchased and in a farmhouse I have built on this Island.'

4 Alice Brayton, *George Berkeley in Newport* (Newport, Rhode Island, 1954), has given the best account of farmhouse turned country manor; see especially p. 31. Benjamin Rand's *Berkeley's American Sojourn* (Cambridge, Mass., 1932), the most ambitious book to date concerning the philosopher's stay on the east coast of colonial America, merely devotes a few lines to Whitehall's interior; see p. 22.

5 Antoinette F. Downing and Vincent J. Scully, Jr., *The Architectural Heritage of Newport, Rhode Island, 1640–1915*. Second Edition—Revised (New York, 1967), p. 440.

6 cf. A. D. Ritchie, op. cit., pp. 2–26.

7 Henry St. John Bolingbroke, *Philosophical Works* (Philadelphia, 1841), II, 140–41.

8 See in particular Mara Vamos's sensitively intelligent study, *Pascal's 'Pensées' and the Enlightenment: the Roots of a Misunderstanding*, SVEC (Oxfordshire: The Voltaire Foundation), 97, 1972.

9 Jean Le Rond d'Alembert, *Éléments de philosophie*, I (Paris, 1821), p. 184.

10 This view is perfectly reflected in vol. II of *Le Grand Dictionnaire Historique* of Louis Moréri (Paris, 1759) where under the entry of 'Berklei (George)' we read: 'Il goûta beaucoup les systêmes du père Malebranche touchant l'existence des corps, & enchérit même sur lui dans son traité des principes de l'entendement humain' (p. 386).

11 Early and mid-century translations into French are as follows: *Alciphron ou le petit philosophe contenant une apologie de la religion chrétienne contre ceux qu'on nomme Esprits-Forts*, traduit par E. de Joncourt (Paris, 1734), 2 vols., to which is appended a translation of the *New Theory of Vision*; ibid. (La Haye, 1734), 2 vols. *Recherches sur les vertus de l'eau de goudron, où l'on a joint des réflexions philosophiques sur divers autres sujets importants*, traduites de l'anglois par D.-R. Boullier, avec deux lettres de l'auteur (Amsterdam, 1745). *Extraits des Recherches sur les vertus de l'eau de goudron* (Amsterdam, 1749). *Nouvelles réflexions sur l'eau de goudron*, traduites de l'anglois (Paris, 1752). *Dialogues entre Hylas et Philonous contre les sceptiques et les athées*, traduits par l'abbé Jean-Paul Gua de Malves (Amsterdam and Paris, 1750). *Caractéristiques de l'état politique du royaume de la Grande-Bretagne sur le pied qu'il est aujourd'hui*, ouvrage traduit sur la 4e édition de l'anglois (The Hague, 1759).

12 This is particularly true of Jean Le Clerc's 30-page résumé and analysis of the *New Theory of Vision* in *Bibliothèque choisie pour servir de suite à la Bibliothèque universelle*. Année M.DCCXI, tome 22, Première partie, Nouvelle Edition, revue et corrigée (The Hague, 1734).

13 David Funt, *Diderot and the Esthetics of the Enlightenment*, Diderot Studies, 11 (Geneva, 1968), p. 42. The unwary student could also be led astray by the printers' error in Charles Dédéyan's useful *L'Angleterre dans la pensée de Diderot* (Paris, 1957–1958), where we read that Jaucourt, not Joncourt, had translated Berkeley in 1734; such a statement, if true, would have been rich in possibilities. On the same page we are told that the account of Cheselden's operation was available to the *philosophes* in 1748; it appeared twenty years earlier, in 1728.

14 Number 402, for the Months of April, May and June, 1728. VII. *An account of some Observations made by a young Gentleman, who was born blind, or lost his Sight so early, that he had no Remembrance of ever having seen, and was couch'd between 13 and 14 Years of Age*. By Mr Will. Chesselden [*sic*] F.R.S. to Her Majesty, and to St Thomas's Hospital.

15 *Anatomy of Criticism*: *Four Essays* (Princeton, 1957), p. 23.
16 In the *Bibliothèque des livres* (Moscow and Leningrad, 1961), p. 74, we learn that the only Berkeley work we are sure he possessed was the 1750 translation of the *Three Dialogues between Hylas and Philonous,* for which, see footnote 11.
17 cf. H. F. Hallet's article, 'Dr Johnson's Refutation of Bishop Berkeley,' in *Mind: a Quarterly Review of Psychology and Philosophy,* Vol. 56, N.S., No. 222, April, 1947, p. 10: '[. . .] the opposition of Berkeley and Johnson reduces to a divergence between two theories of the nature of the human body, and its relation to the mind with which it is united.'
18 Indices of the Beuchot and Moland editions of the *Œuvres complètes,* and of the thoroughly indexed Besterman edition of Voltaire's *Correspondence.*
19 See Ira O. Wade, *Voltaire's 'Micromégas'*: *a Study in the Fusion of Science, Myth and Art* (Princeton, 1950), pp. 82 and passim.
20 William Eddy, *Gulliver's Travels*: *A Critical Study* (Princeton University Press, 1923), p. 99.
21 This passage is from *The Works of George Berkeley,* edited by A. A. Luce and T. E. Jessop (London, 1948), II, 88, and is cited by Harry C. Morris in his article, 'The *Dialogues of Hylas and Philonous* as a Source in *Gulliver's Travels,*' in *Modern Language Notes,* 70, No. 3, March 1955, pp. 173–5. Mr Morris could have quoted additional lines that would also have suggested the *Dialogues* as the 'most probable source' for Swift's development of this imagery on the very large and the very small.
22 op. cit., p. 92.
23 Professor Wade does not list Berkeley among the possible influences on *Micromégas* but, by coincidence, in his study he entitles his chapter four, 'Great and Small'.
24 Édition Flourens, II, 100–16. References are to the M. Flourens edition of the *Œuvres complètes de Buffon* (Paris, 1853–1855).
25 *Œuvres* (Lyon, 1756), I, v–vi.
26 In his quite remarkable *Jeunesse de Diderot* (Paris, 1939), pp. 271–2.
27 Such essays as *The Analyst,* questioning Newton's system of belief in fluxions and addressed to 'an infidel mathematician,' and the ironic *Defence of Free-Thinking in Mathematics* as well as the already mentioned *De Moto,* are all distrustful of mathematical hypotheses which are, in Berkeley's judgment, unstable, and cannot bear close scrutiny in the order of things.
28 Lois Strong Gaudin in *Les Lettres anglaises dans l'"Encyclopédie'* (New York, 1941), pp. 197–201.
29 See especially pp. 236–8, and p. 278 of *Jean d'Alembert, 1717–83,* by Ronald Grimsley (Oxford, 1963).
30 I, 304–5 of the Assézat-Tourneux edition of Diderot's *Œuvres complètes,* hereafter referred to as 'A.T.'
31 *Essai,* Part I, sect. 6. *Œuvres philosophiques de Condillac,* texte établi et présenté par Georges Le Roy, I (Paris, 1947), is used and will be indicated by *Œuv. phil.,* I.
32 Charles Dédéyan, in his study on Diderot (op. cit.) has himself added to the list, also calling attention to the *philosophe* utilizing Berkeley as late as 1769 in a well-known passage of the *Entretien entre d'Alembert et Diderot*: 'Et pour donner à mon système toute sa force, remarquez encore qu'il est sujet à la même difficulté insurmontable que Berkeley a proposée contre l'existence des corps. Il y a un moment de délire où le clavecin sensible a pensé qu'il était le seul clavecin qu'il y eût au monde, et que toute l'harmonie de l'univers se passait en lui' (A.T., I, 118).
33 That Jean-Jacques Rousseau, in mid-career, well on the outer edges of the philosophic movement in France, should have been fascinated by Berkeley's idealistic position comes as no surprise. In a letter to M. de Franquières (15 janvier 1769), he wrote: '[. . .] tandis que toute la philosophie moderne rejette les esprits, tout d'un coup l'évêque Berkeley s'élève et soutient qu'il n'y a point de corps. Comment est-on venu à bout de répondre à ce terrible logicien? Otez le sentiment intérieur, et je défie tous les philosophes modernes ensemble de prouver à Berkeley qu'il y a des corps.'

8

An Eighteenth-Century Student of Medieval Literature: Bernard de La Monnoye

JOHN FOX

Bernard de La Monnoye was one of the most learned French scholars of the late seventeenth and early eighteenth centuries, renowned in his own day for his poetic skill, his command of several languages and his knowledge of the literary history of France. Born in Dijon in 1641, he was educated at the Collège des Jésuites there, and after studying law at the University of Orleans, returned to Dijon to become a barrister. His true interest lay in writing and in the study of literature, and he soon took advantage of his modest fortune to devote himself entirely to such pursuits. In 1671 he won the first prize for poetry ever awarded by the French Academy, and carried off the same prize on no fewer than four subsequent occasions. He was elected to the Academy in 1713, and died in 1728.

Indefatigable annotator of his many books, lover of amusing anecdotes and witty epigrams whose clever trivialities reveal a taste curiously at variance with his true abilities,[1] he produced little himself,[2] but his abundant marginalia and glosses were to leave their imprint on diverse works by other writers, some published in his own lifetime, such as P. Bayle's *Dictionnaire historique et critique,* some which did not appear until many years after his death. He was in many ways suited to be an editor of other people's works, and even more, to be a sort of prompter of other editors. His preparation of an edition of the poetry of Melin de Saint-Gelais has been referred to by L. Gossman in his *Medievalism and the Ideologies of the Enlightenment.*[3] More germane to Gossman's subject, but unmentioned by him, are editions of several late medieval authors projected by La Monnoye and left in rough draft form. They first receive mention in the *Journal Litéraire* [*sic*] for January–February, 1714: '. . . M. de la Monnoye prépare une Edition des plus célébres [*sic*] de nos anciens Poëtes François, tels que *Villon, Coquillart,* la Farce de *Patelin* etc. Il revoit ces Auteurs sur les Editions les plus exactes, et les plus anciennes et les enrichit des Notes Critiques et Historiques' (p. 232). La Monnoye was seventy-three years old at the time! Two years later M. de Sallengre expressed regret that these editions had still not appeared.[4] That of Villon's poetry had to wait over a century and a half before it was published, while

the draft of La Monnoye's edition of Coquillart's works, which never got into print, has
recently been identified by the present author amongst the early editions of Coquillart's
poems in the British Museum.[5] I have not so far found traces of La Monnoye's proposed
edition of *Pathelin*, if, indeed, it ever existed.

The draft of La Monnoye's edition of Villon was identified by Gustave Masson in the
British Museum in 1858[6] and published nine years later by Pierre Jannet.[7] There is no reason
to doubt this identification, though since he was emending the text of the 1723 edition, La
Monnoye must have begun this work at least nine years after the preliminary announcement
in the *Journal Litéraire,* and within five years of his death in 1728. The flyleaf preceding the
title page carries the following handwritten addition: 'L'Histoire et Les chefs de la Poesie
francoise avec la liste des Poetes Provencaux et francois accompagnée de remarques sur
leurs [*leurs* crossed out and replaced with *le*] caracteres [not corrected] de leurs ouvrages.'
Evidently the Villon edition was intended as part of a far more ambitious undertaking.
Even this surviving portion was not to be limited to Villon, for to the main title *Les Œuvres*
[corrected to *Poesies*] *de François Villon* has been added in ink 'et de ses Disciples' and a piece
of paper has then been stuck in with the following inscription: 'Reveuës sur les differentes
Editions Corrigées et augmentées sur le manuscrit de M. le Duc de Coislin et sur plusieurs
autres, et enrichies d'un grand nombre de pieces avec des notes historiques et critiques.' Of
these notes there is no sign, and the 'Additions manuscrites intitulées autres poésies qu'on
croit de françois Villon' to be inserted near the end of the volume were either never completed or have become dissociated from it and appear to be lost. The notoriously unreliable
text of the Coustelier edition has been extensively corrected by La Monnoye, and the
bottom of every page, as well as that of the pieces of paper glued in, has been initialled.
Everything was left ready for the printer, and as Jannet wrote: 'Pour toute la partie du
texte établie par La Monnoye, je n'avais qu'une chose à faire: suivre la leçon adoptée par
lui [. . .]'[8] This confidence was well placed, for La Monnoye's method was sound: the
manuscript from which he drew many of his emended readings, that belonging to the
Duc de Coislin (now BN f. fr. 20041) is precisely the one which A. Burger selected as
recently as 1957[9] as deserving to form the basis of a new critical edition to replace the best
one currently available,[10] which is based on a rather loose eclectic method. It is a surprising
fact that certain of Burger's proposed emendations simply restore the reading that La
Monnoye had chosen almost two and a half centuries earlier.[11] Inevitably, several of La
Monnoye's corrections are no longer acceptable, but even so his treatment of Villon's text
is a remarkable testimony to his scholarship.

The copious annotations in the British Museum copy of the 1532 edition of Coquillard's
poetry are clearly in the same hand as the emendations of the Villon text.[12] These are not
only textual corrections, but also involve the addition of handwritten footnotes to which
numbers have been assigned, showing that this too was intended for publication, an
intention also revealed by several references to a preface and a vocabulary, although these
are not included in this actual volume and are not in the possession of the British Museum.[13]
One of the anecdotes given in the manuscript notes begins: 'Il est juste de mettre ici ce
qui est arrivé il y a six ans [. . .]'.[14] These last words are crossed out and replaced with

'en 1716'. Therefore La Monnoye was working on this edition in 1722,[15] a little earlier than on his Villon edition, but also several years after the original announcement in the *Journal Litéraire*. The notes, hitherto largely unexplored, provide a rich fund of information on many matters, mainly historical, and are particularly detailed on legal affairs and on universities and their customs, La Monnoye having studied law and having practised for a short time at the bar, as we have seen. Many terms of Coquillard's vast and sometimes abstruse vocabulary receive comment, and the survival of certain of them in various regions is noted. Comparisions are made, as is fitting, largely with authors and works of the fifteenth and sixteenth centuries, a much quoted one being *Le Champion des Dames,* whose author, Martin le Franc, is never named, though he is referred to on one occasion as 'un poète plus ancien que Coquillart'.[16] Favourite authors include Villon, Charles d'Orléans and Clément Marot. The *Arrêts d'Amour* are named, but not their author Martial d'Auvergne, while Guillaume Crétin receives a passing reference, and two notes reveal a good knowledge of the *Farce de Pierre Pathelin.* A reference to the author of the *Roman de la Rose* as Guillaume de Meun (p. 80) does not inspire confidence in La Monnoye's knowledge of earlier medieval literature, and similar doubts are raised by a rather vague note on the romances of chivalry: 'La plus part des anciens Paladins ou chevaliers errans ont eu des historiens; et l'on a fait même des chroniques de chevaliers qui n'ont jamais existé, quelques uns de ceux qui ont esté reellement, n'ont souvent fait des actions de valeur et n'ont pris le party de la chevalerie qui étoit autrefois l'employ des gentilshommes les plus distingués qu'afin d'avoir occasion de faire faire leur histoire et d'y faire inserer toutes les actions qu'ils auroient souhaité de faire'.[17] That La Monnoye had read some works in manuscript form is revealed by his studies of Villon's text, but his reading of medieval works was clearly based mainly on printed editions. An interesting note summing up his knowledge of the religious theatre prior to 1541 is here quoted *in extenso*:

'C'étoit l'usage anciennement de representer en comedie tous les Mysteres de la Religion. Cela se faisoit principalement aux grandes festes et ces comedies duroient quelquefois 8 jours. L'hostel de Bourgogne destiné aujourd'huy pour la Comedie Italienne, servoit de Theatre à ces representations. Elles se faisoient sous la direction d'une confrerie de la passion. Et c'est pour cela que sur la grande porte de L'hostel de Bourgogne a Paris on voit encore les Instrumens de la passion. Mais ces representations furent supprimées en 1541 par un arrêt du Parlement. Voicy les comedies de ce genre qui sont venuës à ma connoissance: *l'ancien Testament* in folio. 2° La Patience de Job in 12°. 3° *L'annonciation* in–folio, et qui est assez rare. 4° *Le mystere de la passion* in fol. et in 4° peu commun. 5° *La vengeance de la passion.* 6° *Le mystere du mauvais riche* in 12° peu commun. 7° *Les actes des apostres,* il y en a deux differens l'un in 4° et l'autre in folio. L'in folio est le moins rare. 8° *L'apocalypse* qui se trouve ordinairement a la fin des actes in folio. 9° *Le mystere du bien et du mal avisé.* Je ne l'ai vu qu'une seule fois et meme en manuscrit. 10° *Le mystere St. andré* 12° assez rare. 11° *Le miracle de la sainte hostie* arrivé aux carmes des Villettes in 12°. 12° L'histoire de St. Christophle in folio, assez rare. 13° L'histoire de St. Dominique.[18]

Increasing attention has recently been devoted to the post-Renaissance revival of interest in medieval literature.[19] Coming as he did between Pasquier and Fauchet on the one hand, and La Curne de Sainte-Palaye and Le Grand d'Aussy on the other, La Monnoye is clearly worthy of closer study than he has hitherto been accorded. The unpublished material that he has left is a rich treasure accumulated in the course of a very long life devoted to literature and which has not yet yielded up all its secrets.

NOTES

1 The following is a characteristic example:

> Prêtre
> La prêtrise me désespère,
> On a beau me la proposer.
> Hé quoi! Si l'Eglise est ma mère,
> Comment pourrai-je l'épouser?

2 The *Noëls bourguignons,* a collection of carols in his native dialect, the first series of which was published in 1700 under the pseudonym Gui-Barôzai (=Bas rosés, a nickname applied to the Burgundian *Vignerons* because of their wearing of this attire) are his chief title to fame. His fellow-Burgundian J.-M. Morin has criticised him severely for having written them: 'Des Noëls en patois! . . . Quand on est latiniste, helléniste, italianiste etc. . . . et académicien! . . . Mais ce sont là des vétilles!' (*La Monnoye et ses Noëls bourguignons. Examen critique de cet ouvrage en forme de réquisitoire,* Dijon, 1905, p. 91). The truth is that La Monnoye, like so many scholars, was better as a critic than as a creative writer.

3 Baltimore, 1968, p. 13. Characteristically, this edition was never actually published by La Monnoye himself, but his notes were incorporated in P. Blanchemain's three-volume edition of Melin de Saint-Gelais's poetry, Bibliothèque Elzévirienne, 1873. Blanchemain's introduction includes a biography of La Monnoye and an account of his work on this poet.

4 *Poésies de M. de la Monnoye de l'Académie Françoise,* avec son éloge, publiées par M. de S***, The Hague, 1716, p. xxxix, footnote.

5 Paris, Galiot du Pré, 1532, BM Catalogue no. C. 107. a. 9.

6 This is a copy of the 1723 Coustelier edition and bears the catalogue no. 241. f. 17.

7 *Œuvres complètes de François Villon suivies d'un choix des poésies de ses disciples,* édition préparée par La Monnoye, mise au jour, avec notes et glossaire par M. Pierre Jannet (Paris, 1867).

8 op. cit., p. xxi.

9 In his *Lexique de la langue de Villon précédé de notes critiques pour l'établissement du texte* (Geneva-Paris).

10 By A. Longnon, revised by L. Foulet, published in the C.F.M.A. series, 4th edition, 1932.

11 Both agree, for example, that *Le Testament,* l. 34 should read 'Pour l'ame du bon feu Cotart' in place of 'Et pour l'ame' or 'Par l'ame'; l. 82, 'Lors que le roy me delivra' in place of 'Que le roy me delivra'.

12 The British Museum catalogue, influenced no doubt by Masson, attributes the Villon emendations to La Monnoye, but does not identify the author of the notes added to the Coquillard text.

13 They are to be found in the Bibliothèque Nationale, f. fr. 25448–25450. I am indebted for this information to Dr M. J. Freeman, whose edition of the poetry of Guillaume Coquillard is soon to be published by Droz, Geneva.

14 The full text of the anecdote, which has a real La Monnoye flavour about it, is as follows: 'Il est juste de mettre ici ce qui est arrivé en 1716 au lieutenant de Police de Paris. Un manant se vint plaindre a luy, qu'il avoit trouvé sa femme sur le fait; et qu'il venoit luy en demander justice. Sur le fait, dit le magistrat, qui ne savoit quelle justice luy rendre; ouy sur le fait, monseigneur, elle est ici: elle vous le dira elle meme. Elle entra, et avoua la chose a demi entre ses dens. Y a t'il un verrouil à ta porte, dit le grave et refrogné magistrat; non, monseigneur repondit le manant. Tient Voyla un ecu, fais en mettre un; et toy, dit il, à la femme, tient toujours le verrouil fermé. L'escu tint lieu d'arret et il n'en fut point appellé' (note 107, inserted immediately before p. 63).

15 Was it the appearance of the Coustelier edition in the following year that discouraged La Monnoye from pursuing this project? This seems unlikely since Coustelier merely reproduced the text of earlier editions, without notes or glossary. La Monnoye's, had it been published, would have been far superior.

16 p. 38, note 68. The page references which La Monnoye gives for his quotations from *Le Champion des Dames* suggest that he was using the 1530 edition (Pierre Vidoue, Paris).

17 p. 113, note 45 (second numbering).

18 Note 135 opposite p. 158.

19 In addition to L. Gossman's work, already referred to, one may also cite Professor C. E. Pickford's Inaugural Lecture, given in the University of Hull in 1966, and entitled *Changing attitudes towards medieval French Literature,* also the PhD thesis of G. J. Wilson on Le Grand d'Aussy, inspired by that inaugural and which it is hoped will be published in the near future.

9

The Prince de Ligne and the Exemplification of Heroic Virtue in the Eighteenth Century[1]

BASIL GUY

In the first edition of a small volume entitled *Fantaisies Militaires,* published by Charles-Joseph, prince de Ligne, in 1780, we read:

Fussiez-vous du sang des héros, fussiez-vous du sang des dieux, s'il y en avait; si la gloire ne vous délire pas continuellement, ne vous rangez pas sous ses étendards. Ne dites point que vous avez du goût pour notre état [de soldats]. Embrassez-en un autre, si cette expression froide vous suffit. Prenez-y garde, vous faites votre service sans reproche, peut-être. Vous savez même quelque chose des principes; vous êtes des artisans; vous irez à un certain point, mais vous n'êtes point des artistes. Aimez ce métier au-dessus des autres à la passion. Oui, passion est le mot. Si vous ne rêvez pas militaire [. . .], quittez vite un habit que vous déshonorez.[2]

Thanks to the urgency of its tone, this passage is not without importance, above all when we realize the very special meaning which the author would attach to the words: *héros, gloire, honneur, passion.* And not excepting the fact that this volume appeared anonymously under the false imprint of a little-known village in Bohemia—the modesty of which is almost without parallel at a time when most experienced authors were attempting to woo the public with poems on strategy, tactics, and the art of war in general, not to mention dull treatises and long, duly edited for the amusement of polite society—the special quality of this exhortation requires at least a few words to place its theme in historic perspective before the particular contribution of the Prince de Ligne to a discussion of heroic virtue in the eighteenth century can be fully appreciated.

Heroism is one of humanity's more enduring idealizations. Dating from at least the eighth century B.C., the notion and the term found their first literary expression in Hesiod when he attempted to describe an era 'filled with the deeds of a godlike race of men who are called heroes', in order to trace their descent from Olympus, through Homer, to his own day. This famous interruption in the poet's review of 'the four ages of mankind' (gold, silver, bronze, and iron) occasioned the subsequent consecration of the term: the heroic age.[3]

As a man possessing the virtues of nobility, the hero, because of his over-riding self-control, became a 'model for emulation', one of the recognizable hallmarks of civilization as Hegel claimed, 'who undertakes and accomplishes a complete enterprise in consistent reliance upon his personal resources and initiative.'[4] Furthermore,

the hero is the ideal individual type whose being is centred in [. . .] 'pure', and not technical values—and whose basic characteristic is natural distinction of body and soul. The hero may be noted by a superabundance of intellectual will, concentrated in a struggle against the instincts. This is what constitutes the greatness of his character.[5]

The hero's role is therefore twofold. In the first and most usual acceptance of the term, he is actively engaged as doer; in the second, he is to be seen possessed of a special intelligence as thinker which contributes equally to the success of his undertakings, informing and guiding them so that the outcome is as much dependent on the one as on the other force.

Yet, because of a transfer of meaning in *topoi* that originally indicated *fortitudo et sapientia*, courage and wisdom, like Vergil's 'arms and the man . . .', modern ideas about heroes and heroism are a far cry from what the Ancients intended or their public understood. Viewed in this light, Olivier (in the *Song of Roland*) may be seen not merely as a complementary figure to Roland, but as a hero in his own right. And, thanks to the stabilizing—if not stultifying—influence of Christianity, such an ideal remained generally unchanged in Europe until, roughly, the seventeenth century.

Since that time, both in life and in literature, the hero has been found wanting, disintegrating, and even 'demolished'. Paul Bénichou has proved that Corneille's ideal was effectively dead by the end of the seventeenth century,[6] notwithstanding Napoleon's dictum that France owed its sense of glory under the Revolution and Empire to Corneille.[7] But then, we might ask, what had happened, so that after some one hundred and fifty years heroes and heroism re-appear, rising like a phoenix from the ashes? The intervening period of the eighteenth century has frequently been charged with being 'inglorious' and Vauvenargues's the only name cited as adding some lustre to the concept in that time. Yet even this last author may be viewed as one of Lanson's 'attardés et égarés', a throwback to neo–classical modes of thought, leaving still unanswered the question: Did the ancient ideal disappear entirely?

Given the general development of such commonplaces as constitute the proper study of the history of ideas, it would hardly seem likely. And such is, indeed, the case. For, just as the hero had been transformed, by Corneille's time, into an idealization of the social conscience, so, by the time of the Revolution, that vision had been itself transformed and given another interpretation, untoward and less obvious perhaps, but of considerable import for succeeding generations. Old ideals never die—nor even fade away—they are refurbished, reconstructed if need be, and continue to endure, despite the vagaries of that humanity which they serve to illustrate.

One such mutation may be seen in the work of those writers from the seventeenth century whom we normally consider the defenders of the classical canon, especially Boileau. But there are others, not least of whom that Bossuet who bore witness to a changing perspective as he proclaimed:

Loin de nous les héros sans humanité. Ils pourront forcer le respect et ravir l'admiration comme font tous les objets extraordinaires, mais ils n'auront pas les cœurs. Lorsque Dieu forma le cœur et les entrailles de l'homme, il y mit premièrement la bonté, comme son propre caractère et pour être la marque de cette main bienfaisante dont nous sortons. La bonté devait donc faire comme le fond de notre cœur, et devait être en même temps le premier attrait que nous aurions en nous-mêmes pour gagner les autres hommes. La grandeur qui vient par-dessus, loin d'affaiblir la bonté, n'est faite que pour l'aider à se communiquer davantage. [. . .] Reconnaissons le héros qui, toujours égal à lui-même, sans se hausser pour paraître grand, sans s'abaisser pour être civil et obligeant, se trouve naturellement tout ce qu'il doit être envers les hommes ; comme un fleuve majestueux et bienfaisant, qui porte paisiblement dans les villes l'abondance qu'il a répandue dans les campagnes en les arrosant, qui se donne à tout le monde, et ne s'élève et ne s'enfle que lorsqu'avec violence on s'oppose à la douce pente qui le porte à continuer son tranquille cours. Telle a été la douceur, et telle a été la force du Prince de Condé.[8]

Thus did Bossuet further refine the notion of heroism by situating martial virtue in the framework of rational conduct, exceptional valour in terms of unexceptional humanity. Undoubtedly the situation—a state funeral—no less than the man—le grand Condé—determined his view in this instance. Yet so pervasive was the attraction of this new ideal that we can easily find other examples of it even in the less grandiose reflexions of a La Bruyère. Because this author is too familiar to need quoting *in extenso,* we would point out merely that in his chapter *Du mérite personnel,* after contrasting the military hero with the great man, who may be 'de tous les métiers', the moralist writes as follows: 'Il semble que [le héros] soit jeune, entreprenant, d'une haute valeur, ferme dans les périls, intrépide ; que [le grand homme] excelle par un grand sens, par une vaste prévoyance, par une haute capacité et par une longue expérience. Peut-être qu'Alexandre n'était qu'un héros et que César était un grand homme.'[9]

Most likely the names 'Alexandre' and 'César' are used by La Bruyère instead of Condé and Turenne, which it would have been rather impolitic to vaunt—and criticize—in this manner at Chantilly. After all, the hireling author did not want to bite the hand that fed him. For, if we read the text aright, we realize that there *is* criticism here, particularly in the negative of exclusion applied to the Hellene: 'Alexandre *n*'était *qu*'un héros'. This one phrase gives us a clue to La Bruyère's real meaning. More than that, it indicates how, starting from almost the same premises as Bossuet, the author of the *Roland,* or even Vergil, he develops an element that henceforth would undermine the notion of *le héros* more and more, until that notion would be changed almost beyond the recognition of Homer and Hesiod, not to mention Bossuet and La Bruyère.

Now, if we return to the quotation from Ligne's *Fantaisies Militaires* with which we began, we note that his contribution to the subtle transformation of the Cornelian hero into that of Napoleon is significant. And, though the example of the Prince de Ligne in the development of this notion has often been overlooked, he was himself a 'model for emulation', not only by reason of his birth, but also because of his talent, first as a military hero, then as the creator of heroic character in works of literature. Such a coupling of both word and deed is rare at any period, but, in the eighteenth century, heroism of thought and action in the life of one man was a singular occurrence that requires consideration, 'a veritable phenomenon', as Ligne's first—and best—critic, madame de Staël, would claim, saying:

'[. . .] la civilisation s'est arrêtée en lui à ce point où les nations ne restent jamais lorsque toutes les formes rudes sont adoucies, sans que l'essence de rien soit altérée [. . .].[Le privilège de la grâce chez lui] ne touche à rien assez rudement pour blesser [. . .] et jamais elle n'ébranle la vie qu'elle embellit.'[10]

But what was this life? A few details should enable us to gauge more exactly the role of hero played by the Prince de Ligne and so arrive at a better understanding of heroism in his works.

Born in 1735 to one of the most illustrious names of the Austrian Netherlands, Charles-Joseph de Ligne came from a family that had ever been in the forefront of their peers, whether as diplomatists or as soldiers. His grandfather, father, and uncle were all Marshals of the Empire, and it was in the military that Charles-Joseph grew up, after a confused and confusing education at the family seat of Belœil, not far from the scene of Fontenoy. As a youth he had been present at the siege of Brussels, just as later he participated in the Seven Years' War. Although he was married in 1755 to an heiress of the house of Liechtenstein, domesticity did not keep him from gaining a reputation as a soldier. After receiving his baptism of fire at Kolin in 1757 and a battlefield commission at Hochkirch in the next year, Ligne participated in the Austrian victory of 1759 at Thiennendorf (or Kunersdorf, depending on the sympathies of the historian one reads), as later he participated in the occupation of Berlin. The peace of 1763 brought enforced leisure and the opportunity to return to France where he had once carried news of the battle of Maxen and had begun those amorous exploits for which he was formerly best known. Indeed, he would thenceforth travel to Paris for about six months of each year and was ultimately admitted to the intimacy of Marie-Antoinette and Count d'Artois, the future Charles X. Meanwhile, his obligations as a prospective father-in-law took him to Poland and Russia, where he soon became an admirer of Catherine the Great. In 1787, he was included in the party organized by Potemkin to visit the newly-conquered territories of the Crimea, which ended with Catherine's Second Turkish War. In this campaign, Ligne fought as a colonel on the Russian side at Elizavetgorod and Ochakov. He later joined the Imperial forces before Belgrade where his military career touched its zenith when he was rewarded for valour with the cross of Maria Theresa and the rank of Commander in the military order of the same name. After 1789, Ligne was little by little removed from the centres of power, and under Leopold II and Francis II was no more than a cipher in the military and political life of the times because he had been implicated in the Belgian revolt of that year. With the invasion of the Low Countries by the armies of the French Revolution, he lost all his holdings there and was forced to live in straitened circumstances in Vienna, relieving the tedium of existence by writing and by visits to his family and friends in Bohemia. On one occasion or another, he encountered many of the great or near-great of his own day, adding to the list of notables from another generation whom he had known, like Voltaire, Rousseau and Diderot, the names of Casanova, Beethoven, and Gœthe. In 1807, he was given the purely honorific title of Captain of the Emperor's Bodyguard, and in 1808 that of *Feldmarschall*. At this time, he was very much the cynosure of all who passed through Vienna or who lingered for the Congress, including madame de Staël and Talleyrand. Thanks to such as these, he knew once more, if briefly, the same sort of favour that had earlier enchanted him throughout cosmopolitan Europe, and we may assume that he died happy amidst the festivities of 1814.

As this sketch would indicate, Ligne was an experienced and capable soldier, the exemplification of heroic virtue even as it had been touted from antiquity to the eighteenth century. As one of those 'models for emulation' with which we began, he had ever lived with the inspiration of the great military commanders of yore, not to mention those of his own family circle. Although his childhood was given over to 'enfantillages et dérèglements' of one sort or another, Ligne remained (if we believe his memoirs) an indefatigable reader, especially of military history. Heroism then seized upon his mind, and the idea of heroism would scarce leave him thereafter, dreams of battle, great deeds, and a crown of laurel obsessing him even when awake:

[. . .] Je dévorais Quinte-Curce et les *Commentaires* que je trouvai dans une vieille bibliothèque du château de Baudour, et je croyais devenir ce qu'ils étaient. Le siège de Prague [en 1742], la sortie, l'escalade, me tournaient la tête. Cela me remit dans mon ardeur militaire. Je croyais devenir tout au moins un Maréchal de Saxe.

J'étais fou d'héroïsme. Charles XII et Condé m'empêchaient de dormir. Il me semblait que je devais l'emporter sur eux. Je me pâmais sur Polybe, je commentais les *Commentaires* de Folard. On parlait de guerre. J'avais fait promettre à un M. de Chaponais, capitaine dans Royal-Vaisseaux, de garnison à Condé, de m'engager dans sa compagnie. Je serais déserté de chez mon père et, sous un nom inconnu, je me faisais déjà un bonheur inexprimable de n'être reconnu qu'après les faits les plus éclatants.[11]

At the age of fifteen, Ligne composed a work entitled *Discours sur la profession des armes* of which he was still so proud at the end of his life as to include it in his collected works.[12] At seventeen, when he was made standard-bearer and guidon in his father's regiment, he soon had the opportunity to imitate Condé and Prince Eugene, his heroes *par excellence* (*Fragments*, I, 27). His life as a soldier would thenceforth pre-empt all his energies, except for minor activities like flirtations, marriage, or siring a brood of seven children. But the army was more than an abstraction, it was his true family; and war was life itself. Because of the possibilities which they offered of glory and, more especially, of heroism, he had an almost mystical reverence for them both. Thus he succeeded in refining his ideal of heroism through the harsh realities of the garrison and battle, especially in the campaigns of the Seven Years' War, with their surprises, ambuscades, skirmishes and assaults, their cannonades and sorties. None of these, even in their more barbaric aspects, lessened his enthusiasm, however, and later Ligne would recommend this quality to his 'héros en herbe', saying:

[. . .] Que l'enthousiasme monte vos têtes, que l'honneur (si ceci n'est pas un peu précieux) électrise vos cœurs, que le feu de la victoire brille dans vos yeux. Qu'en arborant les masques insignes de la gloire, vos âmes soient exaltées; et qu'on me pardonne si la mienne, qui l'est peut-être trop en ce moment, m'entraîne malgré moi à un peu de déclamation (*Fantaisies*, p. 2).

At the same time, he infused a rather special quality into his enthusiasm: *la sensibilité*. After making him weep over the corpses on a battlefield, his attitude toward heroism would cause him to veer ever more steadily away from the norm which we have noticed thus far. 'Il faut savoir apprécier ceux qui marchent sur le pas des héros et souvent ceux qui en ont la réputation', for, 'de tous les animaux, l'homme est le plus peureux.'[13]

Further proof of what we are saying may be found in the consequences of a minor skirmish from the War of the Bavarian Succession. In the fall of 1778, Ligne was present at an assault on the cloister of Boesigberg, near Münchengratz in Bohemia. He was responsible for clearing the Prussians from their entrenched positions behind the buildings on a height above the troops he was commanding. Although the manœuvre was a success, one of Ligne's lieutenants, an otherwise unknown officer, was killed. Yet so great was the Prince's concern for heroes and heroic virtue that later he could not forbear to have the incident captured by an itinerant painter in the Low Countries. This interesting composition, entitled 'Le Prince de Ligne soignant un blessé, ou, La Mort du Lieutenent Wolff', may still be seen among the collections at Belœil.[14] Undoubtedly influenced by West's painting of the death of another Wolfe, the celebrated British general, before Quebec, the lesser work is a composition of heroic fancy, extremely revealing of the sentimental pretensions and secret ambitions of the Prince, who believed himself first and foremost a military genius and who wanted to be known as a leader beloved of his subordinates and all those who came in contact with him.

The heights of Boesigberg, shrouded in mist, are dimly to be discerned in the upper left, while the right is shaded by a vague effect of woods, with a tree-trunk and fronds. In the middle-distance, a group of soldiers supports a dying officer, extended diagonally along the ground, from the centre to the lower left. To the right, outlined in a uniform of dazzling white, with gold highlights on the buttons and braid, stands the Prince de Ligne. With both hands, he grasps the left hand of Lieutenant Wolff, while he himself is balanced by another form standing to his right, dressed in a dull maroon uniform and hatless, like the Prince, his left hand resting on Ligne's arm and his right on Ligne's shoulder.[15] However derivative the pathos may seem, there is still a trace of realism—both physical and psychological—in the portrayal of Ligne's head. Turned three-quarters to the viewer, it has not, for all the sketchiness, been flattered. The sympathetic gesture, however, is a far more telling manifestation of those humanitarian heroics which Ligne would later describe in a chapter entitled, 'De la sensibilité dans le militaire' (*Préjugés*, p. 147), or characterize in his memoirs, saying: 'J'ai fait attendre des empereurs et des impératrices, mais jamais un soldat' (*Fragments*, I, 64). But since, for a man of his ilk, war is a necessary evil, he conceived of his ideals only in terms of war.

When constrained to inactivity, Ligne was restive, and he lived through difficult days, even in a time of relative peace. Yet his inactivity was only nominal, for he was still able to seek out heroism in the field of diplomacy, sharpening his ideas as well as his pen. As an observer of diplomatic encounters like that of Joseph II with Frederick the Great at Neustadt in 1770, Ligne could fashion more exactly those appreciations of the great military leaders of his day which form, in general, such a valuable part of his memoirs and, in particular, the necessary complement to his military 'fancies' and 'prejudices'. Thus was the Prince able to approach Frederick, Austria's declared enemy, and evaluate his genius with great acumen, despite the crushing defeat he had inflicted on Ligne's own troops at Torgau in 1760. Witness the following parallel:

Cicéron l'orateur, ne croyait pas que César devînt quelque chose. Son air efféminé [. . .], sa coquetterie [. . .]. M. de Voltaire, que je ne crois pas plus brave que Cicéron, mais qui a autant d'esprit, m'a dit qu'il ne s'était jamais attendu à tout ce qu'on a vu du roi [Frédéric]. Il avait l'air de ne pas se soucier de ses affaires, encore moins du militaire. Il polissonnait à la parade avec des jeunes officiers, dessinait dans le sable avec sa canne par distraction quand la garde passait. César et Frédéric lisaient beaucoup au même âge et acquirent la grande connaissance des hommes, à ce qu'on dit. [. . .] César et Frédéric pardonnèrent des outrages [. . .] sanglants, même des perfidies. Le premier ne chercha pas à trouver les auteurs de plusieurs entreprises contre lui; le second n'a pas fait mourir son baron silésien qui voulait nous le livrer. César prit dans le Capitole trois mille livres pesant d'or; Frédéric prit une vaisselle d'or à l'abbaye de Melk. César y substitua une pareille quantité de cuivre doré; Ephraïm de Frédéric s'est servi utilement de ce métal, et l'alliage le soutint contre nos alliés. [. . .] César battu à Durazzo, Frédéric à Kolin, ne songent qu'à consoler leurs armées. Ils s'accusent du malheur de la journée; ils la réparent à merveille. [. . .] On faisait des chansons militaires sur César; les soldats qui appellent Frédéric 'Fritz', nom d'amitié, lui disent les choses les plus fortes, dont il ne fait que rire.

Il aimerait les fêtes et la magnificence, s'il osait; mais il n'a pas la cent millième partie des richesses de César. Il aime aussi les spectacles. L'un et l'autre ont fait servir la religion à leurs desseins. La seule différence qu'il y a entre ces deux demi-dieux, c'est que César fut cocu et assassiné, et que Frédéric ne sera ni l'un ni l'autre.[16]

The same perspicacity at other times made Ligne irritated with the tergiversation and unheroic conduct of his superiors, always excepting Marshals Lacy and Laudhon. His critical remarks would ever spare these two who, in his eyes, were beyond reproach. Their attitudes frequently brought to mind the name and example of heroes from Greco-Roman antiquity (cf. *Fragments*, I, 52), when the mention of near-contemporaries did not suffice, as in this passage from the *Fantaisies*:

Il était bien plus difficile à Turenne d'être un héros quoiqu'il eût aussi de grands avantages; bien plus difficile encore à Luxembourg et à Catinat, et bien plus encore chez nous à quelques généraux que la gloire est venue prendre par la main, pour les faire monter des grades subalternes aux plus élevés, et les placer sur un trône triomphal, entouré de Français, de Turcs, et de Prussiens, soumis à leurs pieds. (*Fantaisies*, p. 92).

To Ligne's great chagrin, however, even such leaders as these did not place him on the winning side in the long, slow, and inexorable march of history. After 1763, he seemed to be Fortune's dupe; great feats of arms, and heroism—as he conceived it—were not his lot. At the crucial moment, armistices always interrupted when victory seemed within his grasp. And when, disillusioned, he did court glory abroad, he went in the wrong direction, thus missing perhaps the greatest opportunity of his career—fighting for the royalist cause in France after 1789. Even though he was highly honoured by the House of Habsburg, his time was past; and although consulted periodically about tactical operations against the Republic or the Empire, he realized that such a compliment was offered simply out of politeness, *pro forma*. He was by then too philosophical to be disarmed, but his normally well-balanced reaction became tinged with bitterness—because of his too-great *sensibilité*.

G

The same quality that he had desired in his heroes, the same would prevent him from paying court to Napoleon at Dresden in 1807 and admitting that this hero of a new era might be other than 'un bandit couronné' (*Fragments*, I, 17). He also refused, because, in addition to destroying Ligne's vision of the hero and his version of *gloire,* the Corsican represented what the Prince considered but a passing influence in European history: Napoleon was attempting to exist outside, above, and beyond a tradition of noble values conceived in reference to a past world and its ideals. Thus did Ligne note the triumphs of the Emperor with anguish and his reverses with glee. When, with subject Europe, he learned of the invasion of Russia and the retreat from Moscow, Ligne clearly foretold the end of Napoleon's career (cf. *Fragments,* II, 59). What he did not foresee was that, willy-nilly, Napoleon and the French experience had indeed changed history, including the values formerly attaching to heroes and heroism.

As we have tried to show, Ligne's own reactionary stance may be considered as partly responsible for this mutation, or at least for contributing to it. Yet, however ephemeral the realm of his activity, there was still another to which he had always aspired—the kingdom of ideas. To this domain he readily gained admittance, toward the end of his life, with publication of the thirty-five volumes of his *Mélanges militaires, littéraires et sentimentaires.*[17]

While it is true that the Prince had always been ready to indulge his weakness for writing, he was never so eager nor so able to exploit this vein of his genius as in the years after 1795, when most of his work was published. To this source does the name of Charles-Joseph de Ligne owe whatever fame now attaches thereto. For Ligne is a perfect example of those authors who are scarce read today, except for a few pages included in anthologies, and whose complete works continue to sleep undisturbed beneath the dust of decades. Undoubtedly, he was ill-advised in attempting to save the least line from his pen, and, undoubtedly, his works do smell of the lamp. Undoubtedly, too, he is alone responsible for having included in the *Mélanges* divers works arranged pell-mell, omitting any sort of classification or index, complicating to excess the task of the modern reader who is soon left wandering through a maze of material. Yet, as one commentator has said:

Au milieu de tant d'essais divers on se demande quel est le trait principal de notre auteur? L'embarras semble grand, pourtant il n'en est rien. Le Prince de Ligne se révèle bientôt comme un esprit observateur et critique; il suffit de la lecture d'un volume pris au hasard parmi ses œuvres pour qu'on le déclare peintre moraliste. Au bout de quelques pages, vous êtes au courant de sa philosophie et de la justesse de son esprit. On entrevoit de la vérité dans le jugement qu'il porte sur les hommes et sur les choses; mais tout à côté le paradoxe se fait jour dans ses définitions et ses portraits. Si vous ajoutez à cela un tour vif et pittoresque dans la pensée, un style gai à phrases courtes et naturellement coupées en maximes, une certaine recherche toujours dans l'idée ou dans l'expression, la pointe du XVIIIe siècle, un véritable abus d'esprit parfois, vous connaîtrez la physiognomie générale de ses œuvres, immense fouillis où sont comme perdus au milieu de paille et de grains de sable, les diamants les plus finement taillés.[18]

Among these gems are four 'memoirs' of military heroes, presented as from the pen of the subjects themselves: Jean-Louis, comte de Bussy-Rabutin (1773), Louis de Bade (1787), Jean, comte de Bonneval (1801?), and Prince Eugene of Savoy (1809).[19] Because of the off-hand way in which he treats the success awaiting such mystifications, it is clear that Ligne did not realize his greatest achievement would be as a moralist, a writer of letters and 'memoirs'. The qualities of all three types are to be found illustrated in these works; but why, for instance, did Ligne, usually occupied with the pleasures of fashionable life, attempt to tackle such difficult genres? Was it uniquely, as he claimed, because, ruined by revolution, this man, so long favoured by Fortune, was forced to sell 'le peu d'esprit qui me reste'? (*Mélanges*, XI [1796], p. 129). Perhaps. But there is more.

Since in the realm of the imagination all things are possible, Ligne was able, through surrogates like Bussy-Rabutin, to satisfy his longing for heroes and even to identify with them to such a degree as to acquire—at least in his own mind—many of their virtues. As the beginning of the Romantic century approached, what was more natural or more satisfying than the story of a Bonneval? How wonderful the life, filled to overflowing, of this 'gentilhomme limousin' who sets out for war immediately after his wedding and works marvels under Vendôme, who, dissatisfied, turns coat and passes to the other side under Prince Eugene, then abandons the Austrian pennon for the horsetails of a pasha of the Great Turk, and ends his career surrounded by wealth and power on the shore of the Bosphorus!

Ligne's narrative is no more than a romanticized biography, but the surprising feature is that the more he seems to veer away from the Muse of History, the closer he draws in style and feeling to modern psychology. The same would be true of all these efforts, some of which, like his *Prince Eugène*, were enormously successful. And even though Ligne was unable to create the eternal characters of a truly universal genius, he did help to change our thinking about such figures through the details of expression and refinement which he brought to the one idea of the hero. In this, his reconstructions are not unworthy of his predecessor, Courtilz de Sandras—or *was* it d'Artagnan?

His success was as much the result of his enthusiasm as of his *sensibilité*. For it was not enough that his heroes were brave; they had to go to the front as to a party, play as it were, the coquette with danger, and astound in the ultimate confrontation with death by a display of sang-froid and gaiety in their prompt and reasoned use of intelligence and will-power. As he himself proclaimed in the 'Avertissement' to the memoirs of Bussy-Rabutin:

Ce Monsieur de Rabutin que vous venez de me céder n'est point le faiseur des allélulias de Louis XIV. Il ne chansonnait ni ne chantait personne. Il ne déplaisait pas à son maître; mais s'il lui avait déplu, il aurait soutenu sa disgrâce avec fermeté. S'il n'était pas flatteur comme son parent sur la fin de ses jours, il n'était pas non plus si difficultueux [sic] que lui. Les grands hommes que nous avions alors dans nos armées l'estimaient. L'autre s'était brouillé avec M. de Turenne; il fit trembler l'Académie française. Celui-ci fit trembler les Turcs. Ils étaient bien braves tous les deux, avaient autant d'esprit à ce que je crois, l'un que l'autre; mais le nôtre était plus soldat. J'entends par là qu'avec des dispositions pour notre métier; plus officier, c'est-à-dire, plus capable d'application. Qu'on le lise, on le verra. (p. 12)

In the same way, we might say that the biographies of Bonneval and Prince Eugene were written with the sword, and that Ligne was ever ready to apply it in defence of both his heroes and his concept of heroism. After all, as we have attempted to demonstrate, he was deeply committed to both. By such close identification of himself with those he is writing about, Ligne arrives at a convincing presentation and tone, surprising in their moral truth, if not in their historical exactness. Thus, in recounting Bonneval's blustering when faced with red tape, Ligne seems so vigorous and inspiring because, for him, Chamillard undoubtedly represented his own *bête noire*, Chancellor Thugut or some other Austrian official of whom he had to complain. And however involved he may have been, his own critical faculties were ever alert to the possibilities awaiting him in the re-creation of an antique ideal. As outmoded as his view of heroism may now seem, it was not yet so old-fashioned that Napoleon could not adapt to it, nor Dumas, nor Stendhal. The secret of this transformation was recognized by Ligne when he wrote: 'Je n'aime pas ces historiens amoureux de celui dont ils écrivent l'histoire; leurs éloges sont fastidieux; l'ombre au tableau est nécessaire.' (*Mélanges*, III [1795], p. 89).

However 'necessary' it may have been, the shadow which Ligne brought to his portrayal of the hero was added nonetheless too late. For, ever and always, the author's training, prejudices and caste militated against the presentation by him of any great captain as *both* thinker *and* doer. (When judged strictly according to these terms, it is rather amusing to note that Ligne himself was probably more 'heroic' than any of his creations.)[20] The term 'hero' may therefore seem vitiated or subverted not only by the Prince's addition of *sensibilité* to its several qualifications, but also by his insistence that the basis for this ideal is to be found only in the soldierly virtues of courage, obedience, enthusiasm, etc. Restrictions like these naturally limit Ligne's appeal to us today, just as they limited his usefulness to his contemporaries. But were any comparison with other interpretations possible, surely it would be founded more than aught else on the terms of the following unexceptional statement from the pen of this 'happiest man of the age':

Il est malheureux [. . .] que parmi ceux qui peuvent juger de l'héroïsme dans ces brillantes occasions de guerre et de combats, il y ait aussi peu de gens qui réfléchissent sur eux et sur les autres, et encore moins de gens qui aient pu déssiller les yeux du monde entier pour nous juger tout de travers. (*Fragments*, II, 431)

Starting from such a premise in his fictionalized biographies, we can see how Ligne, because of his rationalist approach, refused to deal with time-honoured concepts, preferring instead to propound the lessons derived ultimately from his own life and observations. Thus, while working toward a more modern meaning of 'heroic virtue'—that of the wisdom of experience, cleverness, and eloquence, all united in a program for man viewed as both thinker and doer—Ligne strove to substitute one manner of looking at the human condition for another and effectively converted the limited set of values represented by his heroes into a more timely version of the ideal, centred no longer in society but in the self.

The foregoing examination and treatment of heroic virtue as seen by the prince de Ligne has much to teach us. In dealing with a lesser figure from the historico-literary pantheon of the eighteenth century, we may appreciate more exactly what happened in the day-to-day encounters of a time-honoured concept with new ideas and ideals, whereby the notion survived into the succeeding period and even to our own day. However nugatory Ligne's contribution may seem, it is nonetheless important because it is consistent and complete, ringing significant, if minor, changes on a recognized and accepted tone. The muted quality of these changes contrasts the more with the resounding clangour of other eighteenth-century attitudes which appear in greater relief when we take the long-range view; at the same time, it adds to our understanding of heroic virtue generally.

Even though the most remarkable advances in thinking have often been the result of untoward and radical innovations, they are but fits and starts whose origin and ultimate effect depend more on a never-ending habit or mode lying just beneath the level of consciousness than we are wont to admit. And to this continuum belong Ligne and his work. We should not, therefore, attempt to deny him his due, merely because his is not the most startling or innovative representation of heroic virtue, or because he and the epigoni who followed are cast in the shadow of more famous people, where their contribution is seen only to their disadvantage.

Ligne is unique in his time because he acknowledged (albeit implicitly) that earlier ideals were outdated and in need of revision. Even today the meaning of words like 'passion', 'enthusiasm', 'sensibility', and 'humanity' as used by Ligne can be readily identified, and it is they which enable us to follow, in him, their persistence and renewal, whether singly or in conjunction with one another. Such is the signal merit of Ligne's attempt to present the public with a newer model, sometimes subtle, sometimes outrageous, but filled with psychological insights that are no less important for being *sui generis*. Thanks also to the quality of this effort, we can note a changing stance toward matters both military and moral throughout the age when previous norms were being questioned, even as Ligne set pen to paper.

In many of his writings, but especially in his *History of Charles XII* and in *Candide*, Voltaire realized that a hero need not be noble, rich, virtuous, or aught else—save human. Partly because of those events in his own life which inspired Voltaire, the man with a flawed reputation, sponging for a sou or two, obliged to let his honour go by the board, the man who is no more than gull in the garden[21]—that man may indeed have descended from the heights of thought and action, but who could deny his humanity? And, as expressed by such a wit, who could ever, henceforth, forget it? Meanwhile, the same transference may be observed in Rousseau, though applied in quite different fashion, and to a different end. Heroism in the *Nouvelle Héloïse* is further devalued since the author's very norms have reference only to bourgeois ideals. Thus, true heroism is equated with a virtue that lies in the inward and private sphere, emerging as victor from a struggle between conscience and passion. For Rousseau, as for his heroes, the ideal is an achievement of moral, *not* of military, godlike, or any other sort of valour. But nowhere is the ultimate proof of our contention more in evidence than in the works of Diderot, his novels and treatises. And among these last, nowhere more succinctly expressed than in the article 'Héros' from that great enterprise, *l'Encyclopédie*:

On définit un héros, un homme ferme contre les difficultés, intrépide dans le péril et très vaillant dans les combats; qualités qui tiennent plus du tempérament et d'une certaine conformation des organes, que de la noblesse d'âme. Le grand homme est bien autre chose; il joint au talent et au génie la plupart des vertus morales; il n'a dans sa conduite que de beaux et de nobles motifs; il n'écoute que le bien public, la gloire de son prince, la prospérité de l'état et le bonheur des peuples. [. . .] Les qualités du cœur l'emportent toujours sur les présents de la fortune et de la nature; c'est que la gloire qu'on acquiert par les armes est [. . .] une gloire attachée au hasard; au lieu que celle qui est fondée sur la vertu est une gloire qui nous appartient. Le titre de héros dépend du succès, celui de grand homme n'en dépend pas toujours. [. . .] Enfin, l'humanité, la douceur, le patriotisme, réunis aux talents, sont les vertus d'un grand homme; la bravoure, le courage, souvent la témérité, la connaissance de l'art de la guerre, et le génie militaire, caractérisent davantage le héros; mais le parfait héros est celui qui joint à toute la capacité et à toute la valeur d'un grand capitaine, un amour et un désir sincère de la félicité publique.

Though we have had to wait until our own time to appreciate fully the implications of a passage like this, or the conclusion to Diderot's *Deux Amis de Bourbonne,* we are better able to see how they—and their contributions to the notion of heroism—stand out so distinctly against the background to this development furnished by writers like the prince de Ligne. For without such a foil, we would be at a greater loss than ever to comprehend why, by the middle of the nineteenth century, the traditional ideas of heroes and heroism were the object merely of a certain bemusement or perhaps of outright derision. Whatever the individual reasons for, or the expression of, such an attitude, it can be recognized as easily in the hostility that pervades chapter two of Musset's *Confession* as in the recurrent irony with which, throughout the *Chartreuse,* Stendhal refers to 'notre héros'. Even abroad, there is a certain disaffection to be discerned in Thackeray's subtitle to *Vanity Fair,* 'A Novel without a Hero', and in the following quotation from Heine, a man who needed to believe in heroism but who found such an ideal impossible in a century dominated by a free press, representative government, and the bourgeoisie:

The diminution of greatness, the radical annihilation of heroism, these things are, above all, the work of that bourgeoisie that came into power [. . .] through the fall of the aristocracy of birth. In all spheres of life, that bourgeoisie has caused its narrow and cold shopkeeper's ideas to triumph. It will not be long before every heroic sentiment and idea will become ridiculous. [. . .] if indeed they do not perish completely.[22]

So, through the ages, has the concept of heroism changed to reflect the total experience of man. Though the hero of the epics is now one with the poets themselves, representatives of Hesiod's 'god-like race of men' in the present day are not hard to find, for they constitute a recurring phenomenon, no matter how self-conscious their posturing and despondency. The romantic hero of our bourgeois age, paralyzed by doubt, is primarily a rebel against a background to which he is secretly attached, torn between militant desire and a chronic sense of guilt. Yet, like his forbears, this anti-hero is man's projection of himself as he faces the meaning (or meaninglessness) of life, and his role is to challenge the powers that escape human understanding.

Changing concepts of heroism thus reflect basic cultural shifts. And so long as we attempt to project our image through notions like this in order to gain at least a share in eternity via the ephemeral means they offer, heroes and heroism are still essential to mankind. Indeed, we may safely claim that heroic virtue remains one of those constants by which a civilization is known. Our vision of ourselves is so closely linked to our vision of the hero that both become as one. For this reason alone, the problem of the hero is still very much with us—and will be—for it is a problem of definitions. Despite Curtius's claim that a proper study of heroes and heroism is yet to be given to us,[23] we may nonetheless hope to approximate that ideal some day, thanks to a better understanding of exemplars like the prince de Ligne, who

> . . . with natural instinct to discern
> What knowledge can perform, is diligent to learn;
> Abides by this resolve and stops not there
> But makes his moral being his prime care . . .
> More skillful in self-knowledge, e'en more pure
> As tempted more; more able to endure
> As more exposed to suffering and distress;
> Thence also, more alive to tenderness . . .
> [Who] in the many games of Life [plays] one
> Where what he most doth value must be won:
> Who, not content that former worth stand fast,
> Looks forward, persevering to the last,
> From well to better, daily self-surpast.[24]

NOTES

1 The following pages represent substantially the text of a paper read before the AATF on 28 December 1970, at its annual meeting in New Orleans. For the purposes of publication, full bibliographical information is given with the first reference in the notes, thereafter, according to a short-title reference for easy identification in the body of the text. The author's attention was drawn to the following items too late for them to be of use in his presentation: Pierre-Henri Simon, *Le Domaine héroïque des lettres françaises* (Paris, 1963), and Maria Rosa Lida de Malkiel, *L'Idée de la gloire dans la tradition occidentale* (Paris, [1968]).

2 Charles-Joseph, prince de Ligne, *Fantaisies militaires,* edited by Heusch (Paris, 1914), p. 1. Hereafter referred to in the text as: *Fantaisies.* The original edition bears on the title-page: PREJUGES [FANTAISIES] / MILITAIRES / par un / Officier Autrichien. / Tome Premier [Second]. / A KRALOVELHOTA, / MDCCLXXX.

3 Hesiod, *The Works and Days,* v. 156–73.

4 Hegel, quoted in Victor Brombert, (editor), *The Hero in Literature* (New York, [1969]), p. 189.

5 Max Scheler, quoted in Ernst-Robert Curtius, *European Literature and the Latin Middle Ages* (New York, 1953), p. 167.

6 Paul Bénichou, *Morales du Grand Siècle* (Paris, [1960]), pp. 97–111.

7 Brombert, *The Hero in Literature,* p. 268.

8 Jacques-Bénigne Bossuet, *Oraisons funèbres,* 2 volumes (Paris, 1897), II, 68–9.

9 Jean de La Bruyère, *Les Caractères,* 2 volumes (Paris, 1854), I, 184–5.

10 Germaine, baronne de Staël-Holstein, *Lettres et pensées du maréchal prince de Ligne* (Paris-Geneva, 1809), pp. xii–xiii.

11 Charles-Joseph, prince de Ligne, *Fragments de l'histoire de ma vie,* 2 volumes, edited by Leuridant (Paris, 1928), I, 15, 19. Hereafter referred to in the text as: *Fragments.*

12 Published in Charles-Joseph, prince de Ligne, *Mélanges militaires, littéraires et sentimentaires,* 35 volumes. A Mon Refuge . . . et Se vend à Dresde chez les Frères Walther, 1795–1811, X (1796), pp. 5–21. Hereafter referred to in the text as: *Mélanges.*

13 Charles-Joseph, prince de Ligne, *Préjugés militaires,* edited by Heusch (Paris, 1914), pp. 142–3. Hereafter referred to in the text as: *Préjugés.*

14 Reproduced in Charlier-Hanse, *Histoire illustrée des lettres françaises de Belgique* (Brussels, 1958), p. 223. Despite differences in the dimensions of this painting (290 x 334 mm) and West's 'Death of General Wolfe before Quebec' (6' x 7'), mentioned next in the text, the influence of the latter cannot be denied. In addition to the fact that no more than ten years separate their respective dates of composition (1770–ca 1780), West's painting soon attracted considerable attention throughout Europe, thanks to an engraving published in 1771 and widely distributed.

15 Hector de Backer, in 'L'Iconographie du prince de Ligne', *Bulletin de la Société des Bibliophiles et Iconophiles de Belgique* (Brussels, 1919), p. 158, identifies this figure as the prince's eldest son, though on what basis, he does not say; we have been unable to find proof that young prince Charles accompanied his father in this campaign.

16 Charles-Joseph, prince de Ligne, 'Lettre à M. de La Harpe', *Œuvres,* 4 volumes, edited by Lacroix, (Brussels–Paris, 1860), II, 208–11.

17 For details relating to the complex problem surrounding identification of this work, see Hector de Backer, 'Bibliographie du prince de Ligne', *Bulletin de la Société des Bibliophiles et Iconophiles de Belgique* (Brussels, 1914), pp. 179–86, and Basil Guy, 'Contribution à la Bibliographie du prince de Ligne', *Le Livre et l'Estampe* (Brussels, 1970), pp. 7–8.

18 N. Peetermans, *Le Prince de Ligne; ou, Un Écrivain grand seigneur à la fin du XVIIIe siècle* (Liège, 1867), pp. 167–8.

19 The first editions of these works are as follows: *Mémoires sur les campagnes faites en Hongrie par le comte de Bussy-Rabutin* (Paris [no editor], 1773); *Mémoires sur les campagnes du prince Louis de Bade* (Brussels, 1787); *Mémoire sur le comte de Bonneval,* in *Mélanges,* XXVI (1802), pp. 3–185; *Mémoires du prince Eugène de Savoie, écrits par lui-même* (Weimar, 1809).

    The success of Ligne's *supercheries* may be noted in the fact that the Bibliothèque Nationale in Paris continues to list the first title under the name of Bussy-Rabutin, and not under that of its true author. On the favour accorded the last-named work, see Hector de Backer, loc. cit., pp. 165–8 and Basil Guy, loc. cit., pp. 15–16.

20 cf. Brombert, *The Hero in Literature,* p. 234.

21 We are indebted for this expression and for part of our interpretation here to Roy Wolper, 'Candide—Gull in the Garden?' *ECS,* III, 2 (1970); pp. 256–77 passim.

22 Heine, quoted by Brombert, *The Hero in Literature,* p. 267.

23 Curtius, op. cit., p. 169.

24 Wordsworth, 'Character of the Happy Warrior'.

10

Beaumarchais and the Early Balzac

D. R. HAGGIS

L'invention, c'est d'emprunter. Balzac, *Les Ressources de Quinola.* Acte III, Scène 13

In the oration delivered by Victor Hugo on 21 August 1850 at the cemetery of Père Lachaise on the occasion of Balzac's funeral we find the words: 'Tous ses livres ne forment qu'un livre [. . .] livre merveilleux [. . .] qui prend toutes les formes et tous les styles, qui dépasse Tacite et qui va jusqu'à Suétone, qui traverse Beaumarchais et qui va jusqu'à Rabelais.'[1] It may surprise us to find that, when Hugo associates the name of a French dramatist with that of Balzac, the first name that occurs to him is that of Beaumarchais rather than that of Molière. But Hugo was right, of course, in discerning the presence of Beaumarchais in Balzac's work: he is one of the French writers to whom Balzac most frequently makes reference—only Voltaire and Rousseau, among the writers of the eighteenth century, are referred to more frequently[2]—and one whose achievement he aspired, in the early years of his career, to emulate and to rival. 'Ma plume vaut celle de Beaumarchais', he proudly boasts to the Duchesse d'Abrantès in 1833.[3] Like the young Stendhal, Balzac seems to have been convinced at the outset of his career that it was by becoming a dramatic author that he would satisfy his two principal passions: 'l'amour et la gloire'. Even the unfavourable reception given by family and friends to *Cromwell,* his first attempt at tragedy, does not seem to have deterred him from telling Le Poitevin de l'Égreville a few years later that, having studied 'la manière et les procédés de composition dramatique qu'on admirait dans Beaumarchais', he already had it in mind to write 'à la Beaumarchais deux ou trois grands drames qui avaient leur place marquée entre *Le Mariage de Figaro* et *La Mère coupable'.*[4] The hard facts of literary life and his desire to free himself from dependence on his family soon combined, however, to make him pursue his ambition in a different direction: collaboration in the writing of novels, he discovered, was a more promising way than the writing of plays of convincing his family that he could earn his living by his pen.

The change did not put an end to his hopes of writing successfully for the theatre, or to his making plans for plays. One of his most interesting projects from our present point of view concerns a play (a comedy, it would seem) to be entitled: *Le Républicain.* It runs as

87

follows: 'Alceste politique. Figaro *idem*. Ridiculiser la patrie. Grouper autour d'un honnête homme les idées de notre époque personnifiées. Intituler le *Républicain*. [. . .] S'inspirer de Molière et de Beaumarchais, de la plaisanterie âcre de lord Byron, et fondre le tout. [. . .] Exprimer le siècle.'[5] It does not appear to be possible to date this project precisely, but it would seem to belong to the early years of Balzac's career.[6] The interest of this sketch is two-fold. Firstly, it makes clear, not simply that Beaumarchais was very much in Balzac's mind and that he was one of the authors he principally aspired to emulate, but also that the character of Figaro had a particular fascination for him.[7] Secondly, it shows Balzac thinking of creating characters based on *dramatic* models, but making them political figures and placing them in a contemporary political context. The project suggests, in fact, Balzac aspiring to achieve a fusion of a successful imitation of comic and dramatic qualities found in characters created by two of his great predecessors with a realistic evocation of a modern social and political reality—with something, that is, that seems to foreshadow what Balzac himself was later to achieve with outstanding success, not in the drama, but in the novel.

It is fascinating to speculate what kind of a play the execution of this project might have produced. We may pause to wonder, with some of the observations on *Le Barbier de Séville* made by Professor Niklaus in his valuable study of the play in mind, whether Balzac's project does not really imply a fundamental misunderstanding of what might be called the 'paradox' of Figaro. Professor Niklaus reminds us that in writing his first great comedy Beaumarchais follows a convention of eighteenth-century French literature by setting his play in Spain, and he shows that there is a profound but subtle connection between the Spanish setting and the relevance of the comedy to a state of affairs actually obtaining in France. The exotic setting—which is not 'authentic' in a realistic sense—not merely does not *prevent* the play referring to contemporary France; there is a sense in which one may say that it *enables* it to do so in a more radical, and therefore more dangerous, way than it could have done otherwise. 'It is certain that there is no trace at all of the real Spain in this play. Figaro and Almaviva are Spanish by name but French by nature. To insist, against the evidence, on the authenticity of the setting is to misunderstand Beaumarchais's purpose in using it, which is to lull his spectators with unreality and, paradoxically, alert them to social truths they would otherwise have been unwilling to accept.'[8]

Balzac's project for *Le Républicain* reveals, then, two creative impulses: a desire to write successfully for the theatre following in the tracks of Molière and Beaumarchais; a desire to portray his own times, 'd'exprimer le siècle', as he puts it. We may attribute, perhaps, the ambition which the project betrays to satisfy both these impulses in the execution of a single work to the fact that, at the time Balzac sketched the project, his knowledge and understanding both of the true nature of his own gifts and of the character of the times in which he lived were still imperfect and far from complete. The project was not carried out. During Balzac's *années d'apprentissage* as a novelist, however, the example of Beaumarchais clearly remained much in his mind, and, more particularly, the character of Figaro continued to exercise its fascination over his creative imagination. In the second of the novels published by Hubert in 1822 under the pseudonyms of A. de Viellerglé (Le Poitevin) and Lord R'hoone (Balzac): *Jean-Louis, ou la fille trouvée* their influence is especially clear.

Several critics have drawn attention to Balzac's debt to Beaumarchais in this novel, though generally without pressing very far an enquiry into its nature and extent. Though we cannot be certain that the project for the play: *Le Républicain* antedates the writing of the novel, it is not without interest to consider the part played by Beaumarchais's example in the composition of *Jean-Louis*, with the project for the play in our minds.

The persisting presence of Beaumarchais's comedies in Balzac's imagination at the time he was writing the novel is attested by a reference to Basile, another to Bartholo, and the use of a name (Fanchette) possibly borrowed from *Le Mariage de Figaro*, but Balzac's debt to Beaumarchais goes well beyond these superficial references to some of his characters.[9] In another early novel that Balzac was writing just about the same time as *Jean-Louis* or a little earlier, *Clotilde de Lusignan*, he imitated Scott's *Ivanhoe*. The way in which he imitates Beaumarchais, and in particular *Le Mariage de Figaro*, in *Jean-Louis* shows certain striking similarities with the way in which he imitates Scott in *Clotilde*. In the first place, Balzac borrows from his 'source' details, episodes, relationships between characters. In *Jean-Louis* we find a libertine *marquis* (Vandeuil) and his discarded, but weak and forgiving, *marquise* who clearly seem to be modelled on Almaviva and the unhappy Rosine. Vandeuil is appointed ambassador to the English court by the king, just as Almaviva is made ambassador to London in the first act of *Le Mariage de Figaro*. In the third act of *Figaro* a mark from a spatula on the arm of the hero reveals that he is the long-lost son of Marceline; at the beginning of *Jean-Louis*, Maître Plaidanon, the *procureur du Châtelet*, thinks he has discovered his lost daughter in Jean-Louis's sweetheart, Fanchette, when he finds that she has 'une fraise sur le genou'. The hero's uncle in *Jean-Louis* expresses in an address to his nephew sentiments that recall Figaro's song at the opening of *Le Barbier de Séville*; and to describe Courottin, the wily *petit clerc* who serves in turn the interests of Jean-Louis and those of his rival Vandeuil, Balzac uses a phrase that seems to have been suggested by Brid'oison's description of Double-Main, the *greffier*, in *Le Mariage de Figaro*.[10]

Balzac's imitation goes further. He finds in one of Beaumarchais's comedies a central, basic situation which he takes over and uses as a kind of *canevas* on which he embroiders his own story. He borrows the triangular situation in which Beaumarchais involves Figaro, Suzanne, and the Count in *Le Mariage de Figaro* and the theme of the repeatedly delayed marriage. The marriage that is to take place between Jean-Louis, the humble young *charbonnier*, and Fanchette, the *jolie ravaudeuse*, is frustrated by the violent passion that the aristocrat Vandeuil conceives for Fanchette on seeing her at the house of Maître Plaidanon in the first volume of the novel, and it is this infatuation that marks the beginning of the long deferment of Jean-Louis's marriage, and of the preposterous adventures of the hero in his efforts to recover his lost fiancée which fill the greater part of the rest of the book. This is not unlike what Balzac does in *Clotilde de Lusignan*. There, in addition to imitating details found in *Ivanhoe*, he borrows from Scott the central idea of introducing into his story a character who is an illustrious historical figure in disguise and of making him play a decisive role in the action. It is true that the young novelist, missing no opportunity of exploiting popular taste with a view to ensuring a success, makes Vandeuil not only an aristocrat but also a villain who recalls the villains of melodrama, or of the *romans noirs* of the time,[11] and that it is a threatened revelation of his villainy that ultimately brings about his renunciation of the heroine who is thus left free at the end of the book to marry Jean-Louis. It nevertheless seems clear that it was in Beaumarchais's comedy that Balzac found the initial situation which he took as his point of departure.

Balzac's early project for a *play* based partly on an imitation of Beaumarchais appears, as we have seen, to embody two deep-rooted ambitions: the desire to create a comic character imitated from Figaro; the desire to achieve, in creating the imaginary world in which this character operates, a representation of the real, contemporary world—more particularly, of its political character. What becomes of these two aims in the *novel* that he actually writes, and what signs—if any—are there of his having tried to realize them there?

As an attempt to create a character worthy to rival with Beaumarchais's Figaro, madame Delattre judges *Jean-Louis* a failure, and she attributes this failure principally to a problem of style. 'Les qualités essentiellement dramatiques de Figaro rendent sa transposition dans le domaine du roman à peu près impossible', she writes. 'Balzac s'y était essayé dans *Jean-Louis,* mais sans succès [. . .]. Il se rend compte [. . .] que le style de Beaumarchais contribue énormément à rendre ses personnages vivants selon les exigences du théâtre et non celles du roman.'[12]

The question of style is, no doubt, an important one. There are passages in *Jean-Louis* in which Balzac seems quite clearly to be trying to emulate the comic style of Beaumarchais as we find it in the role of Figaro. Here, for example, is an exchange between the Marquis de Vandeuil and Courottin:

— Monseigneur, je n'ai plus qu'une grâce à vous demander.
— Laquelle? dit le marquis impatienté.
— Faites-moi l'honneur de m'accorder cent coups de bâton. Je n'ai pu parvenir à vous voir qu'en promettant la moitié de ce que vous me donneriez à l'un de vos laquais.
    Le marquis rit beaucoup, et lui dit: 'Par ma foi, tu es rusé, et je te protégerai de bon cœur.'

But it takes more than one stylistic swallow to make a fictional summer, and flashes of this kind are rare.[13]

It might seem pointless to look any further for reasons for Balzac's failure than to the fact that the young author of *Jean-Louis* possesses none of the qualities that made Figaro possible: neither Beaumarchais's temperament, nor his experience, nor his talent. Yet it is instructive to look at the results to which his attempted imitation of Figaro in an early work of fiction lead. The role of Figaro seems to have undergone a radical transformation, and a dissociation to have taken place of two aspects of Beaumarchais's character. In conceiving the initial situation of his hero, Balzac, as we have seen, appears to have in mind the situation of Figaro in *Le Mariage de Figaro,* though he makes nothing of the relationship of master and man on which, as Professor Niklaus has reminded us in connection with *Le Barbier de Séville,* so much of the comedy in Beaumarchais depends.[14] But there is another important aspect of Figaro's role. Part of his superiority over his master lies in his greater ingenuity, so that it is the servant who becomes the *machiniste* (to use Beaumarchais's own term) in the play, and this is the aspect of the role that seems particularly to have caught the imagination of the *apprenti romancier*: Beaumarchais suggested to him the use that might be made of a character imitated from Figaro in keeping a story on the move. This aspect of Figaro's role appears to have been in Balzac's mind, not so much in creating the figure of his hero, however, but rather in the creation of the *petit clerc,* Courottin, for it is Courottin who has the happy knack of arriving on the scene at the unexpected but propitious moment, of turning a situation to his own advantage, and who, by acting as a go-between among the characters, furthers the progress of the action.[15] The *situation* of Figaro suggests to Balzac the situation of Jean-Louis; the *function* of Figaro suggests to him the role of Courottin; but in neither of these characters can Balzac be said to approach an imitation of the *personality* of Figaro.

What of the setting in which Balzac places these characters and of the matter of the story this early novel tells? *Jean-Louis,* considered from this point of view, appears as one of the most interesting of the *romans de jeunesse* because of the way in which it represents a stage in Balzac's development. P. Barbéris has said that 'l'intérêt majeur de *Jean-Louis* est d'être, après un roman historique et "noir", un roman de la réalité moderne. [. . .] [C']est le premier livre de Balzac qui épouse et suggère la courbe nouvelle du siècle.'[16] While it might, in a sense, be described as a 'roman historique', the attribution to it of the description: 'roman de la réalité moderne' seems to me more questionable. What, in fact, do we find in *Jean-Louis*? Balzac, indeed, sets his story in a 'realistic' French setting. He dates the action, making it begin in 1788. He sets it in Paris. At the start of the novel, the guests at Maître Plaidanon's *soirée* discuss the convocation of the *États Généraux*; towards the end, the hero's uncle, Barnabé Granivel, becomes a member of the *Assemblée Constituante,* and soon afterwards finds himself in the Conciergerie because he has defended the King before the *Convention*; in the course of the story, Jean-Louis himself leads the people in their attack on the Bastille, and goes off to fight for the cause of liberty in America. But all this localizing of the story in time and place remains almost entirely external, serving simply as a *décor.* It makes a curious contrast with the *matter* of the story, for the story Balzac tells is for the most part a pure extravaganza, a tissue of preposterous improbabilities designed to hold the interest of the reader by their fantastic character and their unflagging pace. 'Ce qu'il y a de plus intéressant dans la peinture de la Révolution', Barbéris says, 'c'est que Balzac nous y montre une immense entreprise de mutation du pouvoir et des richesses. Jean-Louis le charbonnier devient général, Barnabé député, Granivel propriétaire de biens aristo-cratiques; l'astucieux Courottin, jusqu'alors dévoué par intérêt au duc de Parthenay, se demande s'il ne ferait pas mieux, au moment où "les vilains lèvent la tête" de passer du côté de Jean-Louis.'[17] All this is true. But what is also important is the fact that Balzac, at this stage, achieves very little in the way of an organic relation between the matter of his story and the social and political realities of the France in which it is set. We are told that Granivel gets rich; we are not shown how. If Courottin rightly judges the way in which society is moving, the vertiginous speed with which his fortunes improve is due less to the accuracy of his political judgment than to the fact that Balzac creates between the services he renders and the *largesse* with which his masters reward them a disproportion that belongs to the realm of fairy-tale.[18]

All this might seem to have taken us far from the topic of Balzac's imitation of Beaumarchais. Not quite so far, perhaps, as might at first appear. For it is not, I think, entirely fanciful to suggest that a relation may exist between Balzac's indifference in this early novel to the creation of links between his story, his characters, and their historical setting, and the fact that the imitation of Beaumarchais, and in particular of the character of Figaro, is still in his mind. There is an attempt, it seems to me, to preserve in *Jean-Louis* something of the freedom of invention that we find in Beaumarchais's comedies, and something of the comic atmosphere. No single character in Balzac's novel can match Beaumarchais's valet; and freedom of invention takes the form of fantasy and of the improbable and preposterous, rather than of comedy—or of the kind of comedy that Beaumarchais achieves. Yet the brisk pace at which events succeed one another in *Jean-Louis,* the resourcefulness shown by Courottin, intervening in the action, manipulating the other characters, do suggest that the influence of Beaumarchais's example may have been at work, not only in the genesis of this novel, but also in its execution, and perhaps it is an attempt to emulate in the *facture* of his novel some of the qualities that Balzac admired in the work of his predecessor that partly explains why, if the setting of this novel is 'realistic', the matter of its story, for the most part, is not.

The first novel in which Balzac succeeded in representing much more fully the social and political reality of the historical period in which his novel was set was, of course, *Les Chouans,* published seven years after *Jean-Louis. Les Chouans* is a work of particular interest from our present point of view, for in it the character of Corentin makes his first appearance, and M. Bardèche has already drawn attention to the fact that Corentin, in *Les Chouans,* recalls Beaumarchais's Figaro.[19] How does he do so? The similarity of the two names suggests a possible link in the author's mind between Corentin and the earlier Courottin of *Jean-Louis,* and if Corentin may indeed be regarded as a later incarnation of Figaro, it would certainly seem to be through the character of Figaro-Courottin, rather than through that of Figaro-Jean-Louis that his line of descent is to be traced. Beyond the bare fact that Corentin is a man of humble birth who finds his hopes of obtaining the hand of the woman he loves thwarted by the intrusion of an aristocrat, the similarities between the situation and the fortunes of Corentin and those of Figaro appear very shadowy. But when we consider the *function* of Corentin in the novel—his role in the third part, in particular—the suggestion that Balzac may again have had Figaro in mind in creating him seems a good deal more plausible. As the story approaches its climax, it is Corentin, with his ingenuity and talent for intrigue, who plays the part of *machiniste,* holding the threads that bind together the other principal characters and manipulating the movements of the aristocratic lovers.

The differences between the two characters are, of course, hardly less striking than the similarities. Balzac makes Corentin a very different *kind* of character from Figaro: less likable, far more sinister, and motivated, not by zest for life and a spirit of fun, but by jealousy and desire for revenge. But the way Balzac seems here both to imitate and to modify is interesting, because a close link exists between the 'psychology' that Balzac gives to this character and the *éclairage* in which he presents the historical reality with which his story deals. Balzac contrasts the figure of Corentin with that of Commandant Hulot. The two men represent different attitudes towards the defence of a cause, and towards dealing with one's political adversaries. Corentin is a political spy in the service of Fouché, and the means he employs to bring about the capture of Montauran are the devious means of dissimulation and intrigue. Hulot, on the other hand, is all honesty and forthrightness. Though Balzac cannot entirely withhold his admiration for a vast political design like that in which Corentin plays a part, and for a mind like Fouché's capable of conceiving it, he leaves us in no doubt, in those parts of the novel where Corentin and Hulot confront one another, that he regards Hulot as the more sympathetic character and Corentin's attitude and conduct as ignoble.

Balzac's debt to Beaumarchais in *Les Chouans* seems, then, to be confined to an imitation of the *role* of Figaro, of his function as a *meneur du jeu*. The more prominent the place Balzac gives to the representation of an historical reality in his fiction and the nearer he approaches to what was to be his true subject: the portrayal of the recent past and of what Lukács calls 'the present as history', the more difficult—or perhaps impossible?—any imitation of Figaro as a character of comedy becomes. As his understanding of the nature of his own peculiar gifts and of the *kind* of novelist he aspires to become develops, the desire expressed in his early dramatic project to 's'inspirer de Beaumarchais' seems to persist; but imitation assumes a different, and it would seem, much modified, form.

The surviving links between Beaumarchais's Figaro and Corentin, when they are considered in conjunction with what the earlier Courottin of *Jean-Louis* also appears to owe to Figaro, do, however, suggest the seminal role that the example of Beaumarchais seems to have played in Balzac's early creative activity. They do rather more than this. They provide, more generally, just one more illustration of the part that imitation and borrowing played in the early stages of Balzac's career. There seems to be some evidence to suggest that it was only gradually, as Balzac's self-confidence increased, that their role in the major works diminished.[20] André Wurmser, in an important recent study of Balzac, makes the interesting point that, if Balzac's *romans de jeunesse* are generally far removed from the realities of actual life, this is because Balzac began his career as a novelist by adopting a common assumption of his *milieu* and his times: the task of the novelist was not to imitate the 'real' world, but rather to take the reader out of it. Ingenious invention, rather than what we call 'realism', was the aim. 'Horace de Saint-Aubin pensait que ses livres n'avaient rien de commun avec la réalité et qu'au commencement était l'invention', Wurmser writes.[21] This primacy accorded to *invention* did not exclude *imitation* of the novelist's predecessors and contemporaries—imitation as a starting-point for invention. Of such imitation both *Jean-Louis* and *Clotilde de Lusignan* offer examples.

Wurmser seems to suggest, however, that with the writing of *Le Dernier Chouan* all this changed. 'C'est à Fougères qu'est né le romancier réaliste. [. . .] Balzac comprend que c'est le réel qu'on doit imiter et non sa reproduction littéraire. Il s'inspirait de la littérature antérieure, il s'inspirera de la vie contemporaine. Il n'imitera plus que ce qui est.'[22] This, it seems to me, is to overstate the case, for all the evidence of recent study points in the opposite direction: the more closely *Les Chouans* is studied, the more strands appear in it of borrowings—more or less extensive and important—from the work of other writers. Balzac's debt to Beaumarchais in his conception of the role of Corentin is just one of these strands.[23] The interest, indeed, of *Les Chouans* for the student of Balzac lies largely in the way that its composition seems to mark a point in Balzac's career at which, while he appears still to rely quite extensively on imitation and on the borrowing of ideas from others, the novel also prefigures what is to come, because Balzac here succeeds in setting firmly in an historical context the story he creates partly out of the elements he borrows.

*   *   *   *

Recent study of Balzac in France has shown that Balzac's imitations of Beaumarchais did not come to an end with the publication of *Les Chouans,* though his later debt seems to be to Beaumarchais's *drames* rather than to his comedies. Perhaps this was a natural consequence of the emergence of the *romancier réaliste* in Balzac. Professor Laubriet, in his edition of *César Birotteau,* has shown that a scene in the first act of Beaumarchais's play: *Les Deux Amis, ou le Négociant de Lyon,* first played in 1770, bears such a striking similarity to a scene in *César Birotteau* that it seems impossible not to believe that Balzac had Beaumarchais's play in mind when he wrote the novel. Particularly interesting here is the fact that Balzac finds in the scene, not merely a trait that he lends to his *parfumeur*: his severity towards all bankrupts, however their bankruptcy may be brought about, but also (as Professor Laubriet shows) hints in Beaumarchais's dialogue that catch his imagination, and that he develops elsewhere in the novel and in relation to other characters.[24]

César Birotteau was published in December 1837, and the years that followed its publication are the years of Balzac's most serious renewed attempt to write for the theatre. It seems that when he came to make this attempt he aimed to achieve in theatrical form something resembling what he had by this time successfully achieved in the novel. In a letter written in December 1838, he says: 'Il n'y a plus de possible que le *vrai* au théâtre, comme j'ai tenté de l'introduire dans le roman.'[25] René Guise states that *L'École des ménages* (1839) clearly shows the results of Balzac's reflections on the *Essai sur le genre dramatique sérieux*; and that the *point de départ* of *Vautrin* (1839–40) is neither *Le Père Goriot,* nor even the fictional character that Balzac introduces in the novel-cycle, but Beaumarchais's *La Mère coupable.*[26] Only one play by Balzac contains a serious attempt to return for inspiration to the comedies of Beaumarchais and to create a dramatic character imitated from Figaro: *Les Ressources de Quinola* (1842). It is a strange play, a kind of curious hybrid. The world into which Balzac introduces the resourceful Quinola is a Balzacian world far removed from the gay and care-free world in which Figaro operates; the man he serves is no amoral, pleasure-seeking Almaviva, but an inventor at grips with intrigue, cupidity and jealousy, a figure related to Balthazar Claës and David Séchard. A good many of the limitations that prevented Balzac from ever reaching the highest level as a writer for the stage can be found in this play. But most clearly, it suggests the insuperable obstacles that stood in the way of Balzac's ever achieving his early ambition to create in a dramatic work a successful rival to Beaumarchais's Figaro. It was not just that times had changed. Balzac's attitude towards the times in which he lived, and his appreciation of them, were very different from Beaumarchais's. To find in the work of Balzac a character who reflects the temperament of his creator as Figaro does that of Beaumarchais and who, in virtue of the way he does this, serves as a point of reference by which his times are judged, we have to turn to the very different figure of Vautrin.

NOTES

1 *Actes et Paroles*, t. I.
2 See G. Delattre, *Les Opinions littéraires de Balzac* (Paris, 1961), p. 401.
3 *Correspondance* (édition Garnier), II, 342.
4 P. Barrière, *Honoré de Balzac et la tradition littéraire classique* (Paris, 1928), pp. 93-4.
5 D. Z. Milatchitch, *Le Théâtre de Honoré de Balzac* (Paris, 1930), p. 24.
6 Milatchitch gives no date. Barrière, who also quotes the entry from the *Pensées, sujets, fragments*, assigns it with other projects to the years 1820–35.
7 'C'est sur le personnage de Figaro en tant que réussite littéraire [que] se cristallisent plusieurs de ses aspirations personnelles' (G. Delattre, op. cit., p. 184).
8 R. Niklaus, *Beaumarchais: Le Barbier de Séville* (London, 1968), p. 16.
9 P. Barbéris attributes Balzac's borrowing of the name of Fanchette to the title of a novel by Restif de la Bretonne: *Le Pied de Fanchette*. On the authenticity of the early novels see P. Barbéris, *Aux Sources de Balzac: Les Romans de Jeunesse* (Paris, 1965), pp. 27–39. 'Balzac est bien l'auteur de nos huit romans, y compris et en entier *Jean-Louis* que, de très bonne heure, il a revendiqué, bien que paru sous double signature' (p. 38).
10 'Le chagrin ne dit rien, ne fait rien, ne prouve rien, et n'avance à rien' (*J.-L.*, livre III, ch. 4, p. 85). Cf. *BS*, I. 2. 'En attendant, mangeons à deux râteliers. . . voilà la bonne philosophie' (*J.-L.*, livre I, ch. 4, p. 108). Cf. *MF*, III. 13.
11 As M. Bardèche and P. Barbéris have pointed out.
12 G. Delattre, op. cit., p. 185.
13 A. de Viellerglé et Lord R'hoone, *Jean-Louis, ou la fille trouvée* (Paris (Les Bibliophiles de l'Originale) [s.d.]), livre I, ch. 5, p. 169. Elsewhere Balzac invents a rather similar kind of repartee for a character who in other respects owes nothing to Figaro, as in this exchange between the hero's father and uncle:
— Mais alors . . . comment me débarrasser des inquiétudes que cette petite Fanchette me cause?
— En la mariant à Jean-Louis.
— Mais, frère, elle n'a rien.
— Ils s'aiment.
— C'est une fille trouvée.
— Aimerais-tu mieux que ce fût une fille perdue? (*J.-L.*, livre I, ch. 2, pp. 47–8).
14 See R. Niklaus, op. cit., p. 47.
15 The Figaro that underlies the figure of Courottin is the Figaro of whom Suzanne says: 'De l'intrigue et de l'argent, te voilà dans ta sphère' (*MF*, I.1), and: 'On peut s'en fier à lui pour mener une intrigue' (*MF*, II.2), the Figaro we see in the first act of *Le Barbier de Séville* and in the second act of *Le Mariage de Figaro* particularly.
16 P. Barbéris, op. cit., pp. 100–6.
17 ibid., 103.
18 Such hints as there are in *Jean-Louis* of what Balzac was later to achieve in relating an invented story to contemporary social, political, and economic reality are to be found mainly towards the end of the novel: when, for example, Jean-Louis's father defends his son's right to seek the hand of Fanchette-Léonie who has turned out to be the daughter of the Duc de Parthenay, on the grounds that he is now the son of a man of great wealth who, as a result of the Revolution and the Revolu-

H

tionary wars, has been able to buy up the impoverished Parthenay's estates. But Balzac's account of Granivel's enrichment fills a bare half-dozen lines: 'Le père Granivel [. . .] ne s'occupa que du soin d'agrandir une fortune déjà fort honnête; il acheta, vendit, racheta, et revendit, tant et si bien, qu'il se trouva en quelques années possesseur d'immenses richesses.' (*J. -L.*, livre IV, ch. 6, pp. 143–4).

19 'C'est une de ces interprétations de Figaro par lequel [*sic*] Balzac était tenté depuis si longtemps' (M. Bardèche, *Balzac romancier* (Paris, 1940), p. 168).

20 Or 'imitation' took the rather different form of an attempt to 're-work' an idea found in the writings of another novelist—as in *La Muse du Département* or *Le Lys dans la Vallée*.

21 A. Wurmser, *La Comédie inhumaine* (Paris, 1970), p. 84. The pseudonym was, of course, another used by Balzac before publishing for the first time under his own name in *Les Chouans*.

22 A. Wurmser, op. cit., p. 85.

23 Others derive from Mérimée, Scott, and Stendhal. Recently, Professor Hemmings has persuasively argued that 'Marie de Verneuil, his first vibrant feminine creation' might be described as 'a Stendhalian heroine making an exceptional appearance in a novel by Balzac', and that she owes much to Balzac's knowledge of *De l'Amour*. See 'Balzac's *Les Chouans* and Stendhal's *De l'Amour*', in the *Festschrift* presented to the late Professor H. Hunt: *Balzac and the Nineteenth Century* (Leicester, 1972), p. 110.

24 *C.B.* (Garnier, 1964), pp. liv–lvii.

25 *Correspondance,* III, 475.

26 See Guise's interesting pages in Balzac, *Œuvres complètes* (Paris (Les Bibliophiles de l'Originale), 1969), XXII, pp. 636–40.

Two Anti-Novels:
Molloy and *Jacques le Fataliste*

SUSAN HAYWARD

At this point in time, we often hear mention of an artistic revolution currently changing traditional literary genres. The New Novelists claim they are creating a new form for the novel by a calculated destruction of all the classical rules concerning the form of the novel. New ideas on the expression of time, of space and of the consciousness of the author and of that of his created characters are expressed by such writers as Nathalie Sarraute, Alain Robbe-Grillet and Susan Sontag. The goal is to reveal new ways of perceiving the physical world. The objective point of view of the traditional novelist is shown to be a lie and the subjective mode begins.

Amongst all these contemporary novelists, however, there is one author who stands apart by his preoccupation with language and with the metaphysical question of the 'I'. Whereas almost all the other New Novelists have devoted themselves to the renewal of the novel, with the purpose of making it into something revolutionary, Samuel Beckett has devoted himself to the quest of the Mysterious 'I' of mankind by means of a completely new language. Beckett is perhaps the most important author of his time, not simply because he is interested in language as a mode of communication or an expression of the individual, but also because he tries to resolve certain fundamental questions about human kind and our world.

It is perhaps this humanistic orientation of his which permits the present study: for if Beckett belongs to the twentieth century, he none the less resembles other, earlier novelists who dealt with these same questions. Denis Diderot, eighteenth-century author, and Samuel Beckett, modern writer, share the same strong desire to explain man, the same impulse to express the 'I' through a reformed language.

Even upon a first reading, *Jacques le Fataliste* and *Molloy* offer a great number of obvious similarities. From the point of view of plot, both novels present us with two characters who are travelling toward an undefined destination. Moreover, these characters, whilst travelling, tell innumerable stories wherein they attempt to describe their experiences and their personal ideas. The journey in the physical world thus becomes one of a linguistic order also. It is through language, then, and the way in which these two authors manipulate it that Diderot and Beckett call the traditional novel in question.

Before examining the particular manner in which each author questions the role of language and the novel we should examine briefly their general thoughts on the nature of language and its limitations. It is in an article in the *Encyclopédie* that Diderot explains his mistrust of language as a means of intellectual and rational communication. Stressing the emotive aspect of man, Diderot demonstrates the insufficiency of an abstract language:

Par la raison seule qu'aucun homme ne ressemble parfaitement à un autre, nous n'entendons jamais précisément, nous ne sommes jamais précisément entendus; il y a du plus ou du moins en tout; notre discours est toujours en deçà ou au delà de la sensation.[1]

Man, a complicated being, always changing, always moving, cannot express the unique perception he has of himself and the external world through a language that is limited and uniform. And others, because of their particular characteristics, their personal vision of reality, cannot understand him either. Each individual is isolated in his own world because of the insufficiency of a language made up of abstract symbols. Diderot clarifies this problem in *Le Rêve de d'Alembert*:

Toute abstraction n'est qu'un signe vide d'idée. On a exclu l'idée en séparant le signe de l'objet physique et ce n'est qu'en rattachant le signe à l'objet que la science redevient une science d'idées. [...] Lorsque, après une longue combinaison de signes, vous demandez un exemple, vous n'exigez autre chose de celui qui parle, sinon de donner un corps, de la forme, de la réalité, de l'idée au bruit successif de ses accents, en y appliquant des sensations éprouvées.[2]

Language divorced from the real experience of an individual can only express the intellectual side of man, to the exclusion of his spiritual essence. A form of communication of a subjective order is thus one of the main goals of Diderot.

Approximately two hundred years later, Samuel Beckett will voice this same mistrust of abstract language as well as the same desire to expose the unique side of an individual. In an essay, 'Dante ... Bruno. Vico ... Joyce', Beckett vehemently attacks the language of abstraction as a literary form:

The form that is an arbitrary and independent phenomenon can fulfil no higher function than that of stimulus for a tertiary or quaternary reflex of dribbling comprehension.[3]

Like Diderot, Beckett feels that intellectual abstraction as a means of communication is separate from man. Beckett lauds Joyce's *Finnegan's Wake* for the following usage of language:

We notice that there is little or no attempt at subjectivism or abstraction, no attempt at metaphysical generalization. We are presented with a statement of the particular.[4]

Beckett's attitude, as well as that of Diderot, toward a complete expression on the part of the individual comes through quite explicitly in their theatre. There the instantaneous quality of language, and the sound and rhythm of the spoken word acquire significant importance. It is no longer the sense of the word that dominates, but its sonority, its evocative quality. Furthermore, these two authors limit the role of the spoken word in their plays, stressing gesture, the most fundamental form of communication and thus the more true of the two. With Beckett this tendency culminates in the plays *Actes sans paroles I, II,* where physical language completely suppresses intellectual language. A similar development also occurs in Diderot's last plays where body movement, mime, and passion-ate cries dominate articulated communication.

Even though Diderot and Beckett share certain ideas on language and its limitations, the basis for their attitudes is nonetheless somewhat different. Beckett's artistic effort in his novels is above all to reveal the 'I'; the essential element of a human being that is im-prisoned by the temporal and spatial limits of his body and the outside world. This 'I', a fairly mystical entity, inhabits the dark regions of man, the interior space that is out of chronological time and spatial reality. The 'I', escaping as it does established rules of human life, rules of cause and effect, of life and death, cannot possibly express itself by the means of a language that is rational, logical and temporal. In the Beckettian universe, time without reason constitutes a source of pain for the 'I', for the passage of inexplicable time denies the present, the only temporal notion known by this 'I'. Language intensifies this pain, because of its temporal characteristics. The search for the 'I' via the spoken word—the central preoccupation of Beckett's *Molloy*—is thus bound to fail.

Diderot does not preoccupy himself so much with a metaphysical conception of mankind. Rather, he stresses the emotive side of man which has become suppressed by a Cartesian dialectic. To the doctrine of determinism (a philosophy that reduces existence to an inevit-able series of cause and effect without explanation) he opposes the idea of the mystery and uniqueness of the individual, his emotions, his feelings and his perceptions. Given that the elements of sensuality and irrationality in man are not expressible by language in its present state, another form of communication, one that is more subjective and personal, must be created.

Both authors, then, are seeking to break the constraints of a rational language (albeit Beckett's goal is more metaphysical) in order to unveil a specific aspect of mankind that is out of the range of the spoken word.

In *Jacques le Fataliste* and *Molloy,* the questioning of language necessarily becomes a questioning of the novel also. By starting his novel in a fairly surprising manner, Diderot warns us early of his attitude toward this novel and to the genre of the novel as a whole. He asks both himself and the reader questions about the two principal characters, Jacques and the master, meanwhile refusing to provide any answers:

Comment s'étaient-ils rencontrés? Par hasard, comme tout le monde. Comment s'appelaient-ils? Que vous importe? D'où venaient-ils? Du lieu le plus prochain. Où allaient-ils? Est-ce que l'on sait où l'on va?[5]

In his role as creator of the novel, Diderot destroys his omniscient position, thus revealing that he does not wish to create a novelistic illusion. This voyage of Jacques and his master—a voyage which seems to be the central focus of the novel—is shown to be a literary artifice that allows Diderot to expose certain ideas of a literary and philosophical order.

Beckett uses the notion of the voyage in a similar manner. Molloy tries to rejoin his mother, apparently to resolve some old problems. In the second half of the novel, it is now Moran who is voyaging, this time searching for Molloy. But these characters, who never obtain their physical goals, lack psychological depth, and exist only as a mouthpiece to Beckett's linguistic and metaphysical preoccupations.

Molloy is written in the first person singular, a stylistic procedure that supposedly renders the characters of a novel more plausible, and more human even. The interior monologue of *Molloy* is, however, rather special. Even though the 'I' of this novel is not the standard third person who comes between the author and the reader, this 'I' is different from the author in that it is, in some way, a pseudo-'I'; it is the observer, the subject, the conscience of Beckett, and, at the same time, the observed, an object examined by the author. A kind of schizophrenia on the part of the author can be observed here. The 'I' that expresses itself, or rather, that tries without much success to express itself, undergoes a metaphysical evolution. It lives in a dimension beyond linear time and space, withdrawing more and more from the physical world to enter into its spiritual self. This 'I' is not of our world; it seems like a fictitious creation that Beckett uses to reveal certain metaphysical and philo-sophical notions of his. This 'I' does none the less express the existential anxiety felt by Beckett himself.[6] In this way, Beckett objectifies his 'I', separates it from himself, which enables him to analyze it in a more profound way than that offered by introspection. He creates then, a third, transparent person: a combination of his thoughts and his emotions, an independent entity, independent that is from the creator.

Diderot's way of introducing himself into his novel seems simpler and more direct than Beckett's procedure. The reason for this might be found in the fact that as an author of the eighteenth century he was without the sophisticated psychoanalytical knowledge and tools currently at Beckett's disposal. Diderot is therefore obliged to establish a clear relationship with his novel and his characters.

Diderot often intervenes in *Jacques le Fataliste,* either to comment on what has just happened, or to quite simply question the reader. At one stage during Jacques's story, when he is relating a conversation between the doctor and his host, Diderot declares:

Telle fut à la lettre la conversation du chirurgien, de l'hôte et de l'hôtesse; mais, quelle autre couleur n'aurais-je pas été le maître de lui donner, en introduisant un scélérat parmi ces bonnes gens? Jacques se serait vu, ou vous auriez vu Jacques, au moment d'être arraché de son lit, jeté dans une fondrière? Pourquoi pas tué? Tué, non. J'aurais bien su appeler quelqu'un à son secours, ce quelqu'un aurait été un soldat de sa compagnie: mais cela aurait pué le *Cléveland* à infecter. La vérité, la vérité![7]

Diderot intervenes, interrupting the even flow of the story by introducing himself into his fictitious creation. By his interventions, he awakens the reader's doubt, prohibits him from believing the story by continually questioning its so-called verity. These interventions also indicate a specific attitude on Diderot's part toward the novel. He refuses to give in to the logical rules of the novel which demand a clear continuity, a developed plot, a beginning, a crisis and a dénouement. Diderot allows himself, in his role of an individual separated from the literary process, to express himself as much and as often as he wishes. His digressions and interventions thereby constitute an unforeseeable itinerary toward freedom, a revolt against literary forms that are static, beautiful and perfected.

From another point of view, these digressions reveal Diderot's continual effort to attain truth: by introducing himself into the text itself, he removes the traditional distance between reality, nature, the external world and the lie of art.[8] The irregular aspect of nature and its multiple transformations are manifested in the very form of the novel where the author tries to smash the perfection, and thereby the lie, of a work of art. By offering the reader other possibilities, as far as the content of the novel is concerned, Diderot evokes the notion of relativity in this world, the absence of absolute ideas. Moreover, by his hesitant expression, by the contradictions and revisions that we can perceive in the above quotation and elsewhere, Diderot stresses the impossibility of telling the truth and the insufficiency of language.

Whereas in *Jacques le Fataliste* it is the author who questions the verity of the novel, in *Molloy* the characters themselves seek to attain this ideal. Thus, Molloy and Moran stutter and falter rather than speak, and never succeed in finding the right words to explain their ideas or to describe a particular event; instead they contradict themselves constantly: 'je . . . non, je ne peux pas le dire. C'est-à-dire je pourrais le dire, mais je ne le dirai pas, oui, il me serait facile de le dire, car ce ne serait pas vrai.'[9] The outcome, quite naturally, is that the reader can trust neither the author, nor his characters, nor his novel. The novel is thereby shown to be a fabrication, an illusion, a lie. Since the language is no longer *logos,* is no longer capable of expressing the truth, only fictions can be created.

This absence of an author in *Molloy* also points to certain philosophical preoccupations of Beckett's. Through the intermediary of the character, Beckett communicates obliquely with the reader. He renounces the position of power and the responsibility of the omniscient author and endows his literary creations with a superior kind of self-confidence. Molloy and Moran live therefore in a world where God, the creator, is abolished. They lack an explanation to their existence but are subject to the temporal and spatial limits of the physical world. Without an omnipotent god, the world created by Beckett is ruled by a series of unfathomable causes and effects, of births and deaths. In this world without escape, the only freedom possible for a human being is a limited one and one that is completely controlled by the physical forces of reality. Molloy explains this freedom in this way:

Moi j'avais aimé l'image de ce vieux Geulincx, mort jeune, qui m'accordait la liberté, sur le noir navire d'Ulysse, de me couler vers le levant, sur le pont. C'est une grande liberté pour qui n'a pas l'âme des pionniers. Et sur la poupe, penché sur le flot, esclave tristement hilare, je regarde l'orgueilleux et inutile sillon. Qui, ne m'éloignant de nulle patrie, ne m'emporte vers nul naufrage.[10]

There is a similar notion of freedom in *Jacques le Fataliste,* where determinism and freedom are clearly opposed. Whereas the sentence repeated throughout the novel: 'cela était écrit là-haut' indicates the determinist aspect of Diderot's thinking there is also a consistent effort to denounce fatalism, to liberate man. From a structural point of view, the intervention of the author (of which we have already spoken) is a way of attaining this goal; from the point of view of the characters, Jacques, who is for the most part the spokesman for the determinist doctrine, tries to fight the series of causes and effects. At one point in the novel, he explains his desire to stop talking, to stop the fatalistic chain, meantime telling us yet another story; his freedom then is limited to making criticisms:

Un jour, un enfant, assis au pied du comptoir d'une lingère, criait de toute sa force. La marchande, importunée de ses cris, lui dit: Mon ami, pourquoi criez-vous?
— C'est qu'ils veulent me faire dire A.
— Et pourquoi ne voulez-vous pas dire A?
— C'est que je n'aurai pas si tôt dit A, qu'ils voudront me faire dire B.[11]

This paradoxical conflict between the desire to stop talking, to bring the eternal prattling to an end and the need to keep on talking, to continue to tell stories is present in both *Molloy* and *Jacques le Fataliste*. At the bottom of this apparent contradiction lies the problem of language. As we have already seen, both authors reject logical language, a means of communication that is incapable of expressing certain fundamental aspects of man, the 'I' according to Beckett, or nature, truth, according to Diderot. Because the literary effort is doomed to failure, by the very nature of this language, one wonders why Beckett and Diderot, since they are aware of the impossibility of bespeaking the 'I' or the truth, try none the less to write novels wherein nothing of any significance occurs except on the linguistic level.

To a certain extent these authors attempt to resolve the problem by approximation: they destroy the logical aspect of language (and it is especially with Beckett that language borders on madness, a surrealist form) and the novel, with the hope of getting closer to the inexpressible and irrational element in man. Despite the effort of both authors, man still remains an enigma, a mathematical division without a finite answer, that of 'vingt-deux par sept'.[12] The non-rational work of art however will bring the novelist and his reader a little closer to that truth.

A further examination of *Molloy* and *Jacques le Fataliste* reveals that these stories also represent a way of passing time. Beckett, Diderot, and their respective characters devote themselves completely to this end. Both Molloy and Moran are writers working on their journals; Jacques and his master entertain themselves by recreating in speech form their past experiences. Living as they do in an incomprehensible universe, where each cause has its necessary effect, where time passes, bringing them ever closer to the ultimate reality: death, where no individual ever succeeds in discovering the truth of his own existence or the physical world, these characters lack a reason for living. Their lives end up by being nothing more than a long painful wait in an incomprehensible world. In order to diminish this existential suffering, they give themselves over entirely to the telling of stories, to the creating or repeating of fictions, all in an effort to forget the real world. Molloy explains this need to tell, to say anything and even nothing:

Ne pas vouloir dire, ne pas savoir ce qu'on veut dire, ne pas pouvoir ce qu'on croit ce qu'on veut dire, et toujours dire, ou presque, voilà ce qu'il importe de ne pas perdre de vue, dans la chaleur de la rédaction.[13]

Story-telling thus becomes an effort to escape the absurdity of existence; but the act of story-telling also serves as a proof of existence, and is thereby reassuring. Moran and Molloy use the literary genre of the journal; by creating literature, they affirm that they are functioning, living beings. In *Jacques le Fataliste,* however, where dialogue replaces the written form, we find an important relationship between the two speakers, Jacques and his master.

The couple, a creation of Beckett's in *En Attendant Godot* and of Diderot's in this particular novel, reveals certain central aspects of human relationships. Each partner in the couple Estragon/Vladimir, and in Diderot's couple Jacques and the master, needs the other for either psychological or material reasons. Jacques, who loves to speak, has the perfect listener in his master, whose main interest is listening. Each partner serves as a witness to the other's existence by recognizing his presence and his actions. The relationship between the two is based on the human need not to be isolated from the exterior world. While realizing the impossibility of communicating in a significant and profound way, because of the very nature of language, Jacques and his master continue to talk to each other, to dupe one another. This conversation between the two illustrates the basis of their relationship:

Jacques: Vous avez un furieux goût pour les contes!
Le Maître: Il est vrai; ils m'instruisent et m'amusent. Un bon conteur est un homme rare.
Jacques: Et voilà tout juste pourquoi je n'aime pas les contes, à moins que je ne les fasse.
Le Maître: Tu aimes mieux parler que te taire.
Jacques: Il est vrai.
Le Maître: Et moi, j'aime mieux entendre mal parler que de ne rien entendre.[14]

Story-telling serves yet another purpose. When Beckett, Diderot and their characters narrate, they become involved in a creative world. By trying to create, to invent, they escape the real world and enter a fictitious universe created according to their needs and personal ideas. By the means of language, these two authors and their characters try to become creators and usurp the role of an omniscient god who is absent from their world. The limitations of language however prevent the accomplishment of this goal, as Molloy says:

Et que je dise ceci ou cela ou autre chose, peu importe vraiment. Dire, c'est inventer. Faux comme de juste. On n'invente rien, on croit inventer, s'échapper, on ne fait que balbutier sa leçon, les bribes d'un pensum appris et oublié, la vie sans larmes, telle qu'on la pleure. Et puis, merde.[15]

Given the impossibility of explaining or justifying life by means of words, the characters of *Jacques le Fataliste* and *Molloy* use other games with a view to achieving the same goal. The references to mathematical properties which occur frequently in both novels reveal another way to pass time and to give meaning to human existence. Apart from the famous incident where Molloy regulates the distribution of his sucking-stones, there are several examples of this logical and ultimately comical way of looking at the exterior world. Molloy, when speaking about an extremely banal subject, stresses the absurdity of examining life scientifically:

Un jour je les comptai. Trois cent quinze pets en dix-neuf heures: soit une moyenne de plus de seize pets l'heure. Après tout, ce n'est pas énorme. Quatre pets tous les quarts d'heure. Ce n'est rien. Pas même un pet toutes les quatre minutes. Ce n'est pas croyable. Allons, allons, je ne suis qu'un tout petit péteur, j'ai eu tort d'en parler. Extraordinaire comme les mathématiques vous aident à vous connaître.[16]

In Diderot's novel, Jacques and his master also pursue intellectual games of a mathematical order. The master passes his time taking snuff, looking at his watch and listening to Jacques. When Diderot describes these occupations of the master, he employs a style very similar to Beckett's:

Puis il cherchait sa montre à son gousset, où elle n'était pas, et il achevait de se désoler, car il ne savait que devenir sans sa montre, sans sa tabatière et sans Jacques; c'étaient les trois grandes ressources de sa vie qui se passait à prendre du tabac, à regarder l'heure qu'il était et à questionner Jacques; et cela dans toutes les combinaisons. Privé de sa montre, il en était réduit donc à sa tabatière, qu'il ouvrait et fermait à chaque minute, comme je fais moi, lorsque je m'ennuie. Ce qui reste de tabac le soir dans ma tabatière est en raison directe de l'amusement, ou inverse, de l'ennui de ma journée. Je vous supplie, lecteur, de vous familiariser avec cette manière de dire empruntée de la géométrie, parce que je la trouve précise et je m'en servirai souvent.[17]

The ironic tone of both passages indicates immediately that Beckett, Diderot and their characters do not believe in scientific or mathematical analysis as a way to self-awareness. For indeed, by looking at physical reality in an ordered and rational fashion, by putting each phenomenon in its proper category, by regulating the superficial level of human existence, we resolve nothing insofar as the mystery of man is concerned. All we are doing by playing such intellectual games is passing time.

The obsession with objects on the part of both Diderot's and Beckett's characters is also linked to this need to give a meaning to life. The objects, being inanimate things, are beyond the reach of the destructive forces of chronological time. Even though the objects disintegrate as time goes by, they do not know the profound anxiety of man confronted by an ever-changing reality. Without feelings, emotions, life, these objects represent a complete separation from the painful and negative aspects of human existence. Thus, when the master plays with his snuff-box, or when Molloy counts his pockets and his stones, or even when Moran takes care of his bees, they are all attempting to escape this existential suffering. By placing their objects in a logical order, one that is numerical and comprehensible, these characters transpose their personal need for order to a world of objects. The object becomes then an extension of the individual, the means whereby he satisfies his dominant desire to order his irrational world.

These series, these lists of mathematical properties, these complicated enumerations of objects and their appearances also offer us the basis of both Diderot's and Beckett's humour. By describing any event or thing in a scientifically exaggerated way, these two authors reveal the insufficiency of logic, mathematics and science as a total explanation of existence. The strict rigidity of logical reasoning becomes absurd as soon as one is dealing with fundamentally human questions. This juxtaposition of the everyday, of the banal with the scientific is what produces laughter. In the description of a conversation between Jacques and his master, Diderot ridicules this type of reasoning. The exaggeration of logic ultimately causes it to transcend the rational and to enter the realm of the irrational, the absurd, the comic:

Et les voilà embarqués dans une querelle interminable sur les femmes; l'un prétendant qu'elles étaient bonnes, l'autre méchantes: et ils avaient tous deux raison; l'un sottes, l'autre pleines d'esprit: et ils avaient tous deux raison; l'un fausses, l'autre vraies: et ils avaient tous deux raison; l'un avares, l'autre libérales: et ils avaient tous deux raison; l'un belles, l'autre laides: et ils avaient tous deux raison; l'un bavardes, l'autre discrètes; l'un franches, l'autre dissimulées; l'un ignorantes, l'autre éclairées; l'un sages, l'autre libertines; l'un folles, l'autre sensées, l'un grandes, l'autre petites: et ils avaient tous deux raison.[18]

From a structural point of view, the symmetrical form of this discussion and the repetition of certain phrases must strike us. Symmetry, an artistic concept that aims for perfection, a finished form, underlines the ridiculous aspect of this conversation, where the subject-matter itself quite understandably resists concrete, final definitions. The accelerated rhythm toward the end and the repetition also intensify the irony of this discussion.

These same humorous elements appear frequently in *Molloy*, a metaphysical and yet down-to-earth and often very funny novel. At one point on his journey, Molloy attacks a perfect stranger in the forest. This surreal act, without logical motivation, or explainable cause, coupled with the way in which it is described, shows an obsession with symmetry, an attention directed to apparently meaningless details, and a series of repetitions:

Je dégageai donc prestement une béquille et lui assénai un bon coup sur le crâne. Cela le calma [. . .]. Voyant qu'il respirait toujours, je me contentais de lui envoyer quelques chaleureux coups de talon dans les côtes. Voici comment je m'y pris. Je choisis avec soin mon emplacement, à quelques pas du corps, en lui tournant bien entendu le dos. Puis bien calé entre mes béquilles, je me mis à osciller, en avant, en arrière, les pieds joints, les jambes serrées plutôt [. . .]. Je me balançai, voilà l'essentiel, avec une ampleur toujours grandissante, jusqu'au moment où, le jugeant venu, je me lançai de toutes mes forces en avant, et partant un instant après en arrière, ce qui donna le résultat escompté. [. . .] Je me reposai un peu, puis me relevai, ramassai mes béquilles et allai me mettre de l'autre côté du corps, où je me livrai avec méthode au même exercice. J'ai toujours eu la manie de la symétrie.[19]

These two passages indicate certain humorous elements central to both novels but they also constitute a central aspect of their structure as a whole. Structurally speaking, *Molloy* is a symmetrical novel *par excellence*. The novel falls into two parts, each presenting the story of an individual on a journey. Molloy, expelled from the womb, is searching in a fairly disorganized way for his mother, the image of the return to the womb. His journey, which also seems like a metaphor of the search for self, takes place even at the level of language, in the grey region of his mind. As he withdraws more and more from the physical world, Molloy finally finds himself in his mother's room, a kind of womb. He does not achieve his ultimate goal which is to escape completely from reality by returning to the maternal region out of linear time and space; but, because of his psychological or mystical journey, he has come closer to his essential 'I'. In the second part of the novel, where Moran journeys in search of Molloy, the reader meets with a fairly ordinary man, a good petit-bourgeois who busies himself with all the material questions of daily life. But, as he searches for Molloy he progressively disintegrates. By the end of his journey and the novel, Moran has become the Molloy of the beginning of the novel: a being separated from reality, living in his mind only, wanting nothing more than to journey, to search for his 'I'. The end of the novel is thus the beginning. Most of the action has been on a linguistic plane. All the descriptions, the stories and gestures of the novel were no more than pastimes. The characters merely turned in circles, coming and going, but never arriving anywhere.

Even the language of this novel goes in circles, similar to the whole structure. Molloy and Moran repeat the same stories, make the same stops, returns and starts. They never reach any definitive conclusion. The faltering language and the circular structure of the novel create a simultaneity of past, present and future. Chronological and linear time, a great source of suffering in the real world, is finally done away with in this novel. The characters, turning in circles in a universe that is out of time and thus out of space, plunge ever deeper into their innermost part: their minds. The structural circularity of *Molloy* is transformed into a spiral that goes up and down in turn, that comes close and then moves away from the intrinsic 'I'. The infinite spiral and the journey without end become, in the final analysis, an eternal waiting.

These stylistic effects, repetition, stopping and starting, are also employed in *Jacques le Fataliste*. Diderot's personal intervention prevents the logical continuation of Jacques's stories. At one point, however, Jacques gives up his role as narrator and the master starts relating his own stories. In the end, though, neither the characters nor the author ever finish their stories.

As far as philosophical questions are concerned, nothing definitive is said either. The conflict between determinism and humanism which troubles Diderot and his characters remains unresolved. Diderot, Jacques and his master have solved nothing by their talking; the fundamental questions about their existence are left without a conclusive answer. They state nothing—except the impossibility of stating anything.

Thus *Jacques le Fataliste* and *Molloy,* from a structural point of view, lack definitive limits. The mystery of man remains incomprehensible, and ever inexpressible through words. Both novels could go on indefinitely, without achieving their ultimate goal. The babbling goes on into infinity.

Et moi, je m'arrête, parce que je vous ai dit de ces deux personnages tout ce que j'en sais.—Et les amours de Jacques? Jacques a dit cent fois qu'il était écrit là-haut qu'il n'en finirait pas l'histoire, et je vois que Jacques avait raison. Je vois, lecteur, que cela vous fâche; eh bien, reprenez son récit où il l'a laissé et continuez-le à votre fantaisie, ou bien faites une visite à Mlle Agathe, sachez le nom du village où Jacques est emprisonné; voyez Jacques; questionnez-le: il ne se fera pas tirer l'oreille pour vous satisfaire, cela le désennuiera.[20]

Alors, je rentrai dans la maison et j'écrivis. Il est minuit. La pluie fouette les vitres. Il n'était pas minuit. Il ne pleuvait pas.[21]

NOTES

1 Herbert Josephs, *Diderot's Dialogue of Gesture and Language*: 'Le Neveu de Rameau' (Ohio State University Press, 1969), p. 13.

2 ibid., p. 15.

3 Samuel Beckett, 'Dante . . . Bruno. Vico . . . Joyce' published in: *Our Exagmination Round His Factification For Incamination of 'Work in Progress'* (London, 1972), p. 13.

4 ibid., p. 22.

5 Denis Diderot, *Œuvres Romanesques*, Classiques Garnier (Paris, 1959), p. 493.

6 The word 'existential' is used here in a strictly literal sense, without any reference to Sartre's existentialism.

7 Diderot, p. 526.

8 Herbert Dieckmann, *Cinq Leçons Sur Diderot* (Geneva-Paris, 1959), p. 128.

9 Samuel Beckett, *Molloy,* Éditions 10/18 (Paris, 1971), p. 23.

10 Beckett, *Molloy,* p. 66.

11 Diderot, p. 710.

12 Beckett, *Molloy*, p. 84.
13 ibid., p. 35.
14 Diderot, p. 650.
15 Beckett, *Molloy*, p. 40.
16 ibid., p. 39.
17 Diderot, p. 516.
18 ibid., p. 513.
19 Beckett, *Molloy*, pp. 111–2.
20 Diderot, p. 777.
21 Beckett, *Molloy*, p. 234.

12

Rousseau's English Pension[1]

R. A. LEIGH

An English contemporary of Rousseau's, in a work published in 1755, produced this definition of the word 'pension', in which, it is fair to say, lexicographical objectivity was at least
partially eclipsed by political rancour:

Pension. An allowance made without an equivalent. In England it is generally understood to mean any
payment given to a State hireling for treason to his country.

Johnson's embarrassment, seven years later, at the offer of a pension from George III
is as well-known as the soothing assurances which enabled him to accept it: the pension was
offered for meritorious service already rendered, and not in expectation of future subser-
vience, much less treason. Whether, in fact, it influenced his conduct in the Wilkes affair
or in the dispute with the American colonies, is something which lies beyond the scope of
this paper.

However, Johnson's definition, suitably transposed, or modulated into a remoter key, does
serve to highlight Rousseau's dilemma, or rather the series of dilemmas in which the threat
of royal patronage placed him. For, like all self-respecting history, the history of Rousseau's
English pension was preceded by a long pre-history which moulded and conditioned it.

I

This pre-history begins, in so far as any pre-history can be said to begin, with Rousseau's
'conversion'. By that I don't mean either of his two conventional conversions to a different
form of christianity: I refer to the great spiritual crisis which changed the course of his life
on the road to Vincennes in October 1749. The main impact of this conversion I shan't
attempt to deal with here: it gave him a new insight into society and into the predicament
of contemporary man, seen as wretched, depraved, sick and enslaved, when he was destined
by nature to be happy, good, healthy and free. Such considerations would lead us to the
discussion of Rousseau's ideas which were shortly to produce, from 1750 to 1762, a whole
series of electrifying masterpieces. It is the other aspect of this conversion which concerns
us here: its visible impact on his contemporaries. For Rousseau decided that it was his duty
to live his philosophy, and not simply to write about it; and this, the cynic might be tempted
to say, constituted his greatest mistake. It led him to the complete repudiation of conventional methods of ordering one's existence, or furthering one's interests. In particular, from

now on, dedicated poverty was to replace careerism: a poverty deliberately fostered and maintained as the price of independence, integrity and a serene conscience, the highest good. To keep your hands clean, you had to stay out of the game. The secret of happiness and peace of mind was not, as even decent people had thought, to earn enough to satisfy your wants: that was the path to servitude, since most wants were artificial. Freedom meant reducing your wants to the minimum. Then you would not need to work more than a few hours a day and could not be enslaved. It was a message which fell uneasily on the ears of an acquisitive age devoted, then as now, to pleasure, status-seeking and conspicuous consumption. But Jean-Jacques put his doctrine into practice. He gave up his lucrative sinecure as cashier to a financier, and took to copying music at a few pence a page for a couple of hours every morning. As a visible sign of his 'réforme', as he called it, he gave his watch away, since only a busy slave needed one, and refused to wear the genteel insignia of wig, sword, lace cuffs and ruffles. A plain dealer in plain functional clothing: that was J.-J. He was aided in his resolve by having all his shirts stolen whilst out at a concert.

The effect of this doctrine, preached and practised, in mid-eighteenth-century Paris can scarcely be imagined. Mid-eighteenth-century Paris was the capital of venality and luxury, of a demoralising and widespread scramble for wealth, of stupefying disparities in living standards. Perhaps nothing like it had been seen since the days of imperial Rome, or would be seen again before star-spangled Hollywood of the low-tax era. But Paris was also the capital of patronage and sycophancy. Rousseau's behaviour and scathing *obiter dicta* were resented not only by the large tribe of men of letters whose headquarters were Paris, and who felt they were being got at (as indeed they were). His remarks also attracted the attention of the Government. From D'Argenson's diary we learn that Rousseau had proclaimed that a man of letters should take the triple vow of poverty, liberty and truth: an intolerable contradiction of official policy. A prominent courtier suggested he should be thrashed, and a little later, when Rousseau had outraged national pride by his satirical onslaught on French music, he was on the point of being expelled from France altogether. He was publicly insulted, burnt in effigy and couldn't go out without a bodyguard. Even before that point was reached, his good faith was being constantly assailed by a horde of pamphleteers and by the anonymous authors of clandestine news-letters. They denounced his campaign against corruption as envy or misanthropy, and his 'cynicism' (in the sense of being a disciple of Diogenes) as a profitable pose; they even declared that his disinterestedness and poverty were a sham, a blatantly hypocritical attempt to attract charity. However, Jean-Jacques did make one or two temporary converts, including oddly enough D'Alembert, who put forward in an early essay on *Les Gens de Lettres* somewhat similar ideas on patronage, though of course diluted with his usual tact and prudence.

The first acid test of the authenticity of Rousseau's newly adopted attitudes came with the unprecedented success of his operetta *Le Devin du Village,* first produced before the Court at Fontainebleau on 18 October 1752. The occasion was a triumph; the King went round for days on end croaking its catchy tunes in his cacophonous wheeze, and commanded a second performance. Madame de Pompadour arranged a third, in which she herself took part. A contemporary diarist records that the King spent over 150,000 francs on the operetta, including, I suppose, special gratuities for the cast and orchestra. Everyone thought Rousseau's fortune was made and his future assured. After the first performance, the master of ceremonies, the duc d'Aumont, asked him to stay on at Court until the next day, in order to be presented to the King, who was expected to grant him a pension. Instead, after a sleepless night pondering his decision, Rousseau left early in the morning. A celebrated passage in his *Confessions* gives the reasons, not necessarily in hierarchical order. Rousseau suffered from a painful bladder complaint which made it necessary for him to urinate frequently and at short notice. He was afraid of having to hang about waiting for the King in the long gallery at Fontainebleau, of being imprisoned in the crowd of courtiers and of disgracing himself in public. (This went on for many years: in December 1764 when Boswell came to see him at Môtiers, he found him with a catheter inserted, and complaining that he needed 'un pot de chambre à tout instant'). Then again, there was his timidity and lack of aplomb. When the King spoke to him, he would have to reply. He owed it to himself and to the world, not simply to mumble a few elegant commonplaces like anyone else, but to wrap up in a graceful expression of gratitude some profound or useful truth, or even an apt exhortation which a monarch could take to heart. But it was futile to prepare such a speech in advance. He was sure to forget it: nor could he trust himself to rise to the occasion on the spur of the moment. Just as imperative, on a different level, was the fact that to accept such a pension was incompatible with his principles and his personality. It was not simply that this advocate of austerity was a republican and an enemy of the wealthy and powerful. It must be remembered that in eighteenth-century France, you didn't get your pension by presenting a book at the post-office or having your bank account credited. In fact, to be granted a pension and to get it paid were two very different things. It wasn't so much that the Treasury was nearly always empty. No doubt it was, although the Court always behaved as though it were full. The point was that no one ever knew how much money was available at any given moment. There was no budget, and no accounts. All that was known for certain was that there wasn't enough to go round, and this led to a constant scrimmage to get what there was. Pensions were usually secured on particular funds or on the product of particular taxes. Once you got your official letter specifying the amount and the fund, your troubles began. In order to turn your grant into hard cash, you had to dance attendance on the civil servants in the appropriate department at Versailles. As a result, the ministerial offices there were besieged by an army of pensioners, despairing or determined, all pressing for payment. What you got, if anything, depended entirely on your own standing, the names you could drop and the patrons you could rely on. Even then, you couldn't be sure you would be paid regularly. Now, the fire-power of a scruffy, down-at-heel eccentric, and a foreigner at that, demanding payment in a Genevese drawl, flying into a rage at the slightest impertinence, real or imagined, of the jack-in-office, was likely to be strictly nil. Soliciting for Jean-Jacques would be a fruitless humiliation.

Even without a pension, of course, the Court performances of the *Devin* brought Rousseau quite a lot of money: a hundred *louis d'or* from the King, and fifty from madame de Pompadour (which he had to be bullied into accepting, and for which he thanked her in four lines of the most tortuous and equivocal prose he ever wrote). He also received

1200 francs from the Opera, for public performances, and three hundred from his publisher
Pissot for the score, with a promise of another two hundred in books, which it is not clear
was ever honoured. All in all 4500 Fr.—much more than for any other work of his, with
the single exception of *Émile*—an ironical comment on eighteenth-century values, one
might be inclined to think: but would it be any different today?

Rousseau's sidestepping of royal favour had a significant epilogue. A few days later, as
he was about to dine with madame d'Épinay, a cab drew up outside the house, and the
passenger, his friend Diderot, motioned to him to get in. He was thereupon treated to a long
lecture on the subject of his precipitate departure from Fontainebleau. The luxury of
indulging his principles, Diderot declared, was no doubt eminently satisfactory for J.-J.
All right: let him live on bread and water if he wanted to. But why must his dependants,
Thérèse Lavasseur and her mother, be made to suffer? He owed it to them to go back on
his decision, and try to obtain the pension which the Court was still prepared to grant.
Jean-Jacques, of course, disagreed, the discussion grew heated and they parted. Diderot's
officiousness had produced one of the first and certainly one of the most ominous cracks in
their friendship, the earliest recorded sign of what was to develop in the course of time into
a complete break with the *philosophes*.

II

That in brief is the story of Rousseau's first royal pension. Chapter Two in this pre-
history took place ten years later, almost to the day. In June 1762, shortly after the publication of *Émile*, on hearing that the *Parlement de Paris* had not only condemned the book but
issued a warrant for his arrest, Rousseau departed hastily from Montmorency and took
refuge with friends at Yverdon, in the pays de Vaud, then governed by Berne. There he
learned with incredulous dismay that his own native city of Geneva had gone one better
than the *Parlement de Paris*: it had condemned both *Émile* and the *Contrat social* to be burnt
by the common hangman, and had decided, in a secret decree communicated to the French
government but not to the public or Rousseau's family, to arrest the author if he set foot
on the territory of the Republic. This example was soon followed, with varying degrees of
severity, in Holland, in the Austrian Netherlands, and in Vienna itself. But the worst blow
fell when the Bernese authorities ordered the prefect of Yverdon to expel Rousseau.
On 9 July he crossed the mountains on foot and moved into a house in the village of
Môtiers, in the principality of Neuchâtel, whose nominal sovereign since 1707 was the
King of Prussia. In 1762, of course, that meant Frederick the Great. One of Rousseau's
first acts on arrival was to throw himself on the mercy of the Governor of the Principality,
the Jacobite George Keith, hereditary Earl Marshal of Scotland.[2] The Scotsman, who was a
humane, liberal and enlightened free-thinker, with a strong anti-clerical bias, and an even
stronger sense of humour, immediately adopted Jean-Jacques more as a son than a protégé,
gave him temporary asylum and dispatched to Frederick, in his halting French, an urgent
appeal for confirmation. Frederick was then actively engaged in winding up the Seven
Years' War by a campaign which was to secure for him, once and for all, the possession of
Silesia. He had just defeated the Austrian Field-Marshal Daun in a bloody engagement at

Burkersdorf, and was preparing to lay siege to Schweidnitz, which the Austrians had to evacuate within a fortnight or so. Frederick replied to Keith's letter on 29 July 1762 from his camp at Ditmansdorf, no doubt booted and spurred, and with the sound of the Austrian cannon still reverberating in his ears. In his own hand and in his own inimitable French, he wrote:

Donnons Mon cher Milord Azile au Malheureux, ce Rousseau est un Garsson Singuillér, filosofe Cinique, qui n'a que La bissace pour tout bien, il faut L'Empécher tans que cela se poura d'ecrire, par ce qu'il traite Les Matieres Scabreuses qui Exsiteroient des Sensations trop Vives dans Vos Tetes Noeuf-chateloises, et ocasionneraient des Clameurs de tout Vos pretres enclins a La Dispute et plains de fanatissme.

This reply of Frederick's, which reached Milord Maréchal a fortnight later, placed him in a quandary. He knew Rousseau well enough to realise that he would never agree to purchase immunity at the price of being gagged. He therefore sent him a carefully edited version of Frederick's remarks, softening the royal command into a casual hope, and adding that he had already assured the King that Rousseau intended in any case to give up writing. The pill was softened, then: it was also sweetened by a honeyed introduction: 'J'ay reponse du Roy qui est fort aise de donner azile a la vertu persecutée' (Frederick had said nothing about virtue, persecuted or otherwise). However, Rousseau declined to swallow the pill, even softened and sugared. He answered stiffly that he could not consider himself bound by what had been merely the expression of an intention, and wished to reserve his position. Milord Maréchal replied, with his usual tact, that the King had not laid down any *express* condition, and reported further to Frederick, no doubt dropping a hint about Rousseau's financial difficulties. This letter has been lost, but Frederick's reply is extant, once again written from an armed camp (1 September 1762, from Peterswalde), and once more in his own hand. It contains a long passage on Rousseau, of which I shall quote only the beginning:

Je Vois que nous penssons de Meme, il faut Soulagér ce pauvre Malheureux, qui ne peche que par avoir des Opinions singuilleres Mais qu'il croit bonnes, je vous ferai remettre 100 ecus dont Vous aurez la bonté de Luy faire donnér ce qu'il luy faut pour Ses bessoins, je crois En luy donnant Les Chosses en Nature qu'il Les acceptera plus tot que de L'Argent, si Nous n'avions pas la Guerre, Si nous n'etions pas ruinéz je lui ferai batir un hermitage avec un jardin, ou il pouroit vivre Come il croit qu'ont vecus nos premiérs peres, j'avoue que mes idées sont ausi Diferentes des Sienes qu'est Le fini de L'Infini.

This was followed by a whole page or more of astringent criticism of Rousseau's ideas, which Frederick evidently knew only at second or third hand. He ended by recalling a well-known anecdote, almost legendary, which illustrated Rousseau's indifference to money and which contrasted sharply with the attitudes of most of the men of letters with whom Frederick had had to deal. The King commented:

Ce grand Desinteressement est sans Contredit le fond Esensiel de la vertu, ainsi je juge que Votre Sauvage a les mœurs aussi pures que L'Esprit inconsequent.

This letter, like the first, again placed Milord Maréchal in a difficult position. He had seen enough of Rousseau by now to know that it would be virtually impossible to give effect to his royal master's instructions without mortally offending his protégé. And in fact, the

fiasco of his friendship with madame d'Épinay had made Jean-Jacques even more determined than ever to accept nothing from anyone. Milord Maréchal persuaded madame de
Boufflers, one of Rousseau's most powerful and influential friends, to intervene: her reward
was an elaborate sermon and a magisterial rebuke. He then approached Rousseau personally,
with the disconcerting result that the Sage of Môtiers resolved to train his fire on the King
himself. Jean-Jacques was perhaps not sorry to avail himself of the opportunity he had
renounced in the case of Louis XV of delivering to a crowned head a useful and edifying
homily. It was easier of course to do so in writing and at a distance: having no common
frontier with his Swiss principality and having no troops on its territory, Frederick was
forced to rule it with a very light rein. And so, on 1 November 1762, not without trepida-
tion, Rousseau wrote to the King:

Sire,
Vous êtes mon protecteur et mon bienfaiteur, et je porte un cœur fait pour la reconnoissance: je veux
m'acquitter avec vous, Si je puis.
    Vous voulez me donner du pain: n'y a-t-il aucun de vos Sujets qui en manque?
    Otez de devant mes yeux cette épée qui m'éblouït et me blesse. Elle n'a que trop bien fait Son Service,
et le Sceptre est abandonné. La carriére des Rois de vôtre étoffe est grande; vous étes encore loin du
terme. Cependant le tems presse, et il ne vous reste pas un moment à perdre pour y arriver. Sondez
bien vôtre cœur, ô Frederic! Pourrez-vous vous résoudre à mourir Sans avoir été le plus grand des
hommes?
    Puissai-je voir Frederic le juste et le redouté, couvrir enfin Ses Etats d'un peuple heureux dont il
soit le pére, et Jean Jaques Rousseau, l'ennemi des Rois, ira mourir de joye aux pieds de Son Trône.

    Understandably, Frederick was slightly peeved by Rousseau's exhortations. He wrote to
Milord Maréchal on 26 November, from Meissen:

Il faut avouér que l'on ne sauroit poussér le desinteressement plus loin qu'il le fait, c'est un grand pas a
la Vertu, si ce n'est La Vertu meme;
    Il veut que je fasse La paix, le bonhome ne sait pas la Dificulté qu'il y a d'y parvenir, et S'il Conoissoit
les politiques avec les quels j'ai a faire, il Les trouveroit bien Autrement intretables que les filosofes
avec les quels il s'est brouillé.

    Frederick's offer to Jean-Jacques soon leaked out, partly owing to indiscretions at Potsdam,
partly through Milord Maréchal, who in the hope of strengthening Rousseau's position,
advertised the intended benefaction, and made the King out to be more generous and more
favourable to Jean-Jacques than he actually was. Rousseau's refusal also became widely
known, and was widely admired and widely criticised. These facts have some bearing on
the rest of the story. For the moment, however, let it be simply noted that this second
opportunity of a royal pension had been side-stepped like the first.

                                        III

    We now leap forward another three or four years, to the strange events of 1766 and
1767.
    The story of Rousseau's English pension is embedded in the tragi-comedy of his quarrel
with Hume. It would take us too long to attempt at this point to digest this enormous

red-herring: but so much nonsense has been written on the subject that a few words of explanation are indispensable.

In one sense there never was a quarrel between Rousseau and Hume, in the sense of a personal confrontation, and that was basically the trouble. It was all done by correspondence. I think it was John Donne who said, 'Sir, more than kisses letters mingle souls': one of the most misleading half-truths ever perpetrated. There was certainly no mingling of souls in the correspondence between Hume and Rousseau, but rather, in the modern cant phrase, a classic dialogue of the deaf. The trouble started with the press campaign against Rousseau which began after his arrival in England in January 1766. He was always far more sensitive to public opinion than he ever admitted. It is no doubt significant that he has written so revealingly, and in such a modern way, on the distorting effect of 'opinion' on personality. Indeed, his sensitiveness in this respect was a powerful factor in his decision to write his autobiography. Deeply disturbed by the pin-pricks of various journalists, he began to wonder who could be responsible for the change in tone and attitude of the press towards him since his arrival in England. Hume came under suspicion because of his friendship with the *philosophes,* who were Rousseau's enemies; but more particularly because of his un-demonstrative character which made it impossible for him to rise to Rousseau's standards of sensibility or to respond to his emotional advances. After all, what are you, a phlegmatic Scot, a placid philosopher and a civil servant into the bargain, to say or do when, à propos of nothing in particular, one of the most celebrated writers of the day jumps on your lap, flings his arms around your neck, wets your cheek with his tears and sobs out an incoherent entreaty in a foreign language? In these circumstances, Hume's embarrassed mumble, 'Quoi! mon cher monsieur! Eh! mon cher Monsieur!', was bound to seem somewhat inadequate. Hume did not understand (how could he?) that Rousseau was looking for a sign of that genuine affection which would be a proof of Hume's innocence. Then again, for Hume, Rousseau, after all, was only one pebble on a busy man's beach, whereas Rousseau expected from all his friends complete devotion and absolute priority. With him, it was always all or nothing. After his initial suspicions, from which he himself at first recoiled in horror, and repudiated with shame, he set Hume a series of carefully devised tests, which the bewildered Scot quite naturally failed miserably. This was the position at the end of March 1766. The rest was inevitable. In Rousseau's eyes, Hume had proved to be the ring-leader of a conspiracy to entice him to England where he would be isolated, friendless and helpless: where his reputation would be undermined and his character besmirched, and where, held up repeatedly to public ridicule and contempt, he would, in the end, be completely discredited. As in the case of all paranoiac delusions, everything which Hume said and did could be made to provide evidence of his guilt: and ironically enough, his very efforts to help Rousseau could be construed as so many attempts to gain his confidence in order the more effectively to destroy him.

As early as July 1762, soon after the condemnation of *Émile,* on first learning of Rousseau's plight, and in the mistaken belief that he was coming to England, Hume had suggested the possibility of official recognition of the fugitive's genius. With an enthusiasm for the enlightenment and culture of 'Farmer George' which is apt to seem somewhat strange today, but which was widely shared in the 1760s and even later, he wrote to madame de Boufflers:

We are happy at present in a king [George III had come to the throne on 25 October 1760] who has a taste for literature, and I hope M. Rousseau will find the advantage of it, and that he will not disdain to receive benefits from a great monarch, who is sensible of his merit. (1 July 1762)

Madame de Boufflers had promptly conveyed a hint of this to Jean-Jacques (10 September 1762), but nothing further had been done since Rousseau had decided to stay at Môtiers.

A few years later, when Rousseau, after much hesitation, had agreed to come to England, Hume, who had offered to accompany him on the journey and settle him in a suitable place of residence, raised the question again, but this time more definitely, in a conversation which must have taken place at Calais between the 8th and the 10th of January 1766. He asked Rousseau point-blank whether he would accept a pension if offered, assuring him that consent could not possibly endanger his much-prized independence. But Jean-Jacques raised a different objection. He feared that acceptance might be construed as a slight on Frederick, whose offers he had refused, and for whom he had subsequently experienced strong feelings of respect and gratitude, since the King had tried to screen him from the full blast of the bigotry of the Neuchâtel clergy. He therefore said he would have to consult Milord Maréchal, who had retired to Potsdam and who, as a favourite of Frederick's, was in a good position to take soundings. Hume lost no time in reporting this conversation to Conway, then Secretary of State for the Southern Department in Rockingham's administration.[3] Conway's career is a striking demonstration of how to get on in life without doing anything in particular.[4] But although a mediocre soldier and a colourless statesman, Conway was a kind and helpful person: and this story will show that he must also have been an exceptionally patient one. Within a few days of Rousseau's arrival in England, and certainly before 12 February 1766, he raised the matter with the King. The grant was approved in principle, and the amount fixed at £100 per annum (Johnson had had £300). However, Rousseau was such a controversial figure that the King wanted the award kept secret, in order to avoid adverse comment. A series of minor delays followed, which contributed inadvertently to the coming contretemps. Before taking the matter any further, it was decided to await Milord Maréchal's report.[5] By the middle of March his blessing had been received: but the actual signing of the warrant had to be put off through Conway's illness. In the meantime, Rousseau had left the grocer's shop in Chiswick where he had been trying to pick up a little English, and had gone down to Wootton in Dovedale, on the border between Staffordshire and Derbyshire, to live in a lonely house belonging to Richard Davenport, a gouty, free-thinking Johnian who was a great admirer of Émile.

Only one thing now held up the pension: Rousseau had begun to go out of his mind. His suspicions against Hume had hardened into certainty, and he was already in an agonizing state of panic and despair. Oblivious of all this, Hume went ahead, and put the finishing touches to his handiwork by asking Conway to find out whether it was to be a Treasury pension or one from the Privy Purse. Conway took the King's instructions on this point on 2 May, and came back with the news that it was to be paid from the Privy Purse. All that was needed now was Jean-Jacques's formal acceptance: and Hume, with a sigh of relief after a difficult job well done, wrote off to Wootton asking for it the very next day.

Rousseau did not condescend to reply to the traitor; but sent instead to Conway a strange letter which no one could understand and which everyone misinterpreted. In it, after expressing his deepest gratitude and respect for the King, Rousseau begged Conway to defer the pension until better days. His mind was affected by a deep sorrow, and he thought it wiser to postpone all important decisions until he felt able to cope with them. One sentence was particularly enigmatic:

Loin de me refuser aux bienfaits du Roi par l'orgueil qu'on m'impute, je le mettrois à m'en glorifier, et tout ce que j'y vois de pénible est de ne pouvoir m'en honorer aux yeux du public comme aux miens propres.

This was intended to be a covert allusion to the press campaign which he considered had dishonoured him. (Later, Rousseau explained that being absolutely determined not to be under any obligation to that villain Hume, he was at his wits' end to find a decent pretext for refusing.) Knowing nothing of all this, Hume and Conway put their heads together and decided that what Rousseau meant was that he objected to the pension's being kept secret. Having arrived at this erroneous conclusion, Hume was understandably angry. For Rousseau had not only consented to the condition of secrecy, but had even welcomed it as a guarantee of the King's good faith: it was proof, he had said, that the favour was not conferred out of ostentation or vanity. Conway thereupon asked Hume to overcome Rousseau's imagined objection to the condition of secrecy, and on 17 May Hume wrote Rousseau a gentle and tactful letter of expostulation, which was far from expressing the irritation he felt. Receiving no answer, Hume took it upon himself to ask Conway to cut the Gordian knot by making the pension a public one; but Conway not unnaturally insisted that Rousseau must agree in advance, in order to avoid exposing the King to the risk of a second refusal. In answer to a further pressing letter from Hume, Rousseau at last condescended to reply, in a letter blazing with scorn and contempt, accusing Hume of perfidy and treachery. And when Hume indignantly demanded details of his alleged misdeeds, there came the notorious missive of 10 July 1766, as long (Hume put it ruefully) as a three-shilling pamphlet, enumerating all his crimes and the corroborative evidence. It was this letter which convinced Hume that Rousseau was either mad or wicked, and led eventually to the publication of his *Concise and Genuine Account* of their quarrel (French text, October 1766: English text, November).

At the beginning of September the position was explained to the King, and there the matter seemed to rest. It rebounded, however, in the New Year, when, after the adverse publicity he had received in Hume's *Concise Account*, Rousseau decided to demonstrate his good faith and to silence criticism by asking for the pension to be granted, provided it could be done without Hume coming into the negotiations. Conway refused to budge without Hume's agreement, which was given. The long-suffering King consented, and at the end of March 1767 Rousseau sent a formal letter of thanks. Thereupon he was pressed, through Davenport, to nominate an agent to receive payment. This Rousseau, who had no intention of claiming the money, repeatedly put off doing. He had made up his mind to leave England, partly because he believed his life was in danger here, and partly, as he said later, to avoid accepting the pension. On 1 May he left Wootton suddenly, and on the 3rd turned up at the White Hart Inn at Spalding. Hitherto, no one has been able to explain why Rousseau went to Spalding or how he got there. An unpublished document tells us that, having made up his mind to leave England, Rousseau laid a ruler over the map, decided that Boston was the nearest port to Wootton, and made tracks across country. On arrival at Spalding, he discovered that there were no ships leaving Boston for France, and wrote off to Davenport saying he would return if he would have him back. But of course, postal communication between Spalding and Wootton was hopeless. The letters all got stuck at Ashburn. It would have been far better to route them through London. On his side, Davenport, laid low by the gout, persuasively implored his guest to return, in a letter worthy of Mr Woodhouse:

I never was at Spalding, but have always understood it to be one of the most cursed disagreeable places in England. I can't conceive what motive could possibly make you go there, and all that flat country is reckoned very unwholesome especially for those who are not natives—for God's sake return out of it as soon as you can.

By then, however, Rousseau was at Dover, ready to embark. On arrival in France, he went into hiding at the urgent request of his protector, the Prince de Conti, in order to avoid arrest by the *Parlement de Paris* under the old warrant of 1762.

Meanwhile, Hume, convinced by now that Rousseau was more to be pitied than blamed, had gone on pressing Davenport to get Rousseau to nominate an agent to receive payment, and on 1 August 1767, from France, Rousseau did so, thinking that the money would never be paid outside England. (French pensions were hardly ever paid if the beneficiaries left the country). Much to his astonishment, in the middle of December 1767 he received a draft for £50 (two quarters). As he explained in a letter to madame de Verdelin, he had always regarded the pension as a sort of carrot intended to keep him in England: he hadn't dreamt for one moment that it would be paid on the Continent, and he was at first not at all keen on maintaining this link with a country where he had been so unhappy. However, on thinking things over he had decided to accept it, because it released him from other irksome obligations (17 December 1767).

And that, it would seem, was that.

IV

But it wasn't. Whilst a guest of the Prince de Conti at the château de Trie, near Gisors in Normandy, Rousseau's mental torment intensified, but his suspicions changed direction. He no longer believed that Hume was the ringleader of the conspiracy against him, but that he was merely a tool, perhaps an unconscious tool. The real culprits were in France. He was thereupon struck by a scruple about his English pension. He had spoken ill of England and the English; unjustifiably, he now believed. Before he could decently take George III's money, it was his duty to apologise and be assured that he was forgiven. The question was, how was that to be done?

At this point there flits across the stage a mysterious figure, not previously identified. Twice in Rousseau's correspondence passing reference is made to a certain comte de Rochefort. No one has explained who he was, and how he came into the picture; and a reader of the correspondence might be forgiven for assuming that he must have been some French notability whose aid Jean-Jacques had tried, in vain, to enlist. Not a bit of it: 'le comte de Rochefort' was not a Frenchman at all, but an Englishman, the Earl of Rochford, then British ambassador to Versailles. Rochford, the fourth earl, was a professional courtier, diplomat and politician. His grandfather was a Dutchman who had come over with William of Orange (the family name was Nassau de Zuylestein). In July 1766, after a number of other diplomatic posts, he had been appointed Ambassador to Versailles. Frivolous, extravagant and obtuse, he must have been one of the worst we ever had there. For instance, he was completely bamboozled by Choiseul over French intentions in Corsica, and was still sending home soothing assurances at the very moment that the French were landing troops in the Island. In October 1768 he was recalled and appointed Secretary of State for the Northern Department under Grafton. These dates are useful because they help to fix those of two important Rousseau letters which have been lost, though their existence and even their content can now be firmly established. In the first, written no doubt in January or February 1768, he explained that he felt he had done England an injustice by his abrupt departure and by the various harsh things he had said about the country in unguarded moments. He wished to make reparation and begged for an assurance that his apology was accepted. On receiving no answer from Rochford, Rousseau wrote to him again in April, saying that because his apology had been ignored he could no longer accept his pension, though he still felt deep gratitude to the King. Once again, he received neither an acknowledgement nor a reply. There is, of course, no mention of this affair in Rochford's despatches, which are devoted either to long accounts of his pleasant chats with Choiseul or else to the minutiæ of diplomatic etiquette and precedence. And Rochford's private papers have disappeared, since his direct line petered out in illegitimacy. No doubt he dismissed Rousseau's appeals as the gibberish of a time-wasting crank. He himself was shortly to receive a pension of £1000 a year (Public Record Office): and the North papers in the Bodleian show that for the single year 1769–1770 he got through some £13,500, some of it on secret service account, but most of it probably in liquidation of the expenses of his Paris embassy. To such a man, all this fuss over pocketing a mere £100 a year must have seemed quite incomprehensible.

The story leaked out, especially after Rousseau's return to Paris in June 1770, and various kind souls, concerned by Rousseau's poverty, tried to make him change his mind or else to force the money on him, willy nilly. The most spectacular result of these efforts, probably due to Louis Dutens, was that in April 1771 someone brought Rousseau a banker's draft for 6.000 francs, representing three years' arrears, which after a long and tedious wrangle he declined to accept. The aid of Charles Burney was also enlisted about this time,[6] but this attempt too came to nothing, for different reasons. Three or four others, friends or busybodies, intervened at various times, again to no effect. One thing is clear from the scanty official Secret Service and Privy Purse records. Rousseau's pension was never suspended or cancelled. From a document printed in George III's correspondence and other evidence, it is virtually certain that the money went on being transferred to an agent: and the Royal Archives at Windsor show that part at least of the arrears was eventually paid to Thérèse Levasseur after Rousseau's death: one year certainly, and most likely four.

Towards the end of Rousseau's life, a much more sustained attempt to get him to accept his pension was made by some English admirers of his. Brooke Boothby, who had known him at Wootton, visited him in Paris in 1776 and 1777, and was appalled to discover that this elderly couple, one of them infirm, were trying to live on £55 a year, and keep an indispensable maid-servant into the bargain. Rousseau had been obliged to give up copying music, which until then had helped to keep their heads above water. His savings (which in 1767 still amounted to something like 2.000 francs, about £100) had long since melted away. Boothby learned from Rousseau's own lips the story of his dealings with Rochford, and managed to extract from him a promise to accept the pension if Rochford or some other member of the government could be induced to acknowledge Rousseau's apology. Towards the end of December 1777, Brooke Boothby met Patrick Brydone in Lausanne. On hearing the story about Rochford, Brydone, who was then bear-leading Lord North's sons on the Grand Tour, told Boothby that he had more than once heard North say that he wished Rousseau would take the money. Accordingly, Boothby and the second Earl of Harcourt, an enthusiastic disciple of Rousseau's, planned to get North to write a suitable letter. Harcourt was reluctant to approach North direct, as he had kept away from Court since the death of his father, whose memory he fancied the King had slighted. He therefore asked his friend, the second Viscount Palmerston,[7] to do so, in a letter published in 1957 by Mr Brian Connell from a transcript of the original at Broadlands (the letter is misdated by eight years and wrongly attributed to Harcourt's father):

In consequence of the permission you gave me, I now trouble you with a letter about Rousseau, which I fear will appear very tedious because I must necessarily enter into a long detail of his present situation, but Lord North being a good-natured man, as well as a man of letters, when he knows the distress Rousseau labours under, will I doubt not feel glad to do himself the honour of extricating him from them. [. . .].

If you could state these circumstances to Lord North and could prevail on him to take the trouble of only writing two or three lines merely to say that the pension formerly granted should be paid to his order, that he had heard that Rousseau's declining to receive it had arisen only from delicacy, and that his motives for that refusal required no apology, such a letter, my dear Lord, would satisfy completely poor Rousseau's sensibility and be the means of his passing the remainder of his days in ease and comfort. So good a work would be a worthy object of your humanity to exert itself in, and I shall be not a little happy if you can succeed. Should you be able to procure this letter, I have means of getting it conveyed to him. The pension is £100 per annum.

PS. Pray do not let this transaction be made public, as that circumstance would perhaps prevent it being of any use, for a thousand eyes[8] would be told and ridicules given.

Early in 1778, then, Palmerston obligingly took the matter up with Lord North, no doubt verbally, and, strange as it may seem, the Prime Minister actually did write such a letter. He was then immersed in all the difficulties stemming from the war with the American colonists. Burgoyne had capitulated at Saratoga in October 1777, and France was about to enter the war against Britain (6 February 1778). But he still found time to pen a few polite words to soothe Rousseau's feelings. Harcourt thereupon forwarded the letter to Boothby. Boothby wrote to Jean-Jacques several times, but, receiving no reply, sent Rousseau North's letter early in June 1778 by the hand of Sir John Lambert, an Anglo-French banker, as the war with France had made the post unreliable. Unfortunately, Lambert did not set out for Paris immediately, and when he got to the French capital some six weeks later it was too late. Rousseau had collapsed and died on 2 July. The papers were all returned to Boothby, who got North to send £400 to Jean-Jacques's 'widow'. Of the £1200 due to him under the grant, Jean-Jacques had received exactly £50.

V

The last word may perhaps be left to Fanny Burney, who was present in the Drawing-Room at Buckingham Palace when George III rather unexpectedly turned the conversation to Voltaire and Rousseau. Speaking of Voltaire, 'he cried: "I think him a monster, I own it fairly." He next named Rousseau whom he seemed to think of with more favour, though by no means with approbation'. He had heard several anecdotes 'all charging him with savage pride and insolent ingratitude. Here, however, I ventured to interfere; for, as I knew he had had a pension from the King, I could not but wish His Majesty should be informed that he was grateful to him. And as you, my dear father, were my authority, I thought it but common justice to the memory of poor Rousseau to acquaint the King of his personal respect for him—"Some gratitude, sir", said I, "he was not without. When my father was in Paris, which was after Rousseau had been in England, he visited him in his garret, and the first thing he showed him was your Majesty's portrait over his chimney". The King paused a little while on this; but nothing more was said of Rousseau'.

It would be pretentious to add to an anecdote, however extended, anything in the nature of a moral or a conclusion. But perhaps I may be permitted to say just this: One hard fact emerges from this account: Rousseau's disinterestedness, his attachment to his principles. Some commentators may prefer to explain this fact by ascribing to him motives which are not to his credit. But the fact remains a fact, and the commentators' reconstruction of his motives remains conjecture. I have often wondered why such a simple and apparently respectable attitude has given such offence to so many people, both among his contemporaries and since. Perhaps the answer may be, to adapt the words of the poet, 'How smart a lash that fact doth give our conscience'. It is perfectly true that almost everything that Rousseau said or did after 1752 was a direct or oblique reproach to most people. And he aggravated this misdemeanour by his 'holier than thou' attitude: by the assumption, which gradually hardened into an intense conviction, that he was a small, flickering candle-flame of integrity in a dark and wicked world. And of course, he refused to compromise with life. Those who believe that life is essentially a succession of judicious compromises cannot fail to condemn him.

NOTES

1 This paper is a slightly revised version of a talk originally given to the Johnson Society in December 1971. It would have been incongruous to overload the text with a large number of notes and references. Most of the supporting evidence has been or will be printed in my edition of Rousseau's correspondence.

2 At the same time, he drafted a haughty letter to Frederick himself, whom he disliked. It was never sent. The gist of it was incorporated into the letter to Milord Maréchal, as Keith was called.

3 Henry Seymour Conway (1719–1795). He switched the following year to the Northern Department. Hume was on very good terms with him, and became his secretary when William Burke followed the other Rockingham Whigs into opposition (1767).

4 He had been a somewhat incompetent general, and had incurred the anger of George III over the Wilkes affair. His most notable contribution to politics was to propose the repeal of the Stamp Act. He stayed on under Pitt, to the annoyance of the other Rockingham Whigs, and resigned only in January 1768. He did not return to office again until 1782, when he served under Shelburne after the fall of Lord North. Eventually he became a Field Marshal.

5 It should perhaps be explained that by now Keith had recanted his jacobitism, made his peace with George III, no doubt through the good offices of Frederick, and had the attainder repealed and his family estates restored.

6 Burney (who had long been an admirer of Rousseau, and who had translated *Le Devin du Village*) had visited Jean-Jacques in Paris and had been well received.

7 Palmerston, the father of Victoria's Foreign Secretary and Prime Minister, was originally a Rockingham Whig who had occupied minor ministerial office continuously since 1765, in all the various administrations—no mean feat.

8 Perhaps a misreading for 'lyes'.

13

Lesage and the Spanish Tradition: *Gil Blas* as a Picaresque Novel

JENNIFER LONGHURST

Gil Blas de Santillane, although written in French by a French author, seems at first glance a Spanish work, for the setting, the characters, the atmosphere and indeed a large proportion of the actual contents, are all derived from Spain. Since the time of the Renaissance the literary and social life of France had been influenced by Spain, and this influence was perhaps at its greatest at the time Lesage conceived *Gil Blas.* Throughout the seventeenth century, from the time of Rotrou and Pierre Corneille onwards, French dramatists and novelists had looked to Spain for the inspiration and plots of their works, and Lesage began to write in a literary climate which accepted the tradition of translations, adaptations and frank copies of Spanish works.

Lesage's first venture into the world of letters was in the form of a translation from the Greek: *Lettres galantes d'Aristénète* (1695). His next work, five years later, was a translation of some Spanish *comedias,* and for the following thirty-six he was to be working almost continuously on works translated from, based on, or adapted from the Spanish. Of his non-theatrical works only two—*Beauchêne* and *Orlando innamorato*—were not inspired, directly or indirectly, by Spain.[1] Of those works inspired by Spain the longest, and the one to which Lesage devoted many years, is *Gil Blas de Santillane.*

Given the social and literary background of the day, it is not surprising that Lesage should have turned repeatedly to Spain for help in the composition of his works. What is more surprising is that a book written by a man who had never crossed the Pyrenees should be so 'authentic' in details of Spanish life, customs, history and geography that many Spaniards—eminent scholars among them—believed the work to have been written by one of their compatriots, and accused Lesage of translating an unpublished Spanish manuscript and passing it off as his own work.[2] This accusation is doubtless the greatest measure of Lesage's success in his attempt to make the novel seem truly Spanish by constantly reminding the reader of the setting of the book and the nationality of the characters.

The first and most facile method of achieving this local colour is by a sprinkling of Spanish words, words for which Lesage could have easily found a French translation, had he so desired; in fact he sometimes does use the French word too, and we thus find both *Dame*

Léonarde and *Señora Leonarda, écuyer* and *escudero*. There are other Spanish words of which an exact rendering would be more difficult—*olla podrida, picaro, gracioso*—but these are in the minority. When Lesage uses Spanish words it is usually because he wishes to introduce a Spanish note in an essentially French text, rather than because the Spanish content renders a French version difficult. Wherever possible he gives the characters their Spanish titles: *alguazil, alcalde, apuntador, corregidor, señor caballero, licenciado*. The surnames which Lesage gives his characters also add to the general Spanish effect; yet so many of them are either rather commonplace—Rodríguez, Martínez etc.—or comically appropriate to the person's trade—a doctor is called Sangrado, a pickpocket is called Buenagarra, a grocer is called Muescada—that they merely serve to make the work seem self-consciously Spanish.

A more authentic note is struck whenever Lesage has occasion to introduce references to Spanish institutions and traditions, and Gil Blas's dealings with *alguaziles* and *corregidores* show that Lesage was conversant with the duties of both officials, and many more besides. Two other aspects of the novel contribute to the Spanish background, one siting the story in space, the other in time. On the physical plane, Spain is present in the itineraries followed by Gil Blas and his companions, for Lesage gives precise and accurate details of every journey made, telling us exactly where his hero rested and where he stopped to eat. The lists of successive towns and villages on Gil Blas's route as he travels through the Peninsula make the reader acutely aware that the scene is Spain. When he is settled in one town for any length of time the main buildings and districts of the city take over to some extent the role of maintaining the reader's awareness of the Spanish context, but in effect the background becomes much less obtrusive, and it is all too easy, despite the liberal sprinkling of Spanish vocabulary, to forget that the novel does not take place in France.

There are constant evocations of Spanish history in the novel, with references to specific historical events which help us to work out the chronology of Gil Blas's life.[3] The accuracy of the historical details was in fact one of the main pieces of evidence used by those who claimed *Gil Blas* to be a Spanish work, and it is these details, rather than the superficial use of Spanish words in the text, that strengthen the illusion that the story takes place in Spain.

It is obvious therefore that in writing *Gil Blas* Lesage made a conscious effort to produce a novel with a strongly Spanish ambience and flavour; but was he also trying to write a work that continued the picaresque tradition? And if this really was his aim, how far did he succeed? The critics have widely diverging views on this point.

Charles Dédéyan has no doubts at all:

Nous devons nous arrêter au roman picaresque, en retracer les origines, le développement, l'évolution et l'influence, pour mieux comprendre ce qu'a voulu faire Lesage en écrivant *Gil Blas*.[4]

That *Gil Blas* is a picaresque novel is for him so much of a foregone conclusion that he makes little attempt to prove or illustrate his belief, merely contenting himself with re-asserting that

Nous sommes avec *Gil Blas* dans la tradition picaresque du *Lazarillo,* tant par le héros que par la philosophie qui se dégage de cette existence mouvementée.[5]

R. Laufer, on the other hand, who has equally strong views on the subject, denies that *Gil Blas* has anything in common with the Spanish picaresque tradition:

Lazarillo, Guzmán, le Buscón, Marcos de Obregón, Estebanillo González se sont confondus en un seul personnage, ni bâtard, ni chrétien, ni sage, ni bouffon, qui, né petit-bourgeois de province, apprend à connaître le monde, s'élève par ses talents de rédacteur aux premiers emplois dans les ministères et finit ses jours châtelain de village, anobli, opulent, vénérable.[6]

Stuart Miller shares Laufer's views, and concludes: 'I have shown that *Gil Blas* is not a picaresque novel.'[7] But if it is not picaresque, why then did he include it as one of the eight 'classic examples of the picaresque' in a work entitled *The Picaresque Novel*?[8] It is not altogether clear on what grounds Miller bases his conclusions, for he seems to contradict himself on occasion, saying, for example, that *Gil Blas* shows 'fundamental modifications of the usual picaresque plot and pattern'[9] whilst earlier he had asserted that 'those countervailing plot patterns that we find do not substantially change the tone of the picaresque.'[10]

Miller, like Laufer, has excluded *Gil Blas* from the picaresque genre on the basis of its non-conformity with features found in certain picaresque novels (e.g. the illegitimate origins of the protagonist), whilst ignoring the fact that not all Spanish picaresque novels conform to all the criteria that have been applied *a posteriori* to the genre by later critics. A genre is not after all a set of rigid rules; it is a literary convention and has the flexibility of all conventions. Furthermore, a genre must necessarily undergo changes if it is to develop at all, and to insist that any deviation from the norm automatically excludes a work from a genre is to kill the possibility of development and originality within that genre.

This view of a fluid and continually developing genre appears to be held by A. A. Parker; for him, Lesage, in writing *Gil Blas,* has not opted out of the picaresque tradition but merely extended it in a new direction, so that it fosters 'the aristocratic cult of propriety, decorum and social gentility in literature.'[11] Parker enumerates the various aspects of the novel which have undergone changes at Lesage's hands, and attributes them to Lesage's acceptance of eighteenth-century values and his application of these values in the life he allows his fictional creation to lead. With this assertion I cannot but agree, but must reject the conclusion drawn from these facts, namely that 'the originality of Lesage within his tradition is only a descent to the superficial and commonplace.'[12] What I shall attempt to show in this paper, therefore, is, firstly, that *Gil Blas* is a picaresque novel, and secondly, that it has its own value within the picaresque stream.

One cannot assert categorically that Lesage set out with the intention of writing a picaresque novel; one can see, however, that he intended to create a novel in which picaresque elements would not seem out of place, for he included in *Gil Blas* a considerable amount of material derived directly from specific Spanish picaresque novels.

The *Lazarillo de Tormes* is not a fecund source, although there are a couple of reminiscences of the *Lazarillo* to be found in *Gil Blas*. On the whole there are vague similarities to be perceived, especially in Scipion's tale, where the same atmosphere is evoked. Lesage's debt to *Guzmán de Alfarache* is slender, too; perhaps he did not want to spoil the effect of his own translation of the book.[13] In general terms there are nevertheless many similarities between Gil Blas and Guzmán: both are determined to make their way in life, and start by directing their steps to Salamanca; their fortunes vary between being servants and acting as confidants to various important people; as their fortunes change, so do the company they keep and the women they court. Each has a devoted if somewhat roguish servant. Yet despite these similarities only one episode in *Gil Blas* would seem to be derived directly from Alemán's novel. Guzmán, whilst in Italy, tricks a Cardinal into taking pity on him and introducing him into his household. Here he has the chance of abandoning the picaresque life and settling down to honest work as a servant. He rejects this opportunity and exploits the Cardinal's kindness in order to steal from him. In *Gil Blas*, Scipion similarly and fraudently inspires pity in an archbishop and becomes a fortunate member of a happy household. Yet a life of security does not appeal to him, and he invents and executes an outrageous trick which robs his benefactor of valuable jewellery.

La pícara Justina, the first picaresque novel with a female protagonist, is of considerable interest to students of *Gil Blas.* The basic characters of both Camille and Laure can be seen in Justina, but the main interest lies in the fact that this book, like Lesage's novel, is set in the immediate entourage of Rodrigo Calderón and his master the Duke of Lerma. What is more, it is a *roman à clef,* many characters being thinly disguised portraits of members of high society and the court circle of the time. It is a pity that we do not know if Lesage was aware of these allusions to contemporary society; he had, however, already shown in *Le Diable boiteux* that he realized the satirical possibilities of including such characters in a novel.

La vida del buscón, with its distorted realism and grotesque caricatures, would seem to have little in common with *Gil Blas.* Yet the life of Raphaël, and more particularly his attitude and outlook on life, is very much akin to that of Pablos de Segovia—that of a rogue who both delights and takes pride in his trickery. Pablos's feelings of insecurity constantly lead him to seek praise as a reassurance of his superior abilities. Gil Blas, too, is sometimes motivated by a desire for praise, for example when he reveals to Don Gonzale Pacheco the ruses of his mistress Eufrasia.

Lesage had obviously read the picaresque novels of Castillo Solórzano, for we can easily find characters and episodes reminiscent of these works in *Gil Blas.* In *Las aventuras del bachiller Trapaza,* for example, the relationship between Trapaza and Eufrasia is similar to that of Gil Blas and Laure, with the girl appearing and disappearing throughout the story, at times abetting the protagonist in his schemes, and bearing him an illegitimate daughter. The book which relates the adventures of this daughter, *La garduña de Sevilla,* suggested several episodes to Lesage, including the one involving the Alchemist, but above all there is the false hermit who hides robbers in his cave and whose adventures are closely paralleled by Raphaël and Ambroise in their hermit's cave.

Of the Spanish picaresque novels, one had more influence on *Gil Blas* than the rest combined: Vicente Espinel's semi-autobiographical work *Marcos de Obregón.* Lesage's contemporaries realized this, and at first *Gil Blas* was dismissed as a mere translation from the Spanish, or at best a fairly close adaptation. While it is now recognized that *Gil Blas* is not a translation, the fact remains that *Marcos de Obregón* formed a not inconsiderable source of material for Lesage. The main episodes of *Gil Blas* taken from Espinel's work are:

1. The Prologue.
2. The beggar who persuades Gil Blas to give him alms by threatening him with a gun.
3. The fellow-traveller at the inn who, by flattery, tricks Gil Blas into paying for his meal.
4. The trick played by the muleteer to disperse the male travellers so that he can seduce the young bride.
5. The robbers' underground hideout.
6. The trick played on Gil Blas in the *hôtel garni* by Camille, Raphaël and Ambroise.
7. Raphaël's kidnapping and his adventures in Barbary.
8. The story of the *garçon barbier* and Doña Mergelina.

These incidents directly derived from *Marcos de Obregón* form almost one-eighth of Lesage's novel. While this represents a substantial amount of material, considering the length of *Gil Blas,* it is by no means the major part of the work—far more is *not* derived from *Marcos de Obregón.* Yet the influence of Espinel's work is perhaps even greater than is apparent. The prologue, containing as it does advice from Lesage, colours the reader's whole attitude to the book, and his reaction to what he reads; it thus plays a capital role in the reader's interpretation of the work.

The next five episodes, from the false beggar to the adventure in the *hôtel garni,* are important steps in the development of the character of Gil Blas. They mark, in fact, his passing from childhood to adulthood. When he leaves home he is naïvely optimistic about his chances of success in the world; his various encounters dispel his illusions one by one, until at the end he says:

Je me serais alors défié de la chaste Suzanne (p. 557),

and a little later he is more explicit:

De sage et posé que j'étais auparavant, je devins vif, étourdi, turlupin (p. 650).

Determined to trust only himself, he is at last mentally equipped to survive in the rough world in which circumstances have placed him. He realizes, when falsely imprisoned for brigandage, that life does not follow moral laws. One can be punished or rewarded without having deserved either:

Malgré mon innocence, je serai peut-être trop heureux de sortir d'ici pour aller aux galères (p. 540).

There are therefore no absolute values; the most important considerations are to survive, at the expense of others if necessary, and to avoid being preyed upon by fellow men. The best thing to be is not honest but *débrouillard.* Up to this point Gil Blas has been the *trompé.* He has learnt a hard lesson and now becomes the *trompeur.* This volte-face in his attitude to life has come about as a direct result of the experiences Lesage adopted from *Marcos de Obregón.*

Of the other two episodes taken from *Marcos de Obregón,* Raphaël's story is useful in that it provides elements which were popular ingredients of the novel at that period: pirates, kidnapping, slavery in North Africa, *reconnaissances,* etc. Had this material not been readily available in *Marcos de Obregón* it is quite probable that Lesage would have invented

K

it—*Le Diable boiteux,* for example, introduced all these themes. The story of the *garçon barbier* provided a good opportunity for the introduction of local colour in the running of a Spanish household, with *escuderos, dueñas,* guitar serenades and the like. It is also, in Lesage, a fairly interesting, psychologically motivated story. The inclusion of this tale as part of the life-story of Fabrice also served to lengthen the book, and Lesage, being one of a new generation of novelists who were paid according to the amount they wrote, was always anxious to increase the length of his novels.[14] It is evident that Lesage derived much benefit from his reading of *Marcos de Obregón,* and he had cause to be grateful to Espinel.

Apart from these specific borrowings from particular works, in *Gil Blas* Lesage conserved many of the traditional aspects of the Spanish picaresque novel, or at any rate elements which are common to a great many of them. Of the traditional elements of the Spanish picaresque, one of the more easily recognized is the concentration of the action and the interest upon one character, the picaro. In the majority of picaresque novels the name of the protagonist figures prominently in the title, indicating his importance as an individual rather than as a member of any group.[15] In *Gil Blas* there is not so much attention focused on the protagonist as in the other picaresque works, for he is not always either acting in the episodes or directly involved in their outcome, but spends instead quite some time listening to the life-histories of characters whom he meets. This is a technique whereby Lesage forges links between two forms of narrative which remain separate in several Spanish novels: the main narrative and intercalated tales. There are of course many more intercalated tales here than in any Spanish picaresque novel (*Guzmán de Alfarache,* the longest of the Spanish novels, has four), but the precedent is there for Lesage to follow. An attempt is made to integrate the interpolated tales into the main plot by making the protagonists of the tales also characters in *Gil Blas* who relate their own story. On occasions Gil Blas himself moves into the plot of the intercalated novel, as when he rescues Don Alphonse's fiancée. Miller says that in such instances 'the romance and picaresque worlds become subtly fused,'[16] but this is not really so: we abandon the picaresque world on entering the world of the intercalated novel. They remain separate but contiguous, and the characters can move from the romantic sphere into the picaresque sphere and back again. Despite the sidetracking of the reader's attention, Gil Blas remains the main character, for the interest is not diffused on a group of characters throughout the work, but is merely diverted from the hero for a short period, returning to focus on him again with an intensity often heightened by the suspense engendered by the waiting period.

The Spanish picaro is usually left to fend for himself at a relatively early age, and from then on has to live off his own wits. He may be forced to do this because his parents abandon him, or he may leave home by chance to better his living conditions or his prospects, as did Guzmán, Marcos and after them Gil Blas. Gil Blas is not forced to make his own living as soon as he leaves home, for he is sent out well provided with money, but when he is left destitute after his spell in prison it does not occur to him to return home for help. Instead he sets out to make his own way in life as best he can. There has certainly been no preparation in his upbringing for the way of life he now has to lead, and in this respect he is at a disadvantage compared with those Spanish picaros who came from impoverished or even dishonest families and had therefore had ample opportunity to learn from their parents' example.

Gil Blas is fortunate, however, in that his character and manners commend him to people he meets, who are therefore often willing to help or protect him. His *entrée* to employment is nearly always by recommendation, and recommendation not usually by someone who has known him all his life, but by someone who has met him lately and been impressed by his merits. The Spanish picaro, from an early age, had to stand on his own two feet and learn to rely on no-one but himself. Gil Blas, on the contrary, is never left destitute and alone with no-one to help him, or left to cope with a situation that is beyond his control. The help he receives may be minimal, as when the *chantre* gives him a very small amount of money to enable him to travel to Burgos, but it solves his immediate problems. The Spanish picaros would have been overjoyed had their problems been solved as easily as are those of Gil Blas, though it would be true to say that they too benefit from an occasional helping hand.

Social snobbery is also a marked picaresque trait, and Gil Blas is no exception to the rule. The picaro usually springs from a humble or even criminal background, a background of which he is sometimes bitterly ashamed.[17] Denial of his origins is expressed when Pablos writes to his uncle: 'No pregunte por mí, ni me nombre, porque me importa negar la sangre que tenemos'.[18] Gil Blas similarly makes no attempt to contact his parents once he has achieved some measure of success, and is extremely embarrassed when he is visited by someone from his village. When finally he goes to visit his parents, and his mother relates her life, he says:

Elle [. . .] me dit [. . .] une infinité de choses que je n'aurais pas été bien aise que mon secrétaire eût entendues, quoique je n'eusse rien de caché pour lui (p. 1033).

A concomitant of the picaro's rejection of his origins is his desire to become a member of the nobility, a desire finally achieved by Gil Blas. But long before this, he twice disguises himself as a nobleman, thus following in the footsteps of both Guzmán and Pablos. Both set themselves up as members of the aristocracy whenever their finances permit it, but the money runs out too quickly, or else they are unmasked by a former acquaintance. The picara is no less inclined to seek social standing—Teresa de Manzanares, having abandoned her profession of actress and high-class prostitute (the two usually went hand in hand), uses her money to elevate herself to the upper classes, but is recognized by a former theatrical colleague. (In some ways both her career and her aspirations are mirrored by those of Laure in *Gil Blas*.) The Spanish picaro, when playing the nobleman, is aware that he is in fact of a lower class, mainly because the fear of discovery is always with him. For Gil Blas things go differently, and there comes a point in his life when he truly believes himself to be socially superior to most other people. When Scipion arranges for him a marriage with the daughter of a wealthy goldsmith, he says:

La fille d'un orfèvre! [. . .] as-tu perdu l'esprit? Peux-tu me proposer une bourgeoise? Quand on a un certain mérite, et qu'on est à la cour sur un certain pied, il me semble qu'on doit avoir des vues plus élevées (p. 981).

Gil Blas has faithfully followed his Spanish predecessors in aspiring to join the nobility;

the difference is that the Spanish picaros are not allowed to succeed, whereas Lesage permits his hero to become a real aristocrat with *lettres de noblesse* to prove it.

Throughout the novel Gil Blas changes from one master to another, serving them in a variety of roles, from scullion to intendant. His masters are continually changing as for one reason or another he is forced to leave. Only rarely is the change of master made by a voluntary decision on his part, because he does not like the position or feels he could do better elsewhere. Some external event forces his hand and leaves him with but one course of action to follow, or at best little choice in the matter. Of his earliest masters, Sedillo dies, he leaves Doctor Sangrado when threatened by a man whose fiancée had died in his care, the squire dismisses him for befriending unsavoury characters, and the *petit-maître* is killed in a duel. He does leave the actress voluntarily, in a moment of moral revolt against the way of life she leads, but his next master dismisses him, and he is forced to leave the Marquise de Chaves by the threats of a jealous rival. One of the basic elements in the vast majority of picaresque novels is precisely the existence not of one master but of a series of masters, and so in this respect *Gil Blas* conforms to the main trend of the genre.

Closely linked to the continual changing from one master to another is the peripatetic existence traditionally adopted by the Spanish picaro. He moves not only horizontally, that is on a geographical plane, but also vertically, associating to varying degrees and for varying lengths of time with different strata of society. On leaving home, Gil Blas's goal is Salamanca, but for this he soon substitutes Madrid, which then becomes the base to which he returns after his stays in other cities in Spain. On his travels around Spain he covers quite a large amount of territory, taking in Burgos, Valladolid, Salamanca, Valencia, Granada, Segovia, Oviedo and Toledo, as well as many smaller places.

Gil Blas, like the Spanish picaro, also moves through the different levels of society. He associates with all classes of people from robbers and thieves to dukes. The number of different types of people he meets and lives with is quite extensive, covering all types of servants and employees, various ecclesiastical offices, a doctor and different echelons of nobility. He differs from the Spanish picaros in one respect, in that he tends to associate with the upper classes more freely than they are able to, but the basic pattern of moving from milieu to milieu is the same.

All the Spanish picaros, at some time or other during their picaresque careers and to a varying extent, have recourse to subterfuge. For some, especially the girl picaras, it is the main source of their livelihood; for others it is something to be used when circumstances demand it. Gil Blas's first incursion into illegality is made unwillingly, when he accompanies a band of robbers on an expedition, but he subsequently steals with no apparent qualms of guilt. In this first section of the work, in which Gil Blas's life-style is perhaps more typically picaresque than later, his acts of dishonesty, although not infrequent, are usually of a fairly minor nature. Most of his crimes could be described as petty—he cheats Sangrado out of some of the fees, steals clothing from the *petit-maître,* and keeps quiet when the intendant Rodríguez cheats his master. When Gil Blas's crimes are of a more adventurous nature, he is never the instigator; he merely falls in with plans made by some acquaintance. Fabrice invents the ruse whereby they steal the jewellery and candlesticks from Camille and her companion; Ambroise conceives the plan for tricking Samuel Simon, and it is Laure who claims Gil Blas to be her brother, thereby allowing him to live at the expense of the Marqués de Marialva. The only audacious plan Gil Blas forms and executes all on his own is his escape from the robber's cave.

During this period of his life, Gil Blas's activities are on occasion illegal, but his crimes are usually relatively minor, with a few exceptions, and he does not benefit greatly from them. Once he becomes the confidential secretary of the Duc de Lerme, *privado* of Philip III, new vistas of dishonesty are opened up to him. Once again, Gil Blas himself does not realize what opportunities he has to make money, and it is his master who suggests that he should accept bribes for favours requested. But once Gil Blas realizes how easily money can be made in this way, he becomes extremely greedy. During this period of his life, Gil Blas's dishonest practices are on a very large scale and earn him enormous profits. It is questionable whether his actions are technically illegal, for he never misappropriates State funds, and paying for favours and offices was a common procedure at the time. This may well be social satire on the part of Lesage, showing how his hero can make a great deal of money by practices that are ethically wrong, yet not actually illegal. Gil Blas's dishonesty, because of this technicality, is not on the same plane as that of Pablos or Guzmán, yet morally he sinks to a low pitch; many of his actions mirror theirs, but in a higher sphere of society, with deceit playing a prominent part in the majority of his activities.

An important prerequisite of the picaresque novel is that it should be realistic. Realism, when associated with the picaresque, has often been understood to mean reality at its harshest and most cruel, but the fact is that many picaros at some time or other during their careers live very comfortably; several are even successful in the material sphere, and they are therefore not continually subjected to all the rigours of life. So whilst for many picaros poverty and hardship loom large, these are not rigid and unchanging characteristics of the picaresque novel. Realism can therefore, in the context of the picaresque novel, have two meanings: firstly, the rejection of romantic ideals, and secondly, the absence of supernatural devices. The picaresque novel was originally conceived as the antithesis of the sentimental novel, and as such it expresses a reaction against those unrealistic themes and concepts which are so often found in pastoral novels and novels of chivalry. Lesage makes no deliberate attempt to dissociate his novel completely from the traditions and conventions of the past, for as we have seen, the romantic intercalated novels are to a certain extent integrated into the main text. These sections form but a minor part of the work as a whole, however, and Lesage avoids the extravagances and extremes that are to be found in the more exotic novels. Nowhere in the plot does Lesage have recourse to the supernatural or the fantastic. Magic devices which resolve a section of the action; fairytale adventures with giants, wood-nymphs and the like; coincidences so improbable as to border on the marvellous—these should not be present in any work with claims to reality, and Lesage has rejected them all in writing *Gil Blas*. Both fantasy and the supernatural being completely absent from the work, there is no incident which makes the reader doubt the validity of the basic fictional situation, that is, that Gil Blas is relating the events of his life as they really happened. In addition to the realism of the content, the setting too is realistic, located in a precisely defined area rather than in some imaginary kingdom, and in this, too, Lesage follows the example of the Spanish picaresque authors.

Fate and Fortune often play a fairly considerable role in the traditional picaresque novels. The picaro himself is ruled by Fate, or at least there is evidence of some unpredictable exterior influence on his life. Moreover, the picaro is aware of the extent to which he is at the mercy of Fate and accepts philosophically those sudden reversals of fortune which may result. Gil Blas, like his predecessors in the picaresque tradition, would seem to be governed by Fate on occasion; at least that is his explanation for many of the events in his life which run contrary to his expectations:

Mais la destinée que j'avais à remplir ne me permit pas de faire un plus long séjour dans la maison de cette dame (p. 750).
Mais le ciel disposa de nous autrement (p. 843).

Fate can thus play an important part in the plot structure of the novel, initiating new episodes and closing episodes whose novelistic value has been exploited to the full. It can thereby lend an air of suspense to the novel, as the reader is aware that anything might happen at any time, that the relative security or penury of the hero is not to be regarded as permanent, for Fate will always intervene in the course of events and add a new impetus to the tale.

The plot structure of the Spanish picaresque novels tends to follow a well-defined pattern closely allied to the wanderings of the picaro himself. This typically picaresque structure, the *roman à tiroirs,* is essentially fragmented, the work being divided into a succession of episodes which have no apparent causal connection and do not serve to illustrate a single specific theme. (*Guzmán de Alfarache,* if one accepts the view that it contains a religious thesis, comes closest to being monothematic, but the plot structure itself still remains episodic). Usually the various episodes and tales of the novel are linked only by the presence and the character of the hero. In Lesage's novel, this structure is a faithful reflection of the life of Gil Blas himself, which is not a steady progression towards any one goal, but rather an endless series of new beginnings. In general, these new beginnings occur when Gil Blas takes up new employment, and each successive episode thus usually involves entering some new milieu. The people with whom he is in contact at any point in his life have no relation to those he knew formerly, the only stable and constant element throughout being the presence of the protagonist. His life is thus a series of connecting boxes: he leaves one to enter the next, and finds himself cut off from his past life. There may be reminders of what has passed as former acquaintances cross his path again, but rarely does he make any attempt to retain any connection with his past.

In many Spanish picaresque novels the structure is so loose, and there is often so little justification for the arrangement of the episodes as found in the work, that the chronology could be disturbed by the re-arrangement of the episodes without causing undue disruption of the work as a whole, or depriving a particular event of any significance. In *Guzmán de Alfarache* and *La vida del buscón,* however, one can easily detect a measure of conscious planning on the part of the author in so far as the development of the character of the protagonist is concerned. Although the episodes themselves may in many cases offer no particular reason for their chronology, there are nevertheless stages in the psychological development of the hero: in his awareness, his reactions, his outlook. In *Gil Blas* we find three separate cycles of episodes corresponding to the three stages of development of Gil Blas's character. The first cycle, that of the 'innocent' Gil Blas, ends with his stay in prison in Astorga, when he realizes that there is very little justice in life. The second cycle, that of the 'picaresque' Gil Blas, is also closed by a prison sentence, for it is his imprisonment in the tower of Segovia that decides him to renounce the life of luxury and amorality that he had been living and return to the country. The final cycle is that of the 'reformed' Gil Blas, and stretches until the end of the book.[19] Although there can be no interchange of episodes between these cycles, because of the psychological inconsistencies that would result, within any one cycle the episodes could be re-arranged to a certain extent, for they are very loosely knit. There is, in the novel as a whole, no definite progression to a logical dénouement. In each episode the action is complete in itself and therefore has its own individual dénouement; we cannot, however, assign each episode to a specific place in the plan of the whole novel because there is no overall plan to which individual episodes are subordinated. There is, in the second cycle, a certain progression to be seen, for Gil Blas rises in status as he moves from post to post, but there is little interdependence between any two actions, with few episodes relying on events in a previous episode to motivate their action. Since there emerges no mysterious order or coincidence to bind the events together and bring them to a definite conclusion, the work, from the point of view of the action, becomes no more than a record of fragmented happenings. The novel is thus open-ended and, like so many of the Spanish picaresque works, could be continued at the author's will. For a book such as this, with the traditional structure of the picaresque novel, the only definitive conclusion can be the death of the picaro; as long as he is alive there always remains the possibility that he may set out again and continue his adventures. Many of the Spanish picaresque novels ended with the promise of a sequel, which was on occasion written by a different author, and Lesage himself wrote two sequels to *Gil Blas*, for the first version contained only the first six *livres*. Death as an ending would in any case be highly problematical in a first-person narrative.

The influences, both direct and indirect, of the Spanish picaresque on *Gil Blas* may be detected in the various aspects which I have outlined, yet there are other aspects which cannot be explained purely in terms of Spanish predecessors. Whilst adopting many of the techniques of the Spanish picaresque novel and adhering to the mainstream of the genre, *Gil Blas* nevertheless contains some deviations and innovations which show that Lesage was not intending to produce a mere replica of the Spanish novels, but was also concerned with adapting it to his conception of contemporary French taste, thereby adding a new dimension to the classification.

The typical Spanish picaro is a child of poor and usually dishonest parents, who is sent out into the world at an early age to fend for himself. This description is by no means applicable to Gil Blas, for his parents, while being relatively poor, are honest, and they are certainly not members of the very lowest classes of society—his mother was a *petite-bourgeoise* and his father was employed as an *écuyer*. Instead of his parents abandoning him to the mercy of the world as soon as they possibly could, Gil Blas was brought up carefully; he was taught first by his uncle, then by 'le docteur Godinez, qui passait pour le plus habile pédant d'Oviedo' (p. 498). The *écuyer* and his wife obviously tried to do their best for their child, and his education included instruction in Greek, Latin, logic and rhetoric. Few of the picaros had any schooling, but in many ways the upbringing and education received by Gil Blas are very reminiscent of those of Marcos de Obregón, which only confirms Lesage's debt to Espinel's work.

In most of the Spanish picaresque novels, we are shown mainly, but not exclusively, the very lowest strata of society. The bourgeoisie is only infrequently met, and as for the upper classes, they are barely glimpsed. Fleeting contact with the nobility is sometimes made when the picaro manages to pass himself off temporarily as a gentleman—Pablos courting Doña Ana is an obvious example. On the whole, however, the emphasis is laid on the lower classes—thieves, prostitutes, beggars, servants and students.

Gil Blas follows the example of his Spanish predecessors by moving between different milieux and social classes, but he does not, as do the Spanish picaros, spend most of his time with the lower classes. Indeed, contacts with the dregs of society are rather the exception, since Gil Blas quickly gains employment in noble households. Moreover, when we do meet the lower classes, we are shown the least sordid aspects of their life, in striking contrast to the emphasis laid by the Spanish picaresque authors on the harsher side of life. The robbers are not wearing rags, but are dressed magnificently, and eat and drink very well; the servants are not half-starving and ill-treated, for they falsify the account books so that they eat only the best. Peasants and actors are also shown living well and enjoying themselves. Lesage paints the lower classes at moments when their luck is running high, never when they are down and out. Some Spanish novels, notably *Guzmán de Alfarache, La vida del buscón* and *Estebanillo González,* quite clearly paint an unduly bleak picture by overstressing and exaggerating the more sordid features of society. Lesage moves in precisely the opposite direction.

In *Gil Blas* the view of society is wider than in the Spanish novels, with the emphasis on the upper strata, although the picture, like that in the Spanish novels, is not a flattering one. But there are two important differences between the Spanish picaro's view of high society and Gil Blas's view. The first difference is that Gil Blas is always actively involved in each of the environments described, he is not merely looking at them from the outside, longingly. The second point is that, within the particular scene, he is usually placed where it is possible for him to be fully aware of all that is happening to the heads of the household. Within society, the emphasis is on the higher ranks; within a particular house, we usually learn more of the activities of the master than of those of the servants.

Gil Blas is in many respects a lucky picaro because he obtains the material and social success that his Spanish predecessors only dreamt of. Despite the setbacks which are a consequence of the influence of Fate on his life, he rises throughout his career. Indeed his very setbacks always turn out to be fortunate, for if he loses money he suddenly acquires a much larger sum, and if he loses his job, the next job is much better. Throughout his life he always finds protectors and helpers, unlike the Spanish picaro, who for most of the time had to cope single-handed with the blows of Fate. His masters are of increasing social status:

he begins by serving robbers and ends by serving Olivares. Not only are his masters of increasing importance, Gil Blas's own position rises in successive households, from scullion to private secretary. On his final return to Court his social standing would seem to be no higher than previously, but he has advanced on the moral plane. For Gil Blas progresses not only materially but morally too, and this is yet another innovation brought by Lesage to the picaresque tradition. Gil Blas is thus differentiated from the Spanish picaros by being a reformed picaro. It is true that Guzmán de Alfarache also decides to renounce his former evil life, thus illustrating the religious thesis of the work that man can choose to conquer evil; we are not, however, told anything of his new, righteous, life, for the book ends with his renunciation. Gil Blas is the only picaro whom we see in action after his decision to leave the picaresque way of life. This is not a moral decision based on religious teachings, since it involves only a decision to renounce court life and retire to the country. Nevertheless, this decision marks the watershed in his life because it is the philosophical attitude to life engendered by simple pastoral pleasures together with philosophical readings which brings about the change in his moral outlook and the consequent new way of life that can only be conjectured in the case of Guzmán.[20]

Gil Blas differs also from his Spanish predecessors in that he, unlike them, escapes from the social class into which he is born. The Spanish picaro tries to make himself into a gentleman but invariably fails, whereas Gil Blas is allowed to succeed. The Spanish picaro is never a true gentleman, he merely manages to assume the outward appearance of one for a period of time, and his fear of being unmasked shows that he is aware of the falsity of his position. He strives for social recognition and longs to enjoy the comforts of a life of ease, seemingly unaware that there are other aspects to a noble life. The Spanish authors condemn this superficial concept of nobility and take steps to ensure that the picaro's aims are frustrated. Gil Blas, on the contrary, is made to acquire the mind and attributes of a gentleman. He receives a classical education, is well versed in literary matters and has a taste for philosophical reading, these being some of the qualities which render him mentally fitted to take his place with gentlemen as an equal. Because he is psychologically a gentleman, he is eventually permitted to become one socially, and the final seal of approval is thus set on his new status when the king presents him with his *lettres de noblesse*.

In conclusion, one must say that *Gil Blas* is undoubtedly a picaresque novel, for the author made a conscious effort to include those elements which traditionally were part of the life of the picaro, and the work thereby conforms to the main conventions of the genre. At an early age the protagonist is forced to fend for himself, relying entirely on his own wits to earn his living. Trickery plays an important part in his early struggle to make his way in life. Gil Blas adopts a peripatetic existence, moving freely both horizontally through Spain and vertically through society. Closely allied to these wanderings is the structure of the book, the plot being essentially both episodic and open-ended, thus allowing for the possibility of a continuation. The novel is realistic in the sense that it is strictly non-fantastic, the author never having recourse to the supernatural in order to develop or resolve an element in the plot. Fate plays a large part in the life of the protagonist, and he is constantly blown hither and thither by events over which he seemingly has little control. In its realism, in its episodic-type plot, in its emphasis on the effect of Fate, and in a host of other details, *Gil Blas* is a close relative of the Spanish picaresque novel.

At the same time as he accepts these conventions and makes use of them in his work, Lesage also moves with flexibility within the accepted formula, so as to incorporate certain innovatory features. Socially, Gil Blas moves on a higher plane than the Spanish picaros, firstly because he does not spring from a sordid background, secondly because throughout the work the emphasis is mainly on the upper echelons of society, and finally because Gil Blas himself becomes a nobleman. His dishonest activities rise in status with him, and his vices are those of a courtier. Despite this, he is morally superior in that he makes a decision to reform, and carries through that reform successfully. The ideals of Gil Blas are those of an eighteenth-century gentleman, his final aim being not to amass as many riches as possible, but rather to live as an *honnête homme* and achieve happiness. He is above all a lucky picaro, not only because of the social and material success he achieves at the end of the novel, but because, though at the mercy of events, things always turn out well for him and he always finds benefactors and protectors.

I cannot agree with Professor Parker that *Gil Blas* reveals only a superficial and common-place version of the picaresque. Rather than an attempt to tone down the less acceptable aspects of Spanish picaresque novels, the innovations in *Gil Blas* are the product of the positive philosophy of optimism and happy fate that was beginning to emerge in eighteenth-century France. This roseate view pervades the whole work: not only the life of the protagonist, but also the life of other characters, so that we are shown by and large only the brighter side of things and events, and there is less interest in the life of the underdog. From this optimistic philosophy there springs directly the author's attitude to his protagonist. The Spanish picaresque author disapproved of his hero, was opposed to his every aspiration and therefore condemned him to failure in all spheres. In *Gil Blas*, Lesage feels sympathy both for the protagonist and for his aims, and therefore allows him to succeed, to rise socially, morally, and materially. The aims of Gil Blas are on the whole markedly similar to those of the Spanish picaros; Lesage, by his sympathetic attitude towards his protagonist, makes of Gil Blas a fulfilled picaro.

NOTES

1 The non-theatrical works based on Spanish texts are: *Don Quichotte* (1704), *Le Diable boiteux* (1707), *Gil Blas* (1715–35), *Don Guzmán d'Alfarache* (1732), *Estevanille Gonzalès* (1734) and *Le Bachelier de Salamanque* (1736).
2 For a summary of the 'question de *Gil Blas*' see F. Cordasco, 'Llorente and the originality of *Gil Blas*', in *Philological Quarterly*, 26 (1947), 206–18.
3 For example, 1621: 'On dit que Philippe III ne vit plus, et que le prince son fils est sur le trône'; 1640: mention is made of the revolt of the Catalans. See *Gil Blas* in *Romanciers du XVIIIe siècle*, Bibliothèque de la Pléiade (Paris, 1966), Vol. I, p. 1113 and p. 1179. All subsequent references to *Gil Blas* are to this edition.
4 *Lesage et Gil Blas* (Paris, 1965), p. 53.
5 ibid., p. 507.
6 *Lesage ou le métier de romancier* (Paris, 1971), p. 14.
7 *The Picaresque Novel* (Cleveland, 1967), p. 132.

8 ibid., p. 4.

9 ibid., p. 50.

10 ibid., p. 10.

11 *Literature and the Delinquent* (Edinburgh, 1967), p. 121.

12 ibid., p. 125.

13 Yet he did not hesitate to borrow extensively from *Gil Blas* when writing *Le Bachelier de Salamanque*.

14 The second version of *Le Diable boiteux* in 1726 was nearly twice as long as the first, mainly because Lesage added a large number of intercalated novelettes.

15 One of the reasons why the *Roman comique* and the *Roman bourgeois* can be excluded from the picaresque is that the emphasis is on a group of people rather than on an individual.

16 op. cit., p. 18.

17 It is not true, however, as Laufer says (op. cit., p. 12), that all Spanish picaros are bastards. It is partly on this mistaken assertion that he bases his conclusion that Gil Blas, not being a bastard, cannot be called a picaresque hero.

18 Quevedo, *La vida del buscón* in *La novela picaresca española*, ed. Valbuena Prat (Madrid, 1966), p. 1123.

19 The stages in the life of Guzmán are similar: innocence, delinquency, reform; but with the difference that the second stage, as far as the narrative itself is concerned, takes up most of the book, with very little space devoted to the period of reform. Nevertheless, the autobiography itself, because of the way it is written, is an act of reform. The writing of the book is part and parcel of the final stage of development of the character.

20 One should perhaps point out that Grimmelshausen's *Simplicissimus,* which antedates *Gil Blas* by nearly half a century, also offers a reformed picaro. But in the original version the period of reform is again very short.

14

Who were the *Philosophes?*

J. LOUGH

The study of ideas in eighteenth-century France is not always facilitated by some of the terms employed by those engaged in this occupation.[1] The now fashionable term 'Enlightenment' (or in French 'les Lumières') poses many problems; the fact that it has only recently become fashionable may not even be clear to some readers of these pages. When I was an undergraduate (admittedly this takes one back to the first half of the 1930s), the term was virtually confined to use in a German context as a translation for 'Aufklärung'. The parallel, but very different movement in France was generally known as 'le mouvement philosophique', and that is what I was billed to lecture on for several years in post-war Cambridge. It is significant that the 1950 edition of *Chambers's Encyclopædia* has no article on the Enlightenment; it does not even give it an entry in the index. The *Encyclopædia Britannica* (1959 version) devotes only a few lines to this subject; while it does record a recent trend towards applying the term to England and France, it stresses the German context in which the word is generally used:

ENLIGHTENMENT, in German *Aufklärung,* a term used to designate a period of great intellectual activity in the cause of general education and culture, including the preparatory self-emancipation from prejudice, convention and tradition. The name is applied primarily to the movement in 18th-century Germany which was inspired by the so-called popular philosophy of Lessing, Mendelssohn, Reimarus and others. It is sometimes extended to include the England of Locke and Newton and the France of Condillac, Diderot and Voltaire.[2]

Nowadays all that is changed. We have, for instance, a general work like Professor Norman Hampson's *The Enlightenment* (1968) or a more specifically French study in Professor J. H. Brumfitt's *The French Enlightenment* (1972). There remains the difficulty of deciding which thinkers of the period were 'enlightened' enough to qualify for study in such general works. Convenient as the term 'Enlightenment' is, one is not by any means certain that it covers the same writers and thinkers as the term *philosophe*.

  A specifically French term which continues to give trouble is *encyclopédiste*. It is at least a couple of generations since a well-known French scholar protested against the abuse of this term—its use as a kind of synonym for *philosophe*. He insisted quite rightly—though, of course, vainly—that it should be given the meaning which it had for contemporaries from the moment it was coined in 1751: that of contributor to the *Encyclopédie* of Diderot and

D'Alembert. There are, however, several difficulties here. Does one include among the *encyclopédistes* the almost completely new team of contributors got together by Robinet, the editor of the *Supplément,* in the late 1760s and early 1770s? More serious is the uncertainty surrounding the authorship of about two-fifths of the articles in Diderot's *Encyclopédie.* The name of Helvétius, for instance, has often been listed in the past among contributors to the work, but while one can definitely state that so far there is no evidence that he ever wrote a line for it, no one can guarantee that he was not an anonymous contributor, since for all we know the vast numbers of unsigned articles could have been the work of several dozen, indeed several hundred anonymous writers. All we can do is to confine the use of the term *encyclopédiste* to those writers who are known to have been enlisted by Diderot and D'Alembert—and possibly, though not, one feels, very usefully—by Robinet. But on any reasonable interpretation of the term *philosophe,* a high proportion of Diderot's contributors simply cannot be considered to have belonged to that camp.

The term *philosophe* is in constant use by all of us who speak or write about eighteenth-century France. We are continually declaring that 'X was a prominent *philosophe*', that 'the *Philosophes* thought this' or that 'the *Philosophes* rejected that'; but when one asks oneself the question 'Who were the *Philosophes*?', one does not find it all that easy to produce a satisfactory answer. When the question is discussed by a group of people, the result tends to be somewhat confusing. It is, however, through such discussion that some sort of rough working agreement can be reached.

If one tries to discover what contemporaries understood by the term, singularly little assistance can be derived from the dictionaries of the period. The fourth edition of the *Dictionnaire de l'Académie Française* which appeared at a date (1762) when the special sense of the term which we are concerned with was clearly in current use offers merely the following:

PHILOSOPHE, s.m. Celui qui s'applique à l'étude des Sciences, & qui cherche à connoître les effets par leurs causes & leurs principes. (Pythagore est le premier d'entre les Grecs qui ait pris le nom de Philosophe. Les anciens Philosophes. Les Philosophes Grecs. Les différentes sectes des Philosophes. Les Philosophes païens. Philosophe Stoïcien. Philosophe Platonicien. Philosophe Cynique. Philosophe Moral. Philosophe Chimique. Un grand Philosophe. Un célèbre Philosophe. Un des premiers Philosophes de son temps.).

On appelle aussi *Philosophe,* Un homme sage, qui mène une vie tranquille & retirée, hors de l'embarras des affaires. (Il s'est retiré pour toujours à la campagne, c'est un Philosophe, un vrai Philosophe).

Il se dit aussi quelquefois absolument d'Un homme qui, par libertinage d'esprit, se met au-dessus des devoirs & des obligations ordinaires de la vie civile & chrétienne. (C'est un homme qui ne se refuse rien, qui ne se contraint sur rien, & qui mène une vie de Philosophe).

Dans les Colléges, on appelle *Philosophe,* Un écolier qui étudie en Philosophie.

Les Alchimistes se donnent le nom de Philosophes par excellence. Ainsi en termes d'Alchimie, on dit, *L'or des Philosophes,* pour dire, L'or des Alchimistes, la poudre de projection.

It is not surprising if we can derive nothing for our purpose from these definitions and examples; they simply reproduce the text of the 1694 edition.

Even the 1798 edition, most of which was prepared before the Revolution, adds nothing except the not very helpful:

Philosophe, s'emploie quelquefois adjectivement, comme dans ces phrases: Un Roi Philosophe; un Poëte Philosophe; une Femme Philosophe.

The entry PHILOSOPHIQUE, however, does contain an addition which brings us rather nearer to the sense of the word with which we are concerned here:

On appelle *Esprit philosophique* par excellence, Un esprit de clarté, de méthode, exempt de préjugés et de passions. *L'esprit philosophique n'exclut pas l'éloquence, et il la rectifie beaucoup. Cet ouvrage est écrit dans un esprit très-philosophique. L'esprit philosophique a paru devenir l'esprit général des Nations de l'Europe.*

Yet even that does not take us very far.

Some assistance may be derived from the obviously hostile definition given under the heading PHILOSOPHE in the 1771 edition of the *Dictionnaire de Trévoux*:

Dans le monde, on décore aussi du nom de *Philosophes,* ces prétendus esprits forts, qui, plus par air & par une espèce de libertinage d'esprit, que par dépravation de mœurs, se mettent au-dessus des devoirs & des obligations de la vie civile & chrétienne, & qui, affranchis de tout ce qu'ils appellent préjugés de l'éducation en matière de Religion, se moquent des pauvres humains, assez foibles pour respecter des loix établies, & assez imbéciles pour n'oser secouer le joug d'une très-ancienne superstition.

However, not only is this definition far from objective; it also places a rather excessive stress on the *Philosophes'* hostility to orthodox Catholicism.

One turns next for guidance to a man to whom it would be extremely difficult to deny the title of *philosophe,* namely Voltaire; but though in his *Dictionnaire philosophique,* published in 1764 at the very height of the struggle between the *Philosophes* and their opponents, one does find an article PHILOSOPHE, neither in its original form nor in its later additions is there the slightest attempt at offering a definition of what Voltaire and his contemporaries understood by the term in its mid-eighteenth-century context.

If one goes next to another writer of the time whom few people, one suspects, could fail to consider a *philosophe,* Diderot, it is notorious that his *Encyclopédie* offers singularly little help in the obvious article, PHILOSOPHE. As it is unsigned, it was reprinted in nineteenth-century editions of Diderot's works; but as Naigeon pointed out nearly two hundred years ago, it is simply a boiled down version of an essay in the *Nouvelles libertés de penser,* published in 1743.[3] The work itself, which we can now fairly confidently attribute to Dumarsais,[4] was in all probability written somewhat earlier than that; it appears to owe a great deal to Bayle (Dumarsais was born in 1676) and it cannot by any stretch of the imagination be said to offer an adequate definition of the outlook on the world of men like Voltaire and Diderot.

The most useful definition of the outlook, aims and methods of the *Philosophes* is that furnished by Condorcet, writing in 1793, in a well-known passage in the ninth epoch of his *Esquisse.* Although born thirty years after Diderot and very nearly half a century after Voltaire, he can scarcely be denied the title of *philosophe.* Writing in the midst of the most radical phase of the Revolution, he gives a much more comprehensive view of what a *philosophe* stood for than does the *Encyclopédie* article, even though he does not actually use the term at this point. The passage in question opens with the well-known words:

Il se forma bientôt en Europe une classe d'hommes moins occupés encore de découvrir ou d'approfondir la vérité, que de la répandre; qui, se dévouant à poursuivre les préjugés dans les asiles où le
clergé, les écoles, les gouvernements, les corporations anciennes les avaient recueillis et protégés,
mirent leur gloire à détruire les erreurs populaires, plutôt qu'à reculer les limites des connaissances
humaines.

After describing the aims of the movement and the methods used to propagate its outlook
on the world, he sums it all up in the war-cry: 'Raison, tolérance, humanité'.[5]

It is clear that for Condorcet the 'esprit philosophique' embraced a very wide area of
thought and feeling. The whole outlook on the world of a *philosophe* will be based on
reason; thanks to this guide he can think things out for himself, discard all prejudices and
reject authority and tradition. In religion it is bound to lead him to reject orthodox Catholicism, but whatever his final attitude may be—whether he be deist, agnostic or atheist—
he will preach the virtues of toleration and denounce intolerance and fanaticism wherever
they appear. The *philosophe* is definitely outward-looking. He will examine critically the
society in which he lives and the government of his day, attacking all forms of tyranny and
unnecessary restrictions on freedom, including the particularly important freedom of the
press. He will denounce all forms of inhumanity such as war, miscarriages of justice,
barbarous punishments and negro slavery. If Condorcet cannot enlist the support of the
main body of the *Philosophes* for his belief in the indefinite perfectibility of the human race,
it could be said that they at least saw the *possibility* of some degree of future progress if
only men would use their reason to the full, discard harmful prejudices and cultivate the
virtues of toleration and humanity.

So far we have accepted, along with Condorcet, two older and more illustrious figures—
Voltaire and Diderot—as being *philosophes*. But when one thinks of eighteenth-century
French writers, other names besides theirs immediately spring to mind. What of
Montesquieu, for instance? Although he died in 1755, he was only five years older than
Voltaire. This raises the question: How far back in time does one go in bestowing the title
of *philosophe*? What about Fontenelle, who lived to be nearly a hundred and died two years
after Montesquieu? Dare I put forward the name of Bayle, especially when in recent years
so much scholarship has been devoted to trying to prove that he was after all a pretty
orthodox Calvinist? It seems to me that to call Bayle a *philosophe* is to rob the term of most
of its meaning; however, it is a fact that in the passage from Condorcet quoted above he is
named along with Fontenelle, Voltaire and Montesquieu.

Fontenelle too appears to me very much a precursor. He was after all born in 1657
(he was Pierre Corneille's nephew) and, despite his great age which enabled him to outlive
Montesquieu, his active career as a writer fell in the period between the 1680s and the
1720s. Although Abbé de Saint-Pierre, born the year after Fontenelle, was the author of a
Projet de paix perpétuelle and the *Discours sur la Polysynodie* and the creator of the word
bienfaisance, he must surely also be treated as a precursor. Montesquieu offers more of a
problem. Although Condorcet sharply attacks his attitude to politics, he names him next to
Voltaire in the *Esquisse*. There is no doubt that many of the ideas set forth in the *Lettres
persanes* were extremely bold in 1721; Voltaire was disgusted to discover that he could not
get away with the same sort of thing thirteen years later in his *Lettres philosophiques*.[6]

And it is clear that his *Esprit des Lois* exercised a profound influence on the political outlook of the *Philosophes*. It cannot be without significance that D'Alembert devoted fourteen large folio pages of the *Encyclopédie* to his *Éloge de M. le Président de Montesquieu*. One thinks of him none the less as a precursor rather than as a *philosophe*. However, one can perhaps close for the convenient formula—'a *philosophe* before the *Philosophes* had formed a party'.[7]

A fourth name—that of D'Alembert—has now slipped into the discussion of the writers of the time whom we can accept as *Philosophes*; his is surely a name which one cannot leave out. But so far there has been no mention of an illustrious name one immediately thinks of when one's mind turns to the thinkers of eighteenth-century France, to many (though not to me) the greatest of them all—that of Rousseau. Can he be regarded as a *philosophe*? The answer must surely be: Yes, up to a point. After all, as late as 1760 that arch-enemy of the *Philosophes*, Palissot, brought Jean-Jacques on to the stage of the Comédie Française under the most transparent of disguises in his satirical comedy, *Les Philosophes*. However, by that time Rousseau had clearly broken with the *Philosophes*, as his later writings, especially *Émile*, were soon to show.

What of another member of Diderot's circle in the early 1750s, the expatriate Friedrich Melchior Grimm? Undoubtedly, down to 1773, his *Correspondance littéraire*, both through his own contributions and those of Diderot, did a great deal for the diffusion of the ideas of the *Philosophes* in northern, eastern and central Europe. Yet by 1781, as we now know from the *Lettre apologétique de l'abbé Raynal*, Diderot had come to realize that there was now a gulf between his ideas and those of one of his oldest friends: 'Mon ami, je ne vous reconnais plus; vous êtes devenu sans vous en douter peut-être un des plus cachés, mais un des plus dangereux antiphilosophes. Vous vivez avec nous, mais vous nous haïssez.'[8] In any case, not only was Grimm a foreigner, but from the 1770s onwards he was very much of a globe-trotter, unlike another German who, after he was naturalized in 1749, spent virtually the whole of the rest of his life in France and especially in the famous mansion in the rue Royale, butte Saint-Roch (now known more prosaically as the rue des Moulins), Baron d'Holbach.

Nobody, one feels, is likely to challenge the application of the term *philosophe* to the author of the *Système de la Nature*, nor for that matter to his neighbour in the rue Sainte-Anne, Helvétius. Yet if one consults the standard works on eighteenth-century French thought, one occasionally finds the term applied to some rather surprising names. Lanson, for whom I continue to feel a most unfashionable admiration, particularly for his work on the eighteenth century, manages to enrol even Vauvenargues, who died in 1747 at the age of thirty-two, for his chapter on 'le mouvement philosophique'. Surely his outlook and interests were very different from those of such contemporaries as Diderot and D'Alembert.

A much more illustrious figure, Buffon, is also sometimes included among the *Philosophes*. It is true that he had his clashes with the Sorbonne and, more important, that the early volumes of his *Histoire naturelle* had a great influence on *Philosophes* like Diderot, as can be seen in several of his *Encyclopédie* articles, starting with ★ANIMAL. Yet not only did Buffon never produce the article NATURE which the editors announced with a great flourish of trumpets in the preface to their second volume; he spent most of the year on his estate at

L

Montbard, only coming to Paris to pay some attention to his duties at the Jardin du Roi. Important as Buffon is in the history of ideas in eighteenth-century France, he seems to have held himself deliberately aloof from the *Philosophes*. Another prominent scientist of the time whose name occurs to one as a possible candidate for the title is Maupertuis, but, although his mathematical and scientific pursuits covered a very wide field, it is difficult to see how he can be included among the *Philosophes*.

Another important thinker of the time—indeed Lanson calls him 'le philosophe des philosophes'—Abbé de Condillac, is sometimes included among the *Philosophes*. There is obviously no doubt about his influence on men like Diderot and Helvétius, but he too appears to have held himself aloof from the whole movement. It would generally be agreed that his influence on the *Idéologues* was even greater.

They too raise a problem, as they are generally regarded not only as the disciples of Condillac, but also as the spiritual heirs of the *Philosophes*. That being so, one is bound to ask where one draws the line between *Philosophes* and *Idéologues*. So far in our list of *Philosophes* we have applied the term to two men as far apart in age as Voltaire who was twenty-one when Louis XIV died and Condorcet who was in the prime of life when the Revolution broke out in 1789. Men like Cabanis (b. 1757) and Destutt de Tracy (b. 1754) were only a dozen or so years younger than Condorcet and yet they generally bear a different label. And what of Volney (b. 1757) whose *Les Ruines* was published in 1791? These are questions which must be left to scholars more learned in *Idéologie*.

Condillac had an elder brother who is numbered among the more radical political and social thinkers of the time, Abbé de Mably. Yet, interesting as he is as a writer, his semi-communistic ideas would seem to mark him off from the distinctly 'liberal' trends of thought associated with the *Philosophes*.

A more important figure, Turgot, is also sometimes held to have been a *philosophe*. He was certainly much admired by the party and was on friendly terms with several of its members, including (despite the gap in age) Condorcet. He contributed—anonymously since he was a high civil servant—five articles to the *Encyclopédie*; yet these can scarcely be held to seek to 'détruire les erreurs populaires', to use Condorcet's phrase. A man of extremely wide interests, he made his principal contribution in the field of economic thought, and although his dismissal from the post of *Contrôleur général* in 1776 was felt by men like Voltaire and Condorcet to be a catastrophe for France, he could scarcely be regarded as the representative of the *Philosophes* in the government at Versailles. Although there are five solid volumes of his collected works, nowhere in them does one find him writing anything approaching what one might call propaganda for the outlook of the *Philosophes*.

A more likely candidate for the title is a writer who achieved European fame fairly late in his career (he was an exact contemporary of Diderot) with his *Histoire philosophique et politique des établissements et du commerce des Européens dans les deux Indes*, Abbé Raynal. His connection with the *Encyclopédie* in the years before its publication is somewhat mysterious: in 1748–1749 he drew quite a large sum of money from the publishers, but not one single article bears his signature. It is notorious that Diderot contributed many of the inflammatory purple passages in successive editions of the *Histoire philosophique*. There is a case for including Raynal among the *Philosophes,* especially in view of Diderot's defence of him against Grimm in his *Lettre apologétique*.

So far we have identified six writers of the time (or seven if we include Raynal) as *Philosophes*. Arranged in order of age, they are Voltaire, Diderot, Raynal, Helvétius, D'Alembert, D'Holbach and Condorcet. Fortunately, unlike our colleagues in the Renaissance field who have to wrestle with the problem posed by the uncertain membership of the group of poets known as the Pléiade, we are not confined to any stated number of writers in our search for names. In a sense, the difficulty is to know where to stop, to decide how well-known one had to be as a writer before one was considered to be a *philosophe* or indeed whether one needed to have served the cause of enlightenment by publishing anything at all.

The question has been asked: Were there any women *philosophes*? The 1798 edition of the *Dictionnaire de l'Académie Française* does admit of the possibility when it gives the example of 'une Femme Philosophe'. Only one woman is known to have written articles for the *Encyclopédie*—perhaps to be identified as the sister-in-law of the Chevalier de Jaucourt—but all she contributed was a small number of articles on women's fashions, scarcely enough two centuries later to clear the editors of a charge of anti-feminism. Even though her life came to a tragic end as early as 1749, it is possible to consider madame Du Châtelet as an example of a 'femme *philosophe*'. Yet, despite her connection with so eminent a member of the movement as Voltaire, her intellectual interests were mainly mathematical and scientific, and her other writings are merely the brief *Discours sur le bonheur* (published posthumously) and the bulky manuscript of the *Examen de la Genèse* which cannot be attributed to her with complete certainty. If in our search for 'femmes *philosophes*' we consider women who, unlike madame Du Châtelet, lived through the main struggle between the *Philosophes* and their opponents, we might do well to look at the ladies whose *salons* have kept their name alive two centuries later. Obviously madame Du Deffand, madame Geoffrin and madame Necker could scarcely be regarded as 'femmes philosophes'. Baronne d'Holbach does not seem to have shared her husband's intellectual interests; she was apparently more interested in other men than in ideas; but mademoiselle de Lespinasse, although she left behind little but a collection of letters, does appear to have shared the outlook of the writers and thinkers who frequented her modest *salon*.

If one felt compelled to follow the fashionable trends in scholarship, at this point one should hasten to enrol among the *Philosophes* the man whose outlook on the world seems to some recent writers to be the be-all-and-end-all of eighteenth century French thought—'le divin Marquis' in person. Yet although Sade was undoubtedly influenced by the writings of the *Philosophes,* there does not seem to be any reason why one should attach all that much importance to the products of his addled brain.

There are a considerable number of writers, not so far mentioned, whose works are not only familiar to scholars today, but also sometimes enjoyed considerable notoriety or even popularity in eighteenth-century France. They may perhaps be most usefully examined according to their date of birth.

Dumarsais poses an awkward problem. Though he lived to furnish well over a hundred articles to the first seven volumes of the *Encyclopédie*, he was born as far back as 1676, thirteen years before Montesquieu whom one is tempted to exclude, partly because of the date of his birth, and to treat as a precursor. There seems little doubt that Dumarsais was a convinced freethinker, but there are considerable problems when one seeks to determine exactly which of the works attributed to him in the eighteenth century came from his pen. His contribution to the *Encyclopédie* was almost exclusively grammatical. There seems every reason to regard him as a precursor rather than as a *philosophe*.

A very different writer—a wealthy bourgeois, mayor of his native Dinan, *secrétaire perpétuel de l'Académie Française* and Voltaire's successor as *historiographe du roi,* Duclos—has some claim to be regarded as a *philosophe*. It is true that the three articles which he contributed to the *Encyclopédie* are of no great significance, and his *Considérations sur les mœurs* (1750) can only with difficulty be made to reflect, however indirectly, the new ideas current in the middle of the eighteenth century. On the other hand he was on friendly terms with many of the *Philosophes* (and even with Rousseau) and he is said to have been not altogether without responsibility for the gradual infiltration of the *Philosophes* into the Academy. Yet he was a man of too independent views to be classed among their number.

In the same year as Duclos (1704), was born a very retiring figure—the younger son of an old family of *noblesse d'épée* with strong Protestant affiliations, which led to his being educated abroad in Geneva, Cambridge and Leyden and to his entering, not the army, but the medical profession—the Chevalier de Jaucourt. It is difficult to see how it would be possible to deny the title of *philosophe* to the man who wrote getting on for a quarter of the *Encyclopédie,* even if in private men like Diderot and D'Alembert spoke of him as a boring old compiler. It is, of course, perfectly true that, in the words Voltaire applied to a very different contemporary, 'Il compilait, compilait, compilait', in his efforts to supply Diderot with thousands of articles on almost every subject under the sun. I certainly lay no claim to have read all of his 17,000 articles; yet I have read enough of his prose to know that on occasion he was capable of expressing ideas of his own and, more important, that, within the limits imposed by the official censorship and later by Le Breton, he used every opportunity to put forward the ideas of the *Philosophes,* one would guess from a fairly moderate standpoint.

In the very same year was born another writer, one whom it is rather difficult to place since his main works fell in the period before 1750 and were composed either in Holland or later at the court of Frederick the Great where he spent a good twenty years—the Marquis d'Argens. He certainly had his contacts in Paris and presumably must rank as a *philosophe*. Whether the same can be said of another writer who was born in the same decade (in 1709), published one of his works while in exile in Holland, and ended his life not long afterwards at Frederick's court, La Mettrie, is more doubtful. While Voltaire's public references to him were relatively mild, he could scarcely be called one of his admirers; neither Diderot nor D'Holbach who might have been expected to be sympathetic towards his materialism, mentions him more than once in his writings, and both attack his ethical ideas with the utmost vigour. 'L'auteur qui vient tout récémment de publier l'*Homme machine*', wrote D'Holbach in a footnote to the *Système de la Nature,* 'a raisonné sur les mœurs comme un frénétique.'[9] In his *Essai sur les règnes de Claude et de Néron,* Diderot devoted a whole page to a violent attack on La Mettrie's ethical views. Its tone can be judged by the last two sentences:

La Mettrie, dissolu, impudent, bouffon, flatteur, était fait pour la vie des cours et la faveur des grands. Il est mort comme il devait mourir, victime de son intempérance et de sa folie; il s'est tué par ignorance de l'art qu'il professait.[10]

It seems fairly clear that none of these three writers was willing to recognize La Mettrie as a *philosophe.*

Among writers born in the following decade, along with Diderot, Raynal, Helvétius and D'Alembert, was Toussaint whose *Les Mœurs* caused a scandal when it was published in 1748; the work was burned by the hangman and Toussaint retired for a while to Brussels. He was one of the original members of the 'société de gens de lettres' of the *Encyclopédie* and he contributed a good four hundred articles on legal matters to the first two volumes. Thereafter, however, he furnished only two articles each to Volumes III and IV, and that was apparently the end of his collaboration. As his signature—(H)—appeared at the end of the article AUTORITÉ which came immediately after the unsigned AUTORITÉ POLITIQUE and AUTORITÉ *dans les discours & dans les écrits,* he was publicly accused of being responsible for the subversive political article, a charge which he also publicly rebutted in 1765 in the *Gazette littéraire de Berlin.* By that time he had secured a teaching post in Frederick's Military Academy. Round about 1750 he was certainly closely associated with Diderot, but his activities as a *philosophe* seem gradually to have fizzled out.

A very different writer born in the same decade was the Marquis de Saint-Lambert, who is chiefly remembered today because of the way he impinged on the love-life of both Voltaire and Rousseau. Yet in his time he contributed sixteen anonymous articles to the *Encyclopédie,* and some of these, in particular GÉNIE, INTÉRÈT (*Morale*), LÉGISLATEUR and LUXE, are of considerable interest. After resigning from the army he composed a poem, *Les Saisons,* which, if not highly thought of by contemporary critics including Diderot, did contain, both in the text and the notes, a number of quite outspoken attacks on the abuses of the Ancien Régime. I find that I once described him in print as a *philosophe* and I see no reason now to recant this view, though clearly he was not of particular importance in the whole movement.

To this decade there also belongs a man who, after a somewhat unsuccessful literary career in Paris, did a great deal for the diffusion of the ideas of the *Philosophes,* both inside France and in Europe in general, Pierre Rousseau, known as 'Rousseau de Toulouse' to distinguish him from Jean-Baptiste and Jean-Jacques. First from Liège and then, when the authorities there became difficult, from Bouillon, on the French frontier, he published his *Journal encyclopédique* which, despite both its local and French censors, was permitted a certain degree of freedom. He must presumably rank as a *philosophe,* though one of fairly moderate views.

Sedaine, the author of *Le Philosophe sans le savoir,*[11] was also born in this decade. He clearly stood much closer than Pierre Rousseau to the group of *Philosophes* in Paris, but, although his most famous play, and some others of his, clearly reflect the ideas put about by the *Philosophes*,[12] he was not exactly at the heart of the movement.

Moving now into the next decade, among contemporaries of Baron d'Holbach we meet first Boulanger, the author of *L'Antiquité dévoilée* and of *Le Despotisme oriental,* both of which appeared some time after his early death in 1759. He also contributed four lengthy articles to the *Encyclopédie*. Although very much a spare-time writer—he retired shortly before his death from the post of Inspecteur des Ponts et Chaussées—he must surely be reckoned among the *Philosophes*.

To the same age-group belongs Alexandre Deleyre. His life-span was a much longer one since not only did he sit in the Convention along with Condorcet, but, unlike him, he survived the Terror and ended his days under the Directoire as a member of the Conseil des Cinq Cents. His *Analyse de la philosophie du chancelier Bacon* received a terrific boost from Diderot at the end of the article, ÉPINGLE, which he furnished for the *Encyclopédie*; but his other contribution to this work, the outspoken article, FANATISME, is much more important. It was fiercely attacked by contemporary critics of the *Encyclopédie*. In the mid-1750s when he was writing these works, Deleyre appears to have been on friendly terms with both Diderot and Rousseau. However, a great deal of his life was spent far from Paris and much of it abroad, at Liège, for instance, where for a time he wrote for the *Journal encyclo-pédique,* and at Parma where he held the post of librarian. In other words, his connection with the circles of the *Philosophes* in Paris seems to have been relatively short.

In contrast, two writers who belong to the same age group—Marmontel and Morellet (the first of these married a niece of the second)—were certainly much involved in the circles of the *Philosophes,* as we can tell from the memoirs which they both left behind. Marmontel contributed a number of articles, mainly on literature, to Volumes III–VII of the *Encyclo-pédie,* though he prudently withdrew from the enterprise when it began to run into trouble in 1757. However, he later made a substantial and apparently well-paid contribution (over a hundred articles) to the *Supplément*. One or two of his articles in Diderot's *Encyclopédie,* in particular GLOIRE and GRAND, are mildly radical in tone, but Marmontel was very much the second-rate writer determined to 'get on', both by earning money with his pen (his *Contes moraux* met with considerable success) and by exploiting to the full the possibili-ties of securing literary patronage offered by the Ancien Régime, particularly in the eighteenth century. An Academician in 1763, he succeeded D'Alembert as *secrétaire perpétuel,* and in the meantime he had followed Duclos as *historiographe du roi*. As one might expect from a man whose prosperity was so bound up with the continuation of the Ancien Régime, his memoirs show what a bitter blow the Revolution was to him.

Abbé Morellet was much more of a *philosophe* and, as his nickname 'Mords-les' shows, a polemical writer. He was recruited as a theologian to the *Encyclopédie* from Volume VI to replace Abbé Mallet. It is true that he is only known to have written six articles, all of them in Volumes VI and VII, but some of these, especially FATALITÉ and FOI, were severely criticized at the time by orthodox writers. Morellet, it is well known, spent six weeks in the Bastille for having published a biting attack on Palissot's *Les Philosophes*. As a pamphleteer he served the cause of the *Philosophes,* and he was also the translator of Becca-ria's *Traité des délits et des peines.* He must certainly be counted among the minor *Philosophes.*

Two other academicians born in the 1730s, Thomas and Suard, must presumably be added to the list of minor *Philosophes,* Thomas for his series of *Éloges* which he used as a vehicle for the ideas of the party, and Suard, at least the young Suard, for his journalistic activities. It is well known that his election to the Academy was annulled by the authorities in 1772 because of his connections with the *Philosophes* and that he had to be elected a second time after the death of Louis XV before he was allowed to occupy his *fauteuil.*

A more important figure in the history of ideas in eighteenth-century France is the Chevalier de Chastellux. The views on the perfectibility of man which he put forward in *De la Félicité publique* (1772) have often been compared with those of Condorcet in his *Esquisse.* If it is true that Chastellux's views on the future progress of man are very vague when set beside those expressed by Condorcet in the X^e *époque* of his *Esquisse,* there seems every reason to consider him one of the younger generation of *Philosophes.*

There is also a case for considering La Harpe to be one of the party, at any rate down to his change of heart in the Revolution; but a much more definitely committed member was the man he once rudely described as 'le singe de Diderot', Naigeon. Among his two-and-a-bit contributions to the *Encyclopédie* is the astonishingly bold article UNITAIRES, into which he managed to work his own materialistic and atheistic outlook. He and his younger brother were responsible for the editing and publication of the mass of subversive writings which D'Holbach poured forth in the 1760s and 1770s. In addition to editing the works of Diderot and writing the first biography of him, he continued to purvey the ideas of the *Philosophes* in the three massive volumes devoted to *Philosophie ancienne et moderne* in the *Encyclopédie méthodique* which were published in the 1790s.

To sum up, to the names of Voltaire, Diderot, Raynal, D'Alembert, Helvétius, D'Holbach and Condorcet one could add, from among the secondary writers of the period between, say, the 1740s and the Revolution, another fifteen or so names of *Philosophes* of varying degrees of importance and of commitment. The difficulty is to know where to stop. No doubt one could think of fairly obscure writers of the time who might be held to deserve the label, and in any case it could not be held that it was necessary for a man (or a woman) to be a *writer* before he (or she) qualified.

It goes without saying, one hopes, that the views tentatively advanced in these pages are not given out as *ex cathedra* judgements. The only reason for putting them down on paper is to bring out into the open a question which lurks at the back of one's mind whenever one speaks or writes about eighteenth-century French thought.

NOTES

1 This contribution was first composed to be read as a paper at the 1973 conference of the British Society for Eighteenth-Century Studies. In its present form it owes a great deal to the discussion which followed.

2 Just to be different *OED* (the relevant part was published as far back as 1891) states under EN-LIGHTENMENT: 'Sometimes used (after German *Aufklärung, Aufklärerei*) to designate the spirit

and aims of the French philosophers of the 18th c., or of others whom it is intended to associate with them in the implied charge of shallow and pretentious intellectualism, unreasonable contempt for tradition and authority, etc.'

3 See Herbert Dieckmann, *Le Philosophe. Texts and Interpretation* (Saint Louis, 1948).

4 See A. W. Fairbairn, 'Dumarsais and *Le Philosophe*', *Studies on Voltaire and the Eighteenth Century*, Vol. 87 (1972), 375–95.

5 *Esquisse d'un tableau historique des progrès de l'esprit humain*, edited by O. H. Prior (Paris, 1933), pp. 159–61.

6 It is not easy to decide what exactly Voltaire meant in 1734 by 'philosophiques' or what Diderot meant by the word twelve years later in his *Pensées philosophiques*.

7 R. Shackleton, *Montesquieu. A Critical Biography* (Oxford, 1961), p. 390.

8 *Œuvres philosophiques*, edited by P. Vernière (Paris, 1956), p. 630.

9 Part II, Chap. 12, note 80.

10 *Œuvres complètes*, edited by J. Assézat and M. Tourneux (Paris, 1875–7), 20 vols., III, 218.

11 It is possible to argue about the meaning of the word 'philosophe' in the title. Writing in December 1765 in his *Correspondance littéraire* (VI, 445), Grimm emphatically asserts that it has the sense which we are concerned with here: 'On a beaucoup critiqué le titre. Si M. Vanderk n'est pas un véritable philosophe, qu'on me dise ce que c'est qu'un philosophe. Or il l'est certainement sans le savoir.'

12 In the preface to his edition of *Le Philosophe sans le savoir* (Paris, 1929), p. 9, F. Gaiffe even goes so far as to speak of the play as being 'née d'une idée: réhabiliter le nom de Philosophe bafoué par Palissot (Comédie des *Philosophes*, 1760)'.

15

Un magistrat «âme sensible»: le président Dupaty (1746-1788)

ROLAND MORTIER

On se méprendrait singulièrement sur les mobiles et sur les objectifs des penseurs du dix-huitième siècle en les confinant a priori dans l'ordre de la pure raison. Certes, l'époque elle-même s'est tenue pour *éclairée* (ou en passe de le devenir, grâce à l'effort de ses porte-parole les plus qualifiés) et elle s'est présentée délibérément au regard de la postérité comme une ère de réflexion critique et de renouveau scientifique. En se disant *philosophique,* et en élargissant considérablement ce concept, le siècle s'est cru le détenteur d'une sagesse nouvelle, mieux adaptée à la réalité humaine parce que coupée de tous les absolus, y compris celui d'une pure raison. Mais jamais il n'a entendu se cantonner dans un discours théorique ou se mettre au service d'une rationalité intégrale, qu'il s'efforce au contraire de contenir dans des limites précises en accordant leur juste part à l'émotion, à la sensibilité, aux passions, à toute la vie profonde des sensations et de l'intériorité. En définissant l'imagination «la folle du logis», Malebranche reste fidèle à l'orthodoxie cartésienne bien plus qu'il n'annonce la couleur des temps futurs. Diderot est plus représentatif de son époque lorsqu'il proclame: «La raison se traîne, l'imagination vole: mettez la raison sur les ailes de l'imagination, elles voleront ensemble partout où il faut dissiper l'ignorance et détruire les erreurs».[1] Comme l'a fort bien dit Robert Niklaus, «the Age of Enlightenment is the Age of Reason and the Age of Sensibility in one. This truth is reflected in all the cultural activities of the period [. . .]. No careful critic can afford to neglect either element».[2] Nous voudrions illustrer cette remarquable convergence du propos critique et réformateur d'une part avec la sensibilité expansive et l'amour des hommes d'autre part, par l'exemple d'un écrivain un peu oublié, mais qui eut son heure de gloire, le président Dupaty.

La vie de ce magistrat se confond pratiquement avec son œuvre, l'une et l'autre mises au service d'une réforme de la jurisprudence inspirée par l'horreur d'une législation archaïque et de coutumes barbares. Toute sa carrière est vouée à cet amour pratique des hommes, à ce pragmatisme généreux qui se réclame de la doctrine de Montesquieu, de l'exemple de Voltaire, de la sensibilité effervescente de Diderot. Mais le cas de Dupaty est exemplaire à d'autres égards encore: il montre la pénétration des lumières à l'intérieur de la bourgeoisie fortunée et des milieux parlementaires, si hostiles en général au courant «philosophique»; il éclaire les liens entre la vie politique et le monde littéraire dans la seconde moitié du siècle ainsi que la lente progression des idées réformatrices; il illustre enfin la diffusion d'une certaine rhétorique de la sensibilité et son utilisation à des fins pratiques, concrètes et positives.

Nous ne retracerons pas en détail les événements qui jalonnent une existence qui fut courte, mais bien remplie, et nous nous bornerons à en dégager les étapes les plus marquantes.[3] Charles-Marguerite-Jean-Baptiste Mercier Dupaty[4] naquit à La Rochelle, le 9 ou le 10 mai 1746, du second mariage de Charles-Jean-Baptiste Mercier Dupaty avec Louise-Elisabeth Carré de Clam.[5] La famille avait accumulé une importante fortune dans les plantations de St Domingue, où Charles (le père) était né en 1720; très tôt cependant, il avait quitté l'île avec sa mère, devenue veuve en 1723 et bientôt remariée à Paris. A son mariage avec la fille d'un trésorier de France, Charles s'était fixé à La Rochelle où il avait obtenu la survivance de la charge de son beau-père. Après un bref retour à St Domingue, où il siégea au Conseil supérieur de la colonie, il s'établit définitivement à La Rochelle, dont il devint successivement échevin et premier conseiller perpétuel. Sa qualité de notable et ses curiosités scientifiques (il avait commencé des études de médecine avant d'entrer dans l'administration) lui valurent d'être élu très jeune à l'Académie de La Rochelle (1744) où il présenta des mémoires sur des problèmes d'agriculture et d'élevage (culture des moules, des huîtres, sucreries, canne à sucre). Il mourut à La Rochelle le 27 mars 1767.

Son fils Charles-Marguerite avait commencé par suivre les traces paternelles. Ayant fait ses débuts littéraires à dix-sept ans, il entrait à l'Académie de La Rochelle à dix-neuf ans, et en devenait le directeur à vingt ans. Foudroyante progression, qui n'était pas uniquement le résultat de son mérite.[6]

A la fin de 1765, l'académicien de dix-neuf ans prononçait un discours *Sur l'utilité des lettres*; l'année suivante, un *Éloge du chancelier de L'Hôpital* assez révélateur de ses tendances politiques et de son adhésion précoce au mouvement «philosophique».[7] Toujours en 1766, il fut chargé, en sa qualité de directeur de l'Académie, de haranguer le nouvel intendant de l'Aunis, Sénac de Meilhan,[8] qu'il admonesta d'un ton tranchant et peu conforme aux usages, en lui réclamant du pain pour les pauvres et de la justice pour tous.

Sous la pression du milieu familial, il avait dû reprendre la charge de trésorier de France à La Rochelle,[9] mais il ne l'avait fait qu'après avoir été menacé de déshérence (1764). C'est que le jeune homme rêvait de jouer un rôle actif dans l'État et qu'il espérait bien se pousser dans les milieux littéraires. Il se sentait en tout cas appelé à de plus hautes destinées. Aussi s'arrangea-t-il, à la mort de son père (1767), pour obtenir des lettres de vétérance—à vingt et un ans!—après quoi il quitta La Rochelle pour Bordeaux et la trésorerie pour une seconde carrière, cette fois de magistrat. Le 10 février 1768, il était reçu avocat général au Parlement de Bordeaux; l'année suivante, il devenait membre associé de l'Académie locale, fondée en 1712, et dont la réputation était très étroitement liée à la gloire de Montesquieu.[10]

Le jeune Mercier Dupaty avait su faire parler de lui en dehors de l'Aunis et de la Guyenne en posant au mécène «philosophe», adepte de Montesquieu et de Voltaire. En 1767, il avait fait les frais d'une médaille en or destinée à récompenser le meilleur éloge du bon roi Henri IV, ce qui devait lui valoir la bénédiction du patriarche de Ferney, enchanté de voir ses idées se répandre dans la magistrature de province.[11] Il avait fait la preuve de ses curiosités

cosmopolites en lisant à l'Académie de La Rochelle des *Réflexions sur la littérature allemande* qui
s'inscrivaient dans une veine récemment ouverte par Turgot, puis en 1769 une imitation de
l'*Élégie écrite dans un cimetière de campagne* de Thomas Gray, très à la mode en ces années.
Il avait marqué son entrée à l'Académie de Bordeaux en instituant un prix pour le meilleur
éloge de Montesquieu. Décidément, ce jeune magistrat manifestait d'excellentes dispositions
pour la cause «philosophique», et il faisait un usage aussi spectaculaire que généreux de sa
grosse fortune. On savait, à Bordeaux, qu'il collaborait au *Mercure,* qu'il correspondait
avec les célèbres «philosophes» de Paris, qu'il se signalait par ses idées libérales et par son
hostilité envers les jésuites et envers l'absolutisme. Bientôt, on le retrouvera entouré d'une
petite cour d'avocats aux idées avancées, dont certains feront une brillante carrière politique
dans les cercles Girondins, comme Vergniaud ou Garat.

Il apparaît comme l'inspirateur d'une tendance libérale qui va s'élargissant dans la magistrature, et dont l'avocat général de Grenoble, Michel Servan, est alors la plus célèbre
illustration. Au nom d'un idéal de justice et de raison, il s'élève contre les empiètements
du pouvoir central (représenté à Bordeaux par le duc de Richelieu), contre la chasse sournoise
aux protestants, contre les abus de toute sorte d'une jurisprudence archaïque et d'une
magistrature trop sensible aux pressions extérieures. Sa rencontre avec Diderot, née d'un
concours de circonstances, va arracher à celui-ci des cris d'admiration dans une belle lettre
adressée le 22 septembre 1769 à Sophie Volland.

Le jeune ménage Dupaty était venu à Paris à la fin de l'été de 1769 et y avait assisté à
une des ultimes représentations du *Père de Famille.* Peu habituée à un tel spectacle, la jeune
femme (dont c'était la première sortie publique) avait été prise de peur devant un geste
menaçant de Saint-Albin et avait poussé un cri aigu qui avait troublé le déroulement de la
pièce. Mais laissons ici la parole à Diderot lui-même:

Cela m'a valu la visite de son mari, qui a grimpé à mon quatrième étage pour me remercier du plaisir
et de la peine que je leur avais faits. Ce mari est avocat général au parlement de Bordeaux. Il s'appelle
Mr Du Paty. Nous causâmes très agréablement. Lorsqu'il s'en allait et qu'il fut sur mon palier, il tira
modestement de sa poche un ouvrage imprimé[12] sur lequel il me pria de jeter les yeux avec indulgence,
s'excusant sur sa jeunesse et la médiocrité de son talent.

Le voilà parti. Je me mets à lire, et je trouve, à mon grand étonnement, un morceau plein
d'éloquence, de hardiesse et de logique. C'était un réquisitoire en faveur d'une femme convaincue
de s'être un peu amusée dans la première année de son veuvage, et menacée aux termes de la loi de
perdre tous les avantages de son contrat de mariage.

J'ai appris depuis que ce même magistrat adolescent s'était élevé contre les vexations du duc de
Richelieu, avait osé fixer les limites du pouvoir du commandant et de la loi, et fait ouvrir les portes des
prisons à plusieurs citoyens qui y avaient été renfermés d'autorité. J'ai appris qu'après avoir humilié
le commandant de la province, il avait entrepris les évêques qui avaient annulé des mariages protestants,
et qu'il en avait fait réhabiliter quarante. Si l'esprit de la philosophie et du patriotisme allait s'emparer
une fois de ces vieilles têtes-là, ô! la bonne chose! Cela n'est pas aisé, mais cela n'est pas impossible.
Lorsque je revis Mr Du Paty, je lui dis qu'en lisant son discours, ma vanité mortifiée n'avait trouvé
de ressource que dans l'espérance que, marié, ayant des enfants, la soif de l'aisance, du repos, des
honneurs, de la richesse le saisirait et que tout ce talent se réduirait à rien. Vous auriez souri de la
naïveté avec laquelle il me protestait le contraire. (Diderot, *Correspondance,* éd. G. Roth, t. XI,
22 septembre 1769)

Certes, Dupaty n'était pas aussi naïf que Diderot le pensait, et il ne lui était pas indifférent de se savoir approuvé et soutenu par le directeur de l'*Encyclopédie*. N'avait-il pas été salué déjà par Voltaire comme un des hommes appelés à «débarbariser» la France? Dans une lettre personnelle datée de Ferney le 27 mars 1769, l'auteur de *La Henriade* le félicitait de son admirable discours à l'Académie[13] et saluait en lui un des esprits novateurs et audacieux en qui il mettait ses espoirs:

Vous avez signalé à la fois, Monsieur, votre patriotisme,[14] votre générosité et votre éloquence. Un beau siècle se prépare, vous en serez un des plus rares ornements; vous ferez servir vos grands talents à écraser le fanatisme qui a toujours voulu qu'on le prît pour la religion. Vous délivrerez la société des monstres qui l'ont si longtemps opprimée en se vantant de la conduire. Il viendra un temps où l'on ne dira plus: les deux puissances,[15] et ce sera vous, Monsieur, plus qu'à aucun de vos confrères, à qui on en aura l'obligation. [. . .] Travaillez, Monsieur, à nous débarbariser tout à fait. (Best. 14573)

S'il avait connu plus intimement le jeune magistrat, sans doute eût-il conclu sa lettre par un «Écrasons l'infâme»; il se contenta, pour cette fois, d'espérer qu'on graverait un jour une médaille en son honneur.

Le nom de Dupaty allait reparaître dans la correspondance de Voltaire à la fin de 1769 et au début de 1770 à propos d'une représentation à Bordeaux de la tragédie *Les Guèbres*, qu'on venait d'interdire à Lyon (23-x-1769, à Lacombe, Best. 14982). Voltaire n'hésite pas à se réclamer de l'appui de Dupaty dans une lettre au gouverneur de Guyenne, le duc de Richelieu, à qui il le présente comme un «jeune avocat général qui pétille d'esprit et qui déteste cordialement les prêtres de Pluton», d'ailleurs un «idolâtre de la tolérance» (20-iv-1770, Best. 15301). Le 25 juin (Best. 15436), il le décrit au même Richelieu comme «un franc Guèbre» qui s'arrangera pour autoriser la représentation de sa pièce. Il ne semble pas se douter de l'opposition sourde, puis violente, qui existait entre les deux hommes, représentants d'intérêts contradictoires et de groupes sociaux antagonistes.[16]

En effet, le moment était venu, pour Dupaty, d'entrer enfin dans la grande histoire. Enhardis par leur victoire sur les Jésuites, les parlementaires avaient osé défier le pouvoir central en prenant fait et cause pour leurs collègues bretons, que le procureur général de Rennes, La Chalotais, avait dressés contre le duc d'Aiguillon. Dupaty incita ses confrères bordelais à se montrer irréductibles dans la défense de leurs prérogatives, en s'inspirant de la théorie des «pouvoirs intermédiaires» chère à Montesquieu. Aussi lui revint-il de rédiger, le 13 août 1770, des remontrances au Roi, conçues dans un esprit de résistance ouverte. Le choc devait aboutir à la chute de Choiseul et à la venue au pouvoir du triumvirat Terray-Maupeou-Aiguillon. Le gouvernement, se sentant défié, réagit avec promptitude et sa riposte fut très dure. Le 25 septembre 1770, Dupaty était arrêté dans sa résidence de Clam, en Saintonge, et enfermé près de Lyon au château de Pierre-Encise. Les protestations du Parlement entraînèrent sa libération, mais il fut astreint à rester en résidence surveillée à Roanne où il s'occupa à lire et à commenter Beccaria. Libéré complètement au printemps de 1771, il rentrait aussitôt au Parlement, mais pour très peu de temps puisqu'en septembre 1771 tout le corps des parlementaires bordelais se voyait condamné à l'exil, en raison de sa coalition avec les réfractaires du Parlement de Paris. Dupaty devait, pendant trois ans

1771–1774), mener une existence obscure à Muret.[17] Du moins ses mésaventures lui avaient-elles valu de connaître, pendant quelques mois, les fumées de la gloire et les agréments de la popularité.

Voltaire, pourtant favorable aux réformes de Maupeou, s'émut vivement du sort de son jeune protégé, comme en font foi plusieurs lettres de la fin de 1770. Écrivant à d'Alembert, il s'inquiète de l'arrestation d'un «jeune philosophe» dont les seuls délits sont d'aimer la tolérance, la liberté et Henri IV (20-x-1770, Best. 15690). A son correspondant F. L. C. Marin, il dit «s'intéresser infiniment» à l'avocat général de Bordeaux (24-x-1770, Best. 15701). Un peu plus tard, il s'informe à nouveau auprès de d'Alembert: «Je serais très affligé s'il est vrai que mon Alcibiade,[18] dans sa vieillesse, persécute mon jeune Socrate de Bordeaux. Ou je suis bien trompé, ou mon Socrate est un philosophe intrépide. [. . .] Vous me mandez qu'il est gai dans son château [de Pierre-Encise]; mais moi je m'attriste en songeant qu'il suffit d'une demi-feuille de papier pour ôter la liberté à un magistrat plein de vertu et de mérite» (5-xi-1770, Best. 15722). Dans sa réponse, écrite au retour d'un voyage dans le Midi, d'Alembert lui annonçait la nouvelle de l'exil à Roanne (4-xii-1770, Best. 15777). Sur quoi Voltaire s'empressa de réconforter Dupaty en lui annonçant qu'il venait d'ajouter son nom à celui du chancelier d'Aguesseau dans l'édition des *Questions sur l'Encyclopédie* qui s'imprimait à Genève,[19] ajoutant que c'était faire grand honneur à un magistrat janséniste, qui n'était pas, comme lui, à la fois «philosophe et patriote», et l'assurant par surcroît de son zèle, de son estime et de son respect (15-xii-1770, Best. 15797). Quand on songe que la formule s'adressait à un homme de vingt-quatre ans, on se dit qu'elle avait de quoi lui tourner la tête. Dupaty allait d'ailleurs être l'hôte de Voltaire à Ferney en février 1771. Il lui avait, au préalable, adressé une lettre, datée de Roanne le 19 janvier 1771 (Best. 15949), où les mâles déclarations d'indépendance alternent assez fâcheusement avec des grâces maniérées et des prétentions au bel-esprit. Visiblement, Dupaty s'y tortille afin d'être brillant, spirituel et d'étaler ses lectures. Il fallait cependant du courage pour écrire, du fond de son exil: «[les Français] se plaignent d'être esclaves, ils n'ont qu'à dire tous: nous sommes libres, et ils le seront. Mais il faut désespérer d'une nation dont une moitié est payée pour opprimer l'autre, où personne ne connaît ni ses lois, ni ses droits, et où l'on ne sait que persécuter tous ceux qui pensent ou qui font de grandes choses . . . Le projet est formé d'éteindre le flambeau que vous avez allumé. Déjà Séguier a voulu souffler. Ils ne rêvent aujourd'hui que ligue et complot . . .». Mais il se comparait ensuite à Antisthène, inquiet de se voir loué par le peuple, proclamait avec emphase qu'il ne se sentait pas exilé puisqu' «on n'est point en exil où l'on peut penser, sentir et aimer» et assurait Voltaire en conclusion: «Tant que ce cœur battra, vous serez où je suis, et je serai où vous êtes». Tout Dupaty est dans ce mélange de rhétorique et de vigueur, d'ostentation et de sincérité, d'élan généreux et d'affectation encore scolaire. Cet homme qui semble avoir le goût de la bravade, et même du défi, est aussi très sensible au qu'en-dira-t-on. Il versifie dans l'intimité et envoie des poèmes de sa façon à Voltaire (Best. 15820, du 20-xii-1770), mais il le supplie de ne pas les divulguer, parce que la barbarie régnante est telle que le Parnasse, pour un magistrat, «est presque un mauvais lieu» (Best. 16011). On retrouvera plus tard ce souci de ne pas choquer, cette prudence qui correspond à la volonté bien arrêtée de ne pas compromettre une carrière.[20] Au dix-huitième siècle aussi, on pouvait être à la fois opposant et conformiste.

Ses collègues parlementaires n'y furent pas insensibles. Eux qui l'avaient soutenu et suivi dans le conflit avec le gouvernement ne tardèrent pas à lui faire grise mine à son retour. S'était-il trop ouvertement compromis, à leurs yeux, avec les «philosophes»? Le soupçonnaient-ils de se préparer une trop brillante carrière? Méprisaient-ils, au fond d'eux-mêmes, ce riche parvenu? Tous ces éléments ont joué, mais le plus déterminant fut sans doute le coup de barre du pouvoir central au moment de l'avènement du jeune Louis XVI (1774). Les Parlements sont alors rétablis dans leurs prérogatives, mais le gouvernement s'efforce en même temps de coordonner et de moderniser la jurisprudence, ce qui lui concilie aussitôt les faveurs du parti réformateur et des «philosophes». Dupaty, qui avait été l'inspirateur et l'organisateur de la résistance à Maupeou, trouve, à son retour de Muret, un Parlement hostile à toute réforme, bien décidé à reconquérir les privilèges des robins. Les causes de friction, puis de choc, vont se multiplier et le conflit devient ouvert lorsque Dupaty, après une longue attente, finit par acquérir une «survivance» dans la charge de Président à mortier. Toutes les arguties juridiques, toutes les rebuffades, toutes les humiliations publiques seront bonnes pour décourager, puis écœurer, cet ambitieux qui ne possède ni quartiers de noblesse, ni trois générations d'ancêtres magistrats. L'affaire prendra les proportions d'un défi ouvert lancé par les orgueilleux parlementaires au secrétaire d'État Vergennes. Toute la France se passionne pour ce conflit d'autorité. Dans les seuls *Mémoires secrets* de Bachaumont, près de 80 notices sont consacrées à «l'affaire Dupaty», et certaines sont fort longues, reprenant des discours, des mémoires, ou des lettres royales. L'ancien «patriote» de 1770 apparaissait aux yeux des uns comme l'homme-lige du gouvernement, comme une victime de la morgue parlementaire et de l'obscurantisme aux yeux des autres. Que Dupaty ait déplu par son agitation et son goût de la publicité, on n'en saurait douter, mais il incarnait aussi l'ascension d'une bourgeoisie non issue de la robe et son alliance avec un groupe de penseurs hostiles à la religion, ou du moins à son emprise sur la société. Ce renversement d'alliances est caractéristique d'une époque qui vit la venue au pouvoir de Turgot, de Malesherbes, de Vergennes, de Necker. Les épisodes du conflit entre Dupaty et les parlementaires bordelais (ou du moins la majorité d'entre eux) défrayèrent longtemps la chronique. La petite guerre dura des années: elle provoqua une grève des juges, une intervention directe du Roi, l'exil du premier Président; signe des temps: elle s'acheva sur un armistice, le gouvernement chargeant Dupaty de préparer la réforme de toute la justice criminelle et l'envoyant en Italie pour y étudier le problème (1784–85). C'était une manière élégante d'éloigner de Bordeaux le magistrat contesté, sans pour autant le désavouer ou se déjuger. De cette expérience italienne, Dupaty devait tirer la matière de ses *Lettres sur l'Italie*, publiées en 1788, avant une mort précoce qui lui évita peut-être l'échafaud où montèrent son protecteur Malesherbes et ses protégés Vergniaud et Roucher.

Mais la haine des Parlementaires et leur obstination à le chasser de leurs rangs n'étaient pas les seuls titres de Dupaty à la sympathie du public. Comme ses contemporains, il admirait en Voltaire le défenseur des Calas autant que le dramaturge ou le poète. Particulièrement au fait des défaillances de la procédure et de la fragilité des preuves, sensible à la

discrimination qui pesait sur les paysans et sur les ouvriers, Dupaty va mener campagne
pour rouvrir des dossiers criminels douteux et pour revoir des jugements trop sévères. Sa
première intervention se situe à Bordeaux lorsqu'en sa qualité de président de la Tournelle,
il fait libérer—au grand dam des procureurs—un particulier qu'il tient pour détenu arbitraire-
ment (1773). Peu de temps après, il alerte l'opinion dans l'affaire de trois paysans de Chaumont, accusés de vol nocturne avec effraction (à une époque où le vol domestique entraînait
ipso facto la peine de mort), et condamnés au supplice de la roue. Son *Mémoire justificatif
pour Lardoise, Simare et Bradier . . .* (1786, 251 pp. in-4°) fera sensation jusqu'à la Cour, où
Marie-Antoinette s'émeut et envoie de l'argent aux accusés. En 1787, il leur évitera
définitivement l'exécution. Enhardi par ce succès, Dupaty saisit toutes les occasions qui lui
permettront, au prix d'un éclat public, de faire progresser l'idée d'une refonte complète
de la justice criminelle: c'est l'affaire Estinès à Toulouse, puis celle des sept Allemands roués
à Metz en 1769, et qu'il fait réhabiliter. En dépit de l'opposition de la haute magistrature,
il impose au public la conviction de l'urgente nécessité d'une réforme profonde du système
judiciaire français. En 1788, à l'occasion de l'Assemblée des notables, il lance une violente
philippique contre des méthodes désuètes et cruelles dans ses *Lettres sur la procédure criminelle
de la France, dans lesquelles on montre sa conformité avec celle de l'Inquisition, et les abus qui en
résultent* (177 pp. in-8°) qui font de lui une manière de Beccaria français. Sa mort inopinée,
survenue le 17 septembre 1788, l'empêchera de réaliser son grand projet (qui illustre la
volonté de changement qui prévalait dans les cercles dirigeants avant 1789), et aussi de
connaître une Révolution qui lui aurait probablement été fatale.

Il serait intéressant de relire attentivement les œuvres juridiques de Dupaty, dans la
mesure où elles ne se dissocient jamais de son sens de l'humain, de la vérité et de l'équité.
Sa critique de la torture, de la procédure secrète, des châtiments disproportionnés, de
l'inégalité des prévenus devant la loi, tout cela relève de ce que les «lumières» ont de plus
généreux et de plus positif.

Mais tout cela s'enrobe aussi dans une rhétorique qui, avec le recul, donne une impression
d'apprêt et de pose. A l'époque, au contraire, on en approuvait «la grande clarté, la logique
pressante, l'éloquence vigoureuse, la saine hardiesse» (*Mémoires secrets*, 10 mars 1786).
Les milieux maçonniques s'étaient empressés de fêter son courage et son patriotisme: le
16 août 1779, la Loge des Neuf Sœurs le couronnait à l'occasion de sa fête annuelle au
Wauxhall;[21] on y lisait un extrait du chant IX consacré au mois de novembre dans le
poème *Les Mois* du jeune Roucher, où Dupaty était célébré comme défenseur de la liberté,
comme magistrat incorruptible, comme ami généreux:[22]

> Je ne veux confier ce sacré ministère
> Qu'à l'homme vertueux, dont l'éloquence austère
> N'adopte, pour tonner contre l'oppression,
> Ni mot injurieux, ni lâche passion:
> Qu'à l'inflexible honneur il soit resté fidèle,
> Et qu'enfin Dupaty lui serve de modèle.
>
> Peut-être à ce seul mot, Dupaty, rougis-tu?
> Mais à notre amitié bien moins qu'à ta vertu
> Je devais aujourd'hui ce solennel hommage [. . .]

On saura que j'avais pour ami véritable[23]
Un homme incorruptible, intrépide, équitable,
Qui, *sensible aux malheurs par le peuple soufferts*,
Sut braver, jeune encore, et l'exil et les fers.
Poursuis donc, Dupaty, ta course glorieuse [. . .]

En 1786, la même Loge faisait graver son portrait pour rappeler son intervention en faveur des trois condamnés de Chaumont. Après avoir bénéficié de l'appui et de l'admiration de Voltaire et de Diderot, il s'était lié d'amitié avec la nouvelle génération des «philosophes», avec Condorcet tout particulièrement, mais aussi avec Chamfort qui le tenait pour «un des hommes les plus vertueux du royaume, plein d'esprit, de talent et de simplicité» (lettre d'octobre 1775). Protecteur des belles-lettres, il fut le mécène, non seulement de Roucher, mais aussi de Nicolas-Louis François, dit François de Neufchâteau,[24] à qui il trouva un emploi à Saint-Domingue, et qui l'en remercia par un quatrain qui figure au-dessous du portrait de Dupaty dans certaines éditions:

De l'absence et du temps, quel ascendant vainqueur!
Ton buste, ô Dupaty, me console et m'enflâme;
Et la publique voix parle moins à mon cœur
Que ce marbre éloquent où respire ton âme.

A la fin de sa vie, Dupaty devait ajouter à cette double auréole de mécène des lettres et de réformateur des abus la gloire, plus durable encore, de l'écrivain. C'est en 1788 seulement qu'il se décida à publier, après l'avoir retouchée et mise en forme, sa correspondance du voyage italien de 1784–1785. Il mourut trop tôt pour en connaître le succès, qui fut considérable et se prolongea jusque sous la Restauration.[25]

Les *Lettres sur l'Italie, écrites en 1785* ne sont ni un simple récit de voyage, ni un guide touristique, comme les *Délices d'Italie* de Rogissart (1707), comme le *Nouveau Voyage d'Italie* de Misson (1691–1698), ou comme cette encyclopédie de l'Italie ancienne et moderne géographique, économique et artistique qu'est le *Voyage en Italie* de Lalande (1769). Il offre plus d'analogie avec les *Lettres familières* du président de Brosses, et surtout avec les *Considérations sur l'Italie* de Duclos, mais ces deux ouvrages n'ont paru qu'après la Révolution (respectivement en 1799, dans une édition très fautive—qui ne fut corrigée qu'en 1836— et en 1791), et leur style diffère profondément de celui de Dupaty. La ressemblance tient surtout à ce que de Brosses en 1739, Duclos en 1767, et Dupaty en 1785 voyagent en «philosophes», curieux de mœurs autant que de beaux-arts, et qu'ils réfléchissent aux problèmes de retard culturel, de paupérisme, de superstition qui se posent à eux à chacune de leurs étapes.[26]

Le décalage entre les trois auteurs est surtout affaire de sensibilité, de style et de ton. A l'impressionnisme de Charles de Brosses, à la gravité un peu sèche de Duclos succèdent, avec Dupaty, l'exhibitionnisme sentimental et le goût du pathétique. A l'instar de Diderot, de Mercier ou même de Baculard, il affectionne le style exclamatif, le cri entrecoupé de points de suspension, l'ivresse lyrique, la pose extatique, l'épanchement attendri.

Tout le monde n'appréciera pas cette phraséologie, cette rhétorique passablement vaticinante.[27] Les sceptiques et les «rationaux» ironiseront cruellement, comme la vieille marquise de Créqui dans une lettre à Sénac de Meilhan: «Il y joue Montesquieu, comme le singe joue l'homme [. . .] et partout des sensations, des émotions. [. . .] Il faut cependant voir cela, afin d'accroître, s'il se peut, son mépris sur les réputations; car cela réussit.» La Harpe parlera d'un «mélange de bon sens et de faux esprit». D'autres critiqueront la continuelle recherche, l'abus des néologismes, les allures inspirées et une perpétuelle affectation d' «humanité» et de «sensibilité», comme autant de concessions à la mode. Mais c'est précisément en tant qu'expression d'un moment très curieux de la sensibilité en France que ce livre mérite d'être relu. Dupaty y apparaît à la fois comme un généreux réformateur, comme un disciple des «encyclopédistes», comme une âme déjà romantique et comme un esthète néo-classique. Peu d'écrivains sont aussi représentatifs de la synthèse qui était en voie de s'opérer à la fin du siècle, et qui visait à concilier les élans du cœur avec les exigences de la raison.

Dans l'*Avertissement* de l'édition de 1788, l'auteur revendique avec vigueur la qualité d' «âme sensible»:

On reprochera peut-être à l'auteur d'avoir écrit plusieurs endroits avec un certain enthousiasme, avec sensibilité; mais souvent il a écrit en présence même des objets, et il a le malheur de sentir. [. . .] On pourra encore accuser le style d'être quelquefois poétique. Comment décrire un tableau sans en faire un?

Duclos avait mis l'accent sur la malpropreté des auberges, sur la déchéance des Romains (qu'il préférait appeler «les habitants de Rome»), sur la crapule et la filouterie des Napolitains. Dupaty est beaucoup plus disposé à s'attendrir ou à sympathiser. A Toulon et à Gênes, il s'apitoie sur le sort atroce des galériens, à Monaco sur la misère des pauvres. Il fait le procès de l'administration génoise, de la prétendue liberté lucquoise, et réserve toute son admiration au Grand-Duc de Toscane, prince éclairé, moderne et «philosophe», qui a tiré ses états du sous-développement. Les défauts des Napolitains le choquent moins que Duclos, et il est sensible à leur amour des enfants ainsi qu'à leur conception très originale du bonheur de vivre.

Nourri de souvenirs classiques, de Plutarque au *De Viris* et de Cicéron à Horace, il proclame sa déception devant le spectacle d'une Rome humiliée, misérable, ravagée par «la faux du temps, la hache de la barbarie ou le flambeau du fanatisme»(Lettre XLVI). Il s'écrie, après Montaigne, «Non, cette ville n'est pas Rome, c'est son cadavre; cette campagne, où elle gît, est son tombeau; et cette population, qui fourmille au milieu d'elle, des vers qui la dévorent» (Lettre XLIV), et pourtant, de cette ville dont presque plus rien ne subsiste, si ce n'est le Colisée et le Panthéon, le prestige est toujours irrésistible: «la renommée de Rome n'étonne plus, que Rome étonne encore» (Lettre XLVI).

Mais le disciple de Montesquieu cède bientôt la place au contemporain de Delille et de Bernardin. Traducteur de Tibulle et de Properce (dont il intercale des passages traduits de sa plume aux endroits les plus appropriés), il s'attarde volontiers au charme des lieux agrestes, aux plaisirs de la solitude, aux délices de l'imagination. Il s'assied (Lettre L) parmi les fleurs, dans le tombeau de Cécilia Métella, et se laisse envahir par la beauté du site, par le bourdonnement des abeilles, par les souvenirs historiques, et par «mille autres impressions [qui] jetèrent peu à peu mon âme dans une rêverie délicieuse».

La lettre LIV, écrite de Tivoli, est d'une écriture déjà pleinement romantique, qui insiste sur le fracas de la cascade, sur le tumulte des eaux,[28] sur les contrastes saisissants du paysage:

M

mais cette page digne de Chateaubriand s'achève sur une invocation à Horace!

L'adieu à Tivoli (Lettre LV) associera en lui le père de famille, le poète sensible et l' humaniste classique, pour s'achever sur un discours qui tient à la fois de Rousseau et de l'élégiaque Bertin:

Adieu vallon, adieu cascades, adieu rochers pendants. [. . .] En vain vous voulez me retenir; je suis un étranger. [. . .] Mes enfants, il faudra venir vous asseoir sous cet antique olivier. [. . .] Adieu encore, belles ondes [. . .] que je regretterai [. . .] et non pas tous ces marbres, tous ces bronzes, toutes ces toiles, tous ces monuments tant vantés, car vous, vous êtes la nature, et eux, ils ne sont que l'art.

A Frascati, dont les jardins lui paraissent affreusement dégradés, il montre peu de goût pour les jeux d'eaux bizarres auxquels les Italiens se complaisent, et préfère réserver son intérêt aux «aspects romantiques» du site (Lettre LVIII).

Surtout, Dupaty est l'homme des promenades vespérales et solitaires (au Colisée, Lettre LXXIII): aux «premières ombres du soir», il se délecte à voir «la nuit se glisser par les arcades» et à fixer son regard à la plus haute pierre «sur laquelle le dernier rayon du soleil mourait.» Il affectionne (à l'opposé de Madame de Staël[29]) le mystère et les ténèbres des catacombes (Lettre LXIX, aux catacombes de St Sébastien). «J'aime les lieux souterrains,» écrit-il, «là, détachée de tous ses sens et seule avec elle, l'âme jouit alors de toute sa sensibilité, elle s'élève à une hauteur inconnue. On dirait que la route du ciel est sous la terre». Les lieux «affreux» le charment, lorsqu'ils ont une histoire: le paysage sinistre de Paestum parsemé de mares d'eau croupissante, hanté par les corbeaux et les couleuvres, a pourtant «je ne sais quelle horreur, qui me charme», c'est qu'il s'y projette en imagination dans une ville grecque, parmi les Sybarites (Lettre XCVIII). Mais il n'est pas insensible à la variété des couleurs au plein jour: à la Villa Adriana (Lettre LXXI), il ne se lasse pas «de contempler ces ruines, de couleur violette, répandues sous un ciel d'azur, sur des gazons d'un vert tendre.»

L'auteur de la postface de l'édition de 1792, qui signe C*** et qui doit être Condorcet, souligne, dans une lettre du 4 mars 1790, la manière très particulière qu'avait Dupaty d'écrire, de voir, de louer et de voyager. «L'esprit philosophique marchait le premier [. . .] L'esprit littéraire suivait [...] pour traduire les sensations en images et les récits en spectacles. L'esprit magistral [= de magistrat] n'était pas moins occupé à étudier les lois du pays [. . .] à considérer de sang froid les abus, à confronter le langage de la justice avec les habitudes de la barbarie. [. . .] Les ruines de l'antiquité et l'infortune des grands hommes le frappaient d'une sublime terreur. Il devenait peintre et poète aussitôt que compatissant.»

Faudrait-il tenir pour «préromantique» ce produit exemplaire du croisement des «lumières» et de la sensibilité, ce fervent admirateur des anciens? La vérité est plus complexe: Dupaty est réformateur parce qu'il s'intéresse au sort des déshérités et qu'il est «l'ami des hommes»; il se livre aux épanchements les plus poétiques aux lieux mêmes que sanctifie la poésie latine. La critique du système juridique, en cet adepte de Voltaire et de Montesquieu, trouve sa source dans un élan sentimental.[30] Romantique avant la lettre, il ne connaît pourtant d'autre modèle que «le beau idéal». Contemporain de Laclos et de Bernardin, de Parny et de Delille, ce magistrat «âme sensible», ce «philosophe» poète illustre la richesse et la complexité d'une époque trop méconnue de notre littérature, celle qui correspond aux ultimes années de l'Ancien Régime.

NOTES

1 Selon le témoignage de D.-J. Garat dans ses *Mémoires historiques sur le XVIIIe siècle et sur M. Suard,* deuxième édition (Paris, 1821), i. 236.

2 *A Literary History of France: The Eighteenth Century* (London, 1970), p. 389.

3 Pour une information plus complète, on se référera à la notice rédigée par M. Roman d'Amat pour le *Dictionnaire de Biographie française,* Paris, Letouzey, XII (1970), col. 318–320. Riche et détaillée, cette notice est cependant conçue dans un esprit inutilement polémique.

4 On écrivait indifféremment Dupaty et Du Paty au dix-huitième siècle.

5 Les descendants adopteront au dix-neuvième siècle le patronyme Dupaty de Clam, qui fut rendu tristement célèbre par le rôle que joua dans l'affaire Dreyfus le colonel de ce nom, qui est d'ailleurs l'arrière-petit-fils de notre Dupaty.

6 Son biographe, M. Roman d'Amat, affirme que ses parents avaient 80.000 livres de rentes, ce qui constituait une très grosse fortune à l'époque.

7 L'éloge académique était devenu, au dix-huitième siècle, un véritable genre littéraire, où excellèrent Fontenelle, d'Alembert et Thomas. Il était souvent le véhicule de la pensée «philosophique» et réformiste.

8 Le futur écrivain politique et auteur du roman *L'émigré.*

9 La charge était héréditaire dans la famille de la première femme de son père, née Richard des Herbiers.

10 Voir P. Barrière, *L'Académie de Bordeaux, centre de culture internationale au XVIIIe siècle (1712–1792),* 1951, spéc. pp. 44, 66, 118 et 231.

11 «Le bon Dieu bénisse cet avocat général de Bordeaux qui a fait frapper la médaille de Henri IV gravée par Cathelin d'après Cochin. On dit qu'il est aussi éloquent que généreux. Les parquets de province se sont mis depuis quelque temps à écrire beaucoup mieux que le parquet de Paris.» (Voltaire à G.-H. Gaillard, le 23-1-69; Best. 14482).

12 Le *Discours de M. Dupaty, avocat général, dans la cause d'une veuve accusée d'avoir forfait avant l'an de deuil,* 1769, fera aussitôt l'objet d'un article de Diderot dans la *Correspondance littéraire* du 1er octobre 1769, reproduit dans *Œuvres complètes,* éd. J. Assézat et M. Tourneux (Paris, 1875–7) VI, 388–389.

13 Th. Besterman suppose qu'il s'agissait d'un éloge de Henri IV.

14 Il est significatif que Voltaire et Diderot se servent du même terme pour exprimer ce qui est, à leurs yeux, la forme nouvelle de la relation entre l'individu et la collectivité nationale.

15 La puissance spirituelle et la puissance temporelle, ou l'Église et l'État.

16 Il savait pourtant Richelieu hostile aux philosophes et protecteur de Palissot (voir Best. 15436), et peut-être ne se faisait-il, au fond, pas trop d'illusions sur le sort de sa démarche.

17 La fin de cet exil correspond à la mort de Louis XV et à l'avènement d'un gouvernement plus favorable à la pensée des «lumières». Dupaty occupa ses loisirs en rédigeant, pour l'Académie de Bordeaux, un *Éloge de Montaigne* conçu dans une optique très «philosophique» (1772).

18 Le duc de Richelieu (1696–1788), gouverneur de Guyenne et maréchal de France.

19 Éd. Moland, XVIII. 16. Il s'agit du fameux article «Blé», section VI, *Grammaire, morale,* où Voltaire commente le dicton «Ne nous remets pas au gland quand nous avons du blé» et dénonce les archaïsmes intolérables de la société du XVIIIe siècle: «Ne nous gouverne plus dans le XVIIIe siècle comme on gouvernait au temps d'Albouin, de Gondebald. [. . .] Ne parle plus des lois de Dagobert, quand nous avons les œuvres du chancelier d'Aguesseau, les discours de MM. les gens du roi, Montclar, Servan, Castillon, La Chalotais, Dupaty, etc. Ne nous cite plus les miracles de saint Amable».

20 En 1784, Beaumarchais envoya à Dupaty des billets de loge pour la représentation du *Mariage de Figaro,* dont on sait quelle opposition il avait suscitée dans l'entourage du Roi et de la part de Suard, alors censeur royal. Dupaty sollicita l'échange de ses billets de loge contre des billets de

rez-de-chaussée, arguant du fait qu'il se rendait au théâtre avec sa femme et ses filles «qui ont leurs raisons de ne pas se montrer en public». Beaumarchais lui répondit par une lettre cinglante, le 10 mai 1784: «Je n'ai nulle considération [. . .] pour des femmes qui se permettent de voir un spectacle qu'elles jugent malhonnête, pourvu qu'elles le voient en secret. J'ai donné ma pièce au public pour l'amuser et pour l'instruire, non pour offrir à des bégueules mitigées le plaisir d'aller en penser du bien en petite loge, à condition d'en dire du mal en société. Les plaisirs du vice et les honneurs de la vertu, telle est la pruderie du siècle. Ma pièce n'est point un ouvrage équivoque; il faut l'avouer, ou le fuir. Je vous salue et je garde ma loge» (L. de Loménie, *Beaumarchais et son temps,* II, 581). Sainte-Beuve affirme que cet incident était destiné (comme quelques autres) à faire de la réclame pour une pièce qui n'en avait pas besoin (*Causeries du Lundi,* 21 juin 1852, Paris, Garnier, 4e éd., VI, 237).

21 Mais Dupaty plaça modestement ses lauriers sur la tête du jeune Garat (qui venait de composer un éloge de Montesquieu). Garat citera Dupaty dans ses *Mémoires historiques* (éd. 1821, I, 345) à propos de l'affaire des trois hommes de Chaumont, mais sans rappeler l'existence de ces liens personnels.

22 Dans la somptueuse édition illustrée de 1779, publiée par souscription, ce passage se trouve au t.II, pp. 136–137.

23 Roucher, venu à Bordeaux pour y présenter son poème, y avait trouvé un admirateur enthousiaste en Dupaty. Celui-ci lui procura, par ses relations à Paris, le poste de receveur de la gabelle (sans résidence) à Montfort-l'Amaury. On sait que le malheureux Roucher fut exécuté le même jour qu'André Chénier, en 1794.

24 François de Neufchâteau fut ministre de l'Intérieur après Thermidor, comme Garat le fut avant la Terreur. Il est significatif de retrouver à ce poste deux anciens protégés de Dupaty.

25 Quérard en cite une dizaine d'éditions. Celles de 1819, 1824 et 1825 comportent une notice bio-graphique sur l'auteur. L'édition originale de 1788 était anonyme.

26 La seule étude détaillée sur le sujet est, à notre connaissance, l'article de E. Berti Toesca, 'Il Presidente Du Paty alla scoperta dell'Italia', dans *Nuova Antologia,* octobre 1956, 205–218.—Voir aussi J. Bertaut, *L'Italie vue par les Français,* (s.d.), p. 125.

27 Stendhal détestera évidemment le style de Dupaty au même titre que celui de Chateaubriand. Il se gausse des «traits d'esprit du président Dupaty», tout juste bons pour des commis marchands français, et s'indigne que son livre, «protégé par les industriels» ait eu quarante éditions (*Promenades dans Rome,* Firenze, Parenti, I, 91, daté du 11 novembre 1827). Stendhal fait erreur dans son estima-tion, et on voit mal qu'il y ait dans les *Lettres* des plaisanteries pour commis-voyageurs. Chateau-briand, qui aurait dû exécrer en Dupaty le voltairien anticlérical, s'est montré au contraire plus équitable pour son prédécesseur: «L'admiration déclamatoire de Dupaty n'offre pas de compensa-tion pour l'aridité de Duclos et de Lalande, elle fait pourtant sentir la présence de Rome; on s'aperçoit par un reflet que l'éloquence du style descriptif est née sous le souffle de Rousseau, *spiraculum vitae.* Dupaty touche à cette nouvelle école qui bientôt allait substituer le sentimental, l'obscur et le maniéré, au vrai, à la clarté et au naturel de Voltaire. Cependant, à travers son jargon affecté, Dupaty observe avec justesse. [. . .] A la villa Borghèse, Dupaty voit approcher la nuit: «Il ne reste qu'un rayon du jour qui meurt sur le front d'une Vénus». Les poètes de maintenant diraient-ils mieux?» (*Mémoires d'Outre-Tombe,* éd. Levaillant, III, 431–432). A la date où Chateau-briand écrit ses *Mémoires,* il a renié beaucoup d'aspects du premier romantisme et repris goût au dix-huitième siècle, si vilipendé dans *Le Génie du Christianisme.*

28 Déjà la première Lettre, écrite d'Avignon, montrait la fontaine de Vaucluse plus violente et plus contrastée que ne l'avaient représentée Pétrarque et Delille (dans *Les Jardins*).

29 L'auteur de *Corinne* a bien connu Dupaty, grand admirateur de son père, et elle s'est souvenue des *Lettres* dans son roman. Voir C. Pellegrini, 'A proposito della cornice di *Corinne,*' *Mélanges Henri Hauvette* (Paris, 1934), pp. 511–518.

30 Il vérifie ce que disait, trente ans plus tôt, l'article «Foible» de l'*Encyclopédie*: «à mesure que l'esprit acquiert plus de lumières, le cœur acquiert plus de sensibilité.»

16

King Arthur: Style Louis XVI

LYNETTE R. MUIR

Shortly before the fatal battle of Salisbury, in which he receives a mortal wound, Arthur, king of Logres, has a vision of the Wheel of Fortune: 'En cele roe avoit sieges dont li un montoient et li autre avaloient; li rois regardoit en quel leu de la roe il estoit assis et voit que ses sieges estoit li plus hauz'.[1] Soon, however, Fortune turns her wheel and Arthur crashes down 'si felenessement que au cheoir estoit avis au roi Artu qu'il estoit touz debrisiez et qu'il perdoit tout le pooir del cors et des membres'.[2] In this vision, we are told, 'vit li rois Artus les mescheances qui li estoient a avenir';[3] but we may, perhaps, also see in it a figure of the fluctuating fortunes of King Arthur in the succeeding centuries.

Even before the end of the Middle Ages the person of Arthur himself, as distinct from his knights and the Round Table, had undergone a series of metamorphoses, and this is particularly noticeable if we compare the French and English developments in Arthurian romance from the twelfth to the fifteenth century. Even if we ignore, as the medieval writers would appear to have done, the pre-Geoffrey of Monmouth annals and Celtic manifestations of Arthur, it is still notable that on the common foundation of the *Historia Regum Britanniae,* French and English romance constructed two quite separate and independent structures.[4] One of the principal differences between these two towers of Vortigern is the role of Arthur himself. More and more, in the French romances, the king is supplanted by his major knights and especially by the lineage of Ban.[5] Lancelot, the Frenchman, replaces the British Gawain as the dominant knight of the Round Table, and the Welsh Perceval is relegated to second place in the Grail Quest by Galahad who has the double qualification of being Lancelot's son and pure of all earthly taint. In contrast to this tendency, we find in English literature a series of Gawain romances which have no French equivalents, and two verse redactions of the Decline and Fall of the Arthurian Empire, in addition to that contained in Malory. In these English poems, however, Arthur appears less as a figure of romance than as a king of legend, a great British Worthy. The thirteenth-century alliterative *Morte Arthure* contains a version of the Wheel of Fortune episode in which the vision in the *Mort Artu* is elaborated into a pageant of the Nine Worthies. The first six, Alexander, Hector and Julius Cæsar, Judas Maccabeus, Joshua and David, are already on the Wheel and, as Arthur watches, they crash down amid lamentations. Two others, Charlemagne and Godfrey de Bouillon, are busy clambering towards the highest seat, when Fortune herself raises Arthur above them:

> Scho lifte me up lightly with her lene hondes,
>   And sette me softly in the see, the septre me rechede;
> [. . .] Dressid oñe me a diademe, that dighte was fulle faire
>   And syne profres me a pome pighte fulle of faire stonys,
> [. . .] In sygne that I sothely was soverayne in erthe.[6]

It is scarcely surprising that the protagonists of the two great cycles of romance, the *Matière de Bretagne* and the *Matière de France*, should have been brought into confrontation in this way, but whereas in this text the English author is generous in his praise of Charlemagne:

> He salle be crowelle and kene and conquerour holdene,
>   Covere be conqueste contres ynewe;[7]

the same generosity had not been shown towards Arthur by the thirteenth-century French author of the *Prose Tristan* who introduced the emperor Charlemagne into his work, apparently for the exclusive purpose of disparaging the achievements of his predecessor. All the versions of this episode describe how Charlemagne conquered England and saw relics of Arthur and his knights which led him to criticise the king for having achieved so little when he had such warriors: 'Et lors dist que voirement avoit li roys Artus cueur d'enfant qui tant avoit eu aveuc lui de preudommes et de bons chevaliers [. . .] et si n'avoit en tout son eage conquesté que un pou de terre [. . .] qui peust tout le monde par force de chevalerie avoir conquis et mis en sa subjection'.[8] It is surely significant that these episodes begin to appear in the early thirteenth century, at a time when France, under Philip Augustus, was rapidly winning back large areas of territory which had been part of the Anglo-Norman empire when the first Arthurian romances were composed. Not surprisingly this Charlemagne incident is conspicuously absent from the English versions of the Tristan cycles, though it occurs in French, Italian, Spanish and Portuguese.

The revival of classical literature at the end of the Middle Ages may have represented a turn of Fortune's Wheel for Arthur and his knights of the Round Table, but his destruction was neither total nor lasting; in both England and France, indeed, examples of Arthurian works in classical forms are to be found. One example of 'classicised' Arthur is Alamanni's epic, *L'Avarchide*, which appeared after his death in 1556. The subject of this pseudo-Iliad is the siege of Clodasso (Claudas in the *Prose Lancelot*) by the knights of the Round Table, led by Arthur, Lancelot and Galehaut 'who play the parts of Agamemnon, Achilles and Patroclus respectively.'[9] From England there comes Thomas Hughes's pseudo-Senecan tragedy, the *Misfortunes of Arthur* (1558) which is firmly based on Geoffrey and omits any mention of the whole *corpus* of French Lancelot romance.[10] These two works, although they are both classical in form and Arthurian in subject, epitomise the early post-medieval development of Arthurian literature in France and England: the dichotomy between romance and history is firmly established and this sets the tone for the next two centuries. In England, with the exception of reprints of Malory and other standard texts, Arthur appears in the seventeenth century only as a historical figure, usually as a focus for the ideals of Restoration monarchy. Rejected as a worthy epic hero by both Milton and Dryden, though for different reasons, the wretched Arthur fell into the hands of Blackmore whose epics, *Prince Arthur* and *King Arthur,* were denounced by Dryden:

> All the former fustian stuff he wrote
> Was dead-born doggrel or is quite forgot.[11]

Blackmore, whose indifferent qualities as a poet fully justify Dryden's attacks, makes little use of even the historico-legendary material of Geoffrey. His *Arthurs* are political allegory, and it is really only in name that Arthur is involved.[12] Nor is there much more than the names in Dryden's opera *King Arthur or the British Worthy* which describes a victory of Britons over Saxons in which the valour of Arthur only triumphs because of the magic of Merlin. Dryden, too, only triumphs over Blackmore because of the magic of Purcell's music. The text is as banal as the fustian he accused Blackmore of writing.[13]

Not surprisingly, these disastrous attempts to keep Arthur alive as a historical figure caused his almost total disappearance from romantic literature in England, where from Spenser to Scott Arthurian romance is virtually unknown.[14]

English poets of the seventeenth century, seeking a theme for their national epics, tended to consider carefully, even if they sometimes by a fine instinct later rejected, the most famous of the medieval British conquerors, Arthur; their French counterparts had no such problem. For national heroes and heroic poetry there was a plethora of great figures to choose from, led by Arthur's great rival, Charlemagne.[15] Arthur did, however, survive in France even in that most classical century, but almost exclusively as a figure-head, the founder and president of the Round Table. In the post-medieval, as in the medieval period, French romance tended to be more interested in knights than kings. On the heels of *Amadis de Gaule* there followed a great troop of semi-pastoral, semi-chivalrous romances, some of which included Arthurian characters and many of which were indebted to the Round Table for their ideas of chivalry: 'the glorified type of the knight stood out, fashioned after one pattern and expressing a common ideal. [. . .] What accentuated the fondness for these knights of old was the growing realization that modern nobility was on the decline'.[16] The seventeenth century looked back to the Golden Age of St Louis as Chrétien had looked back to the age of Arthur when:

> cil qui soloient amer
> se feisoient cortois clamer
> et preu et large et enorable;
> or est Amors tornee a fable. (*Yvain,* 21–24)

or the author of the *Vie de Saint Alexis* looking back yet further to the 'tens ancïenur' when 'feit i ert e justise ed amur' (1–2).

This habit of looking back to the age of Arthur as an ideal of manners and morals rather than an age of conquest and victory marks a fundamental difference between the English and French attitudes to the *Matière de Bretagne* and explains why the British king survived more readily in France than in England. There were, of course, many among the more erudite who condemned the old romances out of hand: 'Ces histoires faites à plaisir plurent à des lecteurs simples, et plus ignorans encore que ceux qui les composoient'[17] but in the world of chivalry a champion never failed to come forward to defend the accused, and even in seventeenth-century France Romance did not lack her Lohengrin, though the terms in which Chapelain defends the *Lancelot* are less than enthusiastic: 'J'ai lu ce livre [the early printed text of *Lancelot*] et ne l'ai point trouvé trop désagreable; entre les choses qui m'y ont plu, j'y ai vu la source de tous les romans qui, depuis quatre ou cinq siècles, ont fait le plus noble divertissement des cours de l'Europe'.[18]

Chapelain and his followers defended the old romances primarily because they were a valuable source of linguistic information for philologists; he praises the stories, as distinct from the style which he ruthlessly condemns, as being well contrived, but above all he favours reading 'ces vieux romans' because they 'peignent au naturel les mœurs et les coutumes de ces mêmes siècles'.[19]

Chapelain's insistence on the merit of the romances as stories is more important than he realised, since a good story always attracts an audience and it is not surprising that the great Arthurian revival of the pre-romantic period should have concentrated on the story of the Round Table and the adventures of its members rather than on the uninteresting and dubiously historical conquests of its leader. The first great flowering of Arthurian romance had begun in France with Chrétien de Troyes and his coevals, whence it spread all over Europe and it was not then unfitting or surprising that the second blooming should have followed the same pattern, though it is perhaps a little ironical that it should have occurred in the century and the country which saw the great developments of reason, order and enlightenment: eighteenth-century France.

The revival of medieval romance in the eighteenth century in France owes much to the work of La Curne de Sainte-Palaye, who was a notable antiquarian and scholar, probably best known for the ambitious *Dictionnaire des Antiquités*, 'through which he intended to do for the Middle Ages and early modern times what classical scholars had done for Ancient Greece and Rome'.[20] It was unfortunately never completed but the seventy-seven quarto volumes of manuscript (with a further seventeen volumes of *Supplément*) give some idea of the scale and richness of the project.

As part of his source material Sainte-Palaye read the medieval romances and encouraged others to do so and, especially, to publish extracts and summaries of them. He justifies this in the *Mémoire concernant la lecture des anciens romans de chevalerie* printed in 1743.[21] The similarity in many points to Chapelain's *La Lecture des vieux romans* was apparently coincidental: 'après avoir achevé ce mémoire j'ai appris que j'avois été prévenu il y a long-temps par M. Chapelain',[22] and Sainte-Palaye, in fact, goes much further in defence of reading romances than Chapelain had done. He quotes, among many other writers on the subject, an interesting comment by Le Laboureur: 'mais je soutiendrois bien qu'il y a de la honte à un savant de ne les avoir pas lûs, ou de les avoir lûs sans profit', and adds his own conclusion: 'Croira-t-on que le Laboureur ait voulu perdre son temps à des études frivoles?'[23] Emboldened by the support of scholars of the seventeenth and eighteenth centuries who had found in the old romances 'un portrait du vieux temps', Sainte-Palaye sets forth his scheme:

'qu'il me soit permis de souhaiter que quelques gens de lettres se partagent entre eux le pénible travail de lire ces sortes d'ouvrages, dont le temps détruit tous les jours quelques morceaux, d'en faire des extraits, qu'ils rapporteront à un système général et uniforme. [. . .] On pouroit ainsi parvenir à avoir une bibliothèque générale et complète de tous nos anciens Romans de Chevalerie'. In these extracts Sainte-Palaye particularly wishes to see preserved the references of use for history, antiquities, genealogies and geography 'sans rien omettre de ce qui donneroit quelques lumières sur les progrès des Arts et des Sciences'. This severely academic approach is not, however, intended to preclude totally an indication of stylistic, moral or psychological felicities.[24]

This project of Sainte-Palaye's, unlike the *Dictionnaire,* did come to fruition and a great number of medieval works found their way into print, usually in abbreviated form, in the great collections of the second half of the century, especially, of course, in the vast *Bibliothèque des Romans* (more than two hundred volumes in the British Museum edition) which appeared in parts from 1776 to 1789, was restarted in the year VI under the title *Nouvelle Bibliothèque* and continued until 1805. Arthurian works included in the *Bibliothèque* were the *Merlin, Lancelot* and *Saint-Graal,* the *Meliadus* and *Tristan, Perceval le Gallois* and *Perceforest.*[25]

In addition, episodes from these works sometimes appeared in unexpected places. The *Fabliaux ou Contes du XIIe et du XIIIe siècle,* published by Legrand d'Aussy in 1779, contained an episode from the *Lancelot* in which the hero, because he was the faithful lover of Queen Guinevere, was able to break the enchantment of the *Vallon des Faux Amants.* A letter about the *Fabliaux* quotes part of this story as an example of how 'ces vieux auteurs possèdent surtout au plus haut point le secret d'exciter l'intérêt de curiosité'. At the conclusion of the extract the writer adds a comment by one of his friends that is unintentionally ironic: 'On voit bien, dit-il, que ce Vallon-là n'a pas été imaginé dans notre siècle. Jamais on ne le verroit désenchanté. Il seroit plus solide que la Bastille'.[26]

The result of the *Bibliothèque des Romans* and the other compilations far outdid Sainte-Palaye's earlier hopes. People began to read medieval romances for pleasure, not for scholarly profit, so that gradually critics began to distinguish between one romance and another, to consider seriously the relative merits of different versions: 'Jamais notre ancienne littérature fut-elle mieux connue qu'elle ne l'est aujourd'hui par l'*Histoire des Troubadours,* par le *Recueil des Fabliaux,* par les *Annales poétiques* et surtout par la *Bibliothèque universelle des Romans'.*[27] These versions of the romances of chivalry (which the eighteenth century divided into three groups: 'ceux de la Table Ronde, ceux de Charlemagne, et les Amadis. La première classe a occupé pendant deux ans les auteurs d'extraits')[28] were contributed by a number of different writers, but there is no doubt that one man in particular did more than any other writer to popularise the romances: the comte de Tressan, whose 'plume élégante et gracieuse n'a pas peu contribué à embellir la Bibliothèque des Romans'.[29] Tressan's major retellings of romance were republished as a separate work from the *Bibliothèque* and the *Corps d'extraits des romans de chevalerye* appeared in 1782.[30] The only Arthurian romance in this collection is the *Tristan,* probably one of the most typical of Tressan's works; it gives us a very good picture of the world of the Round Table as it appeared in the early years of the reign of Louis XVI, and especially of Arthur himself, who plays an important role in Tressan's *Tristan*.

From the moment of Tristan's first meeting with Arthur, we realise that for Tressan the monarch matters. 'Le chevalier vengé lève alors la visière de son casque; une longue barbe blanche tombe sur sa poitrine. La majesté et l'air respectable de ce chevalier fait soupçonner à Tristan que c'est le roi Artus; ce prince le lui confirme.'[31] This meeting sets the tone for the whole romance. The king is always noble and valiant: 'La haute valeur d'Artus en est émue. Après Lancelot du Lac et Gaalaad, ce grand roi passait pour être le meilleur chevalier de la table ronde'.[32] This attitude to Arthur in no way prevents Tressan elaborating the loves of Lancelot and Guinevere. Arthur, the king, is noble and magnanimous. Arthur, the wronged husband, is not even mentioned. This attitude to the dignity of kingship is emphasised in the episode of King Marc's treachery. The Cornish king takes part in a trial by battle against Amans: 'et quoique lâche et faible, il a le bonheur de le tuer'.[33] Fortunately, one of the judges is suspicious because Marc had refused to take the Oath beforehand: 'il suspend tout, et remet la décision de cette affaire au sage et grand monarque Artus. [. . .] Artus intérroge Marc avec cette supériorité et cette majesté qui fait souvent frémir le crime.' Marc is forced to admit the truth: 'Artus frémit d'indignation; mais, respectant la dignité royale', he merely keeps Marc prisoner at the Court. Later, Arthur forces Marc to be reconciled with Tristan. Although this episode is based on the *Prose Tristan,* the treatment is very much Tressan's own, and he does not, in fact, always feel the need to follow his model faithfully. As a result he becomes the only author of Arthurian romance to bring together Tristan and Yseult, Lancelot and Guinevere: 'pendant quelques temps, les illustres habitants de la cour d'Artus et du château de la Joyeuse Garde, se visitèrent souvent. Nous ne voulons point parler de quelques soupers secrets qu'il y eut entre la belle Genièvre, Lancelot et ces deux amants: et quels délicieux soupers!'[34] We have here moved completely away from 'cette naïveté si ingénue, si attachante' which charmed the eighteenth-century reader in the medieval romances. Tressan fell in love with his own creations and softened many crudities of outlook and behaviour in the romances he retold. 'Il n'est pas nécessaire que le détail supprimé soit répugnant, il suffit qu'il soit dépourvu de noblesse'.[35] To maintain this nobility and majesty, Tressan completely revises the Grail Quest. Now it is a question of a crusade by Arthur's knights to recapture the Saintes Reliques: 'Artus, toujours occupé des plus grands projets, l'était alors de la conquête du Saint Graal'.[36] An advantage of this transformation is that it enables Arthur to share in the Quest and he is urged to do this by the voice of Merlin: 'Quelque puissance secrète le fit arrêter près du tombeau qui renfermait Merlin; alors le grand prophète éleva sa voix: "Roi Artus," dit-il, [. . .] "Ores est-il temps de marcher à la queste du Saint Gréal. Roi Artus, écoutes?" '[37] Perhaps, even at that moment, Tressan's King Arthur heard the sound which was to be the death-knell of eighteenth-century monarchy: the trampling of the mob as it marched not to conquer the Grail but to conquer the Bastille which to the writer in 1779 had seemed so solid. For in Tressan's Arthurian world we can recognise an element of fairy-tale escapism—it is no more real than Marie-Antoinette's Versailles farm.[38] In his portrayal of a world where benign monarchy is supported by knights whose valour is only equalled by their gallantry, Tressan created a new version of chivalry which has for the reader today much of the naïve charm which the medieval tales had for the gilded aristocracy of pre-revolutionary Versailles. Perhaps no other post-medieval writer of Arthurian romance has achieved so vivid a picture of King Arthur as the focal point of a glittering court. This Arthur is not a historical ruler, nor a legendary Worthy, scarcely even a figure of chivalrous romance; he has disguised himself in the latest French fashions, and sallies forth like Haroun al Raschid among, dare I say it, his Arabian knights.

NOTES

1 *La Mort le roi Artu,* edited by J. Frappier, T.L.F. (Paris, 1964), p. 226.
2 ibid., p. 227.
3 ibid., p. 227.
4 Even the vernacular texts most closely associated with Geoffrey, the *Bruts* of Wace and of Layamon, display marked differences of detail and style. Cf. *La Partie arthurienne du Roman de Brut,* edited by I. D. O. Arnold and M. M. Pelan, Bibliothèque Française et Romane (Paris, 1962).
5 It is, perhaps, worth emphasising here that the French cycles are known by the name of the principal knight involved: Lancelot or Tristan, while Malory's compilation retained the king's name—*Morte d'Arthur.*
6 *Morte Arthure or the Death of Arthur,* edited by E. Brock, EETS, OS 8 (1865), ll.3349–50, 3353–4, 3357. The *pome* offered as an emblem of power is reminiscent of the scene in the *Chanson de Roland,* laisse xxix:

> [Rolant] En sa main tint une vermeille pume,
> 'Tenez, bel sire', dist Rollant a sun uncle,
> 'De trestuz reis vous present les curunes.' (386–8)

Arthur's vision of Fortune's Wheel is only briefly mentioned in Malory and the figure of Fortune herself has completely disappeared (Malory, *Le Morte d'Arthur,* Book xxi, ch. 3).
7 ed. cit., ll. 3424–5.
8 *Guiron le courtois,* Bibl. Nat., MS français 355, fol. 66r. For the different versions of this story in the *Tristan* and related texts, see my article: 'Le personnage de Charlemagne dans les romans en prose arthuriens' (*Boletin de la Real Academia de Buenas Letras de Barcelona,* 31 (1965–66), 233–41).
9 M. W. Maccallum, *Tennyson's Idylls of the King and Arthurian story from the XVIth century* (Glasgow, 1894), p. 117. Although Alamanni wrote mainly in Italian, his patrons were the French kings, François Ier and Henri II, so he may be considered part of the French tradition at this date.
10 Maccallum, op. cit., pp. 118–24, and R. Barber, *Arthur of Albion* (London, 1961), p. 138.
11 R. Blackmore, *Prince Arthur* (1695) and *King Arthur* (1697) are discussed in some detail by Maccallum (op. cit., pp. 148–158 and Appendix I, pp. 414–8) and briefly by Barber (op. cit., pp. 140–1).
12 Spenser's allegory of the *Faery Queene* cannot really be considered a part of Arthurian literature though it is significant as evidence of the esteem in which the name of Arthur was held in England. Spencer's Arthur is the epitome of chivalry, 'the glass of fashion and the mould of form', although Arthurian romance had been condemned by Ascham because in it: 'those be counted the noblest Knightes that do kill most men without any quarrell and commit foulest advoulteries by sutlest shiftes' (Ascham, *The Scholemaster,* edited by E. Arber, English Reprints (London, 1869), p. 80). Yet even Ascham conceded that 'ten *Morte Arthures* do not the tenth part so much harme, as one of these bookes made in Italie and translated in England' (ibid.).

13 The recent revival of Dryden's *King Arthur* by the English Opera Group underlined the gap between Dryden and Purcell most clearly. The final tableau, in which the Round Table tilted up as a penny (old) with Britannia posed before it to receive the homage of the 'Valiant Britains', should not be considered a happy variant on the tableau of the Order of the Garter prescribed by Dryden (*King Arthur or the British Worthy* (Cambridge, 1928, based on the text of 1701)).

14 cf. Barber's *Chronological List of English Arthurian Literature* (*Arthur of Albion*, Appendix D). It is noticeable that the texts listed between Malory and Scott's *Sir Tristrem* are concerned only with the pseudo-historical Arthur; though it is true that Percy's *Reliques* include a few ballads under whose rustic guise the romances make their earliest post-medieval and pre-romantic appearance in England.

It is ironical, though perhaps not surprising, that the 'historical approach' of English Arthurian stories never inspired any of the writers to envisage a factual Return of Arthur, although such an eventuality survived long in popular tales and superstitions. Here, France can claim a notable first: Guillaume Apollinaire's *Arthur, roi passé roi futur*, published in the *Mercure de France* (15 avril 1914). The scene is London, in the year 2105, and King George IX is on the throne. Arthur, in the guise of 'un Merveilleux Chevalier d'Airain Étincelant et Magnifique', enters Buckingham Palace and claims the throne. The doctors and armourers having declared the body and armour of the claimant to be of an age consonant with the claim, the finishing touch is given when a telegram is brought to the king: 'Ce télégramme lève tous mes doutes. En voici la teneur: Tombeau Arthur vide'. The king abdicates, Arthur marries the princess 'et la vie reprit son cours ordinaire cette année même, 1914, à la date du 1er avril, où j'écris cette chronique.' For Apollinaire, Arthur's return is nothing but an April Fool's joke. (I am grateful to my colleague Dr Berry for introducing me to this entertaining little story.)

15 A list of such works is given in Edelman's comprehensive study: *Attitudes of Seventeenth-Century France toward the Middle Ages* (New York, 1946), ch. 5.

16 Edelman, ch. 3, pp. 97, 98. The whole chapter is rich in quotations of the seventeenth-century attitude to chivalry and its institutions.

17 P. D. Huet, *Traité de l'origine des romans*, edited by A. Kok (Amsterdam, 1942), p. 195.

18 J. Chapelain, *La Lecture des vieux romans*, edited by F. Gégou, with *Lettre-traité de P. D. Huet, sur l'origine des romans* (Paris, 1971), p. 166.

19 Chapelain, ed. cit., p. 180.

20 L. Gossman, *Medievalism and the Ideologies of the Enlightenment. The World and Work of La Curne de Sainte-Palaye* (Baltimore, 1968), p. 268. In 1752 Sainte-Palaye published one of the first adaptations of medieval texts: his *Aucassin et Nicolette* 'was directed at a sophisticated, aristocratic public eager for the extreme pleasure of artful simplicity' (Gossman, p. 261). The taste for medieval and pseudo-medieval tales in easily read form developed rapidly after 1750. I am most grateful to Dr V. Mylne of the University of Canterbury for a list of such romances drawn from her forthcoming Bibliography of French fiction in the second half of the eighteenth century.

21 *Mémoires de littérature de l'Académie Royale des Inscriptions,* XVII (December 1743), pp. 787–99.

22 ibid., p. 790.

23 ibid., pp. 788–9.

24 ibid., p. 798.

25 Many different writers contributed to the *Bibliothèque des Romans*, including the Marquis de Paulmy and the Comte de Tressan. Paulmy was a bibliophile and his vast personal collection of romances and other medieval works is described in the sixty-five volumes of the *Mélanges tirés d'une grande Bibliothèque*. (I am grateful to my colleague Dr G. Hainsworth for pointing out to me, some years ago, that a copy of this rare work existed in the Leeds City Reference Library.) In his analyses and extracts Paulmy proves himself a more accurate but less stylish writer than Tressan. He describes his procedure in the *Avant-Propos* of the *Roman de Hugues Capet*: 'Nous allons en donner l'extrait suivi sans interruption et sans aucun mélange, ni de réflexions, ni de remarques,

ni de citations de vers dans le langage ancien, nous réservant de mettre à la fin un certain nombre de notes'—quoted by H. Jacoubet, *Le Comte de Tressan et les origines du genre troubadour* (Paris, 1923), p. 322.

26 Métra, *Correspondance secrète, politique et littéraire ou Mémoires* [. . .] *de la littérature*, 10 April 1779. (Original edition, London 1787. Slatkine reprint. 3 volumes, Geneva, 1967.) I am grateful to my colleague, Mr D. A. Coward, for this reference and much other bibliographical assistance. (I was not, unfortunately, able to consult the study of Le Grand d'Aussy by G. J. Wilson: 'Le Grand d'Aussy and the *Fabliaux ou Contes*: an Eighteenth Century Medievalist and his Work', unpublished thesis for the degree of PhD, Hull, 1973).

27 *Mercure de France*, février 1779, pp. 179–83, cited in H. Jacoubet, *Tressan*, p. 191. There were frequent reviews and comments on the *Bibliothèque* and other works in the *Mercure de France*. Many are quoted by Jacoubet who lists and describes all the principal publications of collections of romances: *Tressan*, pp. 186–93.

28 Jacoubet, *Tressan*, p. 192.

29 La Harpe, cited in Jacoubet, *Tressan*, p. 190.

30 For detailed analysis of the different Tressan extracts which made up the *corps d'extraits*, see H. Jacoubet, *Comment le XVIIIe siècle lisait les Romans de Chevalerie* (Grenoble, 1932). This complements his major study of Tressan and his work cited above.

31 *Histoire de Tristan de Léonis et de la reine Yseult*, l'an 7 (1799), 2 vols. in one, I, 130. All quotations are from this edition.

32 ibid., II, 13.

33 ibid., II, 58–9.

34 ibid., II, 123.

35 Jacoubet, *Tressan*, p. 269.

36 *Tristan*, II, 124.

37 *Tristan*, II, 128.

38 'Du rose, du bleu, de la soie, des mouches, de la poudre, des moutons blancs, des rubans, [. . .] nos vieux héros enfin amenés dans nos boudoirs et transformés en talons rouges.' L. Gautier, *Les Épopées françaises*, I, 586 (Paris, 1865). Gautier condemns *M. Paulmy et ses secrétaires* most severely in the revised edition of the *Épopées*: '*La Bibliothèque des Romans* touchant à tout, a tout déshonoré; voulant tout rajeunir, a tout flétri' (*Épopées*, Paris, 1878, I, 472).

17

Dialogue as Narrative in Eighteenth-Century French Fiction

VIVIENNE MYLNE

During the second half of the eighteenth century, upwards of fifty of the new works of narrative fiction published in French were in dialogue-form; that is, they consisted wholly or largely of dialogue,and were printed in the same lay-out as plays, with the names of the characters preceding the remarks attributed to them.[1] This number of *contes dialogués* and *romans dialogués* constitutes something like one-fortieth of all the new works of fiction published in the same period. It is therefore quite a minor phenomenon, barely deserving to be called a vogue. Nevertheless, the continuous flow of such works is a new development. And if we speculate about its causes,we shall be forced, I think, to conclude that it represents a small but significant element in some wider and more general changes.

There have not, to my knowledge, been any comprehensive general studies of the way in which French novelists have handled dialogue, though comments on the subject can be found in works on individual authors.[2] It seems safe, however, to say that up to about 1700, conversation in serious novels—as distinct from comic fiction—tended to be formal and stylised, with relatively long speeches. During the first decades of the eighteenth century, some writers of fiction developed a more familiar or naturalistic style of dialogue, with briefer exchanges between the characters, and in certain cases conversation became noticeably more important as an aspect of the whole work. Two authors who are outstanding in this respect are Challes, in *Les Illustres Françoises* (particularly in the frame passages), and Marivaux in both *La Vie de Marianne* and *Le Paysan parvenu*. As for Crébillon fils, conversation is a crucial element in all his novels and tales.

This increase in the scope and liveliness of dialogue in fiction took place without much theoretical discussion. Marivaux defended his practice, in rather vague terms, only when critics objected to the 'vulgarity' of some of the scenes of *La Vie de Marianne*. It is in Crébillon's *Le Sopha*, published in 1742, that we find one of the first discussions of the contributions that dialogue can make to a story:

—Dites-moi un peu, demanda le sultan, en avez-vous encore pour longtems?
—Oui, Sire, répondit Amanzéi.
—De par Mahomet! Tant pis, répliqua Schah-Baham, voilà des discours qui m'ennuient furieusement, je vous en avertis. Si vous pouviez les supprimer, ou les abréger du moins, vous me feriez plaisir, et je n'en serois pas ingrat.

—Vous avez tort de vous plaindre, lui dit la sultane. Cette conversation qui vous ennuie est, pour ainsi dire, un fait par elle-même. Ce n'est point une dissertation inutile, et qui ne porte sur rien, c'est un fait . . . N'est-ce pas dialogué qu'on dit, demanda-t-elle à Amanzéi en souriant?
—Oui, Madame, répondit-il.
—Cette façon de traiter les choses, reprit-elle, est agréable, elle peint mieux, et plus universellement, les caractères que l'on met sur la scene.[3]

In this exchange Crébillon points out two of the major functions which dialogue can fulfil: conversations can themselves be 'deeds', or events in the plot; and they can serve to portray or characterize the speaker.

Just over a decade later, Marmontel took up the subject, but this time with a specific technical problem in mind. In his article 'Direct' in the *Encyclopédie*, he wrote:

Il n'est aucun genre de narration où le discours *direct* ne soit en usage, et il y répand une grâce et une force qui n'appartient qu'à lui. Mais dans le dialogue pressé, il a un inconvénient auquel il seroit aussi avantageux que facile de remédier. C'est la répétition fatigante de ces façons de parler, *lui dis-je, reprit-il, me répondit-elle*, interruptions qui ralentissent la vivacité du dialogue, et rendent le style languissant où il devroit être le plus animé. [. . .] Quelques modernes, comme La Fontaine, ont distingué les répliques par les noms des interlocuteurs; mais cet usage ne s'est introduit que dans les récits en vers. Le moyen le plus court et le plus sûr d'éviter en même tems les longueurs et l'équivoque, seroit de convenir d'un caractère qui marqueroit le changement d'interlocuteurs, et qui ne seroit jamais employé qu'à cet usage.

This passage may not have been widely read. But Marmontel returned to the subject, with a reference to his *Encyclopédie* article, in the preface to the collected edition of his *Contes moraux*, the first two volumes of which appeared in 1761. In this preface Marmontel drew attention to the fact that he had followed his earlier suggestion by omitting, in the *Contes*, most verbs of speaking. Since this work was a best-seller, we can be sure that this innovation, and his comments, had a wide circulation.

It is much to Marmontel's credit that he put his finger on this precise technical problem of the fiction-writer, and also suggested a feasible solution. When he refers to 'le dialogue pressé', he presumably means conversations made up of short remarks rather than long speeches. I have already suggested that dialogue of this kind became an established feature of French fiction during the early decades of the eighteenth century. Marmontel has thus recognized a development which had not been marked enough to call for special consideration by earlier theorists.

We are now so accustomed to the printing devices which make swiftly moving conversations clear to the reader's eye, that we may not appreciate the difficulties of the eighteenth-century writer and reader. We need to remember that remarks by different speakers were then run on into long paragraphs, not broken up by a new line for each remark by a fresh speaker.[4] And there were no accepted conventions, among French printers, about a typographical sign to indicate a change of speaker. Some English printers, including Richardson, used the dash for this purpose. It was this solution which Marmontel adopted, and which some printers in France still use in preference to *guillemets*.

Marmontel's prime concern is with literary effects: he wishes to exploit the liveliness of short crisp conversational exchanges, while avoiding the monotony which would arise from repeating 'dit-il', 'répondit-elle' at frequent intervals. But he does not advocate using the lay-out common to dialogue-form and plays, let alone substituting dialogue for the standard kinds of narrative. Some of the writers who cast their stories in dialogue-form did however use Marmontel's arguments to explain or justify their practice. Others made the alternative and obvious comparison, between *contes dialogués* and plays.

One of the theorists who discussed the difference between plays-to-be-read and plays-to-be-acted was Chabanon, in a work entitled *Sur le sort de la poésie en ce siècle philosophe* (1764). Chabanon's chief point is that the origins of tragedy can be found in Homer, and he analyses and praises the varied use of dialogue for different situations in the *Iliad*. To support his thesis, he provides 'une version du dernier livre de l'*Iliade* en tragédie'. This is a one-act play, in alexandrines, entitled *Priam au camp d'Achille*. In the preface to this tragedy, he argues that some kinds of incidents or actions are interesting and effective to read, but could not be staged:

Nos sens, frappés de la représentation vivante d'un personnage, ne lui permettent pas d'agir ni de parler aussi librement qu'il eût pû faire si ses actions et ses paroles ne nous eussent été transmises que par un papier muet et insensible. (p. 52)

He cites the behaviour of Lovelace as one example and, in his own tragedy, 'Priam tremblant et suppliant lorsqu'Achille le poursuit le fer à la main' (p. 55). This leads him to the general conclusion:

Si ce trait, et quelques autres que le Théâtre n'admet point, peuvent se soutenir à la lecture, n'est-on pas en droit d'en conclure qu'il peut y avoir deux sortes de Drames, les uns *représentés,* les autres *écrits* (si j'ose m'exprimer ainsi), et que mille sujets incompatibles avec les convenances de la Scene, attacheroient et plairoient sur le papier. (p. 56)

Chabanon's argument is based on scenes which are too horrifying or shocking to be acted out on the stage. Various writers of fiction were to extend the range of elements thought to be unsuitable for stage-plays but appropriate for 'dramatic' works intended to be read.

Antoine Bret, himself a not very successful playwright, produced one of the first volumes of *contes dialogués* to contain a preface discussing the form: *Essai de contes moraux et dramatiques* (1765). He cites both Marmontel and Chabanon, but gives the latter's argument a new twist by suggesting that dialogue-tales are a suitable vehicle for young writers with little of importance to say. He hopes that they will adopt the new genre and thus be persuaded 'à ne plus fatiguer nos théâtres de mille petites fables qui peut-être seroient pour des contes un fond suffisant' (p. viii). It would be preferable for writers without the genius of, say, a Molière, to create 'un conte passable' rather than merely 'une comédie insipide'. The *conte dramatique,* he maintains, offers wider scope in subject-matter and does not call for the skill and ingenuity which a good playwright needs in order to observe the unities and other requirements of the theatre. But Bret is anxious that there should be no confusion between stories of this kind and real drama:

N

Afin que notre amour-propre, si habile à nous séduire, ne pût nous tromper par l'idée d'avoir écrit quelque chose qui fût digne du théâtre, il seroit important qu'on ne fît jamais usage des mots Scène ou Acte, et qu'on se contentât, comme on le fait ici, de séparer toutes les conversations par une simple barre. (pp. x–xi)

During the next decade or so, this attitude is echoed by several authors. There is, it seems, a certain reluctance to equate *contes* with plays. Bricaire de La Dixmerie, in the preface to his *Contes philosophiques et moraux,* explicitly disclaims any attempt to dramatise his own stories:

J'ai plus donné aux descriptions et au récit qu'au dialogue, parce que je voulois faire un conte plutôt qu'une pièce. Il s'en faut de beaucoup que je blâme l'usage contraire; mais j'ignore si l'on doit blâmer l'usage que j'adopte. (p. xii)

Similarly, Costard brought out a work entitled *Les Orphelins* (1767), which is described on the title-page as 'conte moral mis en action en forme de pièce dramatique, en cinq actes et en prose'. But he hastens to state: 'Ce n'est point une comédie que j'ai eu dessein de faire' (p. 3); and he explains his choice of dialogue-form in terms that remind one of Marmontel's remarks:

Pour éviter des longueurs, trop souvent inséparables d'une simple narration, j'ai cru devoir mettre la mienne en dialogue, et sous la forme d'une pièce dramatique. (p. 4)

By the 1780s, however, there seems to be more willingness to dwell on the similarities between dialogues and plays. The editors of the *Bibliothèque universelle des romans* explain their inclusion of a play by Lope de Vega in the following terms:

La Dorotée [. . .] peut tenir au genre dramatique par le dialogue, mais c'est tout; et, par rapport à nous, une pièce en six actes immenses, dont la fable n'est point ordonnée ni circonscrite, dont l'action est nulle, sans intrigue, qui, du reste, est semée d'une foule de poésies en tout genre, et de digressions qui passent les privilèges de l'épisode; une pièce de cette fabrique, disons-nous, ne peut être appellée Comédie, mais un Roman d'un tissu singulier.[5]

And the argument is summed up with the remark, 'Les premières comédies des Espagnols [. . .] ne sont, à leur jugement même, que des Romans dialogués'.

Admittedly, this verdict may depend on what French critics saw as the inadequacies of Lope de Vega's dramatic technique. But a few years later the same periodical published an anonymous story, *L'Homme conséquent, conte dramatique en trois actes,* and described the author's aim as being 'de faire, tout à la fois, un conte qu'on pût lire et une comédie qu'on pût jouer'.[6]

Charles Borde draws the same kind of parallel in his *Discours sur la fiction,* when he argues: 'On peut placer au rang des comédies, les romans qui contiennent des peintures des mœurs, et dont les dialogues sont autant de scènes'.[7] And the final stage of the argument can be seen in comments such as that of the editor of madame de Genlis's *Nouveaux contes moraux*. He justifies filling up the sixth and final volume with two comedies (which had already appeared in the *Bibliothèque des romans*) with the remark: 'D'ailleurs un drame n'est autre chose qu'un roman mis en action'.[8] We may see this evolution in ideas either as a tribute to the growing prestige of the novel, or perhaps as evidence of the declining quality of drama. Whatever the explanation, it seems clear that from the mid-eighties onwards, many critics are willing to see the *conte dialogué* and the *roman dialogué* as being on a par with plays.

The final factor to be taken into account in the development of the *conte dialogué* is, obviously enough, the existence of dialogues as a literary genre. With illustrious models in classical antiquity, various types of dialogue had become established in French as a recognized form of literary expression.[9] One of the most favoured was the *Dialogue des morts*.[10] And a more recent development (though with a paradigm in the Catechism) was the pedagogic dialogue for the instruction of children.

The emphasis, in most works of this kind published before 1750, had been on religious or philosophical ideas, or on information, or criticism of society, literature etc. Narrative elements were often present, but the author's aim was not primarily to tell a story. It is easy to understand, however, that as conversation became more important in novels and stories, some writers would see the possibility of using the dialogue-form to present the whole of a narrative. The first writer of any note to adopt this structure was Crébillon, in *La Nuit et le moment*, which he wrote, it appears, in 1737, the year in which he also completed *Le Sopha*.[11] However, *La Nuit et le moment* was not published until 1755, while *Le Hasard du coin du feu*, probably written some time shortly after 1742, did not appear until 1763.[12] The only other early *conte dialogué* by a major author is Diderot's *L'Oiseau blanc*, composed at about the same time as *Les Bijoux indiscrets*, in 1748.[13] This too was delayed in publication; it came out only in the 1798 edition of Diderot's *Œuvres*. In terms of published works, liable to influence other authors and provoke imitation, the *conte dialogué* could therefore have had little effect before 1750.

With on the one hand, the advent of *contes dialogués*, and on the other, Marmontel's efforts to enliven dialogue by omitting verbs of speaking, we can find, from about 1770 onwards, quite a wide range of possible ways of presenting conversations in fiction.

At one extreme is the kind of *conte dialogué* which contains an absolute minimum of material outside the conversation; description of the characters, and stage-directions about action, are dispensed with or kept to the barest essentials. *La Nuit et le moment* comes fairly close to fulfilling this specification.

Then we have the sort of work which is still *dialogué*, or laid out like a play, but where the writer is more generous with description and interpolated narrative. Nerciat, in *Les Aphrodites* (1793), tends to give each episode a narrative introduction, and supplies in a footnote a description of each new character as he or she appears. (It would seem that *Jacques le Fataliste* should also be classed in this group of novels, but its multi-level use of dialogue really makes it unique.)

In a third category of novel or story, the bulk of the work is presented in the narrative form used for most fiction, but one or more of the conversations are set out in dialogue-form. The best-known work in which this occurs is *Paul et Virginie* (1788). The Vieillard tells how Paul would often come to the pawpaw-tree which Virginie had planted, and undertakes to relate a long conversation they had one day at the foot of the tree. He then adds:

Je vous la raconterai en forme de dialogue, afin que vous jugiez du bon sens naturel de ce jeune homme; et il vous sera aisé de faire la différence des interlocuteurs par le sens de ses questions et de mes réponses.

Despite the last sentence, Bernardin de Saint-Pierre puts 'Paul' and 'Le Vieillard' above their respective remarks. This irruption into dialogue-form breaks up the old man's narrative in a very odd and implausible way. Another strange example of this practice is to be found in a letter-novel, *Le Petit Grandisson* (1787), translated by Berquin from the Dutch original of madame de Cambon. Young Guillaume D***, writing home to his mother, quite frequently reports a conversation in the household where he is staying by presenting it in dialogue-form. It is more usual, however, to find this intermittent use of dialogue-form in short stories, where it is made to emerge from the more conventional presentation of conversation. Here is an example from the *Contes philosophiques et moraux* of Bricaire de La Dixmerie, who, in spite of the disclaimer we have already seen, does utilise quite often the 'dramatic' lay-out for conversations.

Est-ce qu'on aime toujours parmi vous? reprit Charles. Je n'en sçais rien, ajouta la belle Saxonne, mais je soupçonne qu'on aime sans se le dire, et sans se le demander.

CHARLES MARTEL

Mais pour me suivre, ne regrettez-vous point votre patrie?

ISBERGE

Qu'est-ce qu'une patrie? Ne pourrions-nous pas avoir la même, vous et moi?

CHARLES MARTEL

Non; mais vous pourriez habiter la mienne, ou moi la vôtre. (p. 8)

In a fourth group could be set the books by authors who followed Marmontel in trying to make their characters' conversations more vivid by consistently omitting the verbs of speech. This practice did become fairly widespread, especially when, from the 1780s onwards, some printers adopted the convention of starting a new line for a fresh speaker, as well as using dashes. In 1776 Louis-Sébastien Mercier published a novel which contains a good deal of conversation punctuated by dashes to indicate a change of speaker, and he called the work *Jezennemours, roman dramatique,* thus indicating the value attached to this type of presentation.

In a fifth and final group come the writers who continue to observe the traditional methods, still using phrases like 'dit-il', 'répondit-elle' for every alternation of the speakers.

Before going on to discuss in more detail the works which we can classify as true *contes dialogués,* I should perhaps comment on some developments which seem to me to be consequences of the increasing exploitation of fictional conversation.

One such development is a tendency for dialogues which are *not* primarily narrative to become livelier and more naturalistic. The case of Diderot's dialogues springs to mind. One must be careful not to over-estimate the influence of contemporary fiction and its techniques on works like *Le Neveu de Rameau* and *Le Rêve de d'Alembert*. But neither should one ignore the fact that Diderot's first true dialogue was a *conte dialogué*, *L'Oiseau blanc*, and that some of the vigour and onward drive in his more philosophic dialogues comes from the narrative elements which he fuses into the discussion. It seems to me at least possible that he, and others who wrote dialogues chiefly concerned with ideas, may have been influenced to a certain degree by the new importance and effectiveness which conversation had been acquiring in novels and stories.

Secondly, there is a movement in the other direction: discussions which one might have expected, a few decades earlier, to be presented as dialogues, are now given a narrative thread and written as something more akin to a novel. Such works are not numerous, but one example is *Le Baron Van-Hesden ou la république des incrédules* (1762), by Père Michel-Ange Marin. During five ample volumes, we accompany the hero on a boat-trip along the Rhône. He is a young Dutchman who has been influenced by both Protestantism and the new philosophy. The journey is spent in conversations with a Catholic hermit and some other passengers. By the time he makes landfall, Van-Hesden has been persuaded to embrace Christianity and the tenets of the Catholic church. It would be far too strong and flattering to say that Marin has turned the argument into a series of adventures, but the effort to achieve a novelistic effect of narrative is quite evident.

Thirdly, just as there seems to be a certain amount of give-and-take between philosophic or religious dialogues and narrative fiction, so we find a new kind of interchange between fiction and the theatre. Short stories were adapted, more frequently than ever before, as plays or as libretti for the relatively new genre of *opéra comique*.[14]

Marmontel's *Contes moraux*, which some critics had already called 'dramatiques' because of their preponderance of dialogue, were found particularly suitable for this treatment. And the more unusual reverse process also took place: in 1751 there appeared both an anonymous novel, *Élixir du sentiment*, which Mornet describes as 'la mise en roman de la *Cénie* de madame de Grafigny'; and also *La Mère marâtre ou l'injustice vengée* by Dufour, which according to Raynal is 'la tragédie de *Rodogune* mise en récit'. Baculard d'Arnaud wrote and published two versions of the story of Euphémie, one as a *drame* and the other as a novel, the *Mémoires d'Euphémie* (1768). And in the *Bibliothèque universelle des romans* (1784, janvier II), there is an even more curious case: the Comte de Tressan takes a comedy by madame de Genlis, *Zélie ou l'ingénue*, writes forty-four pages of narrative which provide, in more detail, the information in the first three scenes of the play, and then reverts to the original play-text, making cuts however in the more rhetorical and melodramatic passages. Although the explanation of what he has done contains the statement:'L'art de la Comédie est supérieur à celui du Roman', it seems clear that the *roman dialogué* has here carried the day.

A systematic description of all the eighteenth-century *contes dialogués* which I have traced would take too much space and would also make thoroughly tedious reading. I propose therefore to deal with certain cases only. I shall first discuss some examples of bad technique, that is, works where the dialogue-form is either inadequately exploited or should not have been used at all. After this I shall deal with groups of stories which have in common certain kinds of subject-matter; and then go on to various individual works which present some special points of interest.

Just as the vogue of the letter-novel led some writers to choose this form for stories which would have been more effective or plausible in third-person narrative, so the dialogue-form was sometimes used to convey material for which it is not really appropriate. One of the main factors involved is a question of time or tense. Plays and dialogues can offer two distinct kinds of 'event': there are incidents which take place as the play proceeds, in a time-present which the characters live through as they are talking; or there is the 'récit de Théramène' approach, where one character relates events that happened in the past and are now over and done with. If this second type of narrative is used to constitute the whole of a *conte dialogué*, the tale becomes merely an equivalent of an ordinary story or of a memoir-novel, with the addition of an audience to punctuate the recital with comments. To gauge the effect of this, one has only to imagine what *Manon Lescaut* would be like if Prévost had made the Man of Quality and his ward offer frequent observations on Des Grieux's account of his sufferings.

There is a further, practical, complication if such a story is presented in dialogue-form. The narrator may well need to offer conversations which are a part of his tale. Are these conversations also to be laid out in dialogue-form, thus introducing a fresh—and possibly confusing—set of interlocutors? Or should the narrator be made to resort to 'He said', 'She said' in recounting such discussions?

Crébillon has in fact shown how a story following this pattern *can* be effectively organised. *Le Sopha* is an account of Amanzéi's past experiences, related to the Sultan and the Sultana, who comment fairly extensively on the story. The factor which, more than any other single element, makes this technique effective in *Le Sopha*, is that the listeners are strongly charac-terized. The Sultan is comically stupid and the Sultana witty and intelligent. When either or both of them are made to intervene in Amanzéi's recital, the reader is still entertained by the interplay of personalities between narrator and audience. And since Crébillon did not choose to set the work out in dialogue-form, there is never any confusion between the characters whose conversations Amanzéi repeated, and the talk between himself and his listeners.

To see what happens when a less skilful author turns a similar situation into a *conte dialogué*, we have only to turn to the anonymous *Marianne ou la paysanne de la forêt d'Ardennes. Histoire mise en dialogues* (1767). The work consists of Marianne's adventures, related by herself to Ergaste. Unlike Crébillon's audience-characters in *Le Sopha*, Ergaste is colourless and uninteresting. Here is a fairly typical example of his contribution to the dialogue:

MARIANNE

Tous ces menus détails, Ergaste, doivent bien vous avoir ennuyé; mais il falloit arriver par un chemin qui n'est peut-être pas le plus court, mais le plus simple et le plus clair.

ERGASTE

Vous avez raison, Marianne, la premiere chose est de se faire entendre, et toujours de la manière la plus naturelle. (p. 25)

The author of the work clearly realized that Ergaste was an ineffective character. He says, in the *Avertissement*:

Qu'on trouve, si l'on veut, Ergaste un bavard qui ne dit pas grand-chose de bon; on aura raison, c'est un personnage postiche qui ne m'a point intéressé. (pp. vii–viii)

In my view the story, such as it is, would be improved if Ergaste's remarks were deleted, leaving us with a straightforward memoir-novel.

  Marianne will also serve to illustrate another literary shortcoming. Some of the writers who use dialogue-form claim that it can present, through the characters' speech, a more faithful impression of their social background than would a conventional narrative. The author of *Marianne* expresses this notion too:

On n'a eu recours à aucuns manuscrits Chinois, Arabes ou Indiens, &c. pour écrire cette histoire; l'Héroïne elle-même en a dicté les principaux événemens. Cette Héroïne étant une paysanne, on a cru devoir choisir le genre du dialogue, comme le plus propre à conserver cette simplicité, cette naïveté si convenable au genre rustique. (p. vii)

Unfortunately, the author has already explained why he could not fully achieve this aim. In his *Épître à Marianne*, he excuses himself:

Vous y lirez votre histoire, mais vous n'y trouverez point votre style. Vous racontiez, et j'écrivois, mais j'écrivois loin de vous, et ma plume fidèle dans les faits, ne pouvoit répandre dans le récit les grâces naïves de votre esprit et de votre conversation. (p. v)

The extract from the dialogue, cited above, shows that Marianne, in spite of an early plea: 'A peine sçais-je un mot de françois' (p. 2), speaks correct standard French. Sometimes indeed her speech takes on a distinctly literary flavour, as when—paradoxically—she is protesting that she is merely a simple village maiden:

Vous me dispensez donc d'art et de finesse, car je vous avertis que je n'en eus jamais; vous vous contenterez de cette franchise rustique qui correspond si bien à ma naissance et à mon éducation, de cette nature rude et sauvage qui va droit au but, sans s'écarter de son objet. (p. 3)

We may therefore be led to expect, by these opening pages, that there will be no attempt to suggest rustic dialect or uneducated speech. But with a further twist of inconsistency, Marianne is made to report conversations between peasants who utter remarks such as:

Quand on vient nous t'asticoter nous autres, je n'entendons pas de raillerie. [. . .] Tian, regarde, Pierre, disoit celui-ci, elle est malfiguenne jolie dà. (p. 22)

These 'stage-peasant' exchanges create a level of discourse which is markedly different from that of Marianne, herself supposedly a *paysanne*.

In the passage just quoted, Marianne relates the conversation, using verbal forms like 'disoit celui-ci'. But on several occasions there is a switch to dialogue-form for such talk. And when we have four pages set out in this way, for a discussion between Marianne and Antoine (pp. 74–8), the reader may tend to forget that Marianne is supposed to be repeating all this to Ergaste.

Marianne's adventures do not offer anything that is particularly new or enthralling, by the standards of the time: a licentious nobleman tries to seduce her, but she defends her virtue; she goes to Paris, but dislikes what she finds there and returns to marry Antoine and enjoy the simple delights of country life. The main interest of the work may now seem to lie in the various illustrations it provides of how not to write a *conte dialogué*.

However, I may have been too harsh with the author of *Marianne* on one topic, that of dialect. While one may justifiably blame him for not achieving a spoken style which evokes Marianne's origins, we should perhaps be grateful that he did *not* try to write all the narrative in rustic speech. The wearisome effect of a continuous flow of dialect can be appreciated when one reads any of the *poissard* dialogues by Vadé and his emulators. An anonymous volume called *Délassemens nocturnes* (1765) contains one such dialogue: *Le Panier de maquereaux disputé*. The stage directions are in standard French, but the fishwives' conversation contains remarks like:

LA BLONDE

Comme t'es toute essouflée à force de pialler; mais si j'n'avons pas de gueule, en guise d'ça j'ons des poings avec quoi j'te boucherons une fenêtre du visage. (p. 17)

Most of these *poissard* dialogues are only marginally narrative; they generally convey quarrel-scenes, where the interest and amusement lies in the outrageousness of the insults. A modern reader may well become bored after a few pages of such vituperation, and the tedium arises in part from the effort required to decipher the sense. The writer of a *conte dialogué* may therefore need to find some middle way, and to suggest uneducated speech-habits without relying too extensively on dialect-forms.

While *Marianne* might have turned out more satisfactorily if there had been no attempt to present it as a dialogue, there are other works which offer potentially effective dialogue situations but do not exploit them adequately. Something of the kind occurs in an anonymous three-volume novel called *La jeune Nièce ou l'histoire de Suckei Thomby* (1789).[15] The story begins with monsieur and madame Middleton, a prosperous childless couple, deciding to adopt one of the sons of a family retainer. The boy, Benjamin, is sent to school, but does not like the restraints imposed upon him, and suggests to madame Middleton that the child they should be caring for is her own niece. The obstacle to this plan, as madame Middleton points out, is that her husband detests the Irish, and the girl's father is an Irishman. The confident retort is:

BENJAMIN

Laissez-moi faire, Madame, je m'engage à vaincre la répugnance de mon maître. Le père de votre nièce étoit Irlandois; et quand il seroit né à la Chine, seroit-ce une excuse suffisante pour abandonner et méconnoître une innocente enfant? [. . .] Ayez seulement soin de m'appuyer quand j'aurai mis l'affaire en train. (pp. 7–8)

What the reader expects, of course, is a scene which would show Benjamin exerting his powers of persuasion over monsieur Middleton. Instead, the author lapses into ordinary narrative, and merely says:

Benjamin s'acquitta si adroitement de sa commission, que M. Middleton consentit à recevoir chez lui la malheureuse enfant dont il avoit toujours détesté jusqu'à la pensée.

This is clearly a missed opportunity. If an author chooses to build his story on conversations, he should not resort to summary for crucial stages in the plot which depend, precisely, on conversations.

Another blemish which occurs in a number of narrative dialogues is the extensive use— or abuse—of soliloquies and asides. To my mind, these are devices which we may well accept for stage works, but whose artificial or conventional nature is less tolerable in written stories. Costard's *Les Orphelins* is more like a *drame* than a *conte moral* (it resembles *Le Fils naturel* both in tone and in several aspects of the plot); and the opening of the work reads as follows:

L'action se passe dans un salon de compagnie très-simplement meublé.
Nerville seul se promene à grands pas, avec un air d'impatience; ensuite il tire sa montre et dit:
A peine est-il neuf heures. [. . .] (p. 7)

The work contains several other soliloquies, some of them of a page or more in length. Antoine Bret too, perhaps because of his previous experience in writing plays, is fairly lavish with soliloquies and asides.

This brings me to a final reproach against some *contes dialogués*: weak as many of them are, a few of them might actually be more effective if performed as plays than they are as reading-matter. I would take this to be true of *L'Exemple*, the last of the three works in Bret's *Essai de contes moraux et dramatiques*.

This concerns a young woman, the Présidente, who is good at heart but is being tempted to form an extra-marital liaison and to flout her husband's wishes in other ways, such as going to call on Clarice, her sister-in-law. Clarice is in social disgrace because her lover was persuaded by another woman to publish Clarice's love-letters, with cruel comments. In the central scene of *L'Exemple*, Clarice arrives, disguised as a *marchande de modes* (to spare the Présidente's reputation). She tells her own story, and this living example accomplishes what the exhortations of the Présidente's husband and mother had failed to do.

This plot is not strikingly original, but it lends itself to a number of varied scenes, and the arrival of Clarice in disguise could be quite effective in performance. One might argue that

visual effects of this kind are better adapted to the stage than to dialogue-tales in which
the author eschews visual description. Among the total output of *contes dialogués,* a few
do seem to call for a theatrical rendering rather than mere armchair reading.

If we consider the various *contes dialogués* with a view to classifying them by subject-
matter, two main categories immediately become apparent: we may call them, in a vague
but not inaccurate way, the edifying and the unedifying. By the latter term, I mean a group
of works which range from the mildly erotic story, in which the language is, however,
blameless, to the most detailed type of pornography, where the characters' choice of words
is as uninhibited as their behaviour. The dialogue-tales in this group are of course only part
of the flow of works which can be called 'libertine'.[16] As might be expected, a fair number
of the more scandalous *contes dialogués* are also anti-religious and/or anti-clerical; we find
titles such as: *La Religieuse en chemise ou la nonne éclairée* (1763) and *Le Monialisme* (1773).
Indeed there are certain social types who recur with the predictable regularity of characters
in the *commedia dell'arte*: the priest or mendicant friar who seduces women in the houses he
visits, the profligate and debauched abbé, the licentious nun. These are matched on the
secular side by the young *roué*—usually of noble birth—by the sensation-hungry Marquise
or Comtesse, and by the girl of less aristocratic parentage who has become a prostitute or
courtesan. To these we can add the Agnès of the company, the innocent adolescent who is
longing for initiation.
   The themes of the dialogues also follow well-established patterns. There are discussions
and advice on how to be a successful courtesan (where the authors have models in the
writings of Lucian and Aretino); these may contain little or no narrative. There are stories
of the type: 'How I became a prostitute', which are narratives about past events. And
finally we have the dialogue where seduction, copulation etc. are occurring as the conversation unfolds. The literary quality of these works is extremely variable. At the most refined
end of the scale one finds works such as Crébillon's *Le Hasard du coin du feu,* which I shall
discuss later. At the overtly pornographic extreme there are some pieces which are merely
crude sensationalism, but there is also Sade's *La Philosophie dans le boudoir* (a borderline case
where the balance wavers between action and theorizing), and Nerciat's *Les Aphrodites,* in
which the lively characterization and a certain pervasive gaiety combine to give the work
some merit.
   It is very rare for dialogues of this type to contain comments or explanations concerning
their literary presentation. In *Les Écarts du tempérament* (1785), however, Nerciat first puts
forward the overworked claim that this work was found among the papers of a man who
had just died, and then, in his rôle of 'Editor', offers a mock-literary reason for publication:

[. . .] mais chaque personnage a des traits qui semblent avoir été saisis d'après nature, ce qui nous a
paru mériter que cette folie fût publiée. (*Avis*)

The work is referred to as a 'pièce', but Nerciat recognizes that its peculiar nature calls
for special measures:

Ce Drame, de nature à ne pouvoir occuper la scène, ne se pique point d'avoir des formes théâtrales. [. . .] Attendez! puisque vous ne verrez jamais les personnages sur la scene, il est bien d'aider un peu votre imagination et de vous donner une idée de leurs figures. (p. 6)

He then lists the 'Acteurs' and provides a brief description of each of them.

There can be no doubt that the dialogue-form has specific advantages to offer for the writer of either allusively erotic or openly pornographic works. In the first category there is the entertainment to be derived from discreet language carrying a wealth of indiscreet implications; in the second, the titillations or shocks of pornographic episodes can be heightened when the participants themselves describe, or express their reactions to, what is going on. Dialogue exploits, in such cases, the spoken word as concealment, or as revelation.

One would probably not be justified in attributing to the authors of most of these works any serious intention to alter the reader's moral standards. (Sade would be the notable exception.) In contrast to this un-didactic approach, the works I have labelled 'edifying' are all quite obviously intended to influence the reader. The nature of the desired improving effect may vary. The Chevalier, in Maubert de Gouvest's *L'École du gentilhomme* (1754), wants to help his nephew to become a good, honourable soldier. Bret's *L'Exemple,* as we have seen, carries a lesson for the young wife. The commonest theme, however, is the gradual conversion to Christian belief of a protagonist who begins by being ignorant of, or hostile to, religion. Gros de Besplas turns this subject into a death-bed drama in *Le Rituel des esprits-forts ou le voyage d'outre-monde* (1759). Durand, in *Je veux être heureux* (1782), gives a more lively and varied series of conversations which are occasionally quite entertaining. And this type of work also has its *âmes sensibles*: the most notable example is Marie-Françoise Loquet, who wrote both *Entretiens d'Angélique* (1781), and a sequel, *Entretiens de Clotilde* (1788). The latter work was dedicated to the 'demoiselles pensionnaires des Dames Ursulines', and the author urged these young ladies to 'déclamer ces Entretiens dans les jours de [leurs] grandes récréations' (p. iv). The kind of acting ability required can be judged from the passage in which Euphrasie breaks the news that she has been converted (the *points de suspension* are all the author's):

EUPHRASIE

O la plus tendre des mères! votre bonté augmente mon repentir. Perfide! comment as-tu donc pu affliger si longtemps une mère si aimable? O douleur! . . . je n'en peux plus . . . O ciel! mes forces m'abandonnent . . . je me meurs . . . (*Elle tombe évanouie dans les bras de sa mère*).

MADAME DU VIVIER

(*serrant sa fille contre son cœur.*)
O ma fille! ô fruit de mes entrailles! dans quel état te vois-je! Faut-il que le sein où tu reçus la vie. . . Mon cœur . . . mon amour . . . ouvre les yeux . . . chère enfant, reprends tes esprits . . . instruis ta mère du sujet de tes larmes . . . (pp. 106–7)

This kind of speech (and punctuation) is reminiscent of the *drame*. And there are a few *contes dialogués* which show this tendency even more clearly. I have already mentioned, in this connection, Costard's *Les Orphelins*. Another work, which must surely qualify as the most sombre of all the dialogue tales, is *Les Dernières Aventures du jeune D'Olban* (1777), by Ramond de Carbonnières.[17]

The characters include the doom-laden Wertheresque hero who commits suicide; a *bourru bienfaisant* figure, Birk, who, together with the music-master Solfa, introduces elements of comedy and the grotesque in a way to delight Victor Hugo; a Missionnaire who is trying to convert Lali, the young heroine, to Catholicism, but whose love for her goes guiltily beyond mere brotherly Christian affection; and two robbers living in a hut in the forest. The action is set in Alsace, and moves freely between Birk's house, the Missionary's cell, a clearing in the forest, etc. The stage directions are vividly pictorial (D'Olban has assumed the name of Sinval because he fought a duel and is still a fugitive from justice):

SINVAL

(dans une sombre forêt de sapins, sans chapeau, les cheveux sur le visage, l'habit en désordre, deux pistolets à la ceinture). (p. 86)

And Sinval-D'Olban shows in his speeches that he is one of the early Outsider-figures: 'Mon cœur est fermé, Lali; la douleur y repose . . . Si je suis étranger au monde, n'en accusez que mon extrême sensibilité' (p. 22). But he can find comfort in Nature, if not among men; and it is through the pine-woods to the ruined Castle of Honak that (for no very clear reason) he goes to kill himself.

One is, unfortunately, continually tempted towards ribald comment when discussing this work. Yet though it lacks Hugo's evocative skill with language, it foreshadows many of the more striking aspects of Romantic drama. It would have provided an effective opera libretto for, say, Donizetti or Bellini—potentially more moving, and certainly less implausible than *La Somnambula*.

One writer of *contes dialogués* did provide his own music, though not on an operatic scale. This is Moline, whose dialogue, *Le Duo interrompu, conte, suivi d'Ariettes nouvelles* (1766), contains both the words of the songs which Lise's singing-teacher brings for her, and also the music. In a later work, *Les Catastrophes amoureuses ou le retour à la vertu* (1796), Moline again introduced a number of lyrics of his own composition.[18] One occasionally feels that the dialogue itself is being used as a pretext for these verses.

We have by now seen the *conte dialogué* put to many uses. Among all the possible types of fiction, it might seem that the one least suitable for presentation in dialogue-form is the historical novel. Such works generally need to offer a good deal of explanation and description; and the difficulty of suggesting the speech-habits of a bygone age without resorting to 'Gadzookery' is well known. Nevertheless we find Meissner writing not only a dialogue novel set in Renaissance Italy, but also a life of Alcibiades in dialogue. I include these in our discussion of French works because two French versions of *Bianka Capello* were published (both in 1790), and three of *Alcibiade* (1787, 1788, 1789). Clearly the translators and booksellers felt that these works would have more appeal to the French reading public than some other German novels.

One of the translations of *Alcibiade* appeared in the *Bibliothèque universelle des romans*

(1788, avril), where the editor suggests that Meissner, in utilising dialogue, was following the example of Wieland's *Diogène de Sinope*. This is a reminder that several other German authors of the period also resorted to dialogue-form for stories. It is at least possible that the impulse to use dialogue for narrative came to Germany from France. (As far as I have been able to discover, there was no comparable development in England.)

The work which seems to close the eighteenth-century flow of dialogue narratives is Carmontelle's *Les Femmes, roman dialogué*. (Carmontelle died in 1806; the novel was published in 1825). I turned to this with high hopes; some of Carmontelle's *Proverbes* are quite lively, and he also wrote a set of *Conversations des gens du monde* (1786), which are excellent of their kind. Here the author's aim is given as being 'd'apprendre aux Étrangers à parler sans rien dire'. These dialogues are little sketches of family and society life, capturing the casual and even pointless conversations which are often more a demonstration of sociability than a meeting of minds. No lesson or story emerges from the *Conversations*. Even the comic elements are too lightly touched in to be called satire. But Carmontelle succeeds in creating a vivid impression of a certain milieu, with its preoccupations and its characteristic mode of speech. Can he maintain this convincing atmosphere and characterization, and combine with them a story-line strong enough for a three-volume novel? The answer is, unfortunately, no. In *Les Femmes*, the hero, Saint-Alvire, feels that he has exhausted all the pleasures society can offer. His more reflective friend, Dinval, encourages him to take a look at the varying characters of women in 'la bonne compagnie'; and eventually, of course, Saint-Alvire both learns how to love and also discovers the woman who fulfils his ideals. Sadly we have to admit that, like so many eighteenth-century dialogue narratives, this novel is interesting as an experiment, but mediocre as a work of literature.

Rather than end on this dying note, I propose to finish with a brief discussion of some works of merit.

Jacques le Fataliste is so long and complex, and has already attracted so much critical comment, that I can obviously add little of value in a few words. There are nevertheless one or two points which are worth noting here, because they are connected with issues already raised in this article. Firstly, Diderot uses the dialogue lay-out for many of the extended conversations between his main characters—Jacques, Le Maître, L'Hôtesse— and also between characters in the intercalated stories told by these three people and by himself as Narrator. Generally speaking, he avoids confusion by skilful (or whimsical) transitions into, or out of, the dialogue-form. But on one occasion, in the 'Bigre' anecdote, he chooses to substitute the heading 'Moi' for 'Jacques', since Jacques is reporting a conversation in which he took part.[19] Elsewhere, he manages things so that even when Jacques is the narrator, his name is kept as a dialogue-heading; this can be done, for instance, when Jacques participates in a conversation, by laying it out as in ordinary novels, not in dialogue-form.[20] Secondly, the exchanges between the main narrator and the imaginary reader are never presented in dialogue-form. This helps to differentiate them from other dialogue passages (and incidentally saves there being another 'Moi' in the work). A detailed study of how the narrator moves between the various levels of dialogue in *Jacques* would surely demonstrate Diderot's virtuosity in improvisation.

In *La Nuit et le moment*, Crébillon accomplishes the task of showing how a young man, Clitandre, can talk himself, in half-an-hour or so, into the bed and the embraces of a woman he has never courted before. Clitandre's main resource for creating and maintaining an erotic mood is the recounting of some of his previous conquests. Cidalise, whose bedroom is the setting for the dialogue, pursues this topic, and asks for fresh examples, with a lively interest which suggests that she is more of a discreet accomplice to his current designs than an innocent victim.[21] Crébillon here shows, in contrast to a work such as *Marianne ou la paysanne . . .*, how a narrative of past events can be effectively exploited to exert a direct and appreciable influence on the character's present behaviour.[22]

In *Le Hasard du coin du feu*, the challenge Crébillon sets himself is even more complex: Célie, a woman whose lover has just died, is to incite the Duc de Clerval into making love with her; and not only is Clerval indifferent to her, but he is also the lover of her friend and relation, the Marquise. The measure of Crébillon's achievement is that he makes this plot seem plausible and even inevitable.

The first four scenes are used largely to establish the characterization and to supply the facts we need to know. The Marquise emerges as intelligent and a woman of principle; she attaches more importance to true affection than to physical faithfulness, and is happy that Clerval should be 'constant' even if he is not always 'fidèle'. Célie, by contrast, is shallow, flighty and selfish. All this is conveyed in natural-seeming conversation, arising plausibly out of gossip and reflections about acquaintances.

Both the Duke's arrival and the Marquise's departure provide an element which is notably missing from *La Nuit et le Moment*: the outside world with its duties and responsibilities. The Duke is late because of business at Versailles; the Marquise is called away to go and see her ailing mother. In a brief *tête-à-tête* before she leaves, they discuss Célie in unflattering terms which complete our picture of her.

The long scene which then ensues offers a sequence of changing relationships between Célie and the Duke. Not every change is due to talk alone: when he finally possesses Célie, it is partly because she has moved to an armchair in which she reclines 'd'une façon tout à fait négligée'. But before this, she has first taken one of his automatic compliments and exaggerated its significance to a point where he cannot contradict her without discourtesy; and then tried unsuccessfully to make him admit that he loves her, since the uttering of the word 'amour' is the verbal formula she requires in order to justify, in her own eyes, sexual licence. The Duke will not betray his attachment to the Marquise in this way. Having enjoyed Célie's favours, he then manages, by clever talking, to ensure that this *passade* will not have any consequences which might embarrass his relationship with the Marquise. Célie is out-manœuvred emotionally and verbally, and we end by feeling some admiration for the Duke's superior wit and his own peculiar brand of constancy.

Some mention must also be made of the stage-directions which Crébillon uses here in a way that restores the function of the narrator. During the moments of silence between the characters, as when Célie is sulking, there are lengthy analyses of the Duke's thoughts and motives. The style in these passages is notably abstract and remote; Crébillon achieves a distancing effect, so that we are still kept in the position of spectators watching the comedy.

To conclude: while the conversation occasionally offers sentences which seem too complex and well-organised for spontaneous talk, and although there are a few *longueurs,* one kind of battle between the sexes is admirably conveyed in this fireside encounter.

If we leave *Jacques le Fataliste* out of account, as being neither wholly dialogue nor wholly narrative, then the two *contes dialogués* by Crébillon seem to me to be the most effective works of the genre. Crébillon both formulated and followed the two essential rules for narrative dialogue: to organise the conversation so that it convincingly portrays characters, and to make it eventful.

NOTES

1 See the end of this article for a list of such works.

2 For a brief general discussion, see Albert Henry, 'L'expressivité du dialogue dans le roman', *La littérature narrative d'imagination* (Colloque de Strasbourg, 1959) (Paris, 1961), pp. 3–22. This article contains little on eighteenth-century writers, but poses some interesting questions and offers useful bibliographical indications.

3 *Collection complette des œuvres de M. de Crébillon le fils, nouvelle édition* (Londres, 1779), III, 245. All references to Crébillon texts will apply to this edition.

4 In the quotation from *Le Sopha* above, I set out the conversation according to modern usage. One of the complications for those using eighteenth-century texts is illustrated in the fact that the comic oath 'De par Mahomet!' (which is not preceded by a dash in the original) might in theory be either the close of Amanzéi's reply or the beginning of the Sultan's comment. In such cases the reader was forced to make his own interpretation, a need which modern printing conventions have removed. On this subject, see Yves Le Hir, 'Dialogue et typographie', *L'Information Littéraire,* Vol. 13, no. 5 (December 1961), pp. 15–16. M. Le Hir makes some interesting points, but his generalizations should be treated with caution as they are based on insufficient evidence.

5 *Bibliothèque universelle des romans,* 1782, January, I, p. 4.

6 *Bibliothèque universelle des romans,* 1785, October, I, p. 110.

7 Charles Borde, *Œuvres diverses* (Lyon, 1783), II, 252.

8 *Nouveaux contes moraux et nouvelles historiques* (Paris, 1819), VI, 235.

9 See Rudolph Hirzel, *Der Dialog, ein literarhistorischer Versuch,* 2 volumes (Leipzig, 1895); the bulk of this work concerns dialogues in Greek and Latin. On English works, see Elizabeth Merrill, *The Dialogue in English Literature* (New York, 1911).

10 See Johan S. Egilsrud, *Le 'Dialogue des Morts' dans les littératures française, allemande et anglaise,* 1644–1789 (Paris, 1934).

11 Hans-Günter Funke, *Crébillon fils als Moralist und Gesellschaftskritiker* (Heidelberg, 1972), p. 34.

12 Funke, *Crébillon fils,* p. 34, n. 66.

13 For a discussion of *L'Oiseau blanc,* see the article by Janet Osborne and myself, 'Diderot's early fiction', *Diderot Studies,* 14 (1971), pp. 143–66.

14 See Clarence D. Brenner, 'Dramatizations of French Short Stories in the Eighteenth Century', *University of California Publications in Modern Philology,* 33(1947), 1–34.

15 This novel poses some problems of dating and provenance. The preface contains the following phrase: 'l'ayant composé sur un plan nouveau, pour éviter les *dit-il* et les *dit-elle*' (p. 1). But such a plan was by no means 'new' in 1789. So the possibility arises that the novel, which is set in England, might have been written in English in the 1760s, and translated some years later. It does not contain any claim to be a translation, but it would seem in any case to have been written—or translated— by someone with an imperfect command of French. For instance, we find *joindre* used where one

would expect *rejoindre*: 'Miss Thomby les ayant joints' (p. 49); and there are some sentences which read strangely: 'Monsieur Hichinbroocke et miss Thomby l'encourageoient, et il fit publiquement l'amour à miss Hichinbroocke devant toute la compagnie' (p. 163).

16 See Barry Ivker, 'Towards a definition of libertinism in eighteenth-century French fiction', *Studies on Voltaire and the Eighteenth Century*, 73 (Geneva, 1970), 221–39.

17 On this highly individual writer, see C. Girdlestone, *Louis-François Ramond (1755–1827), sa vie, son œuvre littéraire et politique* (Paris, 1969).

18 *Les Catastrophes amoureuses* . . . has been attributed, by Barbier and Quérard, to Pichenot. But the only other publication attributed to the abbé Pichenot is a set of *Poésies sacrées*; and *Les catastrophes amoureuses* of 1796 is an extended version of *Dinville ou les catastrophes amoureuses, histoire vraisemblable par l'auteur du* Duo interrompu (1770).

19 *Œuvres romanesques*, edited by Henri Bénac, Classiques Garnier (Paris, 1951), pp. 698–9.

20 e.g., *Œuvres romanesques*, p. 587.

21 For an outline of how the dialogue proceeds, see Clifton Cherpack, *An Essay on Crébillon fils* (Duke University Press, 1962), pp. 149–59. My only point of disagreement with Cherpack's analysis is that he considers Cidalise to be 'really quite naïve' (p. 155). To my mind, the fact that Cidalise sends her maid away (together with the maid's remarks before leaving) is sufficient proof that she foresees what lies ahead and is willing to co-operate with Clitandre.

22 cf. Funke, *Crébillon fils*, 'Der Bericht eigener Liebeserfolge und das Erfragen der galanten Vergangenheit des Partners hat die Funktion, die Möglichkeiten einer neuen Liaison zu ergründen und, vor allem bei der Frau durch Erregen der Einbildungskraft den Mechanismus der "Selbstverführung" auszulösen. [. . .] Dem gleichen Zwecke dienen die "Geschichten", die Clitandre der schönen Cidalise erzählt' (p. 245).

NARRATIVE WORKS WRITTEN WHOLLY OR LARGELY IN DIALOGUE-FORM AND PUBLISHED BETWEEN 1750 AND 1800

(Library-holdings are indicated as follows: A—Bibliothèque de l'Arsenal; BM—Library of the British Museum; BN—Bibliothèque Nationale. Dates or numbers at the end of an item indicate re-editions before 1800.)

I

WORKS WRITTEN IN FRENCH

1754: MAUBERT DE GOUVEST, Jean-Henri, *L'École du gentilhomme* (Library of Congress); 1761 (BM).

1755: ANON., *Le Mari mécontent de sa femme* (BM).
CRÉBILLON, Claude-Prosper Jolyot de, *La Nuit et le moment* (A, BN); 14, plus 5 in *Œuvres*.

1758: BARRIN, abbé Jean, *Vénus dans le cloître*, first published 1682; 18 re-editions up to 1750; 1758 (BM); 10 more re-editions before 1800.

1759: GROS DE BESPLAS, abbé Joseph-Marie, *Le Rituel des esprits-forts* (BN); 1760, 1762, 1771.

1763: ANON., *La Religieuse en chemise* (BM); 1774, 1775.
CRÉBILLON, Claude-Prosper Jolyot de, *Le Hasard du coin du feu* (A, BM, BN); 1764, plus 5 in *Œuvres*.

1765: ANON., 'Le panier de maquereaux disputé', in *Délassemens nocturnes* (A).
BRET, Antoine, *Essai de contes moraux et dramatiques* (A, BM, BN).

1766: MOLINE, Pierre-Louis, *Le Duo interrompu* (BN); 1767.

1767: ANON., *Marianne ou la paysanne de la forêt d'Ardennes* (A, BN); 1773, 1798.
COSTARD, Jean-Pierre, *Les Orphelins* (BM, BN).

1770: MOLINE, Pierre-Louis, *Dinville* (A, BN). (This is the first part of *Les Catastrophes amoureuses*, 1796).

1771: ANON., *La Rhétorique des putains* (no copy located); 1790 (BM), 1794.

1773: BEAURIEU, Gaspard Gaillard de, 'Le Seigneur bienfaisant', in *Le Porte-feuille amusant* (Univ. of Michigan, VGM).

1776: USSIEUX, Louis d', *Les Deux Sophies, nouvelle françoise* (A, BM).

1777: ANON., *Le Monialisme, histoire galante* (BM).
       CAZALET, Nicolas, 'Les Aveux', in *Les Méprises* (A, BN).
       RAMOND DE CARBONNIÈRES, baron Louis-François-Élisabeth, *Les Dernières Aventures du jeune d'Olban* (A, BM, BN); 1789.

1778: LAFITE, Marie-Élisabeth Bouée, madame de, *Entretiens, drames et contes moraux à l'usage des enfans,* (BN); 1781, 1783.

1779: BASTON, abbé Guillaume-André-René, *Voltairimeros ou première journée de M. de V*** dans l'autre monde* (BN).

1781: DUBOIS-FONTANELLE, Joseph-Gaspard, 'Tête-à-tête conjugal', in *Nouveaux mélanges,* t. II (no copy located); 1785, re-titled *Théâtre et œuvres philosophiques* (BN).
       LOQUET, Marie-Françoise, *Entretiens d'Angélique* (BN); 1782.

1782:· BERQUIN, Arnaud, *L'Ami des enfans* (A, BM, BN); 14, plus about 10 in *Œuvres*, plus numerous editions of extracts.
       DURAND, Antoine-Joseph, *Je veux être heureux* (no copy located); 1829 (BN).

1784: GENLIS, Stéphanie-Félicité Ducrest de Saint-Aubin, comtesse de, *Zélie ou l'ingénue*, adapted by the comte de TRESSAN, in *Bibliothèque universelle des romans,* 1784, January II (BM, BN).

1785: ANON., *L'Homme conséquent*, in *Bibliothèque universelle des romans,* 1785, October I (BM, BN).
       NERCIAT, André-Robert Andréa de, *Les Écarts du tempérament* (BM); 1793.
       SAURIN, Bernard-Joseph, 'Zéphirin et Lindor', in *Les Soirées amusantes ou recueil choisi de nouveaux contes moraux* (A, BN); 1787.

1787: ANON., *La Matinée libertine* (BM, under 'NERCIAT').
       LAFITE, Marie-Élisabeth Bouée, madame de, *Eugénie et ses élèves* (BN); 1787, 1792.

1788: LOQUET, Marie-Françoise, *Entretiens de Clotilde* (BN).

1789: ANON., *La Jeune Nièce ou l'histoire de Suckei Thomby* (BN).

1790: BILDERBECK, Ludwig Benedict Franz von, *Cyane, roman grec* (BM, BN); 1791.

1791: ANON., *L'Eau à la bouche et la pelle au cul* (BN).

1793: NERCIAT, André-Robert Andréa de, *Les Aphrodites* (no copy located); 1864 (BM, BN).

1794: BILDERBECK, Ludwig Benedict Franz von, *Paramythes, imitées d'Herder* (BN).

1795: SADE, Donatien-Alphonse-François, marquis de, *La Philosophie dans le boudoir* (BM, BN).

1796: DIDEROT, Denis, *Jacques le Fataliste et son maître* (BM, BN); 4, plus *Œuvres*.
       MOLINE, Pierre-Louis, *Les Catastrophes amoureuses* (BM). (This is the completion of *Dinville,* 1770).

1797: BENOIST-LAMOTHE, François-Nicolas, *Les Veillées du presbytère* (Harvard).

1798: DIDEROT, Denis, 'L'Oiseau blanc', in *Œuvres,* x (BM, BN).
       LA SALLE D'OFFÉMONT, Adrien-Nicolas Piédefer, 'Les Charlatans', in *Le Mieux* (BN); 1799.

II

WORKS TRANSLATED INTO FRENCH

1760: (?) ARETINO, Pietro Bacci, dit., translator ANON., *La Putain errante* (no copy located); 7; the 1791 re-edition is in BM, BN.

1779: CAMPE, Joachim, translator ANON., *Le Nouveau Robinson,* t. I (Göttingen).
       CAMPE, Joachim, translator ANON., *Le Nouveau Robinson* (Yale); 1783, 1784.

O

1783: CAMPE, Joachim, trans. by Auguste-Simon d'ARNEX, *Le Nouveau Robinson* (BM); 12.

1787: CAMPE, Joachim, trans. by Michael HUBER, *Le Nouveau Robinson* (no copy located); 1793, 1797 (both in Yale).

MEISSNER, August Gottlieb, trans. by Aloys Friedrich von BRÜHL, *Alcibiade* (Lausanne).

1788: MEISSNER, August Gottlieb, trans. by PERRIN DE CAYLA, *Les Quatre Ages d'Alcibiade*, in *Bibliothèque universelle des romans*, 1788, April (BM, BN).

1789: MEISSNER, August Gottlieb, trans. by RAUQUIL-LIEUTAUD, *Alcibiade* (BN), 1792, 1795.

1790: MEISSNER, August Gottlieb, trans. by RAUQUIL-LIEUTAUD, *Bianca Capello, roman dramatique* (BN).

MEISSNER, August Gottlieb, trans. by the marquis de LUCHET, *Histoire de la vie et de la mort de Bianca Capello* (BN: t. III only, Library of Congress).

1798: KLINGER, Friedrich Maximilien, translator ANON., *Les Aventures du docteur Faust* (BM); 1798, 1802 (BN).

1800: NAUBERT, Christiane-Bénédicte-Eugénie, trans. by J.-N.-E. de BOCK, *Les Chevaliers des sept montagnes* (BN).

18

French and English Merchants in the Eighteenth Century: Voltaire Revisited

NORMA PERRY

Voltaire's remarks about merchants in *Sur le commerce,* the tenth of the *Lettres philosophiques,* have long formed part of French and English folklore. Hardly a historian of either country used to fail, in any discussion of eighteenth-century commerce or mercantilism, to cite Voltaire's evidence in support of the contention that in early eighteenth-century France commerce was weakly and despised whereas in the England of the same period it was flourishing and admired, and that further the merchant himself was in England almost a philosopher-prince whereas in France he was regarded as a low and unworthy fellow. Much moreover has been made of the supposed enthusiasm of the English aristocracy for 'business' (on the strength of Voltaire's references to the younger brothers of Lord Townshend and the Earl of Oxford), in contrast to the French nobility's distaste for it. Lanson in his edition gives, as possible sources, quotations from various contemporary writings supporting these points, particularly the last, that members of the aristocracy and the gentry regularly apprenticed their younger sons to trade, although the custom was perhaps declining. Voltaire's further assertion that the *négociant* in France undervalued himself because his calling was treated with such disdain implies of course that the reverse was true in England.

Voltaire's ability to assess with at least a fair degree of accuracy the situation in England and in France has for long never seriously been challenged. And yet one may wonder why, if people are so frequently sceptical of the conclusions drawn on the basis of comparatively brief visits to various countries by even the most reputable of journalists, Voltaire's statements have not been examined rather more closely and indeed critically. Letters such as the tenth of the *Lettres philosophiques* are, after all, simple journalism; and most of us are somewhat suspicious of the instant knowledge of foreign parts presented to us in works which the twentieth century pours out in even greater quantity than the eighteenth. It is true that Voltaire spent nearer three years than two in London, but his interests were many and it is not likely that he could be perfectly informed on all of them. He had, too, the additional disadvantages of knowing almost no English when he arrived—although this he reputedly remedied with miraculous speed—and as I have shown elsewhere,[1] of spending a considerable amount of time frequenting Huguenot expatriates whose native tongue was French, and who, although undoubtedly merchants, were nevertheless, because of their heritage and a certain tendency to commercial inbreeding, not entirely typical of the merchant group. On the other hand, Voltaire had, or so it would seem, an impeccable source of information on merchants in his host and dear friend, the perfectly English and indisputably mercantile Everard Fawkener.

Voltaire's credibility founders, however, if he based his remarks on merchants on erroneous assumptions. What if Voltaire did not, to begin with, know very much about merchants in his own country or in any other? And what if his French and English readers were in general no more clear about the identity, functions and way of life of merchants than he was?

In recent years commentators on Voltaire have sometimes expressed limited reservations about his remarks on England. Peter Gay, for instance, points out that because he was

infatuated with England and resentful against France, Voltaire was not an objective observer, and his account of English society is too uncritical to be wholly accurate.[2]

This historian states (in a footnote on p. 56) that Voltaire's claim that the younger sons of peers did not disdain going into trade

is rather exaggerated: younger sons of peers usually went into the army, the church, or the diplomatic service, and Voltaire's examples are by no means representative.

Gay is still tentative in tone whereas H. J. Habbakuk states very firmly, again referring to Voltaire, that

it was, in fact, extremely rare for a younger son of a peer to go into trade. [. . .] It was only among the gentry with large families that trade was at all a common occupation for a younger son.[3]

And yet J. McManners in his companion piece on France in the same volume (pp. 36–7) clearly accepts the validity of Voltaire's remarks: he says that the tragedy of the poverty-stricken provincial nobility

was that pride prevented them from striking out into commerce, the resource, as Voltaire observe with admiration, of younger sons in England.

As to the status and activities of the merchant in England and France, comparatively little work has been done on the subject, and it is only recently that economic historians have begun, largely because of the quantitative methods of research, to question the assumptions which we have by and large all generally accepted.

It would therefore be unjust to Voltaire to suggest that he was himself to blame if he painted (as I suggest) an inaccurate picture of the status of the merchant in England and France. The whole question of the merchant—beginning from an accurate definition of the word itself—was and is extremely complex. Information *is* now available from the economic historians, but a comparative study of English and French merchants is still lacking; and it would seem that even the best economic historians of both countries are unaware that while they are employed in reassessment in their own country, a similar reassessment is going on on the other side of the Channel. Thus each group, while presenting what they hope is a more accurate description of eighteenth-century commerce in their own country, un-wittingly continues to perpetuate minor myths now exploded in the other.

In additional defence of Voltaire, it ought to be said that the cards were stacked against him as far as possible objectivity of views on the merchant was concerned. He was, after all, a young and in some ways inexperienced man, and there is no reason why he should have the expert knowledge required for such objectivity. Moreover, as I hope to show, there was little likelihood of any other young Parisian of his day having that knowledge. The same was true, in a different way, of his acquaintances in England: the expert knowledge, in a sense, was there, but it was atypical and therefore misleading. Further, the wrong deductions could be drawn from the right material and indeed not only were but long continued to be so drawn. One may perhaps profitably begin from this last point and try to put into perspective a literary work whose significance was incorrectly judged by critics until recently and which would probably have been judged equally falsely by Voltaire.

Voltaire left London in 1729 and thus missed seeing George Lillo's *London Merchant* which was put on in 1731 and as is known was later to inspire several French playwrights. If Voltaire had seen the play (and he was an avid theatre-goer), he would surely have taken it as additional evidence that the merchant was highly respected in England by the upper ranks of society, for the epilogue makes it plain that besides the citizenry of London, the audience included 'fine powdered sparks' in the boxes and people of fashion in the pit. Indeed it is known that all the members of the royal family attended the play at various times during its long first run.[4] It has therefore been taken for granted by critics, as it might well have been by Voltaire, that the chief charm of the play for the audience lay in the character of the high-principled merchant Thorowgood (whose apprentice Barnwell is led astray into the murder of a rich uncle by the fascinating prostitute, Millwood), and in the short panegyrics on the respectability, indeed primacy, of the merchant, which occur in the play, particularly at the beginning of Act II. Bonamy Dobrée in his introduc-tion to the 1948 (London) edition felt that

the obvious and almost comprehensive reason for the play's success is that here at last the newly-risen merchant class, which with its wives and daughters now largely made up the theatre audience, was directly catered for. (p. vii)

He further claimed that

all this chimed in very well with popular feeling during the early years of the great mercantilist era, already sung incidentally by Philips in *Cyder* (1708), Pope in *Windsor Forest* (1713), by Thomson *passim* in *The Seasons* (from 1726), and was before long to be the sole theme of Dyer's *The Fleece* (1757). The sentiments fitted in superbly with the sense of expansion and power that were in the air; they stirred the blood of the bourgeois audience in the same way as the patriotic spirit of Henry V had roused that of the audience in the days of Queen Elizabeth. (pp. ix–x)

All this sounds at first reading quite convincing, but in fact leaves a number of questions unanswered. Did Dobrée feel that the gentry and aristocracy too were charmed by the play's choice of a merchant setting? (He makes no mention of the high-born element in the audiences.) What did he mean by the 'merchant class' which largely made up the theatre audience? Thorowgood is an extremely wealthy, influential and also literate and articulate man—a 'gentleman', one can say; and his peccant apprentice Barnwell is of a similar type and perhaps gently-born, for we learn in Act IV that the uncle whom he is to murder is 'a gentleman of a large estate and fair character in the country where he lives'. Is this what a 'merchant' was, and were the audience indeed all of this type? Further, do polemics make 'good theatre' (for *The London Merchant* quite clearly *was* good theatre) and are they what bourgeois or aristocratic audiences normally seek as their fodder?

The passages in the play which laud or specifically refer to the merchant are in fact short and few. In Act I there is some praise of 'honest merchants' and some financial detail is given. The Act II Scene 1 panegyric consists in Thorowgood's advice to Trueman (the 'good' apprentice) as to the manner in which he is to conduct himself:

I would not have you only learn the method of merchandise and practise it hereafter merely as a means to getting wealth. 'Twill be worth your pains to study it as a science, see how it is founded in reason and the nature of things, how it has promoted humanity as it has opened and yet keeps up an intercourse between nations far remote from one another in situation, customs and religion; promoting arts, industry, peace and plenty; by mutual benefits diffusing mutual love from pole to pole.

To which Trueman later adds that he has observed that 'those countries where trade is promoted and encouraged do not make discoveries to destroy but to improve mankind'. Admittedly this does say much for mercantilism, and implies approval from the mainly bourgeois audience. But in Act I, Scene 2, Thorowgood, in giving instructions to his daughter Maria about the entertainment to be given to the noble lords who are to be his guests, enjoins, 'Let there be plenty and of the best, that the courtiers, though they should deny us citizens politeness, may at least commend our hospitality'. This is a certain indication that others most clearly did not hold the merchant in the esteem in which his own class did. Maria, moreover, makes it plain that the social distinctions implied were very much a part of life, when she comments to her father that 'the man of quality, who chooses to converse with a gentleman and merchant of your worth and character, may confer honour by so doing, but he loses none'. For the main body of the play, the interest, I feel, rests unequivocally not on Thorowgood but on the spicy predicament of young Barnwell who falls prey to his unscrupulous charmer, on the pathos of the mute love for him of the *ingénue* Maria, and on the efforts to save Barnwell made by the blade-straight apprentice Trueman who plays Tiberge to Barnwell's Des Grieux. The appeal of the play, in other words, is much the same as that of *Manon Lescaut* to the unsophisticated; the merchant setting, though important, is nevertheless secondary and may be explained at least partly by Lillo's desire to found a tragedy on a drama of private life (see the dedicatory letter he writes as a preface) and by his own trading background, that of a jeweller in the City of London.

These impressions are reinforced by the 1965 (London) edition of *The London Merchant* by William H. McBurney. His excellent introduction mentions early on that 'both the "low" material and style of the new play made acceptance by the Town highly unlikely', and quotes Colley Cibber who says that Lillo gave the play to the out-of-season company of young actors at Drury Lane preferring that 'it should take its fate in the summer than run the more hazardous fate of encountering the winter critics' (p. 339). The undeniable success of the play at its first run is indeed partly and rightly attributed by McBurney to its serious use of bourgeois and mercantile material, and also to its politcal implications (its setting is Elizabethan but there are topical political references and veiled criticisms of Walpole's foreign policy), as well as to its reassurance of the audience as to the parity of esteem due to both the man of quality and the merchant-gentleman (p. xvi). But this critic asserts that since we know that not only the middle class flocked to the play but also the gentry and aristocracy, 'the appeals of the play were evidently more complex than has usually been acknowledged' (p. xvii). These appeals he sees to be six-fold: first, there was the imitation of the familiar and popular conflicts of love, honour, and friendship found in Dryden, Otway and their successors, especially the extravagant friendship between Barnwell and Trueman; second, there was the highly satisfactory depiction of Millwood, a creature of almost tragic stature, not totally unworthy of comparison with Lady Macbeth and Cleopatra; third, there was Lillo's skill in avoiding the pitfalls of a comic sub-plot without divesting the play completely of humour; fourth, there was the interpolation of an enter-tainment of music and dancing when Millwood invites Barnwell to a *souper intime* in order to seduce him, a type of interlude much in favour with the Town; fifth, its prose seemed refreshingly natural in 1731 (pp. xvii–xxiv). Finally, although it was criticised for its 'lowness', its convincing pathos won the day (p. xxi).

One might well guess, in fact, that *The London Merchant* appealed to the audiences of 1731 for much the same basic reasons that the first melodrama, *Cœlina ou l'enfant du mystère*, appealed to the Parisian audiences of 1800, except that Guilbert de Pixerécourt's play, and his audiences, were possibly more naïve in nature.

The continuing success of the play until late in the century was, however, directly related to its mercantile and minatory content. The pathos wore thin and soon seemed ludicrous to the aristocracy, gentry and upper middle classes, but the play was for long traditionally presented in London at Christmas, Easter, and on Lord Mayor's Day in November, for, as Colley Cibber remarked (op. cit., p. 340), 'it was judged a proper entertainment for the apprentices, &c. as being a more instructive, moral, and cautionary drama, than many pieces that had usually been exhibited on those days, with little but farce and ribaldry to recommend them'.

Thus *The London Merchant,* while apparently seeming to verify all Voltaire's impressions about the status of the merchant in England, can be seen to prove the point hardly if at all. Certainly Lillo claimed that the merchant *was* the equal of the man of quality, but Lillo was of minor artisan-trading stock himself, and in any case the game is given away by those class-conscious remarks of Thorowgood and Maria.

As far as English literature is concerned, one can probably best assess the social position of those in trade by looking at the novels of Jane Austen. It is of course true that her novels were written over three-quarters of a century after the date of the *Lettres philosophiques,* but there is no indication that the situation had changed in any marked manner, as far as social acceptance was concerned, during that time. *Pride and Prejudice* (1813) is the best novel to study because of the interesting range of class in it. Here the distinctions are clear. At the top of the pyramid is Darcy, who is old landed gentry and reluctant to ally himself with the Bennet family because although the father is a gentleman, the mother was the daughter of an attorney, and has a sister who had married her father's clerk and a brother who is in London 'in a respectable line of trade' (p. 23).[5] We may also remember that this last member of the family eventually impresses Darcy creditably because he is a man of sense and some education, unlike his egregiously vulgar Bennet sister. Above the Gardiners (Mrs Bennet's family) but very far below the Darcys come the Lucases whose head, Sir William, was formerly in trade (unspecified) in the local town, Meryton, became its Mayor, and was given a knighthood which 'gave him a disgust of his business' so that he devoted himself thenceforward to being a gentleman (p. 14). And above the Lucases, closer to Fitzwilliam Darcy himself but not of course to his formidably aristocratic aunt Lady Catherine de Bourgh, come the Bingleys, 'of a respectable family in the North of England', whose father had made a fortune of nearly £100,000 in trade, had meant to purchase an estate, but had not lived to do so (p. 12). Bingley has been educated as a gentleman and is a close friend of Darcy. Analysed from another aspect, these groups show that the aristocracy scorn (Lady Catherine) or accept (Darcy) a successful gentlemanly merchant or at least his children (the Bingleys) and scorn the lower mercantile groups; that the Bingleys scorn (the Bingley sisters) or accept (Bingley himself) the Bennets, the Lucases and the Gardiners. Mr Bennet, an individualist and, because of his gentle birth, secure himself of social acceptance, tends to scorn everyone.

Another useful work to cite while speaking of social acceptance, and much nearer in date to the *Lettres*, is *Clarissa Harlowe* (1747–8), which is sometimes referred to as a novel in which a merchant makes an important appearance, without his exact social definition being discussed. Ian Watt analyses the class-structures implicit in Richardson's novel in *The Rise of the Novel* (London, 1957), and points out the following facts (pp. 229–30): Clarissa and Lovelace come from the wealthy landed gentry and have noble connexions, but in Clarissa's case only on her mother's side. Her family is ambitious to rise socially. James, the only son, hopes for a peerage if the family fortunes can be concentrated on him, but Lovelace's courtship of Clarissa threatens his plans, for it may lead James's uncles to divert some of their fortunes to Clarissa. Thus, apart from his personal animosity to Lovelace, James has good economic reasons for persuading his family to force Clarissa to marry Solmes, who is extremely rich but of low birth (and has presumably risen through trade) and will therefore not expect any other dowry with Clarissa than the grandpaternal estate which is already hers. This fully indicates the attitude of the higher gentry to a marriage by one of its daughters to a person in trade. As Watt points out, Solmes is in addition presented as a man 'most unpleasantly typical of the rising middle-class', mercenary, upstart, 'totally devoid of social grace or intellectual cultivation, repulsive physically, and a poor speller to boot' (pp. 229–30). Hardly a characterisation which would seem to accord with Voltaire's impression of what the upper-class English felt about the merchant.

One can also go back to 1722, before Voltaire's English visit, and look at Richard Steele's *The Conscious Lovers* where we again find an honourable and esteemed merchant, Mr Sealand, who is proud of the dignity of his class and thinks it no dishonour to Sir John Bevil in proposing a match between young Bevil and his own daughter Lucinda. But it is made plain that Sir John himself condescends to those who have not the advantage of gentle birth, and Mr Sealand is stung at one point to declare:

We merchants are a species of gentry, that have grown into the world this last Century, and are as honourable, and almost as useful, as you landed Folks, that have always thought yourselves so much above us.

This sort of defensive aggression on behalf of the merchant is shown in other plays, such as Daniel Defoe's *Roxana* (1724), John Gay's *Polly* (published, though not produced because of censorship, in 1728) and the same dramatist's *The Distress'd Wife* (1734), where Barter asks indignantly (or possibly satirically):

Is the name then [of merchant] a term of Reproach?—Where is the Profession that is so honourable?—What is it that supports every Individual of our Country?—'Tis Commerce.—On what depends the Glory, the Credit, the Power of the Nation?—On Commerce.—To what does the Crown itself owe its Splendor and Dignity?—To Commerce.[6]

The eulogy of the merchant in these works does indeed show the upward thrust of the merchant class in the second and third decades of the century in England and it is true that the only French production written in the early eighteenth century and dealing with a similar type, the *traitant*, Lesage's *Turcaret* of 1709, is the reverse of eulogistic. But the discrepancy between what the merchant thinks of himself and what he knows others think of him is apparent in the English plays. It is, in fact, a case of special pleading on the part of dramatists who had reason to polemicise a little. John Lillo was a jeweller in the City of London; Richard Steele, although not of trading stock himself, was for mercantilism and the middle-class way of life by reason of his Whiggish and philanthropic inclinations; John Gay had been apprenticed to a London mercer; Daniel Defoe was the son of a butcher and tallow-chandler and himself a wholesale hosier. The patent indignation of all these men at the *lack* of esteem shown to the merchant is much more suggestive of what the attitudes of people 'in society' were to the trading class, than is any of the praise they place in their merchants' mouths. Defoe in fact deeply resented his not being accepted by the great; this has been attributed to paranoid tendencies on his part but it is, I think, fairer to see it, as does Bonamy Dobrée, as 'a sign that he had misjudged the level to which his trading class had risen'.[7] (The same type of judgement can be made of Voltaire after the Rohan-Chabot affair.)

Defoe's name is an important one to cite in this context, as it was he who published in 1728 his *Plan of the English Commerce* wherein he irascibly but, one feels, impotently shakes his fist against the 'gentry' (including in this group the nobility, the men of arms, the clergy and gentlemen 'unmix'd with plebeian Blood for immemorial Ages') who do not appreciate

Trade and consider it a 'universal mechanism'. His further observations are in a sense very like Voltaire's and could well have furnished the Frenchman with the basis for some of his remarks on merchants:

If they would look a little nearer, they would see themselves not by Practice only degenerating into Trading men, but even their Fortunes, nay, their very Blood mingled with the Mechanicks, *as they call them*; the Necessity of their Circumstances frequently reconciles the best of the Nobility to these mixtures; and then the same Necessity opens their Eyes to the Absurdity of the Distinctions which they had been so wedded to before.

It is with the utmost Disgrace to their Understanding, that these People would distinguish themselves in the Manner they do, when they may certainly see every Day prosperous Circumstances advance those Mechanicks, *as they will have them called,* into the Arms, and into the Rank of the Gentry; and declining Fortunes reduce the best families to a level with the Mechanick.

The rising Tradesman swells into the Gentry, and the declining Gentry sinks into Trade. A Merchant, or perhaps a Man of a meaner Employ, thrives by his honest Industry, Frugality, and a long series of diligent Application to Business, and being grown immensely rich, he marries his Daughters to Gentlemen of the first Quality, perhaps a Coronet; then he leaves the Bulk of his Estate to his Heir, and he gets into the Rank of the Peerage; does the next Age make any Scruple of their Blood, being thus mix'd with the ancient Race? Do we not just now see two Dukes descended by the Female Side, from the late Sir *Josiah Child,* and the immediate Heir a Peer of Ireland? [. . .]

On the other Hand, the declining Gentry, in the Ebb of their Fortunes, frequently push their Sons into Trade, and they again, by their Application often restore the Fortunes of their Families: Thus Tradesmen become Gentlemen, by Gentlemen becoming Tradesmen. I could give examples of this too, but they are too recent for our naming.[8]

Defoe's claims are at once true and not true. The tone of his writing is defensive and over-indignant, obviously aimed at an audience which will take much convincing, and this indicates that his assertions were *not* generally accepted. 'Society', in other words, did not accept the merchant at his own valuation and it let him into its ranks only through the back door. Further, although merchants did, by the acquisition of wealth, become 'gentlemen', they were, as we shall see, much fewer in number than Defoe suggests (Sir Josiah Child, who had in any case died in 1699, was a very unusual man). Lastly, confusion is caused by Defoe's (and other people's) uses of the words 'merchant', 'trading men', 'nobility', 'gentry', 'tradesman', 'business', 'trade', certainly in the modern mind, and quite probably, it seems to me, in the minds of the early eighteenth century.

'Merchant' and '*marchand*' are blanket terms which covered an extremely wide range of middle-class activity in both England and France. In England, the situation is complicated by the use of the term 'in trade' which can mean different things according to one's own social class. To return to *Pride and Prejudice*: Sir William Lucas sounds as though he has been in *retail* trade in a large way, since his small fortune has been acquired in Meryton, away from the main centres of business; Mr Gardiner's 'respectable line of trade' in London is wholesale but obviously not very grand (p. 124); Mr Bingley *père* was clearly a merchant in the important sense of the word, since he made £100,000 (over half a million pounds in modern terms). The Darcys tend to scorn all these groups, but the Bingley children as the second generation of the topmost mercantile group are acceptable to some members of the aristocracy if not to all. Sir William Lucas could condescend to others 'in trade' because he has acquired a very small fortune and a knighthood, but he is many steps below the Bingleys on the social ladder and has no great fortune: *his* daughter, Charlotte, is fortunate to make a match with the dreadful Mr Collins, Lady Catherine's chaplain. All these groups, however, rank considerably higher than the swarm of shopkeepers and small tradesmen whom we also have to designate as being 'in trade'. *Mutatis mutandis,* the distinctions were the same in France. Retail trade in both countries was a 'low' occupation; its practitioners were despised by the other members of the mercantile class; they made fortunes only if they operated on a very large scale or eventually went into the wholesale trade—and they were, even so, socially and economically very far below the true 'merchants' and the French equivalents of these from the *marchands en gros* upwards. In neither society was it normally possible for those in retail trade to make an impact nationally or to climb far up the social scale (except, of course, over a large number of generations by a gradual process of family evolution); in both countries, social ascension and even national influence were possible for those *at the top* of the superior group of 'trading men' whereas the main body of this same superior group remained bourgeois and only locally influential.

Unfortunately, on both sides of the Channel people are by and large victims of the misinterpretations intrinsic to living in certain social groups. It is a sociological truism that members of one social group tend not only to be ignorant of the real nature, life-style, functions and culture of other social groups but also to imagine that they *do* know what other groups are like—in other words, to base their attitudes on an ill-formed stereotype of the group concerned. Social myth takes the place of social reality. The eighteenth-century stereotype of the merchant as far as other groups within the bourgeoisie, and as far as the gentry and nobility were concerned, was undoubtedly that of Molière's *bourgeois gentilhomme.* He was 'in trade' (unspecified) and he was a low fellow; he was coarse-grained (but 'clever' and cunning), boorish, uneducated; he was a 'thruster', he aped his betters, his sole interest after the acquisition of a large fortune was in acquiring a title. He was not Mr Sealand or Mr Thorowgood, he was Monsieur Jourdain and—worse—Mr Solmes.

Such is the persistence of this type of social myth that the twentieth-century stereotype of the 'trading man', although certainly modified, is not in essence vastly different from that of the eighteenth and nineteenth centuries. Because of lack of adequate information (which is indeed very hard to acquire because of the immense variety within any one supposedly homogeneous group), the average person has little notion of the gradations in the practice of trade and thus little idea of the varied personalities and activities of those who engage in it. This is particularly true of the ranges of trade higher than retail. The Grocers' Company of the City of London, for instance, still smacks to the uninitiated of cash and a striped apron (or at best a supermarket) rather than of international dealings in commodities and shares, and the joint ownership in trust of the public school known as Oundle. And, nearing the top of the scale, the stereotype of the successful man of business remains Robert Maxwell rather than the Hon. Angus Ogilvy or even Soames Forsyte. Thus critics have continued to accept as valid what the eighteenth century thought it knew about the merchant, because they themselves often work to a similar stereotype when thinking of merchants. This is why the references to Fawkener in works on Voltaire are vague and even contradictory. We find: 'négociant distingué', 'an opulent English merchant'; 'his father was a mercer [. . .] and his grandfather a druggist'; 'he had been a Turkey merchant and was nevertheless admitted to speak his word in intellectual, even political circles'; 'silk and cloth merchant'; 'he acquired his fortune by the sale of Eastern silks and fabrics'; 'riche négociant de la Cité'; 'un riche «marchand» de la Cité'; and 'ce simple drapier'.[9] None of these descriptions gives a true picture of what sort of 'merchant' Everard Fawkener was, and some are distinctly misleading, to say the least. He was in fact 'gentry', and a member of a distinguished merchant family of the highest importance in the Levant Company and consequently in the City, which dealt on the largest possible scale with all sorts of commercial and financial transactions.[10]

By the French at the time, of course, Fawkener was necessarily seen as a Jourdain figure. The mirth aroused by Voltaire's dedication of *Zaïre* to Fawkener was, in the context of the social myth, completely natural and justified. D'Allainvalle's satire *Le Temple du goust*[11] presents Kafener (Fawkener) to us in Scene 6 'habillé grossièrement, une pipe à la bouche & parlant pesamment', and describes him as 'Capitaine marchand courant de mer en mer'; he smokes incessantly through the scene, speaks in Jourdain-esque manner of his discovery, through the patronage of the god Momus (Voltaire), that he has a genius for poetry, and when at the end of the comedy Momus is struck by Jupiter's thunderbolt for his impertinence in defending Kafener and taking over the Temple, Kafener, seeing his patron disappear through a trapdoor, stupidly comments, 'Voilà Momus à fond de calle', and strolls off still smoking. The satire's chief shafts are aimed at Voltaire's self-conceit and there is no great malice in the jokes at Fawkener's expense. But I do not think that d'Allainvalle took care to choose a comic merchant figure from among several possibilities for his Kafener. Fawkener must be Kafener because a merchant was always a Kafener—on both sides of the Channel. The English would no doubt have reacted in similar manner to the name of a French merchant as the dedicatee of an English play. True, John Lillo had dedicated *The London Merchant* to Sir John Eyles, who was a merchant, but his standing is made irreproachably plain by the addition of the words 'Baronet, Member of Parliament for, and Alderman of the City of London, and Sub-Governor of the South Sea Company', whereas Fawkener is simply 'marchand anglais'. Sir John was a great man in the land and too well known to be covered by the Jourdain stereotype. The same would be true in France of the influential French merchants, although their case is more complicated, as we shall see later. When Voltaire in his *Seconde épître dédicace* (1736) to *Zaïre* asks his fellow countrymen to rid themselves of their prejudices against merchants with the words:

Je jouis en même temps du plaisir de pouvoir dire à ma nation de quel œil les négociants sont regardés chez vous; quelle estime on sait avoir en Angleterre pour une profession qui fait la grandeur de l'État, et avec quelle supériorité quelques-uns d'entre vous représentent leur patrie dans le parlement, et sont au rang des législateurs,

his vision is suffering from the double distortion of not quite accurate information about England and partially unjustified assumptions about France. And he was also unaware that, as we have seen, English apologists for mercantilism were, as he was, making similar pleas against prejudice in their own country. Had any one of these latter spent two or three years in Bordeaux, he might even have been dedicating a play to the great merchant Abraham Gradis and marvelling at how much better things were ordered in France, to the vast amusement of the English.

When speaking accurately of 'merchants', we are dealing on both sides of the Channel with a group which is extremely small numerically in national terms. The vast majority of the so-called mercantile class are of no interest here because they engaged in retail trade and were not influential (except the most successful among them locally) in the way that Voltaire meant, and because they neither came from, nor intermarried with, nor were accepted by, the gentry, and still less the nobility. (These are best called 'tradesmen' in English and '*détailleurs*' or '*détaillants*' in French.) The group we are concerned with were not even the wholesale traders of the internal markets (in France the *marchands en gros*), but those who dealt in wholesale trade in the international markets (*négociants* in France, merchants in England) and whose activities included acting as attorney or commission agents, stock jobbing, loan contracting, shipping, banking, ownership of plantations, exchange broking, insurance, and bullion dealing. Some specialized in a certain branch of trading (in England usually belonging to one of the large merchant associations such as the Levant or East India Companies), but large-scale success usually came with the proliferation of activities and the gradual move from business proper to the realms of high finance,[12] which always involved association with the government of the day. Similarly in France, 'les grosses fortunes, sous l'ancien régime, ont beaucoup moins comme sources le commerce et l'industrie que les opérations financières. Les financiers jouent un rôle de premier ordre dans l'État, pénètrent dans les rangs les plus élevés de la société'.[13] These financiers in France included men of business as well as the *officiers des finances royales,* who, despite the different origin of their 'places' were not, it seems to me, vastly different in type from those men who in England 'bought', by favours rendered or promised, a lucrative office such as that of the Postmaster General, which was well-nigh a sinecure but made its holder a fortune because he could invest the funds allocated for the running of the Post Office, and himself retain the interest. The difference of course was that in France a proportion of the money from the leasing of offices went to the royal purse whereas on the English side it was venal ministers who profited, not by money but indirectly, from the transactions. The financiers were absolutely indispensable to the state in both countries, and I would question Pierre Léon's blanket assertion that they were so much less so in England because of the creation of the Bank of England in 1694.[14] Important though this undoubtedly was, the individual banker was still indispensable, particularly at times of governmental crisis, such as the bursting of the South Sea Bubble, during wars, and so forth. Pierre Simond alone, for instance, the Huguenot merchant-banker whom Voltaire knew in his early days, in April 1783 subscribed £30,000 to the £12,000,000 loan floated by the Bank of England.[15] The same was true of France: when kings needed money in a hurry they got it from the *traitants* or from eminent merchants or businessmen of international repute, frequently from men who like their English *confrères,* were all these things at once; men well known in the young Voltaire's day, such as Samuel Bernard, Legendre, Demeuves, the brothers Crozat, the brothers Pâris; men who prior to 1750 were pillars of the régime and felt at their ease within it.[16] In England they were men like Sir Josiah Child (although he was dead by 1699), Sir Thomas Johnson (of Liverpool), Sir Henry Furnese, Sir Joshua Vanneck, William Beckford, Sampson Gideon.

The men just named were at the very top of the group but there was a whole body of merchants on either side of the Channel, of the type of Pierre Simond and the Fawkeners, who were extremely substantial, highly influential and either greatly respected or greatly despised according to their personalities, life-styles, manner of business and according to the standpoint of the person viewing them. They were generally envied by the lower ranges of the merchant class and therefore often traduced. Some were unjustifiably despised by those above them socially and some were genuinely despicable. They could be used as justifications, either by exception or by conformity to the rule, of belief in the Jourdain stereotype.

The most real distinction between the two national groups, it seems to me, is that whereas in England the merchants operated—and lived—chiefly in London (but also in the great ports such as Liverpool and Bristol), in France the *négociants* were almost to a man in the provinces, in the great trading centres of Laval, Beauvais, Lyons, Marseilles, Bordeaux, Toulouse, Rouen, Nantes and so on.[17] The chief great financiers were in Paris, but they were very few in number and because of their immense influence they were feared and despised, just as, say, Sir Josiah Child had been and William Beckford was to be: stigmatised as a slave of the court in the one case and 'a noisy, purse-proud, illiterate demagogue' (to use Macaulay's words) in the other.[18] In this fact lies a very good explanation for Voltaire's amazement at the type of merchant he knew in London but whose equivalent he could in reality have met had he at that time known the provincial merchant centres as he was later to know Lyons. These men were all much respected by those who knew them as they were doubtless the flower of their kind, but envied by their lesser competitors; and there existed in both countries others of the same group who were shady in their dealings and uncouth in their ways.

It was the former not the latter merchants who were being extolled by writers on both sides of the Channel. I have mentioned earlier the plays written in England in the first three decades of the century, and Defoe's *Plan of the English Commerce* of 1728. The most important work of the half-century in England is Malachy Postlethwayt's *A Dictionary of Trade and Commerce* of 1751 (London), preceded in 1750 by his *The Merchant's Public Counting House*, which still has the apologetic tone of the earlier works. Across the Channel in Paris, the main works comparable to Defoe's and Postlethwayt's had appeared much earlier: Jacques Savary's *Le Parfait Négociant, ou Instruction générale pour ce qui regarde le commerce de toutes sortes de marchandises, tant en France que des pays étrangers* of 1675. This too is an apologia for the *bourgeoisie commerçante* and it has the same sort of defensive note to it that Defoe's *Plan* was to have fifty years and Malachy Postlethwayt's seventy-five years later. Following Savary came Formentin's *Traité du bonheur* of 1706, again in the same tone, but here more confident:

De tous les états de la vie, le commerce est celui qui a le plus de commodités et peut-être le plus d'agréments; un marchand qui vit avec honneur dans sa condition, qui ne vend ni à faux poids ni à fausse mesure et qui se contente d'un gain légitime, trouve non seulement dès ce monde la reconnaissance de sa probité, par la bonne réputation qu'il s'acquiert, mais il se prépare un bonheur éternel pour l'autre. [...] Le gentilhomme et l'officier de judicature ont le pas devant le marchand: mais s'il leur cède cet avantage, il semble qu'il soit dédommagé par le gain qu'il fait sur ses marchandises et par l'importance d'une fortune aussi étendue que celle des autres est bornée. (p. 124)

Louis-Silvestre de Sacy in his *Traité de la gloire* (1715), goes farther than this and far from showing indignation, as Savary did, at the contempt shown by other groups for the *commerçants,* boldly says:

C'est une erreur grossière, que de s'imaginer que l'espérance du gain puisse seule engager dans le commerce et que l'amour de la gloire n'y puisse entrer par quelque endroit. [...] L'amour de l'honneur ou de la gloire peut seul animer, s'étendre et perfectionner le commerce. (p. 92)

Robert Mauzi comments: 'Cette dignité que le commerçant revendique, nul ne songe à la lui contester en ces premières années du XVIIIe siècle, où le bourgeois n'est pas sans prestige.'[19] It would perhaps be truer to say that, as in England at the same time, the merchant was at once granted the respect he desired, and denied it, according to the attitudes of those who discussed him. One last example of the type of writing prevalent in the two countries, making propaganda, for one reason or another, on behalf of the merchant, is Marie Huber's *Le Monde fou préféré au monde sage, en vingt-trois promenades de trois amis* (Amsterdam, 1731), where the character who incarnates the author's ideal of 'le monde sage' is Éraste, a *négociant.*[20]

It seems clear that the ambivalent attitudes to the man of business in the two countries stem directly from his growing success and his socially important rôle. Contrary to popular belief, commerce in France was thriving in the early eighteenth century:

Success in the growing business world, whether in commerce, finance or industry, was largely the result of personal competence, and the success was so striking, and so important in terms of the total economy, that occupational roles in this area won prestige and recognition in spite of the traditional contempt for them. The businessman, like the early knight, was a mere 'self-made man'; nevertheless, his property was such as to command respect regardless of his ignoble heredity. It was through the rise of the world of business especially that the approval of mobility—limited approval to be sure—was introduced into the stratification system of eighteenth-century France.[21]

The notion of extreme social mobility in England and complete lack of it in France has now been discarded, and the pattern looks more similar in the two countries. The line between the nobility and the rest was not as sharply drawn as T. S. Ashton, for instance, believed.[22]

In England, as has been said, the notable concentration of merchants was in London and the majority lived *bourgeoisement* in the City, only a few of the very wealthiest living at the 'polite end of town'.[23] Very few of them corresponded to the popular archetype of the man who rose from nothing to a vast fortune. Good luck and judgement helped, but the men best able to make a fortune in trade were already in possession of capital.[24] The privileged group we are discussing lived handsomely, and of these the merchant princes differed little from the nobility in habits of life, living in equal state, spending huge sums on furniture, food and servants,[25] whereas the rest simply lived in substantial houses in a substantial manner. They tended to marry within their occupational group, often in order to expand their enterprises and acquire capital,[26] but there was also at the higher levels a general desire to move upward into the gentry, and this was achieved by early retirement, the acquisition of an estate and intermarriage with the higher social group. The picture has, however, been exaggerated. It was only the very wealthiest who could marry their daughters into the aristocracy. It is true that such as Sir Peter Delmé, Huguenot and Lord Mayor of London, Everard Fawkener's brother-in-law, became the father-in-law of the 1st Lord Ravensworth and that Voltaire's acquaintance Pierre Simond married his two daughters into the aristocracy; it is also true that some great merchants bought large estates and that some acquired titles. But 'the barriers to social advancement were still formidable', and the gate to advancement was 'a narrow gate and difficult to pass'.[27] The estates which the merchants bought were usually small, and on the fringes of London, in Essex, Surrey, Middlesex, to which they eventually moved and finally retired completely. As to great estates, they could be bought only if landowners were willing to sell and not only did very few of these come on the market but very few individuals could make enough money even in a life-time to buy a great estate.[28] In the mid-eighteenth century it took a capital outlay of about £30,000 to buy a comfortable residence and an estate worth £1,000 a year, an investment which enabled one to enter the ranks of only the middling gentry.[29] It was difficult to acquire a title even with an estate purchased. The peerage was a small body until the burst of new creations in 1784. From 161 temporal peerages in 1704, the number rose only to 182 in 1780. The majority of creations were only to replace extinct peerages. The largest single group of men ennobled consisted of those who had performed notable services to the state (Walpole, Pitt, Speaker Onslow; eminent lawyers such as Cowper, Harcourt and Macclesfield; famous soldiers and sailors such as Cadogan, Cobham, Hawke and Rodney). There was none who had been actively engaged in trade nor any financier, until Robert Smith was made Baron Carrington in 1796. 'The great merchants were rewarded less lavishly, by baronetcies and Irish peerages.'[30]

   The chief way for a great merchant to improve his social status and political influence was really by alliances through marriage and, as Habbakuk says, although London society was open to 'the amusing, the talented and the able, [. . .] the marriages of a class are a better index of its social feelings than the composition of its dinner parties' (p. 19). And the marriages between the aristocracy and the bourgeoisie were between aristocratic sons and bourgeois daughters, not *vice versa*. Even here there has been exaggeration of the trend because such marriages were always much publicised. Of these, Habbakuk says:

No one has yet calculated their frequency, but it is evident from the terms of the settlements on such marriages that considerable material gains were necessary to induce the great families to contract them, and when relevant statistics are available, we may perhaps find that actresses were not much less common than bourgeois heiresses. The contemporary attention which mésalliances commanded is proof of their rarity rather than of their frequency. (p. 19)

As to the supposed cross-fertilisation caused by the entry of the younger sons of the gentry and the aristocracy into 'trade', the picture has been distorted, and myth perpetuated. Habbakuk, in the phrase already quoted, is convinced that it was 'extremely rare' for the younger son of a peer to go into trade and cautiously states that 'it was only among the gentry with large families that trade was at all a common occupation for a younger son' (p. 19). The significant word here is 'large'. It is generally agreed that the pattern was for the elder son to inherit the estate, the second to enter the army, the third the church, the fourth the navy. Habbakuk further points out that 'offices were, par excellence, a way of providing for younger sons' (p. 7). The solicitations of great men by fathers, mothers and other loving relations, solicitations on behalf of their offspring and connexions for governmental posts, court offices, pensions, annuities and for lesser posts in the Customs, Excise and Tax offices, pullulate in the correspondence of the eighteenth century. These possibilities would take care of the younger sons of most families. When Sir Lewis Namier describes the situation thus:

The eldest son inherited the family estates, the second, third, or even fourth, were placed in the Church, in the army or navy, at the bar, or in some government office, but the next had usually to be apprenticed to a merchant, and however great the name and wealth of the family, the boy baptised Septimus and Decimus was almost certain to be found in the counting house,[31]

he is grossly oversimplifying. The infant mortality rate in the eighteenth century[32] made it unlikely that enough children survived to maturity for any Septimus or Decimus to be seventh or tenth in more than name, and in any case such numerical first names were usually based on total numbers of children, not on those of sons and daughters separately. Thus, Namier's hypothetical Decimus might well be the last of six brothers and four sisters of whom only three brothers and two sisters survived. Moreover, the families of the peerage at that time seem to have been much smaller on average than Namier's statement would suggest.[33] And the fact that Voltaire was able to cite the younger brother of the Earl of Oxford, Nathaniel Harley, as having been a factor at Aleppo, proves even less than such an isolated instance would normally prove, since Harley died at Aleppo in 1720, when Everard Fawkener was himself a factor there.[34] It is a clear case of the natural but misleading tendency to draw general social conclusions from particular information furnished by members of one's own circle.

The pattern in France roughly parallels, I think, that in England, provided that one remembers that only the financiers were in Paris and that the great merchant families were in the provinces. The lower orders of the merchant class lived as simply, or possibly more simply, than their English equivalents, but the chief merchants lived luxuriously, as luxuriously as great nobles and often more luxuriously than the provincial nobility. The financiers, particularly the *fermiers généraux,* were hated for their profits and reproached for their humble origins but, like the English merchants who seldom, if ever, rose from rags to riches, many had begun as financial agents (for example, Bouret who became *trésorier général de la maison du roi*). Grimod de la Reynière later in the century had a financier as father although he had a *charcutier* as grandfather (much to his mother's discomfort).

P

Lallemand de Retz, Live de Bellegarde, d'Arnoncourt, all *fermiers généraux* in 1726 when Voltaire went to England, were sons of substantial and respected families.[35] Financiers with enormous fortunes made great display of their wealth and were consequently despised (as was William Beckford in England); they had splendid country homes on the fringes of Paris, at Passy, Auteuil, Vanves, Ivry, Puteaux, but despite what was said of them frequently showed every indication of good taste.

According to Henri Sée (p. 162), there was a tendency for the wealthy merchants to retire and live on their incomes, unlike their English equivalents, who all, Sée suggests, founded merchant dynasties, but the same tendency of course was prevalent in England too. Pierre Léon points out that:

Le bourgeois tend à s'évader de sa classe. [. . .] Pour beaucoup, l'entrée dans la noblesse et l'acquisition de fiefs provoquent la rupture avec l'ancien état. L'officier, l'homme de loi, le négociant résignent leurs charges et vont vivre sur leurs terres.

He utters, however, the same warning as G. E. Mingay did about social ascension for the Englishman:

Le bourgeois n'oublie pas la barrière invisible, maintenue avec une délicate fermeté, qui le sépare de la classe vraiment dominante. Les mœurs et les préjugés sont, à ce point de vue, plus résistants que les lois, et la fusion est rarement complète. (p. 641)

The same author describes (p. 643) the power exercised by the greatest of these men. Samuel Bernard, for instance, was exercising in France during Voltaire's young manhood the same sort of power as Sir John Barnard and Sampson Gideon in England. Bernard in 1709 was trying to establish a National Bank of the type later advocated by Law; he was charged with diplomatic and political missions, and in fact he worked with the government in all the important measures of the day. Although accused of corruption, ostentation, vulgarity, he held an important salon in Paris, attended, for instance, by Cardinal de Rohan. He married his daughters to noblemen, one to a Molé, and the other to the Marquis de Mirepoix, giving with the second the enormous dowry of 800,000 *livres*; similarly, the vicomte de Rohan-Chabot later married Mademoiselle de Vervins, the grand-daughter of a cloth-mercer.[36] Such misalliances seemed as scandalous in France as they were in England and were presumably roughly as frequent.

In the provinces, the great merchants shared local social honours with the nobility, particularly perhaps the great shipping magnates of the chief seaports such as François Bonaffé of Bordeaux who was reputed to have ended with a fortune of fourteen million *livres,* and Abraham Gradis of the same town (the son of an impecunious Marrano merchant) who was received at Paris as an equal by courtiers as well as financiers.[37] These were the equivalents of the men in England who were so successful that the roads of social ascension were open to them. As in England, money was invested in estates because as in England land-ownership was the supreme symbol of the noble style of life. By the eighteenth century the great ship-owners of Saint-Malo, the Baude, Magon and Danycan families, for instance, had estates all over Brittany.[38] By this method, a man could of course acquire a spurious particle to his name which, while it fooled nobody, nevertheless in time helped him on the way up the social ladder; E. G. Barber cites (p. 95) the prosperous merchant J. B. Accarias of Die, in Dauphiné, who thus became Accarias de Sérionne. Otherwise, one could buy an office for its social advancement rather than for its lucrative nature, since the highest of these offices conferred immediate nobility and still others gave it after a period of perhaps twenty years. This seems to me the rough equivalent of the knighthoods, baronetcies and Irish baronies and earldoms 'bought' in England at the same time. Two of Samuel Bernard's sons, for instance, became *président du parlement* and *maître de requêtes,* thus reaching the higher ranks of the *noblesse de robe.*[39] This *savonnette à vilain* by which one cleaned up one's ancestry became inordinately expensive as the century progressed and, again, fooled no one at the time—but neither did a newly acquired baronetcy or Irish barony in England. Then there was the direct sale of letters patent of nobility by the monarch. Pierre Goubert thinks that the eighteenth century showed more restraint here than did the seventeenth, and that '*lettres d'anoblissement* went only to influential merchants, high-ranking soldiers, and the more loyal servants of the crown' (p. 181), but E. G. Barber instances the 1,200 payments for *lettres d'anoblissement* made between 1732–1748 in Paris alone.[40] Just as in England a wealthy man *could* become a gentleman by living like one long enough, so in France it was possible for a *roturier,* or at least his son, to become noble by a gradual process of *vivre noblement*; but Goubert points out that it was still advisable for the man of fortune to speed up the process by buying a sound ennobling office (p. 186). He categorically supports the idea that money was the key to social evolution (p. 188), which of course was exactly the case in England too.[41] He gives interesting examples of the provincial ascension patterns (p. 189). Apparently twenty-seven out of the fifty-eight gentlemen who were convened to elect the noble representative for the Bailiwick of Beauvais in 1789 belonged to families ennobled during the course of the century, nearly all of them by purchase of the office of *secrétaire du roi.* Among them were sixteen members of the families of Danse, Regnonval and Michel, all of whose grandfathers or fathers had been serge and linen merchants in the previous century. Similarly, of the three hundred or so noblemen created in eighteenth-century Brittany, the largest group consisted of big businessmen: every one of the great families of ship-owners, financiers and slave-traders is accounted for on the list; we find the names Danycan, Magon, Trouin, of Saint-Malo, Michel, Grou, Piou, Montaudouin of Nantes and so forth.

Pierre Goubert, in another work, *Familles marchandes sous l'Ancien Régime: les Danse et les Motte, de Beauvais* (Paris, 1959), shows in the two families named what appears to be a very typical provincial pattern. The Motte family in general tended to *vivre bourgeoisement,* apparently either happy not to aspire to nobility or preferring to spend their money on other pleasures (comparable to the substantial English merchants who lived out their days in the City, eschewing the lure of the 'polite end of the town'); they spent their money on wines, silver, jewellery, furniture, expensive musical instruments, refused to buy land, remained '*des négociants-nés*'. But one of them, Lucien, had ambitions for his line. A dowry of 35,000 *livres* (at a date when the largest dowries did not usually go above 20,000) was given for his daughter Anne to marry a *conseiller du roi*, François Le Febvre; three sons went into the Church and became *chanoines* or better; two sons remained linen-merchants but became *juges-consuls* and *échevins*. The last son, François (1668–1714), in his comparatively short life, rose much higher: he remained in trade but bought the office of *contrôleur au grenier à sel* (thus becoming an *officier royal*); he married Marie, daughter of Jean Le Scellier, *écuyer* and *seigneur* of Hez (thus infiltrating the nobility by marriage), and, unlike the other Mottes, he bought land and a château at Bizancourt (thus acquiring the appearance of noble rank by an illegitimate use of the particle). Similarly, in the Danse family, Lucien (1668–1727), *négociant, juge-consul, échevin,* seems to have remained content with his *haut bourgeois* lot, but his brother Gabriel 'le magnifique' (1659–1732), having amassed a great fortune and lived *bourgeoisement* until the age of fifty-seven, in 1717 was able to buy the office of *écuyer valet de chambre* to the Regent and, licensed, as it were, to *vivre noblement,* then spent his days going the rounds of his various châteaux and *seigneuries* which he bought piecemeal. Far from being held, as Voltaire might have surmised him to be, in low consideration, he and his family were among the most esteemed men in their province. As Goubert says:

Ils deviennent seigneurs, et même châtelains, sans sortir de leur Beauvaisis natal. Dans leur ville même, ils enlèvent tous les postes d'administration, de direction ou de prestige, laïques comme ecclésiastiques. Opulents, possessionnés, influents, cultivés, ils participent, dans leur province alors largement sur le Royaume, aux grands mouvements d'idées qui devaient inspirer la Révolution. (p. 177)

As to the extent to which nobles indulged in commercial activity in the two countries, again the traditional assumptions are now in question. Habbakuk sees the vast majority in England, including even those who owned mines, like the Dudleys, drawing their income mainly from agriculture, as *rentiers* (pp. 6–7). He dismisses the trading peers as few and atypical. Mingay takes a less extreme view but sees the younger sons of peers as making their way mainly in government posts or the professions and 'more rarely' in trade (p.106); however he asserts that the French nobility was much more like its English counterpart than has been thought. He denies that the French aristocracy *as a whole*

neglected their estates, [. . .] thought only of preserving their privileges and feudal rights, and looked with patrician horror on money-grabbing in trade or industry. These charges may be broadly justified if one considers only the limited group of wealthy court nobles, although even the parasitical character of these has been exaggerated; many of them served in government, and some took an important part in coal and iron production, and in commerce and finance. (pp. 281–2)

Pierre Goubert substantiates these assertions, declaring that the supposed 'economic sterility' of the new nobility does not often correspond to reality.[42] He points out that the nobility conferred by the office of *secrétaire du roi* and even by some *lettres de noblesse*

did not involve even a moral obligation to discontinue the 'Grand Commerce' of shipping, the Indies and the slave-trade. There is no known example of any Nantes shipowner calling a halt to his activities as a result of ennoblement.

Secondly, he shows that the oldest noble families engaged in maritime ventures—he instances that shipowner and slave-trader, the father of Chateaubriand. Moreover, the great nobility is not above investing its capital in ships and the Indies: it simply works through dummies or nominees, like the Mountaudouins of Nantes, who acted on behalf of the families of Bourmount and Maurepas. The Charettes (ancestors of the Vendée leader) were lending money against ships sailing for Martinique as early as 1715.

He refers also to the industrial ventures (ironworks, potteries, textile factories) owned by Breton families such as the Andignés, Farcys, Condés, Rohans, Villeroys, Chaulnes, and Pinczon du Sel des Monts. Long before the topmost strata of the nobility moved into industry under Louis XVI, they had already moved into commerce. As in England, the numbers engaged in commercial activity were, I imagine, probably small. But they were important. Goubert refers again to Nantes. Of the two hundred families engaging there in commerce with the Indies, the slave-trade, shipments to the Ile Bourbon, Louisiana, Canada, and the English colonies in America, barely a score were noble. But of 6,300 shipments investigated, at least 1,725 (that is to say 27%) were commissioned by these same noble families. And these were the same sorts of activity in which the noble trading families of England took part, families such as the Norths, whose fourth holder of the barony had a third son, Sir Dudley, who was Treasurer of the Levant Company with interests ranging over the whole of the Middle East.

Finally, as to Voltaire's gratification that his 'ordinary' merchant friend Fawkener should be appointed Ambassador to the Porte, far from this being a sign that the merchant was honoured in his own country as far as England was concerned, it has been a source of puzzlement that *with* his merchant background he was ever appointed. Peers and influential politicians tended to monopolize the highest appointments in diplomacy and 'commercial connexions [. . .] were regarded as a hindrance or even a bar to candidates who aimed at diplomatic careers'.[43] Fawkener's case is complex, and it is difficult to assess the relative importance of factors involved, of which his membership of the Levant Company, the most prestigious of the merchant companies, was only one.[44]

It would thus seem that, during the first three decades of the eighteenth century, when Voltaire was coming to maturity and when he was necessarily formed by the myths as well as by the realities of his environment, the merchant group in France was much more similar to the English group than dissimilar. Its composition was similar, its activities were similar, its position in society was similar. That Voltaire thought otherwise was due to his lack of knowledge of a very complicated subject. Much research has yet to be done on the topic, but the most interesting aspect of all this is that Voltaire's incorrect assumptions have for so long been adduced as proof of those same assumptions incorrectly held by others. It is even possible that because of his enormous prestige his views were, at least in part, the reason that those assumptions were given credence in the first place.

NOTES

1 'John Vansommer of Spitalfields: Huguenot, silk-designer, and correspondent of Voltaire', *Studies on Voltaire and the Eighteenth Century*, 62 (Geneva, 1968), 137–50; 'Voltaire in England: a quarrel with some Huguenot connexions', *Proceedings of the Huguenot Society of London*, 22, 1 (1971), 12–23; 'Voltaire's London Agents for the *Henriade*: Simond and Bénézet, Huguenot merchants', *SVEC*, 102 (Banbury, 1973), 265–99.

2 *Voltaire's Politics*: *The Poet as Realist* (Princeton, 1959), p. 44.

3 'England', in *The European Nobility in the Eighteenth Century,* edited by A. Goodwin (London, 1953), p. 19.

4 Colley Cibber, *The Lives of the Poets of Great Britain and Ireland* (London, 1753), p. 339.

5 This reference and those following are from Nelson's edition of the novel. A similar analysis to mine is given by Dorothy Marshall in *English People in the Eighteenth Century* (London, 1956), p. 57.

6 For these instances from Steele, Defoe and Gay, see Bonamy Dobrée, *English Literature in the Early Eighteenth Century, 1700–1740* (Oxford, 1959), p. 3.

7 ibid., p. 36.

8 *A Plan of the English Commerce* (London, 1728), reprinted by the Shakespeare Head Press (Stratford-upon-Avon, 1927), pp. 8–9.

9 F. Baldensperger, 'Voltaire anglophile avant son séjour d'Angleterre', *Revue de littérature comparée* (1929), p. 47; J. Churton Collins, *Voltaire, Montesquieu and Rousseau in England* (London, 1908), p. 15; N. Mitford, *Voltaire in Love* (London, 1957), p. 39; T. Carlyle, *History of Friedrich II of Prussia* (London, 1869), Part I, Vol. II, 388; J. Parton, *Life of Voltaire* (London, 1881), I, 203; G. Brandes, *Voltaire* (New York, 1936), I, 169; A. Bellesort, *Essai sur Voltaire* (Paris, 1925), p. 50; L. Foulet, *Correspondance de Voltaire (1726–1729)*, (Paris, 1913), p. 59, note; A. M. Rousseau, 'Voltaire et l'Angleterre' (unpublished doctoral thesis, University of Paris–Sorbonne, 1971), p. 139.

10 See my monograph, *Sir Everard Fawkner, Friend and Correspondent of Voltaire*, SVEC, Vol. 133 (1975).

11 *Le Temple du Goust,* The Hague, 1733.

12 See, for England, T. S. Ashton, *An Economic History of England*: *The Eighteenth Century* (London, 1972; first edition, 1955), p. 21; Lucy Sutherland, *A London Merchant 1695–1774* (London, 1962), p. 15; and my article, 'Voltaire's London Agents for the *Henriade* . . .'; and for France, Pierre Léon, 'Les Nouvelles Élites', in *Histoire économique et sociale de la France,* edited by F. Braudel et E. Labrousse (Paris, 1970), II, 611–14.

13 Henri Sée, *La Vie économique et les classes sociales en France au XVIIIe siècle* (Paris, 1924), p. 222.

14 op. cit., p. 624.

15 See my 'Voltaire's London Agents for the *Henriade* . . .', p. 288.

16 Pierre Goubert, *L'Ancien Régime,* t. I, *La Société* (Paris, 1969), translated by Steve Cox as *The Ancien Régime*: *French Society 1600–1700* (London, 1973), p. 247.

17 See M. Reinhard, 'Élite et noblesse dans la seconde moitié du XVIIIe siècle', *Revue d'histoire moderne et contemporaine* January 1956, p. 13. The anonymous author of *Le Négociant patriote* (Amsterdam, 1784), p. 225, quoted by R. Mauzi in *L'Idée du bonheur dans la littérature et la pensée françaises au XVIIIe siècle* (Paris, 1960), p. 288, note, describes Paris as 'cette grande ville pleine de *marchands* et vide de *négociants*'.

18 See H. R. Fox-Bourne, *English Merchants* (London, 1898; first edition, 1866), pp. 231–44 and 342. Vigny used the social myth rather than the social reality when he wrote *Chatterton*. The ludicrous and offensive portrayal of merchants in both Beckford and John Bell is proof of the continued acceptance of the Jourdain stereotype (here with sadistic overtones) in the nineteenth century. Bell, moreover, is a typical example of the confusion between the *marchand, manufacturier* and *négociant* rôles. He is a rich woollen manufacturer and merchant but, impossibly, lives behind the 'shop', where he presumably sells his cloth retail.

19 op. cit., p. 280. The quotations from Formentin and Sacy are taken from R. Mauzi, op. cit., pp. 272 and 280.

20 Cited by Jean Ehrard, *L'Idée de nature en France dans la première moitié du XVIIIe siècle* (Paris, 1963), p. 387.

21 Elinor G. Barber, *The Bourgeoisie in Eighteenth-Century France* (New Jersey, 1967; first edition, 1955), p. 9. This writer makes the point that although eighteenth-century French society was not an 'open-class' system, neither was it a caste system, but stood somewhere between the two extremes.

It was only late in the century that the class-system changed into a caste society, when the old nobility at last successfully resisted the long-standing royal policy of recognition and ennoblement of the bourgeois. The revival and expansion of trade had got under way by 1717. See Warren C. Scoville, *The Persecution of Huguenots and French Economic Development, 1680–1720* (Berkeley, 1960), p. 446, and also Tom Kemp, *Economic Forces in French History* (London, 1971), *passim*.

22 op. cit., p. 20.

23 George Rudé, *Hanoverian London* (London, 1971), p. 55.

24 See W. E. Minchinton, 'The Merchants in England in the Eighteenth Century', *Explorations in Entrepreneurial History*, 10, No. 2 (1957), 62–71; Lucy Sutherland, op. cit.; Richard Pares, *A West India Fortune* (London, 1950), *passim*.

25 J. H. Plumb, *England in the Eighteenth Century*, Pelican History of England, VII (Harmondsworth, 1950), p. 14.

26 W. S. Minchinton, op. cit., p. 68.

27 G. E. Mingay, *English Landed Society in the Eighteenth Century* (London, 1963), p. 26.

28 H. J. Habbakuk, op. cit., pp. 3 and 16.

29 G. E. Mingay, op. cit., p. 26.

30 H. J. Habbakuk, op. cit., p. 18. Financiers were apparently not, even as Irish peers, socially acceptable. In a wireless talk (1 September 1973), the present Lord Carrington referred to his famous ancestor, Robert Smith, a banker, and described how on the latter's first taking his seat in the House of Lords the other peers rose to their feet and left the Chamber in protest, 'because he was in trade'. This was in 1796.

31 *England in the Age of the American Revolution* (London, 1930), p. 9, quoted by W. E. Minchinton, op. cit., p. 62.

32 In families of the peerage, the infant mortality rate dropped from roughly $33\frac{1}{3}$% in the seventeenth century overall, to roughly $25\frac{1}{2}$% in the first half of the eighteenth century. See T. H. Hollingsworth, 'The Demography of the British Peerage', *Population Studies*, 18, No. 2 (1964), Supplement, 1–108 (36, 42).

33 The mean family size in the peerage in the eighteenth century overall varied roughly from 3.5 to 5 children. See Hollingsworth, op. cit., p. 31.

34 See my study, *Sir Everard Fawkener* (n. 10, above).

35 Henri Sée, *La France économique et sociale au XVIIIe siècle* (Paris, 1933; first edition, 1925), p. 156.

36 Elinor G. Barber, op. cit., pp. 103–4.

37 ibid., pp. 28–9.

38 ibid., p. 95.

39 ibid., p. 114.

40 Taken from Franklin L. Ford, *Robe and Sword, The Regrouping of the French Aristocracy after Louis XIV* (Cambridge, Mass., 1953), p. 208.

41 See also J. McManners, op. cit., p. 26.

42 *The Ancien Régime: French Society 1600–1750*, pp. 191–8.

43 D. B. Horn, *The British Diplomatic Service 1689–1789* (London, 1961), p. 250.

44 For a full discussion of the reasons for Fawkener's appointment, see my study, *Sir Everard Fawkener* (n. 10, above).

19

De Sylvain Maréchal à Maiakovski: contribution à l'étude du théâtre révolutionnaire

JACQUES PROUST

Le livre de Marvin Carlson sur le théâtre de la Révolution Française, publié à New York en 1966, et traduit depuis en français, présente, à côté de mérites certains (richesse de l'information, précision dans le détail . . .), deux défauts assez graves: il manque singulièrement de sympathie pour son sujet, et il ne tient pas compte de la *pratique* théâtrale elle-même. A cet égard, il ne comble pas plus l'attente du lecteur moderne que ne l'avaient fait auparavant ceux de Jacques Hérissay,[1] Eugène Jauffret,[2] Henry Lumière,[3] ou Henri Welschinger.[4]

L'une des pièces les plus caractéristiques du théâtre révolutionnaire est sans doute *le Jugement dernier des rois,* de Sylvain Maréchal, représenté pour la première fois au Théâtre de la République, à Paris, le 26 vendémiaire an II (17 octobre 1793). Marvin Carlson lui consacre quelques pages de son ouvrage,[5] mais bien à contre-cœur,[6] et il ne sort pas à son propos du cadre de l'histoire anecdotique: genèse, circonstances de la représentation, accueil de la pièce et du public. Il y a beaucoup plus de détails, souvent pittoresques, dans le livre de Maurice Dommanget sur Sylvain Maréchal.[7] Et l'auteur, au moins, n'éprouve pas d'aversion pour son sujet, bien au contraire!

Ce sujet, cependant, Dommanget l'a manqué aussi bien que Carlson, faute de trouver un point d'où il puisse être vraiment *vu.* Essayer de comprendre *le Jugement dernier des rois,* ou toute autre pièce du théâtre révolutionnaire, en effet, ce n'est pas tant chercher ce que l'auteur y a dit, ce qu'il a voulu dire, ou ce qu'on lui a fait dire. C'est s'interroger sur ce qu'il a réellement *fait,* c'est-à-dire sur sa *pratique,* et éventuellement la théorie de cette pratique. La question étant de savoir si ce qu'il «faisait» était révolutionnaire, je ne connais pas de meilleure méthode d'approche que l'*étude poétique comparée* de son texte[8] et d'un texte qui lui soit effectivement comparable, c'est-à-dire inscrit lui aussi dans une pratique révolutionnaire, mais dans un autre contexte.

Le choix du *Mistère-Bouffe,* de Maiakovski, comme terme de comparaison n'est pas le fruit du hasard. C'est une pièce dont la thématique est très proche de celle de Maréchal, si

215

proche qu'elles ont pu être éditées ensemble il y a quelques années, à Berlin (R.D.A.), en traduction allemande, avec une présentation commune.[9]

D'après Maiakovski lui-même, le *Mistère-Bouffe* fut écrit un mois avant le premier anniversaire de la révolution d'Octobre, et «comblé d'éloges» par Lounatcharski.[10] La première représentation eut lieu à Petrograd le 7 novembre 1918, dans une mise en scène de Meyerhold; elle eut un succès limité. Maiakovski en fit une seconde version. Elle fut créée à Moscou le 1er mai 1921, au théâtre Meyerhold, et publiée le mois suivant.[11] Les traductions allemande et française utilisées ici ont été faites sur cette seconde version.

Le Jugement dernier des rois se passe dans une île déserte qui—Dommanget l'a bien remarqué —rappelle singulièrement *l'Ile des esclaves* de Marivaux. Comme elle, c'est une utopie. Cette île est dominée par un volcan en activité dont le rôle sera décisif au dénouement. Sur un des côtés de l'avant-scène, une cabane ombragée d'arbres, au bord d'un ruisseau, nous situe d'emblée en pleine robinsonnade. Un vieillard vit là depuis vingt ans: il a été relégué dans l'île par l'arbitraire d'un «despote», Louis XVI. Il n'a d'autre société que celle d'une tribu de *bons sauvages,* qui lui apportent régulièrement de la nourriture et à qui, nouveau Vicaire savoyard, il a appris à adorer le soleil.

Un jour—c'est là que commence la pièce—débarque dans l'île un détachement de sans-culottes. Ils sont une douzaine, représentant toutes les nations d'Europe. Ils cherchent un lieu où reléguer leurs anciens rois. La rencontre des sans-culottes et du vieillard est pleine d'émotion. Ils lui apprennent que Louis XVI n'est plus, et que tous les peuples de l'Europe, à l'exemple des Français, se sont libérés de leurs maîtres. Les sauvages venus voir leur ami fraternisent avec les révolutionnaires. Entrent alors les rois: «un à un, le sceptre à la main, le manteau royal sur les épaules, la couronne d'or sur la tête, et au cou une longue chaîne de fer dont un sans-culotte tient le bout».[12] Chacun d'eux est caractérisé aussi fortement par le costume qu'il porte, et par sa démarche, que par les propos qu'il tient ou ce que dit de lui son gardien. Les sans-culottes, le vieillard et les sauvages les laissent maîtres de l'île, où ils ne tardent pas à se disputer, puis à se battre et à s'entredéchirer. L'anarchie atteint son comble lorsque les sans-culottes reviennent pour leur donner des biscuits. Le volcan entre alors en éruption: «le feu assiège les rois de toutes parts; ils tombent, consumés, dans les entrailles de la terre entrouverte».[13]

De son côté, Maiakovski met en scène sept couples de *purs* (le Négus, un radjah, un pacha, etc.), et sept couples d'*impurs* (soldat de l'armée rouge, allumeur de réverbère, chauffeur, mineur, etc.). Ces couples s'opposent à peu près comme le groupe des rois et celui des sans-culottes chez Maréchal.

La scène représente d'abord «le globe terrestre à la lumière d'une aurore boréale».[14] Le déluge, symbole de la révolution, submerge inexorablement la terre, et tous les *purs* se réfugient au pôle. Malgré leur inquiétude, ils sont restés imbus de leur dignité et de leurs droits. Les *impurs* arrivent à leur tour, et en dépit de la tension qui existe d'emblée entre les deux groupes, les *purs* obtiennent d'eux une sorte de trêve pour fabriquer une arche qui les sauvera tous.

Le second acte se passe sur le pont de l'arche. Les continents s'écroulent. Les *impurs,* qui n'ont rien à perdre, n'ont aussi rien à craindre. Les *purs,* au contraire, s'affolent. Ils décident de faire roi le Négus, et d'accaparer à son profit, c'est-à-dire au leur, les provisions de l'arche. Les *impurs* se laissent d'abord berner, mais le «roi» prend tout pour lui, et réconcilie contre lui les *purs* et les *impurs*. Le Négus est jeté par-dessus bord, et les rescapés instaurent une démocratie dans laquelle les treize *purs* survivants sont «ministres et administrateurs»:[15] les *impurs* travailleront pour eux et les nourriront. Ceux-ci ne tardent pas à se révolter, et la plupart des *purs* sont précipités dans l'abîme à leur tour.

Cependant les *impurs* sont travaillés par la faim. Certains ont des visions. L'*homme du futur* vient les prêcher, et leur donner des raisons de lutter. Électrisés, ils décident d'escalader le ciel, par les mâts et les vergues de l'arche.

Le troisième acte se passe dans l'enfer. Les *purs* y parviennent les premiers. Ils n'ont rien abdiqué de leur hargne et de leur cupidité. Arrivent ensuite les *impurs,* hardis, sûrs d'eux. Ils bafouent à plaisir l'autorité des diables et de Belzébuth même. N'ont-ils pas connu l'enfer sur la terre? Découragés, les diables les laissent passer et ils continuent leur montée vers le ciel.

Le quatrième acte a pour cadre le paradis. Dans les nuages, les élus goûtent un confort très petit-bourgeois, que vient troubler le chant sacrilège des impurs:

> Chante, chœur des fusils!
> Grondez, grondez, canons!
> C'est nous, notre Sauveur!
> Notre Jésus, c'est nous![16]

La nourriture éthérée qu'on leur offre ne leur convient pas, et ils commencent à saccager le paradis. Jéhovah est impuissant à arrêter la destruction.

Au cinquième acte, les *impurs* se trouvent regroupés sur une montagne de débris. Ils discutent âprement pour organiser leur travail. Ils dégagent successivement des ruines une locomotive, puis un bateau. Entre les sept couples d'*impurs,* la locomotive et le bateau, se noue un dialogue de plus en plus vif et serré, et l'exaltation croît jusqu'à ce que tout le groupe grimpe sur la locomotive, à la suite du soldat de l'armée rouge.

Sixième acte: «c'est la terre promise».[17] Les *impurs* arrivent devant une immense porte. L'émerveillement les saisit devant les réalités qu'ils découvrent, et qui sont leur œuvre. La porte s'ouvre, et les *choses* entrent: le marteau, la faucille, les machines, les trains, les autos, le rabot, les tenailles, la scie, le pain, le sel, le sucre, le tissu, la botte. Elles ne sont à personne, elles sont à tous; elles sont familières et amicales. Le journalier empoigne la scie, le forgeron le marteau; la couturière saisit l'aiguille. Les machines tournent docilement quand le mécanicien les met en route. Finalement l'auteur, le décorateur, le metteur en scène, les spectateurs eux-mêmes montent sur le théâtre, pendant que le chœur des *impurs* chante une adaptation de l'*Internationale.*

Il existe évidemment entre ces deux pièces de nombreuses similitudes. Elles ont frappé l'éditeur allemand, à tel point qu'elles lui ont fourni presque toute la matière de son introduction. J'ai déjà souligné au passage, dans le *Mistère-Bouffe,* l'opposition fondamentale entre les *purs* et les *impurs.* Elle répond à celle des *rois* et des *sans-culottes* chez Maréchal. Dans un cas comme dans l'autre, c'est une contradiction dynamique, qui se résout par la victoire des révolutionnaires. Dans les deux cas aussi, le ressort dramatique est immédiatement fourni par la situation historique concrète de l'auteur. *Le Jugement dernier des rois,* le *Mistère-Bouffe,* ne sont pas tout à fait des pièces comme les autres: ce sont des actes *politiques.* En octobre 1793, la «prophétie» de Sylvain Maréchal, jouée dans un des théâtres les plus «rouges» de Paris, sert directement le gouvernement révolutionnaire, aux prises avec de graves difficultés extérieures et intérieures. Aussi Maréchal est-il aidé en retour: le Comité de Salut public souscrit pour trois mille exemplaires de la pièce, et donne une allocation de poudre et de salpêtre au Théâtre de la République pour la réalisation de l'artifice final.[18] Maiakovski, de même, considère qu'il fait acte de militant, et peut constamment compter sur le soutien de Lounatcharski.[19]

En 1918, à Petrograd, et encore en 1921 à Moscou, la production théâtrale courante restait classique. Les organisateurs de spectacle préféraient, semble-t-il, jouer et rejouer *Macbeth,* plutôt que d'affronter le risque d'un spectacle *vraiment* révolutionnaire.[20] Et il ne faut pas croire qu'en 1793 les entrepreneurs des théâtres parisiens fussent beaucoup plus hardis. Même au Théâtre de la République, on ne donna jamais la pièce de Maréchal seule— elle était de toute façon trop brève. Il est tout de même significatif qu'à l'affiche on l'ait toujours associée à des spectacles rassurants: *le Méchant, l'Avare, l'Étourdi, les Folies amoureuses, Catherine ou la belle Fermière, Philoctète* . . .[21]

Sur le plan formel, *le Jugement dernier des rois* et le *Mistère-Bouffe* ont en commun un certain irréalisme. Maréchal présente sa pièce comme une «prophétie». J'ai indiqué au passage, en la résumant, deux traits qui l'apparentent à l'utopie et à la robinsonnade. Il faut y ajouter le *naturalisme*: les sauvages adorent le volcan qui surplombe l'île, et le vieillard leur enseigne à adorer aussi le soleil, à qui il fait hommage tous les jours des fruits de la terre. Alors que les hommes laissaient aux rois déportés dans l'île une chance d'y subsister par leur travail, l'éruption soudaine du volcan, symbole parfait de la justice immanente, les anéantit pour jamais.

Ces traits d'irréalisme se remarquent d'autant mieux qu'ils contrastent fortement—en apparence—avec une recherche très poussée de la vérité dans le costume. Maréchal a consacré près de trois pages, en tête de sa pièce, à décrire dans le détail l'habillement des personnages: matières, couleurs et formes, rien ne semble oublié. Pourtant, à y regarder de près, ce souci de la vérité ne vise pas au vrai: il vise au symbolique. Chacun des rois représentés est identifié avec son vêtement et avec ses ornements au point de ne plus être qu'une carapace vide, une brillante marionnette, une figure de jeu de cartes. Les sans-culottes sont aussi typés: il y a l'Espagnol, l'Allemand, l'Italien, le Napolitain, et ainsi de suite. Quant aux indigènes—j'y reviendrai—, ce sont décidément des sauvages de convention: «pantalon et gilet de tricot de soie, clairement tigrée; sandales lacées; perruque et barbe grises».[22]

La fantaisie de Maiakovski est encore plus débridée que celle de Sylvain Maréchal. Le résumé même que j'en ai fait le suggère: le déluge, l'arche renouvelée de Noé, l'enfer, le paradis, la terre promise, c'est à la fois la Genèse, les prophètes, et l'Apocalypse. Le tout traversé d'un souffle allègre de dérision. Le décor du premier acte, par exemple, est décrit en ces termes:

La scène représente le globe terrestre à la lumière d'une aurore boréale. La glace du plancher est traversée par le pôle où se trouve le centre d'une toile d'araignée formée par les câbles des latitudes et des longitudes. Le monde s'appuie sur deux morses placés côté cour et côté jardin. Au milieu, un Esquimau-chasseur, un doigt enfoncé dans la terre, appelle l'autre Esquimau, étalé près de lui à côté du feu.

Dans cet univers de fantaisie, l'Anglais et le Français—chacun avec son drapeau—, le Négus, le Chinois, le Radjah, le Pope, Lloyd George «qui ressemble au morse comme deux gouttes d'eau»,[23] la dame avec ses «innombrables cartons à chapeaux», les esquimaux dans leurs fourrures sont aussi *faux* que les personnages du *Jugement dernier,* je veux dire qu'ils sont *vraiment* conformes au modèle le plus banalement reçu.

Autre point de comparaison, le style. Maréchal n'écrivait point comme Maiakovski, il s'en faut de beaucoup, mais la *pratique* de l'écriture militante conduit nécessairement à la double tentation du lyrisme et du didactisme. Maiakovski y a cédé—épisodiquement— aussi bien que Maréchal. Lyriques: dans *le Jugement,* l'adresse du sans-culotte français à la postérité;[24] dans le *Mistère-Bouffe,* au sixième acte, le chant des machines[25] et celui du mécanicien.[26] Didactiques: chez Maiakovski, certains passages de l'exhortation de *l'homme du futur,* au second acte;[27] chez Maréchal, les discours successifs du Français, de l'Allemand et de l'Anglais au vieillard qu'ils instruisent du cours pris par la Révolution.[28]

Ces ressemblances formelles—et on pourrait en trouver d'autres—ne doivent cependant pas induire en erreur: le contenu de *Mistère-Bouffe* diffère autant de celui du *Jugement dernier* que 1917 diffère de 1793 . . .

La révolution de 1793 était essentiellement politique. Aussi bien, l'objectif avoué des sans-culottes, dans *le Jugement dernier,* se résume-t-il à un déplacement du pouvoir politique: l'Europe avait des rois, elle est devenue républicaine; le peuple, *c'est-à-dire la nation* (française, anglaise, allemande, russe . . .) exerce maintenant la souveraineté qu'avait usurpée le *despote* (Louis, Georges, Frédéric-Guillaume, Catherine . . .). Dans cette perspective, les oppositions de classe ou d'ordre entre les diverses composantes du «peuple» tendent à être effacées, sinon niées. C'est à peine si l'on nomme, en passant, à côté des rois, les«prêtres», les «aristocrates», les «fédéralistes». Ce sont des «méchants», des «égoïstes», les «frelons» de la ruche:[29] caractéristiques morales, plutôt que sociales.

En réalité, le transfert de la souveraineté, des mains du despote à celles de la nation, n'est pas une conquête, c'est une reconquête. L'ordre républicain permet aux peuples de retrouver l'équivalent de l'*ordre naturel,* et les sans-culottes peuvent fraterniser avec les sauvages, comme ils le font en effet à la fin de la scène 3 du *Jugement dernier.*[30]

Cet ordre naturel, l'athée qu'était Sylvain Maréchal n'est pas loin de le sacraliser, dans le culte enseigné par le vieillard aux sauvages, par exemple, mais surtout dans la représentation qu'il donne de la «révolution», comme expression libre et immédiate de la volonté générale d'un peuple illuminé par une évidence rationnelle: «Le peuple français s'est levé. Il a dit: *je ne veux plus de roi*; et le trône a disparu. Il a dit encore: *je veux la république,* et nous voilà tous républicains».[31] Le concept d'*ordre* sous-jacent à cette représentation des choses n'est pas construit autrement que celui qui fondait la monarchie de droit divin: c'est un ordre idéal, abstrait, anhistorique. Seul change l'instrument de la révélation: là l'Écriture et la raison; ici la raison seule. C'est pourquoi *le Jugement* est une pièce aussi anticléricale dans la forme que religieuse dans son contenu: au culte de la nature célébré par le vieillard, répondent le réquisitoire du sans-culotte romain contre les prêtres,[32] et les divers jeux de scène où le Pape est ridiculisé.

1917, contrairement à 1793, est une révolution économique et sociale. Avant d'être des citoyens, les *impurs* de Maiakovski sont des *producteurs,* et la lutte que les *purs* mènent contre eux dès le début de la pièce est une lutte de classe. Les débats ouverts successivement à propos de la royauté, de la démocratie bourgeoise, et du pouvoir soviétique lui-même, ne sont certes pas des digressions, mais ils s'ordonnent toujours par rapport à une question première, qui est celle du pouvoir économique. A terme, la victoire de la commune réalise la meilleure adéquation possible entre l'organisation sociale et politique, et la réalité économique. Ici, le concept de classe prend naturellement le pas sur celui de nation: les *purs* ont besoin d'un drapeau ou d'un costume pour se distinguer, alors que chacun des *impurs* est d'abord mineur, menuisier, boulanger, soldat. Au sixième acte, lorsqu'ils découvrent la terre promise, chacun peut lui donner le nom qu'il veut: Ivanovo, Marseille, Rostov, Manchester ou Moscou.[33]

Pour Maréchal, la Révolution est comme une *illumination*; mais pour Maiakovski, elle est une *route*.[34] L'ordre (provisoire) instauré à la fin de *Mistère-Bouffe* n'est pas la restitution d'un ordre naturel perdu. La libre société des bons sauvages n'y a pas d'équivalent. Les esquimaux même y sont *chasseur* ou *pêcheur*. La route de la Révolution ne conduit pas de l'ordre à l'ordre, mais du désordre à un certain ordre. Elle est, en outre, jalonnée de luttes et chacun des «actes» du *Mistère-Bouffe* en représente une. Enfin cette route n'a pas de terme. L'arrivée dans la terre promise, au sixième acte, est aussi bien le point d'un nouveau départ: «Des millions de volontés appellent la commune aujourd'hui, disait Maiakovski, mais d'ici cinquante ans, peut-être, les cuirassés aériens de la commune partiront à l'assaut des planètes lointaines».[35]

A la conception idéaliste et fixiste de Maréchal—qui, malgré qu'il en ait, débouche sur un naturalisme d'essence religieuse—s'oppose chez Maiakovski une conception matérialiste de l'histoire qui est résolument et radicalement athée. Ainsi, il peut se permettre d'être discret dans l'anticléricalisme (son Pape est assez bénin) et même de présenter, au second acte, des phénomènes de mysticisme qui ne prêtent pas à rire. En revanche, les deux actes qui se passent en enfer et au paradis sont très corrosifs à l'égard des représentations religieuses les plus couramment reçues dans la foi populaire. Mais la scène la plus intéressante, pour comprendre vraiment l'athéisme de Maiakovski, est celle de *l'homme du futur*.[36] C'est une subtile dérision du Sermon sur la montagne, et l'homme du futur est, à la lettre, l'antéchrist. Mais c'est aussi, comme dans la littérature romantique et comme dans la tradition millénariste populaire, le sans-culotte Jésus, qui se réincarne d'âge en âge dans les pauvres de ce monde: «Où est-il?» dit le cordonnier. «Je crois qu'il est en moi», dit le forgeron. «Moi aussi,/ je crois qu'il m'a contaminé», dit le journalier.[37] On n'imagine pas chez l'auteur du *Jugement dernier des rois,* une telle liberté dans la réinterprétation du mythe chrétien.

Les différences que je viens d'indiquer sont à la fois conjoncturelles et structurelles. Elles touchent à la forme aussi bien qu'au contenu, et elles sont la conséquence de deux conceptions divergentes de la pratique révolutionnaire. Mais si l'on admet ce fait, il faut se demander si les similitudes apparues à première lecture en sont réellement. Et pour répondre correctement à cette question, il faut dépasser l'opposition reçue de la forme et du fond, cesser de considérer l'une comme l'expression de l'autre. Car c'est dans sa forme même que la pièce de Maréchal—comme tout texte—prend son sens.[38] Et s'il se trouve que ce sens n'est pas celui qu'il a pensé lui donner, il ne suffit pas qu'il «annonce» par tel ou tel trait Maiakovski pour être aussi «révolutionnaire» qu'il le semble, par exemple, à Trude Richter, son éditeur allemand.

Je me tiendrai, pour faire court, à deux ou trois questions précises, posées par le rôle du *volcan,* par celui des *sauvages,* et par le *discours* des sans-culottes,[39] le *Mistère-Bouffe* ne fournissant plus ci-après qu'un système commode de référence.

On aura déjà noté au passage que le volcan joue un rôle décisif dans le dénouement du *Jugement dernier des rois*: il exprime parfaitement le concept d'ordre naturel immanent qui fonde la pensée politique de Maréchal. C'est pourquoi son activité doit être perceptible dès le début de la pièce, et c'est pourquoi les sauvages l'ont toujours adoré. On peut penser que le réalisme de la mise en scène—la poudre, le salpêtre . . .—était d'autant plus poussé que l'action même (l'éruption finale) était moins vraisemblable.

Car ce volcan est très encombrant. La difficulté de concevoir une mise en scène où il ait sa place d'un bout à l'autre de la pièce et qui rende sa dernière manifestation crédible n'est que l'aspect tangible d'une difficulté plus essentielle. Chez Maiakovski, les éléments naturels sont constamment subordonnés à l'homme, ils ne se substituent jamais à lui. Chez Maréchal, au contraire, l'humanité reste tributaire de la nature, et il y a contradiction entre la prétention—verbale—des sans-culottes à dominer leur destin, et leur résignation de fait devant l'ordre des choses.

Ajoutons qu'à l'époque où la pièce fut créée, en plein combat contre le fédéralisme, le volcan tendait naturellement à figurer sur scène la Montagne.[40] Dans cette «lecture» comme dans l'autre, il reste que le peuple, en tant que force politique, est physiquement absent du théâtre. Il est représenté au premier degré—au sens scénique comme au sens politique—par ces militants exemplaires que sont les sans-culottes, et au second degré par le volcan.[41]

J'ai dit que, dans la pièce de Maréchal, le peuple était physiquement absent du théâtre. C'est vrai du point de vue formel, mais faux du point de vue dramaturgique, si l'on considère que sa *fonction* est remplie sur scène . . . par les sauvages. Dans l'ordre de la nature, les sauvages sont les «aînés» des sans-culottes; ils sont le peuple *au naturel.* Mais ce peuple est passif et muet. Passif, il a besoin d'un instituteur, le vieillard, à la fois pour se garder de l'état monarchique[42] et orienter correctement son culte d'adoration vers la lumière du soleil levant.[43] Muet, il a besoin d'un truchement, le vieillard encore, pour lui expliquer par gestes les événements qui se déroulent sous ses yeux. Par là, les sauvages remplissent aussi la fonction dramaturgique des spectateurs. Ils «représentent» les spectateurs en tant qu'observateurs de la Révolution, comme les sans-culottes de la pièce les représentent en tant qu'avant-garde militante. Il y a donc encore ici contradiction, entre le projet conscient de Maréchal, exprimé dans les propos qu'il prête aux patriotes, et sa *pratique* théâtrale réelle.

Cette contradiction est en grande partie résolue chez Maiakovski: 1°, ses deux esquimaux font partie, comme chasseur et pêcheur, du groupe des *impurs,* au même titre que le mineur et le menuisier, et ils parlent avec la même liberté; 2°, les *impurs* ne constituent pas une délégation représentant le peuple travailleur, ils sont une fraction du peuple lui-même; 3°, au final, les spectateurs montent sur le théâtre avec les acteurs, et participent à l'ultime phase de l'action qu'est l'exécution de l'hymne révolutionnaire.

Sylvain Maréchal, comme d'autres écrivains de son temps, a fait quelque effort pour intégrer au langage dramatique des façons de parler authentiquement populaires, ou liées de très près à l'événement, ou en passe de changer de sens. Cet effort se remarque d'autant plus que certains mots ou expressions sont soulignés dans le texte: embêter,[44] guillotiné,[45] sans-culottes,[46] souverains,[47] sujets,[48] grâces.[49] Maigre moisson, en somme. A la vérité, Maréchal cherche seulement à naturaliser aux moindres frais un langage et un style qui ne sont pas ceux du peuple, mais ceux de ses *instituteurs,* au sens plein que le mot avait à la fin du dix-huitième siècle. Car il n'est pas vrai que le peuple soit le *sujet* des discours qui forment la trame du *Jugement dernier des rois;* il en est tout au plus l'*objet* et à coup sûr le *destinataire*: le vieillard, puis le sans-culotte français, figures et porte-parole de l'auteur, parlent vraiment *pour lui,* c'est-à-dire tout ensemble à son intention, et à sa place.

Ce n'est pas ici le lieu de soumettre à la contre-épreuve la langue et le style de Maiakovski, d'autant que la traduction française, plus encore que l'allemande, affadit beaucoup l'original russe. Mais il paraît évident—même en français—que si la *pratique* de Maiakovski est authentiquement révolutionnaire, comme je le crois, c'est surtout à ce niveau. D'entrée le ton est donné par un prologue, dit par un *impur,* qui n'est pas seulement une présentation mais à la lettre l'emblème de toute la pièce: poétique et familier, gouailleur et grave, libre à l'égard des conventions de l'éloquence politique comme du répertoire dramatique classique, il joue avec les signifiants, au besoin par le calembour, de telle sorte que les rapports généralement admis entre signifiants, signifiés et référents, c'est-à-dire en dernière analyse la relation de l'homme au monde, se trouvent remis en question.

L'instituteur des sans-culottes disait:

Nature, hâte-toi d'achever l'œuvre des sans-culottes; souffle ton haleine de feu sur ce rebut de la société, et fais rentrer pour toujours les rois dans le néant d'où ils n'auraient jamais dû sortir.

Fais-y rentrer aussi le premier d'entre nous qui désormais prononcerait ce mot de *roi* sans l'accompagner des imprécations que l'idée attachée à ce mot infâme présente naturellement à tout esprit républicain.[50]

Dans le *Mistère-Bouffe,* le forgeron dit plus trivialement et plus véridiquement au Radjah:

Eh! Tout pacha que tu es,
N'oublie pas le proverbe turc:
Tout, tout, tout, mais pas . . . cha![51]

Pour faire œuvre révolutionnaire, même dans les limites contraignantes que lui imposait la révolution bourgeoise, il a manqué à Sylvain Maréchal l'audace—alors inouïe—de dire, comme l'*homme du futur* aux *impurs,* dans Maiakovski:

La parole est à vous.
Je me tais.[52]

NOTES

1 *Le monde des théâtres pendant la Révolution* (Paris, 1922).

2 *Le théâtre révolutionnaire, 1788–1799* (Paris, 1869; réimp. Slatkine, Genève, 1970).

3 *Le théâtre français pendant la Révolution, 1789–1799* (Paris, s.d.).

4 *Le théâtre de la Révolution, 1789–1799* (Paris, 1880).

5 P. 176 de l'édition américaine.

6 «One of the most infamous plays of the Revolution» (ibid.).

7 *Sylvain Maréchal, l'égalitaire, l'«homme sans Dieu» (1750–1803). Vie et œuvre de l'auteur du Manifeste des Égaux* (Paris, 1950). La quasi-totalité du chapitre x, p. 259 et suivantes, est consacrée au *Jugement dernier des rois*.

8 Par *texte*, puisque nous parlons théâtre, j'entends non seulement le «livret» de la pièce, mais l'ensemble des «documents» qui rendent compte des conditions matérielles de sa représentation.

9 S. Maréchal, *Das Jüngste Gericht der Könige*; W. Majakowski, *Mysterium buffo*. Herausgegeben, und mit einem Vorwort versehen von Dr Trude Richter. Henschelverlag Kunst und Gesellschaft, Berlin, 1963. Je dois la découverte de cette édition assez rare au dix-huitiémiste polonais Marian Skrzypek, et mon exemplaire lui-même à Ulrich Ricken, de Halle (R.D.A.). Je les remercie ici l'un et l'autre. Dans la suite de cette étude, j'utiliserai la traduction française du *Mistère-Bouffe* parue dans le *Théâtre* de Maiakovski (Paris, 1957).

10 Maiakovski, p. 93.

11 Édition de Berlin, déjà citée, pp. 24, 26, 84.

12 S. Maréchal, *Le Jugement dernier des rois* (Paris, an II), p. 16. C'est à cette édition que je renverrai ci-après.

13 ibid., p. 36.

14 Maiakovski, p. 105.

15 ibid., p. 150.

16 ibid., p. 191.

17 ibid., p. 216.

18 Dommanget, pp. 262–263.

19 Sur les démêlés de Maiakovski avec diverses autorités, avant la représentation des deux versions successives de sa pièce, voir «Tout sauf des souvenirs», dans Maiakovski, pp. 93–96.

20 ibid.

21 Voir la *Gazette nationale*, dans les semaines qui suivirent la création de la pièce.

22 Maréchal, p. VIII.

23 Maiakovski, pp. 114–115.

24 Maréchal, p. 25: «Voilà pourtant les auteurs de tous nos maux! Générations à venir, pourrez-vous le croire!» [etc.]

25 Maiakovski, p. 226:

> Ouvrier, pardon!
> Pardon, ouvrier!
> Vous nous avez forgées,
> fondues,
> montées. [etc.]

26 ibid., p. 231:

> Je n'ai jamais vu faire si jour!
> Mais ce n'est pas la terre,—
> c'est une comète avec une queue de trains luisants. [etc.]

27 ibid., p. 164:

> Ecoutez
> Le Nouveau Sermon sur la montagne. [etc.]

28 Maréchal, p. 9 et suivantes.

29 Maréchal, pp. 11–12. A l'époque où fut créée la pièce, Maréchal n'était pas communiste. C'est plus tard qu'il devait participer à la Conspiration des Égaux aux côtés de Babeuf.

30 Maréchal, pp. 16–17: «Braves sans-culottes, dit le vieillard, ces sauvages sont nos aînés en liberté: car ils n'ont jamais eu de roi. Nés libres, ils vivent et meurent comme ils sont nés».

31 Maréchal, p. 9. Le même processus se renouvelle ensuite pour tous les autres peuples.

32 Maréchal, pp. 22–23.

33 Maiakovski, p. 217:

«Moscou, Rostov ou Manchester,
l'essentiel n'est pas là», dit le journalier.

34 Maiakovski, p. 97. L'auteur écrivait, en tête de la seconde version de sa pièce: «Le *Mistère-Bouffe* est une route. La route de la révolution. Personne ne saurait dire avec précision quelles montagnes nous aurons à faire sauter encore en la suivant».

35 Maiakovski, p. 97.

36 ibid., p. 164 et suivantes.

37 ibid., p. 169.

38 Sur le concept de *forme-sens,* voir les travaux de Henri Meschonnic, et en particulier *Pour la poétique,* I, II, III (Paris, 1970–1973).

39 Ces questions se sont posées effectivement à un groupe d'étudiants et à un comédien-metteur en scène, qui travaillaient avec moi à la réalisation scénique du *Jugement dernier des rois.* Je parle donc ici encore, et plus que jamais, d'une *pratique.*

40 Même chose dans la tragédie de Lemierre, *Guillaume Tell,* qui ne dut certainement une partie de son succès sous la Convention qu'à cette symbolique immanente—et totalement involontaire, puisque la pièce avait été conçue en 1766.

41 Chez Maiakovski, le déluge pourrait jouer le même rôle que le volcan: il symbolise lui aussi la Révolution en marche. Mais ses flots portent les *purs* comme les *impurs.* Les *impurs* fabriquent l'arche, et ils jettent eux-mêmes à l'eau les *purs.*

42 Maréchal, p. 15; «Une fois ils voulaient à toute force me reconnaître pour leur roi: je leur expliquai le mieux qu'il me fut possible mon aventure de là-bas, et ils jurèrent entre mes mains de n'avoir jamais de rois, pas plus que de prêtres».

43 ibid., p. 14. Cf. p. 16.

44 ibid., p. 3.

45 ibid., p. 8.

46 ibid., p. 11.

47 ibid., p. 10.

48 ibid., p. 13.

49 ibid., p. 21.

50 ibid., p. 27.

51 Maiakovski, p. 151.

52 ibid., p. 168.

20

A Supposed Letter of Montesquieu in 1795

ROBERT SHACKLETON

The ex-Jesuit Augustin Barruel was the most influential, though not the first, exponent of the theory that the French Revolution was the result of a deliberate conspiracy of the *philosophes* and the freemasons. Barruel's life was one of peregrination.[1] The banning of his Order in France drove him to Germany, the Revolution (when he had regained France) drove him to England. It was at London that he published his most celebrated work, *Mémoires pour servir à l'histoire du Jacobinisme*. The four volumes of this work did not appear simultaneously: the first two bear the date 1797 while the third and fourth are dated 1798. A letter of eulogy from Burke to the author, dated 1 May 1797, makes it clear that although the first volume had then been read by Burke the second was yet to be published.[2]

The leaders of the conspiracy, for Barruel, were Voltaire, d'Alembert, and Frederick the Great, but he by no means holds Montesquieu innocent. It was indeed from the publication of *L'Esprit des lois* that he dated 'ces spéculations philosophiques sur la liberté et l'égalité' which bred doubt and uneasiness, reshaped French public opinion, weakened the attachment of the French to monarchy, and brought about the horrors of the Revolution.

This argument, which is little more than a rhetorical flourish, leads to a claim, based on the juxtaposition of two passages from the chapter on the English constitution, that Montesquieu's message can be summed up thus:

Français! vous croyez être libres, et vivre en sûreté sous la conduite de vos rois. Votre opinion est fausse; elle est honteuse.[3]

In *L'Esprit des lois,* he discerns the principles which led to the demand for the summoning of the States-General.

He quotes supporting evidence from the *éloge* of Montesquieu by d'Alembert and from Condorcet and infers:

Si Voltaire avait moins avancé la Révolution Religieuse, Montesquieu aurait moins contribué à la Révolution Politique; [. . .] si l'un eût été moins hardi contre l'autel, l'autre aurait moins osé contre le trône.[4]

This singular conclusion distresses Barruel, whose attitude towards Montesquieu is tinged with reverence and admiration; and his torment is made worse by a letter published by a London newspaper above the name of Montesquieu, in which, among other un-welcome things, there is a violent attack on the Jesuits:

Quelle preuve terrible contre Montesquieu ne trouverait-on pas encore dans la lettre publiée sous son nom, dans un journal de Londres, si jamais l'authenticité de cette lettre pouvait être prouvée.[5]

He has not seen the letter himself, and owes the knowledge of its contents to a friend. He appeals in a footnote to any of his readers who may be acquainted at first hand with the letter to communicate its location to him:

Je prie instamment ceux qui pourraient avoir des connaissances plus spéciales sur cette lettre, ou avoir en main le journal dans lequel elle fut publiée, de vouloir bien m'en faire part. Je ne peux pas douter de la véracité de Mr l'Abbé le Pointe,[6] qui m'en a fourni la traduction; je le connais trop bien pour douter le moins du monde, qu'il n'ait vu et traduit la lettre sur un journal anglais qui parut le soir et vers les derniers mois de l'année 1795; mais n'ayant pas mis à cette lettre toute l'importance que j'y aurais attachée, il ne se souvient plus, ni du titre distinctif de ce journal du soir, ni de la date de la feuille qu'il a traduite; ce qui m'a ôté le moyen d'aller à la source, et me réduit à demander à mes lecteurs les instructions qu'ils pourraient avoir sur cet objet, et qu'ils voudraient bien me faire parvenir par Mr Dulau, Libraire à Londres, Rue Wardour.[7]

In 1798 Barruel announced that he had discovered the location of the letter. It is in the *Courier and Evening Gazette* for 4 August 1795.[8] This journal, for the year in question, is exceedingly rare, and the only recorded copy of the number sought (no. 943) is to be found in the Birmingham Reference Library. The text of the letter, which appears on p. 4, is as follows:

A FRAGMENT OF A LETTER FROM BARON DE MONTESQUIEU TO A PRESIDENT OF ONE OF THE PARLIAMENTS OF FRANCE, TRANSLATED INTO ENGLISH

... A time will come, and that time is not far off, when either the Monarchy must fall or the Society (meaning the Jesuits).

The mine is dug, the match is kindled, the fatal moment is on the wing: the persons charged with setting fire to the mine wait with impatience for the signal; and the grand projectors will not fail to give it soon, if not prevented.

Nothing provokes the Society more than the spirit of Freedom, which is lately rising among us. They know perfectly well that the reign of reason, and the reign of despotism, are as irreconcilable as heaven and hell. You may remember the uproar which the Society raised against the *Persian Letters* ...

The *Spirit of Laws* was written with all possible caution but to no purpose. The Society condemned it and insisted that all the rest of the world should condemn it. They exerted all the magic of their craft to prevail with the Court to stigmatise the work, and to banish or Bastile the author.

The office of these Reverend Blood Hounds is to track out every man who endeavours to enlighten his species, to hunt him down by every knavish artifice, and then to devour him.

Let us then for the future whisper our thoughts instead of writing them. It is dangerous to write, and it is of little use to write, when the writer's hand is constrained in the shackles of an ecclesiastical inquisition. Instead of writing let us feel, and let us act.

Let our Parliament fight these Necromancers at their own weapons. Let them oppose cunning to cunning, and system to system, or else all is lost.

We have on the throne a good Prince, but a weak one. The Society are endeavouring all they can to change him from a Monarch to a despot.—If they prevail, I tremble at what must be the consequence, a civil war and seas of French blood floating on every side.

Happy would it be for the French if they were less enlightened! The writings of our neighbours, the English, have given us so strong an idea of Liberty, and so strong a desire to preserve the little Liberty we have, that we shall make the worst slaves in the world.

Confined as we are in the privileges due to the human species, we are infinitely more free than Mussulmen. It will be a long time before we can be brought to reconcile ourselves to the whips and chains of eastern despotism.

If the Society be supported in their pretended zeal against Jansenism, what has not every honest citizen to fear? The little people are now attacked, the great will be attacked in their turn. The Society will point out every man they think fit, as a Jansenite, and by that means expose him to the hatred of the multitude, and the indignation of a fanatical court. Shall this be borne? Shall we be obliged like whining school-boys, to mumble over our Catechisms, whenever we are called upon by the Society?

But the Society is still gaining ground, and the flames of church dissention are still spreading. The Society must therefore be expelled, or France must perish.

We cannot be free all at once. We must then wait with patience, but labour on continually in the cause of Freedom. Since we cannot fly to the height we aim at, let us climb to it.

O that we could but once get rid of these foreign military hirelings! An army of natives might be gained to the side of Liberty, at least a part of them: but foreign troops are kept on foot for this very reason.

An Irish brigade is kept on foot for another reason. These are entertained, because some Ministerial projectors imagine, that they may one day or other facilitate the conquest of Ireland, by their influence on the rest of the natives.

But this is a wild scheme. Was France to invade Ireland, I would wish that the invasion was made not for the sake of France, but for that unfortunate island, where all the miseries, and all the indignities that despotism can invent, are accumulated on the heads of the wretched Roman Catholics.

They are kept in a continual state of nakedness and famine: and what is still worse, the rage of despotism is levelled against the religion and morals of this unhappy people. Perjury, information and apostacy, are not only encouraged, but even necessitated amongst them by acts of Parliament. This does no honour to the Reformed Church. This is Popery under a Protestant disguise.

Zealous as I am for the glory and happiness of my country, I should be sorry that France acquired a foot of ground more than she is already possessed of. We can be happy with what we have; we should be ruined if we acquired more.—We should lose in relative power, whatever we gained in real power, and our government would change into the bargain.

Let us abandon England to her own destiny; she shall fall by her own weight.

This will be the case when the Liberty of the People is invaded.

Oligarchs have in all ages been the mortal enemies of all literary Freedom. Everything written in the defence of Liberty is construed by these men into a libel against themselves.

The English Clergy will not be averse to the dominion of the Oligarchs, because, in fact, they will share in the advantages of it. The Oligarchs will employ all the engines of power and preferment to gain the sanction of religion for their purposes.

It will be good sport to see French Liberty rising in the same proportion that the Liberty of England is falling. Then shall Protestant Jesuitism play the same farce in England, that Popish Jesuitism is now playing in France. Then shall the Advocates for English Liberty be persecuted under the pretext of religion. Then shall every man, who is obnoxious to the ambition of the Oligarchs, have a troop of holy spies at his heels, who shall watch all his motions, pursue him through every maze of privacy and amusement, peep into all his secrets, divulge these secrets to the world, and give him up a sacrifice to the power of the Oligarchs, and the furious superstitions of the populace.

This is our case now in France . . .

[This letter was written a few years before the Baron's death].[9]

The instinctive conviction that the letter is false which may be felt by anyone well acquainted with the works of Montesquieu does not have evidential value for others, and does not make a careful scrutiny of the letter unnecessary. If it was written a few years before Montesquieu's death in 1755, and later than the publication of *L'Esprit des lois* in 1748, it was indited at a time of great Jesuit controversy in France. There survives in fact, though it was not known until 1907, a letter of 9 July 1753, which Montesquieu wrote to an unnamed *parlementaire* on the religious affairs of the time.[10] Certainly there is nothing *a priori* against Montesquieu's having written another letter on the Jesuit controversy to a parliamentary magistrate towards the end of his life.

A number of passages undoubtedly echo views which Montesquieu expressed elsewhere. To see the Jesuits as hostile to the spirit of freedom is perfectly compatible with describing them as 'les familiers de l'Inquisition'[11] and with the sweeping assertion:

Une chose que je ne saurais concilier avec les lumières de ce siècle, c'est l'autorité des Jésuites.[12]

That the idea of liberty comes from England is a commonplace in Montesquieu's thought. Equally characteristic is the reference to the 'whips and chains of eastern despotism'. More persuasive, however, are the prediction that England 'will fall by her own weight [. . .] when the liberty of the people is invaded', and the fear that the French monarchy might degenerate into despotism.

On the other hand, it is not easy to imagine Montesquieu writing openly of the weakness of Louis XV. Whether in private he saw the king as a weakling cannot be known, but it is far from inconceivable; no breath, however, of personal criticism of Louis XV received expression from his pen. He can scarcely be thought of as describing the Jesuits as 'reverend bloodhounds'; although the phrase is found elsewhere in anti-Jesuit polemical writings,[13] it is foreign to the style of Montesquieu. Nor is the suggestion well founded that the Jesuits stirred a storm against the *Lettres persanes*; and their hostility to *L'Esprit des Lois* was less extreme and less active than that of the Jansenists.

To the doubts arising from the foregoing passages should be added others arising from references to Ireland. The prospect of a French invasion of Ireland was not an unreal one in Montesquieu's later years, even after the Jacobite rebellion of 1745.[14] The reference, however, to the unhappiness of the Roman Catholics in Ireland, suffering 'all the miseries and all the indignities that despotism can invest', accords ill with the comment made in *L'Esprit des lois* on the treatment of the Irish by England: 'quoiqu'elle lui eût donné ses propres lois, elle la tiendrait dans une grande dépendance; de façon que les citoyens y seraient libres, et que l'Etat lui-même serait esclave.'[15] Scarcely compatible either is the report of Lord Charlemont, who visited Montesquieu in 1754 and reported, 'I have always found him an advocate for a union between [Ireland] and England.'[16]

These inconsistencies make it improbable that the letter is authentic, but two other passages can be held decisive. The first is the suggestion that the Parlement should fight the Jesuits. Someone with superficial knowledge might attribute this to Montesquieu, thinking of him as a parliamentary magistrate devoted to the privileges of his rank. But Montesquieu was never a *parlementaire outré*, and in the crises of the 1750s believed in the neutrality of the Parlement, and resented its identification with one party. In his letter of 9 July 1753 to a member of the exiled Parlement of Paris Montesquieu insists that the duty of the Parlement is to maintain the constitution: 'cette constitution vous a été transmise et vous devez la transmettre.' He bitterly laments the Parlement's abandonment of neutrality in the conflict between Jesuits and Jansenists in favour of commitment to the Jansenists:

Nous ne pouvons comprendre par quelle fatalité le Parlement, juge naturel de ces choses, se trouve aujourd'hui partie et comment, au lieu d'être à la tête de la justice, il se trouve pour ainsi dire à la tête d'un parti.[17]

The author of these words cannot have urged the Parlement to fight the Jesuits.

The second decisive passage follows the cry against mercenaries:

O that we could but once get rid of these foreign military hirelings! An army of natives might be gained to the side of Liberty, or at least a part of them.

Mercenaries, in other words, are undesirable since they cannot be deflected from their loyalty to their paymaster, but native troops could be won over to an insurrectionist cause. It is flatly inconceivable that Montesquieu expressed this sentiment.

Why should a forged letter have been attributed to Montesquieu in 1795 by an English newspaper? The *Courier and Evening Gazette* was either owned or edited by James Perry, a well-known radical journalist. Moreover, it was favoured in Revolutionary France. The Hon. Robert Clifford, the translator of Barruel's *Mémoires,* describes it as 'ever sounding the praises of the French Revolution' and attributing to it in another matter a pro-French distortion of the news which anyone would find *prima facie* astonishing, declares:

When the reader is informed that an office is established, Rue du Bacq, for the delivery of the *Courier* at Paris, that it is strongly recommended by a creature of the Directory, in one of their periodical papers, while all other English papers but one, are proscribed, his surprise will cease, as it is natural to expect that some return must be made to the Directory by the editor of this paper for so marked a favour, though it were at the expense of truth.[18]

It is in the context of French opinion of the day that the publication of the supposed Montesquieu letter is to be understood.

Numerous attempts were made during the Revolution to reinterpret Montesquieu, presenting him as being at heart a revolutionary, or at least a republican.[19] Roederer, in his *De la députation aux États généraux* of 1788, had already stressed the affinity in Montesquieu's eyes between monarchy and despotism.[20] Philippe-Antoine Grouvelle devotes an entire work to the theme in his *De l'Autorité de Montesquieu dans la Révolution présente* (s.l., 1789). Though greatly admiring his subject, Grouvelle criticises him severely, and in part condemns, in part explains away his monarchical leanings. Quoting Montesquieu's words 'Quoique la manière d'obéir soit différente dans ces deux gouvernements, le pouvoir est le même,' he interprets them as meaning 'Le monarque est [. . .] un vrai despote,' and readily cites Usbek from the *Lettres persanes*: 'La monarchie est un état violent qui dégénère toujours en despotisme ou en république.' His constant aim is to ascertain the 'pensée secrète' of Montesquieu; at one point he sums it up succinctly: 'Monarchie en général est *Despotisme*.'[21]

As prominent a revolutionary as Barère expressed great enthusiasm for the philosopher in his *Montesquieu peint d'après ses ouvrages* (*s.l.,* an V), systematising his classification of governments thus:

Toutes les républiques, quelles que soient leurs formes et leurs organisations, sont filles de la liberté. De même toutes les monarchies et tous les gouvernements d'un seul sont les enfants du despotisme, y tendent ou s'y précipitent sans cesse.[22]

Shortly before this Goupil de Préfelne, speaking in the Conseil des Anciens, firmly attributed to Montesquieu the view that the best government and the only good government was the republic.[23]

Clearly, the contributor to the *Courier and Evening Gazette* was doing what Roederer, Grouvelle, Barère, and Goupil were doing: he was seeking to present to his readers a picture of Montesquieu as a friend to the revolutionary movement. They achieved their end by soliciting the text; he invented the text. The letter which perplexed and distressed Barruel was a fraudulent contribution to a new exegesis of Montesquieu.

The final word should be with Jean-Joseph Mounier, ex-revolutionary and *émigré*, whose treatise *De l'Influence attribuée aux philosophes, aux francs-maçons, et aux illuminés sur la Révolution de France* (Tübingen, 1801) was expressly directed against Barruel. Attacking the conspiracy theory, he writes:

L'illustre Montesquieu même était, disait-on, un conspirateur. Il avait soutenu que le pouvoir judiciaire serait trop terrible dans les mains d'un roi, et qu'il ne devait jamais remplir les fonctions de juge. Un ecclésiastique français, qui a publié à Londres quatre volumes sur les prétendues conspirations, causes de la révolution de France, a trouvé cette doctrine criminelle. Il pense que les hommes ne peuvent être trop assujettis à l'autorité des princes. Il croit révéler au monde l'infamie de Montesquieu, parce qu'il a découvert que ce grand homme désirait la destruction des Jésuites; qu'il les accusait de transformer les monarques chrétiens en despotes, et qu'il voulait du moins conserver à sa patrie le peu de liberté dont elle jouissait. Dans *L'Esprit des lois,* l'un des plus beaux ouvrages que ce siècle ait produits, il y a quelques défauts sans doute, quelques maximes hasardées. Les abus de la monarchie française y sont trop présentés comme des bases essentielles de toutes les monarchies simples: mais il n'y a pas un seul mot qui puisse encourager à renverser, par la violence, l'ordre établi dans un gouvernement quelconque, et surtout à transporter une démocratie sans limites au milieu d'un vaste pays corrompu par les habitudes du luxe et de la mollesse.[24]

These are wise words and give a truer picture of Montesquieu than do either Barruel or the anonymous fabricator of the *Courier and Evening Gazette*.

NOTES

1 See particularly, on Barruel, the article in C. Sommervogel, *Bibliothèque de la Compagnie de Jésus, Bibliographie*, 1 (Bruxelles et Paris, 1890), cols. 930–45, and B. N. Schilling, *Conservative England and the Case against Voltaire* (New York, 1950).

2 *The Correspondence of Edmund Burke*, ed. T. W. Copeland *et al.*, ix (Cambridge and Chicago, 1970), pp. 319–20.

3 *Mémoires pour servir à l'histoire du Jacobinisme* (Londres, 1797–8), 4 vols., ii, p. 72.

4 ibid., p. 90.

5 ibid.

6 The Abbé Lepointe was a fellow clerical émigré who published a *Dissertation historique sur les libertés de l'Église gallicane et l'Assemblée du Clergé de France* (Londres, 1799).

7 Barruel, *Mémoires*, i, pp. 90–1.

8 The note in which the discovery is communicated appears as a footnote on p. 400 of vol. iv of the English translation of the *Mémoires* (London, 1798) and also as an insert among the preliminary pages of vol. vi of the original edition.

9 I am indebted to the Librarian of the Birmingham Reference Library for supplying a xerox copy.

10 *Œuvres complètes de Montesquieu*, edited by A. Masson, 3 vols. (Paris (Nagel), 1950–5), iii, pp. 1465–9.

11 *Pensée* 482 (ed. cit., ii, p. 171).

12 *Pensée* 715 (ed. cit., ii, p. 217).

13 I am indebted to Dr Derek Watts for drawing my attention to a characterisation of Jesuits as *limiers* in Jean Marteilhe's *Mémoires d'un Protestant condamné aux galères* of 1757 (in ed. of Paris, Société des Écoles du Dimanche, 1881, p. 6).

14 *The Gentleman's Magazine* announced in 1755 the rumour of an intended French invasion of Galway (xxv, p. 235).

15 *De l'Esprit des Lois*, xix, 27.

16 F. Hardy, *Memoirs of the Political and Private Life of James Caulfield, Earl of Charlemont* (London, 1810), p. 36.

17 ed. cit., iii, p. 1466.

18 R. Clifford, *Application of Barruel's Memoirs of Jacobinism to the Secret Societies of Ireland and Great Britain* (London, 1798) (also appended to vol. iv of his translation of the *Mémoires*), p. 43.

19 See É. Carcassonne, *Montesquieu et le problème de la constitution française au XVIIIe siècle* (Paris [1927]), pp. 619–31.

20 Carcassonne, op. cit., p. 621.

21 Grouvelle, *De l'Autorité de Montesquieu*, pp. 37, 39, and 67.

22 Barère, *Montesquieu peint d'après ses ouvrages*, p. 63.

23 *Le Moniteur*, xiv, 16 ventôse, an IV.

24 J.-J. Mounier, *De l'Influence* . . . (Paris, 1822), pp. 30–1.

21

The *Lettre sur les aveugles:* Its Debt to Lucretius

CHRISTINE M. SINGH

When considering the development of Diderot's philosophical ideas, an important question and one which has been frequently posed is that of the part played by the ancient atomists in his work. Of these, Epicurus was undoubtedly the most accessible to him, not directly through his own writings, since very little of this has survived,[1] but through Lucretius's poem, *De Rerum Natura.* Scholars have debated, and no doubt will continue to do so, on the exact nature of Lucretius's interpretation of Epicurus's philosophy, on whether he was entirely faithful to his Greek master. However, this does not really concern us here, since it was with Lucretius's poem rather than with Epicurus's extant works that Diderot and other educated men of his time were likely to be most familiar, and it was mainly from this that their first-hand knowledge of Epicurean atomism was derived. The question then becomes one of establishing the role played by *De Rerum Natura* in Diderot's development, and in this study an early but important stage in his career has been chosen, namely, the year 1749, the year which brought him imprisonment in Vincennes for the publication of the *Lettre sur les aveugles,* in which he debated, through the blind mathematician Saunderson, upon such controversial subjects as the existence of God and the origins of the world.

None of the more general works concerning Lucretius's influence on Enlightenment thinkers mentions the existence of a link between the *Lettre sur les aveugles* and *De Rerum Natura.* Fusil,[2] for example, plays down the importance of Lucretius's role in the intellectual development of the French *philosophes* of the eighteenth century; Fleischmann[3] generally follows him to the same conclusion. The name of Lucretius *does* crop up, however, in the works of those critics who have considered the question of Diderot's originality in the *Lettre sur les aveugles.* For it has been argued that Saunderson's death-bed discussion with Holmes is of striking originality and that Diderot, influenced by the discoveries of his contemporaries in fields such as biology and medicine, has here taken a significant step towards a coherent theory of transformism.[4] Counter to this, it has been maintained that the *Lettre sur les aveugles* shows Diderot to be still, in his thinking about the origins of life, at the stage of the atoms plus chance materialism of *De Rerum Natura.*[5] It has even been argued that during the whole of his career Diderot never really progressed far beyond the

233

philosophy of Epicurus and Lucretius.[6] These differences are stark indeed, and in the light of them there is unquestionably room for a new investigation of Saunderson's words with the purpose of establishing clearly the extent of Diderot's debt to Lucretius at this stage of his career.

Saunderson's speech occupies only a small proportion of the *Lettre sur les aveugles,* but it was sufficiently explosive, in spite of its brevity, to occasion Diderot's arrest and imprisonment in Vincennes. He chose to depict a man, about to die, discussing the existence of God with a Protestant minister. At a time when many men are at their most vulnerable, ready to clutch at any straw, ready to grab at any salvation offered to them, Saunderson betrays no fear.[7] His rejection of the existence of an 'être souverainement intelligent', inextricably bound up with the lives of men, brings with it a certain calm in the face of death, when death can be seen simply as part of a cycle of growth and decay undergone by the whole of nature. Indeed, Saunderson appears to fulfil Lucretius's prediction that human fears of the gods and of death will be dispelled through knowledge of the workings of nature:

> hunc igitur terrorem animi tenebrasque necessest
> non radii solis neque lucida tela diei
> discutiant, sed naturae species ratioque.[8]

This early part of the speech,[9] however, is clearly more directly linked to contemporary religious controversy, and to some of the issues raised in the *Pensées philosophiques* than to Lucretius. Whilst 'Un phénomène est-il, à notre avis, au-dessus de l'homme? nous disons aussitôt, c'est l'ouvrage d'un Dieu [. . .]' and

> quippe ita formido mortalis continet omnis,
> quod multa in terris fieri caeloque tuentur
> quorum operum causas nulla ratione videre
> possunt ac fieri divino numine rentur.[10]

express essentially the same idea, the idea itself had already become common property so that a direct link cannot be established. What is more important at this introductory point in the speech is that here Diderot, through Saunderson, brings up once again the question of purpose in the world, of whether the attributes of the natural world point inevitably to the existence of an intelligent God. Whereas in the *Pensées philosophiques,* he was indecisive, putting various points of view without coming to any conclusions, here he rejects as spurious the finalist argument and joins the ranks of the polemicists against religion, attacking those, including himself,[11] whose complacency and vanity make them explain the mysteries of life by an even more mysterious God. There is no direct connexion with Lucretius here, and yet in both it is clear that it is only after the mind has been freed from the constraints of religion and superstition that the workings of the universe and the origins of life can be understood. Lucretius is as a missionary who has seen the light and needs to impart his knowledge to others in order that they may live more fully. With Diderot the feeling is more one of personal discovery than of missionary zeal; ironically, it is through the words of a blind man that he begins to see; the scales fall from his eyes in preparation for the boundless vision of the universe which is to follow.

The second part of the speech takes us back to the beginnings of the world and contains the famous discussion upon monsters. The Académie des Sciences had been interested in explaining the existence of monsters for many years and most anatomists had for a long time been roughly divided into two camps between those who considered monsters to be accidents of nature and those who felt that they must be part of a mysterious divine order. Their interest was linked to the investigation of the reproductive process since they were particularly concerned with those who were born deformed, and the quarrel was closely bound up with the widely held belief in the theory of the 'pré-existence des germes' as a way of explaining how life is passed on.[12] Diderot may well have read the *Mémoires de l'Académie* which dealt in detail with the question of monsters[13] and in addition he would have found a summary of the views of the opposing sides in Maupertuis's *Vénus physique*. However, in spite of the fact that Diderot was probably familiar with contemporary developments in the field of teratology, the only point at which Saunderson mentions monsters found *after* the earliest stage in the earth's history is right at the end of this section of the speech:

«[. . .] mais l'ordre n'est pas si parfait [. . .] qu'il ne paroisse encore de temps en temps des productions monstrueuses. [. . .] Voyez-moi bien M. Holmes, je n'ai point d'yeux. Qu'avions-nous fait à Dieu, vous et moi, l'un pour avoir cet organe, l'autre pour en être privé?»[14]

The real Saunderson was not in fact born blind as is claimed in this passage, but lost his sight as a result of smallpox when he was a baby. Details of this kind are of no consequence to Diderot however, who is in any case using Saunderson as a symbol, and as a mouthpiece for his own ideas; the arguments he uses here are intended to provoke the maximum emotional response and have little regard for accuracy. From what he says it is clear that he is using the fact that monsters continue to exist in his own time only in order to back up those ideas he puts forward about the first beginnings of the earth, which are in turn linked to the question of the existence of an intelligent God. He is interested not so much in contemporary disputes about monsters as in contemporary disputes about the nature of the universe in which monsters are but a detail.

Another way of looking at this much-discussed section of Saunderson's speech is to argue that Diderot, in writing it, was influenced by his earlier reading of Shaftesbury's works and that a section from *The Moralists* may have inspired some of his ideas on the subject of monsters. Whilst not ruling out the possibility of a link between the two, it should be pointed out that Shaftesbury's aim in the passages usually quoted is to *explain* the existence of monsters, to show that they are a necessary part of a benign and ordered nature:

Much is alleged in answer to show why Nature errs, and how she came thus impotent and erring from an unerring hand. But I deny she errs; and when she seems most ignorant and perverse in her productions, I assert her even then as wise and provident as in her goodliest works. [. . .] 'Tis on the contrary from this order of inferior and superior things that we admire the world's beauty, founded thus on contrarieties, whilst from such various and disagreeing principles a universal concord is established.[15]

His monsters are part of the natural order of things, Diderot's are thrown up by chance from primaeval chaos. He is describing a continuous, natural process of which monsters form a comprehensible part, Diderot is more concerned with the beginnings of the world and with the original monsters, most of whom gradually perished. Paul Vernière believes that Diderot and Shaftesbury had a single common source in Lucretius v (837–55),[16] but whereas this is likely in the case of Diderot, it is less easy to substantiate when it comes to Shaftesbury. The context of the *The Moralists* passage is quite different from that of both Lucretius and Diderot, in addition to which, those references which Shaftesbury does make to Lucretius at various points in his works are generally somewhat hostile. There is possibly a connexion between Shaftesbury's description of a natural cycle in which one species preys upon another:

The vegetables by their death sustain the animals, and animal bodies dissolved enrich the earth, and raise again the vegetable world. The numerous insects are reduced by the superior kinds of birds and beasts, and these again are checked by man, who in his turn submits to other natures, and resigns his form, a sacrifice in common to the rest of things.[17]

and the following lines from Lucretius:

> vertunt se fluvii frondes et pabula laeta
> in pecudes, vertunt pecudes in corpora nostra
> naturam, et nostro de corpore saepe ferarum
> augescunt vires et corpora pennipotentum.

but these lines are from Book II (875–8) and not Book v at all. The ideas expressed in these passages are not taken up by Diderot in the *Lettre sur les aveugles,* and do not really find a place in his work until the much later *Rêve de d'Alembert,* where they are used in modified form.[18]

Up to now the influences upon Diderot have been imprecise, a probable interest in contemporary controversies on the subject of monsters, reinforced perhaps by the work of Maupertuis, a possible link with his earlier reading of Shaftesbury. Buffon, too, must be mentioned here, for although the first three volumes of the *Histoire naturelle* were not published until after the *Lettre sur les aveugles,* Diderot knew Buffon and was undoubtedly familiar with many of his ideas before they were published.[19] If, against this background, we turn to Lucretius, a great deal of this imprecision disappears. For the vision of the universe which Diderot, through Saunderson, presents is unmistakably Lucretian in character. Saunderson cries, carried away:

Si nous remontions à la naissance des choses et des temps, et que nous sentissions la matière se mouvoir et le chaos se débrouiller, nous rencontrerions une multitude d'êtres informes, pour quelques êtres bien organisés.[20]

Lucretius too is particularly concerned with 'la naissance des choses et des temps'; almost like a refrain throughout his poem is the conception of original chaos:

> ... sed nova tempestas quaedam molesque coorta
> omnigenis e principiis, discordia quorum
> intervalla vias conexus pondera plagas
> concursus motus turbabat proelia miscens, [. . .]²¹

and of 'la matière en mouvement':

> nimirum nulla quies est
> reddita corporibus primis per inane profundum,
> sed magis assiduo varioque exercita motu
> partim intervallis magnis confulta resultant,
> pars etiam brevibus spatiis vexantur ab ictu.²²

Lucretius, as Diderot, describes the beginnings of animal and human life on earth, a time when there existed both 'êtres bien organisés':

> Quare etiam atque etiam maternum nomen adepta
> terra tenet merito, quoniam genus ipsa creavit
> humanum atque animal prope certo tempore fudit
> omne quod in magnis bacchatur montibu' passim,
> aeriasque simul volucris variantibu' formis.²³

and 'êtres informes':

> Multaque tum tellus etiam portenta creare
> conatast [. . .]²⁴

He goes on to describe creatures which he classes as monsters because of some obvious, external, physical peculiarity; Diderot, with more knowledge of anatomy, describes creatures whose internal organs fail to function correctly. Both are nevertheless agreed that what was important for the survival of a species was that its members should be able to 'subsister par elles-mêmes et se perpétuer'.²⁵ Lucretius goes into the question in rather more detail:

> cetera de genere hoc monstra ac portenta creabat,
> nequiquam, quoniam natura absterruit auctum
> nec potuere cupitum aetatis tangere florem
> nec reperire cibum nec iungi per Veneris res [. . .]²⁶

but the underlying idea is the same in both cases. Both are agreed too that many non-viable creatures perished during the early stages of the world's existence:

les monstres se sont anéantis successivement; [. . .] toutes les combinaisons vicieuses de la matière ont disparu. [. . .]²⁷

> Multaque tum interiisse animantum saecla necessest
> nec potuisse propagando procudere prolem.²⁸

Diderot's ideas are so close to those of Lucretius in this part of Saunderson's speech that it would be difficult to make any claims regarding Diderot as a forerunner of Lamarck or Darwin here without making them for Lucretius as well. For Diderot does not say anything at this point that Lucretius had not said so many years before. He conceives of man having been thrown up by chance, like all the other different species of animals and other beasts. He has not yet reached any clear conception of a link between various species or of one species developing into another. 'Le hasard' governs his universe as it did that of Lucretius, for at this stage in his career he is concerned principally with the destruction of the Christian and deist notion of order, replacing it with a vision of a nature which is completely blind.

The claim that Lucretius was the most important source of inspiration for Diderot here is reinforced as Saunderson's speech goes on to its close. For Diderot lapses into pure Lucretius; indeed, it is almost as if Book II (1044–1170) of *De Rerum Natura* is now open in front of him as he writes. After the sentimental digression during which the entire assembled company begins to weep uncontrollably, Saunderson goes back briefly over what he has said about monsters in the early stages of the earth's age. 'Mais pourquoi n'assurerois-je pas des mondes ce que je crois des animaux?'[29] he asks suddenly. Lucretius too makes this jump from speaking of animals to speaking of planets:

> [. . .] in primis animalibus inice mentem; [. . .]
> quapropter caelum simili ratione fatendumst [. . .][30]

Saunderson elaborates:

combien de mondes estropiés, manqués, se sont dissipés, se reforment et se dissipent peut-être à chaque instant, dans des espaces éloignés [. . .]?

Lucretius also makes the point that combinations of atoms throughout the entire boundless universe must have resulted in other worlds:

> nullo iam pacto veri simile esse putandumst, [. . .]
> hunc unum terrarum orbem caelumque creatum,
> nil agere illa foris tot corpora materiai;
> cum praesertim hic sit natura factus, et ipsa
> sponte sua forte offensando semina rerum
> multimodis temere incassum frustraque coacta
> tandem coluerunt ea quae coniecta repente
> magnarum rerum fierent exordia semper,
> terrai maris et caeli generisque animantum.
> quare etiam atque etiam talis fateare necesse est
> esse alios alibi congressus materiai,
> qualis hic est, avido complexu quem tenet aether.[31]

that nothing is unique:

> Huc accedit ut in summa res nulla sit una,
> unica quae gignatur et unica solaque crescat, [. . .][32]

no created thing eternal:

> quandoquidem vitae depactus terminus alte
> tam manet haec et tam nativo corpore constant,
> quam genus omne quod hic generatimst rebus abundans.[33]

Saunderson refers to 'le mouvement' which 'continue et continuera de combiner des amas de matière'; Lucretius too:

> seminaque innumero numero summaque profunda
> multimodis volitent aeterno percita motu,[34]

In a burst of inspired enthusiasm, Saunderson cries:

O Philosophes, transportez-vous donc avec moi, sur les confins de cet univers, au-delà du point où je touche et où vous voyez des êtres organisés; promenez-vous sur ce nouvel océan, et cherchez à travers ses agitations irrégulières, quelques vestiges de cet être intelligent dont vous admirez ici la sagesse![35]

Lucretius, still in the same section, pleads with his reader to liberate himself from the narrow confines of the earth and to seek to understand the nature of boundless space:

> quaerit enim rationem animus, cum summa loci sit
> infinita foris haec extra moenia mundi,
> quid sit ibi porro quo prospicere usque velit mens
> atque animi iactus liber quo pervolet ipse.[36]

whilst soon after he describes nature, organising herself of her own accord, 'sua sponte', 'dominis privata superbis',[37] without interference from the gods. Saunderson's speech draws to a close in the same way as does Book II of *De Rerum Natura*. He describes the world as a 'composé sujet à des révolutions qui toutes indiquent une tendance continuelle à la destruction; [. . .] une symétrie passagère [. . .]'. Lucretius too describes the process of gradual decay (1131 onwards) and the inevitability of the world's being eventually destroyed:

> iure igitur pereunt, cum rarefacta fluendo
> sunt et cum externis succumbunt omnia plagis,
> quandoquidem grandi cibus aevo denique defit,
> nec fuditantia rem cessant extrinsecus ullam
> corpora conficere et plagis infesta domare.
> sic igitur magni quoque circum moenia mundi
> expugnata dabunt labem putrisque ruinas.[38]

Book II ends with a planter bemoaning his lack of produce, who 'nec tenet omnia paulatim tabescere et ire ad capulum spatio aetatis defessa vetusto';[39] Saunderson ends by exposing

R

Holmes's narrow conception of the nature of the world; neither Holmes nor the planter are able to see things except in terms of their own limited human experience; it is Saunderson and Lucretius who recognise these limitations and endeavour, through imagination, to surpass them in order to achieve a much wider vision of the universe, the first step towards a more profound understanding of it.

This final point cannot be emphasised too strongly—for Diderot this *is* only a first and somewhat groping step; Saunderson's speech does not represent a fully-developed theory of the origins of the world. In fact, it is in this that the most striking difference between him and Lucretius lies; Diderot is exploring, merely suggesting, Lucretius is dogmatic, believing he has all the answers. And yet, in spite of this difference in attitude, the presence of Lucretius is undeniably to be felt in this work of Diderot's. He looks back to the Ancients before he can look forward to the Moderns. As he did so often throughout his career,[40] he uses the Ancients as a basis for the development of his ideas upon questions of vital importance to his contemporaries. For him the legacy left by the literature of the past plays a vital and living part in his understanding of the present.

Though a number of critics have mentioned that Lucretius may have influenced Diderot in his writing of the *Lettre sur les aveugles,* the real extent of the influence has never previously been determined. This study has shown that in at least two-thirds of Saunderson's speech Diderot expresses ideas which are also to be found in Lucretius, that in the 'monster' section he follows Lucretius fairly closely, and that the subsequent and final section is based almost entirely on one hundred and thirty lines at the end of Book II of *De Rerum Natura.* Such a close adherence to another author suggests that Diderot had not made a great deal of progress towards an independent view of the world. That is not to say that Saunderson's speech does not make an impact but its impact comes mainly from the fact that it represents a very powerful and striking piece of anti-religious propaganda. What is important is not what is built up but what is torn down. We must wait for the *Pensées sur l'interprétation de la nature,* and later, for *Le Rêve de d'Alembert,* for Diderot to elaborate and develop ideas which are suggested here. Here, however, the way is laid open, the barriers destroyed. Diderot, through Saunderson, displays all the enthusiasm of a new convert, not to, but away from a belief in God. And who more natural to turn to at such a time than Lucretius, Lucretius who set out to free man from the fear of death and of the gods, and who tried to do so by giving him a deeper understanding of the nature of things?

NOTES

1 The only complete works attributed to Epicurus which have survived are three letters and a collection of 'Principal Sayings'. These are all recorded in Diogenes Laertius, Book x. The work of Gassendi, in the seventeenth century, had done much to rehabilitate Epicurus in the eyes of orthodox Christians and to enable him to be considered in the same way as other ancient philosophers. Nevertheless, Gassendi's work was not easily accessible because of its length and method of presentation,

with the result that the best exponent of Epicurean philosophy, particularly the physical theories, remained Lucretius.

2 Fusil, 'Lucrèce et les philosophes du XVIIIᵉ siècle', *Revue d'Histoire Littéraire de la France*, 34 (1928), pp. 194–210.

3 W. B. Fleischmann, 'The Debt of the Enlightenment to Lucretius', *Studies on Voltaire and the Eighteenth Century*, 25 (1963), pp. 631–43.

4 Jacques Roger, *Les Sciences de la vie dans la pensée française du XVIIIᵉ siècle* (Paris, 1963), pp. 593–4, summarises the opposing positions of critics on this question.

5 Roger, op. cit., p. 594. To those he mentions can be added Émile Callot, *La Philosophie de la vie au XVIIIᵉ siècle* (Paris, 1965), pp. 303–5.

6 Roger, op. cit., pp. 665–8.

7 That is, unless the enigmatic 'O Dieu de Clarke et de Newton, prends pitié de moi' be seen as a faltering on Saunderson's part.

8 The edition of Lucretius's work used throughout is that edited by Cyril Bailey: *Titi Lucreti Cari De Rerum Natura. Libri Sex* (Oxford, 1963, first published 1947). Vol. I. Prolegomena, Text and Critical Apparatus. Translation. *De Rerum Natura*, II, 59–61 in Bailey, p. 238.

9 References to the *Lettre sur les aveugles* are to the critical edition of Robert Niklaus (Geneva, 1963). For convenience, the speech of Saunderson has been divided into three sections:
   (i)   Beginning to 'de l'éléphant et de la tortue'.
   (ii) 'Considérez, M. Holmes [. . .] pour en être privé?'
   (iii) 'Je conjecture donc [. . .]' to end.

10 Niklaus, p. 40; *De Rerum Natura*, I, 151–4. Bailey, p. 182.

11 *Pensées philosophiques*: Pensée XX.

12 For a full discussion of the question, see Jacques Roger, op. cit. pp. 397–418.

13 *Mémoires de l'Académie*, 1740–43. (Published in 1746). Reviewed in the *Journal des Savants*, April 1748.

14 Niklaus, p. 43.

15 Shaftesbury, *The Moralists*, ed. Robertson, reprint 1963 (Gloucester, Mass.), p. 22.

16 Diderot, *Œuvres philosophiques*, edited by P. Vernière (Garnier, 1964), p. 121.

17 Shaftesbury, op. cit., p. 22.

18 Diderot, *Œuvres philosophiques*, edited by P. Vernière, pp. 261–4.

19 For a discussion of the question of the links between Diderot and Buffon in 1749, see Jacques Roger, 'Diderot et Buffon en 1749', *Diderot Studies*, 4, pp. 221–36.

20 Niklaus, p. 42.

21 *De Rerum Natura*, v, 436–9. Bailey, p. 454.

22 *De Rerum Natura*, II, 95–99. Bailey, p. 240.

23 *De Rerum Natura*, v, 821–5. Bailey, p. 474.

24 *De Rerum Natura*, v, 837–8. Bailey, p. 474.

25 Niklaus, p. 42.

26 *De Rerum Natura*, v, 845–8. Bailey, p. 476.

27 Niklaus, p. 42.

28 *De Rerum Natura*, v, 855–6. Bailey, p. 476.

29 Niklaus, p. 43.

30 *De Rerum Natura*, II, 1080, 1084, Bailey, p. 292.

31 *De Rerum Natura*, II, 1052, 1056–66. Bailey, pp. 291–2.

32 *De Rerum Natura*, II, 1077–8. Bailey, p. 292.

33 *De Rerum Natura*, II, 1087–9. Bailey, p. 292.

34 *De Rerum Natura*, II, 1054–5. Bailey, p. 290.

35 Niklaus, pp. 43–4.

36 *De Rerum Natura*, II, 1044–7. Bailey, p. 290.
37 *De Rerum Natura*, II, 1091; 1092. Bailey, p. 292.
38 *De Rerum Natura*, II, 1139–45. Bailey, p. 296.
39 *De Rerum Natura*, II, 1173–4. Bailey, p. 298.
40 He used Terence, Seneca, Socrates and Horace in a similar way.

22

The Clandestine Book Trade in 1752: The Publication of the *Apologie de l'abbé de Prades*

J. S. SPINK

The Archives of the Bastille contain a very copious dossier devoted to the activities of the journeymen printers who secretly printed and distributed, along with other clandestine works, the *Apologie de l'abbé de Prades*, part of which was written by Diderot.[1] The operation was an episode in the campaign of repression undertaken by the police against the secret printing and distribution of opposition literature in the middle years of the century. The campaign itself may be dated from 1748, which was the year of France's defeat at the end of the war of the Austrian Succession, as well as being that of the publication of Montesquieu's *Esprit des lois*. The records of the Bastille show little evidence of any such repression in previous years, whereas after that date the number of arrests of people accused of writing, printing, distributing or possessing copies of banned books, tracts printed without per-mission, and manuscript copies of satires against the King grew constantly. The records of the Parlement de Paris also show that the judges were under pressure from the Crown to take action, and the *Nouvelles Ecclésiastiques* (a Jansenist publication) give ample proof of the way in which the two clerical parties, supporters and adversaries of the Bull *Unigenitus*, vied with each other in their attack on the *Philosophes*, the zeal of the Sorbonne and of the entourage of the Archbishop of Paris being constantly whipped up by the taunts of the Jansenist opposition, ever ready to accuse them of slackness. The first volumes of the *Encyclopédie* were caught by a chill blast which their contents, always prudent and often conciliatory to the point of trimming, by no means suffice of themselves to explain. The poor abbé de Prades, a would-be intermediary between theologians and philosophers, was swept away like chaff before an autumn gale. Some of his teachers had the courage to defend him, but most of them, feeling what was in the wind, drew in their raiment and reviled him. During the whole of the summer of 1752, the *lieutenant de Police*, Berryer, and his henchmen, Rochebrune, *commissaire au Châtelet*, and d'Hémery, *exempt de robe courte*, carried out skilful operations which led to many arrests. As one letter in the dossier we print below states expressly, Berryer was acting on orders received from the minister of Police, the comte d'Argenson, with the object of stopping the publication of tracts relating to 'les affaires présentes de l'Église', an expression which covers Jansenist attacks on the Archbishop of Paris and also the Prades affair.

The abbé de Prades himself had been spirited out of Paris, and then out of the country, by none other than the marquis d'Argenson, the comte's brother, and a former minister for foreign affairs. At the beginning of February he was hidden in the house of the curé of Saint-Sulpice-de-Favières, at Segré, d'Argenson's estate six miles south-west of Arpajon. From there he proceeded to Holland and then, in August 1752, to Berlin, where Voltaire met him on the 18th or 19th of the month. During the summer he composed his *Apologie*, the manuscript of which was in Paris, and in Diderot's hands, by September. At that moment appeared a further condemnation of Prades, after those of the Sorbonne, the Archbishop of Paris, the Bishop of Montauban and the Pope. It was the work of Caylus, the pro-Jansenist Bishop of Auxerre, who turned the attack very pointedly against the *Encyclopédie* and the whole intellectual movement stemming from Locke, Newton and Montesquieu, with jibes, *en passant*, at the Jesuits and the Sorbonne. Directly attacked, Diderot felt obliged to reply, and did so by adding a third part to the work in two parts supplied by the abbé. He was obviously acquainted with parts I and II, when he composed part III—the preface to part III shows that—so it is reasonable to suppose that it was he who handed the manuscripts to the printers. According to Naigeon, the abbé was given credit for this third part also,[2] in spite of its being so well written that a more lively mind and a more skilful pen than the abbé possessed were needed for its composition.

D'Hémery suspected Diderot, and also, though wrongly, d'Alembert, from the first. The dossier no. 11794 of the Bastille enables us to follow the story[3] and to conclude that Diderot received parts one and two of the work in September and handed them to Rainville, one of Le Breton's journeymen printers. He confided the third part to another printer, Prieur, and at the moment of doing so expected it would be ready before parts I and II, as he says in the preface of part III. The abbé's two parts were distributed by 1 October at the latest and it is likely that part III was also available then, although part III was not mentioned before 17 October and it was then mentioned by implication only, the copies found on 1 October being described as 'imperfect' because part III was not included.[4]

Rainville was arrested on 17 October. He denied everything when first interrogated, but later made a complete confession. The first two parts, except for the last six sheets, had been printed by a journeyman printer named Bobin on a clandestine press in the rue Saint-Antoine. The third part and the last six sheets of part II had been printed by Prieur. For part III, Prieur had used great primer fount while bourgeois had been used for the rest, a statement which an examination of the editions bears out. Bobin completed his edition in bourgeois fount following Prieur's text. Rainville confessed all this on 12 November, but d'Hémery had already discovered, by 18 October, that Rainville had sold copies of the incomplete edition to a woman bookseller named La Foliot on 1 October and this fact had been sufficient for Rainville to be imprisoned alone in one of the Bastille's dungeons.

The work was distributed by La Foliot and also by Laurent Prault junior, who was arrested on 4 November. Prault at one time had 80 copies of it and on another occasion spoke of 100 copies at 5 livres 15 sols and another 8 copies at 7 livres 10 sols and mentioned a girl who had 1,200 copies in her possession.[5] The police records do not say that any of these copies were seized and it is therefore possible that they were distributed.

The following documents give details of other enquiries concerning clandestine printing presses and mention other tracts, chiefly of Jansenist inspiration. They are included because they help to give a complete picture of the activities of Berryer, Rochebrune and d'Hémery during the operations carried out in October and November 1752.

ARCHIVES OF THE BASTILLE: Dossier No. 11794

1. *D'Hémery to Berryer, 17 October 1752*
[ff. 20–21] Monsieur,

J'ay l'honneur de vous rendre compte que par les recherches que j'ai faites au sujet des deux lettres qui ont paru imprimées addressées à Mgr l'archevêque de Paris en dattes des 7 et 19 du present mois, j'ai decouvert qu'elles ont été imprimées chez le S. Le Breton sans cependant qu'il [20ʳᵒ] y ait eu part puisque c'est un de ses garçons nommé Rhinville qui les a imprimées à son inscüe et pour son compte; par conséquent il en connoit l'auteur qui est un jeune homme dont je n'ay pu sçavoir le nom.

J'ay tout lieu de croire aussi qu'il sçait ou a été imprimé[e] l'apologie de l'abbé de Prades qui vient de paroitre et que ce pourroit bien etre dans l'Imprimerie de Le Breton, 1°. parce que je soupçonne que Diderot et Dalembert en sont les auteurs, 2°. Parce que Rhinville en [21ʳᵒ] a vendu plusieurs exemplaires imparfaits qu'il avoit surement volés, peut être a l'Imprimeur.

Enfin monsieur, il est certain que Rhinville a imprimé de son chef les deux Lettres en question et qu'il connoit l'auteur et qu'il sçait aussi où a été imprimé[e] l'apologie de l'abbé de Prades, ce qu'il ne manquera pas de dire dès qu'il sera arresté

d'Hemery

Ce 17.8bre 1752.
Apostils by Berryer
Mr Duval [*Berryer's Secretary*]

Il faut que le comʳᵉ de rochebrune interroge sur le champ Rhinville et tire de lui
    1°. s'il a imprimé les deux lettres cy jointes
    2° qui en est l'auteur
    3° qui a imprimé l'apologie de l'abbé de prades ou qui la [sic] imprime
                17.8ᵇʳᵉ 1752

signé le 17.8ᵇʳᵉ 1752
une lettre a M. le Gouverneur de la Bastille pour recevoir le N[omm]é Rhinville Compagnon Imprimeur.

2. *Berryer to Rochebrune, 17 October 1752*
[f. 23]

Je prie Monsieur le Commissaire Rochebrune de se transporter de L'ordre du Roy chés Jacques Rhinville Compagnon Imprimeur au moment qu'il y sera arrêté en vertu des ordres de sa M[ajes]té. a l'effet d'y faire perquisition et la saisie des MMSS. et Imprimés prohibés qui pourront s'y trouver dont il dressera procès verbal.

fait le 17.8ᵇʳᵉ. 1752.
Berryer

3. *Report on search at Rainville's lodging*
[f. 18ʳᵒ] du 17.8ᵇʳᵉ. 1752

   Procès verbal de perquisition chez le nommé Jacques Rainville Compagnon Imprimeur au moment qu'il a été arreté par le S. D'Hemery Et conduit a la Bastille.

   L'an mil sept cent cinquante deux Le mardy dix sept octobre sur les huit heures du soir ou environ nous Agnan Philippe Miché De Rochebrune avocat au Parlement Commʳᵉ Enquesteur et Examinateur au chatelet de Paris

   a la requisition du S. Joseph D'hemery Lieutenant de Robbe Courte Lequel nous a dit qu'il est chargé d'arreter le nommé Rainville Compagnon Imprimeur pour Le conduire a la Bastille et qu'il seroit necessaire de faire une perquisition chez ce particulier afin de connoitre s'Il ne s'y trouvera point d'Imprimés deffendus ou quelques papiers qui puissent Le Convaincre d'en faire la distribution [,] sommes transporté avec le d[it]. Sieur Dhemery Rüe de la Harpe dans une maison a porte cochere de laquelle est principale locataire La Ve. Clermont Et Etant montés au quatrieme Etage de Ladᵉ. maison et entrés dans une chambre ayant vüe sur la dᵉ. Rüe de la harpe, nous y avons trouvé un particulier qui a dit se nommer Jacques Rainville agé de vingt sept [18ᵛᵒ] ans ou environ natif de Paris, compagnon Imprimeur demeurant en la maison Et chambre ou nous sommes; Et Luy ayant fait Entendre le sujet de notre transport, nous luy avons fait vuider les poches de son juste au corps de sa veste Et de sa culotte et les papiers qui s'y sont trouvé[s] ont été mis a part; avons Ensuitte fait en presence dud. Rainville perquisition dans Les tiroirs de sa Commode, dans la ditte chambre et dans un Grenier audessus de ladᵉ. chambre sans qu'il s'y soit Rien trouvé de suspect Et aprés ladᵉ. perquisition faitte nous avons Examiné les papiers trouvé[s] dans les poches dud. Rainville parmi Lesquels avons trouvé un quarré de papier contenant la notte suivante, trente cinq lettres d'un Theologien a 4ˢ. deux cent vingt cinq Reflexions a 4ˢ. Et quatre vingt quatorze Relations a 6ˢ. Et led. Rainville aprés serment fait de dire verité Interpellé de nous declarer ou ont été Imprimés les d. ouvrages Et Combien Il en a distribué[s] et enfin par qui Ils luy ont été Remis, a dit qu'il n'a [19ʳᵒ] distribué aucun des d. ouvrages et que c'est un papier qu'il a trouvé dans la Rue Et qui ne doit point tirer a consequence pour le charger. Interpellé ensuite de parafer la dᵉ Notte a Refusé de le faire; pourquoy avons parafé Led. quarré de papier qui est demeuré annexé à la minutte dud. procés verbal; et attendu les ordres de sa Majesté Led. Sieur D'hemery qui en est porteur s'est chargé de conduire au chateau de la Bastille Led. Rainville qu'il a arreté

   Dont Et de tout ce que dessus avons fait et dressé Le present procés verbal pour servir et valloir ce que de Raison; Et a le dit Sieur Dhemery signé avec Nous, a l'Egard dud. Rainville Il a Refusé de signer de ce Interpellé ainsy qu'il est dit en notre minutte.

                                                                Pour copie
                                                                De Rochebrune

[The rough draft of this report occupies ff. 24–27.]

4. *Paper found in Rainville's pocket*
[f. 17]
trente-cinq Lettres d'un Theologien à 4s
deux cens vingt-cinq reflexions, à 4s
quatre-vingts-quatorze relations, à 6s

5. *Berryer to Rochebrune, 17 October 1752*
[fᵒ31ʳᵒ]

   Je viens de remettre, Monsieur, au Sr. d'hemery des ordres du Roy pour arrêter et conduire a la Bastille un nommé Rhinville Compagnon Imprimeur, dès qu'il y sera arrivé, Je vous prie de vous transporter au Château a l'effet de luy faire subir Interrogatoire de l'ordre du Roy sur les faits qui vous seront donnés par led. Sr. D'hemery, et Nommément luy demander sil a imprimé les deux lettres cy jointes, qui en est l'auteur et la demeure, si c'est luy qui a imprimé l'apologie de l'abbé de Prades et sur la demande de qui il l'a fait, et si ce n'est pas luy, qu'il donne des renseignemens sur cela.

Je suis, Monsieur, votre tres humble et tres obeissant serviteur

Berryer

Ce 17.8ᵇʳᵉ. 1752.

Et vous m'enverrés sur le champ Coppie de l'Interrogʳᵉ. ou votre Minutte s'il étoit pressé d'agir sur les eclaircissemens que le prisonnier donnera.

M. le Commʳᵉ. Rochebrune.

6. *D'Abbadie to Berryer, 17 October 1752*
[f.36ʳᵒ]

A La Bastille, le 17ᵉ.
8ᵇʳᵉ. 1752

Monsieur

J'ai l'honneur de Vous informer que j'ai reçu Le Nommé Rainville, conduit par Le Sʳ. D'hemery. Sur votre Lettre datée de Ce jour.

Je suis avec Respect
Monsieur

Votre très-humble, et
très-obeissant Serviteur
dabadie

7. *First Interrogation of Rainville*
[f.28ʳᵒ]
du 17.8.ᵇʳᵉ 1752.

Interrogatoire subi par Jacques Rainville compagnon Imprimeur detenu de l'ordre du Roy au chateau de la Bastille.

Interrogatoire fait de l'ordre du Roy par Nous Agnan Philippe Miché De Rochebrune avocat au Parlement Commʳᵉ Enquesteur et Examinateur au chatelet de Paris.

Subi par Jacques Rainville detenu de l'ordre du Roy au chateau de la Bastille

En consequence nous etant transporté dans le Gouvernement dud. Chateau de la Bastille ou led. Rainville a eté ammené par le S. Dhemery Lieutenant de Robbe courte, nous avons procedé aud. Interrog[atoir]e ainsi qu'il suit

Du Mardy dix sept octobre mil sept cent cinquante deux, dix heures du soir.

Premierement interrogé de ses nom, surnom, age, pays, qualité et demeure.

a Dit aprés serment de Repondre vérité se nommer Jacques Rainville agé de vingt sept ans natif de Paris Compagnon Imprimeur demeurant a Paris Rüe de la harpe paroisse St Severin.

Interrogé qui est le dernier imprimeur chez Lequel Il a travaillé

a Dit que c'est le S. Le Breton Imprimeur demᵗ a Paris Rüe de la harpe et chez lequel il a cessé de travailler Le treize de ce mois.

Interrogé quelle Raison a porté le S. Le Breton a ne se plus servir du Repondant

a Dit que le penchant qu'il a pour le vin en est la cause [28ᵛᵒ] a luy Representé qu'il ne dit pas la verité et que led. Sieur Le Breton n'a mis hors de chez luy Le Repondant que parce qu'il avoit Imprimé deux Lettres adressées a Monsieur L'archeveque de Paris L'une dattée du sept octobre et L'autre par Erreur du dix neuf du même mois avec le nom d'Amsterdam pour l'Impression.

a Dit qu'il n'a aucune connaissance des d. deux Lettres

a luy Representé qu'il ne dit pas la verité et qu'il a vendu lesd. deux Lettres a differentes personnes.

a Dit que n'ayant point la connoissance desd. deux Lettres Il n'a pu en vendre.

Interrogé combien il a tiré d'Exemplaires de chacune desd. deux Lettres.

a Dit qu'il n'a point connoissance de ce que nous Luy demandons

Interrogé comment se nomme et ou demeure L'auteur desd. deux Lettres

a Dit qu'il ne le Connoit point.

En cet Endroit nous luy avons Representé lesd. deux Lettres Imprimées, et nous l'avons interpellé de nous declarer s'Il ne les Reconnoit pas pour les avoir Imprimées.

a Dit qu'il ne les a point Imprimées et qu'il ne les Reconnoit point.

Interpellé de les parapher a Refusé de le faire

[29ʳᵒ] Interrogé à qui Il a vendu l'apologie de l'abbé de Prades

a Dit qu'il n'en a point vendu.

Interrogé a qui Il s'est adressé pour avoir ladᵉ apologie.

a Dit qu'il ne peut dire une chose qu'il Ignore.

Interrogé par qui ladᵉ apologie a été Imprimée

a Dit qu'il n'en connoit point L'Imprimeur

a luy Representé que lorsque nous Commissaire avons fait perquisition en sa chambre, Il s'est trouvé dans sa poche un quarré de papier contenant la mention de trente cinq Lettres d'un Theologien a quatre Sols, de deux cent vingt cinq Reflexions a quatre Sols et de quatre vingt quatorze Relations a six sols, Laquelle notte Il a Refusé de parafer parce qu'elle est La preuve Evidente qu'il se mêle de vendre et distribuer des Ecrits deffendus, et que lesd. trois ouvrages sont semblables a l'Impression de l'apologie dud. abbé de Prades

a Dit qu'il a trouvé lad.ᵉ notte ou est la mention desd. ouvrages La Semaine derniere dans la rüe sans qu'il puisse dire Laquelle ne pouvant s'en Ressouvenir.

Interpellé de parafer lad.ᵉ notte a Refusé de le faire.

Lecture a luy faite du present Interrogatoire

Et de ses reponses.

a Dit ses Reponses Contenir verité, y a persisté

Et a signé En notre Minutte

Pour copie
De Rochebrune

[The rough draft is on ff. 31–33 and is signed 'Rainville' and 'Rochebrune'.]

8. *D'Hémery to Berryer, 18 October 1752*

[f. 38ʳᵒ]

Monsieur,

J'ai l'honneur de vous rendre compte qu'en consequence de vos ordres, j'ai arrêté et conduit au Château de la Bastille hier au soir le nommé Rinville garçon imprimeur, en vertu de l'ordre du Roy du . . .

Le Commissaire de Rochebrune a prealablement fait perquisition dans une chambre que ce particulier occupoit rüe de la Harpe, ou il ne s'y est rien trouvé de suspect, sinon dans les poches de son habit un quarré de papier sur lequel etoit ecrit ce qui suit. Trente cinq lettres d'un Theologien à quatre sols, deux cent vingt cinq reflexions à quatre sols, et quatre vingt quatorze relations à six sols. Lequel ecrit le dit Rinville [38ᵛᵒ] a dit avoir trouvé dans la rüe, et a refusé de le parapher, ce qui prouve combien il est coupable, il n'a cependant pas voulu en convenir dans l'interrogatoire que le Commissaire luy a fait subir sur le champ a la Bastille; mais pour l'en convaincre, j'ay fait des recherches des endroits ou il avait vendu des Lettres à M. l'archeveque, et ayant sçu qu'il en avoit porté chez la foliot, je me suis transporté ce matin avec M. le Commissaire chez cette femme place du vieux Louvre, qui est convenue de tout et qui a faite [*sic*] une Declaration qui constate que le dit Rinville a imprimé les dᵉˢ deux lettres a M. l'archeveque des 7. et 19. de ce mois, puisqu'il luy en a vendu en differens tems six douzaines de la premiere et trois douzaines de la Seconde, avec trois exemplaires imprimés de l'apologie de l'abbé de Prades, auxquels il manquoit une troisieme partie, et trente exemplaires de la lettre d'un Theologien aux Eveques qui ont ecrit au Roy, de laquelle nous avons même saisi six exemplaires suivant qu'il est constaté par le procés Verbal du dit Commissaire. La foliot nous a assuré qu'elle ne savoit pas dans [39ʳᵒ] quelle imprimerie ces ouvrages avoient été faits, mais que tout ce qu'elle se rapelloit, etoit que Rinville luy avoit dit il y a quelques jours que Simon du Parlement n'avoit pas fait affaire avec luy parce qu'il n'avoit pas voulu luy donner deux cent livres, pour tirer un mil de la premiere lettre a M. l'Archeveque.

Je pense que cette declaration est plus que sufisante pour convaincre Rinville de tout ce qu'on l'accuse, d'ailleurs c'est un homme dangereux, capable de faire les coups les plus hardis.

Les ouvrages cy aprés sont surement de l'imprimerie des d.ᵉˢ deux lettres, que le dit Rinville declarera sans doute, aussi bien que les Auteurs a qu'il a eu directement affaire.

Deux lettres a Mgr. l'Eveque de xxx du premier juin 1752.

Troisieme lettre du neuf juin, touttes deux supprimées par arret du Parlement.

Reflexions Theologiques sur le premier volume des lettres de M. xxx a ses Eleves, petite brochure peu interessante.

[39ᵛᵒ] Relation de la Mission faite a Armes près Clamecy par les R.R.P.P. Jesuites &c. petitte Brochure.

Lettres d'un Theologien aux Eveques qui ont ecrit au Roy.

Apologie de l'Abbé de Prades.

Et deux lettres à Mgr l'archeveque de Paris des 7. et 19. du present mois.

D'hemery

Ce Mercredy 18 octobre 1752.

9. Berryer to d'Argenson, 18 October 1752
[f. 40ʳᵒ]

[draft⁶]

M. le Cᵗᵉ. D'argenson 18. octobre. 1752
M.

Conformement aux ordres que vous m'avés fait l'hʳ de me donner pour faire [les plus exactes] faire d'exactes recherches des auteurs et Imprimeurs qui repandent ⟨journellement⟩ dans le public des Libelles et Imprimés [calomnieux au sujet] [remplis d'Inj.] aussi injurieux que temeraires, au sujet des affaires presentes de l'Eglise, J'ay mis du monde sur la voye pour tâcher d'en surprendre quelques uns, et ayant appris hier qu'un compagnon Imprimeur appellé Rhinville avait imprimé ⟨à l'insçu de son Me. Imprimeur⟩ les 2. dernieres Lettres à M. l'archeveque des 7. et 19. ⟨de ce mois⟩ [octobre] dont la datte de cette derniere étoit prematurée, Je l'ay fait arrêter et conduire a la Bastille ou on a trouvé 2. exemplaires sur luy et Je me flatte d'avoir la preuve [que c'est luy l'imprimeur] que c'est luy qui les a imprimées. Soyés persuadé Mʳ que Je ne negligerai rien pour decouvrir ceux qui se meslent de pareille besogne [et a mesure] que Je les ferai arrêter sur le champ. [Je ne manquerai] et que Je ne vous laisserai point ignorer le succés de mes [demarches] soins sur cela.

Je suis &c.

10. Report on Search at La Foliot's Shop
[f.41ʳᵒ] du 18.8ᵇʳᵉ. 1752.

Procès verbal contenant la perquisition chez la Vᵉ. foliot qui a fait sa declaration au sujet de plusieurs Exemplaires prohibés que luy a vendus le Nommé Rainville Compagnon Imprimeur

L'an mil sept cent cinquante deux Le mercredy dix huit octobre une heure de Relevée ou environ en notre hotel et par devant Nous agnan Philippe Miché De Rochebrune avocat au Parlement Commʳᵉ Enquesteur Et Examinateur au chatelet de Paris.

Est comparu Le S. Joseph D'hemery Lieutenant de Robbe Courte.

Lequel nous a dit que conformement aux ordres de Monsieur le Lieutenant General de police Il requiert que nous nous transportions presentement place du Vieux Louvre chez la Vᵉ. foliot pour en

Recevoir la Sa declaration au sujet de differents ouvrages prohibés que luy a vendus Jacques Rainville compagnon Imprimeur qui fut conduit Le jour d'hier au chateau de la Bastille et a signé en notre Minutte.

Desquelles Comparution et Requisition nous Commissaire susdit avons donné acte aud. S. D'hemery Et en consequence sommes transporté avec luy place du vieux Louvre dans une des Boutiques qui Reignent Le Long de la Rüe fromenteau du coté de la Rüe des orties et nous y avons trouvé Marie Lefort Vᵉ. de Lambert foliot vivant procureur au Baillage de Bailleux elle occupant ladᵉ Boutique ou nous sommes, Laquelle Instruitte du sujet de notre transport et Interpellée de nous declarer quels sont Les ouvrages prohibés que luy a vendus le nommé Rainville Compagnon Imprimeur que le S. Le Breton [41ᵛᵒ] Imprimeur Rüe de la harpe a Renvoyé vendredy dernier quinze du present mois, nous a dit Et declaré que Le dimanche premier de ce mois un particulier paroissant agé de vingt sept à vingt huit ans ou Environ Luy a apporté et vendus [sic] trois Exemplaires Imprimés de L'apologie de l'abbé de Prades auxquels Il manquoit la troisieme partie; que huit Jours aprés ou Environ le même particulier Luy a vendu trente Exemplaires de la Lettre d'un Theologien aux Eveques qui ont Ecrit au Roy. que le mardy dix du present mois d'octobre Led. particulier a vendu a la declarante quatre douzaine[s] de la lettre à Monsieur L'archeveque dattée du sept du mois, Et le treize suivant Il a encore vendu a La Declarante trois douzaines de la Seconde Lettre a Monsieur L'archeveque dattée du dix neuf octobre present mois, que Lundi Seize de ce mois Led. particulier a encore apporté et vendu a la declarante deux douzaine[s] de la premiere Lettre, que led. particulier a qui la declarante a dit dans la conversation que led. S. Le Breton Imprimeur avoit Renvoyé L'un de ses ouvriers vendredy treize de ce mois, luy a répondu que c'étoit Luy même qui avait été Renvoyé et sur les [42ᵛᵒ] questions que la declarante luy a faittes pour sçavoir pourquoy il en etoit sorti, Il a dit que c'etoit par Raport a quelqu' Interest occasionné par Le Livre Intitulé L'apologie de l'abbé de Prades sans s'etre Expliqué plus amplement; ajoutte la Declarante que ce meme particulier luy a Encore dit qu'il S'etoit adressé au S. Simon Imprimeur Rüe de la harpe pour faire Imprimer La premiere Lettre à Monsieur L'archeveque de Paris et qu'il n'avoit point fait affaire avec led. S. Simon qui luy avoit demandé deux Cent Livres pour en tirer un mille Et a signé en notre Minutte.

Et ayant fait perquisition dans ladᵉ Boutique en presence de ladᵉ Vᵉ foliot, nous y avons trouvé six Imprimés in octavo de la Lettre d'un Theologien aux Eveques qui ont Ecrit au Roy pour se plaindre de l'arrêté du Parlement en datte du cinq may mil sept Cent Cinquante deux a amsterdam mil sept cent Cinquante deux Et comme Ladᵉ. Lettre est sans nom d'Imprimeur et sans approbation Et privilege, nous avons saisi sur ladᵉ Veuve foliot lesd. six Exemplaires qui sont demeurés annexés au présent procés verbal.

[42ᵛᵒ] Dont Et de tout ce que dessus avons fait Et dressé Le present procés verbal pour Servir Et valloir ce que de Raison et a ledit Sieur d'hemery signé avec nous Commʳᵉ. Et la Vᵉ foliot en notre minutte

Pour Copie
De Rochebrune

11. *Berryer to d'Argenson*, [*18 October 1752*]
[f. 43ʳᵒ]

[draft].

M. le Cᵗᵉ d'Argenson

Ayant été informé par voye sûre que le nommé Rhinville Compagnon Imprimeur travaillant dans l'Imprimerie du Sʳ. le Breton avait imprimé à son insçû plusieurs Brochures très mauvaises et Calomnieuses au sujet des affaires presentes de l'Eglise j'ay signé un ordre le 17. octobre 1752. pour arrêter led. Rhinville et le conduire à la Bastille.

Monsieur le Comte d'Argenson est supplié de faire expedier des ordres en forme de la datte cy dessus. pour autoriser ceux que j'ay donnés

Apostils
bon p^r les ordres
23.8^{bre} 1752
Mr Dargenson m'a ordonné de faire arrester le nommé Bobin et le Sr Duderes de Villeras et de les faire mettre à la Bastille.
Les ordres pr arrêter Rhinville du 17.8bre. 1752 envoyés a d'hemery et au Gouverneur de la Bastille.

12. *Chevalier to Berryer, 21 October 1752*
[f. 45ro]

De la Bastille Le
21e. 8bre. 1752

Monsieur
Vous trouverez cy Joint un memoire pour Le S^r abbé Mehegan
Le N[omm]é Rainville qui est au Cachot demande avec Instance de vous parler et si vous ne pouvés venir de vous Ecrire, Ce miserable vous demande la grace de le faire sortir du Cachot se flattant que vous serez content de luy, se promettant de vous dire tout ce qu'il scay J'ai L'honneur d'estre avec un profond respect
Monsieur
Votre

13. *Second Interrogation of Rainville*
[f. 49ro] 12 Novemb. 1752.
Interrogatoire de Rainville Compagnon Imprimeur
Interrogatoire de l'ordre du Roy, fait par Nous Nicolas René Berryer, chev, Conseiller d'Etat Lieut. general de Police de la ville, prevôté et vicomté de Paris, commre. du Conseil en cette partie
Au nommé Rainville Compagnon Imprimeur detenu de l'ordre du Roy au Château de la Bastille.
Du dimanche douze novembre mil sept Cent Cinquante deux de Relevée dans la salle du Conseil dud. château.
aprés serment fait par le Repondant de dire et repondre verité
Interrogé de ses nom, surnom age qualité pays profession et Religion
a dit se nommer Jacques Rainville natif de Paris, agé de vingt sept ans, Compagnon Imprimeur, demeurant lorsqu'il a été arreté de l'ordre du Roy rüe de la harpe de la Religion Catholique apostolique et Romaine.
Interrogé s'il n'a pas imprimé deux Lettres? la 1re portant sur le frontispice *Lettre a Mgr l'archeveque de Paris sur La liberté de la Confession du sept octobre*, la seconde, *Lettre a Mgr l'archeveque de Paris du dix neuf octobre dernier.*
a Repondu qu'il en a remis les Manuscripts au nommé Bobin Compagnon Imprimeur et soldat aux gardes qui les a imprimées ne sçait pas dans quel endroit il a fait cette impression, Croit neanmoins que c'est dans une imprimerie clandestine qui apartenoit aud. Bobin, ou du moins a la tête de laquelle il étoit, a entendu dire aud. Bobin que cette Imprimerie étoit dans le faub. St. Antoine dou il l'avoit demenagée dans les derniers Jours du mois de septembre dernier, mais ne sçait point dans quel endroit il l'a conduite, [Croit être sur].
sçait que les deux premiers volumes de l'*apologie de l'abbé de Prades* moins les six dernieres feüilles du second volume ont été imprimées par led. Bobin; qu'a l'egard des six dernières feuilles du [49vo] second volume et de la 3e partie de gros Romain, elles ont été imprimées par Prieur; observe que la 3e partie de lad^e apologie, qui a parû depuis imprimée en petit Romain, a été fait par led. Bobin.
qu'au surplus des Epreuves de la dite apologie étoient corrigées par l'abbé Pestrelle[7] lequel abbé est fort connu du S. le Breton Imprimeur parce qu'il a travaillé a corriger les Epreuves de l'Encyclopédie.
Interrogé par qui luy avoient été remises les dites deux Lettres mentionnées cy dessus.
a Repondu que les Manuscripts luy ont été remis par le S. Duderé de Villeras

Interrogé si led. Duderé de Villeras ne luy en a pas remis d'autres pour imprimer,

a Repondu qu'il luy a vendu une petite piece de vers intitulée *Predictions d'un[e] Jeune Convulsionnaire &c.* qu'il a donnée au nommé Beauvais, Compagnon Imprimeur pour l'imprimer.

Et en cet endroit avons representé au Repondant les deux Lettres imprimées adressées a Mgr l'archeveque mentionnées cy dessus, lesquelles ont été paraphées du Repondant et de nous après les avoir reconnues pour être celles dont il nous a parlé.

Lecture faite au Repondant du present Interrog[atoir]e a dit que les Reponses qu'il y a faites contiennent verité, y a perseveré et a signé.

Berryer   Rainville

14. *Notes by Berryer, 8 October 1752*

[f. 60] Rinville arrêté le 17. octob. 1752.

Lors de son Interrogatoire du 17.8.^bre N'a rien avoüé. a seulement dit qu'il avoit été renvoyé de chés Le Brethon Imprim^r.

Par le second Interrogatoire qu'il a subi le 12. novembre.

Convient d'avoir remis a *Bobin* compag^on. Imprim^r. les deux MSS. de deux Lettres à M. l'archevêque de Paris l'une en datte du 7. octobre, l'autre en datte du 19. octobre 1752, pour les imprimer dans une Imprim^ie clandestine qui a été démenagée du faub. S. Antoine au mois de 7bre. dernier.

Rinville ajoûte que Bobin a imprimé de l'Apologie de l'abbé de Prades ainsi que Prieur, que c'etoit l'abbé *Pestrelle* qui corrigeoit les Epreuves.

que les MSS. des deux Lettres cy dessus a M. l'arch. de Paris luy avoient été donnés par *Duderé de Villeras*.

que Duderé de Villeras luy a encore donné le MSS. Prediction d'une Jeune Convulsionnaire petite pièce en vers [60vo] qu'il a remise à Beauvais pour l'impression.

Rinville a paraphé deux Exemp^res. imprimés des deux Lettres à M. l'arch. de Paris cy dessus mentionnées.

Duderé de Villeras [a theology student], arrêté le 4 Novembre.

Dit, suivant le procès verbal du 4 novembre, Qu'ayant Coppié la plus grande partie d'une ancienne Lettre attribué[e] a M. Paris il appliqua ce qu'il avoit écrit a M. l'archeveque de Paris et luy en fit une Lettre dont il a donné le MSS. a Rhinville pour l'imprimer. qu'ensuite il composa une seconde Lettre a M. l'archevêque remplie d'injures grossieres dont il a donné pareillement le MSS. a Rinville pour l'imprimer.

Est convenu de nouveau par son Interrog^re. du 12.9^bre. des faits cy dessus [61ro] et d'avoir encore composé une piéce de vers intitulée Prediction d'une Jeune Convulsionnaire a M^rs. du Parlement sur les affaires presentes qu'il a pareillement donnée à Rinville pour imprimer

Laurent Prault arrêté le 4. Novemb.

Suivant le procès verbal de perquisition faite chés luy le d. Jour 4. Novembre, on y a saisi

Six Lettres en Reponse a la Req^te. des sousfermiers.

Cinq seconde lettre de M. l'arch. de . . . en reponse a la Lettre d'un Conseiller du Parlement.

Six Oraisons funebres de la Constitution

Dix Mandements de M. l'arch. de Paris

Six Lettres a M. l'arch. de Paris sur la Confession

une prediction d'une Jeune Convuls[ionnai]re

[61vo] Sept Lettres aux RR. PP. Jésuites

six Reponses des Jesuites a cette Lettre

quinze Apocalypses

Trente huit Consultations de 40 Docteurs

Cinq Requestes des soûfermiers

Six Lettres de M^ra les Commissaires nommés par le Roy

deux Relations de la Mission faite a harmes[8]

La deuxieme et troisieme Lettre a M. L'archevêque de . . .

huit Cent de l'Extrait des Registres du Parlement du 21.8ᵇʳᵉ. 1752.

quatre vingt Apologie de l'abbé de Prades.

Plus s'est trouvé des papiers dans les poches de Prault qui ont été mis sous le sçellé.

Par le même procès verbal Prault a dit

que l'Apologie luy a été apportée par une Dame inconnuë, et qu'elle a été imprimée chés *Ballard* et *Lotin.*

[62ʳᵒ] Et que les autres imprimés luy ont été apportés par des Colportᵣˢ. a lui inconnus, et par des Commissionnaires de S. Sulpice, ainsi que trois exemplaires du Remerciement des Colporteurs qui se sont aussi trouvés parmi les Imprimés cy dessus.

Prault dans son Interrogᵣᵉ, du 5.9ᵇʳᵉ. Est convenu de ce qui suit,

Que depuis 8. a 9. mois il a vendu au Palais les Imprimés non revêtus de permission qui ont parû sur les matiéres du tems, et que ceux mentionnés au procés verbal cy dessus du 4. novembre ont été trouvés chez luy.

qu'il a fait imprimer par *Prieur* l'Extrait des Registres du Parlement auquel il a joint les Art. des ordonnances. En a fait tirer deux mille.

qu'il a chargé *Beauvais* d'Imprimer sur la 1ʳᵉ. Edition un mille de la Lettre a M. l'arch. de Paris sur la Confession

[62ᵛᵒ] plus a fait imprimer par le même un mille de l'Apocalypse dont le MSS. luy a été remis par un Jeune homme, qui a demeuré chés Caudet avocat

plus a chargé Gazil compagnon imprimeur de luy faire imprimer quinze cent de l'oraison funebre de la Constitution dont le MSS. luy a été donné par un *Clerc de Procureur* dont il ignore le nom.

dit que la Consultation des 40 docteurs

la Requeste des soufermiers

Et les Lettres pacifiques

luy ont été apportées par un Commissionnaire de St. sulpice dont il ne sçait le nom mais qui porte l'argent des Decimes et vend du coton.

que la seconde Lettre à M. l'archevêque de XXX.

la Relation de la Mission a harmes

Et la 2e et 3e Lettre a M. l'Eve[que] de . . . ont été apportées à *Loüis Roch* son garçon de boutique.

que le d. Beauvais luy a encore

[63ʳᵒ] apporté

La Lettre aux Rˢ P. Jésuites

La Reponse a cette Lettre

La prediction d'une Jeune Conv.ʳᵉ et le Remerciment des Colporteurs qu'une fille d'environ 28 ans. assés jolie luy a apporté Cent Exempʳᵉˢ. de l'Apologie de l'abbé de Prades

que *frevart* compagnon chés Ballard luy a vendu deux Cent Exemp.ʳᵉˢ. du Mandemᵗ. de l'arche[vê]que de Paris.

Et que la Nommée *Blezeau* fille de boutique de Coutellier luy a pareillmt. vendu de la Reqᵗᵉ. des Soufermiers, et de l'oraison funebre de la Bulle.

que le d. frevart qui luy a aussy vendu de la Lettre aux Jesuites, luy a dit qu'elle avoit été imprimée chés *Godichon pere* par le moyen *du fils.*

Et qu'enfin les Manuscripts cy après trouvés chés luy, luy ont été remis sçavoir.

Par le Sʳ. hallé Employé a l'hotel de Lussan Celuy intitulé: Lettre. Ne l'a point fait imprimer, et un autre MSS.

[63ᵛᵒ] intitulé: *Lettre de M. l'abbé V. . . a un Conseiller du Parlement de Paris* ne l'a point fait imprimer.

Par un particulier dont il ignore le nom mais qui est auteur d'un Roman que Boucher fils fait imprimer, un MSS. intitulé: *Apologie de M̄gr l'Archevêque* piéce en vers, et un autre MSS. ayant pour titre: *Lettre a Mylord C. . . sur les affaires de france.*

Par un jeune homme qui a été clerc de Caudet avocat au Conseil (C'est Charron) un MSS intitulé

Clementine allegorie pour servir a l'histoire de ce tems, Et ajoute que l'Apocalypse est du même Jeune homme.

Et enfin par la veuve la forest Papetiere pont St. Michel un MSS. ayant en tête: *Coppie de la 1ʳᵉ sommation faite au Curé de St Jean par M. de Menneville.*

[64ʳᵒ] Charron arrêté le 14. Novembʳᵉ.

A été arrêté sur la declaration de Prault qui dit qu'un Clerc de Caudet avocat, est auteur de l'*Apocalypse* et de la *Clementine*. Et comme on a sçu depuis que ce Clerc se nommoit *Charron* il a été mis a la Bastille.

Par son Interrogatoire du 18. novembre charron est convenu d'etre l'auteur de l'Apocalypse et de la Clementine, et d'en avoir remis les MSS. a Prault qui a fait imprimer le premier

Perquisition le 15. Novemb. chés Beauvais ruë du plâtre St. Jacques pour l'arrêter et saisir l'imprimᵉ. clandestine qu'il tenoit.

On n'a point trouvé Beauvais chés luy ni un particulier qui y devoit être. Ils venoient de se sauver par dessus les Toits.

on n'a point trouvé d'Imprimerie. Il y avoit seulement dans la Chambre la femme de Beauvais et une nommée Normier.

[64ᵛᵒ] Le S. d'hemery s'est assuré de la femme Beauvais pour luy faire dire ou étoit son mary. Il l'a conduit[e] au for-l'Eveque où a onze heures et demie du soir du même Jour, elle a declaré au Commʳᵉ Rochebrune que Prault Libraire au Palais avait donné a son mari et au N[omm]é *Valade* plusieurs MSS. pour les imprimer avec leur imprimerie a Rouleau qui étoit dans l'Enclos de St. Martin des champs, notamment le Mandement de M. l'archevêque de Paris, et que Prault luy donnoit 30 sols par Jour pour porter des Imprimés en differentes maisons.

Perquisition le 16. Novemb. dans l'Enclos de St. Martin des Champs pour y saisir l'imprimerie a Rouleau.

L'on s'est transporté a 9 heures du matin dans la maison indiquée de l'Enclos de S. Martin des champs. On n'y a point trouvé Beauvais, ni son Camarade, ni l'Imprimerie a Rouleau.

Le principal Locataire qui leur loüoit a dit, que le 5. Novembre ils [65ʳᵒ] luy avoient donné brusquement congé, payé le terme sans se donner la patience de prendre quittᵉᵉ et qu'ils avoient emporté leurs meubles et Effets. qu'ils se disoient horlogers.

Le Commissaire et le S. d'hemery Jugeant que la femme Beauvais les avoient trompé[s] se sont transportés au fort l'Evêque a midy et demi pour lui parler et l'interroger de nouveau.

La femme Beauvais a dit, qu'ayant appris que Prault avait été arrêté le 4. Novembre, elle en avoit aussitôt donné avis au Nommé *Valade* pour qu'il avertit son Mari qui couchoit dans S. Martin a l'endroit de l'Imprimerie, de prendre ses précautions. que la verité étoit qu'ils avaient fait transporter leur Presse rüe du plâtre a l'aide du nommé *Coulon* qui faisoit leurs commissions; ajouta qu'ils avaient imprimé l'Epitre a Madᵉ Moysan [65ᵛᵒ] et un autre ouvrage dont elle ne sçavoit pas le Nom.

Perquisition le 16 Novemb. rue du plâtre S. Jacques chés Beauvais pour y saisir une imprimerie.

Le Commissʳᵉ. et le S. d'hemery le d. Jour 16.9ᵇʳᵉ. a trois heures après midi se sont transportés ruë du platre S. Jacques. Ils ont monté au sixieme étage d'une maison dans un grenier qui s'est trouvé ouvert et qu'on a dit etre occupé par Beauvais.

On y a trouvé une petite Presse d'Imprimerie toute montée et un sac de Caractéres. on n'y a point trouvé Beauvais. S'est trouvé dans le grenier deux Epreuves de l'Epitre à Madᵉ. Moysan.

Maubuy arrêté Le 19 Novemb.

Par le procès verbal de perquisition chés Maubuy led.Jour 29. 9ᵇʳᵉ on a trouvé dans sa chambre un MSS. intitulé: *Lettre intercepté[e] écrite à M. . . . Conseiller clerc au Parlement par M.D. Jurisconsulte sur les affʳᵉˢ du tems* qui luy avoit été apporté le matin par le Sʳ *fremont* commissᵉ d'un Receveur de Rentes qui demeure près l'arcade S. Jean pour l'examiner et le corriger, ce qu'il avoit commencé a faire ainsi qu'il en est convenu.

Est pareillement convenu d'avoir composé la Reponse a la Lettre aux R. P. Jesuites, et le Remerciment des Colporteurs qu'il a remis dans le tems a *Beauvais* pour les faire imprimer.

A avoüé par son Interrog[atoir]e du 17. decembre qu'outre la Reponse a la Lettre &c. et le Remerciment &c. dont il est l'auteur, il avoit aussy composé la Reponse a la Requête des soufermiers et qu'il a confié à *Beauvais* les deux premiers MSS. et le troisieme a *Garnier* colporteur.

A Nié d'etre l'auteur de l'Epitre a la Dame Moysan.

Est convenu d'avoir composé en outre deux ouvrages dont il a remis les MSS a un nommé *Valade* pour les faire imprimer, l'un intitulé: *Le Parlem[en]t vengé ou l'impertinent Jesuite puni, Tragicomedie,* et l'autre *Almanach des Ruelles ou Calandrier galant et historique de l'Isle de Cythere.*

Par son second Interrog.e du 26. Jan.r 1753. est convenu d'avoir composé le *Bref du Pape* qu'il a remis à Beauvais pr. imprimer. Beauvais arreté le 5. decembre.

Il a été arrêté dans la Cave d'une maison située ruë au Maire, et dans cette Cave s'est trouvé[e] l'Imprimerie à Rouleau

a declaré qu'il occupoit ce reduit depuis 15. Jan.r, et n'a point voulu dire au surplus le nom de ses associés

Par le procès verbal dressé lorsqu'il a été arrêté, il est dit qu'il imprimoit pour lors le Bref du Pape avec un Rouleau et qu'il y avoit deux pag. de Caractéres composés dud. ouvrage.

S'est trouvé dans lad. Cave le Remerciment des Colporteurs imprimé et deux MSS. l'*almanach des Ruelles* [67ro] et le *Parlement vengé.*

Par l'Interrog.re de Beauvais du 11.Xbre.

Il nie que Prault l'ait chargé d'imprimer de la Lettre a M. l'arch. de Paris et de l'Apocalypse.

Convient qu'il a imprimé la Reponse a la Lettre aux Jesuites et le Remerciment des Colporteurs dont il a vendu les Exemres a Prault, la Ve Amaury, la dlle Blezeau, et la fe. Morel. tous vendants Livres au Palais que c'est *Maubuy* qui luy en a donné les MSS. amené par Garnier Colporteur qui est a bicestre. qu'il les a imprimés en societé avec *Valade* dans une Imprimie qu'ils tenoient dans l'Enclos de St. Martin des Champs.

est convenu qu'ils l'ont démenagée pour la mettre dans un grenier ruë du plâtre St. Jacques immediatement après la prise de Prault.

Se souvient d'avoir imprimé en outre deux mains de l'Epitre en vers a Made. Moysan qu'il a vendus a la Ve. Amaury, fe Morel et a la Blezeau, que c'est Maubuy qui en est l'auteur

que c'est *Valade* qui a donné les caractéres d'impression qui luy ont été fournis par un particulier a qui on donnoit un Ecu de la main de chaque ouvrage imprimé

Que c'est Valade qui entend bien la Caze [67vo] qui arrange les caracteres des Planches

Nie que *Coulon* aye fait leurs Comm[iss]ions

Convient que Valade et luy ont levé l'autre imprimerie de la ruë au Maire dont Valade a aussi fourni les Caractéres par le moyen du part[icul]ier en question qu'il ne connoit pas

que les 2. pag. de caractéres du Bref du Pape composé[e]s trouvées dans l'Imp.ie de la ruë au maire ont été aussi preparé[e]s par Valade

que c'est Valade qui luy a donné les 2. mss. du Parl.t vengé et de l'almanach des ruëlles. ne sçait d'ou il les tenoit.

que n'ayant point d'ouvrage et se trouvant dans la misere il a accepté les proppo[siti]ons que Valade luy a faites d'avoir en société une imprimerie Clandestine. Mais qu'ensemble ils n'ont imprimé que la Rep. a La Lett. aux Jesuites le Remercim. des Colportrs. et l'Epitre a la De. Moysan

que quant a la Lett. a M. l'arch., l'Apocalypse la Lett. aux Jesuites et la Lett. d'une jeune Conv.re dont on luy parle, Valade luy en a fait mystére, Et que si Valade les a imprimés Ça été pendant que luy Beauvais a eû une maladie qui a duré un mois.

The Rainville dossier ends there except for some notes by Berryer (pp. 68–70) concerning the pamphlets mentioned above. It will be seen that Berryer's men had made a clean sweep by January 1753, arresting a whole network of clandestine printers and *colporteurs* and seizing their printing presses. It is clear that in the middle years of the century the police of the book trade in Paris was both efficient and formidable.

S

NOTES

1 See my 'Un abbé philosophe: l'affaire de J.-M. de Prades' (*Dix-huitième siècle*, III, 1971, pp. 145–80), p. 170.

2 'Cet écrit, dont l'abbé de Prades a recueilli tout l'honneur, et qu'on aurait dû d'autant moins lui attribuer qu'on y remarque partout un homme qui a des idées à lui, au lieu que l'auteur de la thèse n'a guère employé que celles des autres, est un modèle de dialectique [. . .]' (*Mémoires historiques et philosophiques sur la vie et les ouvrages de D. Diderot* (Paris, 1821), p. 162).

3 J.-P. Belin was not acquainted with this dossier, so the paragraph he devotes to the subject is ill-informed (*Le Mouvement philosophique de 1748 à 1789* (Paris, 1913), p. 66). Ravaisson, in his *Archives de la Bastille,* vol. XII, (1881), pp. 389–90, 392 and 394 gives the text of items 1, 8 and 12 below from copies of d'Hémery's letters and Chevalier's letters preserved elsewhere and with slight differences; the others have not previously been published.

4 See below, n° 1 and n° 10.

5 Bastille, 1794, ff. 56vo, 53vo.

6 Words crossed out are placed in square brackets, additions in angle brackets.

7 The abbé Pestré is meant.

8 Armes, near Clamecy.

23

Reflections on the Sequel to
Le Paysan parvenu

LEONARD TANCOCK

Professor Niklaus will remember that many years ago, as young colleagues, we shared an amused scepticism about *ex cathedra* pronouncements by learned French professors that an Old French manuscript was written, say, by a scribe of Provençal origin whose mother was German, who had travelled in Italy but was living in Picardy at the time and knew no Greek. In view of that I have no intention of rushing in with assertions about the authorship of the *Suite anonyme* of *Le Paysan parvenu* where revered authorities have feared to tread. Deloffre points out that contemporaries, including d'Alembert who knew him personally, were in no doubt that parts 6, 7 and 8, published in 1756, seven years before Marivaux's death, were not by him.[1] Much of the subsequent confusion stems from the simple fact that the *Œuvres complètes* of 1781 omits the separate preface published in 1756 and 1758 and prints the eight parts as a complete novel, without comment.[2] In 1825 Duviquet hails the sentimental and edifying end as a masterpiece, but what else could be expected from an editor who 'improved' the text of Marivaux to suit the taste of worshippers of Chateaubriand and Lamartine?[3] Thereafter verdicts have depended upon critics' tastes or prejudices. The hallowed critics of my first youth, Sainte-Beuve, Taine, Lanson and Faguet, avoid the issue, but F. C. Green hails as 'exquisite':

the final summing up which is contained in one lapidary phrase. I refer to the passage in which he describes Jacob's return to his fond wife after an interview which he has had with Mme de Vambures. In one sentence Jacob executes himself: 'Plein des mouvements que Mme de Vambures avait excités dans mon cœur,' he says, 'je sautai au cou de mon épouse.' Comment is superfluous.[4]

It would be indeed, were it not that the 'exquisite' example is from part 6, the first part of the *Suite*, in which madame de Vambures appears for the first time. Deloffre himself says: 'En fait, ce sont les cinq premières parties qu'il faut attribuer à Marivaux, et il n'est pour rien dans les trois autres.[5] Recent scholars have been cautious. E. J. H. Greene does not commit himself,[6] neither does Vivienne Mylne, who indeed is not required to do so by the title and subject of her book,[7] while Robert Niklaus, with commendable wariness, relegates to a footnote the remark that the last three parts 'were written by a Dutchman or a Frenchman living in Holland.'[8]

And yet nobody who knew and worked with Professor Green, as I did, could dismiss him as naïve or careless. The object of this essay is to show that X, the author of the sequel, whose work can often be slovenly in style, elementary in psychology and sentimental to the point of silliness, can also sometimes repeat or imitate tricks of Marivaux and produce in short bursts quite convincing bits of pastiche such as the few words quoted by Green above. At this point I propose to commit the crime all academics have at all times condemned in students' essays and examination papers, namely to narrate the story of the plot and, worse still, to use the very words they all write in justification: 'in order to deal adequately with the question we must first, etc.' So here are the bare bones of a sequel overcrowded with incident.

Part 6. La Vallée, as henceforth Jacob will always be called, is seated on the stage of the theatre with d'Orsan and his fashionable friends. He does not take in the play because of the novelty of the situation, the silly behaviour of some of the young fops and above all the attractions and smiles of two lovely ladies in a box. (In this way X disposes of Marivaux's promise at the end of part 5 of a long digression about Paris theatres and actors). After the play, quickly suppressing a twinge of conscience about his wife at home, La Vallée goes off to a party with his new friend and the two ladies. In a quiet room where d'Orsan has tactfully taken him, sensing his embarrassment at not understanding card games, La Vallée tells his friend about his marriage, mesdames de Ferval and de Fécour, the Versailles adventure and the plight of the d'Orvilles. This last story touches d'Orsan's heart. Home at last, La Vallée recounts to his wife all his adventures minus any reference to madame de Vambures, the one of the two ladies who has captivated him, but we are told (in the words that so struck Professor Green) that because his mind was full of that lady's charms his performance as a husband was extremely competent.

Next morning, as he is leaving to see madame de Fécour, his wife complains of feeling unwell (*et pour cause*, one might think, but here X is following Marivaux's hint and preparing us for her early demise). He finds madame de Fécour still in bed, but her brother-in-law Fécour takes La Vallée aside and proposes that he might convey to the d'Orvilles that the husband's job will be guaranteed if the reward is madame d'Orville. La Vallée indignantly refuses to take the message. On his way home he calls at the d'Orvilles' apartment, but learns that the wife is out and the husband seriously ill. At home he finds his brother Alexandre, whose marriage and business as an innkeeper are collapsing because of his wife's fecklessness and extravagance. The La Vallées offer to be responsible for bringing up Alexandre's two boys. D'Orsan arrives and takes La Vallée off to pay their respects to the d'Orvilles.

Part 7. They find the house in mourning for M. d'Orville. D'Orsan expresses sympathy and because he is already falling in love with madame d'Orville he leaves behind a purse of money. A letter follows them to La Vallée's address asking to whom madame d'Orville should return a purse left at her home. D'Orsan replies that neither is responsible, and signs the letter La Vallée. Then he goes off to see M. Bono about a job for La Vallée. The latter sets off ostensibly to see his brother, but on the way calls first on madame d'Orville and persuades her not to try to find out the origin of the purse of money, then goes on to d'Orsan to report. D'Orsan says he is going to have the d'Orville lawsuit reopened.

There is a long scene at Alexandre's inn, where all has gone to rack and ruin. La Vallée takes charge of the two boys, who are sent to boarding school, and then has to stay home for some time because his wife is now chronically ill. After a mysterious absence d'Orsan returns with La Vallée's appointment to a tax-farm, thanks largely, he explains, to the help of madame de Vambures. After a round of courtesy calls they end up at the house of M. Bono, who invites everybody to dinner—a Verdurin-like entertainment, vulgar and ostentatious, during which a foppish young poet reads his own compositions, including a satirical epithalamium on the marriage of madame de Ferval to her Chevalier (part 4), who thus has all her money. The general drift of the poem is that that pious old voluptuary richly deserves to be squeezed dry and thrown away.

La Vallée leaves for Rheims to learn the technicalities of his new position. A month later he hears that his wife has died in Paris and sheds, he assures us, sincere tears. In Paris to settle his wife's affairs, he has an interview with madame de Vambures, who not unnaturally asks why he is in mourning. He confesses all and declares his love.

Having installed his brother in a house in the country, La Vallée returns to his position in Champagne for eighteen months, during which he corresponds regularly with madame de Vambures. At the end of this time he and madame de Vambures are invited to the wedding of d'Orsan and madame d'Orville at the d'Orsan country house. La Vallée is given a permanent position in Paris partly, so d'Orsan tells him, thanks to the influence of madame de Vambures. He rushes to thank her, sees on her table his own letters which she has not been quick enough to hide. She confesses she loves him, but asks for time.

One day d'Orsan comes to ask La Vallée's help for a young man whose uncle's death has left him penniless. The young man is none other than Jacob's former 'young master', the nephew of his first employer (part 1). There is a burst of affection on both sides and the young man, Beausson by name, will be given a position in La Vallée's office. Now that La Vallée is rich and established by his own merits and efforts, and not just thanks to her influence, madame de Vambures consents to marry him. There is a triumphal progress, with the d'Orsans and brother Alexandre, to a country estate belonging to the new madame de la Vallée.

Part 8. The story could well have been left at that point, with the principals happily married and most secondary characters accounted for. But X presumably felt obliged to bring the tale down to the exact time indicated by Marivaux at the outset, when the nephews were referred to as grown men, and so he produced a final part full of improbabilities and crowded with unnecessary incident but having the crazy logic of a Feydeau farce. Here begins the grand pairing-off or killing-off.

Wonderful to relate, La Vallée's wife acquires ownership of her husband's home village and the local manor house. There, in an atmosphere of Rousseau-like rustic rejoicing, La Vallée's sister, the prettiest of all, most surprisingly becomes a close friend of her new sister-in-law. A momentary cloud is the resentment of a haughty local worthy named

Vainsac at having to treat a former village lad as his social superior, but this is quickly disposed of because (a) old father La Vallée reminds him, in a flood of patois, that his grandfather and himself were peasants together and (b) it is revealed that Vainsac and La Vallée's sister are in love. Their marriage coincides more or less with the news of the death of Alexandre's horrible wife in Paris.

Sixteen years pass, and the La Vallées have two sons and a daughter. Beausson is now in a senior position and virtually a member of the family. La Vallée's elder nephew has a position in Beausson's office and the younger wants to be an officer. La Vallée's own sons differ markedly in character, the elder being bright, keen and hard-working, the younger equally intelligent but given to introspection and melancholy. The daughter discourages many admirers and languishes. For a moment, owing to a misunderstanding, La Vallée thinks that it is his elder nephew who is in love with his daughter, and this gives rise to a scene which Marivaux himself would have approved of. Forgetting all his own experience, La Vallée is horrified at the thought of such a misalliance for his daughter, and upbraids his nephew for his presumption. But a short maternal enquiry shows that their daughter does not love her cousin. Thereupon La Vallée calls into play his old skill as an eavesdropper, and overhears in the garden declarations of love between Beausson and his daughter. In due course these two are happily married. Meanwhile it is revealed that the elder nephew and his cousin, La Vallée's elder son, are in love with two sisters who live in Paris. These are none other than the mesdemoiselles de Fécour, nieces of La Vallée's former admirer, whose death has left them immensely rich. In the fullness of time this foursome is happily married also.

This leaves only La Vallée's younger son unaccounted for, the thoughtful, melancholy one. We now learn that at the surprising age of about sixteen the boy has decided to abjure the world and the flesh and enter a religious order, and the boy's mother endorses his decision. The final episode of this crowded sequel is not the least astonishing. The step his son has taken, and some conversation with monks in the house where he is serving his novitiate, give La Vallée very serious doubts about the morality of some of the events of his own youth, and after making over his Paris house and his affairs to his elder son he retires with his wife to the country and the tranquillity of a God-fearing old age. This retirement, we are told on the last page, happened about twenty years ago.

The author of a sequel has to offer plausible solutions or imitations of plot, construction, motivation, manner and style. Marivaux sets X, the anonymous sequellist, a task which he fulfils with an odd mixture of skill and clumsiness. The first and most obvious thing is the difference of attitude between the two towards the technique of construction, particularly as it concerns time and chronology. Of course X's coincidences are no more specious than those of Marivaux, but the manner of dealing with them is quite different. Marivaux never loses sight of the importance of forestalling the reader's scepticism—indeed it is one of his most striking characteristics that he seldom lets himself be caught out, even if it means inventing a very tall story. X, on the other hand, just throws in coincidences unprepared and unexplained, such as madame de Vambures's happening to have recently inherited her husband's native village, and the two boys being in love with nieces of madame de Fécour.

But more significant is the chronology. Marivaux is notoriously vague about details of chronology, and we are never quite certain at any time how many hours or days have elapsed, or just how old Jacob or Marianne may be—Jacob gives himself different ages at times demonstrably only a few hours or a few days apart. One is reminded of puzzlement about the age of Proust's Narrator. But, as in Proust, time in Marivaux moves very slowly indeed, and the infinitely subtle psychological game of chess, spread over many pages and possibly hours of reading, may represent mental processes happening in a mere moment of time. By contrast X usually packs in events and makes his characters rush hither and thither, or suddenly announces that eighteen months or sixteen years have passed, without any action, psychological or otherwise, except the ageing of the people; but he does clearly mark the passage of time. It is possible by a rough calculation to establish that the writer of these memoirs, left by Marivaux at the age of about twenty, must be about sixty.

Similarly in the matter of motivation X is sometimes rudimentary but at others super-ficially skilful, especially at dodging challenges left by Marivaux. The situation at the end of part 5 could be resolved in several ways. Until almost the end of what Marivaux wrote it looks as though all is set for Jacob to lose his wife, achieve a position and wealth thanks to the friendship of d'Orsan and eventually marry madame d'Orville, whose sick husband is clearly not long for this world. But all this is complicated, still in the authentic text of Marivaux, by d'Orsan's showing great interest in madame d'Orville. Which leaves three very interesting possibilities: (a) tragedy, in which La Vallée and d'Orsan, in love with the same woman, become *frères ennemis,* (b) high comedy, with a *Rodogune* situation in which the two vie with each other in self-effacing nobility so that the better man may win, or (c) farce of various kinds, such as the ludicrous situation in *Les Caves du Vatican* in which the two men, in love with the same woman, agree that the winner will not consummate the marriage in order to remain faithful to his dear friend. Faced with these possibilities what does X do? He avoids the whole issue by inventing a new character, madame de Vambures, with whom La Vallée falls in love at first sight and while his own wife is still very much alive. It will thus be simple to kill off madame de la Vallée and M. d'Orville and achieve a delightful foursome who will be happy ever after.

In like manner X avoids other promises made by Marivaux. For example, with his almost infallible skill in anticipating quibbles in the reader's mind, Marivaux is careful, in painting the elaborate portrait of madame de Fécour, to make it plausible by Jacob's hastening to explain that of course he did not take all this in at his first brief meeting with the lady but is filling in the details from his later knowledge of her. But there is little 'later knowledge' either in the novel or the sequel, for after that first short interview Jacob saw her only twice and for short periods when she was ill in bed and usually other people were present. And of course the very last words of part 5 are a promise of a long digression about the Comédie Française and its actors, which X dispatches in a word or two, explaining that La Vallée was too confused by his neighbours and dazzled by the lovely madame de Vambures in her box to take anything else in.

Yet, specious though all that may be, X is in the tradition of the Marivaux novel by making class differences or snobbery the prime motive and indeed the unity of theme right through the sequel, and here, like Marivaux, he goes beyond local social conditions to universal human truth; for whatever we pretend, we are all conscious of class (though many disguise this with the jargons of economics, sociology, psychology and other so-called sciences). At the party, early in part 6, d'Orsan tactfully draws his new friend into a quiet room to save him from the embarrassment of having to betray his ignorance of card games to the fashionable throng;[9] madame d'Orsan *mère* refuses her consent to her son's marriage to a woman from the petty country squirearchy until, after eighteen months, she has recognised the true worth of madame d'Orville; madame de Vambures, though she has confessed her love, will not marry La Vallée so long as he is under any obligation to her, realising that a husband must have the self-respect that comes from a social position due to his own intelligence and character. Contrasted with these wise manifestations of class awareness (only wild ideological romantics like George Sand could imagine that a marriage between the village artisan and the high-born lady could ever survive the boredom of having nothing whatsoever in common except socialist theory) are the absurdities of the dinner party given by the newly-rich Bonos, the ridiculous behaviour of the pompous Vainsac and the stupid snobbery of the nephews who are ashamed of their father and change their name. Finally there is the successful synthesis on X's part of the good and bad and of the universal and local aspects of this fact of life in La Vallée's horror and prompt reaction on learning that his nephew, the son of a peasant, should dare to aspire to the hand of his daughter. This is worthy of Marivaux's own sense of humour, but perhaps Jacob would have justified himself with subtler casuistry than M. de la Vallée. Of course it might be argued on X's behalf that it is a good point and humanly true to make La Vallée fail to learn from his earlier experiences as Jacob. But this is where X fails as a sequellist. He should be imitating his model, and if Marivaux's Marianne and Jacob have one quality which distinguishes them from characters in contemporary fiction (*Les Égarements du cœur* is later, and Crébillon *fils* was not above stealing things from Marivaux or anyone else) it is precisely that they do learn by experience. All the art of Marivaux is there, in the continuous process of self-education and self-adjustment which warns them of dangers ahead and saves them from ever committing the same mistake twice.

In all these generalities about time and construction I have suggested that the reader of the sequel would be justified in saying sometimes that this is rubbish that Marivaux would never have committed to paper, but sometimes that it might possibly be by Marivaux, or if not Marivaux a conscientious and plausible imitator who is sometimes lacking in taste and anxious to show how clever he is. It is tempting to draw up a balance-sheet, listing on one side the 'good' parts and on the other the 'bad'. But it is not as simple as that because, like Jacob himself in parts 1 to 5, this sequel is ambiguous, with some good in the bad and some bad in the good. Nevertheless it is possible to look first at elements which are at least reasonably successful imitations or pastiches of the externals of Marivaux.

Here is a tolerable imitation of the typical Marivaux treatment of the *identification* of love. At the beginning of part 7, d'Orsan tells his friend La Vallée that he feels he is in love with madame d'Orville:

A cette ouverture que crut me faire M. d'Orsan et à laquelle il ne douta pas de me voir prendre part, je ne répondis que par un *Nous y voilà, je m'y attendais!* Il parut étonné de mon exclamation, qui fut sans doute cause du silence qu'il garda.

Il faut pourtant convenir que ce silence pouvait avoir un autre motif, et la suite le fera croire. C'est l'ordinaire du cœur qui, pour la première fois, trouve jour à sortir de son secret, d'être satisfait d'avoir pu faire soupçonner ses sentiments; et, quand il obtient cet avantage, il n'a pas ordinairement la force de passer outre.[10]

Similarly taken over from Marivaux's dramatic technique, as well as from the story of the litigant in part 4, is this little study of jealousy:

Et quel est cet homme si bien intentionné? me demanda le comte d'Orsan avec un visage qui' quoique contraint, semblait me marquer quelque inquiétude.

Je ne me trompai pas à son mouvement; je le pris pour une impression de jalousie, et je crus de mon devoir de ne pas tarder à effacer un sentiment qui faisait ou pouvait faire quelque tort à Mme de Dorville (*sic*) dans l'esprit de ce seigneur. Je ne puis cependant m'empêcher de faire attention à cette bizarrerie de l'homme amoureux: à peine commence-t-il à aimer que tout l'alarme; son ombre seule, vue à l'improviste, est capable de l'agiter. L'amour serait-il donc un sentiment de l'âme, quand tout son effet est d'en déranger l'assiette et d'en troubler la tranquillité? Voilà une réflexion que je fais la plume à la main; car alors, ne voyant que la gloire de la dame dont nous parlions, je répondis sur-le-champ [. . .].[11]

Most people would agree that the weakest part of the sequel is the 8th, in which not only does X multiply mere happenings at the expense of interplay of character until we have a breathless series of events, but he also appears, at first glance, to pander to the fashion of the age, the age that rapturously applauded the vapid *Devin du Village* and loved the sentimental rustic pictures of Greuze. Yet into this idyll there is suddenly thrown a relentless searchlight of psychological realism worthy of the master himself and significantly expressed in the words of an intelligent woman, La Vallée's wife, the former madame de Vambures:

En effet, me disait-elle quelquefois, la conduite qu'on doit tenir à la ville ou à la campagne est bien différente. Dans la première on pense, et la politesse gagne un cœur que la vanité révolte; mais dans la seconde, l'homme, tout entier à son orgueil, se croit resserré mal à propos dans un coin de la terre: son âme, impatiente de ne pouvoir donner carrière à sa vaine gloire, n'attend qu'un objet pour lui faire prendre son essor. Il croit par là se dédommager de l'injustice que lui fait la société.[12]

So much for Jean-Jacques and the uplifting effects of rustic solitude. And the writer of this thought has carefully studied his Marivaux:

On sait, d'après ma conversation chez le président, qu'en parlant j'ai l'usage d'étudier les contenances et les yeux des personnes auxquelles j'adresse la parole.[. . .][13]

Here is an adroit adaptation of the Marivaux 'surprise' theory of love to the rather crude 'nature is always right' theme which X develops in other places:

La jeune dame, dont chaque mot portait dans mon cœur un trait de flamme auquel je me livrais sans songer, (mais quand j'y aurais pensé, mon mariage m'aurait-il détourné? Non, non; c'est la nature qui nous rend amoureux; elle nous entraîne malgré nous, et nous lui obéissons souvent sans y consentir, et le plus ordinairement avec la surprise d'avoir été si loin): cette dame prit la parole [. . .][14]

Or again, here is another pastiche of the Marivaux manner:

Ne parlons point de mon cœur, me dit-elle. Ah! repris-je, c'est le seul bien que j'ambitionne. Votre bouche refuserait-elle de me confirmer le bonheur que j'ai cru lire dans vos lettres?

Et quand cela serait? . . . dit-elle en baissant les yeux. Je sentis tout mon avantage. Si cela était, madame, dis-je avec vivacité, l'état où m'ont mis vos bontés ne me permettrait-il pas quelque espoir? Elle paraissait rêver profondément. Daignez vous expliquer à un homme qui vous adore. Les sentiments que vous m'avez fait connaître, cette indifférence sur les titres, sur les grandeurs, sur la naissance même, tout fait ici l'excuse de ma témérité. Je vous aime, je suis libre: mon nom ne vous révolte point. J'ose vous demander . . . Arrêtez, me dit-elle, ne pensons qu'à votre arrangement; il y a de quoi nous occuper. Quand il sera fini, je vous permettrai de me consulter sur autre chose; mais jusque-là je vous prie de ne m'en point parler.

Ces dernières paroles furent prononcées avec une espèce de timidité qui m'aurait fort embarrassé, si les yeux ne m'eussent au plus tôt rassuré.[15]

But when X introduces one of these plausible imitations he usually does so by taking over intact a theme already developed by Marivaux in the authentic text, and then he spoils it by a serious lapse of taste. Having fallen genuinely in love with madame de Vambures, La Vallée returns, very late, to his elderly wife. There follows a restatement of the theme that no passion can compare with that of an ageing woman deprived of satisfaction by years of pious chastity and, moreover, that this particular woman's young husband proved himself extremely satisfying in bed because he was able to concentrate his mind upon other females with ampler charms:

Venez, mon cher, me dit-elle; vous aurez le temps de me dire le reste. Que Dieu est bon de vous avoir préservé de ce péril! Pendant cette exclamation, j'avais achevé de me déshabiller; et ma chère épouse, oubliant mes dangers et les grâces que j'avais reçues de la Providence, ne pensa qu'à se certifier que son mari existait. Je ne lui donnai pas lieu d'en douter. Que d'actions de grâces ne rendait-elle pas à Dieu intérieurement d'avoir délivré son époux des mains des trois assassins![16]

So far so good as an imitation of what Marivaux had done in part 4. But then follows a shocking piece of bad taste. Whereas Marivaux's Jacob had freely admitted that his sexual performance had been improved by visions of two females, Ferval and Fécour, both built on voluptuous lines but whom he did not love, X's La Vallée goes on to ascribe his physical prowess to thoughts of madame de Vambures to whom, he explains, he has already given his heart, and his explanation is weak in the extreme:

J'avouerai que, si elle avait lu dans mon cœur, elle y aurait découvert que Mme de Vambures méritait de partager sa reconnaissance.[17]

But worse follows, for he then flounders about and loses himself in distinctions he tries to draw between true love and mere lust:

Telle charmante que m'ait paru Mme de Vambures, telle profonde que fût l'impression qu'elle m'avait faite, j'avouerai nûment que les charmes que je goûtais dans les bras de ma femme me rendaient infidèle à l'amour que je sentais pour la première.

Que le cœur de l'homme est incompréhensible! Je n'avais pas quitté le lit, que l'idée de mon épouse céda dans mon esprit à celle de mon amante, et je redevins tout autre.[18]

And then, far, far worse, a mere half-page later on the morning after this night of vigorous love, La Vallée is setting off to see madame de Fécour:

J'allais partir, quand Mme de la Vallée me pria de revenir au plus tôt, d'autant plus qu'elle se trouvait un peu indisposée. Je n'aurais pas cru que cette indisposition, qui ne consistait que dans un léger mal de tête que j'attribuais à l'insomnie [not to be wondered at], allait me préparer bien de l'embarras, en m'ouvrant une nouvelle route pour venir à la fortune.[19]

So that to psychological crudity X adds literary clumsiness by taking up Marivaux's earlier hint that madame de la Vallée had not long to live and turning this into the abrupt statement that, dear reader, we are now about to kill off La Vallée's elderly and unattractive wife so that, after the regrettable nuisance of having to wind up his late wife's affairs, he may speedily find true love and fortune.

It would seem that X had one thing firmly in mind: that Marivaux was a master of subtle and complicated analysis of love and that he, X, must try to stress the illogicalities, the self-searchings and self-deceptions, self-justifications and casuistries to which love gives rise. But as he lacked taste and judgement he sometimes failed to see the nastiness of what he was saying. Shortly after leaving his own sick wife La Vallée pays his call on madame de Fécour and finds her mortally ill. She herself says she may die. Then follows this little scene:

Bannissez, madame, lui dis-je vivement, cette idée qui me pénètre de douleur. Le pauvre enfant, dit-elle, il s'attendrit! En prononçant ces mots, elle avança ses bras vers moi; j'allai au-devant, et je lui imprimai ma bouche sur cette grosse gorge, dont je ne pouvais me détacher, quand un bruit imprévu m'obligea de me retirer.[20]

And the obligatory 'reflection':

Ce mouvement ne peut sûrement point être attribué à l'amour. J'étais touché de l'idée de la mort dont m'avait parlé cette dame, à laquelle j'avais des obligations. La gratitude qu'elle me témoignait pour mon attendrissement fit seule tout l'effet qu'on vient de voir. Il est souvent des caractères d'amour qui échappent, et qu'on donne ou qu'on reçoit par reconnaissance ou par quelque autre motif, sans que le cœur y entre pour rien.[21]

On the face of it this whole sequence of events is horrible and out of place. Yet one wonders whether X, in his anxiety to reproduce the psychological subtleties of his model, is fumbling towards something akin to the pathetic or even the sublime in the apparently grotesque. Love, or at least sympathy and kindness, can be found in the most unlikely places.

Perhaps we are on firmer ground when it comes to the form and style of the sequel. If for brief moments it is possible to recognise features of the psychological landscape that remind one of some of Marivaux's processes, some of the language reads like a parody of eighteenth-century style at its most conventional, heavy and humourless. The two or three examples that follow are by no means the only ones, and their presence here no doubt says as much about the writer of this article as about their intrinsic quality, but they do not seem to me to bear the stamp of Marivaux.

Towards the end of part 7 d'Orsan confesses to La Vallée that he is in love with madame d'Orville and that he thinks his love is returned. La Vallée feels the same about madame de Vambures, but in his case there is the little matter that his own wife is still alive, though (fortunately) her health is deteriorating. Then follows this mumbo-jumbo:

Si je pris part à sa joie comme le méritait l'amitié dont il m'honorait, j'avoue que la réflexion me fit payer cher ce sentiment; car je me représentai que rien ne paraissait me permettre un semblable espoir. Néanmoins, je lui proposai d'aller ensemble chez Mme de Vambures.

On sera surpris que je n'y aie pas encore paru; l'étonnement cessera dès qu'on sera attention qu'ennemi déclaré de toute dissimulation, je devais redouter un tête-à-tête avec cette dame.[22]

Or again, could anything be less convincing than this fragment of conversation between husband and wife after they have been told that their nephew possesses a portrait of their daughter and have a momentary suspicion that the cousins are in love. The wife, who has interrogated their daughter, speaks first:

[. . .] Voilà ce qui doit nous tranquilliser, et la petite personne n'a certainement pas pu m'en imposer.

Ce que vous me dites, répondis-je à mon épouse, s'accorde assez avec ce que m'a avoué mon neveu; mais suivant ce que vous me rapportez, ma fille paraît ignorer la passion qu'elle a fait naître, et cependant mon neveu m'a déclaré qu'elle connaissait les sentiments qu'il avait pour elle.

Je conviens que cette circonstance m'alarme comme vous, reprit cette dame; mais peut-être cet aveu n'est-il que déplacé dans son récit. Je vais suivre le détail de mes découvertes et vous en jugerez . . . J'ai cru m'apercevoir, ajouta-t-elle, que votre fille aimait; mais quel est l'objet de cette tendresse, je n'ai pu le savoir. Ses soupirs m'ont plus instruit que ses paroles.[23]

For formal pomposity this exchange yields nothing to any third-rate imitation of Corneille. But here, a few pages later, comes the grand confrontation scene. La Vallée, determined to have the matter out with his nephew, goes very early in the morning to the young man's bedroom:

Quelle est donc votre conduite, lui dis-je? Ni votre père, ni moi, nous ne vous voyons plus. Conserveriez-vous encore une flamme dont la honte vous empêcherait de soutenir notre présence?

Non, mon oncle, me dit-il. Daignez même m'épargner un reproche dont les charmes de ma cousine sont seuls l'excuse. Vos conseils ont fait une impression sur moi à laquelle je ne me croyais pas capable d'obéir. Je rends justice à votre fille: mais je lui suis infidèle.

Est-ce être infidèle, repris-je vivement, que de devenir raisonnable? mais, si je prends bien le sens de votre discours, un autre objet vous captive: en êtes-vous aimé?

Oui, mon oncle, répondit-il, et votre fils aîné aime dans la même maison.[24]

Although early in his sequel X scorns what he calls the old-fashioned custom of painting portraits of characters in a novel (one of Marivaux's triumphs):

[. . .] peindre les caractères, c'est rebattre ce qu'on a presque toujours dit. Il suffit de les connaître en gros; le détail sort ordinairement du fond du naturel,[25]

yet in due course, after some promises, he treats us to a portrait of madame de Vambures. For all it tells us about the appearance of the lady he might have saved himself the trouble. Consider the utter banality of the descriptive words italicised:

J'ai promis son portrait et le voici naturellement placé. Elle était d'une taille *haute* et *avantageuse*. Ses cheveux châtains étaient si *parfaitement placés* qu'ils semblaient s'arranger d'eux-mêmes pour faire sortir un front majestueux dont la grandeur était tempérée par deux yeux qui, malgré leur *éclat*, paraissaient inspirer la confiance, et manifestaient un *pétillant* dans l'esprit dont la réalité était capable d'enchanter. Je conviendrai que le visage était un peu long, mais ce défaut était réparé par *les plus belles couleurs du monde.* Sa bouche était *mignonne,* et *la mieux garnie* qu'on pût voir. Elle avait la main *charmante* et la gorge *admirable.*

Je ne puis mieux donner une idée de son esprit qu'en avouant avec ingénuité que, dès que j'eus connu la *justesse* de son discernement et la *sagesse* de ses réflexions etc.[26]

In all that has so far been said it might be possible to allege that X tried, however clumsily or unsuccessfully, to imitate his model. But in one aspect he is distressingly wrong. Never did Marivaux try to underline moral issues or the triumph of virtue and confounding of evil. He was far too much of a realist and had far too acute a sense of humour to want to modify plots or warp characters in the interests of morality. It happens that Climal's schemes do not prosper, nor do the elder mademoiselle Habert and her spiritual director succeed, but it is also true that the happy endings for Marianne and Jacob (as far as we can see Marivaux's intentions) are due as much to their intelligence and dexterity as to their virtue. But in 1756 X lived in the age of sentimental virtue, and he does not allow us to forget it. Besides, he had an eye on the sales.

But even in this respect X does sometimes have a good idea. We learn, for instance, at the absurd dinner party given by M. Bono, of the entirely suitable fate of madame de Ferval. This hypocritical old voluptuary has married her Chevalier who, once he has got his hands on her money, has dropped her. Her end is not contrived; like madame de Merteuil some thirty years later, she is hoist with her own petard.

Nothing, however, can excuse the lamentable moral sentimentality of the end or the perhaps unconscious humour of La Vallée's edifying last word. Impressed by the piety of his younger son, who has entered the priesthood, he has himself seen the vanity of his earlier ambitions and at sixty is freed from the thraldom of desire and has found peace in a godly life (with a safe income):

On a dû le reconnaître: personne n'a poussé la fortune plus loin; mais qui étais-je alors? Un cœur tyrannisé de désirs, qui ne sentait point son malheur, parce qu'il n'y faisait point attention; mais ici les souhaits sont étouffés, et je suis heureux, parce que je vois plus clairement mon bonheur. C'est, je crois, la seule félicité qui puisse satisfaire l'homme véritablement raisonnable.[27]

How can the utterer of these pious platitudes be the man who at the same time has written everything that comes before.? For the fiction is that in late middle age the narrator has just written out the full story of his life. What has happened to Jacob's self-knowledge, his sense of humour, his shrewd common sense, his subtlety? Where is Marivaux?

Having for over forty years watched with some amusement the ebb and flow and even complete U-turns of fashionable critical opinion about artists and authors, may I indulge in a little fantasy? Suppose that some piece of irrefutable evidence, such as a letter to his publisher, came to light and proved that the sequel was undoubtedly written by Marivaux himself? Wouldn't it be interesting to watch us all wriggling out of it? Like Aldous Huxley's Miss Thriplow each one would decide to change by rapid but imperceptible degrees from a salamander sporting amid the flames into a primrose by the river's brim.[28] How Marivaux, who spent so much time depicting precisely such exercises in self-adjustment and sail-trimming, would laugh, or rather smile!

NOTES

1 Marivaux, *Le Paysan parvenu*, edited by F. Deloffre (Classiques Garnier, 1965), pp. xxvii–xxxi.
2 *Œuvres Complettes de M. de Marivaux*, de L'Académie Françoise. Tome Huitième. A Paris, Chez la Veuve Duchesne, Libraire, rue Saint-Jacques, au Temple du Goût. M.DCC.LXXXI. 690 pp.
3 In volumes VII and VIII.
4 F. C. Green, *French Novelists, Manners and Ideas* (London, 1928), p. 107.
5 Deloffre, op. cit., p. xxvii.
6 E. J. H. Greene, *Marivaux* (University of Toronto Press, 1965).
7 *The Eighteenth-Century French Novel* (Manchester University Press, 1965). The sub-title of Miss Mylne's book is *Techniques of Illusion*.
8 Robert Niklaus, *The Eighteenth Century: 1715–1789* (London, 1970, being volume 4 of *A Literary History of France*). The note is on p. 109.
9 p. 297. All textual references are to the Deloffre edition.
10 329–30.
11 332.
12 386.
13 409.
14 295.
15 374–5.
16 304–5.
17 305.
18 ibid.
19 306.
20 310–11.
21 311.
22 364–5.
23 416
24 423.
25 293.
26 375.
27 433.
28 In *Those Barren Leaves*, quoted from memory.

Voltaire and the Question of Law and Order in the Eighteenth Century: Locke against Hobbes

ROBERT S. TATE

I am, of course, aware that in choosing as my subject Voltaire on law and order I shall be accused of grasping for relevance. And indeed, in this day of symposia on racism in the eighteenth century and conferences on feminism in French literature, such an accusation would not come as a surprise (in fact, its absence would be a surprise). But the mutual relationship of law and order is one of the classic problems of human existence, and in the Western world philosophers since Plato have felt obliged to incorporate thoughts on this subject into their systems. Today, as we all know, 'law and order' has become a kind of code word for racism, conservatism, and political repression of dissident elements in our society. But those who so use the phrase are not always aware that they may be committing an intellectual lapsus, and that these two terms, far from making comfortable bedfellows, exist in a reciprocal relationship of mutual tension, as I shall attempt to show. In the context of this present-day confusion, it might be well to glance backward to see how this problem was handled in the eighteenth century, and most particularly in the works of François-Marie Arouet de Voltaire.

In studies of Voltaire as a political animal it is still almost *de rigueur* to say that, unlike his contemporaries Montesquieu and Rousseau, he left us no compact theoretical treatise and that we are therefore obliged to piece together a unified picture from a wide variety of scattered, disparate writings. But we have, I think, come a long way since the day the fatuous Faguet launched his famous phrase against our author as thinker: 'Ce grand esprit, c'est un chaos d'idées claires'.[1] I should like to be able to offer, by way of background, a full review of the various attempts that have been made to unravel the mysteries of Voltaire's politics. Such a review would touch upon excellent studies by Gustave Lanson,[2] Henri Sée,[3] Daniel Mornet,[4] Kingsley Martin,[5] Merle L. Perkins,[6] Renée Waldinger,[7] and John N. Pappas.[8] But space does not permit such a survey. Let me therefore content myself with a brief discussion of three of the most important contributions to our understanding of this subject in the past decade or so—those of Peter Gay, René Pomeau, and Theodore Besterman.

In 1959 Peter Gay first published what is still the most authoritative book on this topic, his *Voltaire's Politics: The Poet as Realist*.[9] Moving beyond the work of his predecessor G. Lanson, Professor Gay has laid to final rest the old notion, inherited from the German Romantics through Taine, Faguet and de Tocqueville, of Voltaire as a vapid, airy spirit flitting from issue to issue like a bee from flower to flower, a proponent of 'abstract, literary politics', a misguided believer in 'infallible rationality'. 'These then are the politics of Voltaire', writes Gay in opening his final chapter (p. 309), 'realistic and serious but rarely solemn, reformist and hopeful but rarely abstract', and he makes his point with merciless logic and dazzling lucidity. Yet I can only agree with Theodore Besterman's remark that this is 'a selective biography of Voltaire, not a systematic and technical analysis'.[10] Further-more, Gay has a brilliant thesis which, in my opinion, he pushes too far: his Voltaire is the life-long defender, on *pragmatic* rather than doctrinal grounds, of the *thèse royale* for France, the belief that the central government could best work modernizing reform in spite of the stubborn resistance of decadent nobles and most particularly of the 'reactionary' law courts (*parlements*), the alleged chief spokesmen of the *thèse nobiliaire*. (I shall return to this point shortly, but meanwhile it should be understood that I am not launching a full, frontal assault on Gay's solid study, but only attempting a relatively minor corrective.) In the second volume of his two-volume interpretation of the Enlightenment, Professor Gay has resumed his savage attack on Montesquieu as basically a conservative old toady and on the 'reactionary, selfish, divisive, irresponsible, superstitious, and intolerant' *parle-ments*.[11] Gay definitely writes out of a *parti pris*, namely, that those who opposed the central administration in eighteenth-century France must have been either fools or knaves. He has given us what I am tempted to call the 'Roosevelt-Truman-Kennedy' history of the Enlightenment in its political aspects, a history eminently suited to the liberal, hopeful early 60s but weirdly out of tune with the confused early 70s. His chapter headings are illustrative in this regard. He writes of the 'Recovery of Nerve' in the Enlightenment at a time when many of us are losing our nerve; of the 'Science of Man' at a time when many doubt that man can be studied 'scientifically'; of the 'Politics of Decency' in a time of indecency in politics. His very subtitle—*The Science of Freedom*—sounds odd now that we seem to be undergoing a new 'faillite de la science', and when many feel they are losing their freedoms. How quickly does history sour; but 'revenons à nos moutons'.

In 1963 the eminent Voltairean scholar René Pomeau, author of *La Religion de Voltaire* (1956, 1969), published a useful anthology of Voltaire's political writings.[12] In his admirable 'Présentation' (pp. 7–51), Pomeau corrects Gay's geographical relativism (which has it that Voltaire favoured 'enlightened despotism' for Russia, 'constitutional absolutism' for France, 'liberal republicanism' for Geneva) by positing a doctrinal element in Voltaire's royalism, revolving as it did around three 'centers of gravity': l'antichristianisme, un activisme autoritaire, un humanisme libéral' (p. 36). For Pomeau it is the struggle to 'crush the infamous thing' which gives unity to the vicissitudes of Voltaire's politics. Unfortunately, this critic does not manage to liberate himself entirely from the pernicious label 'despotisme éclairé', any more than had Kingsley Martin writing years before in his *French Liberal Thought in the Eighteenth Century*. Now, to my mind this term constitutes an unstable and unacceptable oxymoron, a *non-sens* in the eighteenth-century context if we choose at all to look through the *optique* of Montesquieu and his followers, for whom 'despotisme' could not possibly be 'éclairé'. But we are dealing here with a compendium of texts, not with a systematic analysis, and the puzzled reader lays it down feeling that something of the chaos remains.

It was perhaps in order to clear up some of the confusion that Theodore Besterman published in 1965 his article on 'Voltaire, Absolute Monarchy, and the Enlightened Monarch', since republished as a chapter of his *Voltaire* of 1969.[13] Besterman states, quite correctly I think, that the twin principles of love of justice and belief in reason underlay all of Voltaire's political activities and that these principles fused into a respect for law as the basis of civilization. Besterman's Voltaire is, as we shall see, the Lockean Voltaire. But this brief study is perforce far richer in suggestions than in solutions; furthermore, Besterman fails to transcend Gay's strong bias against the *parlement*, nor does he deal with the ambiguities involved in Voltaire's conflict with the law courts, which he, unlike Gay, cautiously identifies with democracy!

Studies on Voltaire's politics have not stopped appearing since the publication of Besterman's *Voltaire*. Recently, Jean Sareil has given us highly detailed studies, in the respectable Lansonian tradition, of 'Voltaire et le cardinal de Fleury' and of Voltaire's ill-fated diplomatic mission to Prussia in 1743.[14] But it is so far hard to see what all this digging and picking will lead to by way of general conclusions. Meanwhile, there seems to be room for one more attempt to bring order out of chaos. But I feel compelled to reiterate what I said in opening a talk on Voltaire and the *parlements* at Nancy in 1971: the present essay will not invalidate René Pomeau's remark of 1955: 'Tout n'est pas dit [. . .] sur la politique de Voltaire'.[15]

Now, as Voltaire did not write in a vacuum, it might be well to review briefly some of the other positions in eighteenth-century France with respect to the law and order question. The recent publication by Professor Lester Crocker of a new anthology of eighteenth-century French literature[16] affords us a unique opportunity to get a fresh and composite view of the moral and political thought of the major *Philosophes*. Using Professor Crocker's textbook as a base, I should like to try a little experiment. (And, like any experimenter, whether he be involved with *sciences physiques* or *sciences humaines,* I must be prepared to see the experiment fail.) I believe that the political thought of the French Enlightenment crystallized around two conflicting poles defined by two Englishmen of the previous century, Thomas Hobbes and John Locke, and that it is possible to group the leading *philosophes* into two opposing camps, one basically optimistic and which I shall call 'Lockean', the other essentially pessimistic and which I shall call 'Hobbesian'. (Indeed, I think it would even be possible to challenge Professor Crocker's view, expressed in *Nature and Culture,* of a three-stage chronological development in the Enlightenment from natural law through utilitarianism to moral nihilism in favour of a view which would see two mutually antagonistic currents running in parallel.) I should like to use 'Lockean' and

T

'Hobbesian' as shorthand or symbols, designating rather more tendencies than frozen doctrines. We must be prepared to speak of 'legendary Hobbesianism' and 'legendary Lockeanism' somewhat apart from the literal scripture of their progenitors. One further *caveat* is in order: I shall, of course, be concerned with the political (and to some extent the moral) thought of Locke and Hobbes and not with their total systems, which encompass a logic, a metaphysic, an æsthetic. Granted these limitations, I shall designate as 'Lockean' the following set of assumptions: that man is basically sociable, not antisocial, and that therefore the state of nature tends toward harmony not war; that the function of government is to limit itself to the protection of those human rights deemed natural and inalienable—right of free speech, of worship, *and* of property; that there is an agreement between ruler and people such that if the Prince violates the bargain, the people have the right to overturn him by violent revolution; finally, that there is an *a priori,* rational standard for judging positive or specific laws, so that there may indeed be 'unjust laws'.[17]

Turn the coin over and you have the gloomier face of 'Hobbesianism'—the view that human nature is basically perverted; that in the Great Chain of Beings which runs from the animals through man to the angels and on to God, man is closer to the beasts than to the angels; that therefore the state of nature is a state of war; that men, if left alone, will devour each other and that therefore the all-powerful authority of an omnipotent sovereign is needed to keep order and prevent anarchy; that the people have no right whatsoever to overthrow or even seriously challenge the ruler; and that Justice follows rather than precedes Law, so that Might makes Right and there is no such thing as an 'unjust law'.[18] In the eighteenth century in France it was Thomas Hobbes, far more than Jean Cauvin (whom we know as John Calvin) who was associated with this bleak view of man. We are dealing here of course with eternally 'relevant' questions. Does man have an innate sense of fair play or does he not? These questions are not of course dead to the twentieth century: behind the horrors of Nazism we glimpse the gloomy ghost of Hobbes. In the eighteenth century, as today, the Lockean view generally lent itself to a liberal political position, the Hobbesian to a conservative stance. Given a choice between law and order, the Lockean will, in a crunch, come down on the side of *individual liberties,* the Hobbesian on that of *collective security.*

Now, among the *Philosophes* I would range the following in the Lockean camp: Montesquieu, Diderot, d'Holbach, and Condorcet. Montesquieu hardly needs justification in this respect, for he gave the clearest exposition of the Lockean position of constitutional monarchy in the early eighteenth century in France. He even went beyond the strict empiricism of the master in positing a universal sense of justice in man. 'Voilà, Rhédi,' writes Usbek in the *Lettres persanes,* 'ce qui m'a fait penser que la justice est éternelle et ne dépend point des conventions humaines; et quand elle en dépendrait, ce serait une vérité terrible, qu'il faudrait se dérober à soi-même' (Crocker, *Anthologie,* p. 87). Central to Montesquieu's work is an attack on Hobbes's justification of absolutism (the latter was of course concerned with justifying the Stuarts against Parliament) and an insistence upon the need for power checking power. Where the *président* may be faulted is not, as Voltaire thought, in positing virtue as the principle of democracy and honor as that of monarchies, for he made it perfectly clear that by virtue he meant, not good morals, but a civic or patriotic spirit, and by honour, not personal probity, but respect for rank and privilege; rather he may be faulted for vesting the responsibility for checking central power in certain corporate bodies—the Church, the nobility, the chartered towns, and especially the *parlements* (calculated to arouse Gay's ire)—and for his seemingly so unmodern idealization of feudalism. As one recent critic has put it '[. . .] Montesquieu's ideal was apparently a kind of feudal monarchy tempered by certain parliamentary and individual rights'.[19]

As for Diderot, his case is hardly less ambiguous than that of Voltaire; and this is not surprising, for he was, after all, a complex genius. It may be that some of the articles of the *Encyclopédie* contain bows to an 'enlightened despot', but, as Arthur Wilson has shown,[20] Diderot awoke only belatedly to politics, and when he did, in the late 60s and early 70s, he was thoroughly opposed to despotism in much the same way that Montesquieu was. His *Réfutation* of Helvétius's *De l'homme*, composed in 1773–76 and published in 1875, contains a thoroughgoing condemnation of the 'despote éclairé' *à la Frederick II*, on the grounds that the people must never be lulled into relinquishing their liberties: 'Le gouvernement arbitraire d'un prince juste et éclairé est toujours mauvais'; and he adds in a Lockean vein that the 'droit d'opposition, tout insensé qu'il est, est sacré [. . .]'. (Crocker, p. 416). And his *Observations* on education written for Catherine of Russia (pub. 1920) contain an even more vigorous warning of the dangers of tyranny: 'A mesure qu'un peuple perd le sentiment de la liberté et de la propriété, il se corrompt, il s'avilit, il penche vers la servitude' (Crocker, p. 424). Similarly, the politics of Diderot's good friend and associate d'Holbach can only be termed proto-republican. His metaphysics may have been atheistic and materialistic, but his politics were thoroughly libertarian and Lockean. His two-pronged attack on both Church *and* State is carried out in the name of individual liberties; as Professor Crocker puts it, d'Holbach 'exige la protection des individus et de leurs biens et la liberté d'expression' (p. 516). Finally, this Lockean current culminates at the end of the century in the *Esquisse* of Condorcet, who gives quasi-mathematical expression to the Enlightenment's faith in progress and gradual amelioration through reason, and in the *Déclaration des droits de l'homme* of 1789, a kind of compendium of all the liberal arguments for human dignity and individual rights.

The current of Hobbesian pessimism, passing through the political conservatism, rooted in profound scepticism, of Pierre Bayle, finds full expression in the writings of La Mettrie, Helvétius, Rousseau, and Sade. La Mettrie is ostensibly concerned with metaphysics (i.e., physics) and with psychology (i.e. physiology), but by his radical pessimism as to the nature of man ('En général les hommes sont nés méchants'—Crocker, p. 157) and by his Hobbesian conviction that there is no good or bad apart from what society considers as such,[21] he prepares the way for later visions of a utopian society based on the total conditioning of the individual. Helvétius, who has often been classed among the liberals, takes the progression a step further. In his *De l'esprit* he reduces all human motivation to the single, overriding principle of self-interest (*intérêt*), and in his posthumously-published *De l'homme* (1772) he outlines an essentially anti-humanistic (as Diderot saw clearly) political view based on the acceptance of the inherent perversity of human nature ('Qui soutient la bonté naturelle des hommes, veut les tromper'—Crocker, p. 513) and on the Hobbist proposition that it is power, not justice, which prevails in human affairs: 'L'amour de l'équité est donc toujours en nous subordonné à l'amour du pouvoir' (Crocker, p. 514).

What of Rousseau? Shall we place him in this grim company? We must reiterate what we said about Diderot, namely, that his complex genius prevents him from fitting neatly into any neat *schéma*; but we *can* speak of prevailing tendencies. And in particular, since the work of Talmon and especially of Lester Crocker, we can no longer rest comfortably with the old image of Rousseau as the liberal champion of individual rights. Professor Crocker's writings on Rousseau are controversial, but I think he has won his point, namely, that at the core of *Émile, La Nouvelle Héloïse*, and *Du Contrat social* lies the plan for a totalitarian political system in which the individual must be conditioned, brainwashed, *dénaturé*, so that he will be able to forsake his *moi individuel* and heed only the collective *moi commun*.[22] We used to think that Rousseau had inverted the Hobbist analysis by blackening society in order to justify nature. Since the work of Crocker we must say that, *like* Hobbes, he blackened nature to the end of justifying his 'new' society. For after all, there is little difference between saying that man has become wicked and saying he is naturally wicked, for, as Rousseau states, human *nature* itself has changed. With Rousseau we quit definitively the world of Lockean reformism, with its conviction that better laws can make better people, in favor of a revolutionary utopianism, in which only a complete 're-education' (and the word has here ominous connotations) can harmonize the conflicting demands of nature and culture. Any doubts as to the collectivist and even totalitarian nature of Rousseau's political thought are dispelled by a reading of his proposed *Constitution* for Corsica and his *Considérations* on Poland (Crocker, pp. 683–9), in which the rights of the individual are completely subordinated to those of the state. Without question, however, this current of Hobbesian pessimism finds its final culmination in the moral nihilism embodied in the novels and tales of the Marquis de Sade. In the horrifying world of Sade the only Right is Might and moreover the strong have a *moral duty to nature* to victimize the weak. If, for Malebranche, 'tout est en Dieu', for Sade *tout est dans la nature*. Sade's dicta needed only await post-1933 Germany to find full realization.

Now, moving to the heart of the matter, where shall we place Voltaire in this scheme? I would contend that the problem is not as simple as it may seem, and that there is a tension in his thought between two conflicting tendencies—order versus freedom—which is perhaps never fully resolved. Critics have often taken note of this ambivalence without making a thorough sounding.[23] Was Voltaire really a fence-sitter on this crucial issue, balancing off *le pour* against *le contre,* as Pomeau[24] and others seem to imply? Surely not, we rejoin, probably because we think immediately of Voltaire the Lockean fighter for justice, tolerance, and individual rights as over against the tyranny, both religious and political, of the *ancien régime*. Although Theodore Besterman tells us rather surprisingly that Voltaire probably had not read the *Two Treatises*,[25] and though he uses Locke explicitly rather more for psychological and epistemological than for political purposes, it cannot be denied that Locke was in the very air Voltaire breathed as the great spokesman of the previous century for political and civil liberties. A strain of 'Lockean' Anglophile liberalism pervades Voltaire's thought from one end of his career to the other, and it is by no means easy to relegate this to any particular period or periods. This point hardly needs driving home, but a few examples chosen from an immense field might be useful in providing a frame of reference. Voltaire's anti-monarchical strain found early formulation in a letter he sent from England on 26 October 1726 to his close friend in France: '. . . I am weary of courts, my dear Tiriot; all that is king, or belongs to a king, frights my republican philosophy, I won't drink the least draught of slavery in the land of liberty'. [26] But the profound impact made by English liberties on the sensibilities of the young poet is perhaps most clearly reflected during this period in the eighth *Lettre philosophique* (1734), in which Voltaire, following Fénelon, says that the English king, 'tout-puissant pour faire du bien, a les mains liées pour faire le mal'.[27] We can find expressions of this Lockeanism even where we might least expect it, for example, in the first *Discours en vers sur l'homme* of 1738, containing the following striking vertical image:

> Ce monde est un grand bal où des fous, déguisés
> Sous les risibles noms d'Éminence et d'Altesse,
> Pensent enfler leur être et hausser leur bassesse. (ibid., p. 211)

Consider, too, the case of the *contes*; they hardly provide evidence that Voltaire was a proponent of despotism, however 'enlightened'. Verdun Saulnier was right to call *Zadig* an 'Anti-Versailles', in view of the 'hero's' sufferings at the hands of capricious courtiers; and, as René Pomeau suggests,[28] *L'Ingénu* of 1767 deserves the same label when we think of the poor Huron's frustrations before an impenetrable bureaucracy and of the 'good' Jansenist Gordon's victimization by that dreaded tool of royal despotism, the *lettre de cachet*. Nor do Voltaire's histories really indicate, despite the popular conception, that he was an unreserved admirer of monarchical power. In his first work in the genre, the *Histoire de Charles XII* of 1731, the sad Swedish king is held up rather more as an example to avoid than to emulate; the *discours* which prefaces the text contains a warning to aberrant kings that 'l'histoire est un témoin et non un flatteur', and in the vivid concluding scene describing Charles's violent death, he is held up as a ruler who violated the sacred *via media*: 'il a porté toutes les vertus des héros à un excès où elles sont aussi dangereuses que les vices opposés'.[29] As for the *Siècle de Louis XIV*, generally regarded as his masterpiece in the historical genre, we should remember that for Voltaire it is writers, artists, and scientists who make a civilization great and not courtiers, soldiers, or bellicose kings, although his great admiration for the 'Sun King' cannot be denied.

Over and over again in his later prose writings Voltaire affirmed, often in his quaint English, that to be free is to obey only 'to' the laws.[30] Thus the article 'États, gouvernements' of the *Dictionnaire philosophique* (1764) ends with the following bit of dialogue:

—Dans quel État, sous quelle domination aimeriez-vous mieux vivre? dit le conseiller.—Partout ailleurs que chez moi, dit son compagnon; et j'ai trouvé beaucoup de Siamois, de Tonquinois, de Persans et de Turcs qui en disaient autant.—Mais, encore une fois, dit l'Européen, quel État choisiriez-vous? Le brame répondit: Celui où l'on n'obéit qu'aux lois.—C'est une vieille réponse, dit le conseiller.

—Elle n'en est pas plus mauvaise, dit le brame.—Où est ce pays-là? dit le conseiller. Le brame dit:
Il faut le chercher.[31]

And the astute reader understands that at the end of the search will be found England.
In view of this text I can only agree with René Pomeau (p. 179) as over against Peter Gay[32]
and Fellows and Torrey[33] that the important *A, B, C* of 1768 represents not an expression
of Voltaire's democratic proclivities at the time of his involvement in the *affaire des natifs* in
Geneva but rather a reaffirmation of his admiration for constitutional monarchy *à l'anglaise.*
Finally, in his article 'Gouvernement VI' (1771) of the *Dictionnaire philosophique*, Voltaire
gave perhaps his most explicit articulation of the civil liberties he would desire for France:

Ces droits sont: liberté entière de sa personne, de ses biens, de parler à la nation par l'organe de sa
plume, de ne pouvoir être jugé en matière criminelle que par un *jury* formé d'hommes indépendants,
de ne pouvoir être jugé en aucun cas que suivant les termes précis de la loi, de professer en paix quelque
religion qu'on veuille, en renonçant aux emplois dont les seuls anglicans peuvent être pourvus. Cela
s'appelle des prérogatives. (Pomeau, p. 190)

There is, then, a profoundly Lockean strain running throughout Voltaire's writings.
Ernst Cassirer was particularly sensitive to this side of the author's politics when he wrote:
'The essential concept of freedom for Voltaire is therefore synonymous with the concept
of human rights. [. . .] All of Voltaire's political writings are inspired by this view of
freedom'.[34]
  So much for the 'happy' side of Voltaire's politics, the Lockean side, with its stress on
law over whim. But note, in the passage just quoted above, that Voltaire speaks of 're-
nouncing posts which Anglicans alone can hold'. Why this disturbing *caveat*? Is there a
'darker side' to Voltaire's politics, a side that we might even call 'Hobbesian'? I think there
is, and that it nearly if not completely counterbalances his liberal Anglophilia. But those
who would deny any kinship between Voltaire and the gloomy philosopher of Malmesbury
would seem to find support in an important article on this subject published by Leland
Thielemann in 1959.[35] As Thielemann takes pains to point out, Voltaire refuted all the
central tenets of legendary Hobbism: the natural wickedness of man, the right of the
stronger, the natural state of war, and the justice of convention. But the matter is considerably more complex than this, and Thielemann fails to stress points he himself makes.
Consider again, for example, the case of the *contes*. Whatever strands of political liberalism
they may contain, in general they betray (think of *Candide*!) a grim vision of reality in
which the strong are constantly thrashing the weak and in which the high-minded rarely
get their just deserts, a vision which contemporaries might have called Hobbesian and which
we would call Absurd. As Thielemann aptly notes, Voltaire 'recognized in Hobbist realism
the universe of *Candide*' (p. 247). The wrung-out reader of Voltaire's masterpiece, upon
laying down the volume, can hardly fail to conclude that the state of nature is a state of war.
  Quasi-Hobbesian, too, is Voltaire's oft-expressed pessimism, derived from his historical
studies as well as from his observations of contemporary events, about the common people,
the 'vile canaille', whom he often cursed and about whose capacity for self-government he

had the profoundest doubts. This visceral pessimism about human nature and the related fear of anarchy often seem to have propelled Voltaire to the opposite, potentially Hobbist extreme: an unreserved admiration for the strong personality, *provided* of course that he be enlightened. Thus his theory of history revolves around the notion that only great men, not great laws or great institutions, can produce great things. His four *âges heureux* in Western history were essentially shaped by towering figures—Pericles, Augustus, the Medici, Louis XIV. (His own private hero seems to have been Henri IV, who brought peace and tolerance to a divided kingdom.) This curious respect for efficiency, even perhaps at the expense of due process, led to Voltaire's preference for being governed, as he colourfully put it, 'by a single lion rather than a hundred rats'. This point of view finds its clearest expression in the article 'Tyrannie' (1764) of the *Dictionnaire philosophique* (ed. cit., p. 412): 'Sous quelle tyrannie aimeriez-vous mieux vivre? Sous aucune; mais, s'il fallait choisir, je détesterais moins la tyrannie d'un seul que celle de plusieurs. Un despote a toujours quelques bons moments; une assemblée de despotes n'en a jamais'.[36] (The opening question, by the way, makes this passage a kind of 'Hobbesian' answer to the Lockean article 'États, gouvernements', previously cited.) Note the naïve faith in the malleability of the despot, presumably at the hands of a *philosophe* like Voltaire. We must acknowledge that our author was singularly insensitive to a principle which is almost sacred in the American system: namely, that there is safety in slowness and that more wisdom may perhaps be distilled out of the clash of a hundred heads than out of the ruminations of a single crowned one.

Finally, and most importantly, Voltaire's link to Hobbes may be seen in his thoroughly Erastian views on the relationship of Church and State. No theme, not even that of English liberties, was dearer to the heart of Voltaire than that of the need for complete and absolute subordination of the ecclesiastical estate to the civil order, of which the *parlements*, by the way, were an integral part. As he surveyed recent European history, Voltaire was repelled by nothing more than by the spectacle of the religious wars in France and Germany, and it is reported that on the anniversary of the Saint-Barthélemy he fell physically ill. His temperature rose considerably whenever he contemplated the sad spectacle of Jesuits and Jansenists at each other's throats in his native France. His entire political career is characterized by an appeal for complete authority of the 'magistrate' over all lay aspects of the life of the Church, a campaign which would find its culmination in the Civil Constitution for the Clergy during the Revolution. As with his Lockeanism, we can find evidence of this 'Hobbist' strain of his thought in places we might not expect it, for example, in the *Poème sur la loi naturelle* of 1752 (published in 1756). The poem is addressed to Frederick II (Voltaire was in Potsdam at the time) and the fourth part gives the political ideas of the poet; the sovereign, says Voltaire, must maintain firm and absolute rule over his own house, to keep the sects from squabbling:

> Mais je prétends qu'un roi, que son devoir engage
> A maintenir la paix, *l'ordre, la sûreté,*
> Ait sur tous ses sujets égale autorité.
> [..]
> Le marchand, l'ouvrier, *le prêtre,* le soldat,
> Sont tous également les membres de l'État. (*Mélanges*, p. 287; italics mine)

But this strain in Voltaire's thought, with its stress on order and security, had perhaps found its clearest expression a few years before, in 1750, in a little pamphlet entitled *La Voix du sage et du peuple* which he wrote in support of the finance minister Machault; the latter was engaged (futilely) in a project dear to Voltaire, that of making the clergy pay its just share of the taxes: 'Il ne doit pas y avoir deux puissances dans un État', writes the author in rejecting the Gallican settlement of the previous century. 'Il n'y a pas un seul exemple de trouble et de dissension quand le prince a été le maître absolu de la police ecclésiastique: il n'y a que des exemples de désordres et de calamités quand les ecclésiastiques n'ont pas été entièrement soumis au prince' (Pomeau, pp. 195, 196). Could this not be a translation from Hobbes? Professor Thielemann was right to state: 'Insofar as the French Enlightenment constituted a philosophic effort to separate the jurisdictions of church and state, it can scarcely be concluded that Voltaire's admiration for Hobbes's yeoman service in the secular cause was either forced or factitious' (p. 243). Little wonder then that Voltaire should remark in his *Philosophe ignorant* of 1766 that Hobbes was 'bien dur'—'mais j'ai peur que sa dureté ne tienne souvent à la vérité' (quoted by Thielemann, p. 247). Kingsley Martin was sensitive to this strangely *étatiste* element in Voltaire's politics when he wrote: 'Voltaire indeed never made any attempt to reconcile his doctrine of sovereignty with his theory of natural rights. Whenever it came to the test he supported the State against the individual and *preferred order to freedom*' (*French Liberal Thought in the Eighteenth Century*, p. 137; italics mine).

This does not sound like the old Voltaire we all know. Is Kingsley Martin right? Does he see in Voltaire those same proto-totalitarian tendencies that Professor Crocker finds in Rousseau? Surely not, but . . . I would maintain that he *is* right with reference to one episode of the author's later career, his involvement in the *affaire des parlements* of 1771, and I would now like to take this up briefly. Space does not permit a full review of the protracted struggle, over legal and constitutional issues, between Louis XV and the law courts. Suffice it to say that the conflict reached its culmination in January 1771 when the Chancellor since 1768, the anti-intellectual René de Maupeou, with the behind-the-scenes support of La Du Barry, suppressed the centuries-old *parlement* of Paris and exiled many of the recalcitrant judges to their (often remote) estates in the provinces after confiscating their posts. Six 'superior councils' were soon set up to provide theoretically free justice in the jurisdiction of the old *parlement*. The much-criticized institution of venality, by which the magistrates could buy and sell their offices, was abolished in favor of a scheme for salaried (and removable) judges, and the old practice of *épices* (under-the-bench payments by litigants to their judges) was eliminated.[37] Despite these reforms a great many contemporaries, including many of the *Philosophes,* viewed the *coup d'état* as an example of unadulterated and unparalleled despotism; Maupeou, and behind him the King, was the target of a propaganda barrage of such viciousness as to make one wonder how the monarchy could ever have regained its credibility. The following little ditty which made the rounds at the time will serve as a specimen: 'La France, qui fut longtemps mangée par les loups, l'est maintenant par les poux (i.e., les *maux poux!*)'.[38] What Morellet told his English correspondent on 5 November 1772 captures the mood of the moment and has haunting echoes for us today in the U.S.A.: 'Notre gouvernement n'a jamais été plus ferme et la nation plus soumise'.[39] *Submissive*

Now, Voltaire intervened in this crisis as a kind of high-grade hack for Maupeou, first by producing his *Histoire du parlement de Paris* of 1769,[40] followed up by a series of anonymous pamphlets under such titles as *L'Équivoque, Les Peuples aux parlements,* and *Lettre d'un jeune abbé.* Why did Voltaire support Maupeou, rather much in isolation from his fellow *philosophes*? The reasons are numerous and complex, far too much so to permit treatment here. I hope to probe them in a further study. Tentatively, I can suggest that when we know them they will not be entirely to his credit. But in Peter Gay's analysis Voltaire's support for Maupeou is something like the apotheosis of a hero, his last, noble defence of the *thèse royale* against a corps of privileged, reactionary, obstructionist nobles of the robe (Gay can hardly restrain his anger against the magistrates, calling them 'entrenched, deliberate, habitual criminals' (*The Science of Freedom,* p. 480)). I do not believe that we can be content with this analysis. First of all, it deals too simplistically with a complex nexus of circumstances. Second, it reeks of Marxism, with its emphasis on class warfare as central to history and its hypersensitive nose for 'privileged aristocrats'.[41] As I have suggested elsewhere,[42] the *parlementaire* line was distinct enough from the *thèse nobiliaire* as to be thought of as a separate *thèse parlementaire,* and when Voltaire wrote in his *Mandement du révérendissime père en Dieu, Alexis* of 1765, 'Nous adhérons aux maximes du parlement de France, qui, comme notre sénat, ne reconnaît qu'une seule puissance, fondée sur les lois' (*Mélanges,* p. 765), he was not only voicing his support for the law courts in their protracted struggle with the clergy but was in effect reiterating the 'parliamentary thesis'.[43] Finally, I believe that Gay's label for Voltaire's political position in his conflict with the *parlements*—'constitutional absolutism'—is, like 'enlightened despotism', an unstable and unacceptable oxymoron, which will not hold up under examination; for if the king is subject to constitutional restraints, he is no longer really absolute.[44]

As already suggested, a great many of Voltaire's contemporaries did not see the matter as does Gay, and we should sometimes be prepared to listen to the testimony of astute contemporaries as over against the fine-spun theories of modern historians. Some, such as the compilers of the *Mémoires secrets,* posthumously attributed to Bachaumont, saw an ageing Patriarch, remote from Paris in the mountains near Switzerland and nostalgic for the old days in the 1740s when he had enjoyed playing courtier to the King. Voltaire may have apostrophized the law courts: 'Parlements du royaume! le citoyen qui vous parle n'est ni homme de cour, ni homme de robe, ni d'aucun parti' (*L'Équivoque,* quoted in Pomeau, p. 159), but many of the *philosophe*'s astute observers saw just that, an old 'homme de cour', buttering up Maupeou (in the hope of being able to return to France) as he had buttered up d'Argenson, Frederick, and Choiseul.[45] We know, for example, that he needed the support of Choiseul in his project to establish a free port at Versoix as an answer to Geneva. We know furthermore that the fate of his landed properties was to some extent in the hands of the French government; thus he wrote to Tronchin of Lyon on 13 December 1758: 'La terre de Ferney est moins titrée [than that of Tournay], mais non moins seigneuriale: je n'y jouis des droits de l'ancien dénombrement que par grâce du ministère; mais cette grâce m'est assurée' (*Lettres choisies,* p. 261). Some very definite 'ulterior' motives seem to have been involved in Voltaire's support for Maupeou.

Of course, Voltaire had good reasons for opposing the *parlements*. Certainly, they had burned books (including his own; but they also burned clerical books) and sentenced people to horrible deaths (think of Calas, Sirven, La Barre). Certainly, the judicial system was filled with abuses and corruption. Certainly, the courts exploited the similarity between *parlement* and Parliament to advance their political claims. But beyond all this, there was an aspect of the *coup d'état* which he overlooked (or refused to see), perhaps because he *was* remote from Paris. The fact is that France in the early 1770s was passing through a constitutional crisis somewhat comparable to the one we have just witnessed in the United States. For, as one recent historian has shown,[46] king and *parlement* had existed for centuries in a kind of tense equilibrium, a dependence-independence relationship which required that neither side rigidly overdefine its position. Historically the concept of French monarchy was essentially judicial, and the king *needed* the *parlement* to give an aura of legality to his legislation. Weak *parlements* might acquiesce before strong kings (e.g. François Ier and Louis XIV) and weak kings might bow momentarily before rebellious law courts, but always it was understood that the equation of power was made up of two halves, each indispensable, for the law courts had a vital role to play in making sure that monarchical sovereignty operated *under,* not outside, the law. They exercised their function through their unwritten but long-sanctioned right to review and 'register' government edicts, and to 'remonstrate' against them if they failed to conform to the ancient constitution, an effective veto which could be overridden only by a royal *lit de justice.* Now, in taking the action he did, Maupeou cut the Gordian knot rather than untying it; he smashed the precarious equilibrium by suppressing one side of it. From a narrowly legalistic viewpoint Voltaire may have been right in saying the *parlements* had few solid grounds for posing as the 'Senate of the nation', but the point is that their claims were historically sanctioned by practice if not by a written document. Moreover, in France in the century after the English Glorious Revolution (1688), with the ideas of Locke and Montesquieu in the air, there was a widespread demand for some institutional check on the power of the monarchy, which was thought by many to be sliding into despotism (*vide* Montesquieu); and it was widely held that only the *parlement* could in practice perform this function, as it had for centuries. This is why René Pomeau writes that Voltaire's opinion, 'correcte du point de vue de l'histoire et de la légalité, méconnaît la nécessité d'une représentation nationale.'[47]

To us the interesting question is: What was it about the Maupeou affair that aroused Voltaire's preference, to return to Kingsley Martin's phrase, for order over freedom? I suspect that beyond his ulterior motives and his righteous indignation against the *parlements* lies an answer at the ideological level. So does Peter Gay, but he finds it in Voltaire's espousal of the 'progressive' royal thesis as over against the 'reactionary' *thèse nobiliaire*— a view which in my opinion greatly oversimplifies the politics of the French Enlightenment. Now, as we have seen, the author's 'Hobbesian' fear of disorder and hatred of quarrelling sects posed a threat to his 'Lockean' stress on individual rights and lawful procedure. I believe that he came to perceive the magistrates as a group of fanatical Jansenist sectarians locked in mortal combat with their enemies the Jesuits and posing a danger to the security of the State. Interestingly enough, it is in the writings of d'Alembert, his political correspondent in Paris, that we find the most lucid articulation of this view, and one wonders if the disciple might have influenced the master in this regard. For example, d'Alembert wrote to Frederick in 1766: 'Ces parlements [. . .] sont encore, s'il est possible, plus abrutis que le clergé, par l'esprit intolérant et persécuteur qui les domine. Ce ne sont ni des magistrats, ni même des citoyens, mais *de plats fanatiques jansénistes* qui nous feraient gémir, s'ils le pouvaient, sous le despotisme des absurdités théologiques,'[48] and this theme pervades the Voltaire–d'Alembert correspondence of this period.[49] Now, as I have attempted elsewhere to show (*Petit de Bachaumont*, pp. 184–5, 190, 200, 205), the phrase 'parlementaires jansénistes' reflects an essentially distorted view of the situation, insofar as it was possible to espouse all the tenets of the Enlightenment, *including* a contempt for the religious Jansenists as fanatical *dévots,* and still support the *parlements* in their struggle against what was seen as royal and clerical despotism; in other words, it was possible to drive a wedge between *Jansénistes* and *parlements.* None the less it was out of this false perspective that Voltaire addressed the judges as follows in his *L'Équivoque* of 1771: 'Vous semblez craindre la tyrannie, qui pourrait prendre un jour la place d'un pouvoir modéré; mais *craignons encore plus l'anarchie* qui n'est qu'une tyrannie tumultueuse' (Pomeau, p. 161; my emphasis). I believe that in the *affaire des parlements* Voltaire's stress on Order outweighed his belief in Law, that the 'Locke' in him yielded to the 'Hobbes'. If we wish to preserve our image of him as the Lockean champion of the rule of law, we shall simply have to admit that he 'called this one wrong'.

In an address delivered at the first annual meeting of the American Society for Eighteenth-Century Studies (Cleveland, 1970), Professor Aram Vartanian, speaking of the relationships of science and humanism in the Enlightenment, hit upon an ingenious phrase to characterize Voltaire: 'conservative radical'.[50] Actually, this was the position arrived at earlier by Professor Pappas, in his aforementioned article on 'Voltaire et la guerre civile philosophique', where he showed Voltaire and d'Alembert at odds over tactics in the war against 'l'infâme', the latter preferring a prudent and 'pure' appeal to public opinion for support, the former advocating a *radical* attack on the Church but through an essentially *conservative* method, that of using 'les grands' of the court. 'Conservative radicalism': not a bad phrase; nor a bad stance. Not an unacceptable oxymoron either, unlike 'enlightened despotism' or 'constitutional absolutism'. Professor Vartanian shows how not only Voltaire's politics, but his ethics, his æsthetics, his physics and his metaphysics as well, revolved around a pattern of 'fixity in change,' which involved maintaining a constant overall framework while working localized change within it. Now, insofar as the *parlement* formed a vital component of the structure of government in the *ancien régime,* it was part of the 'fixity' within which 'change' would have to operate. Voltaire, in supporting its abolition by force, violated the sacred *via media,* the 'juste milieu', the golden mean to which he otherwise clung so tenaciously. He in effect betrayed his own philosophy.

As noted earlier, Diderot, if he came late to politics, was by the early 1770s thoroughly committed to a Lockean and anti-despotic political position; it was left to him to articulate the most interesting reaction among the other *philosophes* to Voltaire's involvement in the Maupeou affair, viewed essentially as sordid. Having put into the mouth of 'Lui' in the *Neveu de Rameau* the words 'Certes, tu n'aurais jamais fait *Mahomet,* mais ni l'éloge de Maupeou',[51] Diderot made the following vivid comment on the old Patriarch in a letter to his associate Naigeon in the spring of 1772, when the *coup d'état* was still a leading topic of discussion and concern:

Hé bien, à l'âge de soixante et dix-huit ans, il vint en fantaisie à cet homme tout couvert de lauriers de se jeter dans un tas de boue; et vous croyez qu'il est bien d'allez [*sic*] lui sauter à deux pieds sur le ventre, et de l'enfoncer dans la fange, jusqu'à ce qu'il disparaisse? Ah! monsieur, ce n'est pas là votre dernier mot.

 Un jour, cet homme sera bien grand, et ses détracteurs seront bien petits.

 Pour moi, si j'avais l'éponge qui pût le nettoyer, j'irais lui tendre la main, je le tirerais de son bourbier, et je le nettoierais.[52]

 So let us not be too hard on our Author; all men make mistakes, even the 'best and brightest' among us. Voltaire was not consistent; but it was, I think, Emerson who said that consistency is the hobgoblin of little minds. His contemporaries often berated him for his oscillations and vacillations, but they could praise him for his humanity and tolerance. (When he took his famous Easter communion in the spring of 1768, the *dévots* of France jumped for joy; but their joy was false, for he was never one of theirs.) André Delattre was not wrong to title his volume of 1957 *Voltaire l'impétueux,* but we should remember that impetuosity is not necessarily a sign of weakness. Or, as Diderot put it: 'On est inconséquent: et y a-t-il rien de plus commun que d'être inconséquent?'[53] Voltaire is, to use the current lingo, 'beautiful' because he is alive and changing, not atrophied or petrified. Even with his flaws he has much to teach us; Peter Gay aptly sums up his wisdom as follows: 'life is, has always been, and will always be, hard; man needs courage, patience, and luck to survive at all; but reason, often flouted, is a tough and aggressive force in the world [. . .]' (*The Science of Freedom,* p. 104). Otis Fellows, in a fine piece many years ago in the *Romanic Review,* showed how 'relevant' Voltaire was in post-1944 France.[54] I think we still need Voltaire, with all his warts and blemishes.

 What lessons can we draw from our examination of Voltaire's politics? First, that yesterday's liberal can become today's conservative, or vice versa, and that while standing still. (I am reminded of what a friend of mine at Iowa recently said: that if you cling to sound principles and just hang on through the storms of changing fashion, sooner or later you will come back into vogue.) Voltaire illustrates the point because in his later career he sometimes failed to follow principles he himself had advocated in his youth and even beyond. In the Maupeou affair, yesterday's liberal did become today's conservative.

 Finally, we can draw the lesson that law and order, far from being synonymous, exist in a dependence-independence relationship, a delicate equilibrium analogous to that in which king and *parlement* existed in the Old Regime. Law needs a context of order in which to function; but some bitter twentieth-century history has shown us what order without law can mean. Like a great many precarious equilibria, this one, too, is best respected and not broken.

NOTES

1 Émile Faguet, *Dix-huitième siècle: Études littéraires* (Paris [1890?]), p. 226.
2 *Voltaire*, 6th ed. (Paris, [n.d.]). This little book is still generally regarded as the best brief introduction to the life and work of the author. 'Voltaire sans nul doute est conservateur', Lanson writes provocatively (p. 191). 'Mais il l'est comme l'est tout libéral. Il ne veut pas de bouleversement violent'.
3 *L'Évolution de la pensée politique en France au XVIIIe siècle* (Paris, 1925), pp. 103–33.
4 *Les Origines intellectuelles de la Révolution française (1715–1787)*, 2nd ed. (Paris, 1934), pp. 82–9, 97–100. Mornet barely advances beyond Faguet's 'chaos of clear ideas'.
5 *French Liberal Thought in the Eighteenth Century*, ed. J. P. Mayer (New York, 1963), pp. 132–43. Martin probably did more than anyone else in the Anglo-Saxon world to perpetuate the notion that Voltaire, and the *philosophes* in general, favoured 'enlightened despotism'. (Originally published 1929).
6 'Voltaire's Principles of Political Thought', *MLQ*, 17 (1956), 289–300. Perkins skilfully shows the psychological principles underlying Voltaire's political positions. But his study is abstract and does not satisfy our desire to know more about the author's specific response to problems of law and order. See the same author's *Voltaire's Concept of International Order* (Geneva, 1965).
7 *Voltaire and Reform in the Light of the French Revolution* (Geneva, 1959). Professor Waldinger shows how the *cahiers* drawn up by the various estates early in the Revolution clearly reflect the Voltairean influence. Yet I agree with the strictures expressed by one reviewer of the book, John Pappas, *Lettres romanes*, 15 (1961), 181–4.
8 'Voltaire et la guerre civile philosophique', *RHL*, 61 (1961), 525–49, followed up the next year by his *Voltaire and d'Alembert* (Bloomington, Indiana U. Press).
9 We quote from the paperback edition: (New York, 1965).
10 *Voltaire* (New York, 1969), p. 295, n. 5. This chapter ('Justice and Government, 1750–1774') essentially reprints an earlier article, 'Voltaire, Absolute Monarchy, and the Enlightened Monarch', *Studies on Voltaire and the Eighteenth Century*, 32 (1965), 7–21.
11 *The Enlightenment: An Interpretation*, Vol. II: *The Science of Freedom* (New York, 1969), pp. 465–83. I am pleased to find myself joined in my strictures on Gay's treatment of Voltaire and the *parlement* by K. M. Baker in a review of the second volume, *AHR*, 75 (1970), 1410–14. Cf. a review essay ('Peter Gay's Enlightenment') by James A. Leith in *ECS*, 5 (1971), 157–71.
12 *Politique de Voltaire*, ed. René Pomeau (Paris, 1963).
13 See above, note 10.
14 'Voltaire et le cardinal de Fleury', *Dix-huitième Siècle*, ed. Roland Desné, 2 (1970), 39–76; 'La Mission diplomatique de Voltaire en 1743', *Dix-huitième Siècle*, 4 (1972), 271–99.
15 'État présent des études voltairiennes', *Studies on Voltaire and the Eighteenth Century*, 1 (1955), p. 196.
16 *Anthologie de la Littérature française du XVIIIe Siècle*, ed. Lester G. Crocker (New York, 1972).
17 For a useful recent exposition of Locke's political philosophy see Ira O. Wade, *The Intellectual Origins of the French Enlightenment* (Princeton, 1971), pp. 513–27.
18 There is a good *résumé* of Hobbes's politics, ibid., pp. 267–83.
19 Mark H. Waddicor, *Montesquieu and the Philosophy of Natural Law* (The Hague, 1970), p. 107. On the uses of medievalism in the eighteenth century (which were not necessarily reactionary) see Lionel Gossman, *Medievalism and the Ideologies of the Enlightenment: The World and Work of Lacurne de Sainte-Palaye* (Baltimore, 1968), and my review in *Diderot Studies*, 14 (1971), 365–70.
20 'The Development and Scope of Diderot's Political Thought', *Studies on Voltaire and the Eighteenth Century*, 27 (1963), 1871–1900.
21 He writes in a thoroughly Hobbist vein in his *Discours préliminaire*: 'Puisque la morale tire son origine de la politique, comme les lois et les bourreaux, il s'ensuit qu'elle n'est point l'ouvrage de la nature, ni par conséquent de la philosophie, ou de la raison, tous termes synonymes' (Crocker,

p. 157). As Crocker points out, La Mettrie, like Helvétius, d'Holbach, and Rousseau, lets ethics be absorbed by politics.

22 See, for example, Crocker's *Rousseau's 'Social Contract': An Interpretive Essay* (Cleveland, 1968), and my brief review in *Dix-huitième Siècle*, 3 (1971), 416. The second volume of Professor Crocker's biography of Rousseau, *Jean-Jacques Rousseau: The Prophetic Voice (1758–1778)*, has just appeared (New York, 1973); Vol. I, under the title *The Quest (1712–1758)*, appeared in 1968.

23 Gay, *Voltaire's Politics*, pp. 14–15; Alfred Cobban, *In Search of Humanity* (New York, 1960), p. 164; Lester G. Crocker, *Nature and Culture* (Baltimore, 1963), p. 449; J. H. Brumfitt, 'Voltaire', in *French Literature and Its Background*, Vol. III: *The Eighteenth Century*, ed. John Cruickshank (New York, 1968), p. 7; John N. Pappas, 'Individual Rights Versus the General Welfare in Eighteenth-Century French Thought', *Romanic Review*, 60 (1969), 10. The latter article deals with our very subject, but from a slightly different angle.

24 Pomeau reproduces (pp. 174–7) the article 'Maître' of the *Dictionnaire philosophique*, in which Voltaire poses the chicken-and-the-egg question of whether monarchy emerged from republican anarchy or republics from monarchical despotism.

25 *Voltaire*, p. 298. We should remember that Locke, like Hobbes, wrote out of a specific context: reversing his predecessor, he justified Parliament against the Stuarts.

26 *Lettres choisies*, ed. Raymond Naves (Paris, 1963), p. 26.

27 *Mélanges*, ed. Emmanuel Berl and Jacques Van den Heuvel (Paris, 1961), p. 21.

28 *Politique de Voltaire*, p. 233. *Candide* is, in a sense, surprisingly timid on the subject of monarchical power; but in the Eldorado episode Candide and Cacambo are pleased to learn that the ceremony for greeting the benevolent king is simply a kiss on both cheeks.

29 *Histoire de Charles XII*, ed. Georges Mailhos (Paris, 1968), pp. 32, 238.

30 Article 'Gouvernement VI', *Dictionnaire philosophique*, quoted in Pomeau, p. 189; *Pensées sur le gouvernement* (1752), Pomeau, p. 232; and many other places.

31 *Dictionnaire philosophique*, ed. Julien Benda and Raymond Naves (Paris, 1961), p. 188.

32 *Voltaire's Politics*, pp. 235–8.

33 *The Age of Enlightenment: An Anthology of Eighteenth-Century French Literature*, ed. Otis E. Fellows and Norman Torrey, 2nd ed. (New York, 1971), p. 430. Certainly contemporaries saw in the A, B, C a restatement of his fondness for English-style monarchy. See, for example, *Mémoires secrets pour servir à l'histoire de la République des Lettres . . .* (London; 'John Adamson', 1780–89), IV, 164–5 (12 December 1768): 'Quant à la première partie [on politics], le dissertateur prouve l'excellence de la Constitution Angloise et des Loix de ce Gouvernement.'

34 *The Philosophy of the Enlightenment*, trans. Fritz C. A. Koelln and James P. Pettegrove (Boston, 1955), p. 251. Cassirer's comment is significant only by virtue of its typicality. Cf., for example, Sée, *L'Évolution de la pensée politique*, p. 117.

35 'Voltaire and Hobbism', *Studies on Voltaire and the Eighteenth Century*, 10 (1959), 237–58. Thielemann correctly notes that, despite his pessimism, Hobbes was regarded in the eighteenth century as one of the chief progenitors of the secular Enlightenment.

36 cf. *L'Essai sur les mœurs*, with reference to the *parlement*: 'La tyrannie d'un corps est toujours plus impitoyable que celle d'un roi. Il y a mille moyens d'apaiser un prince, il n'y en a point d'adoucir la sévérité d'un corps entraîné par les préjugés'. Quoted in Bastard d'Estang, *Les Parlements de France* (Paris, 1857–58), p. 346.

37 For fuller accounts see Alfred Cobban, *A History of Modern France*, Vol. I (Penguin Book, 1957), pp. 89–94; Gay, *Voltaire's Politics*, pp. 309–30; and my *Petit de Bachaumont: his circle and the 'Mémoires secrets'*, Vol. 65 of *Studies on Voltaire and the Eighteenth Century* (Geneva, 1968), pp. 185–9.

38 Quoted in Bastard d'Estang, *Les Parlements*, p. 497, n. 1.

39 *Lettres de l'abbé Morellet de l'Académie française à Lord Shelburne . . . (1772–1803)*, ed. Lord Edmund Fitzmaurice (Paris, 1898), pp. 9–10.

40 On this work see Nuci Kotta, 'Voltaire's *Histoire du parlement de Paris*', *Studies on Voltaire and the Eighteenth Century*, 41 (1966), 219–30. However, Kotta does little more than rehash the Gay line in a thoroughly unoriginal manner. See also Besterman, *Voltaire*, pp. 486–7.

41 This is not surprising in view of Gay's debt to his Mentor, the late Franz Neumann, a German scholar of decidedly Marxist proclivities, as well as to Dean Franklin Ford of Harvard, whose *Robe and Sword* (Cambridge, 1953) is a powerful statement of the theory that in the eighteenth century the *thèse parlementaire* was merely a subtle version of the *thèse nobiliaire*. But Gay's view is already foreshadowed in Marius Roustan, *Les Philosophes et la société française au XVIIIe siècle* (Paris, 1911), pp. 154–65.

42 *Petit de Bachaumont*, pp. 195–8.

43 On ideological affinities between Voltaire and the law courts see my suggestions in 'Voltaire and the *parlements*: A Reconsideration', *Studies on Voltaire and the Eighteenth Century*, 90 (1972), 1533–5. Gustave Lanson perhaps said more than he meant when he called Voltaire a 'parlementaire' (*Voltaire*, p. 36).

44 cf. Pomeau, p. 51. Pomeau calls Gay's phrase 'heureuse' but I wonder if he is being facetious. Earlier in his book Gay had admitted that 'constitutional absolutism' was a solution only on the level of *rhetoric* (*Voltaire's Politics*, p. 16).

45 See, for example, *Mémoires secrets*, II, 7–8 (11 January 1964); III, 169 (5 April 1767); IV, 273 (17 July 1769); V, 224–5 (11 March 1771), 281–2 (15 July 1771); VI, 28–9 (9 November 1771), 42–3 (17 November 1771); XIX, 5–6 (24 July 1768—addition), 254 (21 January 1771—addition); VII, 218–19 (27 September 1774).

46 J. H. Shennan, *The Parlement of Paris* (Ithaca, 1968), Bk. II ('The Political Institution'). Shennan makes clear that there were two sides to the *parlement*'s activities: the judicial and the political.

47 *Politique de Voltaire*, p. 159. He elaborates (p. 27): 'Il ne suffisait donc pas en 1771 de supprimer ces parlements d'opposition: l'erreur de Maupeou fut de croire que se posait seulement le problème d'une réforme judiciaire. Ce fut pareillement l'erreur de Voltaire. Il loue le système représentatif anglais, mais jamais il n'a osé demander, expressément et avec force, qu'une Chambre des communes soit créée en France: ce qui empêche que sa position dans l'affaire des parlements nous paraisse aujourd'hui entièrement satisfaisante.'

48 Quoted in Roustan, *Les Philosophes et la société*, p. 162. My italics.

49 D'Alembert wrote to his master on 25 September 1762, for example: 'Croyez-moi, point de faiblesse humaine; laissez la canaille janséniste et parlementaire nous défaire tranquillement de la canaille jésuitique, et n'empêchez point ces araignées de se dévorer les unes les autres'. *Voltaire's Correspondence*, ed. Theodore Besterman (Geneva, 1953–65), no. 9917.

50 'Intertextures of Science and Humanism in the French Enlightenment', in *Studies in Eighteenth-Century Culture*, Vol. I: *The Modernity of the Eighteenth Century*, ed. Louis T. Milic (Cleveland, 1971), p. 114.

51 *Œuvres complètes*, ed. Assézat and Tourneux (Paris, 1875–77), V, 398.

52 *Correspondance*, ed. Georges Roth and Jean Varloot (Paris, 1955–70), XII, 55.

53 *Œuvres philosophiques*, ed. P. Vernière (Paris, 1964), p. 529.

54 'Voltaire in Liberated France', *Romanic Review*, 37 (1946), 168–76. Republished in his *From Voltaire to 'La Nouvelle Critique': Problems and Personalities* (Geneva, 1970), pp. 13–21.

25

Le Neveu de Rameau and the Awareness of Mediocrity

P. M. W. THODY

The theme of mediocrity recurs explicitly three times in *Le Neveu de Rameau*: at the beginning of the dialogue, where *Lui*'s disparagement of a merely average competence 'aux échecs, aux dames, en poésie, en éloquence, en musique, et autres fadaises comme cela' sparks off a discussion of the moral infirmities of genius; half way through the conversation, where *Lui*'s acknowledged inferiority to Bouret introduces the idea that 'Les génies lisent peu, pratiquent beaucoup, et se font d'eux-mêmes'; and as an introduction to the closing pages, where the same vision of the instinctive, inborn nature of genius brings *le Neveu* back to his own situation as an unsuccessful composer. By this time, however, the emphasis has changed. The *Lui* of the opening exchanges spoke in personal and emotive terms, voicing an almost uncomprehending envy at the idea of his own mediocrity, and proclaiming his readiness to steal if this would enable him to overcome its more obvious financial and social drawbacks. By the end of the dialogue, however, he can see the matter in more general, almost philosophical terms. The superb explanatory image of *la statue de Memnon* not only gives new life to the hackneyed notion of the star which must preside over each true poet's birth. It is accompanied by an increased awareness on Rameau's part both of what he is and of why he should embrace rather than flee his destiny. The triumphant 'Rira bien qui rira le dernier' comes from a different person than the man who uttered the initial cry of 'J'ai donc été, je suis donc fâché d'être médiocre. Oui, oui, je suis médiocre et fâché', and this change is more than a symptom of the mobility which stems from Rameau's birth 'Vertumnis, quotquot sunt, iniquis'. It reflects a process of self-discovery and self-realisation that goes on throughout the dialogue, and which finally enables *le Neveu* to accept himself for what he is: one whose escape from mediocrity through conversation, argument, exaggeration, histrionics and mythomania is wholly in keeping with his failure as a creative artist. The explicit references to mediocrity thus draw attention to an important organic theme in the development of the dialogue and its presentation of a particular kind of human being. At the same time, they illuminate Diderot's own problems, personality and final æsthetic achievement.

The attitudes which can be adopted towards the realisation that one is not, in one's chosen profession and favourite activity, really in the top flight, are many and varied.

U

One of them, for example, is brilliantly described in Browning's *Andrea del Sarto*, where the notion that 'a common greyness silvers everything' offers a melancholy, poetic consolation which is at the furthest possible remove from the frenzied pantomimes which enable Diderot's 'misérable râcleur de cordes' to find refuge from his inability to create anything of lasting value.[1] It is nevertheless a reaction to a comparable experience of self-discovery, and one which has analogies with another theme in *Le Neveu de Rameau* that seems at first sight quite unconnected with *Lui*'s sense of artistic failure: *Moi*'s cult of virtue for emotion's sake. Yet within the dominant biographical framework of the dialogue—a pessimistic vision of Diderot's own situation in 1761—*Moi*'s achievements are not perceptibly greater than *Lui*'s. He may have 'foin dans les bottes' and give 'maîtres à sa fille'. But he has little more permanent to his own personal credit as a creative artist than the *Neveu* whose later career has so signally failed to realise the promise offered in 1757 by the *Nouvelles Pièces de Clavecin*. The *Moi* of *Le Neveu de Rameau*, however, has found an answer; and the writer whom Sabatier de Castres was to describe, in 1772, as a 'littérateur qui a fait beaucoup d'ouvrages sans qu'on puisse dire que nous ayons de lui un bon livre', who had lamented in 1761 that 'tandis que je converse avec vous, les années du travail et de la moisson se passent',[2] appears, through one of his guises at least, to have found a solution: goodness. Personal relationships can indeed, on occasion, be a consolation prize for professional inadequacy, and one which the Diderot-Moi of 1761 could accept very readily: they supported the æsthetic which he was so concerned to propagate in his own plays. Yet this consolation is not presented without irony, and one of the most attractive features of *Le Neveu de Rameau* for the modern reader lies in the skill and honesty with which it undermines some of Diderot's own most cherished notions.

Georges May's remark that 'au *Père de Famille* persécuté *Le Neveu de Rameau* doit sa naissance'[3] has, in this respect, a number of different meanings. Diderot revenges himself on his enemies by holding them up to ridicule, while at the same time producing a masterpiece that does possess the dramatic quality which always eluded him when he wrote directly for the stage. At the same time, however, he transcends his own day and age, communicating with the posterity whose verdict he prized so greatly, by criticising himself. His ironic portrayal, through the character he calls *Moi*, of what Georges May quite rightly dubs as the 'pontifiant père de famille', does more than underline how impossible it is to counterbalance professional failure by a facile indulgence in the virtues of private life. In the moral debate which plays so important a part in the overall structure and final significance of *Le Neveu de Rameau*, it enables *Lui* to win hands down. The felicific calculus by which *Moi* attempts to justify conventional morality has no real answer to the objections which *Lui* is made to base upon the observation of man and society as they really are, and the very style in which the arguments for middle class virtue are presented underlines the intellectual weakness of the case made out for it. It is 'le malheureux' to whom the practitioner of virtue extends a helping hand, not a specific, particularised individual; it is the pleasure of offering advice—'on ne donne rien si libéralement', as La Rochefoucauld observed—which most attracts *Moi* to the activity of doing good; and it is the comfortable glow of moral superiority that he most envies in the story of the man who pours out his opulence on those whom he now compels to acknowledge that they cannot do without him. The self-confident assertion that 'C'est un sublime ouvrage que *Mahomet*; j'aimerais mieux avoir réhabilité la mémoire des Calas' inevitably assumes a more suspect tone from its position in the midst of this self-indulgent evocation of effortless beneficence, and invites the writer to make a clearer distinction between Diderot himself and the *Moi* of the dialogue.[4] Both, indeed, could weep at the recital of generous deeds; but only the latter regarded the comforts of virtue as adequate in themselves to satisfy the human mind. The Diderot who wrote in the *Réfutation suivie de l'ouvrage d'Helvétius intitulé 'L'Homme'* spoke in very different tones when he confessed that 'un violent désir de découvrir, d'inventer, interrompt mon sommeil pendant la nuit, me poursuit pendant le jour' and lamented that he had spent fifty years waiting in vain for the 'heureux hasard' which would entitle him to call himself a genius.[5] The reluctance which we feel to take *Moi* at his own valuation is consequently linked to more than our modern suspicion of tears as a viable source of authentic morality. It is part of the recognition, suggested by the texture and atmosphere of the dialogue, of an obvious but essential truth: that only through artistic achievement can artistic mediocrity be conquered; and only through the writing of *Le Neveu de Rameau* can the sense of failure lying behind it be overcome.

This implied recognition that the achievements in one sphere of human activity are very rarely transferable to another, that even genuine services to one's family and friends cannot outweigh the knowledge of one's professional shortcomings, is nevertheless only one aspect of *Le Neveu de Rameau*. It is, after all, *Lui* and not *Moi* whose problems occupy the forefront of the stage through most of the dialogue, and *Lui* whose mediocrity is openly acknowledged and described. *Moi* is less sensitive to the modesty of his own attainments, and his possibly unconscious response to the problem serves mainly to highlight the more important theme of the dialogue: *Lui*'s awareness of his own mediocrity, and his reaction to it. For it is a mistake to assume, because *Lui* is so defiant in his belief that 's'il importe d'être sublime en quelque genre, c'est surtout en mal', and because this so closely echoes Diderot's much quoted 'Je ne hais pas les grands crimes', that *le Neveu* has actually achieved some greatness in evil-doing. If he had possessed an ounce of either Bouret's genius or his ruth-lessness, he would not now be reduced to making *Moi* pay for the lemonade. For all the contempt he expresses towards them, he is himself not far from being 'une espèce', and the very incident which has led to his most recent misfortune is proof of how he is, himself, 'également gauche dans le bien et dans le mal'. He nevertheless both assumes and transcends his mediocrity by what he describes, immediately after the tale of the 'renégat d'Avignon', as his 'art'. This is not, as his present penury again makes clear, that of actually being a 'renégat d'Avignon'. If he were, he would be enjoying the notecase, purse and jewels of his victim, and would not be borrowing a pinch of snuff from a neighbour. It is the art of telling stories about what has or might have happened in the past, of reliving a heightened, mythical, but æsthetically satisfying version of experience through the dramatic presenta-tion of it to an audience. Like Malraux's Clappique, he lives by the stories he tells, by the image of himself which he compels other people to contemplate, by the amazement which he delights in provoking, by the artistry which—precisely because he lacks the ability to cast it into the permanent and perfect mould of a work of art—he puts into playing out the role or series of roles which he has chosen to perform. Occasionally, like all those who exist primarily for other people, he varies or forgets the part he is playing, matching in the poses he strikes the 'inégalité de ton' which so contrasts with the measured diction of *Moi*'s pronouncements. Thus, 'La paix chez soi' is obtained at one point by thundering like Jove; and at another by quietly acquiescing in whatever his 'chère moitié' decides to do. Even on the more important topic of musical education, he seems unable to decide which attitude to strike. Music leads to nothing, and he would wring the neck of his 'petit sauvage' if his son showed any disposition for it. Yet, at the age of eight, Angélique Diderot is already four years behind in what he clearly regards as the essential art of learning the harpsichord. Admittedly, his ideas are consistent on the more important topics of ethics, the theatre, general education and the iniquity of *le cher oncle*. But it is the opportunity to flaunt them in conversation which really interests him, and without an audience he is nothing. Like the 'homme sociable' of the *Discours sur l'Inégalité, le Neveu* 'ne sait vivre que dans l'opinion des autres'; and it is, again in Rousseau's phrase, 'de leur seul jugement qu'il tire le sentiment de son existence'.

It is undoubtedly one of Diderot's greatest achievements as a creative writer to have transformed a person who must, in real life, often have been a disappointment or a bore into a permanently fascinating individual. For it is, alas, only rarely that the great 'characters' of the literary, intellectual or academic world come up to scratch when we meet them. The performing artist who has no physical instrument on which to exercise a specific and objectively discernible technique is too dependent on the accidents of social intercourse ever to guarantee a predictable and repeatable performance. Like the alcoholic fiancé in Christiane Rochefort's *Le Repos du Guerrier,* who could invent the most marvellous novels until the moment came for actually putting them down on paper, the real Rameau's nephews are always going to be brilliant elsewhere.[6] This is not, of course, a problem peculiar to mythomaniacs. Diderot himself noted two qualities characteristic of a good conversation which are both equally applicable to *Le Neveu de Rameau*. On the one hand, there is the mysterious unity which brings about the situation where 'tout se tient', and where nothing is ever wholly irrelevant; and, on the other, there is the extreme difficulty of retracing the steps by which one subject leads to the next, and whereby this unity grows quite spontaneously from the bringing together of several minds. The virtual impossibility of reproducing the intellectual excitement which can, in favourable circumstances, accompany either a conversation or a virtuoso performance by a verbal exhibitionist such as *le Neveu,* obviously constituted a major æsthetic challenge to Diderot; and it is this challenge which helps to explain why he took so much care over the composition of *Le Neveu de Rameau.* It was not only because he wished to have the last word in the argument over *Les Philosophes* that he revised the dialogue so frequently and perhaps, if Paul Vernière's recent arguments are valid,[7] wrote it all out again in his own hand as late as 1783. The belief that 'la vengeance est un plat qui se mange froid' would certainly fit in with the immense confidence that Diderot had in posterity, and help to explain why he made no attempt to publish what is undoubtedly, in many respects, a polemical work. The future could be trusted to give Palissot and his minions their just deserts, and show the editor of the *En-cyclopédie* to have had right on his side[8]. But what really mattered, for Diderot the writer, was the creation of a work of art that did precisely what *le Neveu* himself had so signally failed to do: use his talents for conversation, buffoonery and anecdote to create a 'bel ouvrage'. It is this, rather than the vituperative portrait of the 'ménagerie' which con-stitutes Diderot's final revenge; and his achievement is all the greater in that it can be seen as a triumph not only over his enemies but over himself.

The similarities between Diderot and *le Neveu* are, of course, obvious and well-known; the same loud voice, the same delight in conversation, the same obsessive paternal love, the same taste for digression, the same vitality, the same extreme changeability, the same relish for argument, the same indulgence in pantomime and play-acting. 'Quand je me rappelle le souvenir de Diderot', wrote Meister, 'l'immense variété de ses idées, l'étonnante multiplicité de ses connaissances, l'élan rapide, la chaleur, le tumulte impétueux de son imagination, tout le charme, et tout le désordre de ses entretiens, j'ose comparer son âme à la nature, telle qu'il la voyait lui-même, riche, fertile, abondante en germes de toute espèce, douce et sauvage, simple et majestueuse, bonne et sublime, mais sans aucun principe dominant, sans maître et sans Dieu',[9] and the description could well apply—if such a being were conceivable—to a successful and respectable version of *le Neveu*. Indeed, one of Diderot's most recent biographers, Yves Benot, goes so far as to claim that 'le bavardage et la dispersion, avant d'être le fait du Neveu, sont d'abord les traits dominants de Diderot', and to write that it is 'Diderot qui parle au lieu d'agir, mais surtout au lieu d'écrire et de composer'.[10] That there was a Neveu de Rameau in Diderot is scarcely open to doubt, and Jean Fabre's thesis that the dialogue was born partly out of Diderot's regret that he had not, in his own personal life, kicked over the traces quite so fully as Jean-François Rameau—or Jean-Jacques Rousseau—remains the most comprehensive *hypothèse de lecture* to Diderot's one completely uncontested masterpiece. What is equally evident is that Diderot himself experienced something of the same discontent at what he felt, on occasion, to be his own inadequacy as a creative artist. There is more than a hint of this in another of the examples which he gives in the *Réfutation,* for when he writes: 'On sent si bien ce qu'on peut et ce qu'on ne peut pas, qu'enfermez-moi à la Bastille et dites-moi: "Vois-tu ce lacet? Il faut dans un an, dans dix ans d'ici, tendre le cou et l'accepter, ou faire une belle scène de Racine . . ." Je répondrai: "Ce n'est pas la peine de tant attendre; finissons, et qu'on m'étrangle sur-le-champ" ', it is difficult not to recall the central place which Racine occupies in the discussion on genius in *Le Neveu de Rameau*.[11] Yet whereas *le Neveu,* faced with the dis-covery that 'au bout de ma ligne, je lis que je suis un sot, un sot, un sot', gives himself over to the easier delights of argument and anecdote, Diderot perseveres. The multiple revisions to which he subjected *La Religieuse,* like the care with which he wrote out the final version of *Le Neveu de Rameau,* are both part of a victory which he won in solitude over the side of his personality which Madame Necker epitomised when she wrote that he was 'le Garrick de la philosophie' and added—rather unkindly—that 'son plus grand talent consiste en la pantomime'.[12]

On at least one occasion, moreover, the Diderot of whom the Abbé de Vauxcelles wrote that 'il avait de l'esprit chaque fois qu'il perdait la tête', whom the Président des Brosses described as a 'faiseur de digressions perpétuelles', did experience the same difficulty as *le Neveu* in putting down on paper the ideas which had seemed so brilliant when all he had done was think about them. 'Ce n'est pas que le soir', he wrote to Sophie in September 1768, 'quand je me couche, je n'aie la tête remplie des plus beaux projets pour le lendemain. Mais le matin, quand je me lève, c'est un dégoût, un engourdissement, une aversion pour l'encre, la plume et les livres', and on that occasion he too proceeded to find consolation in paying visits, listening to music and wasting some three hours talking.[13] The volume and quality of Diderot's work are more than sufficient proof that this was a temptation to which he yielded only rarely, but it was nevertheless an aspect of his own experience which helps to explain not only why he made no attempt to publish *Le Neveu de Rameau* but why he did not even tell anybody he was writing it. What better reply could be imagined to his own self-doubts and his own proclivity to 'le bavardage et la dispersion' than a work composed in silence and written out with no recourse to voice or audience? 'Voilà ce que c'est', exclaims *le Neveu,* 'de trouver un accoucheur qui sait irriter, précipiter les douleurs et faire sortir l'enfant', and the mediocrity of Jean-François lies precisely in the fact that he cannot create alone. By writing *Le Neveu de Rameau* in isolation, not only without a midwife, but without even a passive listener, Diderot finally proved to himself how wrong his critics were and how unfounded, in the last analysis, was the notion that he too, as Madame Necker suggested, might be a mere gesticulating buffoon.

The æsthetic value of *Le Neveu de Rameau* nevertheless goes far beyond its dismissal of Diderot's self-doubts. It is not an introspective, solipsistic work, but one that raises an immense variety of universally interesting problems. The awareness of mediocrity is only one theme among many, and no study of the dialogue can even enumerate, let alone exhaust, all its riches. Yet there is one more feature of *Le Neveu de Rameau* which is linked to the preoccupations examined here, and that is its extraordinary atmosphere of vitality and even of happiness. Partly, of course, the happiness is Diderot's own. He has written his master-piece, and the truculent 'Rira bien qui rira le dernier' is more than a challenge to the future to see where justice lay in the *querelle des philosophes*. It is an assertion of artistic triumph, and the expression of a victory in the only realm that matters to a writer: that of æsthetics. But it is also the reflection of a fundamental generosity of spirit, in that it gives to Diderot's personal and philosophical enemy the last word in a dialogue where his vitality and im-pudence have already been allowed to carry the day in style, originality and argument. For it is *Lui*'s language which is rich in imagery and imagination, not *Moi*'s more ponderous and measured tones. It is *Lui* whose vision of man and society reflects Diderot's most original speculations, and anticipates Marx, Darwin, Nietzsche, Pavlov and Freud. It is *Lui* who asks the important questions about genius, morality, education, heredity, music and the nature of artistic creation. It is *Lui* whose love for his child is spontaneous, absolute and potentially tragic; and *Lui* whose respect for this child's individuality, however ironically expressed, which brings out the stifling and over-protective nature of the cocoon in which *Moi* seeks to insulate his daughter from reality. It is *Lui* who sees himself and others as they really are, and whose ability for self-criticism again underlines the static, unsatisfactory nature of *Moi*'s beliefs. For as *Moi* passes from the detachment of the observer 'qui écoute et démêle son monde' to the disturbed state of the indignant contender who can answer argument only by abuse—'C'est que vous êtes un fainéant, un gourmand, un lâche, une âme de boue'—*Lui* continues to grow in self-awareness and self-confidence. He may indeed be a second-rate musician. But at least he knows it, whereas *Moi* is so fixated in his own attitudes that he has almost forgotten what it is like to feel inadequate. *Lui* has, moreover, chosen a solution to his own mediocrity which is in every way in keeping with what he is. He has a gift for parody and pantomime, and he uses it. Neither the strictest observer of the parable of the talents nor the most enthusiastic reader of the *Supplément au Voyage de Bougainville* could do more. He is not, of course, a Diderot. He has not transcended his failings by the creation of a work of art that expresses and goes beyond them. But what he is, he is; and if it is the fate of the buffoon and mythomaniac to wait for the next listener before achieving the realisation that he is 'toujours le même', it is a fate which he accepts. After all, the possibility of a Diderot preserving him for posterity could never be excluded; and there has never been anything to prevent artists' models from being happy.

NOTES

1 See *Men and Women* (1855), Browning's *Poetical Works* (OUP, 1940), pp. 432–5. It is improbable that Browning knew Diderot's dialogue, and Andrea is, of course, very different from *Le Neveu*. He has, after all, painted two hundred pictures. But he *feels* himself inferior to the greatest artists of his time, and adopts an attitude towards experience which enables him to place this feeling in a satisfactory emotional and biographical context.

2 Quoted by Jean Fabre from the 1781 edition of *Les Trois Siècles de la Littérature* (*Le Neveu de Rameau*, édition critique, Geneva, 1963). The 1761 quotation is from the *Éloge de Richardson*, *Œuvres Esthétiques* (Paris, 1959), p. 48.

3 See 'L'Angoisse de l'échec et la genèse du *Neveu de Rameau*', *Diderot Studies*, 3 (Geneva, 1961), pp. 285–305.

4 This point is very clearly made in notes 151–155 of Jean Fabre's edition.

5 *Œuvres Complètes de Diderot*, ed. J. Assézat, (Paris, 1875–7), Vol. II, pp. 369–70.

6 See *Le Repos du guerrier* (Paris, 1958), pp. 223–7.

7 See *Histoire littéraire et Papyrologie: à propos des autographes de Diderot*, RHLF, 1966, pp. 409–418.

8 For the view that *Le Neveu de Rameau* can still be meaningfully interpreted as a polemical work, see Chapter 8 of Hilde H. Freud's *Palissot and 'Les Philosophes'*, *Diderot Studies*, 9 (Geneva, 1967): '*Le Neveu de Rameau*, Diderot's belated reply.'

9 Jacques-Henri Meister, *Aux Mânes de Diderot*, in: Diderot, *Œuvres Complètes*, Vol. I, pp. 369–70.

10 Yves Benot, *Diderot, de l'athéisme à l'anticolonialisme* (Paris, 1970), p. 29.

11 op. cit., p. 342.

12 Quoted by Benot, op. cit. p. 100.

13 Sec the letter dated 10 September 1768 in *Lettres à Sophie Volland*, ed. Babelon (Paris, 1938), p. 178.

26

Les Liaisons dangereuses:
d'une morale des faits à une morale de
la signification

P. VERNIÈRE

Quand l'heure approche de quitter une œuvre et un auteur, c'est-à-dire de refouler l'œuvre dans cette bibliothèque intérieure qu'on appelle «culture» et de refouler l'auteur dans ce cimetière de notre souvenir où quelques amis perdus côtoient tant d'indifférents, il est essentiel de se demander, à propos des *Liaisons dangereuses,* ce que fut le but de Laclos, le sens et la signification de son roman, et de délimiter avec vigueur les intentions conscientes de Laclos et la part magique d'une œuvre qui, au-delà des mots, nous poursuit et nous hante. Tous les biographes de Laclos ont été frappés par l'espèce de disproportion qui existe entre l'officier d'artillerie, avec son apparente médiocrité, et la puissance de l'œuvre. Ni l'homme, dans la mesure où il nous est perméable, ni la carrière littéraire ultérieure, dans ses «ratages» et les velléités ambitieuses de secrétaire de Philippe-Égalité ou de secrétaire aux Jacobins, ni la vie de famille, bourgeoisement tendre, n'offrent les issues normales qui puissent non pas expliquer mais seulement rendre probables les rapports qui traditionnellement s'établissent entre une œuvre et son auteur.

C'est Marcel Proust, dans le *Contre Sainte-Beuve,* qui s'est élevé le plus vigoureusement contre cette tradition critique qui délaissait «le moi profond» de l'auteur pour sa vie socialisée, et faisait de l'œuvre un épiphénomène naturellement explicable.

Les *Liaisons dangereuses* sont un des meilleurs exemples qui puisse vérifier l'opinion de Proust. Nul doute que Laclos ait voulu faire un grand livre et les notes de Tilly semblent véridiques: «Un ouvrage qui fît du bruit et qui retentît encore sur la terre quand j'y aurai passé».[1] Mais cette exigence, emphatiquement exprimée, de succès littéraire et mondain, ne rend pas l'œuvre plus claire. Notre propos serait d'aborder le problème qui trouble les rapports de Laclos et de la critique depuis presque deux cents ans: celui de la morale, ou plutôt de la signification morale des *Liaisons.* Il s'agit là beaucoup moins d'interprétation ou de casuistique que de faits: depuis la controverse de Laclos et de madame Riccoboni en 1782 jusqu'aux jugements les plus récents, nous n'avons pas à prendre parti, mais à ramasser des opinions et à analyser une œuvre. Nous verrons rapidement que l'essentiel n'est pas de discerner si les *Liaisons* peuvent avoir une influence morale heureuse et malheureuse, si une société donnée doit recourir à un «Index» pour se protéger; mais si les *Liaisons* ont un sens, et si ce sens a été perçu et voulu par l'auteur. Au delà d'une *morale des faits* qui va interpréter une intrigue, une histoire, des personnages, une société donnée, la difficulté réelle sera d'apprécier le *degré de connivence* qui lie l'auteur et ses personnages. Balzac est lié à Vautrin et nous voyons mal dans quelle mesure madame de Merteuil peut être fille de Laclos au même titre que sa fille selon la chair, Catherine-Soulange. Allons plus loin encore: dans quelle mesure cette connivence est-elle consciente?

Mais n'allons-nous pas atteindre un «moi profond» que Laclos, écrivain des «lumières» apparemment épris de moralité et de progrès humain, ne tenait pas à voir apparaître au seuil de sa conscience?

C'est ainsi que la *morale des faits,* tirée d'une œuvre et de la connaissance extérieure d'un être, fait place à une *morale de la signification* qui tient compte, au delà d'une interprétation sociologique dont jouent avec aisance Roger Vaillant ou André Maurois, d'une dimension de profondeur, celle où un auteur n'est plus responsable de son œuvre parce qu'il n'est pas entièrement responsable de son être. Il ne s'agit pas de «démasquer» Laclos qui probablement s'est cru moral et vertueux, mais de soupçonner derrière une œuvre ambiguë un inquiétant personnage qui peignait trop bien le mal pour n'avoir jamais subi ses atteintes et ses tentations. Même si la réussite ne récompense pas notre effort, il nous paraît nécessaire de reconnaître dans les *Liaisons* «ce reflet de flamme souterraine» que Lucien Maury évoquait à propos du *Diable amoureux* de Cazotte.

I. UNE POLÉMIQUE D'AVRIL 1782

Revoyons d'abord une polémique d'avril 1782 entre Laclos et une de ses amies, madame Riccoboni, d'ailleurs beaucoup plus âgée que lui, mais romancière célèbre des *Lettres de Fanny Butler* et de *Juliette Catesby* (1757 et 1759). Cette vieille dame, un peu prude, alors âgée de 69 ans, ancienne actrice de Marivaux, mais entichée de morale et de féminisme, avait accepté l'adaptation par Laclos d'une de ses nouvelles, *Ernestine,* qui devint en 1777 un scénario d'opéra-comique. C'est un échange de huit lettres. Des quatre missives de la vieille dame nous pouvons résumer ainsi les arguments essentiels: le roman donne une idée révoltante des mœurs et du goût de la nation française; madame de Merteuil est un monstre à qui l'auteur prête trop d'agréments et de charme; l'auteur ne prévoit aucune punition juridique à l'égard de ces monstres: «On vous reprochera toujours de présenter à vos lecteurs une vile créature, appliquée dès sa jeunesse à se former au vice, à se composer un masque pour cacher à tous les regards le dessein d'adopter les mœurs des prostituées»; en fin de compte, «tant de dépravation irrite et n'instruit pas, vous en avez trop dit et nul ne croira à votre affectation de moralité. Vous serez marqué socialement par la noirceur du monde que vous avez peint, même s'il existe.»

Avec une exquise politesse, Laclos se plaint de la sévérité du jugement, mais sans hargne et sans se départir d'une totale courtoisie.

En quoi consiste sa réponse? D'abord les Merteuil existent et Laclos prétend qu'il ne pourrait effacer aucun des traits de son monstre «sans mentir à sa conscience, sans taire au moins une partie de ce qu'il a vu»: «Serait-ce donc un tort d'avoir voulu, dans l'indignation de ces horreurs, les dévoiler, les combattre, et peut-être en prévenir de semblables?» A ses yeux le réalisme porte en lui sa propre morale.

Quant à l'art, il ne saurait masquer, mais renforce au contraire par contraste «l'impression d'horreur que le vice doit toujours exciter». Madame de Merteuil comme le Tartuffe de Molière est un personnage symbolique que l'auteur voue à l'indignation publique: «J'ai rassemblé, dit-il, dans un même personnage les traits épars du même caractère:la dépravation féminine jointe à l'hypocrisie». Tous ces cas sont vrais, on les retrouve dans la nature et dans la société. D'ailleurs la meilleure preuve de la réussite, n'est-ce pas le bruit que fait ce livre, et qui révèle «la salutaire indignation publique»?

Débat banal sur la moralité de l'art et sur lequel Racine avait tout dit dans la préface de *Phèdre*: «catharsis», purgation des passions et des vices, punition exemplaire des méchants. Mais le problème est de savoir si Laclos croit vraiment aux arguments qu'il avance. A le lire, on le sent surtout flatté du bruit qu'il excite, de son succès. Vis-à-vis de madame Riccoboni, qui n'a pas l'indulgence de la vieille madame de Rosemonde, il parade comme un coq, joue au moraliste et même au pamphlétaire social puisqu'il souligne «ce que le rang et la fortune permettent d'ajouter à ces vices infâmes». L'artilleur nous paraît pour l'heure «un Savonarole de boudoir».

II. ACCUSATIONS D'IMMORALISME

Or, en deux cents ans, la critique n'a pas cessé de prendre les *Liaisons* pour un ouvrage des plus dangereux. Par extension Laclos a passé pour un auteur cynique et un personnage démoniaque.

Il est difficile dans un concert d'ajouter sa propre voix. Comment interpréter un homme qui, au travers d'une période tourmentée et d'une carrière politique orageuse, s'était fait beaucoup plus d'ennemis que d'amis? Tâchons cependant d'instruire le procès.

Meister, en avril 1782, dans la *Correspondance littéraire* envoyée en Europe à une trentaine de princes et de têtes couronnées, insiste sur la moralité du dénouement:

«Après avoir présenté à ses lecteurs des personnages si vicieux, si coupables, l'auteur n'a pas osé se dispenser d'en faire justice. Aussi l'a-t-il fait. M. de Valmont et Mme de Merteuil finissent par se brouiller, un peu légèrement à la vérité. Mais des personnes de ce mérite sont très capables de se brouiller ainsi. M. de Valmont est tué par l'ami qu'il a trahi. La conduite de Mme de Merteuil est enfin démasquée. Pour que sa punition soit plus effrayante, on lui donne la petite vérole qui la défigure affreusement. Elle y perd même un œil et, pour exprimer combien cet accident l'a rendue hideuse, on lui fait dire au marquis de ° ° ° que la maladie l'«a retournée et qu'à présent son âme est sur sa figure».

«Toutes les circonstances de ce dénouement», ajoute Meister, «n'occupent guère que 4 ou 5 pages. En conscience, peut-on présumer que ce soit assez de morale pour détruire le poison répandu dans quatre volumes de séduction, où l'art de corrompre et de tromper se trouve développé avec tout le charme que peuvent lui prêter les grâces de l'esprit et de l'imagination, l'ivresse du plaisir et le jeu très entraînant d'une intrigue aussi facile qu'ingénieuse? On rencontrerait à Paris peu de liaisons aussi dangereuses pour une jeune personne que la lecture des *Liaisons dangereuses* de M. de Laclos».

Même son chez Laharpe en 1782 dans sa *Correspondance littéraire* envoyée au czarevitch Paul de Russie, le fils de Catherine II: «L'erreur, volontaire sans doute, de Laclos est d'avoir donné pour les mœurs du siècle ce qui n'est au fond que l'histoire d'une vingtaine de fats et de catins qui se croient une grande supériorité d'esprit pour avoir érigé le libertinage en principe et fait une science de la dépravation». Des atrocités gratuitement révoltantes, des horreurs absurdes, voilà le fond de l'ouvrage. Enfin la conclusion est postiche: «La plus honnête femme peut être défigurée par la petite vérole et ruinée par un procès. Le vice ne trouve donc pas ici sa punition en lui-même et ce dénouement sans moralité ne vaut pas mieux que le reste».

Le témoignage de Tilly est intéressant; c'est un authentique libertin qui prend Laclos pour un cynique. Dans une interview donnée à Londres en 1791, alors qu'il accompagnait le duc d'Orléans, il essaie de saisir son secret. Pour lui, Laclos est un corrupteur conscient, d'autant plus dangereux que son livre est techniquement excellent. «C'est l'ouvrage d'une tête de premier ordre, d'un cœur pourri et d'un génie du mal» . . . «un de ces météores désastreux qui ont apparu sous un ciel enflammé à la fin du XVIIIe siècle».

Nous pourrions citer encore plus de vingt témoignages anciens, de la marquise de Coigny, de madame de Genlis (à vrai dire son ennemie), de Montjoie, de Rétif de la Bretonne, de Dumont, de madame de Staël, tout aussi violents. Mais si l'on considère que de Baudelaire à Malraux la réhabilitation de Laclos se déroule sur un plan esthétique et philosophique, mais jamais sur le plan moral, un tel «consensus» est assez effrayant. Lorsque Baudelaire écrit: «Livre de moraliste aussi haut que les plus élevés, aussi profond que les plus profonds», pense-t-il à autre chose qu'à la valeur psychologique et métaphysique de l'ouvrage? N'ajoute-t-il pas: «Caractère général sinistre . . . La détestable humanité se fait un enfer préparatoire». Et s'il admire Laclos, c'est à cause de la «postulation satanique» qu'il lui suppose. Laclos est pour lui un alibi dialectique.

Beaucoup plus étrange est l'espèce d'effroi que conservent à son égard bon nombre de critiques modernes. Ils y voient un livre terrible et singulier qui dépasse de loin les réalités sociologiques. Je ne vois pour croire à la valeur morale des *Liaisons* qu'Émile Dard et André Maurois, «biographes naïfs». D'ailleurs si les *Liaisons* n'étaient qu'un pamphlet contre la noblesse dépravée des années 1780, quel intérêt autre qu'historique aurions-nous à le lire? Or le livre vit et terrifie. Limitons-nous à deux réactions significatives: celle d'André Suarès en 1923:

«Jamais livre n'a plus outragé la part sensible de l'homme. Les *Liaisons dangereuses* sont le seul livre dangereux . . . parce qu'il n'en est sans doute pas un autre qui tienne si peu compte du sentiment et qui ose l'exclure à tel point de la passion qu'elle n'a plus rien de commun avec la sensibilité. Livre redoutable, livre qui attente à la vie».

Celle de Jean Giraudoux en 1932: «Même aujourd'hui les *Liaisons dangereuses* demeurent le seul roman français qui nous donne l'impression du danger».

Mais après tous ces témoignages accablants, dans le procès posthume fait à l'œuvre de Laclos, il est temps de revenir aux faits, c'est-à-dire à l'œuvre elle-même.

III. LA MORALE DES FAITS

Peut-on lire encore d'un œil neuf les *Liaisons* après tant de commentateurs et de gloses? Si l'on consulte les personnages, il est aisé d'opposer le monde traditionaliste de madame de Volanges et de madame de Rosemonde au monde sans foi ni loi de madame de Merteuil et de Valmont. Un monde de faiblesse et d'indulgences, mais aussi d'erreur, de duperie, d'incapacité psychologique, fondé sur un christianisme usé et ritualiste, sans force ni efficace, qui n'impose même pas le respect, voici le premier. Madame de Volanges, certes, se méfie de Valmont, mais son aveuglement vis-à-vis de sa fille dépasse toute mesure. Elle est celle qui «se refuse à croire au mal». Quant à Rosemonde, après la mort de Valmont, son «neveu chéri» en qui elle ne voyait qu'un charmant coquin, que dira-t-elle sentencieusement à Danceny (Lettre CLXXI)?: «Si on était éclairé sur son véritable bonheur, on ne le chercherait jamais hors des bornes prescrites par les lois et la religion».

Je me refuse à croire que Laclos ait fait siennes ces platitudes et que madame de Rosemonde soit comme dans les comédies de Molière «le sage de la pièce». L'aveuglement et la sottise des «honnêtes gens» dans les *Liaisons* prouvent à coup sûr que leur honnêteté est contestée par Laclos et qu'en tous cas il ne s'assimile nullement à leur sort ou à leur idéal. Faut-il aller plus loin? Voyons quelques personnages secondaires. M. Bertrand, par exemple, intendant de Valmont qui regrette que son maître n'ait pu obtenir secours religieux et aide spirituelle au moment de sa mort (Lettre CLXIII), mais se réjouit cependant qu'il ait pu bénéficier de l'extrême-onction. Présentation dérisoire où Laclos semble se moquer du bon apôtre. Autre exemple: le Père Anselme qui, par sa niaiserie plus qu'humaine, permet l'entrevue ultime où madame de Tourvel cèdera à Valmont. Car il se croit l'intermédiaire de la grâce divine au moment même où il n'est qu'un inconscient entremetteur. Dérision encore de la part de Laclos. C'est le cas de dire que «les voies de Dieu sont impénétrables» surtout lorsqu'elles sont machinées par l'officier artilleur.

Passons à la Présidente: c'est une «prude», une «dévote», une «convertisseuse» prise au piège. Elle épie et fait épier Valmont, elle se réjouit de sa «bonne action» au village; elle le défend contre les allégations de madame de Volanges. Même lorsqu'elle saura les desseins de Valmont, sans équivoque possible, elle s'attendrira aux nouvelles de sa «fausse maladie». Elle croira à sa «fausse conversion»; elle n'hésitera pas à partager la niaiserie du Père Anselme. Pécheresse, elle jouira de son péché en le racontant à madame de Rosemonde. Elle ne mourra pas de sa faute, mais de la certitude de n'être plus aimée. Désespérée, damnée donc. Ce n'est qu'à l'heure finale qu'elle pardonnera à Valmont après d'ailleurs avoir appris sa mort. Cette vie et cette mort soi-disant chrétiennes sont encore une dérision. Pensons à la mort de madame de Mortsauf dans le *Lys dans la vallée* et nous saisirons la distance. C'est volontairement que Laclos a associé l'erreur et l'échec, voire même la bêtise, à une vision chrétienne de la vie.

Il éprouve bien sûr une certaine tendresse, comme Valmont d'ailleurs, pour sa chère Tourvel. Plus tard, sous la Révolution, il en vantera le charme à son épouse. Mais pour cet esprit géomètre, pour ce philosophe des lumières, il est évident que la morale ne s'appuie pas sur une transcendance religieuse, ni même sur la «loi naturelle» chère à Voltaire. Dans ce roman qui n'est pas un pamphlet anticlérical ni un conte voltairien mais qui prétend à l'authenticité, le visage donné aux tenants de la morale traditionnelle, le rôle que ceux-ci jouent, les paroles qu'ils prononcent, équivalent à une véritable «profession de foi» de la part de Laclos. Or, le résultat est grave, c'est de détourner la sympathie du lecteur vers le monde des forts, celui de Valmont et de la Merteuil, qui sont attirants par leur force et séduisants par leur intelligence. Qui voudrait de cette morale sanctionnée par l'échec, cette morale des «esclaves», pour parler comme Nietzsche? Par le mépris évident que le romancier porte à la morale traditionnelle, il semble que, sans en être pleinement conscient (et c'est le problème que nous ne pourrons éluder), il valorise intellectuellement et esthétiquement l'univers fuligineux de ses héros du mal. C'est ce prestige démoniaque que les moralistes sont en droit de lui reprocher, même s'il n'en est pas pleinement responsable.

Voilà pourquoi il n'est pas inutile de revenir sur la conclusion des *Liaisons* dont la plupart des commentateurs depuis Meister et Laharpe contestent la légèreté. C'est Laclos lui-même dans sa polémique avec madame Riccoboni qui évoque le précédent de *Tartuffe*. Comme Molière, il punit en quelques pages les méchants: la mort de Valmont, l'œil perdu de madame de Merteuil et son visage grêlé; l'exil des faibles, Cécile et Danceny, et leur refuge chrétien: Malte et le couvent des Carmélites. Nous avons vu le sens qu'il faut donner à la conclusion «chrétienne» de madame de Rosemonde et au pardon «chrétien» de la présidente. Tout ceci sonne faux. De même que Tartuffe devait triompher, logiquement et même légalement, de même la conclusion des *Liaisons* nous paraît postiche. En évoquant *Tartuffe* Laclos l'avoue implicitement.

Mais voyons de plus près: nous voudrions éliminer les raisons psychologiques qui donneraient quelque vraisemblance au duel final de Valmont et de la Merteuil: plus que l'idée, leibnizienne en fin de compte, que le mal se détruit lui-même (et que rien dans l'œuvre de Laclos ne permet de lui attribuer), c'est plutôt l'idée d'un sinistre règlement de comptes entre complices qui prévaudrait.

Cependant les faits, qui, ne l'oublions pas, sont choisis par l'auteur et imposés par lui, nous orientent vers une autre interprétation. Laclos, dans une société athée qu'il jalouse mais dont il partage l'idéologie, développe une morale aristocratique de l'honneur qui est pour l'heure le véritable substitut de la morale chrétienne défaillante. Morts ou vifs, Valmont et la Merteuil sont «déshonorés», et par là privés d'existence légale dans leur milieu. Ils n'ont pas respecté la loi et les usages de leur classe. Le jeu libertin, nous l'avons vu, veut la connivence des victimes, et la connivence de la société. Ils sont allés trop loin. La vraie punition, il faut la voir dans la scène du théâtre des Italiens: la Merteuil est huée et Prévan applaudi. Prévan est et demeure le héros de la société libertine, l'inimitable joueur qui triomphe des «Inséparables», qui amuse mais ne tue personne. Ainsi Valmont et la Merteuil sont éliminés. L'épée de Danceny a rétabli l'ordre.

Or cet ordre est aristocratique. Ni l'État qui intervenait dans *Tartuffe* sous les traits de l'exempt parlant au nom du roi, ni l'Église ridiculisée par l'affaire du Père Anselme, n'y sont mêlés. Mais qui ne voit que s'effondre dès lors la thèse historico-politique de Roger Vaillant? Celle d'un Laclos bourgeois dressé contre les aristocrates? Il est essentiel au contraire de constater que Laclos conserve et justifie la morale de son milieu, ce milieu militaire d'officiers de carrière avec les sanctions de l'honneur, la pratique du duel, notamment, et cela au détriment de toute morale fondée sur une transcendance religieuse, sur une transcendance de l'État ou de la Société, et même de toute morale «philosophique» de l'intérêt général. Pour mesurer l'originalité de Laclos, il nous suffira de comparer la conclusion des *Liaisons* avec le dénouement chrétien de *Manon Lescaut* ou avec les commentaires philosophiques que Diderot apporte, dans *Jacques le Fataliste,* à l'histoire de madame de la Pommeraye.

Le vrai problème de Laclos, en 1782, n'est peut-être pas tant d'apprécier la moralité de son œuvre que de discerner la signification des *Liaisons:* problème qui requiert moins l'analyse rigoureuse des textes qu'une psycho-analyse, hélas chanceuse, de l'auteur.

IV. UNE MORALE DE LA SIGNIFICATION

Nous pourrions émettre deux doutes et par là-même terminer le débat. D'abord, il suffirait de mettre en cause la sincérité de Laclos: ensuite il suffirait de décréter que les œuvres littéraires n'ont aucune signification.

Nous ne pouvons accepter un tel aveu de défaite, qui serait en fin de compte un désaveu de l'intelligence. Sur le premier point, il nous paraît évident que Laclos est un homme «rusé» pour qui les *Liaisons dangereuses* sont à la fois, comme pour tant d'auteurs, «une fin» et «un moyen», une fin en ce qu'ils y ont mis leur cœur et leur talent, un moyen en ce qu'ils en espèrent le succès et la gloire. L'œuvre des *Liaisons* reflète cette double ambition, mais cette ambiguïté ne saurait nous faire croire que Laclos n'est pas sincère. Laclos est sincère comme Rousseau est sincère dans les *Confessions* et dans les *Rêveries.* Laclos peut croire qu'il attaque vraiment une société corrompue symbolisée par Valmont et la Merteuil. Laclos peut croire à la valeur morale de sa conclusion. Toute sa vie ultérieure plaide en faveur de sa bonne foi. Sa vie ultérieure, certes, mais sa vie intérieure? Cette face cachée de soi-même qu'aucun miroir ne révèle? Diderot, moins pudique ou plus franc, sentait qu'en lui-même végétait un être inconnu et dans son *Essai sur les femmes* reconnaissait d'étranges profondeurs. La critique littéraire a-t-elle le droit d'aborder ces rives inconnues? Nous en sentons le risque, mais nous prenons le risque. Le principal est celui de nous bâtir un Laclos de fantaisie et de substituer au Laclos de Baudelaire et au Laclos de Malraux un nouveau mythe. Pris entre une critique positiviste «universitaire» qui, devant le mystère d'un homme et d'une œuvre est contrainte d'avouer son échec et une critique «divinatoire» dont les intuitions peuvent être illusoires, il faut conserver la tête froide et l'esprit lent.

1 *Le problème du mal*

Nous pensons que le meilleur moyen d'aller plus avant ou plus profond est d'aborder le problème du mal dans les *Liaisons* et de se demander comment Laclos le pose et comment il le résout. Je voudrais d'abord faire mienne l'introduction de M. Versini en répétant ses propres termes: «Comment aborder», dit-il, «la présence du mal dans les *Liaisons dangereuses,* sujet de prédilection pour une critique nourrie de philosophie? Ferons-nous de «l'enfer glacé» des *Liaisons* un jalon sur la pente d'une descente aux Enfers qui conduirait à «l'enfer fuligineux» de Sade? et de Valmont un précurseur des damnés romantiques, ou de la marquise une «sœur luciférienne» de Rimbaud? Rattacherons-nous le roman à une tradition «féroce», l'insérerons-nous dans une chaîne du pessimisme cruel qui irait de Racine et du jansénisme à Baudelaire en passant par Duclos et Sade? Ou admettrons-nous de voir en Laclos un chrétien masqué animé d'une profonde croyance au péché originel selon l'idée de derrière de Baudelaire?[2]»

La première explication pourrait être historique. C'est Albert-Marie Schmidt, dans un article fondamental de la *Revue des sciences humaines* (avril-septembre 1951) intitulé «Duclos, Sade et la littérature féroce», qui a montré en quoi depuis Racine la cruauté morale animait une certaine littérature. Racine, en livrant Junie et Britannicus, Hippolyte et Aricie aux persécutions de monstres, écrivait par avance les *Crimes de l'amour* de Sade. Sans aller jusque là, car dans les *Liaisons* la torture demeure morale, on ne peut nier qu'une conception matérialiste et déterministe du monde pose différemment le problème du mal. Un ami de Voltaire, le marquis d'Argens, pousse le système jusqu'à l'absurde dans ses romans, peu connus de nos jours mais qui firent scandale, la *Thérèse philosophe* de 1740 et les *Ressources de l'amour* de 1752. Tout est bien dans le monde, y compris le mal que Dieu a voulu comme le reste. Bien plus, le mal est nécessaire à l'équilibre du monde et c'est le triomphe de la vertu qui détruirait l'ordre. Le mal se confond avec la «nature». Dans cet univers que Diderot animera dans *Jacques le Fataliste* ou *le Neveu de Rameau*, l'homme déterminé par ses sensations et ses passions n'est plus responsable de ses actes. Le vice et la vertu dépendent du tempérament, de la fibre originelle. Dans cette optique, Valmont et la Merteuil sont des êtres naturels qui ne sauraient pécher; Cécile n'est plus «l'ordure originelle» selon Baudelaire, mais cette naturelle «machine à plaisir» que la marquise reconnaît précocement en elle. Valmont et la Merteuil ne sont pas plus coupables que le marquis des Arcis ou madame de la Pommeraye mis en scène par Diderot.

Rien n'autorise une telle interprétation de Laclos et des *Liaisons*. Laclos n'est pas un métaphysicien et nous ne le surprenons jamais en train d'absoudre ses héros en invoquant l'harmonie préétablie de Leibniz ou le déterminisme biologique cher à Diderot. S'il y a connivence entre Laclos et Valmont, elle n'est jamais avouée.

Certains auteurs ont cru qu'une notion métaphysique du mal présidait à l'interprétation des *Liaisons*. C'est le cas d'un livre récent, *Das Böse in den Liaisons dangereuses,* qui est dû à M. Helmut Knufmann (Munich, 1965). Laclos s'inscrirait dans une tradition chrétienne qui irait de Saint Thomas à Kant; il serait donc comme tant d'autres, un chrétien qui s'ignore. Nous n'aurons aucune peine en lisant les *Liaisons* à détruire cette étrange illusion. Laclos est un homme des lumières et sur ce point nullement plus croyant que ses deux héros. Aucune dimension dualiste ou théologique ici. Le mal n'est pas une essence métaphysique, mais une réalité physique, terrestre et humaine. Le péché originel de la tradition chrétienne est un mensonge, une fable de primitifs. Mais si Laclos, comme les philosophes de son temps, comme Rousseau lui-même, rompt avec le péché originel, comment admettrait-il la réalité du démon? Valmont tient à laisser à la Présidente la crainte du péché pour rendre sa victoire plus belle, et non pour l'emporter sur un Dieu qu'il ignore. Sur ce point, l'univers de Valmont est celui de Laclos, un ciel vide de Dieu.

Mais si le mal n'est pas d'origine métaphysique, les humains sont donc seuls responsables?

Et c'est dans la perspective des théories de Rousseau, beaucoup plus que dans le sens déterministe de Diderot ou du baron d'Holbach, que s'inscrit notre auteur. Plus que la nature humaine, c'est la société civile qui est coupable. Il y a effectivement une critique de la société dans les *Liaisons,* ne serait-ce que le «danger des liaisons»; Fréron le fils, le futur terroriste, félicitera Laclos, dans son article de l'*Année littéraire,* de son courage pour avoir révélé «les excès monstrueux dont la société est tous les jours plus coupable» (1782).

Le mal *ontologique* pour parler comme les philosophes s'est donc dégradé en mal *sociologique* dans la pensée laïque optimiste du dix-huitième siècle. On peut dès lors soutenir qu'un des sens du roman, qu'un des desseins de Laclos, est de dénoncer une perversité sociale: le danger des liaisons est un scandale pour ceux qui comme Laclos veulent fonder le bonheur des hommes sur le *bonheur des liaisons,* c'est-à-dire sur une sociabilité harmonieuse.

Nous pensons qu'une telle interprétation qui est celle de M. Versini est judicieuse mais insuffisante. Sous prétexte de rallier Laclos à l'univers de Rousseau c'est faire bon marché des «structures mentales» du dix-huitième siècle qui demeurent encore, quoiqu'on fasse, des structures «chrétiennes». Rappelons-nous *Candide* et l'épisode du bateau hollandais coulé sous les yeux du héros de Voltaire. Dieu a fait périr le pirate, mais c'est le «diable» qui a noyé les autres. C'est le langage de Laclos qui permet dans les *Liaisons,* comme celui de Voltaire dans *Candide* ou dans *La Bible enfin expliquée,* de retrouver les structures anciennes.

2 *Parodie ou sacrilège?*

Or la trace la plus évidente de ces structures, c'est le goût constant des héros de Laclos pour la parodie chrétienne, que nous pouvons à volonté interpréter comme un jeu verbal ou comme un blasphème: donnons quelques exemples: Tout un registre parodique d'images religieuses s'étale dans la lettre IV, de Valmont à madame de Merteuil: «Depuis que nous séparant pour le *bonheur du monde,* nous *prêchons* la *foi* chacun de notre côté, il me semble que dans cette *mission* d'amour, vous avez fait plus de *prosélytes* que moi. Je connais votre *zèle,* votre ardente *ferveur*; et si ce *Dieu*-là nous jugeait sur nos *œuvres,* vous seriez un jour la *patronne* de quelque grande ville, tandis que votre ami serait un *saint* de village. Ce langage vous étonne, n'est-il pas vrai?» Et plus loin: «Vous serez saisie d'un *saint respect* et direz avec enthousiasme, Voilà l'homme selon mon cœur».

La Merteuil comprend fort bien ce langage. Elle s'en fait à son tour une spécialité. C'est la parodie évangélique de la lettre CXIII: «Ce sont les miettes de pain tombantes de la table du riche: celui-ci les dédaigne, mais le pauvre les recueille avidement et s'en nourrit. La pauvre Présidente reçoit ces miettes-là». Dans la lettre CXXI, la Merteuil prie Dieu qu'il ait Danceny en sa sainte et digne garde. Ailleurs elle bafoue le confesseur de Cécile (Lettre LI), comme Valmont bafoue le Père Anselme. La lettre LXXXI tout entière n'est qu'une parodie d'examen de conscience, d'un exercice spirituel ou d'une confession.

Mais le blasphème est plus net encore dans la lettre XXIII où Valmont se trouve transformé en un saint dont la Présidente fait le panégyrique, ou dans la lettre XXI qui relate la fausse bienfaisance: Valmont devient une «image de Dieu», aux pieds de laquelle ses obligés tombent à genoux ou deviennent des «intercesseurs» à qui il demande de prier Dieu pour la réussite de ses projets!

Il est donc raisonnable de voir autre chose qu'un jeu dans ce langage chrétien. La lettre VI est encore plus significative: «J'oserai la ravir au Dieu même qu'elle adore . . . Je serai vraiment le Dieu qu'elle aura préféré», ainsi que la lettre XCVI: «Les ferventes prières, les humbles supplications, tout ce que les mortels dans leur crainte offrent à la divinité, c'est moi qui le reçois d'elle». Badinages voltairiens selon M. Versini? Je ne crois pas. Le langage de Valmont, comme celui de Voltaire d'ailleurs, dans *La Bible enfin expliquée*, est susceptible d'une explication plus profonde. Les «à la manière de» ne sont des plaisanteries que pour les naïfs et révèlent au contraire de curieux refoulements. Le goût évident du sacrilège, que les libertins de Duclos et de Crébillon ne partageaient pas, révèlent à notre sens un Laclos peu connu. L'artilleur n'a pas évoqué le diable comme Faust ou comme l'Alvare de Cazotte dans le *Diable amoureux*. Il n'a jamais cru à sa présence réelle. Mais il est probable qu'il n'en a jamais oublié la valeur symbolique.

V. CONCLUSION

Cette digression sur le langage nous permettra peut-être d'atteindre le vrai Laclos. On a souvent abusé des interprétations psychanalytiques et de ce qu'on appelle la psychologie des profondeurs. Avec Laclos, chez qui l'obstacle l'emporte sur la transparence, c'est notre dernier recours. Voici donc nos conclusions où nous voudrions voir autre chose qu'un nouveau mythe de Laclos aussi anachronique ou subjectif que les autres.

Nous pensons qu'au delà de la morale évidente ou apparente des *Liaisons dangereuses*, où le vice est comme il se doit puni, au delà de cette signification banale qui ferait de cet étrange ouvrage un catéchisme de sociabilité, une honnête mise en garde des jeunes filles en rupture de couvent ou des jeunes épouses esseulées qui, un soir d'été, ont eu trop chaud dans un parc, il y a dans les *Liaisons* une autre dimension à faire valoir. Nous pensons qu'il y a entre ses personnages les plus odieux et Laclos une certaine connivence et qui dépasse l'esthétique. On l'a dit de Racine à propos de Néron ou d'Athalie, de Milton à propos du diable. Pourquoi la refuser à Laclos? Il y a chez lui, en lui, je ne sais quelle admiration pour ses héros qui va au delà de l'indulgence du créateur pour ses créatures. Sur quels points insister? En voici quelques-uns:

—Le mal est séduisant.

—La volonté de puissance est chose grisante.

—Réduire les autres à sa merci augmente le sentiment que l'on existe et exalte le moi.

—Détruire autrui, c'est s'enrichir.

—Avilir autrui est une joie.

—La vie n'a qu'un sens: l'affirmation de soi.

—La morale des forts s'oppose à la morale des esclaves et des imbéciles.

—Dieu est mort, tout est permis.

Nous ne pensons pas néanmoins que cette connivence soit totale ni qu'elle soit avouée. Elle est en grande partie inconsciente. Laclos, nous l'avons vu, s'est probablement cru moral et vertueux. Mais les *Liaisons* sont autre chose qu'un livre de morale. Par delà l'intrigue, les faits, le dénouement, ce livre ambigu révèle sur son auteur et donc sur la nature humaine, de bien curieuses lumières. En un sens Laclos devient alors le principal personnage de son roman. Il est probable que les *Liaisons* lui ont permis de libérer ses propres démons, que grâce à ce livre il put devenir un honnête homme, bon père et bon époux. Mais les démons sont-ils jamais conjurés? Et les contemporains, ceux qui l'ont rencontré et côtoyé, et qui virent en lui un homme «noir», en sentaient peut-être encore la présence.

NOTES

1 Édition de la Pléiade, p. 708.
2 Versini, op. cit., p. 319.

27

Montesquieu and the Theatre

MARK H. WADDICOR

With his reputation for coldness of temperament[1] and his intellectual approach to human problems both personal and political, the author of *De l'Esprit des lois* would not, at first sight, appear to have been an enthusiast of that domain of the passions, the theatre, and even less of the sentimental kind of drama that characterized the eighteenth century. The *Lettres persanes* would seem to confirm this impression. Rica, in the letter he writes about the Parisian theatre, says almost nothing about the plays performed there: his irony is centred on the histrionic talents of the audience and the agility of the *souffleurs de chandelles* (*Lettres persanes,* 28, N.I, iii, 59–61, Pl. I, 172).[2] The librarian who shows Rica the books in a Parisian convent defines poets as 'ces auteurs dont le métier est de mettre des entraves au bon sens, et d'accabler la raison sous les agréments', and so he is hardly being complimentary when he describes dramatists as 'les poètes par excellence'; admittedly, they are 'les maîtres des passions', and he says he *esteems* them, but he is surely being rather unenthusiastic when he simply says that 'les comiques' 'nous remuent si doucement' and that 'les tragiques' 'nous troublent et nous agitent avec tant de violence' (*L.p.* CXXXVII, N.I, iii, 275–276, Pl. I, 337). If neither Rica nor the librarian represents completely Montesquieu's personal view, it is still significant that the latter should use such language. The same indifference seems to be found in a passage written near the end of Montesquieu's life, in a letter to Helvétius: 'je n'ai pas de grandes connaissances sur les choses du théâtre' (11 February 1749, N.III, 1179). It is perhaps for reasons such as these, together with the fact that his three major works seem far removed from the world of make-up and make-believe that is the theatre, that Montesquieu's biographers and critics have accorded little or no attention to what is quantitatively and even qualitatively a relatively important aspect of his work.[3] Altogether, he makes over a hundred references to the theatre, some short, some amounting to several pages; no cultured Frenchman of the eighteenth century could completely neglect this aspect of his civilisation, and in the case of Montesquieu many of his observations are coloured by his temperament and by his social and political theories.

It is true that critics have drawn attention to the dramatic qualities of his work: the *Lettres persanes* have been compared to a tragedy;[4] le président Hénault claimed to find in the *Considérations sur les causes de la grandeur des Romains,* among other qualities, certain 'beautés du dramatique' (N.III, 1129); Montesquieu himself admits that his early dialogue

Sylla et Eucrate (1724) was inspired by 'Quelques scènes de Corneille' (P. 1948, Bkn. 90, N.II, 590, Pl. I, 998); he adds: 'J'étois jeune, et il falloit être bien jeune pour être excité à écrire par la lecture du grand Corneille et par la lecture de cet auteur qui est souvent aussi divin que lui' (ibid.,)—pride rather than shame is surely the sentiment behind this *boutade* of the ageing *président*,[5] and it suggests that in his youth he had a passion for the theatre.

Further evidence of this passion is his play *Britomare,* one of his earliest works,[6] written while he was at the Oratorian Collège de Juilly, between 1700 and 1705. While the Oratorian schools did not encourage drama to the same extent as the Jesuits, they in fact produced more plays in French than the Jesuits. The subjects chosen by the Oratorians included not only Biblical history, but also Roman and even French history, and although the majority of the plays were somewhat static, they attracted large audiences. The fact that this theatrical activity in the collèges was condemned again and again by the Assemblée générale of the order is merely proof of the fondness for drama on the part of individual *régents*.[7] Montesquieu's own efforts at writing a play may well have been encouraged, like those of Voltaire, by his teachers.

Montesquieu destroyed most of *Britomare,* the subject of which was taken from La Calprenède's *Cléopâtre,* but certain fragments of the play are preserved in *Pensée* 359 (Bkn. 477). While they are too short to enable us to judge his handling of plot and character, and while certain lines are mediocre,[8] most reveal considerable skill in the handling of the alexandrine, for example in this passage where Élise expresses her love, with comparatively little of the preciosity that sometimes mars the work of the classical dramatists:

> Vous avez sçu me vaincre après tant de combats,
> En un mot, je vous aime, et je n'en rougis pas.
> Il falloit en rougir quand mon âme insensée
> En osa concevoir la première pensée;
> Il falloit en rougir quand le cruel poison
> Laissoit à mon esprit un reste de raison;
> Que, tantôt abattue et tantôt triomphante
> Je défendois encore ma liberté mourante.
> Mais sans faire aujourd'hui des efforts superflus,
> J'aime, j'ose le dire, et je n'en rougis plus.

Similarly, the long tirade in which Pharate tells how the gods started punishing him for his crimes only when he had repented of them:

> Lorsque je me baignois dans le sang de mes frères,
> Les dieux, ces justes dieux, ne m'étoient point contraires; [. . .]
> Mais depuis que, perdant mon audace première
> Arbate, j'ai voulu faire un pas en arrière, [. . .]
> Depuis ce temps fatal, ma funeste innocence
> N'a fait pleuvoir sur moi que haine et que vengeance.
> Sans cesse malheureux, toujours persécuté
> J'ai senti tout le poids de la divinité.

Cornelian influence is to be seen in the strophe pronounced by Elise:

> La mort est un cruel tourment,
> Qui, pour adorer Britomare,
> Ne me laisse plus qu'un moment.

Antithèses are frequent and are handled with considerable talent:

> Et ce héros terrible à mon esprit confus
> Montre autant d'ennemis qu'il fait voir de vertus.
> (N.II, 144–146, Pl. I, 1030–1031)

If Montesquieu had felt inclined to develop his gifts in this direction, it is not impossible that he should have followed in the steps of the Norman lawyer,[9] whose comparatively calm life, lack of interest in his professional activity, and concern for matters moral and political find a reflection in Montesquieu himself.

During the years he spent in Paris, after 1708, ostensibly gaining legal experience following his three-year course in Bordeaux, Montesquieu had ample opportunity to develop his love of the theatre. In the letter of 1749 to Helvétius, quoted above, where he disclaims any knowledge of drama, he nevertheless continues: 'dans ma jeunesse je devins fol de *Rhadamiste*' (N.III, 1179). Crébillon's tragedy *Rhadamisthe et Zénobie,* with its somewhat obscure plot, violent and rather improbable passions, and forceful verse, was first produced, with great success, in December 1711, and it is not implausible to suppose that Montesquieu attended an early performance that kindled a fire of enthusiasm already prepared by reading the same dramatist's earlier tragedies: *Idoménée* (1703), *Atrée et Thyeste* (1707),[10] and *Électre* (1708). *Rhadamisthe et Zénobie,* like the plays of Corneille and Racine, contains a mixture of political and amorous intrigue: Montesquieu was already at this time interested in the lessons taught by Roman history,[11] but it can hardly be said that the conflict in *Rhadamisthe,* between Rome and 'Ibérie', is of primary importance to the plot, which in addition has no clear moral or political implications; nor do any of the characters arouse the kind of pity we accord to Cinna or Curiace, or the admiration we feel for Auguste. Probably, the young Montesquieu was above all affected by Crébillon's verse and melodramatic effects. His admiration for Voltaire's rival did not wane, since, in the same letter, he says 'j'irai aux Petites-Maisons pour *Catilina*'. In this tragedy, produced in December 1748, the moral, political and human issues are much clearer, and it is easier to understand his admiration.

In spite of that admiration, he does not appear to have attended a performance of *Catilina*[12]—he was in Bordeaux at the time—but the correspondence and the *Pensées,* as well as the published works, frequently bear witness to his interest in the plays and operas[13] written and produced during the first part of the eighteenth century. The twenty-eighth *Lettre persane* shows that he was well acquainted with the French theatre during the Regency. From the *Spicilège,* it is evident that he attended[14] *L'Oracle de Delphes,* a play first performed in December 1722, and that he appreciated its 'philosophic' message if not its dramatic qualities (*Sp.* 333, N.II, 776–777, Pl. II, 1299). He attended the *première* and later performances of La Motte's *Inès de Castro* (6 April 1723), and he keenly followed public and critical reaction (letter to Sarrau de Vésis, 25 May 1723, N.III, 742; *P.* 143, Bkn. 916, N.II, 46–47, Pl. I, 1249–1250) thus continuing, in more serious fashion, the social observations of the *Lettres persanes,* but he was also clearly sensitive to the play itself.[15]

His interest in drama was accompanied by an acquaintance with the leading dramatists of the age. He came to know La Motte soon after seeing *Inès,* if not before, when he started frequenting madame de Lambert's salon,[16] and there he also met Marivaux, whose *Mère confidente* (first performance, May 1735) he probably saw (*P.* 950, Bkn. 939, N.II, 269, Pl. I, 1253), and whose comparison of Corneille and Racine, given before the Academy, of which he was also now a member, he heard and admired (letter to madame Dupré de Saint-Maur, 1749, N.III, 1259–1260).

During his travels in Italy (1728–1729), Montesquieu made a point of studying the opera in Rome, aspects of which he describes in considerable detail (*Voyages,* N.II, 1111–1113, Pl. I, 680–681; *P.* 388, Bkn. 963, N.II, 152, Pl. I, 1258) particularly the question of *castrati,* and the great emphasis placed on spectacle and on violence; he also attended an opera in Milan, but it does not seem to have made any impression on him (N.III, 913); and while in Venice he discussed dramatic theory with the scholar Antonio Conti (*Sp.* 464 and 465, N.II, 814–815, Pl. II, 1336–1337). In Italy, his attention was not confined to opera, since he attended a performance of La Motte's *Romulus,* which he found 'détestable' (*P.* 2153, Bkn. 54, N.II, 646, Pl. I, 986 and *Voyages,* N.II, 1113, Pl. I, 680). While Montesquieu was in England, Fontenelle wrote to him (as well as to other influential people) asking him to accord his protection to mademoiselle Sallé, a *danseuse* who had just been dismissed from the Opéra in Paris, and who had come to London (N.III, 940). There is no record of Montesquieu's having acted upon Fontenelle's request, but the secretary of the Académie des Sciences obviously considered Montesquieu to be not only interested in helping the victim of an injustice but also sympathetic to the cause of the theatre.

On his return to France, in spite of his increasing work on the *Considérations,* then on the *Esprit des Lois,* his interest in the theatre did not wane. During his researches for the *Esprit des Lois,* he came across a translation of a Chinese play, *L'Orphelin de la maison de Tchao*:

Je trouve cette pièce intéressante, l'intrigue bien amenée, bien suivie. Elle donne une idée des mœurs du pays, et il me semble que le vrai moyen de donner cette idée serait de traduire le théâtre chinois. (*Sp.* 554, N.II, 846–847, Pl. II, 1368),

showing once more that his attitude to drama was neither purely æsthetic, nor purely sociological. Although Montesquieu was less critical of the play than Voltaire was to be,[17] both philosophers are preoccupied with the sociological aspect of the piece. Two letters of 1748, one from Montesquieu to Duclos, the other from Hénault to Montesquieu, record his attendance at the private performances of comedies at the hôtel de Brancas: no doubt the sociological interest was not entirely absent even here (N.III, 1124–1125, and 1140–1141).[18] In 1749, he was reporting to Aydie on Voltaire's forthcoming *Électre* (N.III, 1267). One may assume that these scattered references give evidence of only a fraction of Montesquieu's attendance at the theatre. While he was clearly not such an enthusiast as Diderot, Rousseau, or Voltaire, he took more than just the interest of an *honnête homme* since he combined the talent of a social historian with a keen sensibility and acute powers of observation and intelligence. The latter quality is revealed in his observation on the art of acting:

Ce qui fait un bon comédien, ce n'est pas de donner à son visage les mouvements convenables dans le temps que l'on récite les vers; c'est de les faire paroître avant: car la plupart du temps les vers récités ne sont que l'effet de quelque passion nouvelle, qui a été produite dans l'âme. Il faut donc faire paroître cette passion. C'est en cela que Baron excelle toujours. (*P.* 242, Bkn. 987, N.II, 99, Pl. I, 1265)

For all his interest in the theatre, his admiration of certain *comédiens,* and in spite of the fact that he may even have had social contact with them,[19] he never abandoned a certain disdain towards the theatre and actors. Admittedly, he absolved the modern theatre from the condemnation of the Church:

Les excommunications des Pères ne peuvent tomber que sur l'ancien théâtre où les pantomimes dansoient tout nus, où l'on immoloit du sang humain aux Dieux, où l'on se prostituoit en l'honneur de Vénus, et rien n'absout plus le nôtre que les apostrophes des Pères (*Sp.* 361, N.II, 782, Pl. II, 1305).

Clearly, he would have sided with Voltaire and d'Alembert against Rousseau on this question. Nevertheless, his knowledge of the theatre of Ancient Rome, which was often a school of cruelty (*Sp.* 161, N.II, 727, not in Pl.),[20] as in the case of gladiatorial combats, which are a kind of spectacle and entertainment, or of immorality (*Considérations,* 15, N.I., iii, 452, Pl. II, 149, and 17, N.I., iii, 476, Pl. II, 168) helped to foster in him an attitude that was perhaps also a result of his social status. There is a revealing passage in his description of England, telling an anecdote about an English nobleman who, for a wager, acted on the stage. Montesquieu comments: 'Jouer une piece pour attraper mille guinées, et cette action infâme n'est pas regardée avec horreur?' (N.III, 288–289, Pl. I, 880). Although one cannot be sure that Montesquieu is not just condemning the nobleman's greed, there is also an implication that acting is an 'action infâme'. A similar note is struck when he describes how Justinian's reign was marred by the fact that he had 'pris sur le théâtre une femme qui s'y étoit longtemps prostituée' (*Considérations,* 20, N.I, iii, 499, Pl.II, 187). He found the fact that Nero acted on the stage 'extraordinaire', though he was not shocked by Louis XIV's dancing in ballets, because 'les danses venoient des tournois [. . .] et avaient une belle origine' (*P.* 311, Bkn. 1201, N.II, 132, Pl. I, 1301). For Montesquieu, actors are paid entertainers, not social equals, but this did not prevent him from admiring their art.

Montesquieu's love of the theatre has many sources: kindled by reading and seeing the plays of Corneille and Racine, sustained by his admiration of Crébillon, as well as by his sociological investigations, it was also perhaps nourished by a certain atmosphere of libertinage associated in his mind with the theatre: in the letter recommending mademoiselle Sallé, Fontenelle found it necessary to warn Montesquieu that 'vous n'aurez que sa danse' (N.III, 941), and in a passage of the *Essai sur le goût,* we see Montesquieu reflecting—from personal experience, perhaps?—on why an actress who has appealed to us on the stage also charms us in her dressing room (N.I, iii, 628, Pl. II, 1252)[21]. But the *Essai sur le goût,* which was begun in about 1728,[22] is also proof of another very important aspect of his character which has a bearing on the present study: his interest in æsthetics. Montesquieu did not consider himself to be only a political philosopher: witness the surprising number of observations on Italian art in the *Voyages* and in the *Pensées*,[23] and his reply to d'Alembert, who had asked him to write the articles 'Démocratie' and 'Despotisme' for the *Encyclopédie*:

J'ai tiré, sur ces articles, de mon cerveau tout ce qui y étoit [. . .]. Ainsi, si vous voulez de moi, laissez à mon esprit le choix de quelque article [. . .]. Il me vient dans l'esprit que je pourrai prendre peut-être *Goût* et que je prouverai bien que *difficile est proprie communia dicere*. (N.III, p. 1480)[24]

As one of the highest manifestations of eighteenth-century culture, the theatre occupied a predominant place in Montesquieu's æsthetic writings, if not in the *Essai sur le goût* itself. Montesquieu's dramatic theories are to be found partly in the *Essai,* but mainly in his notebooks, and he does not set them out in systematic form. Nevertheless, a clear system emerges.

In several places, he turned his attention to the origins of tragedy in Greece. He saw it as a kind of 'divertissement' accompanying the wine-harvest—that is, as a social event (*De la manière gothique,* N.III, 281, Pl. I, 971). He commented on the rapidity 'avec laquelle les Grecs ont passé du mauvais à l'excellent' in their drama, contrasting it with what he considered to be the slow progress of the French theatre before Rotrou and Corneille (ibid., and *P.* 128, Bkn. 462, N.II, 42–3, Pl. I, 1023). Remaining somewhat aloof from the 'Querelle',[25] he believed the dramatists of the seventeenth century had succeeded in equalling those of Antiquity (*P.* 118, Bkn. 452, N.II, p. 40, Pl. I, p. 1021). Like Voltaire, the relativism of his taste was limited: he despised the Medieval and Renaissance theatre, and he accepted without question the 'règles d'Aristote' which 'sont encore des règles pour nous aujourd'hui, et, malgré le changement de mœurs, nous ne pouvons en départir' (*De la manière gothique,* N.III, 281, Pl. I, 971), though one wonders how he could have argued that *Rhadamisthe et Zénobie,* with its wicked main characters, is in conformity with those rules. He accepted, too, the unities, which he ingeniously explained in a rationalistic manner:

Les trois unités du théâtre se supposent les unes les autres: l'unité du lieu suppose l'unité du temps: car il faut beaucoup de temps pour se transporter dans un autre pays; ces deux unités supposent l'unité d'action: car, dans un temps court, il ne peut y avoir qu'une seule action principale. (P. 2076, Bkn. 821, N.II, 637, Pl. I, 1225)

The explanation is somewhat formalistic and today we tend to subordinate the unities of time and place to that of action. He similarly applied a rationalistic explanation, suggested to him in Italy by Antonio Conti, to the rule of the five acts (*Sp.* 465, N.II, 814–815, Pl. II, 1337).

As regards the nature of tragic experience, he appears to have believed in the Aristotelian theory of catharsis, while laying more emphasis on fear than on pity: Crébillon is

le véritable tragique de nos jours parce qu'il excite [. . .] la véritable passion de la tragédie, qui est la terreur. (P. 68, Bkn. 920, N.II, 22, Not in Pl.)[26]

It is here that the paradox of the preacher of political moderation fascinated by violence and cruelty on the stage, becomes most apparent.

Like the classical theorists, he believed that the subject–matter of a tragedy was relatively unimportant, compared with its ability to present passions which move us (P. 127, Bkn. 461, N.II, 42, Pl. I, 1023) and to give a 'spectacle du cœur humain' (P. 118, Bkn. 452, N.II, 40, Pl.I, 1021). Provided that in offering such a spectacle they respect historical facts and do not commit anachronisms, modern dramatists can write tragedies which rival those of the Greeks (Fragments of the *Essai sur le goût*, N.III, 531–532, Pl. II, 1261).[27]

He considered this rule of *vraisemblance* to be less important in the new pseudo-tragic genre invented by 'Nos modernes', opera, since its principal aim is simply to stir the emotions (P. 119, Bkn. 453, N.II, 40–41, Pl. I, 1021). Nevertheless, 'Je ne pouvois souffrir en Italie de voir Caton et César chanter des ariettes sur le théâtre', hence the superiority of French opera, from the point of view of subject matter, since it is usually based on fables or novels rather than on history (Fragments of the *Essai sur le goût*, N.III, 532, Pl. II, 1261). While the French language is more suitable for tragic diction, since 'le tragique a besoin de force' (P. 415, Bkn. 778, N.II, 159, Pl. I, 1215),[28] Italian music is far superior to French, in opera:

Il me semble que, dans la musique françoise, les instruments accompagnent la voix, et que, dans l'italienne, ils la prennent et l'enlèvent. La musique italienne se plie mieux que la françoise, qui semble roide. (P. 327, Bkn. 961, N.II, 136, Pl. I, 1258)

Montesquieu's conversion to Italian music dates from his stay in Italy, which was more or less contemporary with Rousseau's first visit there. The two men, so opposed in temperament and outlook, nevertheless shared a taste for music that expressed emotion.

Montesquieu also paid considerable attention to the nature of comedy. He accepted that 'le ridicule jeté à propos a une grande puissance' (P. 2147, Bkn. 725, N.II, 646, Pl. I, 1196), and regretted that modern comedy tended to concentrate on 'le ridicule des passions' rather than on 'le ridicule des manières' (P. 817, Bkn. 823, N.II, 239, Pl. I, 1225–1226)—a condemnation of Marivaux, perhaps? Like Voltaire, he believed that all the good comic subjects had already been taken: 'Il faut une nouvelle nation pour former de nouvelles comédies' (P. 287, Bkn. 822, N.II, 120, Pl. I, 1225).

He had much to say, in the *Essai sur le goût* and the accompanying fragments, on the precise causes of the pleasure that comedy gives us. He claimed that it results from our 'malignité naturelle', for example from our 'plaisir de voir un homme dans une erreur où nous ne sommes pas', or 'à voir un homme plus embarrassé qu'il ne devroit l'être'. The other main cause of the effect comedy has on us is 'l'aversion que nous donne pour de certains personnages l'intérêt que nous prenons pour d'autres', and the good dramatist will skilfully keep alive this interest and this aversion till the play reaches its conclusion (Fragments, N.III, 533–534, Pl. II, 1261–1262). Another important element in comedy is of course surprise and suspense; Montesquieu's discussion of these elements has no particular originality and is rather laboured and commonplace (*Essai sur le goût*, N.I, iii, 625, Pl. II, 1249–1250).

In his theorizing about the æsthetic side of drama, Montesquieu in fact can lay no claim to the originality of a Diderot. He was an explainer, a commentator: had he set out his theories in a systematic form, he would have produced, from the æsthetic point of view, a competent and ingenious treatise. His judgements of the dramatists of his own day are similarly revealing of his own tastes, without having any great intrinsic value. Of Voltaire's drama, he says practically nothing: he did not like the man, and was unwilling to make the effort to appreciate his plays,[29] even though they conform quite closely to his own criteria, by their observance of most of the classical rules, and by their appeal to the emotions, and though they are not so dissimilar from the tragedies of Montesquieu's idol and Voltaire's rival, Crébillon. For Montesquieu, Voltaire is too mild:

Voltaire se promène toujours dans des jardins; Crébillon marche sur les montagnes. (P. 1460, Bkn. 930, N.II, 421, Pl. I, 1252)

Another tragic writer, Houdar de la Motte, Montesquieu's 'favori' according to Bulkeley (N.III, 748), pleased him, as we have seen, by an appeal to the emotions, especially in *Inès de Castro* (P. 143, Bkn. 916, N.II, 46, Pl.I, 1249–1250). On the great tragic writers of the classical age, Montesquieu's comments are disappointing:

Il y a dix ou douze tragédies de Corneille et de Racine qui ne permettent jamais de décider: celle qu'on voit représenter est toujours la meilleure. (*Sp.* 373, N.II, 785, Pl. II, 1307)

Pensée 1948 (Bkn. 90) does establish a kind of hierarchy: Corneille is 'grand', Racine is 'souvent aussi divin que lui' (N.II, 590, Pl. I, 998), while the *Essai sur le goût* perhaps reverses that hierarchy as regards style: Corneille's 'vers' are 'pompeux' (the term is not necessarily pejorative), Racine's 'naturels' (N.I, iii, 636, Pl.II, 1258). Like Voltaire, he was both fascinated and repelled by Shakespeare: 'Quand vous voyez un tel homme s'élever comme un aigle, c'est lui. Quand vous le voyez ramper, c'est son siècle' (P. 1307, Bkn. 890, N.II, 394, Pl. I, 1244).[30] He admired Molière for his 'gaieté' and his 'plaisanterie' (P. 1533, Bkn. 886, N.II, 442, Pl. I, 1244) but seems to have preferred the more refined and sentimental comic style— 'le comique noble'—of Nivelle de la Chaussée (*Sp.* 574, N.II, 852, Pl. II, 1373).

If Montesquieu can lay little claim to originality in his æsthetic judgments on drama, the same cannot be said of the way in which he used the theatrical production of different ages and nations to help reveal the character and traditions of each people, as part of his attempt to relate that character and those traditions to laws and institutions. His attitude to literature is partly defined in *Pensée* 2086 (Bkn. 81):

J'aime à lire un livre nouveau après le jugement du public; c'est à dire que j'aime mieux juger en moi-même le public que le livre. (N.II, 638, Pl. I, 996)

P. Barrière is right to say that 'un pareil point de vue révèle plutôt le sociologue et l'historien que le véritable critique',[31] but this *Pensée* does not give a complete picture of Montesquieu's interest in the theatre since it is abundantly clear that he had an æsthetic and emotional reaction to drama as well. Nevertheless, it is the sociological point of view that makes his comments original: he is above all concerned with the way in which the theatre reveals the nature of different peoples.

In the case of the Greek theatre, he claimed that it was as much a cause, as an effect, of *mœurs*: the Greek 'horreur pour l'inceste' came from the theatrical representations of the fables of Thyeste and Œdipus (*P.* 1766, Bkn. 359, N.II, 527, Pl. II, 1091). The Greek leaders also used public games, which are a kind of spectacle, to inculcate military virtues (*Considérations*, 5, N.I, iii, 389, Pl. II, 99), and they used music to prevent those virtues from becoming merely barbaric (*Lois*, IV, 8, N.I, i, 52, Pl. II, 272). The Romans, on the other hand, though they had gladiatorial combats to inspire ferocity in their soldiers, did not temper such spectacles with any antidote. This observation leads Montesquieu to reflect on the different manner in which the modern Frenchman and the ancient Roman regarded physical exercise: for the former, it has no aim other than 'les agréments', for the latter it 'faisait part de l'art militaire' (*Considérations*, 2, N.I, iii, 361–362, Pl. II, 76–77). In his notebooks, Montesquieu also compared the ancient Romans with those of his own day, showing that the same climate that used to produce an 'esprit belliqueux', now, because of certain 'causes morales' (understand: Christianity), only makes the Italians love stage-fights and spectacle (*P.* 1296, Bkn. 1389, N.II, 358, Pl. I, 1328–1329, and *Voyages*, N.III, p. 1113). Similarly, he notes that the temperament of different nations makes theatre audiences react quite differently to the same play (*Lois*, XIV, 2, N.I, i, p. 308, Pl. II, p. 476). Generally, he believed that the theatre could only reflect the moral attitudes of the audience, and that it could not successfully go against those attitudes (*Lois*, XXV, 2, N.I, i, 108, Pl. II, 737); hence, in spite of what he said in *Pensée* 2147, he in effect abandoned the classical idea of the theatre as a moral influence.

This attitude is clear from his remarks on La Motte's *Inès de Castro*, which are the starting-point for a series of reflections on the cynicism of a large part of the theatre-going public of the 1730s: when faced with a scene from *Inès* where family feelings are displayed, many members of the audience laughed. Montesquieu sees this behaviour as the result of a reaction on the part of his contemporaries against what seems to them the excessive and almost mindless sentimentality of previous generations, and he relates this change of attitude, of which it is clear he does not approve, to a change in *mœurs*, in that children in the upper classes are no longer brought up by their parents (*P.* 143, Bkn. 916, N.II, 46, Pl. I, 1249–1250). We see here the beginnings of the reaction against intellectualism and cynicism that was to set in later in the century. Montesquieu's observations remind us of Rousseau's outburst against parental indifference, at the start of *Émile*, although it can hardly be said that Montesquieu was particularly fond of children[32]—it was the social consequences of the education of his time that he deplored.

Observations such as these could only be made after seeing a performance of a play. However, as a provincial, Montesquieu, unlike Voltaire, did not have much real contact with the live theatre until his late teens, when he came to live in Paris, but he was already familiar with it through his reading. At first, the theatre was a passion; at the time of the *Lettres persanes*, he adopted a mocking attitude towards it, but he soon realized that it formed an important element in his intellectual, social and æsthetic experience, and his enthusiasm did not wane, even at the end of his life. But when we consider that, by 1746, his eye disease had become acute[33] and that he could not any longer—if he ever did[34]—appreciate the theatre as a spectacle, we must surmise that his interest was emotional and intellectual rather than visual[35].

NOTES

1 See M. H. Waddicor, *Montesquieu and the Philosophy of Natural Law* (The Hague, 1970), p. 165, n. 77 and p. 180, n. 15.

2 Abbreviations:

L.p.	=	*Lettres persanes.*
Considérations	=	*Considérations sur les causes de la grandeur des Romains, et de leur décadence.*
Lois	=	*De l'Esprit des Lois.*
P.	=	*Pensées.*
Bkn.	=	The analytic order assigned to the *Pensées* by H. Barckhausen in his edition (1899, 1901), and followed by the Pléiade edition.
Sp.	=	*Spicilège.*
N.I, i N.I, ii N.I, iii	=	*Œuvres complètes de Montesquieu*, publiées sous la direction de M. André Masson (Paris, 1950) (a photographic reprint of the 1758 edition of Montesquieu's works, which had three volumes), Vol. I.
N.II	=	*Œuvres complètes de Montesquieu*, etc., (Paris, 1950), Vol. II.
N.III	=	*Œuvres complètes de Montesquieu*, etc., (Paris, 1955), Vol. III.
Pl. I & Pl. II	=	*Œuvres complètes de Montesquieu*, texte présenté et annoté par Roger Caillois, Bibliothèque de la Pléiade (Paris, 1949–1951), Vols. I and II.

3 Vian does not discuss the question at all (*Histoire de Montesquieu* (Paris, 1878); P. Barrière (*Un Grand Provincial, . . . Montesquieu* (Bordeaux and Paris, 1946), pp. 501–2 and 512–13), devotes only a few lines to the question. R. Shackleton deals exhaustively with the possible social contacts Montesquieu had with the writers and dramatists of his day, but the scope of his study does not permit him to analyse the question of their influence on Montesquieu (*Montesquieu, A Critical Biography* (Oxford, 1961)). E. P. Dargan, (*The Æsthetic Doctrine of Montesquieu* (New York, [n.d.], pp. 114–145) says little of interest.

4 e.g. R. F. Reilly, 'The Structure and meaning of the *Lettres persanes*', *SVEC*, 66 (1969), p. 98.

5 This *Pensée* dates from after 1748.

6 It is the first work in Shackleton's 'Bibliography of Montesquieu', in op. cit., p. 400.

7 P. Lallemand, *Histoire de l'éducation dans l'ancien oratoire de France* (Châtillon-sur-Seine, 1888), pp. 326–339. C. Hamel, *Histoire de l'abbaye et du collège de Juilly* (Paris, 1868), p. 224 + n. 2, cites a condemnation of theatrical performances in Oratorian schools, made by the Assemblée générale of 1717. It refers specifically to Juilly as an example of how literature should be taught, by 'des exercices académiques'. But the condemnation does not state that no theatrical performances had taken place at Juilly.

8 Though Shackleton is perhaps being rather severe when he says that 'it is not for intrinsic reasons' that the destruction of the play by Montesquieu is to be regretted—most of the lines that remain (admittedly, they are probably the best) are not so mediocre as the one he cites, op. cit., p. 7.

9 'Montesquieu aurait sans doute pu faire en ce genre de bonnes œuvres de second plan' (P. Barrière, op. cit., pp. 18–19).

10 He had certainly read *Atrée et Thyeste* by 1734–1738, the probable date of *P.* 1099 (Bkn. 779), N.II, 300, Pl.I, 1215–1216, where he comments on a line of Crébillon's play in a way that reveals sensitivity to the *finesses* of the associations and sonorities of poetic language.

11 The *Discours sur Cicéron*, with its praise of tyrannicide, probably dates from 1709, N.III, 15; cf. however Shackleton, op. cit., pp. 20 & 401.

12 'Je suis un admirateur sincère de *Catilina* [. . .]. La lecture m'a tellement ravi que j'ai été au cinquième acte sans trouver un seul défaut, ou du moins sans le sentir' (N.III, 1179).

13 A letter, probably of 1725, shows him about to go to a performance of an opera (N.III, 776).

14 The play was not printed, see n. to N.II, 776.

15 The play 'n'a réussi qu'à force d'être belle. [. . .] Il y a un second acte qui, à mon goût, est au-dessus de tous les autres. [. . .] Je me suis plus senti touché les dernières fois que les premières' (P. 143, Bkn. 916, N.II, 46–47, Pl. I, 1249).

16 Probably in 1724: Shackleton, op. cit., p. 57.

17 *Essai sur les mœurs* (Paris, 1963), ch. 155, II, 397–398. Voltaire based the plot of *L'Orphelin de la Chine* (1755) on this play.

18 cf. Shackleton, op. cit., p. 181.

19 The actress Adrienne Lecouvreur was a guest at madame de Lambert's salon: Shackleton, op. cit., p. 56.

20 This *Pensée* was transcribed by Montesquieu from a *recueil* lent to him by Desmolets: N.II, LXVIII.

21 There is also the actress who asks Rica for his protection: she regrets being no longer able to 'supplement' her *pension* now she is older (*L.p.* 28, N.I, iii, 61–62, Pl. I, 173). In *P.* 2104 (Bkn. 988), however, Montesquieu condemns la Camargo because her dancing merely titillates 'les gens grossiers' (N.II, 642, Pl. I, 1265).

22 Shackleton, op. cit., p. 408.

23 The latest work on Montesquieu's writings on painting and sculpture is: J. Ehrard, *Montesquieu, critique d'art* (Paris, 1965).

24 Here, Montesquieu was up against his rival Voltaire, who in fact supplied 'Goût': the unfinished *Essai sur le goût* was printed as a supplement.

25 *P.* 111, Bkn. 445, N.II, 37, Pl. I, 1018: 'J'aime à voir les querelles des Anciens et des Modernes: cela me fait voir qu'il y a de bons ouvrages parmi les Anciens et les Modernes'.

26 Montesquieu subsequently deleted these lines from this early *Pensée*. They are still revealing of his attitude at the time (1721–31).

27 Though in an early *Pensée*, he claimed that 'presque toutes les bonnes situations sont prises par les premiers auteurs' (*P.* 287, Bkn. 822, N.II, 120, Pl. II, 1225).

28 Montesquieu makes a number of observations on poetic language, for which he had a sensitive ear. In particular, he contrasted the qualities of the French and Italian language (*Sp.* 473, N.II, 817, Pl. II, 1339–1340). He also offers commentaries on various lines of poetry, both Latin (*P.* 1680, Bkn. 878, N.II, 500–502, Pl. I, 1239–1240), and French (*Sp.* 378, N.II, 785, Pl. II, 1308).

29 e.g. *P.* 2233, Bkn. 933, N.II, 664, Pl. I, 1252: 'Je disois que Voltaire étoit un général qui prenoit sous sa protection tous ses goujats'. Also *P.* 1593, Bkn. 1364, N.II, 455, Pl. I, 1325, which seems to refer to Voltaire. On the other hand, Montesquieu did side with Voltaire against Rohan: *Sp.* 913, N.II, 912–913, Pl. II, 1431–1432).

30 cf. *Lois*, XIX, 27, N.I, i, 444, Pl. II, 583: 'Leurs poètes auroient plus souvent cette rudesse originale de l'invention, qu'une certaine délicatesse que donne le goût'.

31 op. cit., p. 491.

32 'Naturellement je n'aime pas les enfants' (Letter of 1725 [?], N.III, 778).

33 J.-M. Eylaud, 'Montesquieu et ses yeux', in *Études sur Montesquieu, Archives des Lettres modernes*, no. 116 (1970), p. 7.

34 See his disdainful remarks about the Italians' love of theatrical spectacle and scenery, *Voyages*, N.II, 1111–1112, Pl. I, 679–680.

35 This study was already in proof when publication of the following was announced: H. Lagrave, A. Lebois, and H. J. Tarraube, *Études sur Montesquieu: Montesquieu personnage de théâtre et amateur de théâtre, Archives des lettres modernes*, No. 151 (1974).

28

Testimonies of Persecution: Four Huguenot Refugees and their Memoirs

DEREK A. WATTS

Of all Louis XIV's acts of government, none was as momentous and as far-reaching in its effects as the Revocation of the Edict of Nantes. Certainly neither the King nor his zealous advisers could have clearly envisaged the consequences, even the more immediate, of the document he signed on 18 October 1685. On the religious plane, the high hopes entertained by many, such as Leibniz, of an early reconciliation of the Christian Churches were dashed, indeed destroyed for over two centuries. Public opinion in the Protestant countries, already inflamed by the *dragonnades* which had begun in France four years earlier, reached a fever pitch of indignation, and a European Grand Alliance against Louis XIV, unthinkable only a few years previously, now seemed imminent. The Elector of Brandenburg broke with Versailles at enormous cost to his exchequer in lost subsidies. In Holland, William of Orange triumphed over the moderates who advocated peaceful co-existence with France; and in England James II, whose reckless pro-Catholic policies seemed to emulate those of Louis XIV, courted disaster by convincing many of his subjects that they would be the next victims of Popish intolerance. When the inevitable happened, there were three thousand French Huguenots among the army which disembarked at Torbay on 5 November 1688, and installed William on the throne of England at the price of just one small combat. Michelet once reproached Macaulay for having neglected the part played by these French veterans, many of whom later fought like tigers at the Boyne, urged on by Schomberg's cry: 'Allons mes amis! Rappelez votre courage et vos ressentiments: voilà vos persécuteurs!' Estimates of the number of Protestants who left France between 1680 and 1700 have varied enormously, between two and eight hundred thousand. The lower figure seems the more probable; this would represent little more than one per cent of the total population, and so recent historians have challenged the traditional claim that the Revocation was an unmitigated economic disaster for France. Nevertheless, thousands of the refugees were among the country's wealthiest, most industrious and most enterprising citizens, and they took with them not only their fortunes whenever possible, and their creative energies, but also their technical skills: industrial secrets and manufacturing processes that had hitherto been exclusive French possessions were now disseminated abroad. Many others among the exiles were men of great intellectual, spiritual or scientific distinction, such as Pierre Bayle, Pierre Jurieu, Jacques Basnage, Jacques Saurin, Denis Papin and Abraham de Moivre. The flourishing expatriate communities they helped to found in England, Ireland, Switzerland, Brandenburg, Scandinavia, Russia, America and above all Holland, became (as is well known) an important factor in French intellectual life in the eighteenth century. Although Voltaire complained of the improprieties of their 'refugee French', all the *philosophes* were indebted to the Huguenot exiles for a constant supply of stimulating, and often subversive, information and ideas. These same communities ensured the diffusion of French culture abroad. One of the reasons why the French language attained such prestige through-out eighteenth-century Europe was that so many autocrats, from Frederick the Great and Catherine of Russia down to the pettiest princelings, had had a Huguenot tutor or governess.[1]

The personal testimony of a number of Huguenot refugees has been published, either as historical source material or for the purpose of edification; but little attempt has been made so far to assign these writings a place in literary history—in the evolution of what is in-creasingly regarded in France as a literary genre, with its own rules and conventions, namely memoirs. This is the aim of the present article, for which I have chosen the four men whose accounts of their tribulations seeem most clearly to belong to what has been called 'la préhistoire de l'autobiographie':[2] Jean Migault, Isaac Dumont de Bostaquet, Jacques Fontaine and Jean Marteilhe.[3]

Jean Migault represents the humblest among the Protestant refugees. He was a village schoolmaster at Mougon, on the border of Saintonge and Poitou; he was also a lay reader in the local chapel, and in addition a part-time notary until 1681, when Protestants were forbidden to hold such offices. Between this year and 1686, his village was subjected to three successive waves of *dragonnades,* during which the brutal soldiery, egged on by the local *curé,* persecuted those Protestants who refused to abjure, and systematically destroyed their property. For most of this period, Migault and his eleven surviving children (his first wife died in 1683) were dispersed in various hiding places in isolated farmsteads and hamlets. The protection of a Huguenot nobleman, M. d'Olbreuse, afforded them a brief respite, but he too was soon arrested and exiled; whereupon the Migault family hid in a dark, damp cave, and were kept alive for weeks only by gifts of food and clothes sent in by friends. Arrested in La Rochelle, where he was trying to arrange a passage on a foreign ship, Migault was imprisoned in a dungeon so small that he could not lie down in it. Here, in his distress on learning of the plight of his family, he signed a promise to abjure. Once released, he turned all his attention to means of escape. The Migaults' first attempt to embark, at Pampin near La Rochelle, failed miserably: some of the party got lost in the darkness, chaos ensued and they all narrowly escaped arrest. But on the same beach, on 19 April 1688, Migault, having borne each of his younger children on his shoulders through rocks and waist-deep water, reached a longboat which took them all to a ship bound for Holland. They disembarked at Briel on 8 May, having survived fearful storms; the next day, their hearts overwhelmed with joy and gratitude, they heard the great Jurieu preach in Rotterdam. Migault later re-married, and spent his last years in Emden, where he died in 1707, aged sixty-two or sixty-three.

Migault's *Journal*[4] was composed soon after his arrival in Holland, and a postscript was added in 1702. It is an utterly unpretentious document, the work of a man who is clearly embarrassed at his own lack of literary skill—the spelling is disconcerting even by the standards of the time—and it was intended solely for the eyes of his own family. Yet the very simplicity of the style radiates a sincerity which makes Migault a convincing and at times moving witness to the horrors he had endured. His *Journal* presents one of the most detailed and (despite the lack of narrative skill) eloquent accounts to be found of the cruelties of the *dragonnades*.[5] It includes a number of picturesque *tableaux*, such as this evocation of the family's final departure from Mougon:

A l'instant nous partîmes, et cheminâmes toute la nuit, n'ayant qu'une monture chargée de quatre personnes, savoir votre bonne mère qui tenoit Elizabeth entre ses bras, Pierre et Marie étoient chacun dans une basse[6] dont je m'étois fourni à cet effet: les deux aînées et moi étions à pié. (pp. 102–3)

There are some moments of wry humour, for instance this comment on the morning after a night of *dragonnades*: 'Le jour étant venu, toute la paroisse se trouva être changée de religion' (p. 83). Migault is at his most eloquent when describing the intense shame he felt for the moment of 'weakness' in which he had signed a promise of abjuration (pp. 162–6). His account of the two embarkation attempts is genuinely exciting to read, though it must be admitted, here as elsewhere, that it is the matter rather than the style that holds our attention.[7]

Isaac Dumont de Bostaquet, on the other hand, was for much of his life by far the most prosperous of our *mémorialistes,* and he would have remained so but for two disasters: a fire which destroyed his mansion at La Fontelaye in 1673, followed twelve years later, when he had almost recovered financially, by the Revocation. Dumont came from a family of Protestant noblemen long established in Normandy, and he was a man of considerable substance; in 1687, when the crisis finally came, he was fifty-five years old; nevertheless, he did not hesitate to abandon all his possessions save a few gold pieces, and most of his family— he married three times and had nineteen children—in order not to forsake his faith. He reached Holland after a hazardous journey, and placed his sword, his one remaining asset, at the disposal of William of Orange whom he served in England and later in Ireland. He fought at the Battle of the Boyne and at the less successful siege of Limerick. William granted him a pension, which enabled him to settle in modest comfort with his wife, first in Dublin, and finally at Pontarlington, County Kildare, where he died in 1709. It was through an Irish acquaintance that Macaulay learned of the existence of Dumont's manuscript, just in time to use it for chapters XIV and XVI of his *History of England*;[8] this revelation led to its publication in 1864 by two historians of French Protestantism.[9]

Dumont wrote his memoirs in successive stages: the first half in April 1688, soon after his arrival in Holland, and the rest in shorter instalments, notably at Greenwich late in 1689, and in Dublin in 1693. The whole manuscript was entitled *Registre,* and indeed it contains a largely factual account of Dumont's life, written solely for the benefit of his descendants. This is how he concludes the first half of his narrative:

Voilà, mes chers enfants, un abrégé de tout ce qui s'est passé dans ma vie de biens et de maux, jusques au temps que le ciel par un effet de sa divine providence et de son secours que j'ai expérimenté dans cette longue course que j'ai déjà faite, m'a amené dans cet asile où, à l'abri de mes persécuteurs, je puis en repos repasser sur les divers événements qui me sont arrivés et qui me rendent un exemple sensible de l'inconstance des choses du monde; et comme les douceurs et la tranquillité de la vie que je mène sont le fruit de ma retraite, je veux vous en laisser un mémoire exact et sincère, et vous donner un patron pour éviter ce que j'ai fait de mal et imiter ce que j'ai fait de bien.[10]

Because of his meticulous factual presentation of the details of his existence, Dumont is a valuable source of information on the style of life of a prosperous French country gentleman in the late seventeenth century. He writes at length about his financial affairs, and in particular about the legal wrangles in which nearly every birth, death and marriage in his family seemed to involve him.[11] Thus his memoirs begin in a low key, but with the coming of the *dragonnades* to Normandy, followed by Dumont's escape to Holland and his enrolment in the Dutch army, the perspective gradually broadens, and the central sections contain some quite accomplished narrative and descriptive passages. In particular one is impressed by the graphic account of the fire which destroyed La Fontelaye; by Dumont's brisk narrative of his first, unsuccessful attempt to leave France—almost all the Huguenot memoirs include at least one such passage, rich in suspense, of the kind which inspired Michelet's eloquent panoramas;[12] and by his vivid though rather fragmentary account of the Battle of the Boyne.[13] It is both vivid and fragmentary, precisely because Dumont writes as an eye-witness, and does not attempt to be an historian. Of the English campaign of 1688–9, he declares:

Comme je ne prétends point faire l'histoire de cette grande entreprise que de ce qui me concerne, je laisse ce soin aux plumes mieux taillées que la mienne à instruire la postérité de cet événement si surprenant. (p. 199)

Towards the end, Dumont tends to overload his story with factual detail, and to become too laconic for the reader's pleasure to endure undiminished. Dumont is not a conscious stylist, and only a few of his descriptive passages are really notable, as is this evocation of the Dutch fleet's arrival in Torbay:

Ce lieu donc nommé Torbay fut l'endroit où nous abordâmes. Il sembloit que la nature l'eût fait exprès pour nous recevoir: cette baie, en forme de croissant, s'avance dans la terre assez avant; elle a au lieu où nous mouillâmes de hautes montagnes garnies de rochers fort escarpés; elle est fort spacieuse et peut contenir un très grand nombre de vaisseaux; notre flotte, quoique très nombreuse, n'en occupoit qu'une petite partie; le fond y est admirable pour ancrer, et les côtes qui l'environnent de trois côtés font que les vaisseaux y sont très en sûreté. Ce fut, dis-je, dans ce lieu que notre grand prince et toute l'armée abordèrent. Le ciel, qui l'avoit heureusement conduit, continuant ses faveurs, rendoit la mer si tranquille que cette baie paroissoit un grand étang; le soleil, qui étoit sur son couchant, brilloit avec tant d'éclat que l'on eût dit qu'il avoit peine à perdre de vue notre héros; cependant, voulant aller promptement rendre compte dans l'autre hémisphère de cette grande entreprise, il laissa le soin à la lune d'éclairer notre descente.
    Le prince le premier mit pied à terre, et son régiment des gardes grimpa les rochers avec une diligence extrême et se campa sur le haut, dans une petite plaine qui y étoit. Comme nous n'avions pas vu le

débarquement de ces troupes, pour n'être pas de l'avant-garde, nous ne savions si c'étoient amis ou ennemis; mais nous reconnûmes bientôt que c'étoient de nos troupes; toutes les autres, à mesure que les vaisseaux avoient jeté l'ancre, étoient portés à terre dans des chaloupes et prenoient leurs postes. On n'entendit que tambours et trompettes; la nuit, calme au possible, obligeoit les échos à y répondre, ce qui, augmentant le bruit de guerre, faisoit un effet merveilleux. (pp. 192–3)

The conventional allegories are obviously seventeenth-century, but there is here and there just a hint of pre-romantic sensibility. Dumont is a shrewd observer of the countries he passes through: he seems somewhat amazed by the English passion for gambling (p. 260), and his first impression of Devonshire life is of the quantities of tobacco consumed by the inhabitants:

Nous remarquâmes avec plaisir la manière de vivre de ces insulaires, et comme ils sont adonnés au tabac, hommes et femmes, jusques aux enfants; nous ne pûmes voir sans rire que l'hôtesse de la maison, qui étoit jeune et assez jolie, donnant à téter à son enfant et fumant en même temps, donnoit sa pipe à tirer à ce petit quand il quittoit son sein. Il la prenoit et la portoit à sa bouche et faisoit tous ses efforts pour fumer. Nous avons vu à peu près que tous ces peuples de l'Ouest en usent de même.[14]

Though Dumont is an attentive observer of life around him, his memoirs are not exclusively the work of an extrovert; as he recalls the principal joys and sorrows of his eventful life, he relives moments of intense personal emotion. This is how he describes his grief at the death of his second wife:

Quiconque a aimé avec la plus forte passion que l'on puisse sentir, réfléchisse sur ce que je fis dans ce triste état; j'aimois, si j'ose dire, dans l'excès cette digne et charmante épouse; une possession de dix à onze années ne lui ayant rien ôté de sa beauté, n'avoit point diminué mon amour. Son humeur douce, et d'une complaisance pour moi achevée, les avoient fait couler avec une rapidité si extrême que le jour même qui précéda sa mort, nous nous étions protesté tendrement que nous ne nous étions pas aperçu de leur nombre.
Si la douleur d'une perte si sensible m'avoit pu mettre dans le même tombeau, j'aurois reçu la mort avec une joie sans pareille: je ne pouvois me séparer de cette chère femme que la mort n'avoit point rendue moins belle: ses yeux, les plus beaux que l'on pût voir, sembloient me regarder, et sa bouche, aussi vermeille que jamais, semblait sourire.[15]

However, Dumont rarely over-indulges his emotions: this may be due to his Huguenot austerity, or to a sober sense (which just as many Catholics shared) of the fragility of human life and the unfailing bounty of Providence;[16] these in fact are the underlying themes of this quite distinguished set of memoirs.

Jacques Fontaine of Jenouillé, near Royan, was an exemplary Huguenot; in fact he was the epitome of almost everything posterity has come to associate with the Huguenots. He was born in 1658, into a family whose Protestant traditions already went back four generations; his father had abandoned the *particule de noblesse* out of humility. After his father's death in 1664, he would dearly have liked to abandon his studies and become an apprentice, but almost every male Fontaine was, or had been, a clergyman, and he was too terrified of his mother to even suggest such apostasy:

Comment faire une telle proposition? J'avais été dédié au saint ministère avant que d'être conçu;
mon père avait été ministre; j'avais trois frères ministres, un qui était mort proposant, deux beaux-
frères ministres, deux oncles du côté de ma mère ministres; et de lui dire que je voulais déroger,
c'était lui arracher le cœur, et changer la meilleure des mères en une lionne à qui on a dérobé ses petits
et l'animer de rage contre moi. Elle m'avait toujours tenu chez des ministres, apparemment dans
l'attente que j'apprendrais à être ministre comme les apprentis des forgerons deviennent forgeurs en
forgeant et voyant forger. (pp. 115-6)

Although he completed his degree course successfully at the Collège de Guyenne,
Fontaine had no time to be ordained before the persecution began in earnest. He advocated
resistance, and soon found himself under arrest, charged with illegal assembly, and subsequently with having caused his fellow-prisoners to refuse to abjure. He conducted his own
defence in so spirited a fashion that his conviction by the Présidial de Saintes was quashed
on appeal by the Parlement de Guyenne. Having failed to rouse his co-religionists to armed
resistance, he decided to emigrate, and with a party that included his sister, his god-daughter
and his fiancée, he ran the gauntlet of the coastal patrols and joined an English ship which
reached Appledore on 10 December 1685. For a while Fontaine lived on Devonian charity;
he and his fiancée each refused a highly advantageous match, and they were married in
Barnstaple in February 1686. Six months later, his attempts to trade with France having
brought him no lasting profit, he entered the service of a rich landowner near Bridgwater,
but soon left it, for he found a servant's lot too humiliating. He then opened a general stores
in Bridgwater, and subsequently in Taunton, where he set himself up as a weaver as well.
In both these trades he was outstandingly successful, in particular with an expert imitation
of the calimanco weave originally manufactured in Norwich. His success in fact aroused
the envy of other traders, and as a result he was prosecuted for alleged malpractices. The
case was contemptuously dismissed by the Recorder; nevertheless this unpleasant episode,
together with the fact that his weaving secrets had been divulged, induced Fontaine to
give up commerce and soon to emigrate to Ireland. He had already been ordained a
Presbyterian minister, having refused despite strong financial inducements to enter the
Church of England, because of his anti-episcopalian convictions. He was appointed to
a living near Cork, where he arrived in December 1694; the stipend was negligible, and so
he was again obliged to live by his own resources, which now included teaching, weaving
and fishing. But prosperity proved much harder to come by on Ireland's rugged shores: the
occasional large catches of fish were wasted because Fontaine, owing to the lethargy or ill-
will of his associates, was unable to get them to market quickly enough, and his weaving
business was killed by an Act of Parliament which prohibited the export of woollen goods
from Ireland. He moved to Bearhaven, where repeated forays by French pirates forced
him to turn his home into a fortress, and it was finally ransacked and destroyed by raiders
in 1708. However, Fontaine was awarded £800 compensation, which enabled him to
move to Dublin, where he bought the lease of a large house—going cheap because it was
reputed haunted—which he turned into a school. He was no longer rich, but he supported
himself and his family with teaching until he was too old and ill to work any longer. It
was then, after the death of his wife in 1721, that Fontaine wrote his memoirs, with the aid

of notebooks and family documents he had preserved. He set to work in March 1722, with remarkable energy for a sick man, for by 21 June he had completed not only his text, but a holograph copy of it destined for those of his children who had emigrated to Virginia.[17]

Fontaine is not, alas! a master of French prose: when he composed his memoirs, he had not heard his mother tongue spoken in its natural context for thirty-six years, and although his syntax is still passable, his vocabulary has become contaminated with anglicisms.[18] He has however plenty of racy expressions of his own, which contribute to the principal quality of these memoirs: the force of the personality, the richness of the self-portrait. Once again, this is a work destined solely for the family circle; it is a monument to the solidarity of the Fontaine clan, and its author intended that it should help to preserve and strengthen that solidarity.[19] The first hundred pages are devoted to his Protestant ancestors and their collaterals, beginning with his great-grandfather who became a martyr to his faith. Throughout, Fontaine portrays himself as a man of austere and intransigent piety, a stern but practical moralist who has helpful advice to offer as well as admonitions. At times, despite his expressions of loving concern, we have glimpses of a forbidding patriarch.[20] There is however a gentler side to Fontaine's personality. In particular he has left us an account of his childhood which is more detailed and more absorbing than almost any to be found in French autobiographical writing before Rousseau. The seventeenth-century *mémorialistes* in particular had tended to pass over the first decade of their lives, and often most of the second, as rapidly as possible; but Fontaine tells us at some length of his attempts at the age of four to preach like his father, and of his imaginative meditations during his sixth year of life about the structure of the heavens (pp. 101–5). Soon afterwards, he was sent to his cousin's school at La Rochelle for instruction; here he was frequently whipped, but he now recalls these chastisements with a certain gaiety:

Entre écoliers, nous nous entretenions du nombre des coups que notre maître nous donnait à chaque fouettée, qui étaient copieux, et souhaitions ardemment d'en savoir le nombre, car on ne pouvait pas compter les uns pour les autres, parce qu'il fouettait toujours ou après l'école ou du moins dans un lieu à part. [. . .] Nous souhaitions fort que quelqu'un comptât les coups qu'il recevait; mais c'était presque l'histoire des rats qui délibéraient d'attacher le grelot au cou du chat. Personne ne se trouvait assez hardi pour l'entreprendre. Quelque difficile que l'entreprise me parût, cependant, ayant bonne opinion de la force de mes résolutions, je m'offris à les compter. Je n'eus pas le loisir de m'ennuyer beaucoup en attendant que l'occasion se présentât, car elle revenait souvent. Ma coutume était que d'abord que le maître me donnait le signal de mettre les chausses bas, je le faisais avec des cris et des exclamations qui ne sentaient du tout point l'enrouement. Je commençai à mon ordinaire aussitôt l'ordre reçu; mais il n'eut pas plus tôt commencé à frapper, que, ne pouvant pas compter (ce qu'il fallait faire tout bas) et crier, je me tus tout à coup. Le maître, surpris de ce nouveau prodige, me regarde en face et, ne voyant nul changement dans mon visage, il refrappe le second coup du meilleur de son courage. J'étais empressé à compter et lui cachais que je comptais. Son étonnement s'accrut comme mon silence continuait; il frappa un troisième coup de toute sa force, qui ne fut pas capable de me faire écarter dans mon compte, mais me força à rompre le silence, de sorte que je m'écriai d'une voix d'autant plus violente qu'elle avait été longtemps retenue: 'Trois!' 'Ha!' dit-il, 'coquin, tu comptes? Compte, compte, compte donc!' Je m'écartai, il faut que je le confesse; mais je ne perdis pourtant pas toute ma peine, car je suis persuadé qu'outre le nombre ordinaire, il me fit présent de plusieurs coups par-dessus le marché. (pp. 106–7)

Needless to say, such treatment did not turn Fontaine into a scholar, but eventually he acquired a highly eccentric but gifted tutor named M. de La Bussière, who fired his enthusiasm, and of whom he has left a vivid and affectionate character-sketch (pp. 119–20).

Fontaine's own self-portrait is developed throughout his memoirs, thanks to a number of careful analyses of his state of mind at critical moments of his life,[21] but above all in the many passages which testify to his resourcefulness, his commercial flair and inventiveness, his optimistic conviction that God helps those who help themselves. No sooner had he bought his first loaf of Devon bread than he saw the possibility of lucrative exports of cheap English grain; unfortunately he had no capital, and his scheme failed through the inefficiency or deceit of those in France whose aid he was obliged to enlist (pp. 228ff.). The success of his shop in Taunton was due to the exploitation of what would now be called 'loss-leaders' (pp. 230–3). He taught himself weaving from scratch (p. 249), yet ended by inventing a special loom that could be operated by a cripple (p. 281). His energy was inexhaustible, and he does not hide his contempt for the *esprit routinier* of Taunton commerce (pp. 275–6). In all these material successes, as in the disasters that overtook him, Fontaine sees the hand of Providence.[22] He claims to have had a prophetic dream that prevented two of his sons from drowning at sea (pp. 300–3). Describing how all his family except himself escaped injury during a gun battle against pirates, he exclaims in his quaint language: 'Béni sois-tu, ô mon Dieu, qui refusas le billet de logement à toutes les balles qui volaient autour de nous comme la grêle!' (p. 352). One can well imagine some of Fontaine's American descendants, more than a century later, praising the Lord and passing the ammunition.

Apart from this vigorous self-portrait, Fontaine's work contains in ample measure the by now familiar ingredients of the Huguenot memoirs: a circumstantial account of the *dragonnades* and other forms of persecution that the Protestants suffered; and some lively narratives, which make good reading despite the limited literary skill, of arrest, imprisonment, escape and armed combat.[23]

The palm, however, must be awarded to the man who did not get away. Jean Marteilhe's *Mémoires d'un Protestant condamné aux galères de France pour cause de religion, écrits par lui-même*, were first published in 1757;[24] they are familiar to historians of French Protestantism and of naval warfare, but they have never achieved a place in the annals of French literature,[25] which seems a pity, for there are not all that many works of fiction written in the eighteenth century which make more absorbing reading than this true story. Michelet once described Marteilhe's work as 'un livre du premier ordre par la charmante naïveté du récit, l'angélique douceur, écrit comme entre terre et ciel'.[26]

The author was born at Bergerac in 1684, of parents whom he describes as 'bourgeois et marchands'. He was barely sixteen when he decided, together with a friend named Daniel Le Gras, to flee from the ferocious *dragonnades* organised by the Duc de La Force, who seemed to be taking revenge on his own Huguenot ancestors. The fugitives actually succeeded in crossing the border near Mézières, but they inadvertently re-entered French territory—the frontier being at this time in a state of flux—whereupon they were denounced, arrested and sentenced to the galleys for life. (This was the mandatory punishment for Huguenots caught while attempting to escape from France.) In January 1702, Marteilhe's family's appeals having finally proved fruitless, he was sent to Dunkirk, and spent over six years chained to the deck of the galley *La Palme,* which was from time to time engaged in operations against the English and Dutch fleets. In 1708, he was gravely wounded in a combat with an English vessel; he recovered and returned to his ship the next year, but he was found to be incapable of rowing, and so he was employed first in the ship's pantry, then as secretary to the captain. Unfortunately for Marteilhe and his fellow prisoners, the English annexation of Dunkirk resulted in the transfer of the French galley fleet to the Mediterranean; the convicts were bundled across France, and subjected once again to all the horrors of the chain-gang; they arrived in Marseilles early in 1713. Only a few months later, however, Marteilhe and several of his fellow Protestants were released as a result of high-level interventions, including (he tells us) a personal appeal from Queen Anne. The last pages of his narrative describe the triumphant journey of the liberated prisoners across part of Protestant Europe, with a civic welcome in every town from Geneva to Amsterdam, where Marteilhe set sail on a mission of thanks to the Court of St James. Little is known for certain about his later life. According to Oliver Goldsmith in 1758, Marteilhe was 'still alive, and known to numbers, not only in Holland but in London.'[27] He is said to have settled at Kuylenberg near Utrecht, to have married a French refugee named Bernardine Halloy in 1719, and to have lived to the age of ninety-three; but more than one Marteilhe escaped from France after the Revocation,[28] and the evidence needs to be carefully sifted. According to one source, a daughter of this ex-galley-slave married an English admiral![29]

Unlike the other memoirs we have examined, Marteilhe's account is confined more or less to the period of his tribulations, that is from 1700 to 1713. His tale is an appalling one, yet at moments it approaches the sublime; it is certainly enthralling to read. Even before he reached his galley, Marteilhe was lucky to emerge alive from the foul dungeon—the infamous Cachot de la Sorcière in Lille—into which he had been cast (pp. 86–90). No sooner had he embarked than he witnessed the gruesome punishment known as the bastinado—a flogging with a strip of cow-hide, the victim of which rarely survived twelve strokes without permanent injury, though Marteilhe says that a sentence of fifty or eighty strokes was not uncommon (pp. 98–101).[30] But perhaps the most hair-raising passage of all is this description of the Tournelle prison in Paris, which was used as a 'marshalling-yard' for galley-slaves:

On nous fit entrer dans le vaste mais lugubre cachot de la grande chaîne. Le spectacle affreux, qui s'y présenta à nos yeux, nous fit frémir, d'autant plus, qu'on nous allait joindre aux acteurs qui le représentaient. J'avoue que, tout accoutumé que j'étais aux cachots, entraves, chaînes et autres instruments, que la tyrannie ou le crime ont inventés, je n'eus pas la force de résister au tremblement qui me saisit, et à la frayeur dont je fus frappé, en considérant cet endroit. Ne pouvant en exprimer toute l'horreur, je me contenterai d'en donner une faible idée. C'est un grand cachot, ou pour mieux dire, une spacieuse cave, garnie de grosses poutres de bois de chêne, posées à la distance, les unes des autres, d'environ trois pieds. Ces poutres sont épaisses de deux pieds et demi, et sont rangées et attachées de telle sorte au plancher, qu'on les prendrait à première vue pour des bancs, mais qui ont un usage beaucoup plus incommode. Sur ces poutres sont attachées de grosses chaînes de fer, de la longueur d'un pied et demi, et à la distance les unes des autres de deux pieds; et au bout de deux de ces chaînes est un collier de même métal. Lors donc que les malheureux galériens arrivent dans ce cachot, on les fait coucher à demi, pour que la tête appuie sur la poutre. Alors on leur met ce collier au col; on le ferme, et on le rive sur une enclume à grands coups de marteau. Comme ces chaînes de collier sont distantes les unes des autres de deux pieds, et que les poutres en ont la plupart quarante de longueur, on y enchaîne vingt hommes à la file, et aux autres à proportion de leur grandeur. Cette cave faite en rond est si grande, qu'on peut y enchaîner de la manière susdite, jusqu'à cinq cents hommes. Il n'y a rien de si affreux, que de voir l'attitude et la posture de ces malheureux ainsi enchaînés. Car figurez-vous, qu'un homme ainsi attaché, ne peut se coucher de son long, la poutre, sur laquelle il a la tête, étant trop élevée; ni s'asseoir et se tenir droit, cette poutre étant trop basse; si bien que je ne puis mieux dépeindre la posture d'un tel homme, qu'en disant qu'il est à demi couché, et à demi assis, partie de son corps sur les carreaux ou planchers, et l'autre partie sur cette poutre. (pp. 254–6)

There were still worse horrors to come during the journey to Marseilles, but mercifully for the reader, Marteilhe relates them rather more briefly (pp. 267–74). Yet his account is not an unrelieved tale of woe; there are plenty of diverting anecdotes and even a few comic episodes.[31] A few of his persecutors are revealed to be unexpectedly humane and even charitable. The Turkish slaves in particular are mostly gentle and kindly (except for the Moors), and Marteilhe's opinion on this subject echoes that of Montesquieu and Voltaire: 'Ce sont ces gens que les chrétiens nomment barbares, et qui, dans leur morale, le sont si peu, qu'ils font honte à ceux qui leur donnent ce nom' (p. 207). The narrative also includes some vivid accounts of naval engagements, in particular of the galley's unfortunate encounter with an English frigate, whose incredibly courageous and resourceful captain turned out, when finally captured, to be 'un petit homme tout contrefait, bossu devant et derrière'.[32] It was in this action that Marteilhe received the wound that in the end may have saved his life. This is how he describes the events immediately preceding his wounding:

On a vu que, lorsque la frégate que nous attaquions eut esquivé l'abordage et qu'elle nous eut jeté ses grappins et attachés à son bord, nous étions exposés au feu de son artillerie, chargée à mitraille. Il se rencontra donc que notre banc, dans lequel nous étions cinq forçats et un esclave turc, se trouva vis-à-vis d'un canon de la frégate, que je voyais bien qui était chargé. Nos bords se touchaient; par conséquent ce canon était si près de nous, qu'en m'élévant un peu, je l'eusse pu toucher avec la main. Ce vilain voisin nous fit tous frémir; mes camarades de banc se couchèrent tout plat, croyant échapper à son coup. En examinant ce canon, je m'aperçus qu'il était pointé, ce qu'on appelle, à couler bas, et que, comme la frégate était plus haute de bord que la galère, le coup porterait à plomb dans le banc, et qu'étant couchés, nous le recevrions tous sur nos corps.
    Ayant fait cette réflexion, je me déterminai à me tenir tout droit dans le banc, je n'en pouvais sortir, j'y étais enchaîné, que faire? Il fallut se résoudre à passer par le feu de ce canon, et comme j'étais attentif à ce qui se passait dans la frégate, je vis le cannonier avec sa mèche allumée à la main, qui commençait à mettre le feu au canon sur le devant de la frégate, et de canon en canon, venait vers celui qui donnait sur notre banc; j'élevai alors mon cœur à Dieu et fis une courte prière, mais fervente, comme un homme qui attend le coup de la mort. Je ne pouvais distraire mes yeux de ce canonnier, qui s'approchait toujours de notre canon, à mesure qu'il tirait les autres. Il vint donc à ce canon fatal, j'eus la constance de lui voir mettre le feu, me tenant toujours droit, en recommandant mon âme au Seigneur. (pp. 151–2)

Marteilhe was the only survivor of this incident among the eighteen galley-slaves in his section; knocked unconscious, he was left for dead and narrowly escaped being cast into the sea with a load of corpses (pp. 156–7). But such extreme forms of suffering were exceptional.

The world of the galley as he describes it was a rather topsy-turvy place; the régime, like many tyrannies, was arbitrary, inefficient and corrupt: brutality and degradation were naturally the rule, and yet the most unexpected privileges could be obtained at a superior's whim, and above all for a bribe.[33] There was even a ship's orchestra largely composed of convicts![34]

Such a tale as Marteilhe has to tell scarcely needs the resources of art in order to rivet the reader's attention. Is he in fact to any degree an artist? His style has been described as unadorned, naïve, direct, recalling Defoe in its 'graphic simplicity'.[35] But Marteilhe was not a simpleton, and he alone among our *mémorialistes* seems to have been writing consciously for publication.[36] The narrative is several times interrupted by entertaining digressions, which are unfolded rather in the manner of the classical novel.[37] The earlier episodes are fairly skilfully presented, but later on the narration becomes rather confused on several occasions, and there are interruptions and recapitulations which may indicate that Marteilhe did not write his memoirs at a single attempt.[38] He shows some psychological insight, and he has given us one or two vigorous satirical portraits, notably of a Jesuit who tried to persuade him that he was not a victim of religious persecution in the strict sense of the term; this preposterous individual is almost worthy of the *Lettres provinciales* (pp. 287–92). Some episodes, such as this account of the galley's activities during the siege of Ostend, are narrated with a certain dexterity, and enlivened with touches of irony:

Pendant les trois jours qu'on bombardait cette ville, nous allions la nuit, sans feu ni lumière, nous fourrer avec nos six galères parmi la flotte des alliés, pour tâcher d'enlever quelque navire de transport ou galiote à bombe, mais il n'y eut pas moyen d'y réussir. Nous n'eûmes que le plaisir de voir le plus beau feu qu'on ait jamais vu. (p. 123)

Such indeed, despite many blemishes, is the quality of Marteilhe's narrative that the reader soon finds himself asking questions about its degree of authenticity. How did Marteilhe acquire some of the information he gives? Could a man who had spent in such a gruelling manner those years of life that are usually decisive as regards literary formation, have written this narrative exactly as it was published in 1757? According to well-founded traditions, it was the celebrated Huguenot preacher and theologian Daniel de Superville, who had already played some part in securing Marteilhe's release,[39] who urged the ex-prisoner to record his experiences on paper, and then 'corrected' his manuscript; but Superville died in 1728, and it was his son (also named Daniel) who supervised the publication of these memoirs after an inexplicable delay of thirty years.[40] One cannot help wondering exactly to what extent either of these men may have revised Marteilhe's text. Only one addition to the text was acknowledged in the 1757 edition, and that concerns the nefarious activities of the Lazarist priests, who allegedly devised every means of tormenting the Huguenot galley-slaves and preventing their release (p. 216). But the book contains many similar accusations against both the Lazarists and the Jesuits, and some passages of moralising or of anti-Catholic propaganda which, together with the two pages of general introduction, sound very much like editorial interpolations.[41] However, these add up to only a small proportion of the total text, and our (admittedly sparse) knowledge of the genesis of this text gives us no strong reason to doubt the authenticity of the rest. Nobody, certainly, could have invented very much of Marteilhe's story, nor acquired his expert technical knowledge of the running of a galley without years of personal experience.[42] Whether every word of the text is Marteilhe's or not, the *Mémoires d'un Protestant condamné aux galères* are from several points of view a remarkable achievement, which deserves to be more widely known.

These four sets of memoirs obviously have much in common—three of them especially, for Marteilhe's narrative contains as much chronicle as autobiography, and it has been included here partly on account of its undeniable quality. These testimonies were all inspired by experiences of a similar order. They all contain at least some of the themes, and bear witness to some of the qualities, that we have come to expect of Huguenots. The French Protestants, we are told, are still notable for the strength of their family ties and traditions.[43] All our authors confirm this impression: Marteilhe's family moved heaven and earth (as indeed did other Protestants) in their vain efforts to alleviate his suffering; Fontaine urges his children to set up a mutual aid fund which would lead if required to a virtual pooling of their wealth.[44] They are all deeply versed in Scripture, and their narratives often abound in Biblical allusions and quotations; the Psalms are particularly in evidence.[45] These men all preach and observe an austere code of morals, though this does not rob them of practical realism or of a sense of humour. Above all, their unshakable faith in Divine Providence sustains them perpetually; they justify its seemingly contradictory workings with earnest ingenuity, though a more sceptical modern reader may now and again find their explanations a little Panglossian.[46] Finally, they were all obviously men of outstanding mental stamina and resourcefulness, the salt of the Huguenot earth.

Do their memoirs make any positive contribution to the evolution of the genre? In two respects, it may be said that they do. First, in the completely personal nature of their testimony. None of our authors attempts to be an objective historian, their standpoint is that of the eye-witness; the passages in Marteilhe that appear to depart from this rule may well be editorial interpolations. Secondly and above all, the experience of exile has clearly shaped the standpoint from which they envisage their past. Their lives have been cut in two, or in more than two, as a result of persecution and flight. Not that they experience much nostalgia for their *ingrate patrie*; only Dumont, when he evokes the idyllic days of his youth, and Migault when he envisages the eventual return of his children to a more tolerant France, give a hint of this emotion.[47] However, all of them are still haunted by the experiences they relate; they seek to define themselves *against* this past, to justify their revolt against persecution and to underline its exemplary value.[48] Migault, Fontaine and Dumont all address their immediate offspring, but with the obvious hope that their message will be conveyed to a more distant posterity; Marteilhe, more explicitly, intends that his narrative should bear witness before the world to the beliefs for which he suffered so much. Thus our four authors, each in his particular way, have served the cause of Protestantism, but also that of autobiographical literature.

NOTES

1 On the background covered in this paragraph, see particularly: J. Orcibal, *Louis XIV et les Protestants* (Paris, 1951), pp. 147–58; R. Stephan, *Histoire du Protestantisme français* (Paris, 1961), pp. 159–82; W. J. Stankiewicz, *Politics and Religion in Seventeenth-Century France* (Berkeley, 1960), pp. 162–242; Warren C. Scoville, *The Persecution of Huguenots and French Economic Development, 1680–1720* (Berkeley, 1960), passim; Ch. Weiss, *Histoire des réfugiés protestants de France depuis la Révocation de l'Édit de Nantes* (Paris, 1853), 2 vols, passim.

2 P. Lejeune, *L'Autobiographie en France* (Paris, 1971), pp. 54ff. (The intended implication of this phrase is that true autobiography began only with Rousseau.) Lejeune mentions briefly two of our authors, Dumont de Bostaquet and Fontaine, on pp. 61–2.

3 There exist other Huguenot memoirs containing accounts of persecution, which for various reasons I found less suitable for inclusion in this study, e.g. Jean Rou, *Mémoires inédits*, edited by F. Waddington (Paris, 1857); *Les Larmes de Jacques Pineton de Chambrun* (The Hague, 1688): the press mark of the British Museum copy, omitted from the General Catalogue, is 4632.aaa.9; Jean Cavalier, *Mémoires sur la Guerre des Cévennes*, edited by F. Puaux (Paris, 1918); and *Mémoires de Jacques Bonbonnoux, Chief Camisard et Pasteur au Désert*, edited by J. Vielles (En Cévennes, 1883).

4 It was first published in an English version (*A Narrative of the Sufferings of a French Protestant Family* [. . .], London, 1824). Subsequent French editions (1825, 1827, 1840, 1854) were a re-translation of this, though the 1854 edition incorporated some additional material found in one of the two MSS on which N. Weiss and H. Clouzot based the excellent critical edition they published in 1910 for the Société de l'Histoire du Protestantisme Français. All my quotations and references are taken from this edition.

5 pp. 65–144, passim.

6 'Petite cuve en bois servant à transporter la vendange au pressoir, à dos de cheval'—Editor's note.

7 pp. 191–207, 222–30.

8 Macaulay, *The History of England from the Accession of James II,* edited by C. H. Firth (London, 1914), IV, 1679, note. Had he discovered Dumont's manuscript sooner, Macaulay might not have incurred Michelet's reproach mentioned above.

9 Edited by Charles Read and Francis Waddington (Paris, 1864). A useful modern edition, from which all my quotations and references have been taken, has been published in the collection *Le Temps retrouvé*, edited by M. Richard (Paris, Mercure de France, 1968). Virtually nothing is known of Dumont apart from his memoirs: the pages devoted to him by Samuel Smiles (*Huguenots in England and Ireland* (London, 1876), ch. 12) and the brothers Haag (*La France Protestante,* second edition (Paris, 1886), v, col. 772–8) are entirely based on his own testimony.

10 pp. 146–7; cf. 23 (title), 72, 279.

11 pp. 35–6, 41–2, 46–9, 58–9, 69–70, 122, etc.

12 *Histoire de France*, XIII, *Louis XIV et la Révocation de l'Édit de Nantes* (Paris, 1860), chapter 23, pp. 351 ff.

13 pp. 76–81, 113–9, 234–8.

14 p. 194. Dumont was much pleased with his stay in Exeter; the bustling prosperity of the city impressed him, though he found it rather shoddily built compared to the Dutch towns he had recently lived in. It was in Exeter Cathedral that he had his first contact with the Anglican liturgy, the Popish trappings of which repelled him despite the 'voix charmantes' of the choir (p. 198).

15 pp. 71–2. Cf., for intensity of personal emotion, pp. 44–5, 52–6, 60–2, 134–5, 154–6, 160–2, 256–9.

16 See below, p. 330.

17 See *Mémoires d'une famille huguenote*, p. xv. It was this copy that eventually provided the authentic text, published by the Société des Livres religieux in Toulouse (1887, reprinted 1900). All my quotations and references are taken from this edition. Earlier editions were English adaptations, beginning with an abridged text (New York, 1838), dedicated to the 'two thousand descendants

of this exemplary Christian [. . .] who are now living in the United States'; this was followed by an enlarged but still incomplete translation (New York, 1853 and 1872; London, 1874), which was then translated back into French (Toulouse, 1877). Prosper Mérimée published a sympathetic review of the 1853 edition in the *Revue des Deux Mondes* of September 1853 (pp. 1005–14), which was reprinted in his *Mélanges historiques et littéraires* (Paris, n.d.), pp. 301–18.

18 There are some quite picturesque ones, e.g. *gratuité* for *bienfait* (p. 125); *tantaliser* for *harceler* (p. 166); *rapture* for *ravissement* (p. 202); *grosseur* for *épicier* (p. 264); and *tenants* for *locataires* or *métayers* (pp. 304, 320, 342).

19 See below, p. 330.

20 pp. 37–44, 293–4, 379–82, 390.

21 e.g. pp. 141, 212–3, 228.

22 pp. 231, 239, 260, 297, 341, 373–7.

23 e.g. pp. 133ff., 218–27, 323–31, 344ff.

24 Rotterdam, J. D. Beman et fils. A Dutch translation was published the same year, followed quickly by an English version (London, 1758), by one 'James Willington', who in fact was Oliver Goldsmith. There were further editions in French published at the Hague in 1774 and 1778; the latter supplied for the first time all the names that had been left blank in the original edition for fear of reprisals. More recent complete editions in French: edited by H. Paumier (Paris, 1864 and 1881); and by Gaston Tournier (Publications du Musée du Désert en Cévennes, 1942). This last is virtually unobtainable outside France, and so all my quotations and references are taken from the 1881 edition. In 1957 the Folio Society published an excellent English adaptation (unfortunately abridged and re-arranged) by Kenneth Fenwick, entitled *Galley Slave*.

25 Marteilhe's name is not mentioned by either Lanson or Cioranescu.

26 *Histoire de France*, ed. cit., XIII, 324.

27 *Memoirs of a Protestant* (London, 1758), Translator's Preface, p. vi.

28 Another Jean Marteilhe was married in the Savoy French Church, London, in 1711, and a son of his was baptised in 1716 at Les Grecs Church. See D. C. A. Agnew, *Protestant Exiles from France,* third edition (Edinburgh, 1886), II, 105, 122.

29 See the Introductions to the various editions listed above: also A. J. Coquerel, *Les Forçats pour la Foi* (Paris, 1886), pp. 88–9; and a notice in the *Quarterly Review,* cxx, No. 239 (July 1886), p. 63.

30 Marteilhe's account is fully confirmed by Jean Bion in his *Relation des tourments qu'on fait souffrir aux Protestants qui sont sur les galères de France* (London, 1708), pp. 29–32. Bion was a Catholic chaplain on a galley belonging to the same squadron as Marteilhe's; as a result of his experiences, he deserted and became a Protestant. See: Pierre M. Conlon, *Jean-François Bion et sa « Relation des tourments . . . »* (Geneva, 1966).

31 e.g. pp. 5–6, 58–60, 183ff., 258, 287–92, 298–300.

32 p. 148. According to Fenwick, his name was Jermy (*Galley Slave,* p. 103, note).

33 see pp. 103–5, 242–3, 259–61, 264–6, 394–6.

34 p. 411. This detail is confirmed by Bion, *Relation des tourments,* p. 8.

35 See the passage of Michelet quoted above, and the notice in the *Quarterly Review* already referred to, p. 42.

36 See pp. 2–3, 5, 183, 208, 246, 274.

37 See pp. 36ff., 66ff., 171–83, 183–202, 246–9.

38 e.g. pp. 221ff.; cf. p. 426. See K. Fenwick's comments in *Galley Slave,* p. 12.

39 See P. Fonbrune-Berbinau, 'La Libération des forçats pour la foi en 1713 et 1714', *Bulletin de la Société de l'Histoire du Protestantisme français,* 38 (1889), 225–38.

40 There are some handwritten notes to this effect in some old editions, such as the British Museum's copy of the 1757 edition. One of the rare letters by Marteilhe that have been preserved offers some supporting evidence (see Gaston Tournier's introduction to the 1942 edition, p. 14). On Daniel de Superville and his son, see Haag, *La France Protestante,* IX (1859), pp. 326–8.

41 pp. 1–2, 25–6, 48, 160–1, 216–8, 284–5, 292ff.

42 There is a long appendix, much valued by naval historians, entitled *Description d'une galère armée et sa construction* (pp. 347–432).

43 Émile Léonard, *Le Protestant français* (Paris, 1953), pp. 7–9.

44 Marteilhe, pp. 92ff., 158–64, 259–67; Fontaine, pp. 37–44, 379–80.

45 This is most striking of all in the memoirs of Jean Rou (see above, note 3), ed. cit. 1, 29, 75, 83, 88–9, 92–3, 166–7, 264, 268, etc. Cf. R. Stephan, *Histoire du Protestantisme français*, chapter 18: 'Y a-t-il un style protestant?'

46 e.g. Fontaine, pp. 368–9.

47 Dumont, p. 45: 'Jamais on ne pouvoit mener une vie plus douce et plus divertissante [. . .] que la nôtre'; Migault, pp. 45, 241, 271; but see also p. 239.

48 cf. P. Lejeune, *L'Autobiographie en France*, p. 62.

29

A Cosmopolitan Country Clergyman:
Louis Dutens

P. J. YARROW

Elsdon is a little Northumbrian village, on the western side of the Simonside Hills, a few miles south of the Cheviots, four miles from Otterburn (where the famous battle was fought), twenty-five miles from Alnwick (the seat of the Duke of Northumberland), and thirty miles from Newcastle. Even today, the visitor sees nothing but a village green, bordered on two sides by a few houses, and on the north by the church, behind which rises an ancient pele tower, Elsdon Castle or the Vicar's Pele; until 1962, this was the vicarage. In 1801, says Eneas Mackenzie,[1] there were sixty-four houses and a resident population of 267; and in 1821, according to John Hodgson,[2] the whole parish—some twenty-one miles by five in extent—contained 333 houses and 1,855 persons.

To Elsdon, in the autumn of 1765, the most unlikely rector in the history of the parish came to take possession of his new living, worth over £400 a year, and in the gift of the Earl (later Duke) of Northumberland, who had purchased the lordship of Redesdale in 1750. He was a swarthy[3] but dapper Frenchman of thirty-five, who had never 'acquired a sufficient knowledge of the English language, to read or converse in it without any offensive intermixture of the foreign idiom'.[4] In society, he exaggerated the oddity of his English for comic effect;[5] but it seems to have been odd enough in all conscience:

There is still remembered a very singular attempt of his to illustrate and explain one of the inexplicable mysteries of church doctrine. In one of his discourses on the subject, he said—'My very goot friends, there be three time—one time past, two time present, and three time to come; and them three time be all one time'.[6]

Mr Dutens's parishioners were at first hostile, but his good humour soon won them round.

The parishioners of Elsdon expressed much dissatisfaction when they learnt that a foreigner was established as their minister, and on his first visit to take possession of his benefice, his appearance confirmed the dislike; but in preaching the first sermon, the discontent rose to clamorous opposition, one and all declaring they had not understood a single word of his discourse, and a petition to the bishop for relief was the theme of every tongue. Although well informed of all that was passing, he appeared to know nothing of the matter, but freely mixed among the people with the most winning and cheerful condescension, and in going round the parish, he personally invited to dine with him, at the Old Castle, as many of the higher class as his table would accommodate. On the appointed day, as they arrived, they were shewn into a room, and when the whole had met, he entered the room with expressions of the utmost surprise at seeing them there, declaring that he had no reason to expect the honor of a visit from any one of them on that day.—One of them very warmly appealed to himself if he had not in person invited them to dine with him. 'Oh, yes!' returned the clerical humourist, 'Oh yes! my very goot friend, I did invite you, and you, and you, to my dine, but you all say, every one of you say, you no understand one word I speak. Oh ho! very goot, when I preach you from my pulpit, you no understand my speak, but when I invite you to my goot dine, you very well understand!' It was instantly perceived that the play off was a good-humoured joke upon themselves, and a hearty laugh at each other was the prelude to the dinner bell. By similar practices of pleasing chearfulness, he in turn conciliated his parishioners, and still more by being commendably moderate in the exaction of his tithes.[7]

Mr Dutens's previous career had been no more ordinary than was his person. Born in Tours, on 15 January 1730, of a French Protestant family, he made up his mind, at the age of fifteen, to leave France, the Archbishop of Tours having caused a younger sister of his to be placed in a convent and converted to Catholicism. Some years later, he carried out his resolution, and came to England, where his uncle was established as a jeweller in Leicester Fields, London, bringing with him letters from Miss Pitt—with whom he had become intimate at Tours—to her brother, the future Lord Chatham, and to Lord Barrington. He was admitted to Pitt's house on intimate terms, until Pitt learned from his sister (June 1752) that Dutens had boasted that she was willing to marry him. Dutens, in fact, was deeply in love with her companion, Miss Taylor, now back in London; but, as he had no money and no prospects, her mother persuaded him to return to France for a while, and, during his absence, carried her daughter off into the country. Dutens fell ill in Tours and began to think seriously about religion.

On his return to England, he found, with his uncle's help, a post as tutor to the son of Mr Wyche, a gentleman of scholarly and scientific interests who spent half the year in London, and half at Goadby Marwood in Leicestershire. Ashamed of his ignorance, Dutens began to study seriously: he read Latin; Mr Wyche taught him Greek; and he also learnt Italian, Spanish, and Hebrew. After the death of his pupil, he remained with the family as tutor to the second son. He also devoted much attention to a deaf and dumb daughter, who returned home at this time. With considerable ingenuity, he learnt how to communicate with the neglected girl, taught her to write, succeeded in explaining to her such concepts as God, thought, and the mind, and won her affection—to such an extent that she fell in love with him and wanted to marry him.

At that moment, Lord Bute's brother, Stuart Mackenzie, about to depart for Turin as envoy extraordinary, required a secretary and an almoner; the dual post was offered to Dutens, who took holy orders for the purpose (1758). This was the beginning of a lifelong friendship between Dutens and that Darby and Joan, the kind, benevolent, upright, good-humoured, sensible, and studious Mackenzie, and his loving, but foolish, wife, Lady Betty, a daughter of the Duke of Argyll. When, on the death of the Duke of Argyll in April 1761,

Mackenzie was recalled to succeed his uncle and father-in-law as Lord Keeper of the Privy Seal in Scotland, Dutens remained in Turin as chargé d'affaires until May 1762.

Il est certain que ma situation devenoit singulière: né François, élevé en France, je me trouvois ministre du roi d'Angleterre à une cour étrangère, en tems de guerre avec la France.[8]

On his way back to England, he was instructed to stay in Paris for a while in case he might be of use in the peace negotiations then in progress. There, he sat next to Sterne at a dinner given by Lord Tavistock, where Sterne, not knowing who his neighbour was, launched into an imaginary, comic description of Mr Dutens; was received by madame de Boufflers; and, at her house, made the acquaintance of the prince de Conti.

Back in England, he entered Stuart Mackenzie's household as secretary, and was granted a pension of £250 a year by the government. He returned to Turin in April 1764 for a further year as chargé d'affaires. He received a visit from Edward Gibbon on 28 April, introduced him to the Countess of San Gillio's salon the following day, presented him at court on 3 May, and obtained permission for him to visit the citadel and the arsenal. 'Dutems nous a eté très utile. Je suis très très content de ses procedès', wrote Gibbon in his diary.[9] In January 1765, it was James Boswell's turn to be presented by the chargé d'affaires —to the King of Sardinia in the morning, and to the French ambassador's wife, madame Chauvelin, in the afternoon. On that occasion, Boswell found himself in a predicament which he lacked the address to carry off. He was given the task of handing madame Chauvelin to her coach, but a dispute over precedence arose between her and another lady.

I was simple enough to be tossed from the one to the other, as I did just what I was bid; while the rogue Dutens enjoyed my perplexity. [. . .][10]

★   ★   ★   ★

However incomprehensible his parishioners may have found his sermons, it does not appear that he inflicted many on them. As he never mentions Elsdon by name in his memoirs and seldom refers to it, it is not easy to estimate how much time he spent there; but Hodgson's statement that 'he frequently resided'[11] is perhaps more true of his later than of his earlier years, and can scarcely refer to more than brief visits.

After his induction, 'ayant rencontré à Newcastle M. de Mackenzie, qui venoit d'Écosse, j'eus le plaisir de l'embrasser et de revenir à Londres avec lui'.[12] In the first part of 1767, he is living in London with Stuart Mackenzie (in Hill Street), and receiving packets from the French correspondents of Rousseau, then in England. These he took to Rousseau's host, Davenport, who sent them on to Rousseau. Rousseau's books having been sent after him, Davenport sought Dutens's help in disposing of them. The upshot was that Davenport bought Rousseau's set of the *Encyclopédie*, and that Dutens took the rest of Rousseau's books, about a thousand in all, which he housed at Elsdon; for these, valued at £65, he undertook to pay an annuity of £10 until Rousseau's death or his own.

In London, Dutens called on the Duke of Northumberland to thank him for the living (it was Mackenzie who had brought Dutens to the Duke's notice). An invitation to dinner led to his becoming a firm favourite with the Duke and the Duchess, who entrusted their younger son, Lord Algernon Percy, to him—first for a visit to France lasting four or five months in 1767, and then for a Grand Tour of Europe from 1768 to 1771. In the course of their travels, Dutens and his charge were admitted into the best society everywhere. Dutens made the acquaintance of Sir Horace Mann and Lord Cowper in Florence, and that of Beccaria in Milan; saw the Young Pretender in Rome; was presented to the Pope, to the King and Queen of Naples at Caserta (by Sir William Hamilton), to the Elector and Electress of Saxony in Dresden, and to the Prince and Princess of Orange at the Hague; called on Voltaire at Ferney, and on the poet Haller in Berne; saw Marie-Antoinette at Linz on her way to Paris to marry the Dauphin; obtained—with difficulty, and by dint of flattery—an audience with Frederick the Great; and dined with the Duke of Brunswick along with Gustavus III of Sweden (two hours after Dutens's arrival in Brunswick). He spent nearly a year (1770–1) in Vienna, where he was presented to Empress Maria Theresa and Emperor Joseph II, frequented the salon of Kaunitz, met the prince de Ligne, accompanied the court to Pressburg, and played chess with von Kempelen's automaton there. Lady Mary Coke, Lady Betty Mackenzie's sister, saw him in Vienna, playing loo with Kaunitz in the British ambassador's house after dinner. He played for high stakes and lost eight hundred ducats during his stay, she reports.

During the carnival there was no young Man here of twenty years of age that lanched so much into all the pleasures as him, setting up till three & four o'clock in the morning; had he been obliged to this, to have attended Ld Algernon, it wou'd have been very different, but he had no other motive then to amuse himself, for Ld Percy always went home at eleven o'clock.[13]

He took a lodging for Lady Mary with an overpowering, incurable stench and a plague of bedbugs and lice; she never forgave him.

Nor was this his last visit to the continent. He accompanied the Duke and Duchess of Northumberland to Spa in 1772, and, apart from a brief visit to England, lived in France from then until 1776,[14] staying with madame de Boufflers in Paris, and with the duc de Choiseul at Chanteloup, where he spent the happiest days in his life;[15] frequenting mademoiselle de Lespinasse, d'Alembert, and their circle; discussing ancient medals with abbé Barthélemy (to whom he owed his introduction to the duchesse de Choiseul), and hearing him read the *Voyage du jeune Anacharsis*; prevailing on Conti to give Diderot a pension; making the acquaintance of Beaumarchais and the chevalier d'Éon; and, as the official representative of the French Protestants (or some of them), presenting a memorandum to Malesherbes, urging the government to allow their births and marriages to be recorded by notaries instead of Catholic priests (November 1775). On 10 February 1776, madame du Deffand writes to Horace Walpole: 'Je passai la soirée avec lui [le prince de Conti] chez l'Idole [madame de Boufflers], avec Mmes de Luxembourg, de Cambis et M. Dutant'; in April, Dutens—she spells his name correctly by now—has translated a letter of Horace Walpole's for her.[16]

In 1777 and 1778, he toured Italy with the Mackenzies. In 1779, he was living in retirement in Elsdon, when Bute's eldest son, Lord Mountstuart, was appointed envoy extraordinary to Turin; Dutens accepted an invitation to go with him, and twice took his place. On leaving Turin in 1781, he travelled in Italy until 1783, being received in Florence with marks of favour by the Grand-Duke of Tuscany; and then spent a year in France renewing old friendships, before returning to England. During this period abroad, he tells us:

Je voyageois toujours dans une bonne chaise de poste angloise, où j'avois un bureau portatif pour mes papiers, et nombre de livres favoris en différentes langues; au moyen de quoi je me trouvois établi, comme dans mon cabinet, quelque part où je fusse obligé de m'arrêter. Les auteurs que je préférois, autant par goût que pour ne pas oublier les langues que j'avois pris tant de peine à apprendre, étoient, en hébreu, la Bible; en grec, Plutarque, Démosthène, Longin, quelques morceaux détachés de Platon et Xénophon; en latin, les Catilinaires de Cicéron, Tacite, César, Horace et Virgile; en françois, Racine, Télémaque, le Discours préliminaire de l'Encyclopédie par d'Alembert, l'Essai sur le Beau du Père André, les Poésies de Rousseau, de Deshoulières, la Conversation du Maréchal d'Hocquincourt avec le Père Canaye de St.-Evremont, et le Voyage de Bachaumont et La Chapelle; en anglois, quelques ouvrages de Pope, d'Addisson, de Thompson; en allemand, l'Agathon et le Diogènes de Wieland; en espagnol, Don Quichotte et la Diane de Gil-Polo; en portugais, le Camoëns; en italien, l'Arioste, le Tasse, et Pétrarque. J'ajoutois à ces ouvrages de goût le Dictionnaire historique en neuf volumes *in-8°* les Tablettes historiques et chronologiques de Lenglet-Dufresnoy, et quelques Dictionnaires d'histoire naturelle et des sciences exactes.[17]

When he was not abroad, he devoted much of his time to the Duke and Duchess of Northumberland and, after the Duke's death in 1786, to Mackenzie and to another friend, Craufurd. He lived mainly in London, where he had a large circle of acquaintances, and

his domestic expences were always on a very limited scale. The invitations he received to dinner in the full season, were perpetual, and there were many considerable houses, at which a place was always left for him, without the formality of previous notice.[18]

He was admitted to the parties of the Prince of Wales, until he forfeited the Prince's good graces by his book on the King's illness (1789). Sometimes he would stay with the Mackenzies at Petersham (during the Revolution he went there every summer to help them entertain the French émigrés who had settled in Richmond nearby) or with the Earl of Bute at Luton or in Hampshire.

Some of his friends he owed to his travels and his service abroad. Having known Sir Horace Mann in Florence, he called on Mann's friend, Horace Walpole, on 12 February 1786. Mann wrote to Walpole from Florence on 10 March of that year:

As to Mr Dutens, with whom I lived in a degree of intimacy as an agreeable companion, he has travelled much, and has had opportunities of being acquainted with the principal people of many great courts, particularly in that of France. [. . .] He has an excellent memory, and possesses many curious anecdotes, so that he is a very pleasant and most agreeable companion. [. . .][19]

In May 1786, at a concert at Mrs Cosway's, Dutens introduced Horace Walpole to Earl Cowper;[20] in February 1787, he borrowed Christine de Pisan's life of Charles V for him.[21]

The chevalier d'Éon was another old friend. To satisfy the curiosity of Lady Lovaine, Lord Algernon Percy's wife, Dutens invited mademoiselle d'Éon to his house in December 1786—the chevalier was then passing as a woman—to meet her. Lady Lovaine, who had given birth to a child in Dijon, asked mademoiselle d'Éon if she had ever been there; mademoiselle d'Éon replied: 'I have been there, but did not lie in there, *car je suis vierge, et pour que les vierges accouchent, il faut qu'elles aillent à Jérusalem*'. 'It was impertinent to Lady Louvain, and worse in a clergyman's house—but women of fashion should not go aboard Amazons', comments Horace Walpole.[22]

It was no doubt through having met Sir William Hamilton in Italy that Dutens came to be a witness—along with Sir William's cousin, Lord Abercorn—at the wedding of Sir William with Emma Lyon in Marylebone parish church on 6 September 1791.[23] So grateful was Lady Hamilton to Dutens that she wrote to Romney from Caserta on 21 December:

As you was so good to say you would give me the little picture with the black hat, I wish you would unfrill it, and give it to Mr Duten. I have a great regard for him; he took a deal of pains and trouble for me, and I could not do him a greater favour than give him my picture. Do, my dear friend, do me that pleasure, and if there is anything from Naples command me.[24]

The picture was duly sent. The acquaintance, renewed in 1801 after Lady Hamilton's return to England, was terminated by Dutens, who disapproved of her conduct.[25]

Dutens, it must not be forgotten, *was* Rector of Elsdon, and had a more serious side to his nature. Hodgson tells us that Dutens 'was much respected in the parish, to which he was one of its greatest benefactors on record'.[26] It was owing to his efforts that, in 1793, a chapel of ease was built, by voluntary subscription, at Byrness—in his parish, but ten miles from Elsdon. It was endowed with £1,750; and, not only did Dutens contribute £1,200 of this sum himself, but he also provided a curate there, 'who should teach, if required, 12 poor children of the neighbourhood, gratis'.[27]

Occasional glimpses of Dutens's life in Northumberland are afforded by his letters. Newcastle delighted him. On 16 December 1767, he wrote to his cousin, Frederick Dutens, of London:

[. . .] d'ailleurs je vous avoüe que Newcastle est une ville charmante et où je suis accueilli on ne peut mieux; Je suis invité tous les Jours à dinner en Compagnie et à souper. ils ont toutes les semaines une assemblée, un Jour; un autre Jour un Bal; un autre Jour un Concert; vous y trouvez 40, 50, 60 Femmes, dont 20 seront des Beautés qu'on admircroit à Londres.

A letter to Jean-Jacques Rousseau written in Newcastle on 10 February 1768 is equally enthusiastic: he is sure that, if Rousseau had come to Newcastle, he would never have left it, and adds: 'Savez-vous, mon cher Monsieur, que Newcastle est le lieu qui vous convient [. . .]?' On 17 December 1767, he went to Elsdon, whence he wrote to Frederick Dutens again on 27 December:

Je suis dans les montagnes par dessus la Tête, et dans la neige jusqu'au Cou. Jamais cette campagne ci n'a eû si bonne mine, je la compare à une Laide, qui met du Rouge, qui cache les Defauts et lui préte quelques agrémens. Cela a pourtant ses Inconveniens, ce matin j'ai eté obligé de mettre mes Bottes pour aller à l'Eglise, Et j'en ai eû jusqu'aux genoux. Voila qui est fait pour un Mois ou Six Semaines, Je vais aller à Newcastle, y passer ce tems là afin de donner aux Ouvriers, que j'ai mis à l'ouvrage ici, le tems de mettre en execution mes Instructions; peu à peu je m'arrengerai.[28]

The Vicar's Pele had previously been shared by rector and curate. Dutens—this may be what the workmen mentioned in the letter to his cousin were to do—built a separate house for the curate, and took over the whole tower for his own use. Hodgson's description of it allows us to form some idea of Dutens's life in Elsdon.

Till Mr Dutens's death, the first [i.e. ground] floor consisted of a dark vault spanned by one arch, in which, in former times, the rector's cattle were housed by night; a circular stone staircase still leads to the upper rooms, on the first of which was a kitchen and servants' apartments flagged with stone; and above these another room, fitted up as a lodging-room and study, the bed being in a large recess, with closets on each side, one of which served as a wardrobe, and the other for more general purposes: in 1810, it contained the Greek and Latin authorities for Mr Dutens's 'Discoveries of the Antients attributed to the Moderns', copied by himself with great beauty and correctness, and very methodically arranged. His books were mostly ponderous folios, in French and the antient languages. Here Mr Dutens lived, and entertained his company during his residences at Elsden. Formerly, there were two low rooms above, each containing four chambers one partly destroyed by heightening this; and the other is the present garret.[29]

Life in Elsdon was, perhaps, less idyllic than the modern townsman might be inclined to suppose, since—sometimes, at least—Dutens suffered from its seclusion.

Our post is so irregular that I have not heard one piece of news nor seen any newspaper from town since that of the 28th. past, so that I have not the least idea of what passes in the world, and whether we are at peace or war, and who is dead or alive. A few lines also on these subjects would be a charity and I know you like to do good actions. I wish I had anything to say from hence in exchange worth your reading, but it would be in vain for me to attempt thinking of producing something from this barren part of the world,

he wrote to Lady Lovaine in June 1790.[30] However, Elsdon cannot have been too bad, since two years later he refused a rich living in Surrey in exchange:

I feel attached to my old wife, in spite of wrinkles, perhaps because I think I have done it some good and mean to do more.[31]

Louis Dutens had begun writing plays and verse before he was ten, and, at the age of eighteen or so, he had had a tragedy on the subject of Ulysses's return to Ithaca successfully performed at Orleans. He was to write no more plays, though he published some verse in later life; but he was a prolific writer. In 1766, he published a two-volume work, the full, self-explanatory title of which is: *Recherches sur l'origine des découvertes attribuées aux Modernes, où l'on démontre que nos plus célèbres philosophes ont puisé la plûpart de leurs connoissances dans les ouvrages des anciens; et que plusieurs vérités importantes sur la religion ont été connues des sages du Paganisme.* This was attacked by Voltaire—who, however, seems to be confusing it with *Le Tocsin*—in a letter to Chastellux of 7 December 1772 (which Chastellux, Dutens tells us, read in the salons), and in the article 'Système' of the *Questions sur l'Encyclopédie* (1774).[32] Condorcet also attacked it:

Je ne sçais s'il y a beaucoup d'érudition dans l'ouvrage de Mr Dutens, contre les modernes, mais je sçais qu'on y trouve bien peu de philosophie, & surtout une grande ignorance des sciences naturelles. [. . .][33]

Dutens's next venture was an edition—the first collected edition—of the works of Leibnitz, in six volumes (1768). The following year, *Le Tocsin,* an attempt to combat atheism, theism, and deism, was published in Rome; it was later published in Paris, and its title changed to *Appel au Bon Sens.* In 1775 appeared a guide book, *Itinéraire des routes les plus fréquentées.* This work, the plan of which was suggested by Bute and Mackenzie, 'passe pour l'ouvrage le plus utile en ce genre qui ait paru jusqu'ici', says Dutens.[34] It contains a reference to Elsdon: 'Pays de Montagnes, mais où l'on fait de grandes ameliorations'.[35] In 1779, he published Rousseau's notes on his copy of Helvétius's *De l'Esprit,* one of the books Dutens had bought twelve years before (*Lettres à M. D . . . B . . . sur la réfutation du livre De l' Esprit, d'Helvétius, par J. J. Rousseau*). Another guide book followed in 1787: *L'Ami des Étrangers qui voyagent en Angleterre.* Dutens wrote on other subjects, too, including precious stones, current events in England and France, and numismatics—his interest in this subject having been aroused by the collection of Greek medals belonging to the Venetian family Ruzini, given to him by the Duke of Northumberland.[36]

All this literary and scholarly activity did not pass without recognition. In 1775, Dutens was elected a foreign associate member of the Académie des Inscriptions et Belles-Lettres and a Fellow of the Royal Society; in 1784, he was made a corresponding member of the Accademia delle Scienze of Turin; in 1786, he was appointed historiographer royal, and in 1804, along with Dr Burney, librarian of the Royal Institution.

The scholar may consult some of the works just mentioned, but the only one that can be said to survive is his *Mémoires d'un voyageur qui se repose,* written between 1775 and 1805, and published in three volumes in 1806. Dutens himself recognizes that the book might have been better if he had been less charitable, but it is entertaining, interesting as an account of the author himself, and a useful source of information about his age. As he says,

Peu d'hommes, je crois, ont été autant que moi dans le cas de voir, d'approcher, de connoître intimement tant de personnages illustres, dont les caractères se trouvent consignés ici, et qui ne le seront peut-être jamais aussi fidèlement dans l'histoire.[37]

His memoirs are like a roll-call of eighteenth-century celebrities; they deserve to be reprinted.

*   *   *   *

Of Dutens's last years, little is known. He had lost his best friends—Lady Betty Mackenzie died in 1799, and her husband in 1800, leaving him £15,000; but he seems to have led an active social life until the end.

I was well acquainted with monsieur Dutens, and had frequent opportunities of witnessing how completely, in every respect, his well dressed circular *peruque* was a sort of personification of his mind. He had talents—such as ingenuity, upper-form learning, and a vivacious spirit of research and of expression. These were all arranged in precise order, (like the curls of the said peruque) and were obedient at a moment's call. He was therefore loquacious in company, and had the best possible opinion of his own conversational powers. Yet he seemed to be impressed with a conviction that his talents were not so fully appreciated by the male, as by the female part of his auditory; and he was always 'making play' to sustain his expiring reputation with the former, by every possible effort to elicit applause from the latter! Thus, on the announce of dinner (as I have often witnessed) it was 'a marvel' (so Caxton would have expressed it) to see our Octogenarian,

> . . . of amber snuff-box justly vain,
> And the nice conduct of a clouded cane,

looking complacently around, to select some favourite *bas-bleu* to take his arm, and join him in leading off the descending procession to dinner. He was indeed a sort of literary 'Sir Plume;' and a more deter-mined courtier, in domestic life, was never imported from the country which gave him birth. What is droll, he had the living of Elsdon, one of the dreariest spots in Northumberland, and fancied that no one was such a favourite with his congregation as *himself*; because that congregation seldom or never saw his countenance, or, when seen, could not exactly comprehend the language which he uttered! He was one of the heartiest men, for his time of life, that I ever beheld; but then he had all the advantages of lettered ease—a gently-rolling chariot; a well-aired, rather than a well furnished, house; a society which kept good hours, and a reputation which rather made him sought after than otherwise. His activity continued almost undiminished to the last; and I have seen him at the semi-gothic mansion of a well known Baronet,[38] situate not very many furlongs from Putney Bridge, exercise the queue at the billiard-table with surprising alacrity and success. He might be said to have almost had a presenti-ment of his dissolution; for not many weeks before his death he called upon all his friends, in the said 'gently-rolling chariot,' to return them their letters: and himself not long afterwards expired with scarcely a struggle or a groan.[39]

He died at his house in Mount Street, London, on 23 May 1812.

Louis Dutens had an interesting life, though he has no claims to greatness. His mind lacked originality, and he was something of a snob and a tuft-hunter. An unkind critic wrote that

in all the arts of subservient assiduity and persevering cajolement, after personal aggrandizement, he was well qualified for the head professorship in the lucrative school of Sir Pertinax Macsycophant.[40]

But this is unfair. He liked the way of life of wealthy noblemen; but he maintained his independence of judgment, valued his freedom, and declined to become the permanent, salaried companion of the Duke of Northumberland. The motto of his *Mémoires,* taken from Horace, is:

> Dulcis inexpertis cultura potentis amici,
> Expertus metuit.[41]

He had many good qualities. He must have had charm, and he was a good companion, lively, amusing, and good-humoured. He 'possessed an infinite fund of small talk', and

the ease and polish of his accomplished manners, the smile of cheerful gaiety that ever played on his countenance, and the unremitting display of all his faculties, useful or entertaining, [. . .] made him at all times an amusing, and frequently a very useful, resident in a great man's family.[42]

He had more solid qualities, too. He performed his diplomatic duties with efficiency and integrity, and in all the circumstances of his life displayed ingenuity and resource. He was fond of reading and scholarly. Above all, he was a kind man. In his desire to please and to oblige, there may at times have been an element of vanity or exhibitionism, but there is no doubt of the genuine kindness; he was generous with his money, and he would take endless trouble to be of use to others.

NOTES

1   *A Historical and Descriptive View of the County of Northumberland* (1811), p. 67.
2   *History of Northumberland* (1827), Part II, Vol I, p. 82.
3   In an article in the *Newcastle Magazine* in April 1823, J. C. relates that an adversary of Dutens called him a 'cream-colored Swiss parasite', and adds that 'the expression, however coarse, was strikingly characteristic' (p. 202).
4   W. Beloe, *The Sexagenarian* (second edition, 1818), Vol. II, p. 102.
5   J. C., loc. cit., p. 202.
6   J. C., loc. cit., p. 203. This is very much like Dutens's explanation of divine foreknowledge in his *Mémoires*, III, pp. 24–5.
7   J. C., loc. cit., pp. 202–3.
8   *Mémoires d'un voyageur qui se repose*, I, 173–4.
9   *Gibbon's Journey from Geneva to Rome, 1764*, ed. G. A. Bonnard (1961), p. 40. See also pp. 12–40 passim, and Gibbon, *Letters*, ed. J. E. Norton, Vol. I (1956), pp. 172, 175.
10 *Boswell on the Grand Tour*, ed. F. Brady and F. A. Pottle (1955), p. 31.
11 op. cit., p. 89.
12 *Mémoires*, I, p. 260.
13 Lady Mary Coke, *Letters and Journals* (1970 reprint), Vol. III, p. 377.
14 It is difficult to reconcile his statements about these years. On 22 January 1773, he was in Paris and presumably on the point of departure, since he had undertaken to carry a 'grand portefeuille à soufflet' from Morellet to Lord Shelburne (*Lettres de l'abbé Morellet à Lord Shelburne*, ed. Lord Edmond Fitzmaurice (1898), p. 19). The dedicatory letter of his *Explication de quelques médailles* [. . .] *grecques et phéniciennes* (London, 1773), is dated London, 1 December 1773. He tells us in his *Mémoires* that he arrived in France in 1774, shortly after the death of Louis XV (10 May).
15 Dutens's impressions of life at Chanteloup may be found in a letter to the Duke of Northumberland published in the *Newcastle Magazine* in April 1823 (pp. 203–4), as well as in his *Mémoires*.
16 Horace Walpole, *Correspondence*, ed. W. S. Lewis, Vol. VI, 1939, pp. 265, 308, 310.
17 *Mémoires*, II, 259–60.
18 Beloe, op. cit., p. 102.
19 Horace Walpole, *Correspondence*, ed. W. S. Lewis, Vol. XXV (1971), p. 627.
20 Horace Walpole, *Correspondence*, ed. W. S. Lewis, Vol. XXV, p. 646.
21 Horace Walpole, *Correspondence*, ed. W. S. Lewis, Vol. XXXI (1961), p. 245.
22 Horace Walpole, *Correspondence*, ed. W. S. Lewis, Vol. XXXIII (1965), p. 548.

23 H. Tours, *The Life and Letters of Emma Hamilton* (1963), p. 93. Like other biographers of the Hamiltons, the author takes Louis Dutens and the Rector of Elsdon to be two persons.

24 Tours, op. cit., p. 96.

25 J. W. Lorimer, 'The Life and Works of Louis Dutens', (Ph.D. thesis (unpublished) of the University of London, 1952), p. 280. This is an admirable piece of work.

26 op. cit., pp. 89–90.

27 Hodgson, op. cit., p. 89.

28 The letters to Frederick Dutens from Newcastle (16 Dec. 1767) and Elsdon (27 Dec. 1767) are in the Central Library, Newcastle upon Tyne. The passage quoted from the letter to Rousseau will be found in L.-J. Courtois, *Le Séjour de J.-J. Rousseau en Angleterre,* (1911), p. 247, and in Rousseau, *Correspondance générale,* ed. Th. Dufour, Vol. xviii (1932), p. 120.

29 Hodgson, op. cit., pp. 96–7.

30 Lorimer, op. cit., p. 244.

31 Letter to the Countess of Beverley (formerly Lady Lovaine), 25 July 1792, quoted by Lorimer, op. cit., p. 256.

32 Voltaire, *Correspondence,* ed. T. Besterman, Vol. 83 (1963), p. 184; Voltaire, *Œuvres,* ed. Moland, Vol. xx, p. 471.

33 *Seconde Lettre d'un Théologien à l'auteur des Trois Siècles* (1774), pp. 70–1.

34 *Mémoires,* Vol. 1, p. 275. We learn from the *Itinéraire* that Dutens, on his previous journeys, had travelled with an *odomètre* (or 'perambulator') attached to his carriage, recording the distances traversed.

35 p. 3 (1779 edition).

36 *Explication de quelques médailles* [. . .] *grecques et phéniciennes,* dedicatory letter to the Duke of Northumberland.

37 *Mémoires,* Vol. ii, p. 356. In the third volume of the *Mémoires,* Dutens lists the great men of Italy, and adds: 'Ces auteurs vivent la plupart encore aujourd'hui, et je les ai tous vus et fréquentés' (p. 77).

38 Possibly Strawberry Hill, according to Lorimer, op. cit., p. 282.

39 T. F. Dibdin, *The Bibliographical Decameron,* Vol. iii (1817), pp. 92–3. Beloe also says: 'To the very last period of his life he retained his vivacity of intellect, and great activity of body. When turned of seventy, he played billiards with great spirit, and practised all the finesse of the Queue with considerable success.' (op. cit., p. 102)

40 J. C., loc. cit., p. 202.

41 Horace, *Epistles,* i, 18, ll. 86–7.

42 J. C., loc. cit., p. 202.

List of Subscribers

at 21 April 1975

Professor Ian W. Alexander, University College of North Wales, Bangor
Dr E. R. Anderson, University of Edinburgh
Professor L. J. Austin, Jesus College, Cambridge
Dr Richard Bales, Queen's University, Belfast
Professor W. H. Barber, Birkbeck College, London
T. J. Barling, Esq., University of Exeter
Professor Frank Barlow, University of Exeter
M. M. Barr, Esq., Portland, Indiana, U.S.A.
Dr Theodore Besterman, The Voltaire Foundation, Banbury, Oxon
Dr J. D. Biard, University of Exeter
William Brooks, Esq., Exeter
Professor J. H. Brumfitt, University of St. Andrews
Dr K. C. Cameron, University of Exeter
Professor Michael Cardy, Brock University, Ontario, Canada
Professor J. G. Clark, University of Strathclyde
Edwyn and Marie-Thérèse Crowle, Exeter
Dr S. F. Davies, University of Dundee
Peter W. Day, Esq., Highfields, N.S.W., Australia
Professor A. H. Diverres, University College of Swansea
Ms J. Ann Duncan, Newnham College, Cambridge
Dr Enid L. Duthie, Exeter

Professor Ehrard, Riom, France

Professor Jean Fabre, Murat-sur-Vèbre, Tarn, France

Dr A. W. Fairbairn, University of Newcastle upon Tyne

Professor Alison Fairlie, Girton College, Cambridge

Professor A. Graham Falconer, University of Toronto, Canada

Patrick L. M. Fein, Esq., University of Rhodesia

Peter Ffoulds, Esq., University of Birmingham

Dennis Fletcher, Esq., University College of Wales, Aberystwyth

Professor Louis Forestier, Université de Paris X

Professor and Mrs J. H. Fox, University of Exeter

Professor F. W. A. George, St. David's University College, Lampeter

Dr R. J. Godfrey, Gipsy Hill College, Kingston on Thames

Professor Basil Guy, University of California, Berkeley, U.S.A.

Dr A. K. Holland, University of Melbourne, Australia

Dr Eva Jacobs, Bedford College, London

T. G. Jenne, Esq., Exeter

Professor Brian Juden, Royal Holloway College, Egham, Surrey

Professor and Mrs J. D. Jump and Mrs Susan Habeshaw, Bowden, Cheshire

Assistant Professor Emilie Kostoroski-Kadish, Cleveland, Ohio, U.S.A.

Professor Jean-Louis Lecercle, Paris

L. J. Lloyd, Esq., Exeter

Professor J. Robert Loy, City University, New York, U.S.A.

Professor I. D. McFarlane, Wadham College, Oxford

Professor D. McMillan, University of Edinburgh

Professor Jean Marmier, Rennes, France

Michel Martiny, Esq., University College, Cork

Dr Sheila M. Mason, University of Birmingham

Professor Georges May, New Haven, Connecticut, U.S.A.

Professor Gita May, Columbia University, New York, U.S.A.

Professor G. D. Mitchell, University of Exeter

Dr Vivienne Mylne, University of Kent at Canterbury

Jim Poston, Esq., British Embassy, Tel Aviv

Miss Monica Poston, Portland

Professor Anthony R. Pugh, University of New Brunswick, Canada

Dr Malcolm D. Quainton, University of Lancaster

Professor William Ravenhill, University of Exeter

Professor and Mrs T. B. W. Reid, Oxford

Professor John Renwick, New University of Ulster, Coleraine

Professor Pat Rogers, University College of North Wales, Bangor

Marcel A. Ruff, Doyen honoraire, Université de Nice

F. W. Saunders, Esq., University of Manchester

Dr R. A. Sayce, Worcester College, Oxford

Professor Emeritus Jean Seznec, University of Oxford

Dr Robert Shackleton, Brasenose College, Oxford

Dr Marjorie Shaw, University of Sheffield

Mrs Rosemary Smith (née Stonehewer), Lympstone, Devon

Professor J. S. Spink, London

Professor Emeritus W. McC. Stewart, University of Bristol

Dr Anthony R. Strugnell, University of Hull

Norman Suckling, Esq., Hexham, Northumberland

Professor O. R. Taylor, Queen Mary College, London

Professor P. M. W. Thody, University of Leeds

Mrs Yvonne Trotter, Topsham, Exeter

Professor Stephen Ullmann, Trinity College, Oxford

Jacques Vier, Esq., Rennes, France

Professor Jacques Voisine, Université de Paris III

Dr M. H. Waddicor, University of Exeter

Dr R. L. Walters, University of Western Ontario, Canada

Dr D. A. Watts, University of Exeter

Professor D. Williams, McMaster University, Ontario, Canada

Charles Wirz, Esq., Geneva, Switzerland

Dr Barbara Wright, Trinity College, Dublin

Professor Joyce Youings, University of Exeter

Associate Professor Marjorie M. Zeyen, Shaker Heights, Ohio, U.S.A.

The Library, King's College, University of Aberdeen

The Arts Library, University College of North Wales, Bangor

The Library, University of Bath

The Library, Queen's University, Belfast

John E. Robbins Library, Brandon University, Manitoba, Canada

The Library, University of Bristol

The Library, Jesus College, Cambridge

Modern & Medieval Languages Libraries, Cambridge

The Library, University of Dundee

The Library, University of Durham

The Library, University of East Anglia

The Library, University of Edinburgh

The Library, University of Exeter

The Library, University of Glasgow

Niedersächische Staats- and Universitätsbibliothek, Göttingen, Germany

Bibliothek des Romanischen Seminars, Universität Heidelberg, Germany

Brymor Jones Library, University of Hull

The Library, Bedford College, London

The Library, King's College, London

John Rylands University Library of Manchester

Section de Littérature Comparée, Université d'Aix-Marseille III

Bibliothèque de l'Université de Nancy II

Taylor Institution Library, University of Oxford

The Library, Lady Margaret Hall, Oxford

The Library, St. Anne's College, Oxford

The Library, St. Edmund Hall, Oxford

Bibliothèque Universitaire de Perpignan, France

The Library, University of Reading

The Library, University of Regina, Saskatchewan, Canada

Universitätsbibliothek, Saarbrücken, Germany

The Library, University of Stirling

The Library, University of Strathclyde

The Library, University College of Swansea

The Library, New University of Ulster, Coleraine

The Library, University of Warwick

Universitätsbibliothek, Würzburg, Germany